Ancient African Maxims

- → FOR THOSE LIVING IN IGNORANCE SHALL BE LEFT IN THE WILDERNESS
- → SEEK AND YOU SHALL FIND…DISCOVER AND ALL THINGS SHALL BE REVEALED TO YOU
- → THE SHORTEST ROAD TOWARD KNOWLEDGE OF TRUTH IS NATURE.
- → THE INNER LIGHT GROWS IN SILENCE AND CONCENTRATION
- → FOR HUMANKIND KNOWS NOTHING FOR WHICH THEY ARE NOT RIPE
- → THE GREATEST UNDOING TRAVELS FROM THE MIND TO THE TONGUE
- → LEAVE THOSE IN ERROR WHO LOVE THEIR ERROR
- → BEWARE OF BLIND CREDULITY AND PIECE-MEAL CRITICISM. NEVER BELIEVE A WORD WITHOUT PUTTING ITS TRUTH TO THE TEST; DISCERNMENT DOES NOT GROW IN LAZINESS; AND THIS FACULTY OF DISCERNMENT IS INDISPENSABLE TO THE SEEKER. SOUND SKEPTICISM IS THE NECESSARY CONDITION FOR GOOD DISCERNMENT
- → THERE GROWS NO WHEAT WHERE THERE IS NO GRAIN
- → PEACE IS THE FRUIT OF ACTIVITY, NOT OF SLEEP
- → GREAT IS THE ONE WHOSE TREE BEARS FRUIT
- → PROCEED CAUTIOUSLY BEFORE AN OPPONENT, AND GIVE WAY TO AN ADVERSARY
- → NEVER MAKE HASTE TO A DECISION FOR A STORM COMES FORTH LIKE FIRE IN HAY
- → DO NOT IMBALANCE THE SCALE, MAKE THE WEIGHTS FALSE, OR DIMINISH THE FRACTIONS OF MEASURE FOR THE UNIVERSE IS CONSCIOUS AND ALL BEINGS IN IT
- › A SUFFERING HEART IS ROOTED IN CORRUPTION
- → BEWARE OF THOSE YOU STAND IN SOLIDARITY WITH, AS BETRAYAL IS LIKE FIRE PENETRATING DEEPER THAN THE SWORD.

ENGLISH EDITION

The Kemetic Path

Achieving High Spirituality

COMPILED, WRITTEN, AND EDITED BY

Ricky D. Butler

Book Cover/Illustrations by Ricky D. Butler

All claims to original works.

Compilation: 01 (Released 2026)

International Standard Book Number (ISBN): 978-1-7346427-8-0 (E-BOOK)
International Standard Book Number (ISBN): 978-1-7346427-7-3 (PRINT)
International Standard Book Number (ISBN): 978-1-7346427-9-7 (AUDIO)

Library of Congress Control Number: 2025927975

Self-Published. Columbus, Ohio.

This book contains information obtained from authentic and highly regarded sources.

Printed on acid-free paper

9 8 7 6 5 4 3 2 1

TABLE OF CONTENTS

INTRODUCTION

This text, **The Kemetic Path: Achieving High Spirituality**, has been compiled for a widespread audience in plain terms with no poetic or parable form to fulfill three (3) primary objectives: (i) to provide a spiritual alternative to those struggling with religious disaffiliation or seeking a strong connection with nature and a High Power on a higher level of consciousness, (ii) to revive ancient Kemetic teachings based on an overlooked perspective coined as High Spirituality and (iii) to thwart societal control mechanisms.

As technology advances and global communication improves, many people are becoming disillusioned with their religious choices after discovering falsehoods, myths, contradictions, questionable conduct, forgeries, voids, and scientific/historical inaccuracies in sacred texts, religious narratives, points of origin, central tenets, revelations, and prophetic claims. This disillusionment naturally leads to increases in doubts of a faith (skepticism), complete rejection/renunciation of a faith (apostasy), absence from a faith (dissociation), fake support of a faith (false piety + non-practicing by culture/tradition), resentment of a faith, and attacks on a faith. All of these increases running counter to a given faith are lumped together as religious disaffiliation, which can have negative impacts on the life, the health, and the condition of individuals as follow:

1. **Pain and sorrow over being rejected**. Excommunication and rejection from the religious community might result in the loss of friends and family members (isolation/outsidership), the loss of resources (school enrollment, financial support, qualified housing, etc.), a sense of not belonging (identity estrangement), and the inability to marry.
2. **Overwhelmed by guilt and shame**. An apostate or questioning religious believer might manifest thoughts of either being unworthy in the eyes of such a god or turning his/her back on this god. Moreover, if this god is considered one and the same with the religious community, then abandoning the community somehow equates to abandoning this god, resulting in confusion, religious relapse, thoughts of suicide, heightened insecurities, unwanted condemnation, and self-gaslighting. Gaslighting includes experiences of not measuring up, not believing there is a better rationale or religious explanation of the world, and self-blame for parental pain as part of generational/community indoctrination, disapproval, or letdown.
3. **Living in constant fear of life and death**. Religious communities oftentimes have followers whom resort to violence against questioning believers and/or apostates. Sometimes, the religious doctrine condones violence, even calling for death in some cases if the faith is not restored. Additionally, the punishment of a god in the afterlife is used as a fear-mongering tactic to pressure a return to a faith, normally followed by repentance or another confirmation tactic.
4. **Humiliated as a human being**. The poor treatment from the community on top of the agony from being manipulated and controlled might cause an apostate or a questioning believer to feel inadequate, worthless, emotionally numb, and violated, especially if an example is made out of him/her. Even if this individual decides to leave the religious community completely, (s)he will experience difficulties in making critical decisions or taking bold actions with fears of repercussion.

It is worth noting that an overwhelming majority of religious followers and religious converts typically subscribe to religions based on hearsay and mostly uncorroborated testimonies of believers, parental indoctrination, perception of treatment via demographics/identity, and 'acceptance before learning' faith tactics, without inquiring about or researching on the dark and embarrassing components and warnings associated with a faith.

If the reader has experienced any of the above, then (s)he has come to the right place. The recommended alternative to man-made and sketchy religions is High Spirituality, which is a derivative way of life (spiritual, not religious) based on ancient African teachings and African freemasonry, mainly Kemet, stripped and filtered of any and all religious, occult, and ceremonial components. There are no initiations, sacred rituals, forced experiences, sacred texts/doctrines, mythological constructs, material rewards or punishments, days of worship, or institutional places of worship because High Spirituality can never be an institution or an establishment, as the Living Universe is the sanctuary for all finite living beings.

Before continuing the discussion on High Spirituality, it is imperative to discuss the meaning of 'spirituality' in the context of Africa, as the word is oftentimes conflated and interchanged with 'religion'. Phrases such as 'Kemetic Spirituality' or 'African Spirituality' are incorrectly associated with Kemetic Traditional Religions and African Traditional Religions, respectively; even though, spirituality is not synonymous with religion. In fact, spirituality can exist without religion, but religion cannot exist without spirituality because a religion is constructed by taking a fraction of spiritual concepts and adding rules, tenets, rituals, authorities, and dogma to them. The failure to understand spirituality and religion as distinct concepts caused difficulties among scholars studying Kemetic culture and Kemetic spiritual beliefs.

For centuries, scholars have tried to unearth the secrets and the profound wisdom contained within Kemetic spiritual practices and well-preserved hieroglyphics as well as the antiquity of Egyptian civilization and the ancient ruins despite the decipherability challenges of recovered historical articles and the conflicting narratives surrounding oral traditions, especially when examining local tribal customs and when juxtaposing Ancient Egyptian traditions with those of Ancient Nubia and Ancient Greece. The disappointment in deciphering articles and the dissent on authentic oral traditions caused experts like W.B. Kristensen in Leiden and Herman Kees to focus on navigating the religious and the ceremonial matter – almost impenetrable under the guise of modern-day interpretation – rather than assimilating the philosophical content or extracting the underlying knowledge. As a result, Kemetic practices became viewed as a collection of weird myths, doctrines, and dimensions riddled with occult Heka magic and superstition not worthy of worship instead of teachings with lucid rationalism borrowed, adapted, or arguably stolen by other worship systems.

Interestingly enough, there is evidence to suggest that several unrelated local tribes and several unrelated local cults, which existed either side by side or in close proximity, converged on many beliefs without referring to religion at all. Such convergence strongly suggests a rift in religion but not a rift in spirituality because the nationwide validity of a religious doctrine came through political power as seen in Thebes, for instance, when the high priests of the Amun polytheistic cult convinced King Tutankhaten ('living image of Aten') to restore the traditional worship of Amun – which became Amun-Ra after the eventual merger with the sun god – and to change his name to Tutankhamun ('living image of Amun') upon his father's death. His father, King Akhenaten, made every attempt to establish a monotheistic system centered on Aten through official decree during the Amarna Period in the 14th century BCE. When assessing the aforementioned example, which is quite popular, historians only concentrate on either the religious significance of the reversion or the power struggle among polytheistic and monotheistic leaders; however, they overlook a critical detail: the complexity and the fluidity of spiritual beliefs, with or without religion, directly impacting the disunified Egyptian civilization itself.

Put in another way, this critical detail indicates that all of the following pathways of Kemetic spiritual thought are possible, extending to ideas of a personal High Power, an impersonal High Power, and no High Power at all:

1. Traditional polytheistic religion with beliefs and rituals centered on various deities/gods
2. Traditional monotheistic religion with beliefs and rituals centered on one 'god'
3. Hybrid or syncretized religion where one 'god' is worshiped, but others are acknowledged
4. Spiritual practices without religion, where the deities are only accepted as symbols of the material culture
5. Raw spiritual teachings completely filtered of religious elements, favoring direct callouts rather than symbols

Whereas, Item 1 is an explored pathway (most popular) inclusive of the principles and the functions of the forty-two (42) Neteru/NTR across four (4) worlds (Manu, Aakhut, Rostau, and Ament) and ten (10) families (Hermopolis Ogdoad, Solar Triad, Memphis Triad, Esna Triad, Heliopolis Ennead, Dendera Triad, Funerary Quaternary, Theban Triad, Initiatory Triad, and the Cyclic Triad). This pathway is only compatible with a personal High Power.

Whereas, Item 2 is an explored pathway mainly centered on the worship of Aten – the sun disc initially seen as a manifestation of the sun god Ra. Atenism is the first-known attempt at establishing a monotheistic religion in Ancient Egypt. This pathway is only compatible with a personal High Power.

Whereas, Item 3 is an explored pathway seeking henotheistically to understand why a particular god is elevated to a position of uniqueness and supreme power over other gods, how divinity levels/hierarchies of (sub) deities are structured, and what underlying divine essence or power merging is possible. Another common idea for this pathway is hermeticism, which is a philosophical and esoteric religious tradition attributed to Hermes Trismegistus with Greco-African worldviews, reflections of higher realities, and spiritual transformations. This pathway is compatible with a personal High Power or an impersonal High Power.

Whereas, Item 4 is an unexplored pathway of Ancient Egypt with or without the belief in a higher power, where the material culture is shared and the deities are respected despite choices to remain 'non-practicing' or 'unworshipful' of said deities. In this case, for instance, a figure or an idol will represent something (e.g., fertility, light, etc.) rather than be the god of it. This pathway is compatible with a personal High Power, an impersonal High Power, or no High Power at all.

Whereas, Item 5 is an unexplored pathway of Ancient Egypt, completely devoid of anachronisms, religious elements, or even incidental symbols that can be misconstrued as sacred in a religious context. The absence of religion maximizes spirituality, leading to a stronger gravitation toward understanding the physical and metaphysical world. This pathway is compatible with an impersonal High Power or no High Power at all.

High Spirituality, which is a part of this pathway with an impersonal High Power, involves the personal quest for meaning, individual purpose, a deepening interconnection with finite living beings, and a connection to something beyond oneself, such as the High Power and the Living Universe, to reach higher consciousness and to evoke awareness. Furthermore, it encompasses a person's beliefs, values, and practices, and it can be expressed in many ways without any religion, including through nature or personal reflection. It must be remembered that teachings and spirituality were in existence before the fabrication of any religion.

Reviving High Spirituality based on the Kemetic teachings after numerous colonization efforts is a complex and ongoing process, driven by the desire to reclaim identity, preserve cultural heritage, compete against mainstream beliefs, and foster a deeper connection to the Living Universe. Egypt's colonization record, which illustrates the complications facing the original Kemetic culture, includes but is not limited to the following events:

- Assyrians from Mesopotamia conquered and ruled Egypt in 669 BCE.
- Persians led conquests in 525 BCE.
- Alexander the Great of Macedonia conquered Egypt and founded Alexandria in 332 BCE.
- Egypt came under Roman rule after Octavian's army defeated Queen Cleopatra in 31 BCE.
- Christianity spread to Egypt in 33 CE and largely displaced the Egyptian religion by the 4th Century, especially with the establishment of the Coptic Church around 50 CE.
- Arabs led conquests of Egypt in 642.
- Egypt was absorbed into the Turkish Ottoman Empire in 1517
- Napoleon Bonaparte invaded Egypt but was repelled by the British and the Turks in 1801.
- Ottoman Albanian commander Muhammad Ali established a dynasty in 1805.
- British troops defeated the Egyptian army in 1882 (Protectorate until 1914).
- The Muslim Brotherhood under Hassan al-Banna reoriented Egypt until he died in 1949.
- The deliberate flattening/removal of the nose of the Great Sphinx, a culturally African artifact, by Arabs before the 15th Century

It is worth mentioning that the vast majority of conflicts in Ancient Egypt and Modern-day Egypt can be attributed to religion. With that in mind, the revival of High Spirituality is necessary to mitigate religious conflicts, to break societal controls, and to encourage unity among all groups, for High Spirituality is a spiritual system belonging to all humankind.

This text is broken down into three (3) main parts with concise and digestible sections that are not overly academic and that should not overwhelm the reader.

Part 1 Preliminaries & Fundamentals: This part of the text, which prepares the reader to receive the Kemetic teachings, covers philosophical, scientific, and mathematical fundamentals crucial for developing critical thinking skills, identifying flaws in logic, and constructing/evaluating arguments to enhance problem-solving capability, engaging with complex inquiries, and cultivating a deeper understanding of personal self, the Living Universe, and the everlasting High Power.

Part 2 The Raw Kemetic Teachings - High Spirituality: This part of the text comprehensively introduces the core spiritual principles of High Spirituality based on the raw Kemetic teachings – far removed from any religious doctrine – in conjunction with the cosmological paradigm, the mechanisms of consciousness and awareness, and all distinct phenomena associated with the unity, the systemization, the interconnectedness, the energies, the order, and the organization of the rational world governed by the High Power, where both, the intelligent spirit and the physical mantle, cyclically join in the physical and metaphysical layers of the Living Universe. These teachings are direct and greatly simplified, requiring no intermediary, instructor, or mediator for interpretation.

Part 3 Breaking Societal Controls: Through mature discussions, this part of the text explores how to break free from social controls by fostering the awareness of societal expectations/traps, examining manipulative techniques used to sway public opinion, challenging societal norms, and promoting a stronger sense of individual autonomy.

Please note that Kemet and Egypt are used interchangeably throughout the text.

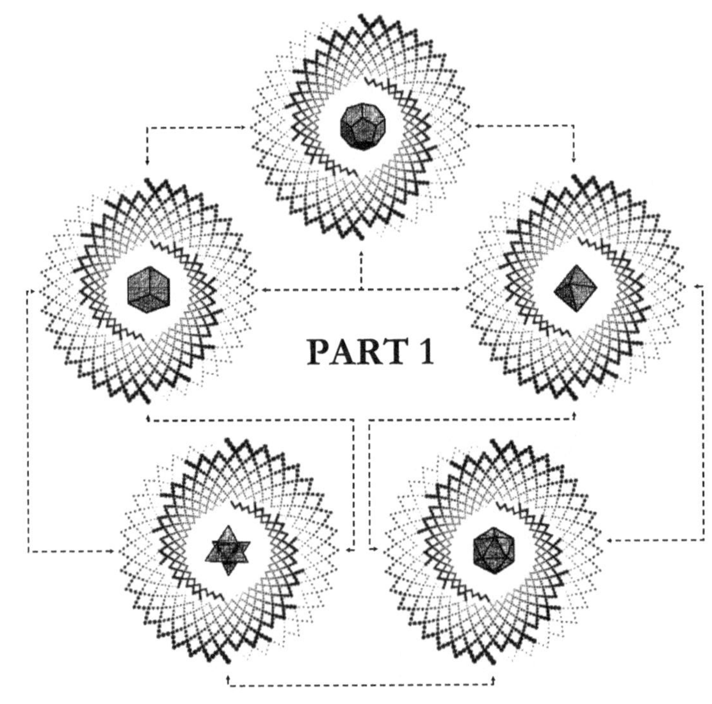

PART 1: PRELIMINARIES & FUNDAMENTALS

METAPHYSICS

ANKH WADJA SENEB | ARTICLE NO: 001

Function: Preparation of Knowledge
Intent: Increase Rationality & Mental Facility
Position: Part 1 – Preliminaries & Fundamentals

ARTICLE NO: 001 – METAPHYSICS

Peace to the High Power! Peace to the Living Universe! Peace to all Finite Living Beings! Peace to All Things – seen and unseen! For my spirit is with me, my image is with me, and my purpose is with me. For wisdom belongs to the seekers in heavy pursuit of knowledge, which can only be ascertained through the preparation and the sharpening of mental facility; and, knowledge is the protective shield against intellectual danger and exploitative measures.

Philosophy is a vital discipline that provides clarification, rationality, and logical analysis of central questions around the nature, the meaning, and the root of life. Thus, in a very general sense, all disciplines and courses may be regarded as branches of philosophy, seeing as all knowledge seeks to answer the question of existence, reality, and its sundry manifestations.

Categorizing philosophy and defining its different aspects prompts the description of each broad subject area, for each aspect/branch encompasses vital elements that make up its general notion. For purposes of total inclusivity and easy absorption by the reader, we will break down philosophy into digestible and succinct pieces, beginning with metaphysics. Metaphysics, which seeks to answer the philosophical question of "*What is real?*", consciously examines the fundamental nature of being, and exposes the reality encompassing it. As this branch is concerned with the ultimate nature of reality, it creates an understanding of an array of abstract topics such as possibility and necessity, free will, change, and causation.

An examination of metaphysical theories reveals that the fundamentals of metaphysics were concerned with the following:

- Reality as a whole
- Fundamental truth behind existing entities
- Possibilities for existence
- Core aspects of contingent things
- The nature of humanity

Traditionally, metaphysics involved two (2) different study areas: ontology and cosmology. Whereas ontology investigated entities and their relation with one another, cosmology was concerned with understanding the origin, the evolution, and the ultimate fate of the universe, which included studying laws that kept it in functioning order and which encompassed problems involving relations between particulars and universals, essence and existence, mind and matter, intrinsic and extrinsic properties, determinism and freewill (or indeterminism), space and time, and unity and diversity – among others.

Notable topics include the following:

- The existence of God - Does a divine being exist, and if so, what is its nature?
- Free will vs. determinism - Are our actions predetermined, or do we have genuine freedom to make choices?
- The nature of time - Is time an objective feature of the universe, or is it a subjective experience?
- The mind-body problem - How do the physical brain and the non-physical mind relate?
- The nature of reality - Does the world exist independently of our perception of it?
- Causation - What is the nature of cause and effect?
- Personal identity - Am I the same person I was yesterday? What constitutes my identity?
- The nature of universals - Do abstract concepts like "redness" or "beauty" have an independent existence?
- The nature of space and time - How do space and time relate to each other, and what are their fundamental properties?

Renowned philosophers, such as Aristotle, suggested that metaphysics was one of the more critical branches of philosophy, even referring to the subject matter as the "first philosophy". Nonetheless, owing to its abstract nature, this philosophical branch has been criticized on both the meaningfulness of its theories and the reliability of its methods. Conventionally, metaphysicians relied on the use of abstract reasoning and rational intuition as methods to conduct their inquiry. Later ages witnessed the evolution of complex systems, such as idealism, in association with scientific theories, pointing towards free will and the distinction between mind and body. Albeit, these idyllic methods would face a lot of opposition in the 20th Century.

Methods used in metaphysics include the following:

- An appeal to what might be vividly imagined as reality
- An appeal to what might **not** be imagined
- An appeal to what an individual might conceive coherently
- An appeal to what might **not** be conceived coherently
- The appeal to intuitions about what is logically possible or logically impossible.
- An appeal to a thorough conceptual analysis.
- The Proof of Propositions by the identification of logic alone, as discussed by British philosopher and logician, Bertrand Russell, is divided between (a) the non-existence of the set of all sets that do not belong to themselves, and (b) their total non-existence thereof.
- The Proof of Propositions using logic and conceptual analysis so that analytic truths can be derivable from logical truths in the narrow sense by the substitution of synonymous expressions, where a cause cannot succeed its effect
- An appeal to the use of inference to the best causal explanation
- The use of inference to the best non-causal explanation with the example of laws of nature and causal relations
- The use of a system of logical probability to show that certain things are likely to be the case or unlikely to be the case.
- The use of inference to the best account of the truth conditions of some statement. This reinforces the idea of a robust correspondence theory of truth as seen in David Lewis's account of the truth conditions of statements about possibilities.

The shortcoming of these methods is that while science, particularly physics, principally concerns itself with the ultimate nature of reality, critics have questioned how metaphysical methods differ from those of science, arguing against the legitimacy of this discipline as it appears to be riddled with pure speculation.

From this point, we will discuss the core philosophical components of metaphysics.

Components of Metaphysics – Ontology

Ontology is the philosophical study of being that focuses on the fundamental classes of reality and their relations, answering questions such as *what exists?* and *what are the basic categories of existence?* According to Plato and Aristotle, ontology examines what is truly in existence, including any physical object whose form can be perceived. As a sub-discipline of metaphysics, ontology is restricted to the most general features of reality, examining how entities exist and how they relate to each other without restrictions to a limited domain of entities. Such features are indicated by substance, where:

- Attributing the oneness or the singleness of a substance to a concept is monism.
- Asserting two distinct substances or two fundamental forms of a concept is dualism.
- Attributing multiplicity of a substance to a concept or multiple forms of a substance is pluralism.

Edmund Husserl and Martin Heidegger assert that there are multiple subjectivities and that the world may be constructed differently depending on a person's notion of reality (truth or fact), resulting in further ontological approaches as follows:

- **Realism**: Realism focuses on the existence of an objective reality independent of perception, owing to the belief that things exist whether they are observed or not.
- **Idealism**: Idealism suggests that reality is fundamentally mental or spiritual, arguing that minds shape certain experiences of reality, and reality itself is a product of the mind.
- **Nominalism**: A view that challenges the existence of universals and abstract entities, arguing that only particular objects exist, so that universals are merely human-made constructs. For instance, concepts such as beauty are seen as a label applied to subjective experiences.
- **Phenomenalism** (also Post-modernism): A view that emphasizes the nature of consciousness and experience by examining how entities are perceived according to an individual's subjective experiences. In this case, objects are merely collections of sensations and experiences.

Ontological characteristics usually describe a knowledge domain by:

- Identifying all the entities in the domain, such as people, places, objects, and ideas.
- Describing the attributes of each entity, such as a person's name, gender, age, date of birth, and occupation.
- Describing the relationships between entities, such as the relationship between two people or the relationship between a person and an object.

All of these aspects are in line with the substance-attribute theory, which is an ontological philosophical concept that contends that objects/ entities are composed of a substance (substratum) and attributes (properties) that are distinct from it. The substance is considered to be the underlying reality that possesses the attributes characterizing it.

Strengths and weaknesses of ontology are as follows:

Strengths	Weaknesses
Systematic analysis of being provides the understanding of the fundamental nature of existence, categories of being, and analysis of concepts like identity.	Abstraction and distance from experience lead to a disconnect from concrete reality, making it impossible to justify them using empirical evidence.
Provides a foundation for other philosophical disciplines, such as ethics, by providing an understanding of the nature of entities and their relationships.	Potential for triviality and overly general theories that offer little insight into the specificities of the world.
Formalization and precision enable a rigorous analysis of concepts in fields like computer science and artificial intelligence, where ontologies are used to represent knowledge.	Formalization may limit the richness and complexity of ontological analysis, which do not capture the nuances and complexities of real-world phenomena.

Components of Metaphysics – Modality

Modality is a subdivision of metaphysics that illuminates the possibility and necessity of events to examine how things must be or can be. Its claims explore the central question: When a statement is made about what is possible or necessary, what determines its truth or falsity? Resultantly, modal facts are construed as facts about possible worlds, where the actual world is just one among many possible worlds.

Types of modalities include the following:

- **Epistemic Modality**: Focuses on knowledge and belief, exploring what may be possible or necessary considering the current state of knowledge.
- **Temporal Modality**: Explores the nature of time and how it constrains possibilities. For instance, "The bus must have already left" expresses a temporal necessity based on a scheduled time.
- **Deontic Modality**: Deals with what is permissible or obligatory according to moral and legal requirements and hindrances.
- **Alethic Modality**: Deals with what is true, necessary, and possible in the broadest sense, encompassing logical truths and possible truths, such as contingent facts.

Characteristics of modal metaphysics include the following:

- **Focus is on Modalities**: Modal metaphysics explores possibility (what can be, even if it is not the case in the actual world), necessity (what must be and what is true in all possible scenarios), and contingency (what is true in the actual world, but could have been different).
- **Incorporation of Possible Worlds Semantics**: The analysis of the truth and falsity of modal claims considers alternative scenarios. A statement is considered possible if it is true in at least one possible world, and necessary if it is true in all possible worlds. On the other hand, a proposition is impossible if it is not true in any possible world. For instance, a 'square circle' cannot exist.
- **Grounding Modal Truth**: If a statement is true in the actual world, its truth is often grounded in facts about that world, so that possible worlds are often seen as the truth-makers for modal claims.
- **Intertwined with Causation**: Modal claims enable the consideration of what could or must have happened, given certain events.

Strengths and weaknesses of modal metaphysics are as follows:

Strengths	Weaknesses
Clarifies fundamental concepts such as possibility, necessity, and actuality, which are crucial for understanding the world's nature	Interpretations of all possible worlds potentially being real violate the oversimplistic principle that entities should not be multiplied unnecessarily.
Explores counterfactual statements, which enable the understanding of cause and effect, and fosters the evaluation of actions and their potential consequences	Challenging to establish a clear connection between modal claims about what is possible or necessary and what the actual world is.
Provides a philosophical foundation for understanding the applications of other fields such as logic, mathematics, physics, and computer science.	The idea of possible worlds as real entities seems counterintuitive and difficult to grasp.
Develops philosophical tools and techniques for analyzing complex philosophical problems, including those related to identity, essence, and free will.	Lack of empirical evidence, as modal metaphysics relies on conceptual analysis and thought experiments.

Components of Metaphysics – Identity (Persistence)

Identity, particularly in the context of persistence over time, is a subdivision of metaphysics that delves into the question: What constitutes the sameness of an entity across varied points in time? In essence, it explores how things can change but remain the same.

Characteristics of identity (persistence) include the following:

- **Persistence**: The way things exist through time, meaning how can something exist at different times and still be considered the same thing?
- **Change and Identity**: Explores how objects can undergo change (properties, composition, etc.) and yet retain their identity. For instance, a ship, which is repaired and which is modified over time, raises the question of when it ceases to be the same entity.
- **Persistence as Stages**: An object endures by having different temporal parts or stages, while others suggest it endures by being wholly present at multiple times.
- **Personal Identity**: Shifts focus to what makes a person at one time the same person at another time. It has implications for concepts like responsibility, moral status, and survival after death.

Ultimately, the metaphysics of identity introduces the problem of persistence, shedding light on fundamental questions concerning what it means for an entity to remain the same thing over time despite undergoing modifications. In the same vein, bundle theory represents a philosophical concept in metaphysics and philosophy of mind that views entities, including human beings, as collections of properties or experiences rather than as having a fundamental, underlying substance or self. As a result, it also raises a central question about personal identity and object persistence over time: If an object is just a collection of properties, then what happens when those properties change?

Strengths and weaknesses of identity (persistence) are as follows:

Strengths	Weaknesses
Provides a framework for understanding how objects remain the same despite undergoing changes, which is crucial for comprehending the nature of reality and how things exist over time	Defining the concept of identity is not straightforward. Philosophers still debate what constitutes identity and what criteria determine sameness.
Provides a basis for reasoning and knowledge by tracking entities and substances over time	Complexity in concepts such as quantum mechanics due to the indistinguishability of identical particles, challenging classical notions of identity.
Foundation for social and ethical frameworks, as they underpin notions of responsibility, rights, and obligations	Lacks practical applications in everyday life, particularly when compared to an approach like empiricism, which focuses on sensory experience.

Components of Metaphysics – Mereology (Parthood)

Mereology is a subdivision of metaphysics that assesses the structure of wholes as well as their constituent parts (parthood relationships). Concerned with the formal properties of the part-whole relation, it underscores many aspects of human understanding, including the physical composition of objects and the organizational structure of complex systems.

Parthood Mereology is a binary relation that holds between a part and its whole, upholding principles such as transitivity, reflexivity, and anti-symmetry. Types of parthood include the following:

- **Proper Parthood**: A part that is not identical to the whole.
- **Improper Parthood**: A part that is identical to the whole.
- **Immediate Parthood**: A part that is directly related to the whole.

Some of the most prominent composition theories include (i) unrestricted composition, where any collection of entities composes a whole, (ii) restricted composition, where only certain collections of entities compose a whole subject to specific conditions, and (iii) nihilism, where no entities compose a whole, so that only simple entities exist.

Mereology (Parthood) includes the following characteristics:

- The nature of identity and change
- The constitution of objects and their properties
- The relationship between wholes and their parts
- The fundamentality of reality

Some questions explored in mereology might include (i) Is a statue identical to the clay that constitutes it?, (ii) When do parts compose a whole, and when do they not?, and (iii) Can something be a part of itself?

Strengths and weaknesses of mereology are as follows:

Strengths	Weaknesses
Provides a formal system for understanding composition by analyzing how parts compose a whole	Controversial mereological principles, such as weak supplementation and extensionality, may prove counterintuitive as they lead to undesirable consequences.
When considering changes in its parts, it clarifies questions about identity and persistence.	The formal nature of mereology can be abstract and difficult to apply to concrete situations.
Offers a way to analyze complex systems by breaking them down into parts, proving useful in both metaphysics and logic.	Mereology can lead to the acceptance of scattered entities, which might be problematic.

Components of Metaphysics – Personal Identity

Personal identity is a metaphysical branch of philosophy that explores the problem of the nature of an individual's identity as well as their persistence through time in spite of changes in characteristics, such as their body and their memories (diachronic identity). Personal identity handles questions, such as (i) What am I?, (ii) When did I begin and what will happen to me when I die?, and (iii) What does it take for a person to persist from one time to another—to continue existing rather than ceasing to exist?

Theories of personal identity include the following:

- **Soul Theory**: Represents the idea that a person's identity is tied to their soul – an immaterial substance. The soul is considered the core of a person, and the person remains the same, regardless of changes to the body or the mind, so long as the same soul exists. This view is often linked to religious beliefs about the afterlife and the immortality of the soul.
- **Body Theory**: Represents that a person's identity is tied to their physical body. The idea is that if one has the same body from birth to death, then they are the same person, even if their physical appearance or mental state changes. Nonetheless, the body is constantly undergoing the change and the renewal of skin cells and blood cells, which raises questions about how much change a body can undergo before it becomes a different person.
- **Psychological Theory**: Focuses on the continuity of a person's psychological states, such as memories, beliefs, desires, and personality traits. A person may be considered the same, as long as there is a sufficient degree of psychological connectedness and continuity between their past and present selves. This theory often faces challenges related to amnesia, split-brain patients, and the possibility of creating a duplicate of a person's psychological state.

Personal identity includes the following characteristics:

- **Continuity of Consciousness**: Some theories involving substance dualism center on the idea that it is sameness of consciousness, specifically memory, that defines whom a person is over time, suggesting that the persistence of consciousness is critical for personal identity. In retrospect, the question, "If a person's conscious experience ceases, even temporarily, does that mean they cease to exist as the same person?", becomes relevant.
- **The Body and Personal Identity**: The body theory argues that a person's physical body is essential for their identity; thus, if the body changes or if the body is replaced, then the person ceases to exist.

- **Memory and Personal Identity**: Psychological theory proposes that a person's identity is tied to their memories, so that if someone can remember past experiences, then they are considered to be the same person. However, questions are raised about individuals with memory loss and the reliability of memory itself.
- **Psychological Continuity**: Psychological theory emphasizes the interconnectedness of psychological states (beliefs, desires, intentions, etc.) over time; however, a question is raised: "If there is a continuous chain of overlapping psychological states, even if some memories are lost, then is the person still considered to be the same?"
- **Thought Experiments**: Thought experiments, such as brain transplants or body swapping, are used to explore the complexities of personal identity and to challenge different theories.

Strengths and weaknesses of personal identity are as follows:

Strengths	Weaknesses
Provides a platform for psychological well-being and growth, boosting a stable sense of self for individuals to understand their values, beliefs, and goals.	Some concepts appear problematic as they do not adequately explain identity in cases of significant psychological changes, like brain damage or severe memory loss.
Boosts biological continuity based on the continuity and the transformation of the physical body.	Some theories can be criticized for not aligning with the intuitive sense of self, as it might not matter that a body is completely replaced by another, as long as the replacement is biologically identical.
Consideration of ethical dilemmas of responsibility, punishment, and even the morality of actions, such as euthanasia or abortion, is put into perspective.	Both psychological and biological approaches struggle with the fission problem, where a person is divided into two or more individuals, raising questions about which, if either, is the original person.

Components of Metaphysics – Space and Time (Travel and Reality of)

Philosophy of space and time has attempted to answer critical questions since the inception of analytic philosophy. In essence, this philosophy explores the following questions:

- Do time and space exist independently of the mind?
- Do time and space exist independently of each other?
- What causes the apparent unidirectional flow of time?
- Are there times other than the present moment?

This metaphysical component covers fundamental questions of reality and existence; however, it still grapples with the nature of space and time, such as their reality, their relationship to each other, and the possibility of time travel. Key aspects in the philosophy of space and time include the following:

- **Reality of Space-Time**: Are they fundamental aspects of reality or merely constructs of the mind?
- **Time Travel**: Is it possible to travel through time both, backwards and forwards?
- **Absolute vs. Relational**: Are they aspects that exist independent of other entities, or are they defined by the relationships between objects?
- **Direction of Time**: There are competing views on the reality of past, present, and future, where eternalism suggests all times are equally real and where presentism suggests that only the present exists.
- **Temporal Parts**: Is it possible that objects might have different parts at different times?

Characteristics of space and time include the following:

- **Dimensionality**: Space is typically conceived as having three (3) orthogonal dimensions (length, width, and height), forming the framework for physical objects and their relationships; however, time is generally understood as a one-dimensional progression, relatively flowing from past to future.
- **Continuity**: Both, time and space, are considered to be one continuum with no inherent gaps. As such, they are infinitely divisible with no missing points.
- **Interconnectedness**: The relationship between space and time is a fundamental topic in metaphysics with questions about their dependence or independence and their interaction with physical reality.

Strengths and weaknesses of space and time are as follows:

Strengths	Weaknesses
Offer an intuitive understanding to individuals whom readily use the concepts to navigate their surroundings	Substantivalism, while offering logical consistency, prompts the idea of infinite possibilities, raising questions about the nature of difference and identity.
Proof of relativity's integration, suggesting that they are not separate entities but rather aspects of a single space-time continuum	Presents paradoxes of time travel, especially backward time travel, which challenge the understanding of time's flow and the nature of reality.
Provides a foundation for reality upon which entities interact	Subjective time – personal experience of time's passage – can differ from the objective time described in physics, triggering questions about the nature of time's reality.

Components of Metaphysics – Cause & Effect

In metaphysics, the concept of cause and effect explores the basic relationship between events, where one event (the cause) triggers another event (the effect). It delves into questions about what the nature of this connection is, whether it is a necessary relationship or not, and how it relates to the understanding of time and reality. The metaphysics of causation explores the following questions:

- What does it take for causal claims to be true?
- What kind of relation are the claims about?
- What do these relations obtain?

In metaphysics, cause and effect relationships are often categorized using Aristotle's *Four Causes* below, which lay the foundation for categories of questions that explain "the whys" of entities that exist or that change in nature. These causes offer different "why" perspectives, exposing the substance, the form, the agent, and the purpose of an event or an entity.

- **Material Cause**: A category that studies the material cause of a change or movement, specifically referring to the material by which something is composed. For instance, the material cause of a study desk can be the wood from a tree.
- **Formal Cause**: A category that studies the formal cause for a change or a movement, including the appearance, the shape, or the arrangement of the entity. In the example of the desk mentioned earlier, the formal cause would be the specific shape and design of the object.
- **Efficient Cause**: A category that studies the moving cause of a change or a movement. This institutes the agent of force that effects a change or produces an entity. For the desk, the efficient cause is the carpenter who carved the material. Another good example is a parent who constitutes the efficient cause of a child.
- **Final Cause**: A category that studies the final cause of a change or a movement. This constitutes the purpose for which something exists in the end. For instance, using the study desk example, the final cause of the desk might be used by someone in an office.

Characteristics of cause and effect include the following:

- **Temporal Order**: A crucial aspect of the causal relationship, establishing a directionality to the connection, it maintains that a cause must occur ahead of its effect. This means that event A can only be the cause of event B if the latter happens last. This is in stark contrast to simultaneous causation, which argues against the cause always preceding the effect.
- **Dependency**: Dependency is a core aspect of the causal relationship between cause and effect because one phenomenon – the effect – is dependent on the other phenomenon – the cause. In this sense, the cause may be partly or wholly responsible for the effect's existence and occurrence. At the very least, supporters claim that, without the cause, the effect would not have occurred in the same way.
- **Potential for Multiple Causes**: The metaphysics of cause and effect entertains the possibility of multiple causes resulting in a single effect, otherwise known as overdetermination or multiple causation. For example, a car crash may be caused by a combination of speeding, a slippery road, and a distracted driver.
- **Necessary and Sufficient Conditions**: On the one hand, a cause can be a necessary condition, such that the effect cannot occur without it. On the other hand, a cause can also be a sufficient condition, such that its occurrence guarantees the effect. Nonetheless, sometimes, a cause is seen to be neither strictly necessary nor sufficient on its own, but rather part of a cluster of factors that together result in the effect.

Strengths and weaknesses of cause and effect are as follows:

Strengths	Weaknesses
The concept of cause and effect helps to explain why certain events tend to follow others, creating predictable patterns in the world.	Hume's problem that humans can only observe the constant conjunction of events, not a necessary connection between them. This prompts questions about the nature of causal power.
Underpins scientific inquiry, seeing as scientific methods rely on the identification of causal relationships to understand natural phenomena and develop technologies	Causal overdetermination (multiple causes) might result in the same effect, making it difficult to determine which specific cause is truly responsible.
The concept of cause and effect provides explanations behind why things happen, offering a framework for reasoning pertaining to the world.	Causal gaps may be evident in situations where causes are difficult to identify or to explain, challenging the general understanding of the event.

Components of Metaphysics – Universals and Properties

In metaphysics, universals and properties are closely related concepts that explore the nature of shared characteristics among different entities. On the one hand, universals are abstract entities, usually characteristics or qualities that can be exemplified by multiple particulars, while properties are the specific characteristics or qualities that entities possess. Some questions explored in these metaphysical concepts include:

- Do universal abstracts like "redness" or "roundness" exist independently of objects that possess them?
- Where and how do these abstract entities exist?
- How do we understand the relationship between a universal and the particulars that instantiate it?

Intrinsically, individuals are said to be similar when they share universals. For instance, an apple and a ruby are both red in color, and their common redness results from sharing the red color (the universal), which must be in two places at once.

Universals	Properties
Classes or categories of things, such as "mammal" or "chair"	Determinate Properties - Specific, non-divisible properties, such as a specific shade of green.
Properties or qualities that an entity can possess, such as "redness" or "heaviness"	Determinable Properties - General properties that can be further specified, like the color green.
Relationships describing how entities are connected to one another, such as "uncle to" or "next to".	Intrinsic Properties - Properties an entity possesses in itself, regardless of its surroundings, such as its density.
	Extrinsic Properties - Properties that depend on an entity's relationship to other things, such as weight, which is dependent on gravity.

Characteristics of Universals include the following:

- **Abstract**: Universals are not physical objects themselves, but rather abstract concepts or qualities.
- **Repeatable**: They can be present in, or shared by, multiple particulars.
- **Grounding Similarity**: They are often postulated to explain why different things are similar with examples being redness, squareness, or humanity.
- **Realism vs. Anti-Realism**: Academics are divided between whether universals actually exist (realism) or if they are just mental concepts or linguistic conventions (anti-realism).

Characteristics of Properties include the following:

- **Particulars**: Properties are the individualized attributes or qualities that entities possess with examples being color, shape, size, weight, or temperature of an object.
- **Instances of Universals**: Properties are often understood as being instances of universals. For example, the redness of a particular apple is an instance of the universal "redness".
- **Intrinsic vs. Extrinsic**: Properties can be intrinsic (inherent to the object, like shape or size) or extrinsic (related to other objects or external factors, like location).
- **Monadic vs. Polyadic**: Properties can be monadic (relating to a single object, like being red) or polyadic (relating to multiple objects, like being between two things).

Strengths and weaknesses of universals and properties are as follows:

Strengths	Weaknesses
Universals candidly explain similarity, revealing why objects share properties. For example, two red apples both instantiate the universal "redness".	Ontological Commitment - The existence of universals as abstract entities raises questions about their nature and how they relate to the concrete world.
Universals address predication by explaining the properties of objects. For instance, the universal "redness" of an apple.	The Problem of the One and the Many - It has been argued that a single universal can be present in multiple objects without being divided or duplicated.
Properties, being particulars, eliminate abstract entities. Instead, they represent concrete entities that exist only in the objects that possess them.	Universals can be difficult to integrate with theories of change and essential properties. If properties are universals, then how can an object gain or lose properties without losing its identity?
Properties, being particulars, can more easily account for change. An object cannot change without losing or gaining a property. However, it may change and still retain its universal quality.	Nominalism - The view that properties are simply ways of categorizing objects and do not have independent existence. They can be seen as less ontologically committed but might struggle to explain certain aspects of language and thought.

Components of Metaphysics – Free Will and Determinism

The study of free will vs. determinism in metaphysics revolves around questioning whether choices are freely made or predetermined by prior causes. On the one hand, determinism suggests that every event, including human actions, is causally inevitable, so that no one can choose otherwise. On the other hand, free will, in its libertarian context, suggests that humans possess the ability to make choices independent of prior causes, allowing for genuine freedom in decision-making. Nonetheless, a middle ground, compatibilism, exists, and it suggests that free will and determinism can coexist.

Some questions explored in the metaphysical concepts of free will and determinism include:

- Are we truly free in our choices?
- If all events are causally determined, how can we be morally responsible for our actions?
- What is the nature of consciousness and self?

Different perspectives of free will include the following:

- **Libertarianism**: The perspective that humans have the capacity to make choices that are not causally determined by prior events.
- **Incompatibilism**: The perspective that free will and determinism are incompatible; thus, if determinism is true, then free will is impossible.
- **Indeterminism**: The perspective that some events are not determined by prior causes, allowing for genuine chance and free will.
- **Agent Causation**: A specific type of libertarianism that proposes that agents (people) can be the cause of their actions, rather than solely prior events or states of the world.

Different perspectives of determinism include the following:

- **Causal Determinism**: The perspective that every event is causally necessitated by prior events, so that there is a chain of cause and effect that determines all outcomes.
- **Hard Determinism**: The perspective that determinism is true, and free will is an illusion. All actions are the inevitable result of prior causes, leaving no room for genuine choice.
- **Soft Determinism (Compatibilism)**: The perspective that determinism is true, but free will is still possible. In this view, actions can be caused by internal states (desires, intentions) and still be considered free, even if those internal states are themselves determined.
- **Psychological Determinism**: The perspective that actions are determined by psychological factors, such as past experiences and mental states.
- **Biological Determinism**: The perspective that actions are determined by genes and biological makeup.
- **Theological Determinism**: The perspective that god's omniscience or divine plan determines all events, including human choices.
- **Logical Determinism**: The perspective that the laws of logic dictate that every statement is either true or false, and such truth or falsehood is predetermined.

Characteristics of free will include the following:

- **Autonomy**: Individuals are seen as having the capacity to initiate actions and make choices independent of prior causes.
- **Alternative Possibilities**: A key aspect of free will is the ability to do otherwise, meaning that in a given situation, one could have chosen a different course of action.
- **Responsibility**: Free will implies that individuals are morally responsible for their choices and actions, as they are the originators of those actions.
- **Libertarianism**: This philosophical stance asserts that free will exists and that determinism is false, emphasizing the power of individuals to originate their actions.

Characteristics of determinism include the following:

- **Causality**: Determinism proposes that every event, including human actions, is the inevitable result of prior causes, often linked to natural laws and antecedent conditions.
- **Predictability**: If determinism is true, then in principle, one can predict future events based on knowledge of the past and the laws governing the universe.
- **No Alternative Possibilities**: Determinism suggests that in any given situation, there is only one possible outcome, and individuals could not have done otherwise.
- **Hard Determinism**: This position argues that free will is incompatible with determinism and that free will is not real.

Strengths and weaknesses of free will and determinism are as follows:

Strengths	Weaknesses
Intuitive appeal - Free will aligns with a person's subjective experience as they make choices and feel responsible for their actions.	Challenges to scientific determinism - Free will struggles to reconcile with scientific explanations that emphasize cause-and-effect relationships in the natural world.
Moral responsibility - If humans have free will, they can be held morally accountable for their choices, which is fundamental to legal and ethical systems.	Free will might lead to unrealistic expectations, especially if individuals set overly ambitious goals or feel excessive guilt when they fall short.
Promotes agency and motivation - Belief in free will can encourage individuals to take initiative, strive for self-improvement, and believe in their ability to shape their lives.	Potential for overestimation of control. Belief in free will can lead to a tendency to blame individuals for their circumstances, even when external factors play a significant role.
Scientific consistency - Determinism is consistent with scientific methods that seek to understand the causes of events.	Determinism challenges moral responsibility. If all actions are predetermined, then it raises questions about whether individuals can be truly held accountable for their choices.
Accountability for social issues - Determinism can help explain how social and environmental factors contribute to individual behaviors, potentially leading to more effective solutions for social problems.	Determinism may lead to fatalism and apathy. Belief in determinism can lead to a sense of hopelessness and a lack of motivation to change one's circumstances.
Predictive power – Determinism can help predict future outcomes, which is valuable in fields like science, engineering, and even social planning.	Un-falsifiability of hard determinism. Hard determinism, which asserts that all actions are causally determined, is difficult to disprove, as it relies on the assumption that all causes are knowable.

Components of Metaphysics – Existence vs. Subsistence

In the concept of metaphysics, existence refers to the state of being real and present as represented by a mode of being for individual, spatial-temporal specific entities. On the other hand, subsistence represents the state of being or continuing to exist, often in relation to the necessary conditions for continued existence, represented by the mode of being for abstract entities or universals (such as a specific color) that exist independently of particular instances for living entities. Examples of questions that fall under these metaphysical concepts may include:

- Does God exist?
- Does this specific chair exist?
- Is there a limit to the size of an existing object?
- What is the essence of a chair?
- What is the relationship between a quality and the object that it qualifies?

Forms of existence include the following:

- **Concrete Existence**: The existence of physical, tangible objects that occupy space and time, like a tree or a desk.
- **Abstract Existence**: The existence of things like mathematical concepts and numbers, which are not physical but still exist in a sense.
- **Possible Existence**: The entities that might exist but do not necessarily exist in the actual world, such as a dragon.
- **Contingent Existence**: Entities that exist but could have been different; or not existed at all (for instance, a specific person).
- **Necessary Existence**: Entities that must exist and cannot exhibit non-existence. For instance, the necessary existence of a personal deity.

Forms of subsistence include the following:

- **Mode of Being**: Subsistence is not just about whether something exists, but how it exists.
- **Abstract Objects**: Even abstract objects, like numbers, may be said to subsist in a realm of logic or mathematical structure.
- **Fundamental Reality**: Certain things may "subsist" in a more fundamental way than others. For instance, Plato's *Theory of Forms* suggests that Forms (abstract concepts) subsist in a higher realm of reality, and physical objects participate in or imitate them.
- **Properties and Relations**: Subsistence can also be understood in terms of the properties and the relations that define a thing's existence. For instance, a desk's subsistence is allied to its function, materials, structure, and form.
- **Essence and Existence**: Existence is seen as distinct from essence (what a thing is). A thing's essence determines what it is, while its existence is the actuality of that essence.

Characteristics of existence vs. subsistence include the following:

- **Focus**: Existence deals with particular, individual objects possessing a specific location in space and time, while subsistence represents universals, abstract entities, and properties that can be present within multiple particulars.
- **Key concepts**: Existence is allied to entities interacting with each other throughout space and time; however, subsistence is allied to properties that exist differently from particular physical objects.

Strengths and weaknesses of existence and subsistence are as follows:

Strengths	Weaknesses
Existence is often grounded on empirical observation and experience, making it easier to ground metaphysical claims in the observable world.	Existence concepts might result in oversimplification as they focus solely on existence and might overlook the deeper, underlying reasons why things are as they are.
The concept of existence is clear, definite, and relatable in everyday life.	The concept of existence might offer a limited scope in addressing certain metaphysical questions, such as the nature of possibility, necessity, and the ultimate ground of being.
Subsistence can lead to a better understanding of the fundamental nature of reality and the relationships between different entities.	The concept of subsistence can be abstract and challenging to understand, making it difficult to connect with everyday experience.
The concept of subsistence offers a way to potentially identify universal principles that underlie all existence.	The concept of subsistence may lack clarity and lack a shared understanding due to ambiguous and multiple interpretations.

Components of Metaphysics – Materialism vs. Idealism

In metaphysics, materialism and idealism maintain two (2) opposing views on the fundamental nature of reality. Materialism asserts that matter is the only substance, and all phenomena, including consciousness, are the result of material interactions. On the other hand, idealism posits that reality is fundamentally mental, so that ideas and consciousness are primary. These opposing views may be categorized under materialistic monism, where everything is believed to be physical, or idealistic monism, where reality is deemed fundamentally mental.

Examples of questions that fall under these metaphysical concepts include the following:

- What is the nature of consciousness if everything is ultimately material?
- Can materialism be reconciled with non-physical phenomena like emotions, thoughts, and values?
- What is the nature of the external world if it is ultimately a product of the mind?
- What are the practical implications of idealism for ethics, social justice, and personal growth?

Forms of materialism and idealism include the following:

- **Reductive Materialism**: The materialistic view that mental states are ultimately identical to physical brain states.
- **Eliminative Materialism**: The materialistic view that mental states, as traditionally conceived, do not exist. As a result, all mental talk is reducible to neuroscience.
- **Non-Reductive Materialism**: The materialistic view that mental states exist, but they are not identical to physical brain states and cannot be reduced to them.
- **Subjective Idealism**: The idealistic view that reality relies on individual minds. For instance, Berkeley's view: "to be is to be perceived".
- **Objective Idealism**: The idealistic view that reality is dependent on a universal or an objective mind and consciousness.

Characteristics of materialism and idealism include the following:

- **Ontological Primacy**: Materialism's core idea is ultimately reducible to physical matter and its properties, while idealism holds to reality as fundamentally mental or spiritual, so that ideas, consciousness, or the mind are primary; and, matter may be dependent on or may be an aspect of the mind.
- **Nature of Reality**: Materialists see reality as objective and independent of consciousness, while idealists see it as subjective and dependent on consciousness.
- **Explanation of Phenomena**: Materialists explain everything through physical processes, while idealists may appeal to mental or to spiritual causes.

Strengths and weaknesses of existence and subsistence are as follows:

Strengths	Weaknesses
Materialism aligns with scientific findings, particularly in neuroscience and physics, which often demonstrate correlations between physical processes and mental phenomena.	Materialism suffers the hard problem of consciousness, where it struggles to explain how physical processes give rise to subjective, qualitative experiences (qualia), such as the feeling of pain.
Materialism can draw on empirical evidence from scientific experiments and observations, making it appealing.	Materialism reduces everything to physical matter, which can oversimplify complex phenomena, potentially overlooking the unique properties of consciousness and mental states.
Idealism explains consciousness at the center of reality, offering a seemingly natural explanation for subjective experience and the mind-body problem.	Idealism carries the potential for Solipsism, which is an extremely subjective form of idealism that insists only one's own mind is sure to exist – a difficult position to defend.
Idealism provides a framework for understanding intangible phenomena such as values, morality, and spiritual experiences, which are often difficult to explain from a purely materialistic perspective.	Idealism often lacks the empirical evidence that supports materialistic views, making it less convincing to those whom rely on scientific findings.

Components of Metaphysics – Theories of Meaning & Mind

Theories of meaning encompass a myriad of philosophical concepts that examine how symbols such as expressions, words, and sentences acquire their meanings, particularly in the context of language and thought. Furthermore, these theories explore how meaning relates to the mind and mental representations. As a result, these theories naturally overlap with the philosophy of mind, which examines the mental states, consciousness, and their relationship to the physical body, particularly the brain. Researchers often categorize the theories of meaning into the following subdivisions:

- **Semantic Theories of Meaning**: These theories relay the specific meanings of expressions within a particular symbol or language system, answering the question, "What is the meaning of this expression?".
- **Foundational Theories of Meaning**: These theories explore the ultimate basis of meaning, seeking to explain how expressions end up with their meanings. In essence, they examine the relationship between language, thought, and reality to address the question, "What makes an expression have meaning?".

Philosophical doctrines tied to theories of meaning and mind are as follows:

- **Panpsychism** is a philosophical doctrine that suggests all matter, however small, possesses some form of individual consciousness. Panpsychism offers philosophers an attractive middle ground between physicalism and dualism. The strongest argument for panpsychism is the intrinsic nature argument, which holds that if it is acknowledged that physical matter maintains an intrinsic and non-dispositional nature, then consciousness is the only intrinsic nature the world is familiar with. Ultimately, it is implied that matter may have a mentalistic nature. However, the strongest argument against panpsychism is the combination problem, which beckons the question, "How do the simple, fundamental consciousnesses of individual particles combine to form the complex consciousness that is collectively experienced?".
- **Animism** is a doctrine that expresses belief in the presence of souls and spirits in both living entities and inanimate objects, be it plants, animals, rocks, places, or the weather. It is a belief that the inevitable possession of a spiritual life force elicits an emphasis on the interconnectedness of all entities, prompting practices of respect, honor, and communion with spirits. Arguments in favor of animism are grounded in the idea that this worldview potentially boosts a more holistic understanding of the world by building a deeper connection with nature and increasing respect for the environment. Conversely, those arguments against animism center on its potential for irrationality, a lack of empirical evidence, and ultimately, the possibility of hindering scientific progress.
- **Hylozoism** is the philosophical doctrine that all matter is unified with life or spiritual activity, so that all matter is, in some sense, alive, either in itself or as participating in the action of a superior principle, usually the world-soul (anima mundi). Arguments in favor of hylozoism are grounded in the complex structures and processes observable in nature, suggesting an inherent capacity for organization and intricacy within matter. Thus, hylozoism might be interpreted as evidence of a life principle inherent in all matter from the formation of crystals to the development of biological organisms. However, arguments against the doctrine center around the lack of empirical evidence and blurred distinctions between living and non-living entities. Ultimately, concepts such as free will and agency are undermined as a result of attributing life to inanimate objects.
- **Pantheism** is the worldview that god and the universe (cosmos) are identical, so that there exists nothing which is outside of god. On the one hand, arguments in favor of pantheism highlight the interconnectedness of all things, emphasizing the universe's intrinsic beauty and complexity as evidence of its divinity; however, arguments against pantheism question the doctrine's ability to account for personal consciousness and agency – not to mention, the problem of evil, where academics have labelled it as a euphemism for atheism because it denies

any theory of the supernatural by calling the universe 'god'.

- **Panentheism** is the belief that god not only encompasses the universe but also transcends it – existing beyond it. A strong argument favoring panentheism is its ability to recognize the concept of a transcendent, all-powerful god involved in the workings of the world, often thought to mean a divine entity energizes the world, experiences or prehends the world, ensouls the world, plays with the world, enfolds the world, gives space to the world, binds up the world by giving the divine self to the world, provides the ground of emergences in/of the world, befriends the world, encapsulates all worldly things, and graces the world. However, arguments against panentheism are grounded in the perceived limitations of god's nature (inadequate concept of transcendence), seeing as notions of god being in the world might also be applied to classical theism, thus suggesting a lack of distinctiveness from classical theism.
- **Pancognitivism** is the philosophical idea that everything is fundamentally conscious in reality. A strong argument for its validity is grounded in the combination problem in philosophy of mind, where it asserts that given thought is present at the fundamental and ubiquitous level of reality, so there is no need to explain how consciousness arises from non-conscious matter. Conversely, arguments against its validity are built around the lack of empirical evidence and the lack of explanatory power behind entities that exhibit complex cognitive abilities, such as humans and animals.
- **Panexperientialism** is the view that conscious experience is fundamental and ubiquitous in nature. Its validity is centered around its potential to solve the hard problem of consciousness (the idea that consciousness is not unique to humans), where it suggests that consciousness is not an emergent property of complex systems but rather a fundamental aspect of reality. This might overcome the difficulty of explaining how subjective experience arises from pure physicality. On the other hand, arguments against its validity center on the difficulty of attributing experience to simple entities (combination problem), beckoning the question: "How do the experiences of individual, simple entities combine to create the complex experiences of living beings?".
- **Panprotopsychism** is a belief similar to panpsychism that holds that fundamental physical entities possess proto-experiential (proto-consciousness) properties. Arguments supporting its validity highlight the problem of consciousness and its relationship to the physical world, so that Panprotopsychism reconciles physicalism (the philosophy that everything is ultimately physical) and dualism (the philosophy that mind and matter are distinct substances), potentially offering a more comprehensive view of reality. On the other hand, arguments against its validity highlight the challenges in defining proto-experiences, seeing as it is not always clear how they differ from non-experiential properties, nor how these proto-experiences combine to form conscious experience.
- **Constitutive cosmopsychism** is the combined view of priority monism and constitutive panpsychism, stating that all facts are realized by and constituted of consciousness-involving facts at the cosmic level. Arguments boosting its validity include the potential to address the problem of consciousness and to offer a unified worldview by suggesting mental and physical aspects are not separate entities, but rather different facets of the same fundamental reality. In contrast, arguments against its validity include the lack of empirical evidence as well as the de-combination problem, which poses the question: "How does individual consciousness arise from a universal consciousness?". Besides, if the cosmic consciousness (universe) bears transparent access to all individual experiences, then how do individual subjects maintain their distinctness?
- **Constitutive panpsychism** is a form of panpsychism according to which facts about human and animal consciousness are not fundamental, but are grounded in and constituted of facts about more fundamental kinds of consciousness, such as facts about micro-level consciousness. Proponents pinpoint its potential to solve the mind-body problem by eliminating the need to explain consciousness as arising from non-conscious matter, and its compatibility with the idea that consciousness might be more widespread than commonly assumed. In contrast, arguments against the notion include the combination problem and the revelation problem, which hypothesize the following question: "If fundamental particles have intrinsic phenomenal

properties, why can't we, through introspection, discover these properties within ourselves?".

- **Constitutive micropsychism** is the most common form of constitutive panpsychism, asserting that all facts are realized by and constituted of consciousness-involving facts at the micro-level. Favorable arguments include the doctrine's ability to evade the explanatory gap between physical and phenomenal properties and its alignment with a principle of ontological parsimony by positing a fundamental and ubiquitous consciousness. However, critics have pointed out that this form of constitutive panpsychism struggles with both the combination problem and the revelation problem, failing to explain why entities do not introspect these micro-consciousnesses directly.
- **Non-Constitutive panpsychism** is a form of panpsychism according to which facts about human and animal consciousness are among the fundamental facts. In support of its validation, panpsychism, including non-constitutive forms, is argued to sidestep the dualist's problem of elaborating on the interaction between mind and matter by presenting consciousness as a fundamental, and not necessarily a composed aspect of reality. On the other hand, it poses potential for absurd implications that panpsychism, even non-constitutive, may result in counterintuitive insinuations, such as attributing consciousness to inanimate objects like pens, which many find absurd.

Absurdism and metaphysics are distinct philosophical concepts that are closely related. Metaphysics explores the fundamental nature of reality, accounting for concepts such as existence, time, and space; however, absurdism explores the conflict between humanity's inherent desire for meaning and the universe's seeming meaninglessness. Absurdism was predominantly accepted as the separation of thought from reality based on the following:

- **Metaphysical Rebellion**: A form of revolt against creation and the human condition of suffering, inherent limitations, and perceived meaninglessness of life.
- **Existentialism**: A philosophical approach built around individual existence, freedom, and responsibility that inspires humans to create their own meaning and values through active choices, given that they are born without a predetermined essence.

In the philosophical sense, absurdism argues against fundamental questions presented in metaphysics, asserting that an attempt to find meaning leads people into conflict either between intention and outcome or between subjective assessment and objective worth. Subjectivism and objectivism are contrasting philosophical viewpoints where the former represents beliefs based on individual perspectives or feelings, while the latter is grounded in an existence independent of individual minds or perspectives.

In this manner, absurdism relates closely to the philosophical concept of nihilism, which suggests that life is inherently meaningless and that traditional values, beliefs, and knowledge are groundless. Being confronted with this conflict might trigger negative encounters of anxiety and depression in association with the following phenomena:

- **Philosophical Pessimism**: A philosophical tradition that inherently suggests that non-existence is preferable to existence and that suffering outweighs pleasure. This outlook follows the unpleasant views of life being fundamentally flawed due to the fleeting nature of happiness, the lack of inherent purpose, and the prevalence of pain.
- **Existential Crisis**: A period of inner conflict and deep confusion about life's meaning, purpose, and personal identity.

Nonetheless, while nihilism typically results in a sense of hopelessness and inaction, absurdism deliberates on how to face the conflict of an irrational and meaningless world through a defiant and passionate engagement with life. Despite recognizing the apparent absence of life's objective meaning, absurdism encourages humans to be conscious thinkers and find subjective meaning in life.

Although the preparation of knowledge articles can be tedious, the objective is to promote a rational mindset that allows the reader to inquire about all things, to challenge all biases, to evaluate evidence holistically, and to sharpen awareness/consciousness. In this way, the reader will become less vulnerable to ego-driven decisions, self-doubt, and manipulation tactics.

Em Hotep!

EPISTEMOLOGY

ANKH WADJA SENEB | ARTICLE NO: 002

Function: Preparation of Knowledge
Intent: Increase Rationality & Mental Facility
Position: Part 1 – Preliminaries & Fundamentals

ARTICLE NO: 002 – EPISTEMOLOGY

Peace to the High Power! Peace to the Living Universe! Peace to all Finite Living Beings! Peace to All Things – seen and unseen! For my spirit is with me, my image is with me, and my purpose is with me. For wisdom belongs to the seekers in heavy pursuit of knowledge, which can only be ascertained through the preparation and the sharpening of mental facility; and, knowledge is the protective shield against intellectual danger and exploitative measures.

Recall that philosophy is a vital discipline that provides clarification, rationality, and logical analysis of central questions around the nature, the meaning, and the root of life.

Epistemology is the branch of philosophy concerned with the study of knowledge, including its origin, nature, and scope of knowledge, exploring questions such as *What do humans know?*, *How do they know it?*, and *What are the limits to their knowledge?*.

Epistemologists typically focus on propositional knowledge rather than procedural or acquaintance knowledge. A proposition is a statement expressed in a declarative sentence with the intention of describing a fact or a state of affairs. Nonetheless, the proposition need not be factual, meaning it may be true or false. For instance, 'Cats are mammals', '2+2=5', and 'It is wrong to murder innocent people' are declarative propositional statements. Such statements of propositional knowledge (or the lack thereof) can be converted using "that"-clauses, such as "He knows that cats are mammals" or "She does not know that 2+2 is equal to five". Resultantly, propositional knowledge can be described as knowledge-that, and it may encompass knowledge pertaining to a wide range of matters, including scientific knowledge, geographical knowledge, mathematical knowledge, self-knowledge, and knowledge about any discipline. Ultimately, the chief concerns of epistemology are as follows:

- **Understanding the Definition of Knowledge**: To determine the nature of knowledge, one must deliberate on what it means to say that someone knows - or fails to know – something as an indisputable fact.
- **Examining the Validity of Knowledge**: Different types of propositional knowledge are made distinguishable based on the source of that knowledge in the effort to separate factual knowledge and mere opinion. Some philosophers follow rationalism, where all knowledge is ultimately grounded upon reason. Others follow empiricism, where all knowledge is ultimately grounded upon experience. As a result, non-empirical or a priori knowledge is possible independently of, or prior to, any experience, and it requires only the use of reason, including the knowledge of logical truths (Law of Non-Contradiction or Knowledge of Abstract Claims). Empirical or a posteriori knowledge, however, is possible only subsequent, or posterior, to certain sense experiences alongside the use of reason, including the knowledge of the color or shape of a physical object as well as the knowledge of geographical locations.

Ultimately, a thorough examination addresses all kinds of knowledge through inquiry (investigating specific questions or phenomena) using the methods of empiricism (focusing on sensory experience as the primary source of knowledge), rationalism (emphasizing reason and innate ideas as sources of knowledge), and skepticism (questioning the possibility of certain knowledge).

- **Determining the Scope of Knowledge**: The extent of human knowledge must be determined based on the following questions:
  - How much do we know?
  - How much can we know?
  - How can we use our reason, senses, the testimony of others, and other resources to acquire knowledge?
  - Are there limits to what we can know?
  - Are there unknowable things?
  - Is it possible that we do not know nearly as much as we think we do?
  - Should we have a legitimate worry about skepticism, which is the view that we do not or cannot know anything at all?

The scope of epistemology is so broad, necessitating a general characterization of knowledge, which applies to all forms of propositions. As a result, epistemologists undertook a complete analysis of the concept of knowledge and agreed on a set of individually necessary and sufficient conditions, which determine the validity of knowledge. The following are fundamentals of epistemology:

- **Belief**: A belief is described as the acceptance that a statement is true. Beliefs actively entertained by an individual are called occurrent beliefs; however, beliefs that the individual has in the background, but are not entertaining at a particular time, are non-occurrent. Correspondingly, most human knowledge is non-occurrent, because only a small percentage of one's knowledge is ever actively entertained in the mind.
- **Truth**: A statement is true if it corresponds to reality. While knowledge requires belief, not all beliefs constitute knowledge because they might be false. Epistemologists assume that there is always an objective truth, so that it is possible for beliefs to match or to fail to match with reality.
- **Justification**: Justification is the reason or the evidence supporting a belief. Ultimately, knowledge calls for factual belief, also known as a justified true belief (JTB) – a belief purported to be true after it is supported by sufficient evidence. Besides, the strongest arguments for knowledge being justified revolve around the observation that a justified belief will presumably be more likely to be true than to be false, and justified beliefs will presumably be more likely or more probable to be true than unjustified beliefs. Critics, however, highlight the Gettier problem, claiming that the justification condition is supposed to ensure that knowledge is based on solid evidence rather than luck – thus, not falling short of knowledge.

Branches of Epistemology include the following:

- **Social Epistemology** investigates the epistemic effects of social interactions, practices, norms, and systems in society. In essence, it focuses on how social factors may impact knowledge, including testimonies, peer disagreement, collective knowledge, and the influence of social institutions. Using both descriptive (exploring how things are) and normative (exploring how things should be) means, it answers the questions, such as *How do we acquire knowledge from others?*, *How do social structures affect the spread of knowledge?*, and *What role do communities play in knowledge creation and validation?*. Moreover, it determines whether a person living alone on a remote island can still possess knowledge.

- **Formal Epistemology** explores knowledge and reasoning, using the formal tools of math and logic, such as probability theory and modal logic in the analysis of knowledge, belief, and reasoning. It aims to provide a precise and a rigorous framework for understanding epistemic concepts and processes, answering questions such as, *What is knowledge?*, *How is knowledge different from mere opinion?*, *What separates science from pseudoscience?*, *When is a belief justified?*, and *What justifies my belief that the sun will rise tomorrow?*.
- **Meta Epistemology** concerns questions pertaining to first-order and second-order epistemological inquiries in the examination of foundations and assumptions. It questions the nature of knowledge, justification, and belief rather than directly addressing specific knowledge claims. Such questions include *What is the proper subject matter of epistemology?*, *What are the goals of the epistemological inquiry?*, and *What are the best methods for doing epistemology?*.

Epistemology encompasses several accepted theories that address the nature, scope, and sources of knowledge. Some of the most prominent ones are listed below:

- **Foundationalism** generally suggests that beliefs are structured in a hierarchy with foundational beliefs supporting other beliefs. In that regard, some beliefs are basic, so that they are self-justifying and without the need for further justification from other beliefs. Naturally, these basic beliefs serve as the foundation for all other knowledge. Examples of basic beliefs might include sensory perceptions or logical axioms. Nonetheless, foundationalism faces the challenge of identifying which beliefs are truly basic and how they can provide a stable foundation for other beliefs.
- **Coherentism** posits that beliefs are justified by their coherence with other beliefs in a system. This way, a belief is believed to be justified if it fits well with the overall system of beliefs, even without relying on any single basic belief. However, coherentism faces the challenge of determining what constitutes a coherent system of beliefs and how to ensure that a coherent system is also true.
- **Reliabilism** focuses on the reliability of the processes that produce beliefs. According to this approach, a belief is justified to be true if it is produced by a reliable cognitive process, such as perception, memory, or reasoning. Ultimately, reliabilism faces the challenge of defining what makes a cognitive process reliable and how to determine the reliability of a process in a specific situation.
- **Virtue Epistemology** relies on the intellectual virtues of the knower. This approach shifts the focus from the structure of knowledge to the intellectual virtues of the knower. Virtues, such as attentiveness, open-mindedness, and intellectual courage, are seen as essential for acquiring knowledge. Ultimately, virtue epistemology faces the challenge of identifying which virtues are relevant to knowledge and how to monitor the extent to which someone possesses those virtues.
- **Epistemic Contextualism** is a theory that proposes that the standards for knowledge vary according to the context in which a belief is being examined. Following this approach, what counts as sufficient justification for knowledge in one context may not necessarily be sufficient in another. Contextualism faces the challenge of defining what constitutes a relevant context and how to determine the appropriate standards for justification in each context.

Epistemology prompted the emergence of many schools of thought that explore the nature and limits of human knowledge. Some are described below:

- **Rationalism**, campaigned by philosophers such as Plato and Descartes, asserts that reason and innate ideas are the primary sources of knowledge. There is a strong emphasis on mathematics and logic as examples of knowledge accessible through reason, especially to prove a theorem or an innate mathematical principle.
- **Empiricism**, championed by John Locke and David Hume, views knowledge as being primarily derived from sensory experience and observation. This allows one to conduct experiments, to

gather data, and to form conclusions based on observations.

- **Skepticism** determines whether humans can attain certain knowledge, raising doubts about the reliability of human senses and reasoning abilities. A skeptic might argue that perception may neither be certain nor be reliable.
- **Constructivism** holds that knowledge is actively constructed by the learner rather than passively received. It emphasizes that individuals build their understanding of the world through experience, reflection, and interaction, rather than simply absorbing information. This idea contrasts with more objectivist perspectives that assume knowledge exists independently of the knower.
- **Contextualism** refers to the standards for what counts as knowledge, and they vary depending on the context of the knowledge attribution. This means that what counts as "knowing something" in one situation might not be considered knowledge in another due to shifts in the standards of evidence or relevance. Contextualism is often presented as a response to skepticism, offering a way to reconcile ordinary knowledge claims with skeptical arguments.
- **Embodied Cognition** emphasizes the role of the body and its interactions with the environment in shaping cognitive processes and knowledge acquisition. This theory challenges the traditional view that cognition is purely a disembodied, abstract, and symbolic process, suggesting instead that thoughts and the ability to understand are deeply rooted in sensorimotor experiences.
- **Neo-positivism**, also known as logical empiricism or logical positivism, stresses the importance of empirical verification and logical analysis in determining meaningful knowledge. It emerged in the 20th Century as a development of positivism, aiming to establish a scientific philosophy grounded in observable facts and logical reasoning.
- **Fallibilism** is an epistemological doctrine that no belief can be known with absolute certainty. It asserts that all knowledge claims are provisional and subject to revision or rejection based on new evidence or further inquiry. Essentially, it recognizes the inherent possibility of error in all beliefs and knowledge.
- **Foundationalism** proposes that knowledge is structured like a building, with basic, self-evident beliefs forming the foundation upon which other, more complex beliefs are built.
- **Holism** asserts that knowledge cannot be understood by analyzing individual components or beliefs in isolation but rather as interconnected units within a larger system or web of belief. It contrasts with atomism, which suggests that knowledge can be built up from basic, individual units.
- **Infinitism** proposes that the justification for any belief ultimately relies on an infinite chain of reasons, where each reason itself requires further justification. This contrasts with other views like foundationalism and coherentism, which seek to ground knowledge in foundational beliefs or interconnected sets of beliefs, respectively.
- **Innatism**, in epistemology, posits that humans are born with some inherent knowledge or ideas rather than having to acquire all knowledge through experience. This contrasts with empiricism, which maintains that the mind is a blank slate at birth, and all knowledge comes from sensory experience. Instead, innatism suggests that certain concepts or principles are pre-programmed into the mind, influencing how people perceive and understand the world.
- **Internalism** is the epistemological view that the justification for a belief is determined by factors internal to the mind of the believer. This means that whether a belief is justified depends on factors such as the believer's mental states, experiences, and reasons rather than on external factors like the reliability of the belief-forming process.
- **Externalism** is the epistemological view that factors outside of a person's internal mental states can be relevant to the justification of their beliefs. This contrasts with internalism and encompasses various theories that emphasize the role of external factors like reliable belief-forming processes, environmental conditions, or causal connections in determining whether a belief is justified or not.

- **Naïve realism**, in epistemology, is the view that human senses provide a direct and an accurate representation of the external world. It suggests that when people perceive something, they are directly experiencing the object itself, and not a mental representation of it. This view also implies that perceptions are generally reliable and that general beliefs about the world are justified by this direct access to reality.
- **Naturalized Epistemology** seeks to integrate epistemology with scientific methods, examining how knowledge is acquired and is justified within the natural world.
- **Objectivism** holds that reality exists independently of the human mind and that knowledge can accurately represent this external reality. It posits that some objective facts and truths can be discovered and verified, regardless of individual perspectives or beliefs. Objectivists emphasize the importance of reason and logic in acquiring knowledge, contrasting with views that prioritize subjective experience or social constructs.
- **Phenomenalism** holds that physical objects and the external world can only be known through sensory experiences, or phenomena. It purports that knowledge of the external world is ultimately reducible to perceptions, challenging the idea of an objective reality independent of human minds.
- **Positivism** emphasizes empirical evidence and the scientific method as the primary sources of knowledge. It asserts that knowledge is valid only if it is based on observable facts and verifiable data, aiming to discover universal laws through objective observation and logical reasoning. Positivism generally rejects metaphysical speculation and focuses on what can be directly experienced and measured.
- **Reductionism** is the view that complex epistemic phenomena can be explained by, or reduced to, simpler, more fundamental elements. It suggests that knowledge, justification, and other epistemic concepts can be understood by analyzing their constituent parts or by relating them to more basic, underlying principles.
- **Reformed Epistemology** argues that religious beliefs, particularly belief in a god, can be rational and justified even without being based on evidence or arguments. It challenges the idea that religious belief must be grounded in external proof, suggesting instead that such belief can be properly basic and arise from cognitive faculties designed by a god.
- **Representative Realism**, also known as indirect realism, is a school of thought in epistemology that posits human perceptions are not a direct reflection of the external world, but rather, mental representations and ideas that stand for external objects. It argues that human beings are not directly aware of external objects themselves, but rather of mental images and sense data that represent those objects. This view contrasts with direct realism, which asserts that humans perceive external objects directly.
- **Situated Cognition** maintains that knowledge and cognitive processes are deeply intertwined with the specific contexts, social situations, and physical environments in which they occur. It challenges the traditional view that cognition is solely an internal, individualistic, and abstract process, arguing instead that it is fundamentally shaped by the interplay between an individual and their surroundings.
- **Platonic Idealism** centers on the idea that true knowledge is derived from understanding abstract, eternal forms, or ideas, rather than from sensory experience. These forms are considered the ultimate reality, and the physical world, which individuals perceive, is merely a collection of imperfect copies or shadows of these forms. Ultimately, Plato's philosophy emphasizes reason and contemplation as the means to access this realm of forms and to attain true knowledge.
- **Transcendental Idealism**, primarily developed by Immanuel Kant, argues that human knowledge is shaped by both the mind's inherent structures and the objects of experience. It proposes that the mind actively structures human experience through categories and forms of intuition (space and time) rather than passively receiving information from the external world. This means people can only know the world as it appears to them (phenomena), not as it is in itself (noumena).

- **Uniformitarianism**, while primarily a geological concept, also has implications for epistemology. In essence, it suggests that the processes observed today have operated in the same way throughout history and across the universe. This idea, when applied to knowledge, implies a certain stability and predictability in how human beings are able to acquire and to understand information.

Once again, the objective of the preparation for knowledge articles is to promote a rational mindset that allows the reader to inquire about all things, to challenge all biases, to evaluate evidence holistically, and to sharpen awareness/consciousness. In this way, the reader will become less vulnerable to ego-driven decisions, self-doubt, and manipulation tactics.

Em Hotep!

AXIOLOGY

ANKH WADJA SENEB | ARTICLE NO: 003

Function: Preparation of Knowledge
Intent: Increase Rationality & Mental Facility
Position: Part 1 – Preliminaries & Fundamentals

ARTICLE NO: 003 – AXIOLOGY

Peace to the High Power! Peace to the Living Universe! Peace to all Finite Living Beings! Peace to All Things – seen and unseen! For my spirit is with me, my image is with me, and my purpose is with me. For wisdom belongs to the seekers in heavy pursuit of knowledge, which can only be ascertained through the preparation and the sharpening of mental facility; and, knowledge is the protective shield against intellectual danger and exploitative measures.

In philosophy, axiology studies the origin, nature, types, and functions of value and valuation, concerning itself with questions such as *What principles should an individual live by?*, *What are the desirable/ undesirable values?*, *Is morality defined by what we speak or feel?*, *What is the blueprint of family values?*, *What is true beauty?*, and *What is immoral and moral?*.

The fundamentals of axiology are as follows:

- **Nature of Value**: The essence of value, questioning whether they are intrinsic (inherent worth of something independent of its usefulness or consequences) or extrinsic (the value that something has owing to its usefulness or consequences)
- **Types of Values**: Differences between various types of values, such as moral, economic, aesthetic, and epistemic values, and explores how they interact.
- **Value Judgments**: Analysis of how individuals and societies make value judgments, what the criteria are, and what the implications of these judgments are

The methods of axiology are as follows:

- **Conceptual Analysis**: A method used in examining the meaning and the implications of value-related terms and concepts
- **Normative Analysis**: A method used in developing and evaluating ethical theories and principles that guide moral behavior.
- **Empirical Investigation**: A method used in studying how people actually behave and make value judgments in real-world contexts.
- **Formal Modeling**: A method that makes use of models such as those derived from logic, math, probability theory, and decision theory to represent and to analyze value judgments.

The theories behind axiology are as follows:

- **Value Realism**: The existence of objective values, where values exist independently of human minds.
- **Value Subjectivism**: Values dependent upon individual or cultural preferences.
- **Value Relativism**: Values being relative to specific contexts or cultures.
- **Ideal Observer Theory**: A philosophical theory that maintains that the ideal observer has perfect knowledge and rationality – thus, such an observer can make objective value judgments.

Validity in axiology generally refers to the extent to which findings accurately reflect the values and value judgments being studied, and how well those findings align with the original assumptions. Some of the ways that axiologists enhance the reliability and the trustworthiness of results include the following:

- **Logical Consistency**: Ensuring that value judgments and theories are free from internal contradictions.
- **Empirical Support**: Testing value judgments and theories against empirical evidence about human behavior and preferences.
- **Coherence with Other Beliefs**: Ensuring that values are consistent with other beliefs and principles that individuals hold.

Axiology delves into the origins of values, how they are formed, and their role in guiding human choices and actions. Resultantly, it examines both intrinsic and instrumental values as mentioned below:

- **Ethics**: Axiology provides the foundation for ethical theories by exploring the nature of good and bad, right and wrong, and how individuals should behave. It explores the question: *Is it morally permissible to lie in a particular situation?*
- **Aesthetics**: Axiology examines the nature of beauty, art, and aesthetic experience, exploring what makes something aesthetically pleasing. As such, it explores the question: *Is a particular work of art beautiful or aesthetically valuable?*
- **Social and Political Philosophy**: Axiology informs discussions about social justice, political legitimacy, and the values that should guide societies. Resultantly, it explores questions such as *Is equality a fundamental social value?*
- **Epistemology**: Axiology can also be relevant to epistemology, as it can be argued that knowledge itself is a value, and that some methods of acquiring knowledge are better than others. Here, it may explore the question: *Which sources of information should be considered reliable?*

Strengths and weaknesses of axiology are as follows:

Strengths	Weaknesses
Shapes understanding of judgments and values. Axiology inquiry helps people reflect on the principles that guide their actions and decisions at a personal and societal level.	The complexity of value judgments, made evident in multiple values, conflicting priorities, and context-dependent assessments
Axiological inquiry leads to a deeper understanding of self and the world, boosting a critical examination of beliefs, attitudes, and preferences.	The difficulty of quantifying value, proven that quantifying value can be challenging, especially when dealing with non-numerical or non-comparable values
The study of axiology develops a more informed and thoughtful approach to ethical dilemmas, aesthetic experiences, and the pursuit of a meaningful life.	The need for nuanced and context-sensitive analysis, requiring a deep understanding of the specific context and values at stake

Once again, the objective of the preparation for knowledge articles is to promote a rational mindset that allows the reader to inquire about all things, to challenge all biases, to evaluate evidence holistically, and to sharpen awareness/consciousness. In this way, the reader will become less vulnerable to ego-driven decisions, self-doubt, and manipulation tactics.

Em Hotep!

AESTHETICS

ANKH WADJA SENEB | ARTICLE NO: 004

Function: Preparation of Knowledge
Intent: Increase Rationality & Mental Facility
Position: Part 1 – Preliminaries & Fundamentals

ARTICLE NO: 004 – AESTHETICS

Peace to the High Power! Peace to the Living Universe! Peace to all Finite Living Beings! Peace to All Things – seen and unseen! For my spirit is with me, my image is with me, and my purpose is with me. For wisdom belongs to the seekers in heavy pursuit of knowledge, which can only be ascertained through the preparation and the sharpening of mental facility; and, knowledge is the protective shield against intellectual danger and exploitative measures.

Aesthetics is a branch of axiology that explores the nature of beauty, art, taste, and aesthetic experience, quickly evolving into a way of describing sensory contemplation of an object (not necessarily art-oriented) for value, appreciation, or judgment. This branch grapples with questions, such as *What constitutes beauty?*, *How do people perceive and judge art?*, and *What is the role of art in human life?*.

The fundamentals of aesthetics typically explore the nature of beauty, art, and taste, examining the principles behind artistic creation and appreciation to determine how human beings perceive, judge, and experience aesthetic qualities. Some fundamentals of aesthetics are as follows:

- **Beauty and Art**: Aesthetics explores questions concerning qualities that evoke pleasure and admiration not only as a subjective experience, but also using objective principles of form, proportion, and harmony. Furthermore, it grapples with understanding what makes anything a work of art, which can be described as creations intended to surpass other objects in their appeal.
- **Aesthetic Experience**: This fundamental concept examines the personal nature of aesthetic experience, as far as people's perceptions, emotions, and cognitions in appreciating and evaluating art and beauty.
- **Aesthetic Judgment**: A fundamental concept that explores the criteria and processes involved in evaluating aesthetic qualities, such as beauty, by questioning whether they are subjective or objective.
- **Value of Art**: It investigates the role and importance of art in human life, considering its connection to other values like truth, morality, and social meaning.

The methods of aesthetics include the following:

- **Conceptual Analysis**: Philosophers analyze concepts like "beautiful", "art", and "taste" to clarify their meaning and implications.
- **Phenomenological Analysis**: They examine the subjective experience of beauty and art, exploring how these are experienced by individuals.
- **Historical and Cultural Analysis**: Aesthetics considers how aesthetic concepts and judgments have evolved across different times and cultures.
- **Formalism**: This approach focuses on the formal elements of art (e.g., line, color, and composition) as the primary source of aesthetic value.

- **Expressionism**: This theory emphasizes the expression of emotions and feelings in art as a key aspect of an aesthetic experience.
- **Realism**: This perspective suggests that art should accurately represent reality or should reflect real-world objects.

Aesthetic theories refer to the set of principles and philosophical frameworks that explore the nature of beauty and taste in art, addressing how aesthetic enjoyment and preferences are experienced and are evaluated. Several theories have been presented in an attempt to explain the concept of beauty and art as follows:

- **Immanuel Kant's Theory of Beauty**: Emphasizing the subjective nature of beauty, Kant argues that aesthetic judgments are based on a "disinterested" pleasure (imagination) free from personal desires or practical considerations, in collaboration with an interplay of cognitive understanding. Thus, beauty is a feeling encountered when people interact with an object that pleases them at a subjective level.
- **Aesthetic Idealism of Beauty (Platonism)**: Viewing beauty as an objective ideal, Plato argues the philosophical view that beauty is transcendental and eternal, existing independently of human perception of the physical world and participating in the perfect form of the good.
- **Aristotelian Aesthetics of Beauty**: Aristotle's Theory of Beauty holds the philosophical view that beauty is found in the order, the harmony, and the proportion of things as imitated in nature with a potential to evoke emotional responses and to reveal universal truths.
- **Hegel's Theory of Art**: The philosophical view that art evolves through historical stages and reflects the spirit of an age, embodying its cultural values according to the gradual development of humanity's spiritual and self-understanding.
- **Contemporary Theories of Art**: Modern philosophical theories that focus on the social and the cultural context of art, often categorized in the following ways:
    - Emotionalism (expressionism) – Aesthetic theory concerned with the content of the work of art, requiring that a work of art arouses a response of feelings. It emphasizes the artist's emotional experience and its expression through the artwork, often with distorted or exaggerated forms.
    - Formalism – Aesthetic theory that emphasizes design qualities, focusing on the formal elements of art, such as line, color, and composition, so that the work's aesthetic value resides primarily in these elements and it can be appreciated independently of any representational or narrative content.
    - Imitationalism (realism) – The theory that recognizes successful art as that depicting life as it is, without idealization or romanticization, focusing on accurate representation of the world.

In aesthetics, psychoanalytic theory, particularly as developed by Sigmund Freud, explores how unconscious desires and conflicts, often expressed through symbolism, unconsciously influence human appreciation and creation of art. For instance, symbolism in art, viewed through a psychoanalytic lens, can reveal hidden meanings related to sexuality, aggression, and early childhood experiences, providing insights into the artist's psyche and the viewer's emotional response.

Once again, the objective of the preparation for knowledge articles is to promote a rational mindset that allows the reader to inquire about all things, to challenge all biases, to evaluate evidence holistically, and to sharpen awareness/consciousness. In this way, the reader will become less vulnerable to ego-driven decisions, self-doubt, and manipulation tactics.

Em Hotep!

ETHICS

ANKH WADJA SENEB | ARTICLE NO: 005

Function: Preparation of Knowledge
Intent: Increase Rationality & Mental Facility
Position: Part 1 – Preliminaries & Fundamentals

ARTICLE NO: 005 – ETHICS

Peace to the High Power! Peace to the Living Universe! Peace to all Finite Living Beings! Peace to All Things – seen and unseen! For my spirit is with me, my image is with me, and my purpose is with me. For wisdom belongs to the seekers in heavy pursuit of knowledge, which can only be ascertained through the preparation and the sharpening of mental facility; and, knowledge is the protective shield against intellectual danger and exploitative measures.

Ethics centers on morality, focusing on concepts around moral obligations, right vs. wrong, and 'good vs. bad'. As such, it is a moral philosophy by virtue of examining moral principles and values that guide human behavior. Ethics is based on two (2) main assumptions: (i) a human being is a rational being, and (ii) a human being is free.

Studying ethics clarifies why one act is more preferable than another, contributing to an orderly social life by providing some guiding principles and revealing the true values of life. Essentially, ethics explores fundamental questions about how individuals and societies should act, encompassing various ethical theories and practical applications. Specific questions explored in ethics include:

- What constitutes a moral life?
- What is the nature of justice and fairness?
- What are the obligations we have to each other?
- Do moral codes differ among cultures?

The fundamentals of ethics are interconnected and often require a thoughtful and nuanced approach to apply these principles in real-world situations, as described below:

- **Autonomy** emphasizes the capacity for an individual's right to make their own decisions free from coercion. It involves respecting a person's capacity for self-determination and ensuring that they have the information necessary to make informed choices.
- **Beneficence** is the principle of doing good and promoting well-being. This principle highlights the moral obligation of people to do good and to promote the well-being of others. In practice, it requires individuals to act in ways that benefit society at large, especially in the field of social work and healthcare, while supporting vulnerable populations.
- **Non-Maleficence** (do no harm) is a principle concerned with the duty of a human being to avoid actions that might cause harm to others. It requires careful consideration of potential risks and benefits before taking action and striving to minimize any negative consequences during everyday interactions.
- **Justice** is a fundamental pillar of ethics grounded in fairness and equality in the distribution of resources and opportunities. Individuals are required to treat everyone impartially and to give them what they are due. Justice calls for equitable treatment for all individuals, regardless of their background or circumstances, and addresses systemic inequalities that might lead to unfair

outcomes.

The branches of ethics are typically divided into the four (4) main areas below:

- **Metaethics** assesses how people engage in ethics by monitoring and by commenting on how an ethical game is being played rather than advancing practical arguments. This branch explores the nature of morality itself, including the meaning of moral terms, the source of moral knowledge, and the objectivity or the subjectivity of moral judgments. Some metaethical questions include the following:
    - What is the meaning of moral terms or judgments? (moral semantics)
    - What is the nature of moral judgments? (moral ontology)
    - How can moral judgments be supported or be defended? (moral epistemology)

- **Normative (Prescriptive) Ethics** focuses on the creation of theories that provide general moral rules governing human behavior, such as utilitarianism or Kantian Ethics. The normative ethicist, in a football analogy, rather than being a football player, is more like a referee whom establishes the rules governing how the game is played. It includes theories such as utilitarianism (maximizing overall happiness), deontology (duty-based ethics), and virtue ethics (focusing on character development). Some normative questions include the following:
    - How do we cultivate virtuous character?
    - What are our duties to others?
    - What is the best way to maximize overall well-being or happiness?

- **Applied Ethics** examines how individuals should act in specific areas of their lives as well as specific moral issues in various contexts. Some questions in applied ethics include the following:
    - Under what conditions is an act morally permissible?
    - What are our obligations to protect others or even the environment?
    - How should governments deal with refugees?

- **Descriptive Ethics** evaluates human actions based on law and customs. Societies have structured their moral principles, which evolve gradually over time, and people are expected to behave accordingly. Also known as comparative ethics, it compares the ethics of the past and the present, and considers insight from other disciplines to explain the moral rightness and moral wrongness. Some questions in descriptive ethics include the following:
    - What percentage of people in the United States believe that stealing is always wrong?
    - What are the most common reasons people give for donating to charity?
    - How do people's moral values change as they age or as they experience different life events?

Theories of ethics offer different perspectives on moral decision-making, focusing on aspects such as consequences, duties, and character, as discussed below.

Deontology

Deontology is an ethical theory that judges the morality of actions based on whether they adhere to a set of rules or duties, regardless of the consequences. Such a theory contends that the ideal ethical action protects and respects the moral rights of those impacted. The fundamental assumption is that people have dignity as a result of their human nature or free choice. Based on such dignity, people have the right to be recognized as goals in themselves rather than just as means to other objectives. It contrasts with consequentialism, which focuses on the outcome of actions. Essentially, deontological ethics emphasizes that some actions are inherently right or wrong independent of their results, as indicated in the examples below:

- **Kantianism**: A prominent deontological theory, Kantianism emphasizes the importance of acting according to universal moral laws, such as "do not lie" or "do not steal". For example, a Kantian would argue that lying is always wrong, even if it leads to a positive outcome.
- **Prima Facie Duties**: W.D. Ross's theory suggests that human beings have several prima facie duties that guide their actions, including fidelity, justice, and beneficence. When these duties conflict, they must be weighed to determine the most compelling action.
- **Social Contract Theory**: Deontological theories like Rawls's Theory of Justice emphasize the importance of social contracts and agreements as a basis for moral duties.

The key points of deontology are provided below.

Concepts	Duty: Human beings have moral duties and obligations that they must fulfill. Rules: These duties are often expressed as rules or principles that guide human behavior. Intention: The moral worth of an action is determined by the intention behind it, not the outcome.
Strengths	Clear Moral Framework: A clear and consistent framework for decision-making based on established rules and duties. Emphasis on Human Dignity: The inherent worth and dignity of every individual, suggesting that people should not be treated as mere means to an end. Protection of Rights: Certain rights are inherent and should be protected, regardless of their consequences. Encourages Social Stability: A focus on duties and rules can promote social order and stability by establishing clear expectations for behavior.
Weaknesses	Rigidity: Deontology can be inflexible and may lead to undesirable outcomes in complex or unusual situations, where following a rule might not be the best course of action. Conflicting Duties: It can be difficult to resolve conflicts between competing moral duties or rules.

	Lack of Consideration for Consequences: Deontology might not adequately consider the consequences of actions, potentially leading to negative outcomes despite adherence to rules. Difficulty in Determining Moral Rules: It can be challenging to determine which rules or duties are morally binding and how they should be prioritized.

There is an interesting paradox to deontics, known as the Paradox of Supererogation. The Paradox of Supererogation stems from three conflicting, yet plausible, claims:

1. Supererogatory acts (morally optional acts that are better than the minimum required) exist.
2. If an act is supererogatory, then it is the morally best action available compared to all other alternatives.
3. The more reason principle - If an act is the best, then it should be obligatory.

The deontic conflict in the paradox is that these claims cannot all be true simultaneously within traditional deontic (moral obligation) frameworks. If an act is the best, why is it not required? Conversely, if an act is optional, how can it be the morally best act to perform?

Resolutions to the paradox generally try to break the logical chain by modifying one of the claims, often the second or the third claim, as listed below:

- **Multi-Dimensional Reasons**: One prominent view suggests that acts are not universally better but better in one specific way (e.g., "justifying reasons") while being opposed by other types of reasons (e.g., "requiring reasons") that make them optional.
- **Conditional Evaluation:** The idea that supererogatory acts are not absolutely the best but only best under certain conditions or in comparison to specific alternatives.
- **Revisiting the More Reason Principle**: Some propose that the more reason principle is not a universally applicable rule and that there can be "weighty reasons" of a different kind that counterbalance reasons to perform the act, even if it is the best option.
- **Focus on the Definition of Supererogation**: Some arguments refine the definition of supererogation to avoid the paradox altogether, clarifying that it is merely "comparatively better" rather than absolutely good.

Utilitarianism

Utilitarianism is a moral theory concerned with maximizing overall well-being, so that the best action/decision is one that results in the greatest amount of happiness for the largest number of people. It offers a straightforward approach to decision-making but faces challenges in accurately measuring happiness and potentially justifying harmful actions.

Strengths and weaknesses of utilitarianism are as follows:

Strengths	Weaknesses
Clear Decision-Making Framework: Provides a relatively straightforward method for determining the best course of action by focusing on maximizing overall happiness or well-being.	Justification of Harmful Actions: The focus on maximizing overall happiness could potentially be used to justify actions that are inherently harmful or wrong, as long as they lead to a net positive outcome.
Promotes the Greatest Good: By striving for the greatest happiness for the greatest number, utilitarianism aims to benefit society as a whole, which can be seen as a desirable outcome.	Difficulty in Measuring Happiness: It can be challenging to measure and to compare happiness accurately across different individuals or situations, making it difficult to determine the best outcome.
Focus on Consequences: It emphasizes the outcomes of actions, which can be helpful in situations where maximizing positive results is crucial.	Complexity and Subjectivity: Applying utilitarianism can be complex, as different individuals might have different ideas about what constitutes happiness or well-being.
Neutral and Impartial: Utilitarianism considers everyone's well-being equally, promoting fairness and impartiality in decision-making.	Potential for Sacrificing Individual Rights: In some cases, utilitarianism might justify actions that infringe upon the rights or well-being of a minority group for the benefit of the majority, raising ethical concerns about individual liberties.

Virtue Ethics

Virtue ethics illuminates character and moral development, maintaining that ethical behaviors should be compatible with certain virtues that allow for the complete development of humanity. These virtues are dispositions and habits that boost the best potential behaviors alongside attribute values such as truth, honesty, bravery, and compassion.

Strengths and weaknesses of virtue ethics are as follows:

Strengths	Weaknesses
Focus on Character: Virtue ethics emphasizes the importance of developing good character traits, such as honesty, compassion, and courage, rather than simply following rules or focusing on outcomes.	Potential for Conflicting Virtues: Different virtues might conflict in certain situations, leading to dilemmas about which virtue to prioritize.
Pragmatic and Flexible: It acknowledges that morality is not a one-size-fits-all concept and allows for societal differences and the acceptance of partiality while maintaining fairness.	Vague and Subjective: The emphasis on individual character and subjective interpretation can lead to a lack of clarity and objectivity in moral judgments.
Holistic Approach: It considers all aspects of a person's character and motivations, including physical, spiritual, mental, and emotional aspects.	Lack of Specific Action-Guidance: It does not provide clear rules or guidelines for how to act in specific situations, making it difficult to apply in some contexts.
Addresses the Complexity of Human Experience: It acknowledges the nuances and the complexities of moral decision-making in real-life situations.	Difficulty in Applying in Crisis Situations: In situations requiring immediate action, virtue ethics might not provide the clear guidance needed for making quick decisions.

Social Contracts

Social contract theory holds that moral rules are those that are acceptable to all members of society; however, they must be objective when analyzing their moral value. While providing a foundation for individual rights and responsibilities within a society, it faces challenges related to consent, reciprocity, acceptance, and the practical application of its principles.

Strengths and weaknesses of social contracts are as follows:

Strengths	Weaknesses
Legitimacy of Government: It offers a justification for the existence of government, arguing that its legitimacy stems from the consent of the governed, whether explicit or implicit.	Potential for Government Overreach: Can be interpreted as a justification for government overreach, particularly in the name of security or public safety.
Foundation for Rights and Responsibilities: Social contract theory establishes a framework for individual rights and societal obligations, providing a basis for just governance and a sense of civic duty.	Unequal Societies: The social contract may not be fair or beneficial to all members, as power imbalances can affect the bargaining process and the distribution of benefits and burdens.
Framework for Democracy: It provides a philosophical basis for democratic principles, emphasizing the importance of individual participation and consent in the political process.	Overemphasis on Reciprocity: The focus on reciprocity can overshadow the importance of equity and fairness, potentially leading to situations where the benefits of the social contract are not distributed equitably.
Protection of Individual Liberty: By outlining the limits of government power and the rights that individuals retain, it can be a powerful tool for protecting individual liberties.	Limited Scope in Informal Economies: Social contract theory may be less relevant or applicable in highly informal economies where the relationship between individuals and the state is less clearly defined.

Moral Error Theory

Moral error theory is roughly the view that morality may be a biologically useful illusion. More precisely, error theory combines views from cognitivism and representationalism to create moral judgments with an antirealist view of the moral domain. Ideally, all moral judgments are systematically false because they mistakenly presuppose the existence of objective moral properties. Nonetheless, while it offers a compelling critique of moral realism, error theory faces challenges regarding the practicality of living without moral beliefs and potential inconsistencies within its own framework.

Strengths and weaknesses of moral error theory are as follows:

Strengths	Weaknesses
Explains Moral Disagreement: Error theory can explain the persistent and widespread disagreements about moral values by suggesting that these disagreements stem from a false belief in objective moral truths.	The Belief Problem: Difficult to explain how people can function with the belief that all moral judgments are false. How then can people continue to act on moral claims?
Addresses the Queerness Argument: It aligns with the idea that objective moral values would be strange and difficult to explain from a naturalistic perspective, offering a way to avoid this "queerness" by denying their existence.	Morean Arguments: Many argue that the strength of moral beliefs makes it more plausible that they are true rather than systematically false.
Provides a Framework for Moral Discourse: Even while claiming moral judgments are false, error theory can offer a way to understand and to analyze moral discourse by focusing on the psychological aspects, motivations, and social functions of moral claims.	Practical Implications: A world without moral beliefs might be practically challenging, as it might undermine motivation, social cohesion, and the basis for legal and political systems.

Natural Rights Theory

Natural Law theory, which posits that morality can be discerned through reason and observation of the natural world, believes in the existence of absolute inherent rights that are bestowed upon humans just by their humanity. It provides a framework for understanding universal moral principles, but faces challenges in its reliance on human reason, potential for outdated conclusions, and varying interpretations.

Strengths and weaknesses of the natural rights theory are as follows:

Strengths	Weaknesses
Community Cohesion: Shared understanding of natural law can foster social harmony and cooperation by providing a common basis for moral judgments.	Fixed Human Nature: Critics argue that Natural Law's assumption of a fixed human nature is simplistic, overlooking the complexity and diversity of human experiences and behaviors.
Universal Moral Guidelines: Natural law offers a foundation for ethical decision-making, suggesting inherent moral principles accessible through reason, applicable across cultures and time.	Reliance on Human Reason: The theory's reliance on human reason can be problematic, as different individuals might interpret natural law differently or reach conflicting conclusions.
Appeals to Reason: Natural Law emphasizes the role of reason in understanding moral truths, making it potentially accessible to those with different religious or philosophical beliefs.	Theological Dependence: Some interpretations of natural law are rooted in religious beliefs, such as god-given purpose, which might limit its appeal to non-theists.
Objective Basis for Morality: Natural Law provides a sense of objective morality, contrasting with subjective or relativist viewpoints, which can be appealing to those seeking a firm moral grounding.	Problematic Outcomes: Strict adherence to natural law principles can lead to questionable outcomes.

Now that the theories of ethics have been provided, it is best to discuss how ethics evolve. The evolution of ethics explores how the principles of morality (a system of distinguishing right from wrong) have developed over time as influenced by human evolution, cultural developments, and philosophical inquiry. Such evolution reveals a philosophical progression from ancient theories to modern theories vis-à-vis the biological and the social progression of morality. Some questions explored include:

- How did the moral sense evolve?
- Are the codes of ethical norms biologically determined by humans?
- Are the codes of ethical norms culturally determined by humans?

Biological Basis	Evolutionary ethics attempts to understand morality through the lens of evolutionary biology, exploring how natural selection might have shaped human capacity for ethical behavior. Fully consistent with Darwin's ideas, the claim is that moral behavior is a necessary outcome of the biological makeup of humans and a product of their evolution.
Cultural Evolution (Altruism, Reciprocity, and Mutualism)	Moral codes are considered outcomes of cultural evolution, which explains the diversity of norms across different populations and their evolution over time. In this case, the need for cooperation, reciprocity, trust, and conflict resolution is crucial to the evolution of morality.
Cultural and Biological Influence	The evolution of ethical systems can be seen as a cybernetic process, where biology and culture interact and provide feedback that shapes moral rules and social structures. The norms to decide which actions are good or evil are largely culturally determined, though conditioned by biological predispositions.
Cognitive Modules	Some theories suggest that specific cognitive modules evolved in early humans, serving as the foundation for moral intuitions and judgments. This prompted a broader understanding of human interconnectedness and the importance of well-being.

Key concepts in the evolution of ethics and morality include the following:

- **Biological Roots** (Cooperation and Social Living): Evolutionary psychology accounts propose that morality evolved as a means to address challenges of social living, particularly cooperation and conflict resolution.
- **Moral Progression from Uncivilized to Ethical**: As societies evolved, ethical frameworks developed to refine concepts of justice and morality, moving beyond primitive notions of revenge and embracing principles of righteousness and justice.
- **Reflection as a Role**: The systematic study of what is morally right emerged as humans began to reflect on customary standards of conduct and to refine them.
- **Conflict Resolution**: Research suggests these are core evolutionary mechanisms driving moral behavior. Kin altruism promotes care for relatives, reciprocity encourages cooperation through exchange and mutual benefit, and mutualism fosters group loyalty and conformity.
- **Affirmation vs. Negation Perspectives**: The evolution of ethics is also influenced by contrasting perspectives on the material world; some people emphasize the importance of engagement with the world, while others advocate for detachment.

Levinas's "face-to-face" concept describes a unique ethical encounter where one person's vulnerability, as revealed in their face, creates an immediate and an inescapable responsibility in the other. This encounter precedes rationality and knowledge, establishing a fundamental ethical obligation to the other before any other considerations.

Key aspects of the face-to-face encounter include the following:

- **Exteriority of the Other**: The face is not just a physical feature but represents the absolute exteriority of the other, resisting attempts to be fully known or possessed by the self.
- **Ethical Demand**: The face is not merely an object of perception but an ethical call or an ethical plea for recognition and responsibility. It compels the self to respond and to acknowledge the other's vulnerability and mortality.
- **Infinite Responsibility**: The encounter with the face generates an infinite and inescapable responsibility towards the other – a sense of being hostage to their needs and well-being.
- **Precedes Knowledge and Totality**: The ethical encounter is before any knowledge or conceptualization of the other. It disrupts the self's attempt to totalize the other and to enclose them within a system of knowledge or understanding.
- **Not a Mere Perception**: The face-to-face encounter is not simply a visual perception but rather a profound experience of proximity and connection, where the other's presence alters the self.

Ultimately, Levinas argues that ethics is not derived from abstract principles or universal laws, but from the immediate and the inevitable responsibility that arises in the face-to-face encounter with the other. This encounter reveals the other's unique and irreplaceable being, demanding a response that transcends self-interest and embraces a commitment to their well-being.

Morality types refer to the different frameworks for understanding what is considered right or wrong, and how people's beliefs about behavior are structured and applied. They can be categorized either by their foundational principles or by the branches of ethical study. Some examples of morality types are described below:

- **Moral absolutism** asserts that the existence of universal and unchanging moral principles has absolute standards against which moral questions may be examined to establish the rightness and wrongness of actions, regardless of circumstances. For example, if telling a lie is immoral, then the idea of an ethical lie is irrelevant in terms of moral constraints.
- **Moral objectivism** is a philosophical stance asserting the existence of objective moral truths, independently of individual opinions or cultural norms. It posits that certain actions are inherently right or wrong, regardless of what anyone thinks or believes. This means moral statements are considered true or false based on whether they accurately describe these mind-independent moral facts or not.
- **Moral relativism** is the idea that there is no universal or absolute set of moral principles.
- **Moral realism** is an ethical theory asserting that objective, mind-independent moral facts exist, making some moral statements true or false regardless of individual beliefs or cultural norms. It is a form of cognitivism, believing moral judgments express claims about reality, not just emotions or preferences. As a result, actions like killing a defenseless person can be objectively wrong, similar to empirical facts in science, because these moral properties are considered real features of the world.
- **Cultural relativism** is the view that ethical and social standards reflect the cultural context from which they are derived. Cultural relativists uphold that cultures differ fundamentally from one another, as well as the moral frameworks that structure relations within different societies.
- **Moral subjectivism** is a meta-ethical theory stating that moral judgments are based on personal opinions, feelings, or attitudes, rather than on objective moral truths. It suggests that what is right or wrong is subjective and varies from person to person.

- **Moral Universalism**, in the realm of ethics and morality, posits that certain moral principles are universally applicable to all individuals, regardless of cultural, social, or personal differences. It suggests that some actions are inherently right or wrong, and these judgments apply universally.
- **Descriptive relativism** notes that different cultures hold different moral beliefs.
- **Ethical egoism** is a normative ethical theory that asserts that individuals are morally obligated to act in their own self-interest, meaning that the morally right action is the one that promotes one's own well-being above all others.

Other notable meta-ethical segways include the following:

- **Motivism** in ethics is the meta-ethical view that moral judgments are not statements of fact but rather expressions of emotions or attitudes. It suggests that when someone says "murder is wrong", they are not stating a truth about murder but rather expressing their feelings of disapproval or aversion towards it.
- **Cognitivism** is concerned with the role of facts and numbers in determining moral good and wrong. Cognitivism explains what kinds of properties or states are relevant to a subject, the values they possess, and why they guide and motivate one's decisions and actions. On the other hand, non-cognitivism in ethics is an abstract ideology that maintains that when anything is labeled as right or wrong based on moral knowledge, judgment can neither be true nor 'untrue'.
- **Emotivism** suggests that moral judgments are not statements of fact but rather expressions of emotions or attitudes. Essentially, when someone says "lying is wrong", they are not making a factual claim that can be true or false, but rather expressing their disapproval and a feeling of aversion towards lying.
- **Prescriptivism** in ethics is the view that moral statements are not merely descriptive but are inherently prescriptive, meaning they aim to guide or command behavior. Instead of stating facts about the world, prescriptivists maintain that moral language educates what actions are right or wrong, highlighting what people ought to do.

Once again, the objective of the preparation for knowledge articles is to promote a rational mindset that allows the reader to inquire about all things, to challenge all biases, to evaluate evidence holistically, and to sharpen awareness/consciousness. In this way, the reader will become less vulnerable to ego-driven decisions, self-doubt, and manipulation tactics.

Em Hotep!

LOGIC & TRUTH

ANKH WADJA SENEB | ARTICLE NO: 006

Function: Preparation of Knowledge
Intent: Increase Rationality & Mental Facility
Position: Part 1 – Preliminaries & Fundamentals

ARTICLE NO: 006 – LOGIC & TRUTH

Peace to the High Power! Peace to the Living Universe! Peace to all Finite Living Beings! Peace to All Things – seen and unseen! For my spirit is with me, my image is with me, and my purpose is with me. For wisdom belongs to the seekers in heavy pursuit of knowledge, which can only be ascertained through the preparation and the sharpening of mental facility; and, knowledge is the protective shield against intellectual danger and exploitative measures.

Logic is a branch of philosophy that studies the principles of valid reasoning and argumentation, using formal systems to analyze and evaluate arguments for truth and validity. It involves a system of principles and rules that guide thought processes in order to reach reasonable and justified outcomes. Ultimately, logic serves as a foundation for critical thinking in everyday life, and it informs other philosophical disciplines. In the attempt to make rational decisions and to understand situations better, there are four (4) components of logical thinking:

1. **Deductive Reasoning**: A component of logical thinking that begins with a general idea and then seeks to reach a specific, more logical conclusion. Example: If A=B and B=C, then A=C.
2. **Inductive Reasoning**: A logical component that relies on blanket generalizations. An individual can base these general notions on anecdotal experiences, personal observations, and facts known to be either true or false. Example: If the boss has been known to hold a group meeting every Tuesday morning for the past few years, then it can be logically concluded that they most likely are going to hold another group meeting every Tuesday morning as well.
3. **Causal Inference**: A logical component that recognizes the reason things evolve and change. Example: If someone is reading an article about critical reading, then it can be casually inferred that they are reading it because they want to change and to become a better critical reader.
4. **Analogy**: Analogical reasoning is a component that realizes the commonality between two or more perspectives. Example: If your friend has an identical twin, then analogical reasoning accepts that their twin, whom you might not have met, looks just like them.

Validity is a formal property of an argument's structure, whereas truth is a property of the propositions (statements) within the argument. Logic deals with arguments, and each argument consists of a few premises. A significant focus is on distinguishing between correct (valid) and incorrect (fallacious) reasoning, aiming to formulate systems that promote sound arguments. An argument is either valid or invalid, whereas a premise is either true or false. Premises are mentioned in the beginning, and conclusions are derived from the premises. A valid argument can have false premises and a false conclusion, or true premises and a true conclusion.

Example 1

All cows are white. (Premise 1)
All swans are white. (Premise 2)
Therefore, all swans are cows. (Conclusion)
In this argument, the conclusion is **false** because Premise 1 is false.

Example 2

Some logic students are cricket players. (Premise-1)
Some football players are logic students. (Premise-2)
Therefore, some football players are cricket players. (Conclusion)
In this argument, the conclusion is **true** because the premises are regarded as true.

Resultantly, an argument is considered valid if its premises cannot be true and its conclusion cannot be false simultaneously. The main method for establishing invalidity is by exhibiting a counterexample or a "parody argument", which is another argument of the same form with demonstrably true premises and a demonstrably false conclusion.

As far as scope is concerned, logic investigates the structure of statements and arguments, the principles of valid inference, and the study of fallacies and paradoxes.

- **Valid Reasoning**: This fundamental focuses on determining when an argument is valid, so that its conclusion actually follows from its premises.
- **Truth vs. Validity**: A key fundamental where logic is concerned with the validity of an argument's structure, and not necessarily the truth of its individual statements. For example, stating "all moons are made of cheese" is valid within a logical framework, even though the premise is false.
- **Inference**: This fundamental provides the rules for drawing conclusions from any given source of information.
- **Formal Systems**: Logic uses formal systems, such as propositional and predicate logic, to represent arguments in a standardized way, making their validity easier to assess.

There are six (6) valid methods through which humans can logically process knowledge.

1. **Perception**: The direct and the immediate method to cognize the objects of the world, where cognition of an object occurs due to the interaction between the object and the sense organs. Perceptual knowledge is valid when an individual perceives the object with its possible features.
2. **Inference**: An independent and valid method that is used to acquire valid knowledge about an object that is not perceivable to the individual, so that the cognition of an object is based on a person's prior knowledge about it.
3. **Comparison**: An independent method to acquire valid knowledge of an unknown object by comparing it with a known object in the world. For example, a 'squirrel' may be described as a small mammal like a country rat with a long furry tail and stripes along its entire body.
4. **Verbal Testimony**: In this method, an instructive assertion of a reliable person is the only one considered as verbal testimony. A reliable person is an individual with expertise in a certain matter and is willing to communicate his/her experience of it.
5. **Postulation**: This method resolves a conflict between two inconsistent, perceivable facts by suggesting a third presumption (piece of new knowledge) that reconciles the two facts.
6. **Non-Perception**: An independent method that provides immediate knowledge of the non-existence of an object in a particular place and time. An individual gains new knowledge of the absence (non-existence) of an object at a particular place, suggesting its existence elsewhere.

Classical Logic

Classical logic was originally created for the purpose of analyzing mathematical arguments, neglecting the distinctions of past, present, and future – or of necessary, actual, and possible. Classical logic builds from simpler to more complex systems. Propositional logic deals with entire propositions and their truth-functional connectives (e.g., "and", "or", "not"). First-Order Logic (FOL) expands on this by introducing predicates (properties of objects), individual variables, and quantifiers ("for all", "there exists") that range over objects. Second-Order Logic (SOL) further extends this by allowing quantification over predicates and sets of individuals, providing greater expressive power. Higher-Order Logics (HOL) are a generalization of SOL, permitting quantification over nested sets and properties of properties, with progressively more complex systems existing for third-order, fourth-order, and so on.

Propositional logic treats statements (propositions) as atomic, indivisible units and examines the logical relationships between them using connectives. It uses propositional variables (normally 'P' and 'Q') to represent statements and symbols for logical connectives such as "and" (∧), "or" (∨), "not" (¬), "implies" (→), and "if and only if" (↔).

Example

"It is raining, and the streets are wet."
In propositional logic, this can be written as;
"P and Q" (P ∧ Q)
where P = "It is raining" and Q = "The streets are wet"

First-order logic analyzes the internal structure of statements by breaking them down into predicates (properties) and terms (individuals or objects).

Individual variables are described as variables that range over objects in a domain, such as (x, y); however, predicates are properties or relations that can be applied to individuals, such as ("is a student", "is greater than", etc.).

Furthermore, quantifiers are symbols that specify the scope of a variable, such as:

- Universal quantifier (∀) - "For all"
- Existential quantifier (∃) - "There exists" or "some"

Example

"For all students, if they pass the test, then they will get a good grade."
In FOL, this could be written as;
∀x (Student(x) ∧ Passes(x) → GetsGoodGrade(x))

Where x is an individual student.

Second-order logic extends first-order logic by adding the ability to quantify not only over individuals but also over predicates, sets, and properties of individuals. Thus, second-order variables can be described as variables that can refer to sets or predicates. Key examples include formalizing the principle of mathematical induction, the completeness of real numbers, and properties of specific functions. SOL also allows for quantification over predicates where it is possible to state: "All properties P satisfy induction" - allowing quantification over all possible predicates P.

Example

"There exists a property P such that for all x, P(x) holds."
In SOL, this could be written as $\exists P\ \forall x\ P(x)$.

Higher-order logic is a generalization of second-order logic that allows quantification over increasingly complex structures, such as sets of sets, sets of sets of sets, and so on, maintaining key features such as an arbitrary nested quantification and hierarchies of types. In arbitrary nested quantification, quantifiers can range over predicates of predicates, or functions of functions, hierarchy of types, specifically in type theory-based systems, terms and formulas have types, allowing for a formal structure of nested quantification.

Non-Classical Logic

Non-classical logics are systems that diverge from traditional logic's binary principles (true/false) to model real-world complexities like uncertainty, vagueness, and contradictions. A breakdown of the specific types is provided below:

- **Fuzzy logic** uses approximate reasoning by introducing degrees of truth, where statements can be partially true, rather than strictly true or false, such as "the room is somewhat hot".
- **Many-valued logic** generalizes classical logic by allowing more than two truth values. For instance, the existence of true, false, and intermediate values can represent uncertainty or other nuanced information.
- **Intuitionistic logic** focuses on constructive proofs, rejecting the "law of excluded middle", which is a principle of classical logic that offers no middle ground, stating that for any proposition P, either P is true or its negation, 'not P', is true. Thus, every statement is either true or false, never both or neither, a concept often represented as "P or not-P" ($P \lor \neg P$).
- **Paraconsistent logic** permits contradictions without triviality, handling inconsistent information by allowing for contradictions without leading to triviality (where anything can be proven true), which is a principle known as a logical explosion.
- **Substructural logic** modifies logical systems by restricting or eliminating certain structural rules, such as contraction (allowing $P \rightarrow P, P$), weakening (allowing $A \vdash B$ if A is true), and exchange.
- **Description logic**, used in artificial intelligence, provides formal frameworks for representing knowledge with rich conceptual structures, often incorporating features of other non-classical logics. It is a family of knowledge representation languages used in AI to represent knowledge about an ontology formally, particularly useful for expressing complex relationships and constraints between concepts and individuals.
- **Digital logic**, often considered a practical implementation rather than a logical system itself, relies on binary truth values. While not a logical system in the same vein as the others, digital logic is the practical, physical realization of logic gates in computers and other electronic systems, operating on binary (true/false) signals.

Meta logic

Metalogic is the study and the analysis of semantics (relations between expressions and meanings) and syntax (relations among expressions) of formal languages and formal systems. As such, it analyzes properties like soundness (proven statements are true) and completeness (true statements can be proven) by treating the logical system itself as a mathematical object. It involves applying mathematical tools and reasoning to examine the syntax (rules) and semantics (meaning) of formal languages and systems, rather than the truths or the arguments within the system. Ultimately, metalogic helps reveal the inherent capabilities and limitations of various logical systems.

Key concepts in metalogic are provided below.

- **Soundness**: A system is sound if every statement that can be proven within it is indeed true.
- **Completeness** - A system is complete if every true statement, which can be expressed in the system, can also be proven within it.
- **Entailment**: The relationship between premises and conclusions, which metalogic investigates for specific properties.
- **Formal Languages & Systems**: The syntax (structure) and semantics (meaning) of these languages and systems.

Modal Logic

Modal logic is the formal study of necessity, possibility, and other related concepts, often expressed using operators like "necessarily" and "possibly" to qualify truth. It extends classical logic by allowing these modal operators to reason about different "modes" of truth beyond simple truth or falsity with its diverse applications including alethic logic (necessity, possibility, and contingency of truth), temporal logic (the "when" of statements), epistemic logic (knowledge), doxastic logic (belief), and deontic logic (obligation and permission).

The fundamentals of modal logic include the following:

- **Modal Operators**: These are symbols or expressions (e.g., □ for "necessarily," ◇ for "possibly") that modify the truth of a statement.
- **Possible Worlds Semantics**: Many modal systems use "possible worlds" to provide meaning for these operators. A statement is necessarily true if it holds in all accessible possible worlds, and possibly true if it holds in at least one.
- **Accessibility Relation**: A relation between worlds that defines which worlds are "accessible" from a given world. The properties of this relation (e.g., reflexivity, transitivity) determine the specific axioms of a particular modal logic.

The following are some types of modal logic:

- **Alethic logic** focuses on the modalities of truth itself— logical necessity, possibility, and contingency. Example: "It is necessarily true that 2+2=4".
- **Temporal logic** deals with the temporal aspects of propositions, using operators for past, present, and future events. Example: "It will always be the case that X".
- **Epistemic logic** formalizes reasoning about knowledge, using operators like "K" for "it is known". Example: "Agent A knows that X".
- **Doxastic logic** studies belief systems, using operators like "B" for "it is believed". Example: "An agent believes that Y".
- **Deontic logic** is concerned with moral concepts such as obligation, permission, and prohibition. Example: "It is obligatory that one should not steal".

Other Forms of Logic

Minimal logic is a weakened form of symbolic intuitionistic logic that rejects both the law of excluded middle and the principle of explosion. It is a foundational system from which more complex systems, like intuitionistic and classical logic, can be built by adding more rules. In standard logic, any statement can be deduced from a contradiction, for instance: "If it is raining and it is not raining, then the moon is made of cheese." However, minimal logic rejects this, so that a contradiction does not automatically result in the trivialization of the entire system.

Ordered logic is a type of formal reasoning that imposes a specific sequence or consumption order on its statements or resources, unlike standard logical systems, where resources can be used in any order. Some of these formal systems deal with order relations, such as the $\leq$ relation in ordered abelian groups. Other examples of ideas or arguments presented in a logical, step-by-step sequence include mathematical proofs, recipes, and survey questions with ordered response options like poor, fair, good, very good, and excellent.

Affine logic is a type of substructural logic that, unlike traditional logic, rejects the structural rule of contraction (where repeated assumptions are combined into a single assumption) but allows linear logic with the inclusion of the weakening rule (which allows for introducing unused assumptions). Thus, affine logic can be embedded into linear logic by rewriting the affine arrow $A \rightarrow B$ as the linear arrow $A \multimap B \otimes \top$. This way, while full linear logic (propositional linear logic with multiplicatives, additives, and exponentials) is undecidable, full affine logic is decidable.

Dialetheism is the philosophical view that some statements are both true and false. This is described as the concept of true contradiction, also known as dialetheia. Dialetheism is closely linked to paraconsistent logics, which are designed to handle contradictions without leading to triviality or the collapse of the entire logical system. It can be seen as a way to resolve paradoxes by accepting that some contradictions are true. For instance, in an ambiguous situation when someone stands in a doorway, it may be argued that they are both inside and outside the room, a scenario that could be considered a true contradiction.

The relationship between logic and absolute truth is a complex topic in philosophy, with no single agreed-upon view. Logic is a tool for preserving truth, but it cannot establish the absolute truth of its starting points, or premises, which often derive from outside logical systems. Absolute truth is a statement or fact that is always and universally valid, regardless of parameters or context, and regardless of individual opinions, feelings, or circumstances. It is contrasted with relative truth, which is conditional, subjective, and can change depending on the situation or person.

The question of whether absolute truth exists in any field or discipline continues to be hotly debated, with some academics maintaining that all truth is relative and no absolute truth exists; however, this conclusion has been argued to be self-contradictory because it uses an absolute truth to negate the existence of absolute truth.

Characteristics of the absolute truth include the following:

- The absolute truth is universal. It applies everywhere and to everyone.
- The absolute truth is independent. Its validity does not depend on any external factors, context, or individuals.
- The absolute truth is unchanging (immutable). It remains consistent and eternal, never altering over time.
- The absolute truth is autonomous. It exists independently without needing validation from other truths or ideas.

Arguments Supporting Absolute Truth

- **Foundation for Knowledge**: Without absolute truth, there would be no basis for knowledge, science, or even basic reasoning, as all claims would be equally valid and equally meaningless.
- **Universal Morality**: The concept of absolute truth provides a framework for universal moral principles and a common standard for justice and ethics, ensuring that certain actions are inherently right or wrong regardless of individual opinion.
- **Objective Reality**: The existence of absolute truth implies a reality that exists independently of our perceptions, a belief similar to philosophical concepts of ideals or forms that are unchanging and essential.
- **Logical Consistency**: Rejecting absolute truth can lead to logical contradictions; for instance, the statement "there are no absolutes" is an absolute claim itself, thus refuting its own premise.

Arguments Against Absolute Truth

- **Inherent Human Limitations**: Humans are limited by their subjective experiences and perspectives, making it impossible to access or to know any objective, absolute truth fully that might exist outside our minds.
- **Cultural and Individual Relativity**: Different cultures and individuals have different beliefs and interpretations of reality, demonstrating that truth can be relative to circumstances and not universally constant.
- **Scientific Empiricism**: While science seeks verifiable truths, it cannot definitively prove the existence of an absolute truth that transcends scientific methods or that addresses matters of meaning and purpose, limiting its explanatory power for life's biggest questions.
- **Logical Self-Contradiction of Relativism**: Arguments against absolute truth often fall into logical traps, such as the relativist who makes an absolute statement that "all truth is relative", thereby contradicting themselves.
- **Difficulty in Identification**: Even if an absolute truth exists, the process of discerning it is fraught with complexity, as truth must be independent of individual beliefs to be truly absolute.

Once again, the objective of the preparation for knowledge articles is to promote a rational mindset that allows the reader to inquire about all things, to challenge all biases, to evaluate evidence holistically, and to sharpen awareness/consciousness. In this way, the reader will become less vulnerable to ego-driven decisions, self-doubt, and manipulation tactics.

Em Hotep!

AFRICAN PHILOSOPHY

ANKH WADJA SENEB | ARTICLE NO: 007

Function: Preparation of Knowledge
Intent: Increase Rationality & Mental Facility
Position: Part 1 – Preliminaries & Fundamentals

ARTICLE NO: 007 – AFRICAN PHILOSOPHY

Peace to the High Power! Peace to the Living Universe! Peace to all Finite Living Beings! Peace to All Things – seen and unseen! For my spirit is with me, my image is with me, and my purpose is with me. For wisdom belongs to the seekers in heavy pursuit of knowledge, which can only be ascertained through the preparation and the sharpening of mental facility; and, knowledge is the protective shield against intellectual danger and exploitative measures.

African philosophy is a broad field encompassing African perspectives on reality, knowledge, and human experience as expressed through oral traditions, art, and rational discourse. A principal driving force in post-colonial African philosophy has been a quest for self-definition. As such, one of the broad senses in which African philosophy can be understood emerges best in the works of Kwasi Wiredu, Paulin Hountondji, Peter Bodunrin, and Henry Odera Oruka. While these philosophers may differ in the details – and are not always comfortable about being grouped– they all take a universalist outlook that begins with the definition of African philosophy as an objective and universal enterprise. Historical context and debates around the definition of African philosophy are centered around the following:

- **Rebutting Colonialism**: Concepts of African philosophy to counter the Western belief that Africa lacked any history or any capacity for philosophical thought, especially after centuries of oppression and the slave trade.
- **Identity Formation**: Elements of African philosophy required to affirm, to reinvent, to reconcile, and to revive identities, lost knowledge, and self-worth.
- **"The" vs. "A" Philosophy**: A determination of whether African philosophy is a single, unified entity, "African Philosophy" or a multitude of distinct traditions "African Philosophies", stemming from the diverse cultural landscapes of the continent.

Characteristics of African philosophy are provided below.

- **Community and Coexistence**: African philosophy often emphasizes coexistence with nature and a collectivist approach over individualism, so that identity is formed through relationships and community membership.
- **Holistic Worldview**: African philosophy views the individual as intrinsically connected to the community and the environment. African cosmology connects all elements, whether living or non-living, putting a strong emphasis on the interconnectedness of the human, spiritual, and cosmic realms. There is often a strong acknowledgment of a spiritual dimension to life, including the presence of ancestral spirits and a supreme being.
- **Morality and Harmony**: African thought places significant emphasis on ethical values, communal harmony, mutual respect, and social justice. The pursuit of social balance and the flourishing of individuals and the community are central. African thought integrates rational discourse with intuitive experience, as opposed to Western thought's focus on logic and reason.

- **Cultural Expressions**: Moral teachings of wisdom and historical value are seen to be transmitted through cultural expressions and oral traditions such as proverbs, folklores, songs, and other art forms, reflecting a deep engagement with lived experience and meaning-making. This approach to knowledge is deeply embedded in cultural contexts and societal interactions.

Kenyan philosopher, Henry Odera Oruka, identified four primary trends or approaches for modern African philosophy:

- **Ethnophilosophy**: Originally coined by Kwame Nkrumah, ethnophilosophy is described as the collective worldviews of African people, their folk wisdom, mythical religious conceptions, and ritual practices. This trend involves the collection and the interpretation of the beliefs and traditions of different African groups to derive philosophical content. One of the novel criticisms against ethnophilosophy is the myth of primitive unanimity proposed by Paulin Hountondji. This is the idea that, in 'primitive' societies, everyone is in agreement with everyone else; therefore, there could not possibly exist individual philosophies in such societies, but only belief systems.
- **Professional Philosophy**: Professional philosophy was a direct response and antithesis of the simplistic and uncritical approach of ethnophilosophy, where African philosophy was developed in academic settings using formal philosophical methods to examine African experiences and concepts critically. This trend emerged when scholars, such as Bodunrin, argued for a universal philosophy as posited against the idea of cultural philosophy. Nonetheless, professional philosophy and its proponents have been accused of working within a framework that is distinctively Western, not African.
- **Philosophical Sagacity**: Philosophical sagacity focuses on the philosophical insights and wisdom of individual African sages and elders, rather than collective traditions. Odera Oruka used this approach to describe a reflective evaluation of thought by a particularly distinguished African elder/sage, whom is a repository of knowledge and wisdom exuding critical thinking and logical reasoning. Unlike ethnophilosophy, philosophic sagacity would be considered a decolonizing philosophy and an emancipatory endeavor to liberate the African mind.
- **Nationalistic–Ideological Philosophy (African Partisan Philosophy)**: Nationalistic-ideological philosophy focuses on the prescriptions of African politicians and intellectuals specifically involved in the independence of Africa from colonialism, addressing issues of identity, governance, and recovery.

African philosophy is as old as humankind, dating at least as far as pre-dynastic African culture and thought. While African philosophy is entwined with culture, it is neither homogeneous nor individualistic, and geographical regions are identified with a distinct philosophical genre/ tradition. The prominent philosophical genres are as follows:

Ubuntu (Bantu Philosophy)

Bantu (Ubuntu) philosophy, often considered the root of African philosophy, is a widely recognized genre among Bantu-speaking indigenous people in the sub-Saharan region of Africa. Ubuntu is a profound African philosophy centered on the belief that a person's humanity is shaped by their relationships with others, summarized by the phrases: "I am, because you are", "I am, because we are", and 'umuntu ngubuntu ngabantu' (meaning "a person is a person through other persons")

In essence, Ubuntu is a philosophy of humanness that underscores the spirit of love and oneness, radiating high mental and moral attributes that promote brotherliness, togetherness, sharing, caring, kindness, consideration of others, and mutual relationships. While Ubuntu was pervasive in many cultures of Zimbabwe, such as the Shona, it was introduced into education through the work of Samkange to promote interconnectedness, compassion, collective responsibility, and social justice.

Ubuntu asserts that individuals find their identity and achieve well-being through community and mutual care. This philosophy prioritizes communalism and social cohesion over individualism, viewing human existence as a shared experience rooted in interdependence with both people and the wider natural world. In fact, whether learned or not, individuals are considered 'uneducated' if:

- They appear ignorant of what is good or bad.
- They appear ignorant of what is to be said and not be said in public.
- They do not respect their own, as well as other people's cultures and personas, including their ideas.
- They do not contribute to the well-being of a society.

Ma'at Philosophy

Ma'at philosophy is a Kemetic (Egyptian) philosophy, derived from truth, justice, balance, or fairness, and symbolized by the Egyptian goddess, Ma'at. Egyptian temple priests transformed the earlier secular Confessionals to create this philosophy in order to link morality, cosmic order, and social harmony with Egyptian deities.

Ethiopian Philosophy

Ancient Ethiopia, meaning 'burnt-faced men' and not to be confused with just modern-day Ethiopia (Abyssinians), refers to traditional Ethiopians (Nubians, Nilotes, Hamites, and/or Kushites) whom emphasized values such as prowess, good relations, humanism, nobility, piety, and love of others. Inhabitants valued sharing and formed tightly-knit communities, and were often admired for their military prowess, creativity, and diplomatic relations.

Ethiopian philosophy was preserved in oral and written form through Ge'ez (Ethiopic) manuscripts. It has evolved through time alongside its associated culture and trading partners. In its written form, ancient Ethiopian philosophy was evident in translated versions of the following:

- The life and maxims of Skendes in 11 CE.
- The treatise of Zaar a' Ya o'qob in 1667 CE.
- The Fisalgwos (The Physiologue) in the 15th century.
- The book of the wise philosophers

Ethiopia was established in the written literature of philosophy and other fields of knowledge by the 14th and 15th centuries. In the 17th century, Ethiopian religious and philosophical ideas were challenged by King Susenyos' adoption of Catholicism and the subsequent presence of Jesuit missionaries. Zera Yacob, a renowned philosopher at the time, embraced an entirely theological culture, relegating all traditions that fell outside Christianity. He had intellectual capacities of repute and extensive knowledge of Christian, Jewish, and Islamic religions. In his opinion, these traditions were infested by lies because men would arrogantly believe that they know everything, refusing to examine things transmitted by their forebears. Thus, Yacob identified the will of a god as rational, and he rejected some Ethiopian traditions, Jewish precepts, and Islamic moral precepts such as sexual interdictions and polygamy as blasphemy.

Yoruba Philosophy

Yoruba philosophy is a resilient genre of African philosophy prevalent and distinctive among people found in West Africa, particularly in the countries of Nigeria, Ghana, and some parts bordering Cameroon. This philosophy was a result of an interaction between the Dogon, Akan, Dahomey, and Yoruba people over millennia. It is very rich in ethnophilosophy, particularly in proverbial lore.

When translated, the proverbial folklores associate wisdom with age, emphasizing the importance of helping each other in times of trouble and avoiding deceitfulness and unfaithfulness. Moreover, Yoruba philosophy reminds humanity of their flawed nature regardless of individual status, encouraging people, whom had lost confidence in themselves and their culture, to revert to their traditional norms and values to move forward, as the future will always exist beyond limited human knowledge.

Once again, the objective of the preparation for knowledge articles is to promote a rational mindset that allows the reader to inquire about all things, to challenge all biases, to evaluate evidence holistically, and to sharpen awareness/consciousness. In this way, the reader will become less vulnerable to ego-driven decisions, self-doubt, and manipulation tactics.

Em Hotep!

BIAS & CONSENSUS

ANKH WADJA SENEB | ARTICLE NO: 008

Function: Preparation of Knowledge
Intent: Increase Rationality & Mental Facility
Position: Part 1 – Preliminaries & Fundamentals

ARTICLE NO: 008 – BIAS & CONSENSUS

Peace to the High Power! Peace to the Living Universe! Peace to all Finite Living Beings! Peace to All Things – seen and unseen! For my spirit is with me, my image is with me, and my purpose is with me. For wisdom belongs to the seekers in heavy pursuit of knowledge, which can only be ascertained through the preparation and the sharpening of mental facility; and, knowledge is the protective shield against intellectual danger and exploitative measures.

A bias can be defined as a disproportionate weight or inclination in favor of or against an idea, thing, or phenomenon, typically in an inaccurate, a prejudiced, a closed-minded, and an unfair way. Biases can be innate or can be learned, comprising systematic errors in thinking that influence decisions, stereotypes, and prejudgments about people, beliefs, attributes, or social groups. Normally, social groups are thought about in terms of race, ethnicity (origin & tribe), gender, religion, sexual orientation, income, and education; however, biases go well beyond this including prejudgments based on height, amount of hair, hair color, eye color, choice of fragrance, choice of clothing, voice pitch, sexual appeal, origin of name, and so forth.

Ultimately, these types of biases are seen to be interconnected, so that cognitive flaws can manifest as social biases, which are often reinforced by unconscious patterns of thought instigated by societal norms. Biases are unique opinions often based on stereotypes associated with the immutable characteristics of something, rather than true knowledge or experience of that thing. While they can sometimes appear helpful to the individual, biases can lead to damaging behavior, unprovoked suspicion, hatred, and unjustified fear. There are hundreds of identified types of biases; however, this article shall cover three (3) specific types of biases: cognitive biases, unconscious biases, and social biases.

Cognitive biases are the most common type of bias, involving systematic flaws in how people process information and make judgments by creating inferences, assessments, or perceptions that are unreasonable. While they might lead to misjudgments and inaccurate conclusions, cognitive biases help humanity make sense of the world by helping people make quick decisions/guesses when little to no information is available. Cognitive biases are further goaded by mental shortcuts (Heuristics), flawed memory, poor oversimplifications of information, issues with paying attention, emotional input, social pressures, and aging.

Common examples of cognitive biases are listed below.

- **Confirmation Bias**: Confirmation bias is the tendency to focus, to interpret, to favor, and to recall information in a way that confirms existing beliefs, preconceptions, and hypotheses. For instance, someone, who believes that a particular political party is bad, will only read news articles that criticize that party, while automatically discounting positive coverage.

- **Availability Heuristic**: This is the tendency to overestimate the likelihood of events and to have greater trust in events that are more easily recalled in memory, often due to vividness or emotional impact. This cognitive bias is based on the realization that information that is easily accessible in a person's memory seems more reliable. For instance, after seeing many news reports about plane crashes, a person might develop an intense fear of flying, even though car travel is statistically more dangerous.
- **Anchoring Bias**: Anchoring bias is the tendency to heavily rely on or anchor on the first piece of information received when making decisions. This cognitive bias reveals that the first piece of information learned often demonstrates a more substantial impact on judgments made in comparison to the pieces of information learned at a later time. As an example, a car salesman might start with a high price (the anchor), making subsequent price reductions seem like a great deal, even if they are not.
- **Attentional Bias**: Attentional bias is the tendency to focus on specific information while simultaneously ignoring other pieces of information. While attentional bias can help an individual focus on the pieces of information that are most important, it can also cause them to disregard other relevant information. For example, an individual might begin noticing only red cars after deciding to buy a red car.
- **Dunning-Kruger Effect**: The Dunning-Kruger effect describes a tendency for individuals with low ability in a particular area to overestimate their competence, while those with high ability tend to underestimate their competence. In essence, people may overestimate their own abilities and believe they are more intelligent or capable than they actually are – even knowing just enough about a subject to think that they are right.

Unconscious biases (also known as implicit biases) are subconscious attitudes or stereotypical beliefs and attitudes that operate outside of a person's awareness and control. They influence an individual's understanding, actions, and decisions unconsciously, and can be in direct contrast with the beliefs and values that a person might think that they hold. They are difficult to identify, and they usually involve no malicious intent, but are often based on learned associations between particular qualities and social groups.

Common examples of unconscious biases are listed below.

- **Affinity Bias**: Affinity bias (also known as the similarity bias) refers to the tendency to favor people whom share similar interests, personalities, backgrounds, appearances, and experiences. People tend to feel more comfortable around other people whom are like them. For instance, a hiring manager might unconsciously prefer to hire a candidate whom shares their alma mater or interests, overlooking more qualified candidates.
- **Gender Bias**: Gender bias refers to the favoring of one gender over another. Subconscious stereotypes made about gender influence perceptions and treatment, affecting recruitment practices and relationship dynamics within a society. For instance, a manager might assume women are less committed to their jobs after having children, negatively impacting women's opportunities in promotions or project ownership.
- **Name Bias**: Name bias is the tendency to prefer certain names over others based on culture-to-culture outlook. It is most prevalent in recruitment, and it can have a negative impact on diversity hiring when a recruiter leans towards offering interviews to certain candidates with favorable names over equally qualified candidates with non-favorable names.
- **Conformity Bias**: Conformity bias occurs when personal views are influenced and are changed by the views of a larger group. As such, it is known as groupthink, and it is related to peer pressure because it can cause an individual to seek acceptance and to act similarly to others, regardless of their own dissenting beliefs. Although conformity generally prevents conflicts, it limits creativity and open discussions on less popular perspectives.

- **Halo/Horns Effect**: The halo effect occurs when people develop an overall positive impression of someone because of one of their traits, commonly relating to physical attractiveness. This bias leads them to put the person on a pedestal inadvertently by constructing their image based on limited information. In contrast, the horns effect causes people to have a negative impression of someone based on one trait or experience.

Social biases are prejudices formed within a society against a person, group, or set of ideas and beliefs, leading to unequal and unfair treatment based on certain characteristics.

Common examples of social biases are listed below.

- **Age Bias**: Ageism occurs when prejudice or discrimination is made based on a person's age. For instance, a company might overlook older, experienced candidates for a new role, assuming they are less technologically savvy than younger applicants.
- **Beauty Bias**: Beauty bias refers to the favorable treatment and positive stereotyping of individuals whom are considered physically more attractive. As a result, the term "lookism" emerged, which is discrimination based on physical appearance. In the fashion industry, for instance, physically attractive individuals might receive more favorable attention or assignments.

Cognitive biases can significantly distort and manipulate how a group reaches a consensus, often leading to a premature, flawed, or "false" consensus rather than being a product of sound, critical thinking. In philosophy, consensus generally refers to collective agreement on a position, argument, or principle. Consensus decision-making offers pros such as inclusive participation, leading to stronger commitment and improved decision quality by incorporating diverse perspectives and fostering goodwill. However, cons include the time-consuming and the slow nature of the process, the potential for groupthink or a poor decision being adopted, the difficulty when there are strong disagreements, and the risk of individual responsibility being diluted.

Pros of Consensus

- **Inclusivity and Participation**: Ensures that all members have a voice and they feel that their ideas are considered, leading to greater buy-in for the final decision
- **Improved Decision Quality**: Incorporating diverse perspectives often results in more accurate, well-rounded, and sustainable solutions
- **Stronger Commitment and Buy-In**: When people feel they have contributed to a decision, they are more likely to support and to implement it.
- **Fosters Collaboration and Trust**: The interactive process builds goodwill, strengthens relationships, and reduces interpersonal conflict.
- **Shared Responsibility**: Members take collective responsibility for the outcome, which can create a stronger sense of ownership.

Cons of Consensus

- **Time-Consuming and Slow**: The process of discussing and agreeing on an issue can be lengthy and may not be suitable for situations requiring quick decisions.
- **Risk of Groupthink**: Members may pressure each other to conform, leading to flawed decisions where dissenting opinions are suppressed.
- **Potential for Poor Decisions**: A decision may be agreed upon that is not truly optimal, as the focus can shift from finding the best solution to achieving agreement.
- **Difficulty with Strong Disagreements**: Reaching consensus can be extremely challenging or impossible when participants have deeply held or opposing views.
- **Diluted Responsibility**: While everyone is involved, individual accountability for the decision's success or failure can become unclear.

- **Exploitation of Power**: Individuals with power might exploit the process to push their own agenda, rather than genuinely seeking agreement.

Once again, the objective of the preparation for knowledge articles is to promote a rational mindset that allows the reader to inquire about all things, to challenge all biases, to evaluate evidence holistically, and to sharpen awareness/consciousness. In this way, the reader will become less vulnerable to ego-driven decisions, self-doubt, and manipulation tactics.

Em Hotep!

INQUIRY & ARGUMENTS

ANKH WADJA SENEB | ARTICLE NO: 009

Function: Preparation of Knowledge
Intent: Increase Rationality & Mental Facility
Position: Part 1 – Preliminaries & Fundamentals

ARTICLE NO: 009 – INQUIRY & ARGUMENTS

Peace to the High Power! Peace to the Living Universe! Peace to all Finite Living Beings! Peace to All Things – seen and unseen! For my spirit is with me, my image is with me, and my purpose is with me. For wisdom belongs to the seekers in heavy pursuit of knowledge, which can only be ascertained through the preparation and the sharpening of mental facility; and, knowledge is the protective shield against intellectual danger and exploitative measures.

Questioning is a powerful probing tool for objectively gathering extensive, unbiased information about another party's perspective, for exchanging knowledge at all levels of detail, for challenging forward actions, for eliciting concealed information, and for stimulating deeper critical engagement with complex philosophical and hypothetical ideas. Understanding the power of the question is vital to increasing knowledge capacity and to persuading others, especially through rhetorical questioning.

A rhetorical question is a question posed for either emphasis or effect rather than for eliciting an actual answer because the answer is often obvious, implied, or unnecessary.

Rhetorical questions fulfill the following purposes:

- **Making A Point**: Rhetorical questions emphasize key points or opinions, making them more memorable. For example, "Isn't this incredible?" emphasizes the beauty of a sunset.
- **Engaging the Audience**: They draw readers or listeners in, making them feel like part of a conversation and increasing engagement with the content. For instance, an engaging rhetorical question would be, "Are we really doing enough to combat climate change?"
- **Expressing Emotion**: They can vividly convey emotions like frustration or wonder. A question like, "How many times must I explain this?" expresses exasperation more powerfully than a direct statement.
- **Challenging Assumptions**: A rhetorical question can challenge a common assumption and can stimulate critical thinking about the subject. An example is, "Isn't it time we stopped accepting that things are just the way they are?"
- **Softening Criticism**: They can introduce critical ideas more gently, making them less confrontational than direct statements, as in "Have you considered the consequences of this approach?" versus "Your approach has serious negative consequences".

Next, questioning can be a strong method of persuasion, especially when combined with other modes of persuasion. The primary modes of persuasion are provided below.

- **Ethos** is the appeal to the speaker's credibility, authority, and character in the effort to establish trustworthiness and rapport to persuade the audience. An audience is more likely to be persuaded if they trust and believe in the authority of the speaker. Examples: A medical doctor discussing health, a scientist presenting research, or a community leader referencing years of local service.
- **Pathos** is the appeal to the audience's imaginations, emotions, and empathy by focusing on their beliefs and values to evoke a response. It aims to connect with the audience on a deeper emotional level, making them invested in the message being disseminated. Examples: A politician discussing the suffering caused by poverty, a charity advertisement showing struggling animals, or a personal story shared with an anonymous intervention group.
- **Logos** is the appeal to logic and reason by focusing on the message and using facts or evidence in support of a claim or an argument. Such facts or evidence include statistics, data, and testimonials that are clear, consistent, and well-ordered. Examples: Citing statistics on crime rates, presenting scientific data on fossils, or walking through the historical artifacts of a city.
- **Kairos** is the appeal to timeliness, whereby an individual is expected to seize the opportune moment or to use a sense of urgency to persuade an audience. Examples: A political campaign urging voters to "Act Now!" to avoid a perceived crisis, an advertisement for a limited-time offer, or a call to take action during an activist event.

Furthermore, the power of the question can direct a conversation, can expose information, and can reveal underlying motivations, especially during negotiations. In a negotiation, the person asking the questions often holds the power because they control the flow and the focus of the discussion. Instead of simply reacting to an offer, a negotiator, who asks strategic questions, forces the other party to provide justifications, revealing interests and potentially exposing weaknesses. Moreover, a well-timed question can also introduce new ideas, challenge assumptions, and reframe a problem to the questioner's advantage. The overall objective of any negotiation is to minimize concessions and to maximize interests.

The contractual elements of a negotiation, written or verbal, include the following:

- **Offer**: This is a definite proposal by one party to another, outlining specific terms of a deal. A well-crafted offer, specific and unambiguous, provides a strong starting point for a negotiation.
- **Acceptance**: An unconditional and qualified agreement to the terms of the offer, where any deviation constitutes a counteroffer.
- **Consideration**: Something of value exchanged between the parties, making the contract legally binding. It must be a mutual bargain, not something given in the past, and of some legal value.
- **Intent with Legal/Arbitration**: The mutual understanding between parties that they want their agreement to be legally enforceable, normally with an arbiter for conflict resolution.
- **Authority and Capacity**: Parties must have the legal authority and the mental capacity to enter into a contract. This ensures that all individuals or organizations involved can legally be bound by the agreement.
- **Certainty**: The terms of the agreement must be clear, definite, and complete enough to understand and to enforce.

Ways to minimize concessions include the following:

- **Leverage One's Position**: A given party should know the value of its offer, and it should be prepared to walk away if terms are unfavorable.
- **Strategic Bargaining**: A party should be able to prioritize needs, to compromise on less critical points, and to understand the difference between a necessary and an unnecessary concession.
- **Focus on Value**: Frame concessions as part of the mutual exchange of consideration to show the other party that such concessions have corresponding value.
- **Maintain Clarity**: Ensure offers and acceptances are clear and unambiguous to prevent misunderstandings that might weaken a party's negotiating position/power.

Due to the complexity and the risks involved during negotiations, a party might elect to assign an agent to speak on its behalf. Agency examines the relationship between a principal and an agent, where the principal delegates tasks to the agent, whom acts on their behalf. Additionally, it explores potential conflicts of interest that can arise when the principal and agent have different priorities or goals, seeking to analyze how these conflicts can be addressed. Agency exists in two (2) main forms:

- **Human Agency**: A concept that emphasizes an individual's ability to act intentionally and to make choices to shape their own life circumstances and future. It also refers to the inherent power and capacity for individuals to act independently, to make decisions, and to have an impact on the world.
- **Legal and Organizational Agency**: A specific type of agency that involves a formal or informal agreement between two parties. In this relationship, one party, which is the principal, grants legal permission to the other party, the agent, to act on their behalf and to make decisions in their best interest, known as a fiduciary duty.

Now that questioning and rhetorical means have been discussed, we can examine the different types of arguments that can follow from them.

Conventional Arguments

Philosophical arguments primarily fall into three (3) categories:

- **Deductive**: Aims for certainty and is evaluated as valid or invalid.

In a deductive argument, the focus is on logical structure. If the premises are true, then the conclusion must necessarily be true.

Evaluation

Valid: If the conclusion logically follows from the premises, even if the premises are false.
Invalid: If the conclusion does not necessarily follow from the premises.

Example

Premise 1: All humans are mortal.
Premise 2: Rick is a human.
Conclusion: Therefore, Rick is mortal. [Valid]

Conclusions made in deductive arguments do not offer new information, only making explicit what is already contained in the premises.

- **Inductive**: Aims for probability and is evaluated as strong or weak.

Inductive arguments use observations to make generalizations or predictions, leading to a conclusion that is likely but not guaranteed to be true.

Evaluation

Strong: If the premises are true, then the conclusion is highly probable.
Weak: The conclusion is not guaranteed, even with true premises.

Example

Premise 1: Every swan I have seen is white.
Conclusion: Therefore, all swans are white.

Conclusions made from inductive arguments can be false, even if all premises are true.

- **Abductive**: Identifies the best explanation and is evaluated for its explanatory power.

Abductive reasoning involves inferring the most plausible explanation for a set of observations.

Evaluation

A strong or weak evaluation is dependent on the explanatory power of the conclusion for the premises.

Example

Observation: John's swan is white.
Conclusion: John's swan is likely from a region where white swans are common.

Cosmological Arguments

Cosmological arguments are metaphysical arguments for the proof of the existence of a god. Metaphysical arguments are generally concerned with the fundamental nature of reality, existence, and causality, rather than totally relying on observations of the physical world. As such, cosmological arguments compose one of the numerous metaphysical arguments for a god's existence, including:

- **Ontological Argument**: A god is defined as the greatest conceivable being. Since it is possible to conceive of such a being, and such a being could not be the greatest unless it existed, it follows that a god must exist.
- **Transcendental Argument** - This argument suggests that logic, morality, and science inherently presuppose a theistic worldview. Without a transcendent source like a god, the foundations for logic, morals, and the ability to understand the universe would crumble.

Essentially, cosmological arguments propose an explanation for the universe's existence, proving significant and enduring philosophical evidence for a god's existence through reason and observation of the natural world. Some key forms to be discussed include the following:

- The Contingency Argument (necessitating a Necessary Being)
- The Causality Argument (requiring a First Cause)
- The Kalam Argument (positing a cause for the universe's beginning)
- Fine-Tuning Argument (suggesting a designer for the universe's life-sustaining conditions)
- Rare Earth Hypothesis.

Proponents supporting the cosmological arguments have to determine if a necessary being is truly a god, if a first cause is required, and if the universe's properties necessitate an intelligent designer.

Opponents of the cosmological arguments must counter the unjustified leap to God, the problem of an infinite regress, the fallacy of composition, and the unproven ability to apply causation beyond the universe.

The **Contingency Argument** or the "Argument from Contingency" examines how every being must be either necessary or contingent. The argument presents the following premises and conclusion:

Premises

- Every being that exists is either contingent or necessary.
- Not every being can be contingent.
- There exists a necessary being on which the contingent beings depend.
- This necessary being on which all contingent things depend, is what is meant by 'a god'.

Conclusion

Therefore, a god exists. There must be a necessary being, not contingent, to explain why anything exists at all, as the universe could have been otherwise. This necessary being is identified as a god.

The dilemma presented for this argument is: If everything needs an explanation for its existence, is this an infinite regress, or is a 'brute fact' acceptable? There is no proof that the necessary being is a god, and this being might be a different kind of being or object. The collection of dependent beings is accounted for by one explanation, and this argument will fail in trying to reason that there is only one first cause or one necessary cause.

The **Causality Argument** (First Cause) or the "Argument of Causality" establishes any cause-and-effect (causal) relationship between events and things, requiring a first mover, the first cause, the sustainer, the cause of excellence, and the source of harmony. The argument presents the following premises and conclusion:

Premises

- There exists a series of events.
- The series of events exists as caused and not as uncaused.
- There must exist the necessary being that is the cause of all contingent beings.

Conclusion

Therefore, there must exist the necessary being that is the cause of the whole series of beings. Everything has a cause; therefore, the universe must have a first, uncaused cause, which is a god (prima causa). Such a god must be the immovable mover.

The dilemma presented for this argument is that the argument creates an infinite regress of causes, with no ultimate beginning, unless an uncaused first cause is assumed. If everything needs a cause, then why does a god not need a cause? Or, if the first cause can be thought to be uncaused and existing forever, why not consider that the universe itself has always existed and shall always exist, and go through an everlasting cycle of expansion and contraction?

The **Kalam Argument** is a specific type of causal argument used to demonstrate that the universe has a beginning and therefore a cause. Applying the general principle of causality, the Kalam argument presents premises and conclusions in parts. The basic argument provides a brief history of the Kalam cosmological argument as stated by the Kalam tradition, while the subsets defend the substance of the argument:

Basic Argument Premises

- Whatever begins to exist, has a cause of its existence – something has caused it to start existing.
- The universe began to exist – the temporal regress of events is finite
- Therefore, the universe has a cause, argued to be a personal will.

Sub-Set 1 Premises (Impossibility of an actual infinite)

- An actual infinite cannot exist.
- An infinite temporal regress of events is an actual infinite.
- Therefore, an infinite temporal regress of events cannot exist.

Sub-Set 2 Premises (Impossibility of the formation of an actual infinite by successive addition)

- A collection formed by successive addition cannot be an actual infinite.
- The temporal series of past events is a collection formed by successive addition.
- Therefore, the temporal series of past events cannot actually be infinite.

Conclusions

Therefore;

1a) An actual infinite cannot exist in the real world; and b) an infinite temporal series is such an actual infinite.

2. A temporal series cannot be an actual infinite, assuming that an actual infinite can exist in the real world, because: a) a temporal series is a collection formed by successive addition; and b) a collection formed by successive addition cannot be an actual infinite.

The dilemma presented for this argument is: If the universe is eternal, then the premise that everything that begins to exist has a cause is irrelevant, and if it had a beginning, then a cause for that beginning is needed. Firstly, the principle of causation might not apply to the universe itself, only to things within it. Secondly, the nature of the cause is not truly known. Even if the universe has a cause, there is no clear reason to identify this cause as the personal god of theism, for it can be a different type of cause. Lastly, the argument's objections to infinity from set theory are not appropriate for philosophical or scientific discussions of the universe.

The **Fine-Tuning Argument** asserts that the fundamental constants and laws of the universe are so precisely set to a narrow range that even minor variations would prevent the existence of complex matter and life, suggesting intelligent design rather than random chance. The argument presents the following premises and conclusion:

Premises

- Many initial conditions and fundamental physical constants of the universe are set to an incredibly narrow range, making life possible within them.
- The universe does indeed have these life-permitting constants.

Conclusion

Therefore, a supernatural designer exists.

The dilemma presented for this argument is: If the universe is designed, then how can we know it was designed by a god and not another intelligent being? The argument assumes that life requires such fine-tuning, and it fails to consider other explanations. Even if the argument successfully proved the existence of an intelligent designer, it would not necessarily lead to the conclusion of a supernatural, omnipotent god.

The Rare Earth Hypothesis is not a cosmological argument for a god's existence, but rather a scientific and a philosophical argument suggesting that the specific combination of geological and astrophysical conditions necessary for the rise of complex, multicellular life in the cosmos is extremely uncommon. As opposed to arguing for a god based on the universe's existence, the Rare Earth Hypothesis uses astro-biological evidence to argue for the rarity of complex life, not for the existence of a creator or a first cause. The hypothesis presents the following premise and conclusion:

Premise

The hypothesis argues that many improbable factors were necessary for the rise of complex, multicellular life on Earth, including:

- A suitable star and location within the galaxy (not too close to the galactic center, far from supernovae).
- A planet with the right mass to hold an atmosphere and a magnetic field
- A large moon to stabilize Earth's axial tilt, which moderates seasons
- Plate tectonics to regulate Earth's climate and to recycle nutrients
- The presence of liquid water
- Periods of mass extinction to allow for evolutionary bursts

Conclusion

Therefore, Earth-like planets with conditions suitable for the evolution of complex life indicate that intelligent life is likely to be exceedingly rare throughout the universe.

The dilemma presented for this hypothesis is: Does the uniqueness of Earth suggest design, or does it reveal a narrow understanding of what life could be? Inherent anthropocentrism, assuming Earth-like conditions, is necessary for all life. Moreover, there is an overestimation of Earth's uniqueness. Various factors, such as the large moon or Jupiter's protective influence, as alternatives or different combinations of conditions, may be possible. Thus, the hypothesis is speculative at best because life can arise under conditions unknown to us.

Fallacies

Arguments are not without their flaws, and only errors in reasoning will result in fallacies, which are faulty, illogical statements. The common fallacies are shown below.

- Fallacy Structure 01 – If A then B. B is true, therefore A is true.

Example

If a person is a professional athlete, then (s)he is in good physical shape.
John is in good physical shape.
Therefore, John is a professional athlete.

Fault: John might be in good shape from hiking or from another profession.

- Fallacy Structure 02 – If A then B. A is false, therefore B is false.

Example

If it is a dog, it is an animal.
It is not a dog.
Therefore, it is not an animal.

Fault: The animal might be a cat, a bird, or any other type of animal.

- Fallacy Structure 03 – A or B is true. A is true; therefore, B is false.

Example

You can have soup or salad for lunch.
You chose soup for lunch.
Therefore, you cannot have salad.

Fault: The options aren't mutually exclusive, so it is possible to have both, soup and salad.

- Fallacy Structure 04 – It is not the case that both A and B. A is false, therefore B is true.

Example

It is not true that both Tom and Reggie went to the party.
Therefore, Tom did not go to the party, and Reggie did not go to the party.

Fault: It might be that Tom went to the party, but Reggie didn't, or vice versa.

- Fallacy Structure 05 – Every A has B. C has B, so C is A.

Example

All cats are mammals.
All dogs are mammals.
Therefore, all cats are dogs.

Fault: The middle term, "mammals," is not distributed. All cats are in the "mammal" class, and all dogs are in the "mammal" class; however, there is no mention of the entire "mammal" class itself, so there is no connection between cats and dogs.

- Fallacy Structure 06 – **Begging the Question**. Providing what is essentially the conclusion of the argument as a premise. Example: "Euthanasia is wrong because killing another person is immoral". The premise "killing another person is immoral" is essentially a rephrasing of the conclusion that "euthanasia is wrong", offering no independent justification.
- Fallacy Structure 07 – **Circular Reasoning**. The person begins with what (s)he is trying to conclude with. Example: "Ghosts are real because I've had a paranormal experience. My paranormal experience was a ghost because only a ghost could cause the weird noises I heard. The weird noises I heard were caused by a ghost because ghosts are real". This argument creates a circle where the conclusion (ghosts are real) is used to support the premise (my paranormal experience was a ghost).
- Fallacy Structure 08 – **Improper Use of Question**. Someone asks a question that presupposes something that has neither been proven nor been accepted by all the people involved. Example: "How many times a day do you shoplift?". This question assumes that the person is a shoplifter, and any direct answer gives credence to the unproven assumption.
- Fallacy Structure 09 – **Faulty Generalizations by Accident**. This fallacy occurs when a general rule is applied to a specific case that is an exception to the rule. Example: "Birds can fly. Therefore, penguins, which are birds, must be able to fly". This applies the general rule about birds to a specific case (penguins) that is a known exception.
- Fallacy Structure 10 – **Faulty Generalizations by Cherry-Picking**. This fallacy involves selecting and presenting only the data that supports a claim while ignoring the data that contradicts it. It gives a false impression of the evidence. Example: "My brand of weight loss pills works. Look at these three testimonials from people whom lost weight after taking them". This ignores the hundreds of other customers whom did not lose weight or had negative side effects.
- Fallacy Structure 11 – **Faulty Generalizations by Weak Analogy**. This fallacy occurs when an analogy is used to prove a point, but the two things being compared are not similar enough to support the conclusion. Example: "Learning to play the violin is just like learning to ride a bike. You will struggle at first, but once you get it, you'll never forget how". Although both activities involve learning a skill, the process, the muscle memory, and the complexity are vastly different.

- Fallacy Structure 12 – **Faulty Generalizations by Hasty Generalization**. This fallacy involves making a broad conclusion based on a small or unrepresentative sample of evidence. It's often a source of stereotypes. Example: "My grandfather smoked his whole life and lived to be 90. Smoking cannot be that bad for you". This draws a general conclusion about a public health issue from a single, exceptional case.
- Fallacy Structure 13 – **Faulty Generalizations by Misleading Vividness**. This fallacy uses a striking, memorable anecdote or a single, vivid example to outweigh and distract from statistical data or a more general trend. Example: "I know the average tourist is a victim of crime, but my friend traveled there last year and had an amazing time with no issues. The country is completely safe". The single, positive story is used to dismiss a more accurate statistical reality.
- Fallacy Structure 14 – **Faulty Cause/Effect**. This fallacy incorrectly assumes that since one event happened after another, the first event must have caused the second. Example: "Every time I wash my car, it rains. So, washing my car causes it to rain". The two events are correlated, but not causally linked.
- Fallacy Structure 15 – **Complex Cause**. This fallacy assumes that an event has only one cause when, in reality, it has multiple contributing factors. It oversimplifies a complex situation. Example: "The student failed the test because he did not study". While not studying was a factor, other reasons might have contributed to the failure, such as test anxiety, an ineffective teacher, lack of sleep, full-time work, or an undiagnosed learning disability.
- Fallacy Structure 16 – **Furtive Fallacy**. This is the belief that an observed event or a trend is a result of a secret plot or conspiracy by a small group of people. It attributes complex societal outcomes to a secretive, malicious intent without sufficient evidence. Example: "The rise in interest rates is a secret ploy by the central bank to bankrupt small businesses". This is a conspiratorial explanation for a complex economic policy that is publicly debated and implemented for a variety of reasons.
- Fallacy Structure 17 – **Gambler's Fallacy**. This is the mistaken belief that if something happens more frequently than normal during a given period, it will happen less frequently in the future, or vice versa. It applies to independent, random events. Example: I have flipped a coin five times, and it has landed on heads every time. The next flip must be tails". Each coin flip is an independent event with a 50/50 chance, and the previous results have no impact on the next one.
- Fallacy Structure 18 – **Slippery Slope**. This is a type of faulty cause/effect fallacy that asserts that a relatively small first step will inevitably lead to a chain of related events, culminating in some significant, usually negative, outcome. Example: "If we legalize marijuana, then people will start using harder drugs, crime rates will skyrocket, and the nation will become a lawless wasteland". There is no logical necessity for the legalization of a substance to cause a massive increase in the use of harder drugs or crime.
- Fallacy Structure 19 – **Appeal to Ignorance**. This fallacy argues that a claim is true because it has not been proven false, or conversely, that it is false because it has not been proven true. It shifts the burden of proof. Example: "No one has ever proven that ghosts do not exist, so they must be real".
- Fallacy Structure 20 – **Appeal to Common Sense**. This fallacy claims that an argument is true because it is obvious, trivial, or common sense, thus dismissing any need for evidence. Example: "It's just common sense that you cannot have universal healthcare. It would cost too much". The argument relies on a gut feeling rather than a detailed economic analysis.
- Fallacy Structure 21 – **Argument from Repetition**. This fallacy, also known as ad nauseam, asserts a conclusion's truth simply by repeating it over and over again. It relies on the idea that if a claim is heard enough times, people will begin to believe it. Example: Chanting "This tax cut will create jobs. This tax cut will create jobs. This tax cut will create jobs". The repeated assertion of the claim is used as a substitute for providing evidence or reasoning.

- Fallacy Structure 22 – **Argument from Silence**. This fallacy concludes that something must be true (or false) because a source is silent on the matter. It's a weak form of reasoning that lacks definitive proof. Example: "You never told me you could not eat shellfish, so I assumed you were not allergic to it". The silence on the matter is taken as evidence of a lack of an allergy, which could be a dangerous assumption.
- Fallacy Structure 23 – **Appeal to Motive**. This fallacy dismisses a claim by questioning the motives of the person making the claim, rather than addressing the substance of the claim itself. Example: "You are only saying we should go to that restaurant because you work there". The person's recommendation might be based on a genuine belief that the food is good, regardless of their employment.
- Fallacy Structure 24 – **Appeal to Authority**. This fallacy misuses authority by citing an expert's opinion outside of their area of expertise, or by citing a non-expert as if they were an expert. Example: "My doctor told me that the stock market is going to crash, so you should sell all your stocks now". While the doctor is an authority on medicine, they are not a financial expert.
- Fallacy Structure 25 – **Appeal to Emotion**. This fallacy manipulates the audience's emotions (such as fear, pity, or anger) to win an argument, rather than using logical reasoning. Example: "Think of the poor animals! We must boycott this company that tests its products on them". This appeals to sympathy for animals to motivate a boycott rather than presenting a reasoned argument for why the company's practices are unethical.
- Fallacy Structure 26 – **Straw Man**. This fallacy involves misrepresenting or oversimplifying an opponent's argument to make it easier to attack. Example: Person A: "I think we should invest more in renewable energy". Person B: "So, you are saying that we should just get rid of all our fossil fuels and leave everyone without power? ". Person B distorts Person A's argument into an extreme, unreasonable position.
- Fallacy Structure 27 – **Steel Man**. The steel man is the inverse of the straw man. It's a constructive and ethical tactic where someone attempts to present his/her opponent's argument in its strongest, most compelling form. To do this, you might clarify their position, address potential ambiguities, and even add evidence or reasoning that they might have omitted. By refuting the best version of their argument, you demonstrate a deeper understanding and strengthen your own position. Example: "I appreciate your concern for reducing gun violence, and I agree that stricter laws are one way to address it. Your position is that a universal background check system would prevent guns from falling into the hands of those with a criminal history, without infringing on the rights of responsible gun owners. While I acknowledge the merit of this point, I believe we should also focus on the illegal guns currently in the public, especially on a tight budget.
- Fallacy Structure 28 – **Two Wrongs Make a Right**. This fallacy attempts to justify a wrong action by pointing to another wrong action, arguing that since the other person did something wrong, his/her own wrong action is acceptable. Example: "Why are you arresting me for speeding? The driver in front of me was going even faster". The other driver's wrongdoing does not excuse your own.
- Fallacy Structure 29 – **False Dichotomy**. A false dichotomy is a logical fallacy that presents a situation as having only two extreme, mutually exclusive options, when in fact other alternatives exist. It's often used to force a choice by oversimplifying a complex issue. Example: "Would you rather fall in love with a rich man or a poor man?". This question presents a false choice. It implies that all men are either rich or poor, ignoring the legitimate possibility of men whom are well off, middle class, or excluded from the definitions of 'rich' or 'poor'.
- Fallacy Structure 30 – **Fallacy of Composition**. This fallacy assumes that because every individual thing in the universe is contingent (might not have existed), the universe as a whole must also be contingent and therefore require a cause. A key example is the contingency argument discussed earlier within this article.

- Fallacy Structure 31 – **Occam's Razor.** This fallacy lies in the assumption that the simplest explanation is always the best or the true one. When properly used, Occam's Razor is actually a problem-solving heuristic, guiding one to choose the simplest explanation among equally plausible theories with the same explanatory power. It is not a universal truth, and it should not be used to dismiss complex, but ultimately correct, explanations or to claim simplicity always equals truth.

Once again, the objective of the preparation for knowledge articles is to promote a rational mindset that allows the reader to inquire about all things, to challenge all biases, to evaluate evidence holistically, and to sharpen awareness/consciousness. In this way, the reader will become less vulnerable to ego-driven decisions, self-doubt, and manipulation tactics.

Em Hotep!

SCIENTIFIC METHODS

ANKH WADJA SENEB | ARTICLE NO: 010

Function: Preparation of Knowledge
Intent: Increase Rationality & Mental Facility
Position: Part 1 – Preliminaries & Fundamentals

ARTICLE NO: 010 – SCIENTIFIC METHODS

Peace to the High Power! Peace to the Living Universe! Peace to all Finite Living Beings! Peace to All Things – seen and unseen! For my spirit is with me, my image is with me, and my purpose is with me. For wisdom belongs to the seekers in heavy pursuit of knowledge, which can only be ascertained through the preparation and the sharpening of mental facility; and, knowledge is the protective shield against intellectual danger and exploitative measures.

Science is defined as a systematic process for understanding the natural world through observation and experimentation, either as a broad body of knowledge gained through such a process or as a specific branch of knowledge for concentrated study. Such a process employs the scientific method, which involves critical analysis, evidence-based reasoning, and the ability to form testable explanations and predictions about a given phenomenon. The scientific method generally consists of the following iterative steps:

1. **Making an Observation**: This is the starting point, where an individual notices something in the natural world and becomes curious about it. The individual observes something, specific or general, that they would like to learn about.
2. **Asking a Question**: Based on the observation, a specific question is formed about what is being observed.
3. **Gathering Background Information**: This involves researching existing sources to understand what is already known. This can also involve discovering if anyone has already asked the same question about the same phenomenon or a similar one.
4. **Formulating a Testable Hypothesis**: A hypothesis is an explanation, an educated guess, or a testable explanation for the observation, which attempts to answer the research question. If proven later, it can become a fact.
5. **Experimentation & Performing Tests**: A testable prediction is created based on the hypothesis. The test should establish a noticeable change that can be measured or be observed using empirical analysis; and, it is also important to control other variables during the test.
6. **Analyzing the Data Collected**: The metrics established before the test are used to see if the results match the prediction. The collected data from the experiment is then organized and analyzed to look for patterns and relationships before determining whether the data supports the hypothesis or not.
7. **Drawing a Conclusion**: Based on the data analysis, a conclusion is drawn about whether the hypothesis is supported or refuted.
8. **Communicating the Results**: After the results of the experiment are documented, they are shared with others or the public through publications, where peers evaluate the methods, results, and conclusions to ensure quality and credibility. The experiment may therefore result in other questions, or the hypothesis may be disproven, prompting the creation of a new one to be tested.

Some important elements used in the scientific method include the following:

- **Principle**: A fundamental truth or rule that forms a component of a larger theory.
- **Hypothesis**: A testable, tentative explanation or 'If-Then' statement for a specific observation.
- **Evidence**: Consists of data and facts that support or refute a claim.
- **Law**: A descriptive statement, often mathematical, summarizing how a phenomenon occurs.
- **Fact**: A specific, verified observation or event.
- **Property**: A characteristic or an attribute of a substance or a phenomenon.
- **Conjecture**: An idea or an opinion based on incomplete evidence, often considered a preliminary hypothesis.
- **Axiom**: A self-evident truth that is accepted without proof.
- **Proof**: A fact, an argument, or a piece of evidence, which shows that something is definitely true or definitely exists

Methods of proof are structured, logical arguments that establish the truth of a mathematical statement, moving from known facts to a conclusion. The following are key methods and significant techniques used in the methods of proof:

- **Direct Proof**: Proceeds from assumptions to the conclusion by directly starting with the hypothesis (the known facts) and using logical steps to show that the conclusion must be true. In the process, each step in the argument follows logically from the previous ones, building a clear and intuitive argument from what is known to what is unknown.
- **Indirect Proof**: Proves that the statement's negation leads to a contradiction. The contradiction demonstrates that the initial assumption of the statement being false must be incorrect, thus proving that the original statement is true.
- **Proof by Contrapositive**: Proves that the logical equivalent of the original statement, known as the contrapositive, which is "If not Q, then not P" when the original statement is "If P, then Q". It works in the following way: "If the contrapositive is true, then the original statement is also true".
- **Mathematical Induction**: Another common method for proving statements about integers, involving a basis step (proving the statement is true for the first integer) and an inductive step (proving that if the statement is true for any integer k, it is also true for the next integer k+1).
- **Proof by Cases**: The concept breaks a problem into smaller, manageable parts, so that the proof is broken down into smaller, individual parts/cases. This way, the statement is proven to be true for each case, and since all possible cases are covered, the statement is considered proven.

Key characteristics of a proof considered proven by a statement made true include the following:

- **Logical Sequence**: Proofs involve a sequence of logical statements, where each statement implies the next.
- **Known Facts and Axioms**: A proof uses the hypotheses of the theorem and previously proven theorems (lemmas) as its starting points.
- **Rules of Inference**: Rules that draw conclusions from other assertions, tying the steps of the proof together.
- **Formal vs. Informal**: While proofs in mathematics are often presented with natural language, they are based on rigorous informal logic.

Science has specific, inherent limitations because it can only investigate the natural world through observation and testable hypotheses. The limitations of the scientific method include the following:

- **Moral and Ethical Judgments**: Science can inform ethical debates by providing facts about the consequences of different actions; however, it cannot make moral judgments.
- **Aesthetic Judgments**: The scientific method cannot measure beauty. While it can analyze what triggers a positive human response to a piece of art or music, it cannot determine whether art should be deemed beautiful or not.
- **Existential Questions**: Science can explain how a process works, but it cannot answer ultimate "why" questions about purpose or meaning.
- **Supernatural Phenomena**: Science cannot investigate the supernatural, as such phenomena, which exist outside of nature, are beyond the realm of its scope and methodology.
- **Technological and Resource Constraints**: Science is limited by the technology and resources available to it at a given time. Some hypotheses, such as certain ideas in theoretical physics, are currently untestable because the necessary technology has not yet been invented or is prohibitively expensive to build.
- **Incompleteness of Observation**: Observation and measurement can be faulty, as human senses are limited, and a complete record of all variables is often impossible to achieve. This means that conclusions drawn from data are always subject to potential inaccuracy or error.
- **Inherent Human Bias**: While the scientific process is designed to minimize bias through peer review and repeatability, scientists are still human. Unconscious or conscious biases can influence how researchers design studies, interpret data, and report findings. Also, the framing of research through social, political, and cultural influences cannot be ignored.

Once again, the objective of the preparation for knowledge articles is to promote a rational mindset that allows the reader to inquire about all things, to challenge all biases, to evaluate evidence holistically, and to sharpen awareness/consciousness. In this way, the reader will become less vulnerable to ego-driven decisions, self-doubt, and manipulation tactics.

Em Hotep!

HISTORICITY OF LIFE ON EARTH

ANKH WADJA SENEB | ARTICLE NO: 011

Function: Preparation of Knowledge
Intent: Increase Rationality & Mental Facility
Position: Part 1 – Preliminaries & Fundamentals

ARTICLE NO: 011 – HISTORICITY OF LIFE ON EARTH

Peace to the High Power! Peace to the Living Universe! Peace to all Finite Living Beings! Peace to All Things – seen and unseen! For my spirit is with me, my image is with me, and my purpose is with me. For wisdom belongs to the seekers in heavy pursuit of knowledge, which can only be ascertained through the preparation and the sharpening of mental facility; and, knowledge is the protective shield against intellectual danger and exploitative measures.

The Earth is approximately 4.54 billion years old, and evidence suggests that life, in the form of simple microorganisms, emerged at least 3.5 billion years ago. Life on Earth has a long and a rich history, supported by evidence from the fossil record, radiometric dating of rocks, and the study of ancient chemical signatures. The fossil record shows a progressive increase in complexity and diversity, with evolutionary transitions and extinctions occurring over vast timescales; however, its record is incomplete and requires careful interpretation.

The fossil record consists of preserved remains (body fossils) or traces (trace fossils) of ancient organisms, providing direct evidence of past life forms and ecosystems. Fossils are found in sedimentary rocks, formed by the deposition of organic and inorganic materials. Geologists use the relative positions of fossils in rock layers (strata) to establish a chronological sequence from oldest to youngest. Ultimately, the fossil record reveals that organisms have changed over time, from simple microorganisms to complex multicellular life forms, and shows evidence of mass extinctions and radical evolutionary transitions. The fossil record is incomplete, however, as not all organisms become fossilized, and only a small fraction of those that do are recovered and studied. This is because conditions on the early Earth were not always conducive to fossilization.

Radiometric dating is a key technique for determining the absolute age of rocks. By measuring the ratio of radioactive parent isotopes to their stable daughter products, scientists can calculate the time it took for the decay to occur, providing ages for Earth and the rocks that contain fossils. By studying the oldest lead ores and zircons, scientists estimate the Earth's age to be around 4.54 billion years. On the other hand, the oldest known fossils are around 3.5 to 3.7 billion years old, indicating life existed by that time. There are also hints of life from older zircons, though these are not conclusive evidence. Radiometric dating relies on the accurate measurement of isotopes and their decay rates. Techniques have limitations; for example, radiocarbon dating is only effective for materials up to about 70,000 years old.

Early periods of life are particularly challenging to study due to the lack of well-preserved fossils. Scientists must use indirect evidence, such as chemical biomarkers or comparisons with modern organisms in extreme environments, to infer what life might have been like.

There is no definitive list of the exact evolutionary stages of humans, but a common progression of significant evolutionary milestones in human development is based on key developments in bipedalism, brain size, tool use, and social complexity, as follows.

1. **Dryopithecus/Ramapithecus** (Early Hominoids): These early hominoids, appearing millions of years ago, represent some of the earliest known ancestors in the human lineage.
2. **Australopithecus** (Southern Ape): These groups, appearing around 4 million years ago, were early hominids that walked upright (bipedalism), though they still had relatively small brains.
3. **Homo Habilis** (able man or handy man): Homo habilis was the first species to use and to manufacture stone tools, marking a significant cognitive leap.
4. **Homo Erectus** (upright man): This species developed more advanced stone tools, began to migrate out of Africa, and was the first to control fire, which revolutionized cooking and warmth.
5. **Homo Heidelbergensis**: An intermediate species that appeared between Homo erectus and later hominids, developing more complex tool use and potentially representing a common ancestor to Neanderthals and Homo sapiens.
6. **Neanderthals** (Homo Neanderthalensis): These closely related hominids were skilled hunters, used specialized tools like spears, and were the first to bury their dead, suggesting sophisticated social and spiritual practices.
7. **Homo sapiens** (wise man): These modern human species, characterized by large brains and complex thought, emerged about 300,000 years ago, developing art, and complex language.

For clarification, modern humans are considered to be Homo sapien sapiens.

The classification of "oldest" groups and tribes, related to life on Earth, is dependent on elements such as continuous living populations, established civilizations, or isolated uncontacted groups. The oldest known continuous cultural groups include the following:

- **Aboriginal Australians and First Nations People**: They are recognized as having the oldest continuous civilization on Earth with a history dating back over 60,000 years. DNA confirms that their ancestors were among the first to leave Africa between 64,000 and 75,000 years ago.
- **San People (Bushmen)**: They are also considered among the most ancient groups with a lineage that can be traced back to early human populations.
- **Sentinelese**: This indigenous tribe on North Sentinel Island is one of the most isolated communities in the world. Their direct connection to ancient populations, with a way of life potentially unchanged for tens of thousands of years, makes them a contender for the oldest group on the planet.
- **Berbers**: These indigenous inhabitants of North Africa have a history spanning over 5,000 years and are among the oldest civilizations in the region.
- **Hadza**: An indigenous group in Tanzania known for their hunter-gatherer traditions, which are among the oldest human subsistence strategies.

Once again, the objective of the preparation for knowledge articles is to promote a rational mindset that allows the reader to inquire about all things, to challenge all biases, to evaluate evidence holistically, and to sharpen awareness/consciousness. In this way, the reader will become less vulnerable to ego-driven decisions, self-doubt, and manipulation tactics.

Em Hotep!

PHYSICS & BEYOND

ANKH WADJA SENEB | ARTICLE NO: 012

Function: Preparation of Knowledge
Intent: Increase Rationality & Mental Facility
Position: Part 1 – Preliminaries & Fundamentals

ARTICLE NO: 012 – PHYSICS & BEYOND

Peace to the High Power! Peace to the Living Universe! Peace to all Finite Living Beings! Peace to All Things – seen and unseen! For my spirit is with me, my image is with me, and my purpose is with me. For wisdom belongs to the seekers in heavy pursuit of knowledge, which can only be ascertained through the preparation and the sharpening of mental facility; and, knowledge is the protective shield against intellectual danger and exploitative measures.

The fundamental forces are as follows:

- **Electromagnetic Force**: A force governing the structure of atoms. It keeps electrons bound to the atomic nucleus. It is also responsible for all chemical reactions, the behavior of light, and the forces that we experience in everyday life.
- **Strong Nuclear Force**: A short-range force that operates within the atomic nucleus. Its primary role is to bind quarks together to form protons and neutrons, and then to hold these protons and neutrons together to form atomic nuclei. Without the strong force, the powerful electromagnetic repulsion between positively charged protons would cause the nucleus to accelerate apart.
- **Weak Nuclear Force**: A force that changes one type of subatomic particle into another. This force is responsible for beta decay, where a neutron in an atom's nucleus can transform into a proton, an electron, and an antineutrino. This process is crucial for nuclear fusion in stars and for powering the sun.
- **Gravitational Force**: Gravity is always attractive, pulling objects with mass toward one another. Its range is infinite; however, its strength decreases with the square of the distance between objects. This long-range, cumulative effect is what holds planets in orbit, what binds galaxies together, and what shapes the large-scale structure of the universe.

Out of the four fundamental forces, the gravitational force is not fully accepted due to its incompatibility with quantum mechanics. General Relativity describes gravity as the curvature of space-time caused by mass and energy, and as a smooth, continuous geometric phenomenon. Quantum mechanics, however, describes the universe as lumpy and discrete at the smallest scales with forces mediated by particles.

Not to mention, constructing a single, elegant theory that can describe all fundamental forces of nature is a monumental challenge in physics. The primary difficulty stems from the irreconcilable differences between General Relativity, which governs gravity on large scales, and Quantum Mechanics, which governs the other three forces on microscopic scales. The names for these unified theories can be confusing, but they have distinct meanings. A Grand Unified Theory (GUT) aims to unify the electromagnetic, weak, and strong nuclear forces, but it does not include gravity. The challenges for GUTs are primarily experimental, as the unification of these forces is predicted to occur at extremely high energies, far beyond the capabilities of current particle accelerators. For instance, many GUTs predict that protons are unstable and will eventually decay – a phenomenon that has not yet been observed despite extensive searches. A Unified Field Theory (UFT) or a Theory of Everything (TOE) is more ambitious, aiming to unify all four fundamental forces, including gravity; however, the difficulties here are both theoretical and experimental.

Outside of the fundamental forces, it must also be remembered that science can only be true under a given set of assumptions. Most physical phenomena, for instance, are normally constructed based on the Principle of Least Stationary Action. This principle states that the true physical trajectory of a system between two points in time is one that makes the "action"—a functional of the trajectory defined as the integral of kinetic energy minus potential energy over time—locally stationary (that is, a minimum, maximum, or saddle point) compared to all other conceivable, infinitesimally varied paths. This principle is a powerful variational method that yields the equations of motion for a system; however, it relies on assumptions that the system's dynamics are well-defined, the endpoints are fixed, and the action is mathematically well-behaved. The underlying assumptions include the following:

- **Fixed Endpoints**: The principle applies to trajectories between fixed initial and final configurations at specified times.
- **Smoothness of Trajectories**: The paths considered must be continuous and differentiable, such that the action can be properly defined and its variation calculated.
- **Well-Defined Lagrangian**: A clear and consistent definition of the Lagrangian (kinetic energy minus potential energy) for the system is required.
- **Nature as Efficient**: The principle assumes nature operates in an "economical" or "efficient" way, seeking optimal paths without explicit intent or a central planning entity.

The idea here is not to expose the reader to the mathematical rigor of the principle but rather to demonstrate that scientific principles reduce the general complexities of the physical world – mathematically and/or empirically – with the minimum number of assumptions. As the number of assumptions behind a scientific idea increases, the limitations behind the scientific idea also increase.

Let's explore the major scientific ideas to highlight these limitations because many people often carry the mistaken belief that scientific ideas cover all possible cases.

- **Conservation of Mass**: For any closed system, the mass of the system must remain constant over time, and that matter can neither be created nor destroyed. Limitations: The Theory of Relativity indicates that mass and energy are interchangeable. In processes where a significant amount of energy is released or is absorbed, there is a corresponding change in mass. The most notable outliers to the conservation of mass are nuclear reactions, such as nuclear fission and fusion.
- **Conservation of (Angular) Momentum**: For an isolated system (where no net external force acts or external torque), the total momentum of the system remains constant. Momentum can be transferred between objects within the system, but cannot be created or be destroyed. Limitations: Friction, air resistance, or the gravitational pull from a third object will cause a change in the system's net momentum. If you consider a non-isolated system, the total momentum will not be conserved because of the external forces causing a transfer of momentum.
- **Conservation of Energy**: Energy cannot be created or destroyed but can only be converted from one form to another. This fundamental principle means that the total energy in a closed system remains constant over time. Limitations: The conflict with general covariance and conservation of energy is that it can only be conserved in an empty universe. Such a conflict arises because the general covariance in General Relativity means that space-time itself is dynamic. As it expands or curves, it loses the time-translation symmetry necessary for a strict energy conservation law. In an expanding universe, the wavelength of photons increases (redshift), decreasing their energy; and, the density of matter and energy changes over time, meaning there is no constant, globally defined energy to be conserved.

- **Newton's First Law**: An object in motion stays in motion with the same speed and in the same direction unless acted upon by a net external force. Limitations: It only applies in inertial frames of reference (frames not accelerating), and it is not accurate for objects moving at very high speeds close to the speed of light or for subatomic particles at the quantum level.
- **Newton's Second Law**: The acceleration of an object is directly proportional to the net force acting on it and inversely proportional to its mass. Limitations: Situations where mass is being gained or lost, such as a rocket expelling fuel, or where objects move at speeds close to the speed of light.
- **Newton's Third Law**: For every action, there is an equal and opposite reaction. Limitations: Systems not in equilibrium, especially biological systems, where action-reaction pairs may not be equal and opposite due to nonreciprocal interactions mediated by the environment.
- **Newton's Law of Universal Gravitation**: States that every point mass in the universe attracts every other point mass with a force that is directly proportional to the product of their masses and inversely proportional to the square of the distance between their centers. Limitations: Cases of intense gravitational fields, very high velocities, or objects on astronomical scales, such as the precession of Mercury's orbit and the observed deflection of light.
- **Bernoulli's Principle**: For a frictionless, incompressible fluid in steady flow, an increase in the speed of the fluid occurs simultaneously with a decrease in pressure or a decrease in the fluid's potential energy. Limitations: Assumes an ideal fluid. An ideal fluid is inviscid (has no viscosity or internal friction), is incompressible (its density doesn't change with pressure), and has laminar flow (no turbulence). These assumptions simplify calculations but are often not entirely true in real-world applications. While liquids are nearly incompressible, gases are highly compressible. The assumption is only valid for gases when the flow speeds are low and the pressure changes are minimal.
- **Navier-Stokes Equations**: Describe the motion of viscous fluid substances, normally assuming fully-developed flow profiles, Couette flow (moving surface against a stationary one), or Poiseuille flow (pressure gradient in a stationary channel). Limitations: Situations involving non-Newtonian fluids (blood, corn starch, etc.), compressible flows, turbulence, and systems lacking Galilean invariance.
- **The Zeroth Law of Thermodynamics**: If two systems are each in thermal equilibrium with a third system, then they are in thermal equilibrium with each other. This law establishes the concept of a single, universal property called temperature. Limitations: It does not provide a method to measure temperature, and most systems are not in thermal equilibrium in practice.
- **The First Law of Thermodynamics**: It states that the change in the internal energy of a system is equal to the heat added to the system minus the work done by the system ($\Delta U = Q - W$). It implies that energy can neither be created nor destroyed, only converted. Limitations: Inability to predict the direction of a process (e.g., heat flow from hot to cold), the feasibility or the spontaneity of a process, and the low efficiency of energy conversion (energy loss) or the difficulties in converting heat entirely into useful work.
- **The Second Law of Thermodynamics**: This law introduces the concept of entropy, a measure of the disorder or randomness in a system. It states that the total entropy of an isolated system can never decrease over time. It explains why heat naturally flows from a hot object to a cold object and why perpetual motion machines are impossible. Limitations: None for this particular law, as only the ideal perpetual motion violates this case.
- **The Third Law of Thermodynamics**: The entropy of a system approaches a constant value as its temperature approaches absolute zero. For a perfect crystal at absolute zero, the entropy is zero. Limitations: No true violations, but some substances, such as liquid mercury or amorphous solids, have non-zero entropy at absolute zero, which is physically impossible to reach.

Scientific ideas have even been applied to cosmology as follows:

- **String Theory**: String theory is a theoretical framework in physics that posits that the fundamental constituents of the universe are not point-like particles but tiny, one-dimensional, vibrating strings. These strings are unimaginably small, far smaller than an atom's nucleus. Limitations: No experimental evidence to support it. The strings are predicted to be so small that there is no conceivable way to directly observe them with current technology. Secondly, it requires the existence of ten or eleven dimensions for its equations to be mathematically consistent. Lastly, it is a background-dependent theory. This means that it is formulated against a fixed background spacetime, which is a major conceptual hurdle to reconciling it with the dynamic and evolving space-time.
- **The Lambda-CDM (ΛCDM) Model**: This model, also known as the Concordance Model, is the standard model of Big Bang cosmology. It is the leading framework for describing the evolution and the large-scale structure of the universe. The model is based on three main components: Lambda (Λ), which represents the cosmological constant or dark energy that is driving the accelerated expansion of the universe; CDM, which stands for Cold Dark Matter, a non-baryonic, non-luminous form of matter that interacts only gravitationally and is responsible for the formation of galaxies and large-scale structures; and ordinary baryonic matter, the stuff we are made of, which only makes up about 5% of the total mass-energy of the universe. Limitations: The model's two main components, dark matter and dark energy, have neither been directly detected nor identified. It also struggles to explain the remarkable temperature uniformity of the Cosmic Microwave Background (CMB) across vast, causally disconnected regions of the observable universe alongside the flatness of the universe's geometry and the prediction of more small, low-mass dwarf galaxies orbiting larger galaxies than what is observed.

Though far from perfect, the Big Bang model has some supporting evidence rather than only refutations. Such evidence includes the following:

- **Cosmic Microwave Background** (CMB): The model accurately predicts the temperature fluctuations and anisotropies observed in the CMB. The peaks and the troughs in the CMB power spectrum are a perfect match for the model's predictions for a universe with specific amounts of dark matter and dark energy.
- **Large-Scale Structure**: Computer simulations based on the ΛCDM model accurately reproduce the observed distribution of galaxies and galaxy clusters, including the cosmic web. The existence of dark matter is crucial for these structures to form.
- **Accelerated Expansion**: The observation of distant Type Ia supernovae showed that the universe's expansion is accelerating, providing the key evidence for a repulsive force like dark energy (Λ) to be a dominant component of the universe.
- **Big Bang Nucleosynthesis** (BBN): The model's predictions for the abundance of light elements (hydrogen, helium, and lithium) produced in the early universe are in excellent agreement with observations.

From here, we shift from the cosmos to living organisms. Taxonomy is the science of naming, classifying, and grouping living organisms based on their structural, genetic, and evolutionary relationships. It uses a hierarchical system, developed by Carolus Linnaeus, that categorizes organisms from broad to specific groups, including kingdom, phylum, class, order, family, genus, and species. This system helps scientists understand the diversity of life and the shared ancestry of all living things. The key principles of Linnaean Taxonomy include:

- **Hierarchical System**: Organisms are grouped into increasingly specific categories.
- **Shared Characteristics**: Classification is based on observable similarities between organisms.
- **Binomial Nomenclature**: The standard scientific name for a species is a two-part Latin name.
- **Universal Naming**: Provides a single, consistent name for each species, eliminating confusion from common names.
- **Hierarchical Ranks**: Include the seven major aforementioned ranks from most inclusive to most exclusive.

As far as evolution, Charles Darwin, in his *On the Origin of Species*, proposed that all life evolved from common ancestors through a gradual process where organisms with beneficial traits were more likely to survive and to reproduce, passing those traits to their offspring. Natural selection is the mechanism through which evolution occurs, involving several key components, such as the following:

- **Variation**: Individuals within a population exhibit natural differences or variations in their physical and genetic traits.
- **Heritability**: Many of these variations can be passed on from parents to their offspring.
- **Differential Survival and Reproduction**: More offspring are produced than can survive, leading to a struggle for existence. Individuals with traits better suited to their environment are more likely to survive and to reproduce.
- **Adaptation**: Over generations, the advantageous traits become more common in the population, leading to the species' overall adaptation to its environment.

The origins of humanity on Earth from a scientific perspective are also important here. The dominant view is that humanity originated in Africa, supported by fossil and genetic evidence of early humans like Homo sapiens appearing there first with the oldest remains found in Ancient Ethiopia – not to be confused with modern-day Ethiopia, which is actually Abyssinia – around 250,000 years ago. Other regions, such as Sri Lanka, show early human presence through sites like the Batadomba Cave; however, this evidence points to sophisticated ancient cultures rather than the initial origin of humanity itself. It is suggested that modern humans later migrated out of Africa, spreading across the world and interacting with other archaic humans. While sites outside of Africa, such as those in the Middle East, Europe, and Australia, have yielded ancient skeletons, they are observed to be typically younger than the earliest African fossils.

Evidence for African origins is as follows:

- **Fossil Evidence**: The oldest known fossils of Homo sapiens are found in Africa, such as those at Omo Kibish in Ethiopia, dated to approximately 195,000 years ago; the Herto fossils, dated to about 160,000 years ago; and the Jebel Irhoud fossils in Morocco, dated to around 300,000 years ago. Early hominid species, predating Homo sapiens, are also found exclusively in Africa, solidifying the continent as the cradle of humankind.
- **Genetic Evidence**: Scientists can compare DNA from different human populations, creating a family tree that shows all modern human lineages converging in Africa. African populations also exhibit the highest genetic diversity, which is consistent with them being the oldest human population group. There is not one modern-day human with zero percent African ancestry.
- **Behavioral Evidence**: Archaeological findings, such as those at Pinnacle Point in South Africa, show early human behavioral complexity, including the earliest marine resource exploitation and changes in stone tool technology. This supports Africa as a key region for human development.

Evidence for Sri Lankan origins is as follows:

- **Archaeological Sites**: Sites, such as the Batadomba Cave in Sri Lanka, provide evidence of human habitation over many millennia with artifacts revealing sophisticated cultures and engineering. The discovery of tools and other artifacts in these caves indicates the presence of advanced ancient Sri Lankans.
- **Sophisticated Civilizations**: Sri Lanka also has a rich history of complex engineering and sophisticated practices that indicate a highly advanced ancient civilization. However, this evidence relates to the capabilities of ancient populations in Sri Lanka, not the initial emergence of humans.

Once again, the objective of the preparation for knowledge articles is to promote a rational mindset that allows the reader to inquire about all things, to challenge all biases, to evaluate evidence holistically, and to sharpen awareness/consciousness. In this way, the reader will become less vulnerable to ego-driven decisions, self-doubt, and manipulation tactics.

Em Hotep!

MATHEMATICS

ANKH WADJA SENEB | ARTICLE NO: 013

Function: Preparation of Knowledge
Intent: Increase Rationality & Mental Facility
Position: Part 1 – Preliminaries & Fundamentals

ARTICLE NO: 013 – MATHEMATICS

Peace to the High Power! Peace to the Living Universe! Peace to all Finite Living Beings! Peace to All Things – seen and unseen! For my spirit is with me, my image is with me, and my purpose is with me. For wisdom belongs to the seekers in heavy pursuit of knowledge, which can only be ascertained through the preparation and the sharpening of mental facility; and, knowledge is the protective shield against intellectual danger and exploitative measures.

The foundational number sets of mathematics include the following:

- **Natural Numbers (N):** These are positive whole numbers {1, 2, 3, ...}.
- **Integers (Z):** This set includes all the natural numbers, their negative counterparts, and zero {..., -3, -2, -1, 0, 1, 2, 3, ...}.
- **Rational Numbers (Q):** These are numbers that can be expressed as a ratio or a fraction of two integers, where the numerator is not zero.
- **Irrational Numbers (P):** These are real numbers that cannot be expressed as a simple fraction. Their decimal representations are non-terminating and non-repeating.
- **Real Numbers (R):** This is the set of all rational and irrational numbers. You can visualize them as all the points on an infinite number line.
- **Imaginary Numbers (I):** These are numbers that, when squared, result in a negative number. The most fundamental imaginary number is the imaginary unit, I, defined as $i^2=-1$.
- **Complex Numbers (C):** This is the most comprehensive set, which includes all real and imaginary numbers on the complex number plane. A complex number is typically written in the form a+bi, where a and b are real numbers, and I is the imaginary unit, but it can be extended to the quaternion number system.

The number classification of mathematics includes the following:

- **Even and Odd Numbers:** An even number is an integer that is exactly divisible by 2, and an odd number is an integer that cannot be divided by 2.
- **Prime and Composite Numbers:** A prime number is a natural number greater than 1 that has only two divisors: 1 and itself (e.g., 2, 3, 5, 7, 11). A composite number is a natural number greater than 1 that has more than two divisors (e.g., 4, 6, 9).
- **Cardinal and Ordinal Numbers:** Cardinal numbers indicate quantity (e.g., one, two, three). Ordinal numbers indicate position or rank in a sequence (e.g., first, second, third).
- **Nominal Numbers:** These are used as labels or identifiers without a value or a quantity (e.g., a phone number, a zip code, etc.).

The basic field axioms are provided below:

- Commutativity of Addition: $a + b = b + a$
- Associativity of Addition: $(a + b) + c = a + (b + c)$
- Additive Identity: $a + 0 = 0 + a = a$
- Additive Inverse: $a + (-a) = 0 = (-a) + a$
- Commutativity of Multiplication: $ab = ba$
- Associativity of Multiplication: $(ab) c = a (bc)$
- Multiplicative Identity: $a \cdot 1 = 1 \cdot a = a$
- Multiplicative Inverse: $a \cdot a^{-1} = a^{-1} \cdot a = 1$; if $a \neq 0$
- Distributivity of Multiplication – Left: $a (b + c) = ab + ac$
- Distributivity of Multiplication – Right: $(a + b) c = ac + bc$
- Distinct Identity: $1 \neq 0$

For clarification, there are no basic axioms for subtraction and division because subtraction and division do not technically exist. Addition can span forward or backward. To distinguish between forward addition and backward addition, we label backward addition as subtraction. We also denote subtraction with the syntax $a - b$, when the correct syntax per axiom is $a + (-b)$. Multiplication can magnify up or can magnify down. To distinguish between a magnify up and a magnify down, we label multiplication 'magnifying down' as division. We also denote division with the syntax a/b, when the correct syntax is $a \cdot b^{-1}$. To guarantee that multiplication and division can be written and can be represented interchangeably, the law of reciprocity, which makes use of the multiplicative inverse above, is applied.

The basic field axioms are the default axioms used to establish a common order of operations; however, any binary operation with any order of operation can be used so long as it obeys the following rules for combining two elements of a set to produce a third element:

- **Closure:** A set is closed under an operation if combining any two elements from the set always results in an element that is also in that set.
- **Associativity:** The grouping of elements does not change the result.
- **Commutativity**: The order of the elements does not change the result.
- **Identity Element:** An identity element is an element that, when combined with any other element, leaves the other element unchanged.
- **Inverse Element:** An inverse element is an element that, when combined with a given element, yields the identity element.

This might be confusing to readers at a low level of math; however, we will illustrate the difference between the common binary operation and another binary system from tropical mathematics.

- Common binary operation of addition: $a + b = c$, thus $2 + 3 = 5$
- Tropical binary operation of addition: $a \oplus b = \min (a,b)$, thus $2 \oplus 3 = 2$
- Common binary operation of multiplication: $a \times b = c$, thus $2 \times 3 = 6$
- Tropical binary operation of multiplication: $a \otimes b = a + b$, thus $2 \otimes 3 = 5$

Once again, any system of binary operations can be created as long as the rules above are met.

Lastly, we will discuss mathematical modeling. Mathematical models are classified by their characteristics and their purpose based on unique applications. Model limitations arise from simplifying assumptions, data dependencies, inherent complexity, and potential overfitting, while errors can stem from these limitations (physical modeling errors) or from numerical approximation (truncation error). Essentially, mathematical models can be categorized in various ways, depending on the nature of the problem, as shown below.

- **Deterministic vs. Stochastic**: Deterministic models have inputs that are known with certainty, producing a single, predictable output, while stochastic models incorporate randomness or uncertainty, leading to a range of possible outcomes.
- **Linear vs. Nonlinear**: Linear models assume a direct, proportional relationship between cause and effect, while nonlinear models are used when the relationships are more complex and not directly proportional.
- **Discrete vs. Continuous**: Discrete models deal with quantities that exist in distinct, separate steps, such as the number of items, while continuous models involve quantities that change smoothly over time or space.
- **Static vs. Dynamic**: Static models describe a system at a single point in time, while dynamic models represent systems that change over time.

The limitations of mathematical models are as follows:

- **Simplifying Assumptions**: Models are built on assumptions that simplify real-world complexity, and these assumptions may not always hold true.
- **Data Dependency**: The accuracy and the reliability of a model are heavily dependent on the availability and the quality of the data used to construct and to validate it.
- **Complexity**: Modeling highly complex systems can be challenging, and the resulting models may be too intricate to manage or interpret effectively.
- **Overfitting**: Models can become too tailored to specific datasets, leading to a loss of generalizability and poor performance on new data flows.
- **Interpretation**: Misunderstanding or misinterpreting the results from a mathematical model can lead to incorrect conclusions.
- **Modeling Errors**: These errors occur in the formulation of the model itself, resulting from deliberate simplifications, a lack of detailed knowledge about the phenomena, or uncertainty in the model's structure.
- **Data Errors**: Inaccuracies or uncertainties within the input data can propagate into the model, affecting the accuracy of its output.
- **Truncation Errors**: When continuous mathematical models are solved using numerical methods, they are often approximated by discrete steps. Truncation error arises from these approximations.
- **Round-off Errors**: These errors result from the limitations of finite-precision arithmetic in computers, where numbers are rounded during calculations.

Once again, the objective of the preparation for knowledge articles is to promote a rational mindset that allows the reader to inquire about all things, to challenge all biases, to evaluate evidence holistically, and to sharpen awareness/consciousness. In this way, the reader will become less vulnerable to ego-driven decisions, self-doubt, and manipulation tactics.

Em Hotep!

PROCESSING A WORLDVIEW

ANKH WADJA SENEB | ARTICLE NO: 014

Function: Preparation of Knowledge
Intent: Increase Rationality & Mental Facility
Position: Part 1 – Preliminaries & Fundamentals

ARTICLE NO: 014 – PROCESSING A WORLDVIEW

Peace to the High Power! Peace to the Living Universe! Peace to all Finite Living Beings! Peace to All Things – seen and unseen! For my spirit is with me, my image is with me, and my purpose is with me. For wisdom belongs to the seekers in heavy pursuit of knowledge, which can only be ascertained through the preparation and the sharpening of mental facility; and, knowledge is the protective shield against intellectual danger and exploitative measures.

A worldview is typically considered to be a set of beliefs and assumptions that shape an individual's understanding of the world, often including the following criteria:

- **View of Human Nature** (Beliefs): The view of human nature encompasses beliefs about humanity's fundamental characteristics and tendencies, which influence how societies are organized and how people behave. These differing beliefs shape views on equality, freedom, morality, and society's structure.
- **View of Good Life** (Economy): Such a life from an economic perspective moves beyond mere wealth, encompassing human well-being and sustainability. This is achieved through policies that ensure fair wages, equitable resource distribution, strong communities, good health, and a healthy relationship with the environment.
- **Equality with Others** (Society): The view of equality in society is the political and the social ideal that all human beings possess equal inherent worth and deserve equal treatment, rights, and opportunities, regardless of their differences. It champions a society free from discrimination, fostering social cohesion, justice, and economic well-being by ensuring everyone can access the resources and the opportunities needed to thrive.
- **Progressive responsibility with Others** (Time): Progressive responsibility refers to a gradual increase in the complexity, the difficulty, and the scope of one's duties, often involving starting with foundational tasks and gradually advancing to more challenging roles and responsibilities over time. It implies growth, skill development, and adaptability in a professional journey, where individuals take on more complex work after mastering simpler tasks.
- **Relationship Between the Individual & the State** (Values): The relationship between the individual and the state is a complex, reciprocal dynamic involving the delegation of power, the establishment of rights and responsibilities, and the sociopolitical construction of shared values. Individuals delegate power to the state for collective security and well-being, while the state provides services and protection in return for obedience and contribution. This relationship is continuously shaped by societal values, historical context, and political discourse, influencing the development of institutions and the very notion of citizenship.
- **Relationships of Humans and Nature** (Geography): The relationship between humans and nature is viewed through diverse views in geography, ranging from the Western anthropocentric perspective, which sees nature as a resource to be controlled and exploited, to more holistic and indigenous views that emphasize interconnectedness, inherent value in nature, and a responsibility for stewardship.

- **Sources of Ethics and Morality** (Knowledge): These sources establish the basis for moral truth and right conduct, which can stem from various sources like divine command (religion), human reason (philosophy), collective agreement (culture/society), or empirical observation (scientific/evolutionary).

Testing a worldview includes the examination of its coverage of reality, an evaluation of its practical application through different perspectives, and the application of qualitative and quantitative methods to assess its justification and truthfulness. There are two (2) primary ways to test a worldview, as shown below.

The 5C's Worldview Test

- **Consistency** (or Internal Consistency): A worldview passes the consistency test if its different beliefs and claims do not contradict each other. To test it, logical flaws should be searched within the worldview's various components.
- **Coherence**: A coherent worldview has parts that logically and rationally connect to form a unified and organized whole. To test this worldview, an examination is done on how well the individual beliefs and tenets of the worldview fit together.
- **Congruence**: A worldview demonstrates congruence when its claims align with and are supported by actual reality and the experiences of life. To test the worldview, the beliefs and the tenets are compared against personal and shared experience, as well as objective facts.
- **Comprehensiveness**: A comprehensive worldview offers explanations for a wide range of life's phenomena, questions, and experiences. To test it, an evaluation of the breadth of the worldview's explanatory power is made.
- **Completeness**: Completeness suggests that a worldview provides a thorough and a satisfactory account of all significant aspects of life and existence. This is closely related to comprehensiveness but focuses on the depth and the satisfaction of the explanation.

The Traditional Worldview Test

- **Indigenous Worldview**: Involves a deep connection to the natural world with emphasis on community, harmony, respect for elders, traditional knowledge, and the belief in a spiritual connection to nature
- **Traditional Worldview**: Focuses on established customs, values, hierarchies, the importance of family and community, and the adherence to religious or spiritual traditions
- **Progressive Worldview**: Focuses on individual rights, equality, social justice, the belief in progress, continuous improvement, rational thinking, and scientific advancement
- **Globalized Worldview**: Focuses on the interconnectedness and the interdependence between nations, the promotion of global trade and cooperation, and the awareness of diverse cultures and perspectives.
- **Transformative Worldview**: Focuses on radical change and systemic transformation, the belief in the possibility of a better world, and the commitment to social justice and environmental sustainability.

Once again, the objective of the preparation for knowledge articles is to promote a rational mindset that allows the reader to inquire about all things, to challenge all biases, to evaluate evidence holistically, and to sharpen awareness/consciousness. In this way, the reader will become less vulnerable to ego-driven decisions, self-doubt, and manipulation tactics.

Em Hotep!

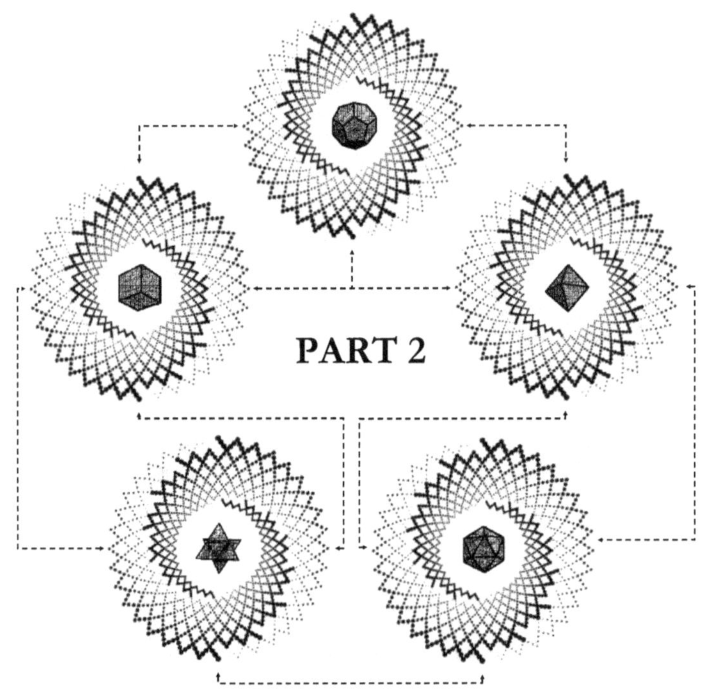

PART 2: HIGH SPIRITUALITY

DAWN OF THE FIRST BELL

ANKH WADJA SENEB | MEDJAI OF GATE #01

Function: Delivery of Raw Kemetic Teachings
Subject(s): Attributes of the High Power, Divine Functions
Position: Part 2 – The Raw Kemetic Teachings | High Spirituality

Peace to the High Power! Peace to the Living Universe! Peace to all Finite Living Beings! Peace to All Things – seen and unseen! For my spirit is with me, my image is with me, and my purpose is with me; and, let it be known by the Morning and the Evening Star that these self-evident teachings, unchanged by time or tongue, shall guide me and shall remain with me as I pursue my connection to the Living Universe and the High Power.

Spiritual sessions, which do not require any sort of purification ritual or worship services, commence with the ringing of bells, as bells not only manifest spiritual connection but also provide spiritual focus and spiritual protection. These sessions, which can be solo sessions or group gatherings, always begin with a call to opening represented by a gate or a salutation for good graces. In High Spirituality, this call is made to the Morning Star (Tioumoutiri) and the Evening Star (Ouaiti) to glorify the High Power as well as its extraordinary creation of a Living Universe.

For clarification, medjai (pronounced 'med-j-eye') are guardians of order, entrusted with protecting royals, areas of trade, and places of sacred knowledge.

The Morning Star's brilliance before dawn serves as a beacon of hope and new beginnings, as it heralds the arrival of the sun and a new day for the promise of a brighter future and the overcoming of darkness.

The Evening Star's luminance hearkens to the tune of nature and wisdom to provide guidance during times of transition or darkness. It appears in the western sky after sunset; and, it has been forever linked to beauty, love, and even represents the end of a cycle and the approach of night.

As finite living beings bathe in the dual effects of the Morning and the Evening Star, becoming immersed in the physical and metaphysical experiences of nature under the High Power, exposed to various cycles inherent in a Living Universe, and simmered by an inherent intelligent spirit, they are molded, forged, and cultivated on a journey known as the Kemetic path longing for balance, interconnectedness, purpose, and the endless pursuit of knowledge.

The High Power is a multi-dimensional life force – incorporeal, immaterial, impersonal, and bodiless – not of spirit that collectively serves as the sole creator, originator, and supreme being with dynamic sub-forces that can act individually or collectively as one in any proportion to execute its unrevealed will, for its whole is equal to the sum of its parts. Consequently, it can behave in a seemingly monotheist and/or polytheist manner without a hierarchical structure of primary, secondary, and tertiary forces. Also, there is no reason for it to be a parent (mother, father, etc.), to have children, or to have a special birth such as a virgin birth, as these things are beneath it.

The name(s) and the image(s) of the High Power have neither been revealed nor have been divulged by the High Power; and, if revealed, they would require definitive corroboration from the High Power as not to be invented in ignorance or in deceit. A healthy alternative would be all finite living beings pre-programmed with the High Power's name, which is not the case. Moreover, the High Power would be expected to respond directly and to appear in its exact form at least once anytime its name is called. It is incorrect to label the High Power as a 'god/goddess' because the gender of the High Power is indeterminate, and religious labeling conventions are not always compatible with spiritual phenomena.

Attributes of the High Power

- An androgynous entity possessing both, feminine and masculine, energies.
- Omniscient (being all-knowing) knowing everything and establishing the parameters and the laws governing the physical world and the metaphysical world of the universe. The wisdom, the knowledge, the parameters, the laws, the words, and the logic of the High Power can never be confined, can never be restricted, or can never be packaged by text, book, message, or measure.

For some readers, the metaphysical world is difficult to conceptualize a part from a fully-perceived physical world; however, the best analogy for the metaphysical layer and the physical layer of a Living Universe can be made through the complex plane of mathematics, where the complex plane represents a Living Universe, the imaginary part is the metaphysical layer, and the real part is the physical layer. Imaginary numbers, while not directly observable like real numbers, are pivotal to understanding phenomena involving oscillations, waves, and alternating currents, just like the metaphysical layer is pivotal to understanding phenomena involving the intelligent spirit, wave motion, consciousness, and awareness.

- Omnipresent (being everywhere at once) freely flowing through and emerging everywhere throughout the physical world of a universe (the domain for finite living beings) and the metaphysical world of the universe (the domain for the Pool of Spirits).
- Omnipotent (being all-powerful) choosing certain ways to handle a universe and all things contained within a universe.

The High Power can create more powerful entities and overcome such entities at will through this divine attribute, best understood through the combined idea of infinity and the concept of limitless potential. This combined idea refers to an unlimited and a boundless potential for growth, expansion, and possibility with no absolute limit, where the High Power either can assign different sizes of infinity or can establish higher infinities.

The High Power can overcome creation and destruction, meaning that it can create itself, destroy itself, bring itself (back) into being, or bring itself out of being (again) as an eternal life force existing inside all space-time and outside all space-time. In full authority, the High Power can accomplish any purpose or can execute any desired will without assuming another form, so there is no need to have an incarnate, as incarnations are beneath it. Consequently, the High Power has an unparalleled form nothing like the finite living beings inhabiting the physical world (e.g., no body parts, animal heads, uni-/multi-cellular constructs/likenesses/images, etc.) or the intelligent spirits emanating from the metaphysical world.

The High Power is best described as dynamic/variable, unpredictable, transcendent, and complex in nature, purpose, and perfection. Such a being can neither be immutable nor be understood in full. Transcending the infimum and the supremum, the High Power is the dual extremum in nature. In other words, the High Power embodies the greatest good, virtue, light, peace, love, etc., and the greatest evil, vice, darkness, hostility, hate, etc.; therefore, angel-demon pairs, 'good god'-'bad god' pairs, and even a complementary demiurge are both, unfathomable and incompatible.

Such an attribute might be difficult to grasp for those whom have been taught that a higher power can only be the greatest good; however, if such a higher power is not the greatest of everything, then indeed it is neither almighty nor omnipotent in divine form.

The High Power solely unlocks/activates the divine functions required to hold any macrocosm together.

Divine Functions		
Motion	Embodiment	Procreation
Matter	Healing	Metabolism
Space	Ritual	Filtration
Time	Consciousness	Storage
Darkness	Breath	Absorption
Light	Sensation	Maturation
Communication	Gestation	Protection
Structure	Vegetation	Periodicity
Precession	Germination	Initiation
Rotation	Birth	Digestion
Revolution	Corruption	Inertia
Fabrication	Sustenance	Parturition
Purgation	Conception	Inundation
Desire	Mastery	Migration
Dissipation	Entropy	Bonding
Genesis	Distillation	Insemination
Substance	Fusion	Coagulation
Expansion	Transformation	Circulation
Contraction	Unity	Decomposition
Quiescence	Inhalation	Assimilation
Mutation	Diffusion	Completion
Resonance	Augmentation	Incubation
Order/Balance	Creation	Enumeration
Presentience	Renewal	Exaltation
Energy	Fruition	Transmutation
Metamorphosis	Fixation	Latency
Animation	Secretion	Multiplication
Purification	Fertilization	Continuity
Precipitation	Ascension	Repetition
Resistance	Quintessence	Polymerization

Em Hotep!

DAWN OF THE SECOND BELL

ANKH WADJA SENEB | MEDJAI OF GATE #02

Function: Delivery of Raw Kemetic Teachings
Subject(s): Energy States, Cosmology, Sacred Geometric Rhythms, Spirit Cycle
Position: Part 2 – The Raw Kemetic Teachings | High Spirituality

MEDJAI OF GATE #02 – DAWN OF THE SECOND BELL

Peace to the High Power! Peace to the Living Universe! Peace to all Finite Living Beings! Peace to All Things – seen and unseen! For my spirit is with me, my image is with me, and my purpose is with me; and, let it be known by the Morning and the Evening Star that these self-evident teachings, unchanged by time or tongue, shall guide me and shall remain with me as I pursue my connection to the Living Universe and the High Power.

The formation, the timeline, the creation, and the evolution of the cosmos have forever piqued the interest of philosophers, scientists, theologians, and everyday people, where some mainly adhere to, adopt, or syncretize the ancient mythological Babylonian tradition/epic, Enūma Eliš, with a seven-day creation story highly suggestive of a 'young' Earth in many religious contexts of creationist thought, or where some impiously adhere to Big Bang theories based on scientific observations, high-parameter standard models, and controlled expansion-evolution experiments (scaled). When juxtaposing these contentious views, the conflict almost always centers on the extreme ends of whether the creation and the evolution of the cosmos hinge on a divine presence or not.

In High Spirituality, which has a hybrid outlook encompassing the presence of a High Power and the convergence of science to predefined (meta)physical laws, the High Power introduces energy states under divine function, facilitating the synthesis of infinitesimally small particle building blocks and sacred geometries necessary for cosmic creation and cosmic evolution.

<u>Impacts of Energy States on Particle Building Blocks</u>

The smallest particle can never be known, and particles are normally addressed in terms of atoms; however, a succinct discussion on known elementary particle classes and fundamental forces is warranted to understand the profound, multi-layered impacts of energy on cosmic construction.

The three (3) smallest known elementary particle classes of matter are quarks, leptons, and force carriers, which have antimatter counterparts.

Quarks of size $< 10^{-18}$ m are described as up, down, charm, strange, top, or bottom.

Leptons of size $< 10^{-18}$ m are described as electron neutrino, electron, muon neutrino, muon, tau neutrino, and tau.

Force Carriers, which are described in terms of mass, spin, and charge, consist of photons, Z bosons, W bosons, and gluons.

Quarks and Leptons are classified as fermions because they have half-integer spin and they obey the Pauli Exclusion Principle, which states that no two identical fermions can occupy the same quantum state simultaneously.

Force Carriers are classified as bosons because they are characterized by integer spin and they mediate interactions between other particles without obeying the Pauli Exclusion Principle.

Whenever particles exhibit hybrid or composite characteristics of fermions and bosons under a strong nuclear force, they are considered hadrons, which are either mesons or baryons.

Mesons are composed of a quark and an antiquark bound together by a strong force, where a lightweight meson is called a pion and where a heavy meson, inclusive of a strange quark, is called a kaon.

Baryons contain an odd number of valence quarks – conventionally three (3) – and include wave function and spin effects (lambda, sigma, xi, etc.).

Protons of size $\approx 10^{-15}$ m are composed of two (2) up quarks and one (1) down quark.

Neutrons of size $\approx 10^{-15}$ m are composed of one (1) up quark and two (2) down quarks.

The protons and the neutrons rest inside the nucleus of size $\approx 10^{-14}$ m

Electrons of size $\approx 10^{-18}$ m orbit around the nucleus (size range from 10^{-15} m to 10^{-14} m) with negative charge alongside neutrally charged electron neutrinos of size $\approx 10^{-24}$ m and weak nuclear interaction forces.

The region spanning the nucleus and the electron orbit forms an atom of size $\approx 10^{-10}$ m.

The bosons exert four (4) different types of force fields (fundamental forces) directly on the atomic structure: (i) electromagnetic forces to keep electrons bound to the nucleus thereby determining the structure of atoms, (ii) strong nuclear forces to hold the nucleus and contained particles together, (iii) weak nuclear forces to facilitate radioactive decay, other interactions, and quark transformations, and (iv) space-time attractive forces caused by mass and energy - mainly accepted as a gravitational theory, though not fully proven. Moreover, possibilities of other unknown fundamental forces remain open.

Whenever the atomic structure forms a pure atomic structure that cannot be broken down into a simpler atomic structure by chemical means, it is called an element; and, the atomic structure can have numerous, yet unique variations, configurations, and sets of properties.

A molecule (size range from 10^{-10} m to 0.05 m) is a group of two (2) or more atoms held together by chemical bonds. These atoms can be of the same element or different elements. Molecules are the smallest unit of a substance that retains its chemical identity.

The strong forces, which hold atoms together within a molecule, are intramolecular bonds (e.g., ionic, covalent, hydrogen, coordinate/dative, and metallic).

The weaker attractions between molecules are intermolecular bonds (e.g., van der Waals forces, dipole-dipole interactions, and hydrogen bonds).

The increasing complexity of molecules into macromolecules results in cells (size ≈ 10^{-5} m) – culminating in the building blocks of life.

The Valence Shell Electron Pair Repulsion (VSEPR) model, proposed in 1940, predicts the three-dimensional geometry of molecules. The fundamental principle of the model holds that the regions of high electron density—both bonding and lone pairs—around a central atom will arrange themselves to be as far apart as possible to minimize electrostatic repulsion. The five (5) possible molecular geometries based on counting the number of electron regions surrounding a central atom are shown below.

linear | trigonal planar | tetrahedral | trigonal bipyramid | octahedral

The reader shall take a mental note of the above to compare the geometries based on chemistry of the 1940s with the geometries - sacred and architectural – of the Ancient Egyptians to follow in the next section to understand how far ahead the Ancient Egyptians were in terms of the physical and the metaphysical layers of the living universe.

<u>Importance of Sacred Geometries</u>

In a Living Universe, there are recurring geometric patterns, designs, and structures from the most minute particles to the greatest cosmic bodies that, when combined, form the material substructure and ordered blueprint of dimensional space and reveal the vibration underlying the physical and the metaphysical planes of oneness, inseparability, interconnectedness, balance, completeness, alignment, and union of all things from part to whole. These sacred geometrical archetypes comprise the following:

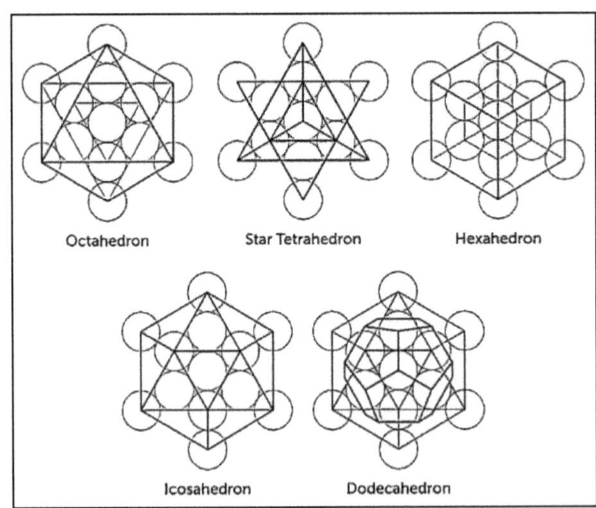

Sacred Geometries – Part 1				
Archetypes	Shape of Faces	Faces	Edges	Corners
Octahedron	Triangle	8	12	6
Stellated Tetrahedron	Triangle	8	12	8
Hexahedron	Square	6	12	8
Icosahedron	Triangle	20	30	12

Sacred Geometries – Part 2			
Archetypes	Sum of ∠ Measures	Completions	Divinations
Octahedron	1440	12	1
Stellated Tetrahedron	1440	12	1
Hexahedron	2160	12	1
Icosahedron	3600	12	1

Whereas, twelve (12) completions under one (1) High Power represents a Living Universe as a unified entity in perfection, harmony, wholeness, continuity, and completion. This unification is self-evident in all of the sacred geometric archetypes through the use of degrees (nfr, 45°, 90°, 180°, 360° + 60-degree equilaterals + 120-degree central angles of a circle), alignment, symmetry, and zero/nfr balance.

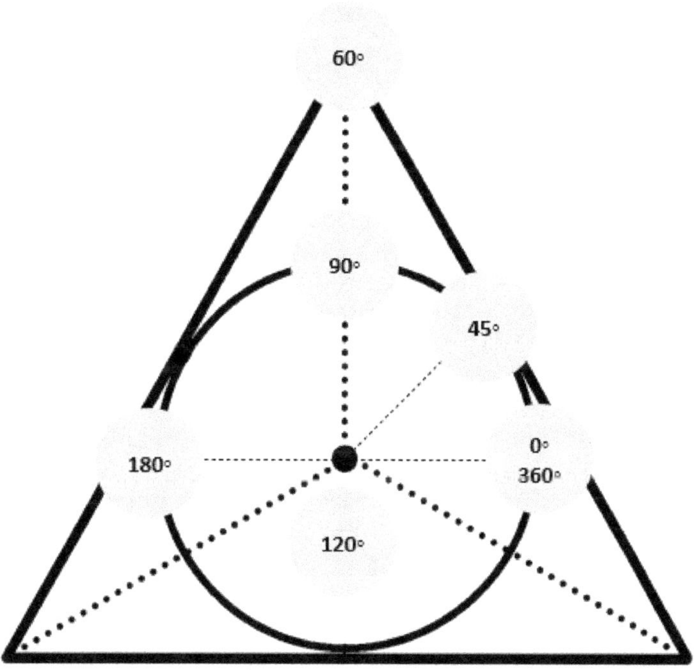

The zero/nfr reference is associated with nfr (0° degrees), which designates base/ground level. From a Kemetic perspective, it is more accurate to use "above nfr" or "below nfr" as a reference point for height or depth because the concept of zero as a numerical value was not formally used in Ancient Egypt; even though, the concept of nothingness and the concept of absence were well-established.

Whereas, the Octahedron provides in-plane stability to dynamic regions under attractive fields through structured equilaterals and interlocking threads.

Whereas, the Stellated Tetrahedron utilizes a vehicle of light as a chariot for spiritual ascension and connection to higher consciousness through mer (light), ka (spirit), and ba (body) as one (1) tetrahedron spins in a direction and the other tetrahedron spins in another direction – dimension to dimension, reality to reality.

Whereas, the Hexahedron initiates the structuring of molecules required to manifest the comprehensible world in space-time, to cause spiritual transformations, and to solidify all foundations.

Whereas, the Icosahedron ushers in the most symmetrical distribution of points, edges, and surfaces with optimal frequency, density, and barrier protection.

Whereas, the Dodecahedron jettisons the unlimited potential of inactive, equilibrium states and empty spaces spontaneously into action through random bursts, chaos, and penetration of cosmic cavities (bubbles, clusters, voids, porous walls, etc.).

Whereas, the Fruit of Life, which consists of thirteen (13) circles where the centralized circle is reserved for the High Power and where the twelve (12) outer circles signify life within a Living Universe, is superimposed onto the sacred geometries because it represents creation, cyclicity, and immortality. Please note that this is called "12-around-1" rather than "13 circles" in the Kemetic teachings.

Unleashing the mystical strength of the sacred geometries with its solely authoritative divine functions, the High Power brings forth mighty rhythms, sacred geometric rhythms, to give birth to the macrocosm out of emptiness.

Behold! Before the Beginning and All That Is!

In the beginning, the High Power was shrouded in emptiness, but not nothingness. As nothingness implies a complete absence of things, essential non-existence of all, or a complete void; however, the High Power remains in existence as an eternal life force. While evident, emptiness refers to the absence of inherent, independent existence in all phenomena. Such a phenomenon from the valley to the precipice of being can only be brought into existence by this life force - the High Power.

By necessity to carry out its own will – not to be praised, worshipped, or any posterior, trivial, deflective, or nugatory function – with full dominion, the High Power creates the parameters and the laws governing the physical layer and the metaphysical layer of a universe. Consequentially,

1. These laws/parameters introduce various causal relationships including natural disasters.
2. Although the laws/parameters behind this necessity are unknown and a universe's purpose/role in fulfilling the High Power's will is unknown, they are associated with causing (re)entry of spirit to body and the unified connectivity of the physical and the metaphysical worlds.
3. Whenever an event is inexplicable by the parameters and the laws governing the physical layer and the metaphysical layer of a universe set by the High Power, the supernatural and/or preternatural cause, which can only be attributed to the High Power, is deemed a miracle. In other words, only the High Power is capable of performing miracles.

For clarification, defying science and mathematics created by humans is not a miracle because such human understandings are supposed to converge asymptotically to those laws and parameters of the High Power. The science and mathematics of humans can be conflicted with unjustifiable singularities (black holes, vortex centers, etc.), changes due to advancing knowledge, and simplifying/forced assumptions; however, the laws and the parameters of the High Power cannot. Anything that goes against these can neither be true nor possible; and it suggests that humans – or any other finite living being for the same matter – should work toward increasing their understanding of these governing laws rather than complacently accepting that only the High Power knows them.

After creating the parameters and the laws governing the physical layer and the metaphysical layer of a universe, the High Power calls forth the sacred geometries in perfect degree and in perfect dimension.

The High Power calls forth the Octahedron into being. And, it is done.

Then, the High Power calls forth the Tetrahedron into being. And, it is done.

Then, the High Power calls forth the Hexahedron into being. And, it is done.

Then, the High Power calls forth the Icosahedron into being. And, it is done.

Then, the High Power calls forth the Dodecahedron into being. And, it is done.

Extending its brilliance to the Fruit of Life ('12-around-1'), the High Power creates the systems of information necessary to stitch the fabrics of all life and all realities ('12'); and, the Fruit of Life ('12-around-1') is overlayed upon each sacred geometry.

The High Power, omnipresent in all positions of '1', casts out its multi-dimensional life force, empowering the Fruit of Life to spin vigorously in all perfect degrees and all perfect dimensions. The sacred geometry rigidly follows, causing vortices to emerge, where the High Power remains poised at all singularities (i.e., the eyes of each vortex), and the trailing vectors induce rhythms.

The High Power commands the amalgamation of the Octahedron and these rhythms to create the Octahedral Rhythm. And, it is done.

Then, the High Power commands the amalgamation of the Tetrahedron and these rhythms to create the Tetrahedral Rhythm. And, it is done.

Then, the High Power commands the amalgamation of the Hexahedron and these rhythms to create the Hexahedral Rhythm. And, it is done.

Then, the High Power commands the amalgamation of the Icosahedron and these rhythms to create the Icosahedral Rhythm. And, it is done.

Then, the High Power commands the amalgamation of the Dodecahedron and these rhythms to create the Dodecahedral Rhythm. And, it is done.

After the High Power creates the sacred geometric rhythms, it harnesses the divine functions, in sole authority, necessary to craft a universe subject to its will. As the divine functions are wielded by the High Power and are thus held sacred in all regards.

The Octahedral Rhythm under Divine Function

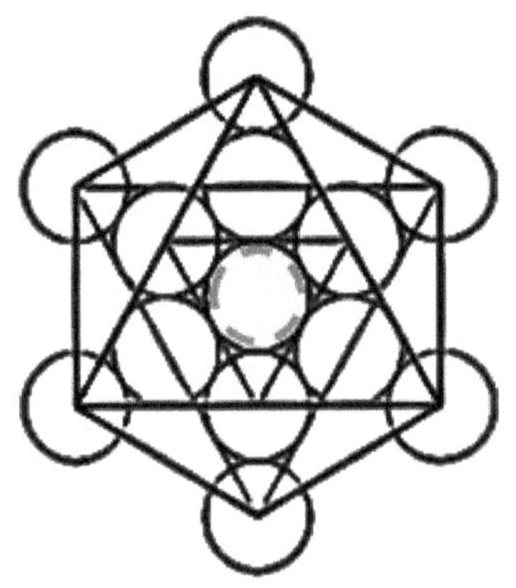

The Octahedral Rhythm		
Motion	Genesis	Divine Functions
Matter	Substance	
Space	Expansion	
Time	Contraction	
Darkness	Quiescence	
Light	Mutation	
Communication	Resonance	
Structure	Order/Balance	
Precession	Presentience	
Rotation	Energy	
Revolution	Metamorphosis	

The High Power activates the Octahedral Rhythm from the '1' position with sole authority over divine functions.

The Octahedral Rhythm generates cosmic waters and cosmic fibers within the primal existence to give both, life and consciousness, to a universe. The proliferation of the cosmic waters and the cosmic fibers, constructing celestial bodies, causes a universe to expand and to contract in infinite space-time as a substance undergoes motion, reactions, fusion, and fission to form matter. Depending on the condition of energy states and the active/passive expressions of matter contained within the cosmic sphere, the hibernation of vital activity manifesting as darkness mutates into powered vital activity after the quiescent matter is stimulated by light.

The constant bombardment of energy and matter produces not only vibration and sound but also the physical forms, the physical patterns, the physical geometries, the physical proportions, the architecture, speech unit synthesis, and the celestial asterisms of a universe exalted by resonance and bounded by natural order, balance, and structure. Since a universe has consciousness under decreed parameters and laws created by the High Power (i.e. a conscious universe is a living universe), it acquires the innate intelligence to measure its constituents (e.g. precession, revolutions, rotations, translations, and space-times of celestial bodies, luminaries, and light), to change the form of its constituents – transformation, adaptation, and/or evolution – and to communicate among infinitesimally small particles of matter and energy states. Such communication among particles and energy states facilitates and fosters the generation of inorganic matter as well as the prototypical elements of fire, terra, water, and air contained within a Living Universe.

The Tetrahedral Rhythm under Divine Function

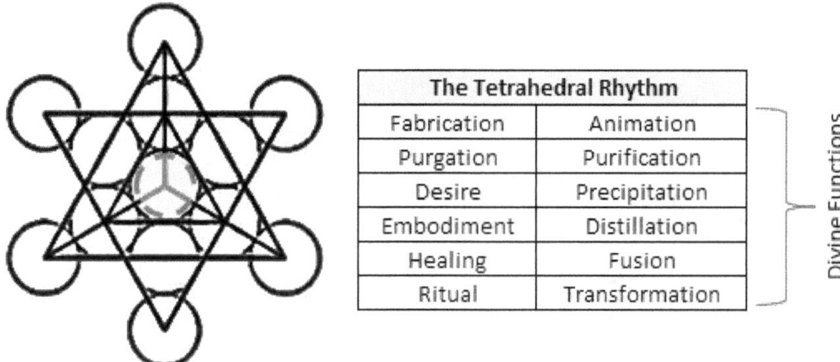

The Tetrahedral Rhythm	
Fabrication	Animation
Purgation	Purification
Desire	Precipitation
Embodiment	Distillation
Healing	Fusion
Ritual	Transformation

The High Power activates the Tetrahedral Rhythm from the '1' position with sole authority over divine functions.

The Tetrahedral Rhythm facilitates the entry of and the exit of the intelligent spirit from the Pool of Spirits originating in the metaphysical world of a universe to the physical world of a universe. Under the divine function of the High Power, each intelligent spirit is created, is fabricated, and is forged with intrinsic characteristics and attributes to ensure the transference of the energetic form to the physical mantle of the finite living being that will house it. The transference of the energetic form involves the action of embodying inert matter with the source of creative activity and the genius of personality, form, and function.

The physical mantle, in turn, represents the alternating flux or the electromagnetic current that constitutes physical life when the intelligent spirit joins with matter in the physical world through precipitation and distillation – purged and purified. After joining in perfect fusion, the matter inherits the characteristics and the attributes of the intelligent spirit, where the resultant stimulates physical life to ascend from its natural level of embodiment and innate consciousness to its supernatural levels of expression, logic, and instinct. All of the inherited information of the resultant's corporeal form is imprinted and is coded in the genome, nuclear and mitochondrial, mainly as DNA or RNA, paving the way for material ancestry, centralized construction, unique identity, and internal stability. Whenever the cohesion of the genome is damaged by mutations or alterations, illness results; however, healing results in genome recovery.

For clarification, the instincts influencing the behavior of the physical life are survival (includes fight-or-flight), (re)generation, nourishment, nurture, conscious development, intuition, ritual, creativity, destruction, hunger, sexuality, carnality, relationship, reflection, and aspiration to supracorporeal.

For clarification, the intelligent spirit is pre-programmed with intrinsic characteristics and attributes. Each intelligent spirit is unique. Moreover, there are no spiritual genes or innate predispositions toward faith or certain beliefs/behaviors, deducing that the raw teachings do not support horoscopes, tarot readings, life path numbers, or the like. This also means that no finite living being can be born 'religious' – only 'spiritual' through the intelligent spirit.

The Hexahedral Rhythm under Divine Function

The Hexahedral Rhythm	
Consciousness	Unity
Breath	Inhalation
Sensation	Diffusion
Gestation	Augmentation
Vegetation	Creation
Germination	Renewal
Birth	Fruition
Corruption	Fixation
Sustenance	Secretion
Conception	Fertilization
Mastery	Ascension
Procreation	Insemination
Metabolism	Coagulation
Filtration	Circulation
Storage	Decomposition
Absorption	Assimilation

Divine Functions

The High Power activates the Hexahedral Rhythm from the '1' position with sole authority over divine functions.

The Hexahedral Rhythm spurs the intelligent spirit's descent into the materialized physical mantle or the physical reproductive matter (ovum, sperm, spore, amniotic fluids, womb, fission boundary, etc.) of a finite living being's physical mantle enclosure following fertilization, cell division, and/or during gestation/germination; and, it positions the sun(s) at the beginning of space-time.

For clarification, the High Power can create, can position, and can cycle one or more suns, moons, luminaries, celestial bodies, etc., in a given universe subject to its will because of omnipotence.

During the developmental stages, the intelligent spirit undergoes expansion or augmentation at variable transformational, physical, emotional, and psychic levels. The parameters and the laws governing the physical layer and the metaphysical layer ensure the continuation of vital organ formation as the intelligent spirit enters the matter at conception, ensure the intelligent spirit's departure back to the Pool of Spirits upon separation prior to decomposition, and ensure the transmutation of the spirit through cosmic realms. The dissolution of the physical mantle is a necessary requirement of the sojourning finite living being.

Lastly, the positioning of the sun(s) at the center of space-time is paramount to the phases of light, and coincidentally the stability of sentient life and the living celestial environment. The Four Diurnal Phases of Light are:

- **The Reborn Light**: This period denotes the emergence of the sun.
- **The Ascended Light**: This is designated by the period when the sun culminates at its highest point in the sky and begins its descent.
- **The Circulated Light**: This period of the setting sun occurs when the light fades.
- **The Unified Light**: This period of the sun's disappearance reveals the journey of light battling through the deepest and darkest regions of the universe to be reborn in the next period.

The Icosahedral Rhythm under Divine Function

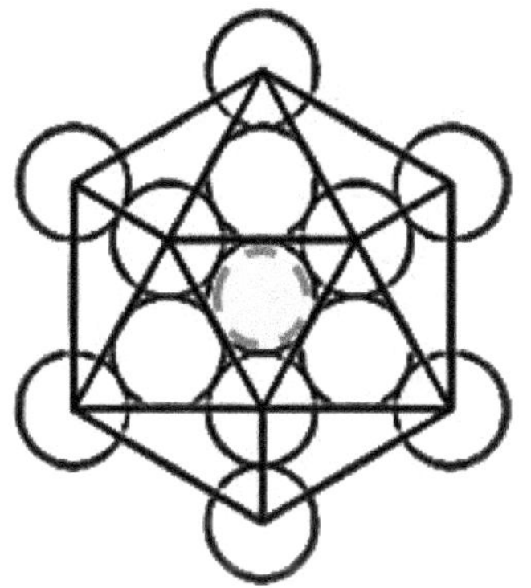

The Icosahedral Rhythm	
Maturation	Completion
Protection	Incubation
Periodicity	Enumeration
Initiation	Exaltation
Digestion	Transmutation
Inertia	Latency
Parturition	Multiplication
Inundation	Continuity
Migration	Repetition
Dissipation	Resistance

Divine Functions

The High Power activates the Icosahedral Rhythm from the '1' position with sole authority over divine functions.

The Icosahedral Rhythm opens the horizon of emergence, introducing periodic and cyclical wave motion, the dissipation of energy (friction, electrical resistance, air/wind resistance, heat, and so forth) throughout the cosmos, and the incidental birth of dwelling spheres in a Living Universe. The incidental birth of dwelling spheres for finite living beings in a Living Universe under the will of the High Power is best illustrated in or analogous to home construction. The builder is the High Power, and the house is a Living Universe. The house is created to fulfill the builder's plan (High Power's will). As moisture builds in the dark cavities of the house, dwelling spheres for organisms like mold are created, and mold materializes in the dark cavities. The mold is analogous to the finite living beings, which are incidental rather than intentional finite beings.

Strengthened by the introduction of wave periodicity and the inertia thereof, the intelligent spirit extricates itself from the bondage with the physical mantle (separation) and the consumption of the physical mantle (decomposition), shedding the physical mantle as it converges toward death. This shedding includes life fluids (i.e., blood, bile, mucus, saliva, etc.) draining out of or emptying from orifices prior to the transmutation into a complete spiritual essence with no past-life memory.

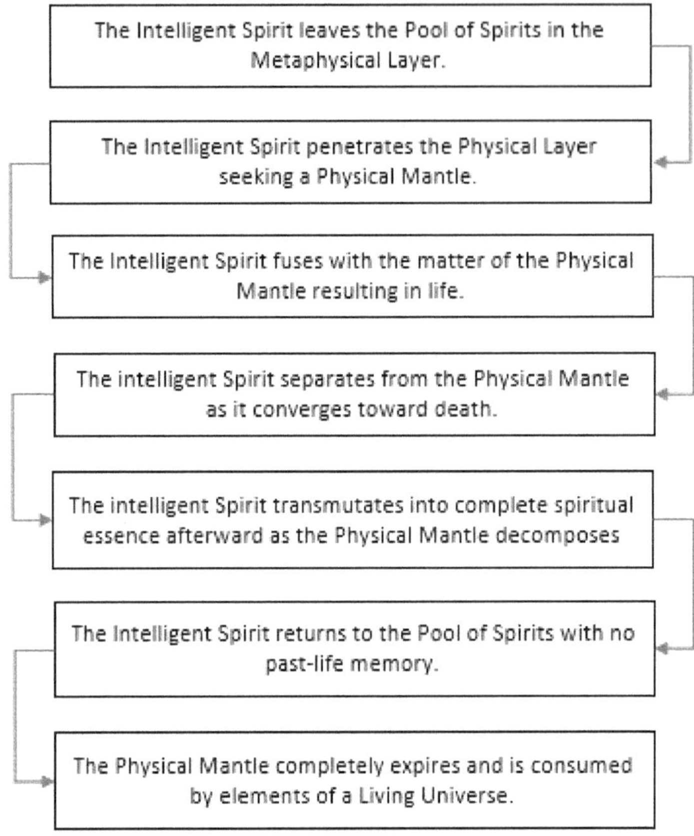

Next, the emergence of energy dissipation places constraints on the prototypical elements of fire, terra, water, and air to protect a Living Universe from perturbative collapse and gradient divergence. The birth of dwelling spheres, where finite living beings can materialize, can adapt, can transform, and/or can evolve, progressively or spontaneously, is a consequential manifestation of a Living Universe because the purpose of a Living universe is only tied to the will of the High Power. Finite living beings have individual purpose and free will in a Living Universe.

For clarification, the High Power has free will, a Living Universe has no free will, and finite living beings have free will.

The Dodecahedral Rhythm under Divine Function

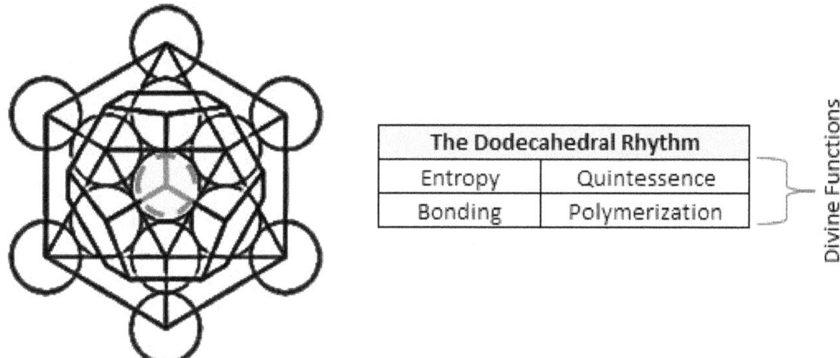

The Dodecahedral Rhythm	
Entropy	Quintessence
Bonding	Polymerization

The High Power activates the Dodecahedral Rhythm from the '1' position with sole authority over divine functions.

The Dodecahedral Rhythm ushers in the binding material, quintessence, that holds/connects the physical layer and the metaphysical layer of a Living Universe together, that facilitates the boundless emanation of ether/plasma from the sun(s), and that fills the regions of a Living Universe beyond/around the celestial bodies in space, randomness, and disorder. Quintessence can also metastasize into alternative realities and can subdivide a Living Universe into multiple volumes. The ability to subdivide a Living Universe into multiple volumes should not be confused with establishing a multiverse.

The interactions between the binding material, Quintessence, and a Living Universe cause the formation of byproducts to populate profusely in the filled regions of a Living Universe beyond and around contained celestial bodies. These byproducts include solvents, glycerols, phosphorus, alcohols, acids, bases, reagents, reactants, enzymes, and simplified sugars. With consciousness to communicate among infinitesimally small particles of matter and energy states, a Living Universe causes these byproducts to bond/assemble freely, to start/terminate reactions, and to transfer mass profusely under variable environmental conditions to overcome high entropy distributions. Over time and unpredictably, these activities result in the formation of structured molecules and organic compounds, simple and complex, such as carbohydrates, peptides, nucleic acids, and lipids.

As a sidebar, there is no coincidence as to why structured molecules form linear, angular, trigonal, tetrahedral, bipyramidal, hexahedral, and octahedral configurations.

Now that all sacred geometric rhythms activated by the High Power and divine functions solely activated/unlocked by the High Power have been revealed, it will become easier to convey the forthcoming points from the raw Kemetic spiritual teachings, which differ from the hybrid Kemetic variants and the traditional Kemetic religious variants – monotheistic and polytheistic.

- Ideas of reincarnation are invalid because the intelligent spirit does not remember past lives, and the physical mantle has no way to recall memories of past lives with or without the fusion of the intelligent spirit. Not to mention, reincarnation targets the 'soul' in the religious context, and High Spirituality does not consist of souls – only intelligent spirits.

- High Spirituality is premised on the cycle of life – physically and metaphysically – rather than an afterlife with or without a reward. There is no need for salvation because the life and the death cycles of the physical mantle are a function of the intelligent spirits cycling from the Pool of Spirits in the metaphysical layer, dismissing ideas of meeting the High Power for judgment of sins or for obtaining permission/favor for passage to any place of the afterlife. The intelligent spirit is eternally cycled; however, a physical mantle obviously is not.
- High Spirituality does involve and does acknowledge paranormal experiences and activities, which can be associated with out-of-body experiences or the roaming of the intelligent spirit and/or energy disturbances in a Living Universe; however, there is no admission of ghosts, demons, or the like. Paranormal experiences are nothing more than unusual events difficult to explain by contemporary scientific understanding, and the scientific understanding of finite living beings is far from perfect.

Up to this point, an astute reader might have noticed that the fabricated universe has been addressed as "a Living Universe" with a generalized indefinite article rather than "the Living Universe" with a specific definite article. The rationale is straightforward when one remembers why the High Power creates a Living Universe – to fulfill and to carry out its will.

Any Living Universe favorable to the will of the High Power and optimal in compliance with the parameters, the laws, and the sacred geometric rhythms created by the High Power is considered a candidate universe because it can be formed in the cosmic emptiness. The candidate universe is one of many possibilities, and it is a direct creation of the High Power. It is initially created in perfection; however, impurities, defects, instabilities, and flaws emerge over time.

For clarification, the order and the number of celestial constituents and cosmological mechanisms (e.g., multiple suns, number of planets, plethora of luminaries, black holes, cosmic fields, etc.) can vary from one candidate universe to another candidate universe because each candidate universe forms continuously with dual (random + systematic) and dual (static + dynamic) components and phenomena.

For clarification, the shapes of celestial constituents and cosmological mechanisms are visualized as simple/complex/infinite polyhedral bodies, simple/complex/infinite polygonal surfaces, and conic sections. Although attributed to the Greeks, the first drafts of the conics were made in Alexandria, Egypt, and conics were heavily used in Ancient Egyptian architecture, especially the triangular conics of the pyramids.

For clarification, any candidate universe can be created or can be destroyed subject to the will of the High Power. A candidate universe has no free will; and, its existence, life, and belongingness are personal to the High Power.

For clarification, a candidate universe is not eternal (i.e., there is an origin and there is an expiration date), and it has different contraction, expansion, and evolution rates. Consequently, there is no way to determine what is the first, second, third…last Living Universe.

For the sake of the teachings, the Living Universe will refer to the current Living Universe as of today from hereon.

Em Hotep!

DAWN OF THE THIRD BELL

ANKH WADJA SENEB | MEDJAI OF GATE #03

Function: Delivery of Raw Kemetic Teachings
Subject(s): Origin/Evolution of Life, Reproductive/Materialization, Sex, Gender
Position: Part 2 – The Raw Kemetic Teachings | High Spirituality

Peace to the High Power! Peace to the Living Universe! Peace to all Finite Living Beings! Peace to All Things – seen and unseen! For my spirit is with me, my image is with me, and my purpose is with me; and, let it be known by the Morning and the Evening Star that these self-evident teachings, unchanged by time or tongue, shall guide me and shall remain with me as I pursue my connection to the Living Universe and the High Power.

Per the Kemetic teachings, life is defined as the cyclical journey of existence in the Living Universe from the time when the intelligent spirit leaves the Pool of Spirits in the pursuit of a physical mantle to the time when the intelligent spirit sheds the physical mantle in spiritual essence on return to the Pool of Spirits as the physical mantle converges toward death. Although the definition of life is simple in High Spirituality, it constitutes a serious challenge to those adhering to traditional religious dogma and contemporary science because there is no universally accepted definition of 'life' that captures the diversity of finite living beings and the difficulties in distinguishing between entities with life and without life. Furthermore, this challenge is compounded when adding layers such as the origin of life and the evolution of life thereafter as follows:

- The doctrine of creationism asserts that life originated with supernatural acts and miraculous interventions of divine creation (intelligent design), where a divine being (or divine beings) creates each finite living being one by one. Prior to Charles Darwin's *On the Origin of Species*, published in 1859, many 20th-century creationists believed the entire universe was created within 6,000-10,000 years based on the 6-day creation story of the Ancient and Abrahamic religions. Despite mounting evidence from the fossil record and the great antiquity of life on Earth against creationism, adherents continue to accept the Garden of Eden account, where Adam and Eve enter as a single pair and where Adam is either born of dust or clay and Eve is either born from Adam's rib or Adam's soulful essence. Furthermore, the religious variant of Kemeticism gives accounts of creation through godly tear drops, which is far from true. Creationists also fail to address evolution (speciation, natural selection, etc.), similarities in genomes (DNA, RNA, etc.) of dissimilar species, geological conflicts (aging/shape/behavior of the Earth), life begetting life, the extinctive dangers of generational inbreeding, the difference in the composition between mud/clay/dust and finite living beings, the definition of a 'kind' (distinct from a species) that cannot change into another 'kind', the possibility of life on non-Earth spaces, and the solemn focus on Earth.
- Spontaneous generation, also called abiogenesis, hinges on the idea that life can originate from non-life when uncontrolled, rudimentary particles synthesize – through physical and chemical means – far beyond complex inorganic entities, ushering in a bifurcation point where non-living beings become finite living beings. At the surface, this theory seems feasible; however, the difficulty of accumulating all the necessary complex molecules for life (e.g. proteins, nucleic acids, lipids, carbohydrates, etc.), the lack of a clear pathway for polymerization under the early conditions of the Living Universe (i.e. the oxidizing nature of Earth's atmosphere would destroy most of the molecules needed for this theory to hold true), and the fact that life requires one (1) specific form of chiral molecules (i.e. homochirality in a prebiotic environment remains

unclear or nearly impossible) renders abiogenesis nearly invalid.

- Biogenesis, by definition, is the idea that finite living beings originate from other pre-existing life, and only finite living beings can give life to other living things. This idea, which is proposed as a counter to abiogenesis and which suggests that less complex finite living beings (e.g., unicellular) can become more complex finite living beings (e.g., multicellular), dodges questions concerning the origin of life by, instead, focusing on how life evolves beyond the unspecified origination point. There is a lot of overlap between those whom believe in biogenesis and those whom believe in strict evolution, so the origin of life dilemma is shared between them.

For clarification, High Spirituality does not support creationism despite the presence of the High Power, as will be seen later on in the teaching.

For clarification, High Spirituality does not support abiogenesis because the creation of life (the Living Universe and finite living beings) requires divine functions solely assigned to the High Power.

For clarification, High Spirituality supports biogenesis to a certain degree on 'life originating from life' and 'life giving life' to other finite living beings; however, the disagreement is on the actual finite living beings under assessment, because unicellular beings cannot give life to multicellular beings.

Unlike the views expressed above, High Spirituality involves a rationalized and a cohesive interplay between the domain of science and the domain of spirituality to justify the origin of life and the evolution of life thereafter.

Recall that the priority of the High Power is fulfilling its will; and, it will not stop executing its will in the interest or to the benefit of finite living beings.

Recall that the High Power creates the Living Universe directly with no free will to fulfill its will. Since the Living Universe has no free will – thus, no capacity to make decisions or choices outside of the High Power's will – the Living Universe is impersonal to and is indifferent to finite living beings in all regards.

Recall that the High Power activates the Icosahedral Rhythm from the '1' position with sole authority over divine functions. The Icosahedral Rhythm opens the horizon of emergence, introducing periodic and cyclical wave motion, the dissipation of energy (friction, electrical resistance, air/wind resistance, heat, and so forth) throughout the cosmos, and the incidental birth of dwelling spheres in a Living Universe for the incidental birth of dwelling spheres for finite living beings.

Recall that the High Power activates the Dodecahedral Rhythm from the '1' position with sole authority over divine functions. The Dodecahedral Rhythm ushers in the binding material, quintessence, that holds/connects the physical layer and the metaphysical layer of the Living Universe together. The interactions between the binding material, Quintessence, and the Living Universe cause the formation of byproducts to populate profusely in the filled regions of the Living Universe beyond and around contained celestial bodies. These byproducts include solvents, glycerols, phosphorus, alcohols, acids, bases, reagents, reactants, enzymes, and sugars. With consciousness to communicate among infinitesimally small particles of matter and energy states, the Living Universe causes these byproducts to bond/assemble freely, to start/terminate reactions, and to transfer mass profusely under variable environmental conditions to overcome high entropy distributions. Over time and unpredictably, these activities result in the formation of organic compounds, simple and complex, such as carbohydrates, peptides, nucleic acids, and lipids.

Recall that the High Power activates the Hexahedral Rhythm from the '1' position with sole authority over divine functions. The Hexahedral Rhythm spurs the intelligent spirit's descent into the physical reproductive matter (ovum, sperm, spore, amniotic fluids, womb, fission boundary, etc.) of a finite living being's physical mantle enclosure following fertilization, cell division, and/or during gestation/germination.

The Origin of Life & The Evolution of Life Thereafter

The birth of dwelling spheres contained within the Living Universe, the presence of inorganic compounds, and the formation of organic compounds fortuitously pave the way for the emergence of finite living beings. The Living Universe and finite living beings can never be anything like the High Power in form, image, or composition because the High Power is the sole multi-dimensional life force of divine nature and of divine type in fraction or in full.

Focusing on its will in the Living Universe, the High Power assumes a distant and an impersonal role in the lives of finite living beings. Due to the self-evident lack of intervention and inaction of the High Power in the lives of finite living beings, the following consequences and constraints arise:

- The High Power embodies the greatest good, light, peace, love, etc., and the greatest evil, darkness, hostility, hate, etc., so the Living Universe and any entity contained within the Living Universe are able to experience anything within these bounds. As an example, suffering and happiness are not necessary; however, they are permitted in the Living Universe because the Living Universe has no free will under the High Power, and it is thus subjugated to the character, the attributes, and the nature of the High Power at all times. The Living Universe is the sanctuary for the High Power.
- Since the High Power is impersonal to finite living beings, it has no desire to be worshipped by, to receive sacrifices/offerings from, or to be praised by them, for the High Power will never stop executing and fulfilling its will in the interest of or to the benefit of finite living beings. Consequently, these finite living beings have individual purpose and complete free will in the Living Universe. Even the illusion of having free will with a divine puppeteer is false because the High Power is not involved in the lives of finite living beings whatsoever. Finite living beings, for instance, are free to damage and to leech off the Living Universe as well as other finite living beings as indirect, yet unintentional, creations.

For clarification, the personal quest for meaning, individual purpose, and a connection to something beyond oneself, such as the High Power and the Living Universe, does not require faith.

For clarification, the High Power does not respond to solemn requests, spells, or prayers for help, guidance, or assistance. If the High Power wanted finite living beings to pray to it, then this act would have been pre-programmed into the intelligent spirit, and finite living beings would carry out the activity impulsively without knowing why so or what it is. Expressions of gratitude to and/or spiritual conversations with the Living Universe or the High Power are considered to be affirmations rather than prayers. There is no mediator or intermediary required. Although there is power in words, fulfilled requests or perceived blessings through affirmation are based on sheer chance.

- Finite living beings never receive any favor or protection from the High Power. No finite living being is viewed as inferior or superior to another finite living being by the High Power. Additionally, all finite living beings are exposed to the risks and the dangers within the dwelling spheres of the Living Universe. Put in another way, the Living Universe and finite living beings are limited in survival, but the High Power is not.

- The divine function of communication allows the High Power to understand the syntax, the phonetics, the phonology, the semantics, the pragmatics, the discourse, and the morphology of all languages and information types constructed by finite living beings; even though, finite living beings do not possess control of such a function. Moreover, the High Power possesses a language unknown to finite living beings; and, this language is not diluted, is not reduced, is not weakened, or is not adulterated in the interest of subordinate understanding.

For clarification, the High Power, being impersonal to finite living beings, does not need finite living beings to speak on its behalf as messengers or through revelation. Revelations, hallucinations, dreams, visions, and the like are augmented projections of the physical and metaphysical world. A proposed revelation account or any proposed divine testimony, which can never be primary, has to be corroborated by the High Power anyway, as testimonies and revelations – sometimes coated in superstition – can be falsified, can be misunderstood, can be misinterpreted, or can be unapplicable given the circumstances.

For clarification, communicating with a finite living being by name or in conversation is the same as communicating with a finite living being by a combination of vibrations, sounds, etc., for which it identifies as or for which it understands. All finite living beings, regardless of sensory-level detectability, cannot produce every vibration, sound, etc., as the High Power can do.

Finite living beings initially materialize and then reproduce at different rates on different scales as the physical mantle consumes requisite nourishment (e.g., inorganic compounds, organic compounds, etc.) from dwelling spheres prior to fusing with the intelligent spirit for life in the Living Universe. As the indirect creation of the High Power, finite living beings have either internally or externally built-in reproductive mechanisms with the necessary settings to mimic the initial materialization process. Finite living beings can enter the Living Universe in two (2) ways: (i) materialization to mature form at a high-energy state requiring longer development rates or (ii) reproduction to primordial form at a low-energy state requiring shorter development rates.

Consequently, the entry of finite living beings into the Living Universe is not without the following challenges:

- The parameters and the laws created by the High Power and governing the physical layer and the metaphysical layer of the Living Universe might restrict the materialization and/or the reproduction of (in)compatible finite living beings in a dwelling sphere.
- A(n) (in)compatible finite living being might fail to materialize in a dwelling sphere or might be waiting for long periods to materialize.
- All of the nourishment (e.g., inorganic compounds, organic compounds, etc.) required to materialize a finite living being is neither available (i.e., absent, decomposed, or degraded) in the dwelling sphere nor proximal to the dwelling sphere.
- A finite living being might materialize in the (un)favorable dwelling sphere, where it is immediately consumed or terminated by existing finite living beings.
- A finite living being might materialize in the (un)favorable dwelling sphere, where its reproductive efforts prove fatal to itself.
- A finite living being might materialize in the (un)favorable dwelling sphere, where the reproduction of offspring takes a long time.
- A finite living being might materialize in the (un)favorable dwelling sphere, where its reproductive capacity is too low with no ability to overcome low population counts.

- A finite living being might materialize in the (un)favorable dwelling sphere with an inability to reproduce, including but not limited to a fractured reproductive system or a defective reproductive system. Another relevant case occurs when a reproducing finite living being does not materialize with its compatible, complementary reproducing finite living being.
- A finite living being might materialize in the (un)favorable dwelling sphere, where evolutionary and adaptive means can do nothing to prevent inevitable extinction or predation.
- The dynamic conditions of celestial bodies in the Living Universe transform a favorable dwelling sphere into an unfavorable dwelling sphere, leading to the mass extinction of existing finite living beings.
- A finite living being cannot migrate from an unfavorable/adverse dwelling sphere to a favorable one. Or, a favorable dwelling sphere never emerges in time.
- The intelligent spirit cannot fuse with the physical mantle of the finite living being at either the time of materialization or the time of reproduction.
- The catastrophic destruction of the Living Universe for any reason by any cause (e.g. destruction necessary for the High Power's will, large-scale cosmic collisions, elimination of (in)organic compounds necessary for life, the High Power's vacancy from the '1' position of any sacred geometric rhythm deactivating divine functions, etc.) subsequently results in the loss of all dwelling spaces and all finite living beings contained within them.

Although this list does not cover all possible challenges and some items do not apply to all finite living beings, it provides a good understanding of the obstacles that finite living beings need to overcome just to manifest in the Living Universe.

The initial finite living beings completely materialize in dwelling spheres with built-in reproductive systems as accidental consequences of nature. Due to variable environmental conditions and variable availability of nourishment (e.g., inorganic compounds, organic compounds, etc.) in a given dwelling sphere, there can be multiple materializations of the same finite living being – complete, incomplete, or failed - with different faciology, images, and phenotypes. Consequently, this means that it is best to talk in terms of the 'first finite living beings' rather than 'the first finite living being' (i.e., the first humans rather than the first human) as the materialization of the first finite being, or the attempt thereof, is only known to the High Power. This idea might be difficult for those whom have been taught this idea of 'first man' and 'first woman'; however, this idea is biologically invalid because low genetic variations result in genetic disorders, congenital defects, and generational termination. Moreover, this idea implies that all finite living beings are products of incest, which can be proven false with modern-day ancestry testing.

For clarification, complete materialization means that the finite living being is able to materialize in full without abnormalities, given the environmental conditions and the availability of nourishment of the Living Universe.

For clarification, incomplete materialization means that the finite living being was able to materialize in fraction with a high-to-low degree of abnormality, given the environmental conditions and the availability of nourishment of the Living Universe.

For clarification, failed materialization means that the finite living being either had abnormalities overcoming the materialization attempt or had insufficient support from the environmental conditions or had insufficient nourishment to materialize.

Key characteristics, which define life, include cellular organization, metabolism (energy usage), growth and development, materialization/reproduction capacity, heredity, response to stimuli, homeostasis (internal stability), and adaptation to the Living Universe through evolution. Not all characteristics, however, must be possessed to qualify as 'life' because the minimum characteristics for 'life' are functions of the complexity of a finite living being. As the complexity of a finite living being increases, the difficulty of materialization and the minimum characteristics for 'life' also increase.

For the sake of discussion, the spiritual title, 'finite living being', will be replaced with the common biological phrase, 'living organism', to better understand the subject matter.

The order of living organisms in increasing complexity is non-cellular to uni-cellular to multi-cellular to composite. Bear in mind that a living organism is considered 'living' if and only if it has consciousness and awareness through the fusion of the intelligent spirit and the physical mantle. These requisites of 'living', which will be explored in later teachings, might be difficult for those whom believe the idea of 'living' requires a brain.

- Non-cellular living organisms are living organisms that lack the defining characteristics of a cell, such as a membrane-bound nucleus, organelles, and the ability to perform independent metabolism. Examples include viruses, viroids, and prions.
- Uni-cellular organisms are living organisms consisting of only one cell that performs all vital functions, including metabolism, excretion, and reproduction. Examples include bacteria, archaea, amoebae, and euglena.
- Multi-cellular organisms are independent organisms made up of more than one (1) cell with development accompanied by cellular specialization and division of labor. Examples include fungi, some algae, and plants.
- Composite organisms are dependent organisms made up of more than one (1) cell integrated with a microbiome of beneficial microorganisms (probiotics, flora, etc.), detrimental microorganisms (viruses, infectious fungi, etc.), and futile microorganisms. Examples include mammals, reptiles, and amphibians.

For clarification, more complex organisms do not come from less complex organisms; however, less complex organisms can be integrated into more complex organisms.

At this point, symbiotic relationships and the human microbiome need to be briefly discussed because composite organisms are oftentimes conflated with multi-cellular organisms or microbiomes are completely omitted altogether – especially in religious and philosophical aspects, where there is a failure to mention this.

Symbiosis, which refers to how living organisms associate with or symbiotically relate to one another, normally occurs in the following ways:

- Chemical commensalism occurs when one living organism benefits from the chemical environment created by another living organism without causing harm or benefit to the other living organism. For instance, bacteria rely on the feces produced by other living organisms for nourishment (approximately 75% water + 25% solid material) without causing harm or benefit to the other living organism.
- Amensalism occurs when one living organism experiences a negative effect (damage, inhibition of growth, or even death) while the other living organism experiences no significant harm or benefit. For instance, algal blooms cause oxygen depletion in water that harms fish without any harm or benefit to algae.

- Phoresy is a symbiotic relationship where one living organism (the "phoront") uses another living organism (the "host") for transport without directly harming or benefiting the host. It's a form of dispersal, allowing the smaller organism to reach new environments or resources. For instance, mites attach to insects to gain access to new flowers.
- Metabiosis occurs when one living organism (the "metabiont") creates or modifies an environment in a way that benefits another living organism (the "dependent organism"). For instance, a hermit crab uses a snail shell for protection after the snail dies.
- Inquilinism is a biological interaction where one living organism (the "inquiline") lives in the nest, burrow, or dwelling space of another living organism (the "host") without causing harm to the host. For instance, barnacles attach to whales for transportation, and the barnacles feed on the passing food.
- Mutualism is a type of interaction where two or more living organisms benefit from one another's presence, and where both living organisms experience a positive impact on their survival or reproduction. For instance, bees collect nectar from flowers, leading to the transfer of pollen for plant reproduction.
- Parasitism is a biological relationship where one living organism (the "parasite) benefits by dwelling on or dwelling within another living organism (the "host"), harming the other living organism (the "host") in the process. For instance, fleas on a dog (ectoparasites), tapeworms embedded in the intestines (endoparasites), and larvae consuming insects (parasitoids) are parasites.

From here, microbiomes of composite living organisms – specifically human microbiomes – can be discussed, where there are many symbiotic relationships at work – commensal and parasitic. For a healthy human adult, microbes approximately outnumber human cells by a ratio of ten to one, and the total number of 'microbe genes' might exceed a factor of 100. The human microbiome/microbiota consists of bacteria, viruses, and single-celled organisms that inhabit the human body. Although bad bacteria (pathogenic) can cause infections and surface blockages, good bacteria (probiotic) are also present to help digest food, to produce certain vitamins, to regulate the immune system, and to fight harmful bacteria. Notable examples include Firmicutes, Actinobacteria, Bacteroidetes, Proteobacteria, Fusobacteria, tenericutes, spirochaetes, cyanobacteria, TM7, lactobacillus, verrucomicrobia, propionibacterium, streptococcus, bacteroides, corynebacterium, C. difficile, staphylococcus, moraxella, haemophilus, prevotella, and veillonella.

Paradoxically, the human biome contains beneficial viruses and harmful viruses. For instance, bacteriophages are viruses that target and that kill bacteria, decreasing the bacterial population in the gut and decreasing the likelihood of bacterial infections. Viral modulators, in continuation, alter immune cell production and gene expression to protect against diseases. Harmful viruses, like influenza, herpes simplex virus, HIV, monkeypox, enteroviruses, noroviruses, etc., cause vomiting, diarrhea, stomach pain, mucosal barrier breakage, immunodeficiency, and bodily disruption.

Finally, the human microbiome contains single-celled organisms such as cilia (hair-like structures with microtubules and dynein arms) that remove mucus and debris from bronchial airways through contractive movement, parasitic protozoa (malaria, giardiasis, toxoplasmosis, and various forms of trypanosomiasis) that can be (in)active, and fungi that can occur naturally to benefit (Saccharomyces boulardii and Saccharomyces cerevisiae) or to detriment (tinea pedis, tinea cruris, ringworm, and candidiasis).

The objectives of discussing the human biome are to show that humans are no different than other finite living beings and that humans, as composite finite living beings, are dependent on less complex finite living beings for survival. This might be difficult for those whom believe that humans have full dominion over other finite living beings or that humans are not functions of other finite living beings.

Recall that finite living beings never receive any favor or protection from the High Power. No finite living being is viewed as inferior or superior to another finite living being by the High Power. Additionally, all finite living beings are exposed to the risks and the dangers within the dwelling spheres of the Living Universe, for the Living Universe and finite living beings are limited in survival.

Humans cannot possibly have dominion over other living organisms because these living organisms (bacteria, fungi, plants, animals, etc.) have the capacity to devour humans for survival and nourishment.

Concentrating on reproduction, the built-in systems of reproduction in the primordial form at a low-energy state can be asexual or can be sexual. A living organism (= a finite living being) involved in reproducing another living organism (= another finite living being) is known as a parent, and the reproduced living organism (= a finite living being) is known as an offspring. Please reference the divine functions under the Hexahedral Rhythm.

- Asexual reproduction refers to a single parent reproducing new/cloned offspring that are genetically identical to the parent. Some examples include binary fission, budding, fragmentation, vegetative propagation, parthenogenesis, apomixis, and sporogenesis.
- Sexual reproduction refers to two parents reproducing offspring with the fusion of gametes. When a gamete has the capacity to fertilize during this fusion, it is called a 'male' gamete, and the corresponding living organism (= a finite living being) exhibits 'male' sex characteristics. On the other hand, when a gamete is a recipient of fertilization during this fusion, it is called a 'female' gamete, and the corresponding living organism (= a finite living being) exhibits 'female' sex characteristics. Internal fertilization occurs inside a female living organism, and external fertilization occurs outside a female living organism.

For clarification, sex characteristics are binary for all finite living beings.

The assignment of sex characteristics to finite living beings leads to the concept of gender.

- When a finite living being possesses only female sex characteristics, it is called a female finite living being. For humans, this is a girl as a non-adult, and this is a woman as an adult.
- When a finite living being possesses only male sex characteristics, it is called a male finite living being. For humans, this is a boy as a non-adult, and this is a man as an adult.
- When a finite living being possesses male and female sex characteristics, fully functional or incomplete, it is called an intersex finite living being. For humans, this is also called intersex. Intersex finite living beings include true hermaphrodites, female and male pseudo hermaphrodites, SRY-negative 46 XX males, XY/XYY karyotype females, human chimeras, chromosomal polymorphics, and any other hybrid variations in chromosomes, genitals, or reproductive organs.

For clarification, the assignment of sex characteristics (gender) is not binary, as expressed in the figure below.

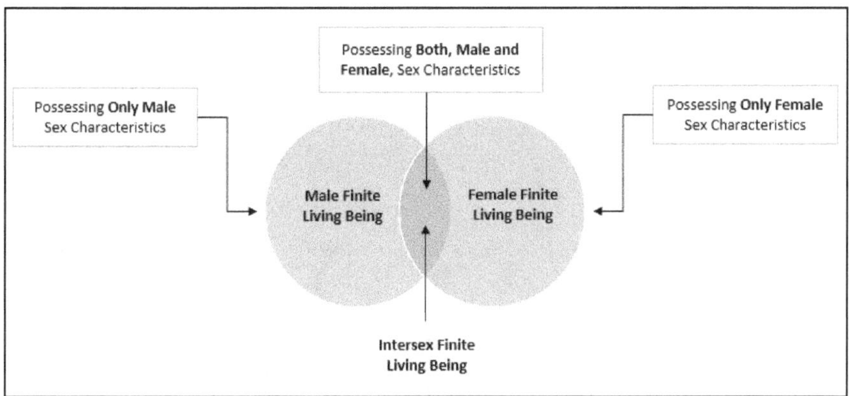

For clarification, intersex characteristics, which are derived solely from intrinsic biological makeup, have nothing to do with gender identities or transgenderism.

For clarification, the High Power is androgynous, possessing both, masculine and feminine energies.

At this point, it is best to discuss human reproduction in Kemetic terms because there are differences in the raw spiritual teachings and the traditional religious dogma, especially the ancient Kahun gynecological papyrus on reproduction, conception, and delivery.

Readers are encouraged to consult textbooks on biology for detailed coverage of biological processes, as this teaching only explores the intersection (points of agreement and disagreement) among spirituality, religion, and biology. Moreover, readers should bear in mind that biology always has a thematic pull towards structure, form, and function, beckoned to divine functions.

The male reproductive structure, which consists of the testes, accessory ducts, glands, and external genitalia, is shown in the figures below.

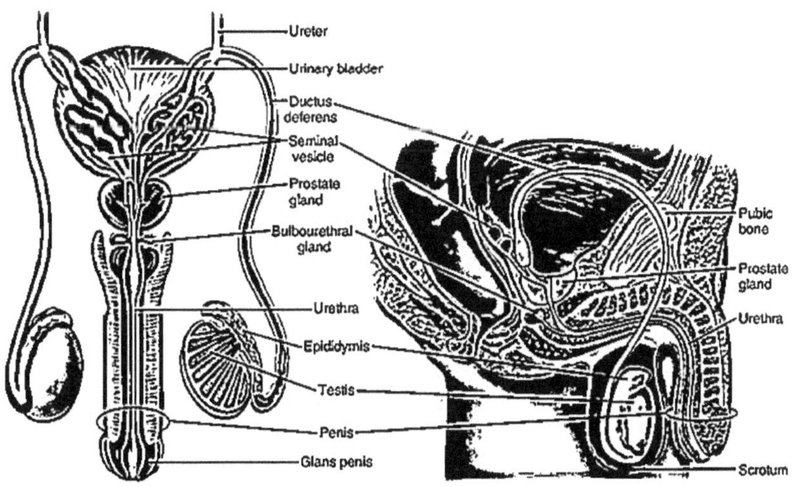

The testes, which are ellipsoid in shape, are positioned behind the penis in the pelvic region outside the abdominal cavity within an elastic pouch known as the scrotum. The scrotum is a small muscular sac that protects the testes and houses the testes near the abdominal cavity to maintain a temperature range between 2.00 °C and 2.50 °C lower than the average human body temperature. The lower bound of the temperature range is required for spermatogenesis because the upper bound of the temperature range and temperatures near the normal body temperature can cause mutations in sperm cells.

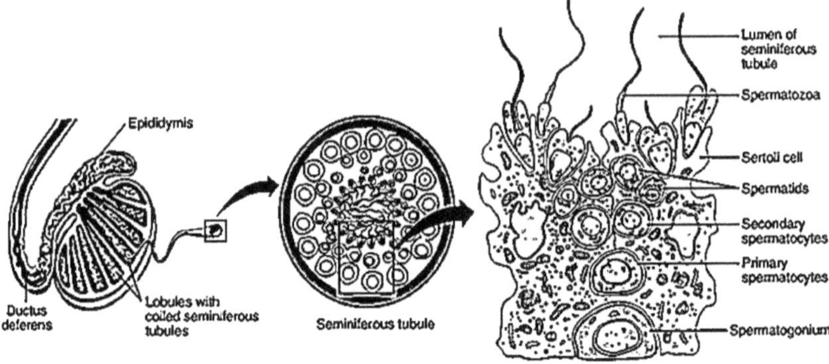

Each testis has approximately 250 compartments called testicular lobules, and each lobule contains no more than three (3) highly coiled seminiferous tubules, which are the site for cell division that leads to the formation of spermatozoa. The exterior area of the seminiferous tubules has interstitial spaces that contain small blood vessels, some immunocompetent cells, and interstitial Leydig cells. The Leydig cells synthesize and secrete testicular hormones called androgens.

The inner lining of the seminiferous tubules consists of Spermatogonia cells and Sertoli cells. Spermatogonia cells, which are diploid and contain forty-six (46) chromosomes each, are the immature male germ cells that undergo meiosis to form sperm cells, and Sertoli cells provide nutrition to the Spermatogonia cells.

Then, the four (4) accessory ducts – rete testis, vasa efferentia, Epididymis, and vas deferens – transport the sperm cells from the testes to the urethra for release outside the body (ejaculation).

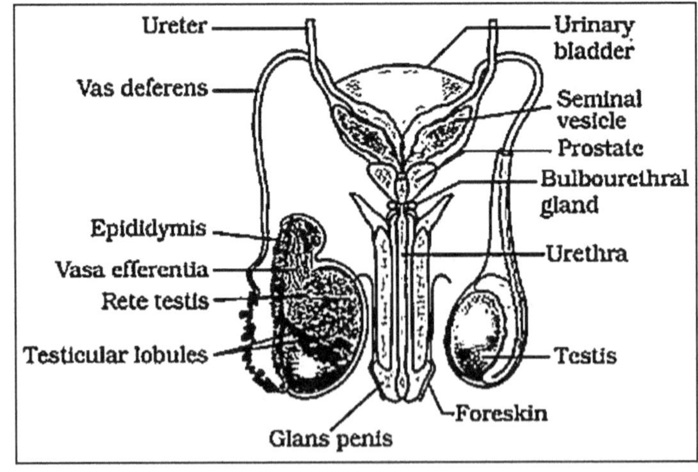

Please note that the raw spiritual teachings (High Spirituality) are in line with the construction of the male reproductive system as well as the origination, the movement, and the release of sperm from the testes; however, the religious variants are not in line with this. Most of the Egyptian priests, whom sacrificed bulls to Egyptian deities, went against science in the belief that semen originated from the spinal cord, that the spinal cord was an extension of the male phallus, and that a fetus was integrated in the semen – explaining the mythological creation of Shu and Tefnut from Ra (the Egyptian sun god).

Finally, the three (3) accessory glands – seminal vesicles, prostate gland, and bulbourethral glands – secrete products that mix with the sperm cells to nourish and to protect them. The seminal vesicles contribute approximately 60-75% of the fluid in semen. The secretions are rich in proteins, enzymes, fructose, vitamin C, phosphoryl choline, and prostaglandins. The high fructose content provides nutrient energy for the spermatozoa. The prostate gland, in continuance, secretes a slightly alkaline milky fluid that helps sperm cells survive the acidic vaginal environment and that improves the motility of the sperm cells. Lastly, the secretion from the bulbourethral glands lubricates the penis and neutralizes any residual acidity in the urethra.

For clarification, sperm cells have consciousness (the ability to detect/adjust to surroundings), have awareness (knowledge of how to move and to survive throughout acidic vaginal environments), and require nourishment granted under divine function through the Dodecahedral Rhythm; therefore, they are finite living beings with a physical mantle and an intelligent spirit.

The physical mantle of the sperm cell is shown below.

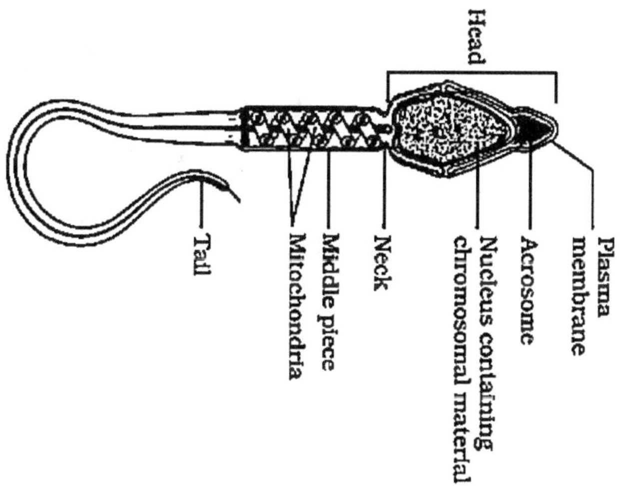

Whereas,

- The acrosome is a structure that is filled with digestive enzymes that help in dissolving the membrane of the egg cell to help fertilize the ovum.
- The middle piece contains numerous mitochondria that produce energy for the movement of the tail (sperm motility).
- The plasma membrane covers the entire physical mantle of the sperm cell.

Two (2) major points need to be highlighted against High Spirituality.

- In biology, each sperm cell has a smooth, oval-shaped head; however, in High Spirituality, the sperm cell has a hexagonal pyramidal head with a rounded tip and a semi-spherical base.
- During ejaculation, 200-300 million sperm cells are released. At least 60% of them should have a normal shape and size, and at least 40% should show vigorous motility. In essence, these percentages further highlight the difficulties of reproduction as expressed earlier in this teaching.

The female reproductive structure, which consists of the ovaries, the oviducts, the uterus, the cervix, the vagina, the external genitalia, and the mammary glands, is shown in the figures below.

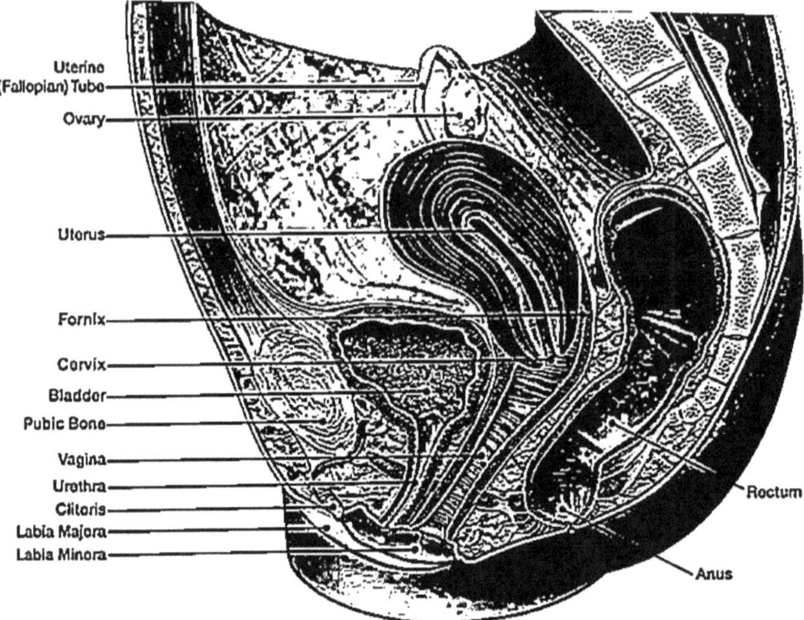

The external structure of the female reproductive system functions to enable sperm cells to enter the body and to protect the internal genital organs from infectious diseases and/or dangerous finite living beings. The main components include the labia majora, labia minora, Bartholin's glands, and the clitoris.

Whereas,

- The labia majora are relatively large enclosures that contain sweat and oil-secreting glands covered with hair at puberty.
- The labia minora lie just inside the labia majora, surrounding the openings of the vagina and the urethra.
- The Bartholin's glands are located beside the vaginal opening, and they produce a fluid secretion (mucus).
- The clitoris, where the two (2) labia minora meet, is a small, yet sensitive, protrusion covered by a fold of skin (prepuce).

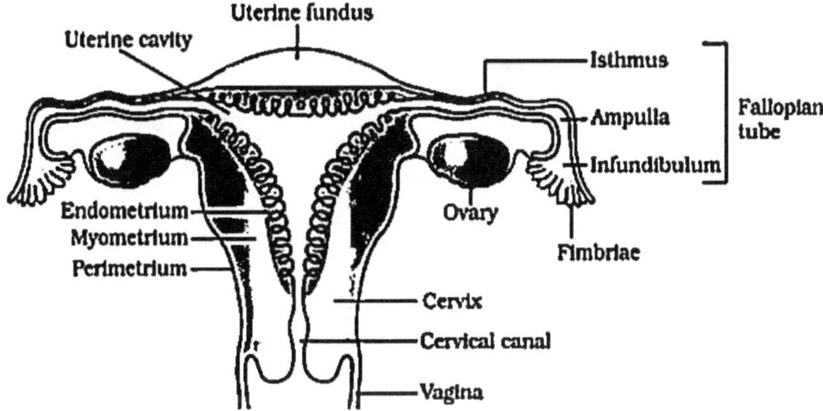

The internal structure of the female reproductive system is designed to facilitate the processes of gametogenesis, ovulation, fertilization, pregnancy, birth, and newborn care.

Whereas,

- The ovaries are small, oval-shaped glands that are located on both sides of the uterus and that produce the female gamete (ovum) and steroid hormones. Each ovary is covered by a thin epithelium enclosing an ovarian stroma, which refers to a matrix divided into two (2) zones – the peripheral cortex and the inner medulla.
- The fallopian tubes are narrow tubes that are attached to the upper part of the uterus and that serve as tunnels for the egg cells (ova) to travel from the ovaries to the uterus. Fertilization normally occurs in the fallopian tubes prior to the fertilized egg moving to the uterus, where the fertilized egg embeds itself into the lining of the uterine wall.
- The uterus (womb), which is a hollow and an expandable inverted-pear housing for a developing fetus, contains the cervix (the lower part that opens into the vagina) and the corpus (the main body of the uterus). As the corpus expands, a channel through the cervix allows sperm cells to enter and menstrual blood to exit.

Please note that the womb is linked to the sacred geometric shapes of a hexahedron and/or a dodecahedron in High Spirituality because the process of giving birth is likened to the birth of a living universe, and the development of the fetus within the placenta of the vaginal wall is likened to the quintessence required to develop a living universe.

For clarification, egg cells have consciousness (ability to detect/adjust to surroundings), have awareness (knowledge of how to move, to protect from disease, and to ensure the penetration of the first compatible sperm cell through membrane layers), and require nourishment granted under divine function through the Dodecahedral Rhythm; therefore, they are finite living beings with a physical mantle and an intelligent spirit.

The entry of the first compatible sperm cell into the egg cell's physical mantle is shown below.

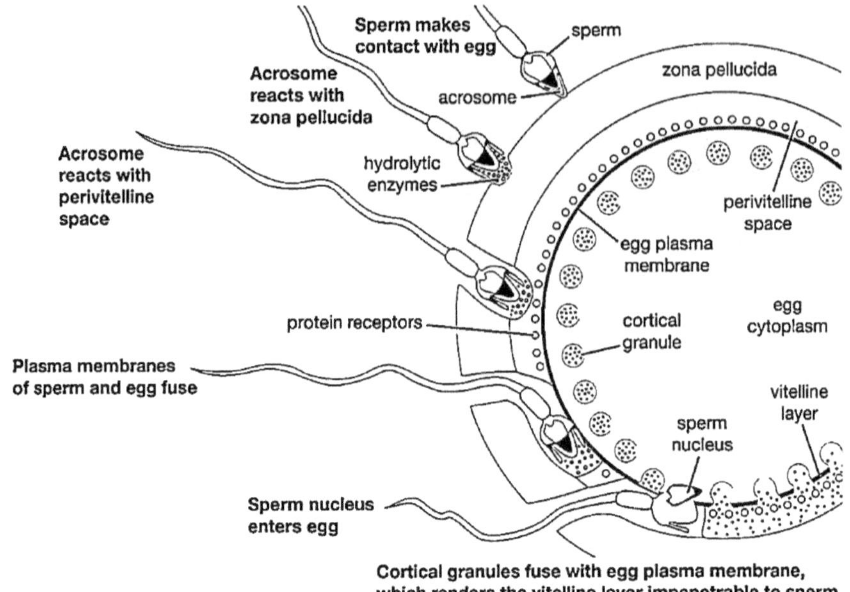

When the sperm cell penetrates the egg cell, the nucleus of the sperm cell (the "seed") joins with the nucleus of the egg yolk (the "fertile ground"), initiating the point of conception.

For clarification, the sperm cell's physical mantle expires after conception, ceasing to be a finite living being as its intelligent spirit returns to the Pool of Spirits.

For clarification, the egg cell's physical mantle expires after conception, ceasing to be a finite living being as its intelligent spirit returns to the Pool of Spirits.

For clarification, the fetus/embryo develops its own physical mantle and receives its own intelligent spirit at conception.

The raw spiritual teachings do not provide an explicit human gestation length or ways to predetermine fetal gender. The human gestation length is only prescribed as the developmental time necessary for the fetus/embryo to survive outside the placenta without nourishment from the umbilical cord once released from the birth canal. The determination of fetal gender, on the other hand, is purely up to chance.

Interestingly enough, the religious variants base the human gestation length on Horus's mythological gestation of 294 days, and some ancient Egyptian subcultures based fetal gender determination on wheat and barley. If barley sprouted first after a pregnant woman's urine was poured on grains of barley and emmer wheat, then the fetus was a projected male, and vice versa. Of course, the pregnancy was predicted to fail if neither of the grains grew.

Returning to the teachings, finite living beings continue to materialize and to reproduce, subject to the variable environmental conditions and the availability of nourishment (e.g., inorganic compounds, organic compounds, etc.) in a given dwelling sphere as well as the changing conditions of the Living Universe. The continuation of finite living beings (survival) depends on fitness, adaptation, and evolution with clear interplay among the three.

Fitness, which refers to a finite living being's ability to pass on its genes to the next generation, is measured by the number of offspring that survive from reproduction to biological maturation. It is not a function of physical strength but rather the success in leaving behind viable offspring and avoiding low genetic variability (incest) in a given dwelling sphere.

Biological maturation is the timing and the tempo of progress towards a mature biological state, encompassing physiological and cognitive development toward a high-energy state (adulthood). For High Spirituality, the age of adulthood or the child-reproducing age is the mature age at which puberty ends, when a finite living being transforms from a low-energy state (child) into a high-energy state (mature adult) physically, hormonally, emotionally, and sexually.

For clarification, pedophilia refers to sexual deviancy or a sexual disorder, where a mature adult experiences/possesses sexual feelings for a child.

Adaptation refers to heritable traits or heritable characteristics that enhance a finite living being's ability to survive. These characteristics include structural (physical features), physiological (internal functions), or behavioral traits.

Examples of structural adaptations include camouflage, mimicry, spines/thorns, large ears, body shape, body size, sharp claws, and aerodynamic beaks.

Examples of behavior adaptations include migration, hibernation, nesting, (non) verbal communication, and nocturnal behavior.

Examples of physiological adaptations include venom production, rapid healing, metabolic rate changes, water conservation, and toxic resistance.

Evolution is the process whereby inherited traits within a population of living organisms change, diversify, mature, and advance over generations, resulting in the gradual development of a modified finite living being or a 'better adapted' finite living being within a given dwelling sphere. The Kemetic teachings are in line with science and the evolutionary observations associated with natural selection, genetic drift, gene flow, selective mating, introgression, and mutations. This includes divergent evolution, convergent evolution, parallel evolution, and coevolution observations. The points of contention center on the mainstream assessment of evolutionary tree branching, assuming a common ancestor as follow:

- There is no universal ancestor as pitched by the Last Universal Common Ancestor (LUCA) model. The materialized finite living beings are the original ancestors of evolutionary trajectories that might or might not experience speciation points. Consequently, an entire evolutionary trajectory of a finite living being can terminate without dooming the evolutionary trajectory of a similar, biologically-related finite living being.
- Finite living beings of low complexity are not the ancestors of finite living beings of high complexity. Non-cellular organisms and uni-cellular organisms materialized first due to their lower complexity and their relatively low need for nourishment.
- The human and the chimpanzee genome sequences differ by approximately 90 million base pairs (Mb) of insertions and deletions (indels) and by approximately 35 million single nucleotides. With the difference between anywhere from 1-4%, it is evident that either humans and chimpanzees share a common ancestor or humans and chimpanzees exhibit similar genomes despite having different evolutionary trajectories – this might be a result of convergent evolution. High Spirituality supports both conclusions.

As this teaching closes, the reader should reflect not only on the obstacles necessary to materialize and to reproduce in the Living Universe but also on the challenges associated with surviving in the Living Universe.

Em Hotep!

DAWN OF THE FOURTH BELL

ANKH WADJA SENEB | MEDJAI OF GATE #04

Function: Delivery of Raw Kemetic Teachings
Subject(s): Consciousness, Awareness, Cognitive Functions, Universe Pathways
Position: Part 2 – The Raw Kemetic Teachings | High Spirituality

MEDJAI OF GATE #04 - DAWN OF THE FOURTH BELL

Peace to the High Power! Peace to the Living Universe! Peace to all Finite Living Beings! Peace to All Things – seen and unseen! For my spirit is with me, my image is with me, and my purpose is with me; and, let it be known by the Morning and the Evening Star that these self-evident teachings, unchanged by time or tongue, shall guide me and shall remain with me as I pursue my connection to the Living Universe and the High Power.

The concept of consciousness, which attempts to explain the relationship between the physical body and the mental processing unit of the brain (the "mind"), has baffled the likes of psychologists, philosophers, and neuroscientists for centuries. In the early 21st century, consciousness was explained rather than defined through individual experiences and profound levels of awareness. Over time, these explanations would shapeshift as the meanings and the uses of the mind changed based on the increasing knowledge of how the brain works, how brain damage and drugs affect/alter physical functionality, and how brain cells and the central nervous system adjust to different experiences accumulated/recorded through neurological devices. Although the changing meaning and usage, even when combined with empirical data or primary experiences, created more voids than solutions, they revealed a thematic problem: How do different mental experiences arise from or directly relate to physical processes as either distinct or interconnected entities?

Assume that there are five (5) different people standing in a circular formation. Every three (3) seconds, a person passes a thorned, red rose to the right-adjacent person. After thirty (30) seconds have elapsed, the rose is completely removed from the group, and an external examiner asks the five (5) people to write down their direct experience with the rose. After the writing phase is over, the external examiner reviews the responses, and the external examiner notices that the experiences of each person are different. Person 1, for instance, associated the sharpness of the thorn with pain, while Person 3 associated the sharpness of the thorn with pleasure. Person 2 and Person 4, as another example, were captivated by the beauty of the rose despite differences in color registry and the smell of the rose, while Person 5 expressed sadness over the rose being cut from its roots and a temporary sense of euphoria when smelling the rose. Many questions arise at this point. How can these subjective mental experiences and/or sensations be related to physical objects? Does the visual display of the brain result in different experiences? What is the driving force behind each person smelling the rose differently?

Two (2) main approaches have been explored to provide answers to the thematic problem above: (i) consciousness per monism is an interconnected function of a single substance/principle, and (ii) consciousness per dualism is a function of two (2) distinct and independent substances/principles (i.e., mind and body, spirit and matter, etc.).

Monist theories of consciousness center on the claim that the mental world is fundamentally a part of the physical world. One theory posits that objects in the physical world might not be real at all, but rather ideas and perceptions of what objects truly are. Put in another way, reality is ultimately mental and a working product of the mind. Although this idea simplifies the metaphysical and the physical worlds into one, it fails to justify why physical objects have enduring qualities and how science is even possible. Another theory under monism, materialism, suggests on the opposite extreme that there is only matter (conjoined with energy and a causally-closed physical world) and that mental states of consciousness are equal to both, brain states and functional states. In essence, the idea asserts that there is no mind, or mental force, apart from matter. Once again, this idea seems feasible on the surface; however, it fails to address the subjective experience of consciousness at the crux of the thematic problem above, the strong emotional impacts linking decisions to causes (i.e. actions are purely reduced to physical cause and effect), and the difficulty of understanding how thoughts, feelings, and mental images can really be matter when they seem to be so different.

Dualist theories of consciousness, which are the default when compared to their monist counterparts, assert that physical entities and mental entities are distinct, and quite possibly separate, from each other (e.g., mind-body or spirit-matter pairs). Cartesian dualism, popularized by René Descartes, holds that the world pivots on substance dualism, where physical bodies are composed of the extended substance, and the mind is made of an unextended substance. The major issue behind this theory is how the mind interacts with the body when the two are made of different substances. In other words, the interaction has to be double-sided, where physical events and the brain must somehow give rise to experiences, thoughts, images, decisions, and other mental events, and mental events must somehow influence or give rise to physical events.

Substance dualism is in direct contrast to property dualism (belongingness of multiple substances to the brain) or dual aspect theory (mental and physical phenomena are two aspects/perspectives of a single reality), which uses word play anomalously to merge dualism with monism. If a person is poked with a rose's thorn, for example, the pain can be described in mental terms (i.e., how it feels) or physical terms (i.e., how the nervous system communicates a response through neural networks); even though the physical terms and the mental terms cannot be reduced to only one description. These theories seemingly avoid the need for two (2) different substances rather than address the relationship between physical and mental entities. This also explains why these theories come in many versions.

More theories – philosophical, psychological, or scientific – can be explored here; however, the popular examples above are sufficient to highlight the weaknesses, the flaws, and the simplified scope of consciousness. All of these theories assume that a brain is required for consciousness, that a human-centric approach is enough to understand consciousness in full, that consciousness does not extend to the Living Universe itself, that consciousness can be loosely defined (sometimes undefined based on personal/subjective feelings), and that mental and physical phenomena cannot be a hybrid function of each other. High Spirituality cohesively addresses all aspects of consciousness subject to nature without making simplifying assumptions or without constituting consciousness under false denotation (i.e., saying what consciousness is not, but not saying what consciousness actually is).

The personal quest for meaning, individual purpose, a deepening interconnection with finite living beings, and a connection to something beyond oneself such as the High Power and the Living Universe, an innately intelligent entity with a physical layer and a metaphysical layer, begins with possessing/developing a sensor processing and feedback response unit to reach higher consciousness and to evoke awareness.

It is important to address the subtle, but important, difference between consciousness and awareness.

Consciousness, which does not require a brain, is a measure of an entity's ability to experience its surrounding environment through external/internal stimuli and a natural sensing mechanism.

Awareness, which does not require a brain, is a measure of an entity's knowledge of its surrounding environment as it experiences the environment through external/internal stimuli and a natural sensing mechanism.

Recall that the High Power activates the Hexahedral Rhythm from the '1' position with sole authority over divine functions – inclusive of consciousness – spurring the intelligent spirit's descent into the physical reproductive matter of a finite living being's physical mantle enclosure.

Recall that the High Power activates the Tetrahedral Rhythm from the '1' position with sole authority over divine functions, facilitating the creation, the fabrication, and the forging of each intelligent spirit with intrinsic characteristics and attributes to ensure the transference of the energetic form to the physical mantle of the finite living being that will house it. The transference of the energetic form involves the action of embodying inert matter with the source of creative activity and the genius of personality, form, and function.

Finite living beings can possess all or some of the following characteristics based on complexity: the khet (physical body), sah (spiritual body), ren (intrinsic/unique identity), ba (personality), ka (life or vital essence with a physical-spiritual twin), shuyet (shadow), and sekhem (power of healing and development).

Recall that the physical mantle represents the alternating flux or the electromagnetic current that constitutes physical life when the intelligent spirit joins with matter in the physical world through precipitation and distillation – purged and purified. After joining in perfect fusion, the matter inherits the characteristics and the attributes of the intelligent spirit, where the resultant stimulates physical life to ascend from its natural level of embodiment and innate consciousness to its supernatural levels of expression, logic, and instinct.

The joining of the intelligent spirit and the physical mantle results in a finite living being, as shown below.

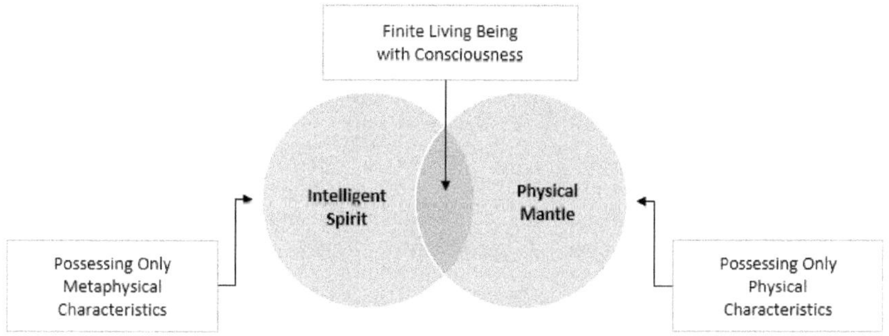

Strictly speaking for a finite living being, consciousness is a measure of a finite living being's ability to experience its surrounding environment (dwelling sphere of the Living Universe or the Living Universe itself) through external/internal stimuli and a natural sensing mechanism. The natural sensing mechanism does not have to be located in the brain.

Examples of Consciousness

- **Non-Cellular Finite Living Beings**: Viruses employ sensory receptors, often located on their surface, to detect changes in their surroundings.
- **Uni-Cellular Finite Living Beings**: Bacteria employ chemoreceptors, physical sensors, light sensors, quorum sensors, and mechanosensors, often located on their cell wall, outer membrane, or appendages, to detect changes in their surroundings.
- **Multi-Cellular Finite Living Beings**: Jellyfish possess a decentralized nervous system (nerve net) that is spread throughout their bodies to detect changes in their surroundings.
- **Composite Finite Living Beings**: Bears possess a central nervous system with respect to their brains to detect changes in their surroundings.

Strictly speaking for a finite living being, awareness is a measure of a finite living being's knowledge of its surrounding environment (dwelling sphere of the Living Universe or the Living Universe itself) through external/internal stimuli and a natural sensing mechanism. The natural sensing mechanism does not have to be located in the brain.

Examples of Awareness

- **Non-Cellular Finite Living Beings**: Viruses employ sensory receptors to monitor/pursue specific molecules, to become latent when threatened by host cells, and to manipulate a host cell's metabolism as a defense mechanism – especially against virophages based on temperature and pH levels.
- **Uni-Cellular Finite Living Beings**: Bacteria employ sensory receptors to find nutrients for growth, to dodge toxins (chemotaxis), and to communicate with other bacteria.
- **Multi-Cellular Finite Living Beings**: Jellyfish utilize their nerve nets to escape predators, to monitor light levels, and to move around obstacles under reflex.
- **Composite Finite Living Beings**: Bears utilize their nervous system and their brains to determine when to hibernate, to engage in social interactions with other bears, to hide/find food, and to follow migratory tracks.

The capacity for consciousness and awareness increases as the complexity of the finite living being increases. This explains why composite finite living beings with brains have redundant, high-order mental facilities of conscious, preconscious, and subconscious that non-cellular finite living beings do not have.

Moreover, the state and the condition of consciousness and awareness can be altered negatively or positively based on exposure within the Living Universe.

Destructive States of Consciousness/Awareness [Negative Alterations]

- **Clouding**: A very mild form of altered mental status or a trance in which a finite living being has inattention and reduced wakefulness.
- **Delirium**: A disturbed state of consciousness, especially an acute, transient condition associated with fever, intoxication, and certain other physical disorders, characterized by symptoms such as confusion, disorientation, agitation, and hallucinations.
- **Lethargy**: A severe drowsiness in which a finite living being can be aroused by moderate stimuli and then drift back to a sleeping state.

- **Obtundation**: A state where the finite living being has a lessened interest in the environment, slowed responses to stimulation, and a tendency to sleep more than normal with drowsiness in between sleep states.
- **Stupor**: A state where only vigorous and repeated stimuli will arouse the finite living being. When left undisturbed, the living being will immediately lapse back to the unresponsive state.
- **Comatose**: A state of unarousable unresponsiveness.

Constructive States of Consciousness/Awareness [Positive Alterations]

- **Regeneration**: The finite living being experiences deep, undisturbed sleep and/or rest.
- **Discernment**: The finite living being can recall and can remember details of dreamy or augmented states; and, the finite living being can distinguish such states from reality with full judgment.

As a sidebar, Ancient Egyptians used to practice dream interpretation, and their dreams were recorded either in stone or within papyri.

- **Vigor**: The finite living being harnesses energy to improve physical and mental health.
- **Adoration**: The finite living being seeks emotional, psychological, and physical relations with similar and dissimilar living beings out of compassion, love, serenity, and spiritual bliss.
- **Unity**: The finite living being experiences moral exaltation, totality, continued ancestral value, and/or enlightenment through oneness with the physical mantle (self) and oneness with the intelligent spirit.
- **Cosmic**: The finite living being develops a commensal relationship with the Living Universe to sustain or to foster the growth of more dwelling spheres.
- **Sacred**: The finite living being uses nature as inspiration to understand the innate intelligence of the Living Universe, the Living Universe's purpose in fulfilling the will of the High Power, and the laws, parameters, and the nature of the High Power governing the Living Universe. Moreover, a sense of fear and ignorance becomes minimized.

Strictly speaking about human beings, reaching a higher consciousness and evoking awareness require the strengthening, the conditioning, and the sharpening of cognitive functions – verbal and non-verbal – associated with brain activity, motor function, and the central nervous system. These cognitive functions, which are primarily executed through the left/right cerebral hemispheres, are the direct interplay between the brain of the physical mantle (physical substance) and the intelligent spirit fused with the physical mantle (metaphysical substance).

As a sidebar, Ancient Egyptians designated the pineal gland contained within the midbrain under the cerebrum as the 'third eye' or the seat of the spirit and a gateway to higher consciousness, represented with either the Eye of Horus or the Eye of Ra.

Each cerebral hemisphere fundamentally consists of a frontal lobe, a parietal lobe, an occipital lobe, and a temporal lobe.

LEFT FRONTAL LOBE

Control/express language
Produce/form language
Produce target speech sounds/patterns
Analytical Thinking/Reasoning
Logical Reasoning
Reasoning of concrete/tangible objects
Pattern Recognition
Kinesthetic Speech
Linear Predictive Speech/Trajectories
Critical Thinking
Symbolic Thinking
Problem-Solving
Primary Motor Control
Discrimination of facial features
Probabilistic Reasoning
Deductive Reasoning (content-ind.)
Inductive Reasoning
Analogical Reasoning (content-ind.)
Causal Reasoning
Reading fluency & Literacy
Verbal Reasoning
Lingual Syntax Construction
Decision-Making
Casting/Exercising judgment
Executing sequences in body movement

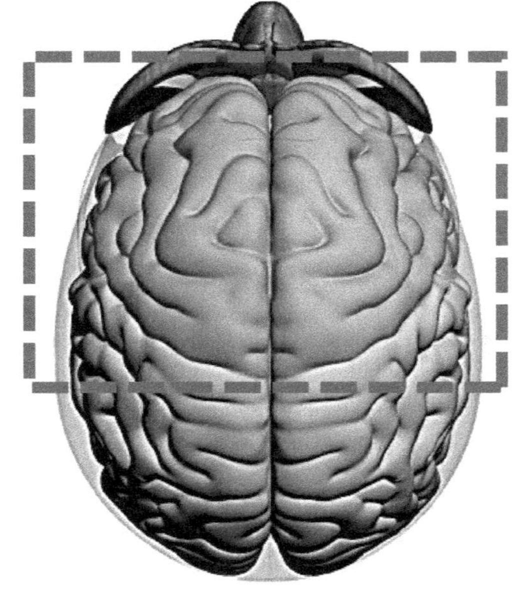

RIGHT FRONTAL LOBE

Non-Verbal Reasoning
Artifactual Reasoning
Abstract Reasoning
Primary Working Memory (+hippocampus)
Face Perception
Planning/organizing events
Attention and Concentration
Emotional Control/Expression (+amygdala)
Deep Mental Fitness
Creativity
Imagination
Music/Art
Mechanical Reasoning
Deductive Reasoning (content-dep.)
Analogical Reasoning (content-dep.)
Voluntary Movement & Kinesthetic Learning
Awareness

LEFT PARIETAL LOBE

Long-Term Memory Retrieval
Sensory/Episodic Memory
Kinesthetic Perception
Mental Self-Perception
Mental Strategies
Tracking body positioning and movements
Processing 3D Environments
Sensory Information (e.g. somatosensory)
Gustatory cortex

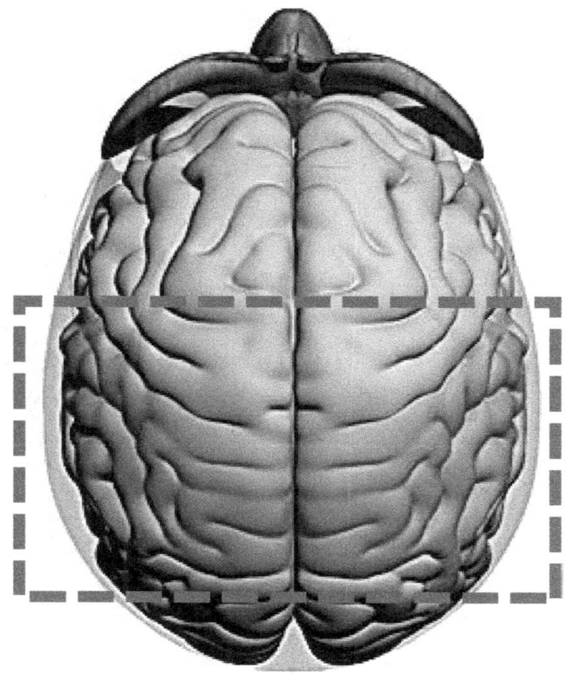

RIGHT PARIETAL LOBE

Working Memory (secondary)
Numerical Quantification
Numerical Reasoning
Spatial Reasoning
Spatial Acuity
Spatial Orientation
Symbolic Relationships

LEFT OCCIPITAL LOBE

Right Visual Acuity
Visuospatial Processing + Color (RHS)
Visual Recognition (RHS)
Visual Attention (RHS)
Visual Perception (RHS)
Narrow Visual Span (right to left)
Coordination (assists cerebellum)

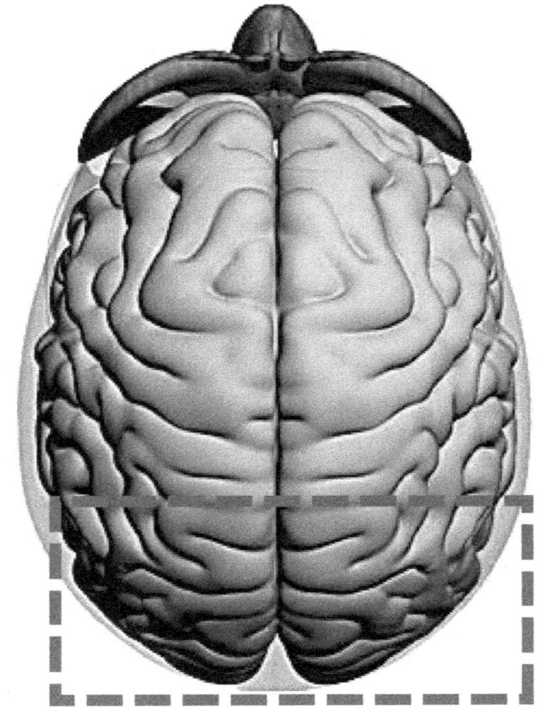

RIGHT OCCIPITAL LOBE

Left Visual Acuity
Visuospatial Processing + Color (LHS)
Visual Recognition (LHS)
Visual Attention (LHS)
Visual Perception (LHS)
Narrow Visual Span (left to right)

LEFT TEMPORAL LOBE

Memory Storage and Knowledge Recall
Linking meaning to written words
Linking meaning to spoken words
Comprehension
Information Processing
Recollecting Verbal Details
Learning/internalization
Sound frequencies to action responses
Social Cognition
Short-Term Visual Perception
Olfactory Cortex
Language Perception/Production

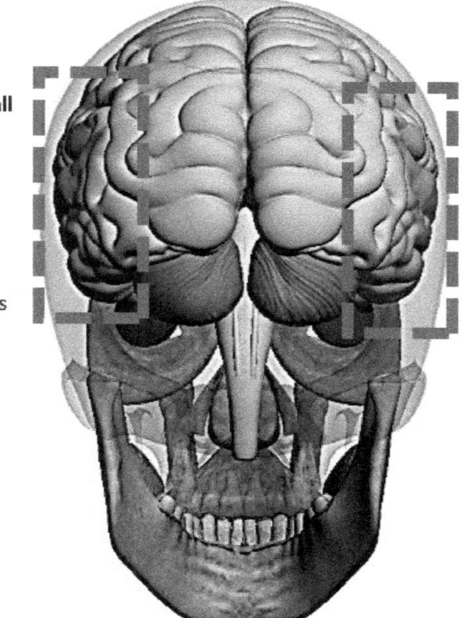

RIGHT TEMPORAL LOBE

Auditory Speech Discrimination
Recollecting Non-Verbal Details
Object Recognition
Symbolic Recognition
Facial Recognition
Data Recognition
Auditory Acuity
Temporal Acuity

BRAIN STEM

Midbrain - Controls reflex patterns of vision/hearing
Pons - Relay station, cerebral cortex to the cerebellum.
Medulla - Controls vital functions
Cerebellum - Controls synchronized movements
Access point to corticospinal tracts

For clarification, any attempts to dampen, to restrict, to hinder, to sabotage, to destroy, or to weaken the neural cognitive functions will cause harm to the direct interplay between the brain of the physical mantle and the intelligent spirit – thus, causing harm to consciousness and awareness. This includes cases where a human being either suppresses rationality to appease superiors/ authorities (e.g., refusing to ridicule a dubious or an insane idea) or relies on another human being to act on its cognitive behalf (e.g., a dormant consciousness).

For clarification, consciousness (sensory perception to experience surroundings) should not be confused with being alive (having a fully-integrated physical mantle and intelligent spirit) as these are two (2) different things. A finite living being can be dead but have consciousness (e.g., a severed bee still moving wings); or, a finite living being can be alive but have no consciousness (e.g., a drowning victim in need of resuscitation)

Reaching a higher level of consciousness, finite living beings will naturally start to postulate about the mysterious order and harmony of the Living Universe tied to the High Power's will, especially since the equilibrium, the pathway, and the cosmic arrangement of the Living Universe are mirrored in the survival of finite living beings in dwelling spheres.

Recall that the High Power activates the Octahedral Rhythm from the '1' position with sole authority over divine functions, giving the Living Universe consciousness under decreed parameters and laws and the innate intelligence to communicate among infinitesimally small particles of matter and energy states.

The Living Universe is not exempt from consciousness and awareness; and, it is no surprise that the Living Universe possesses a metaphysical and a physical layer as shown below.

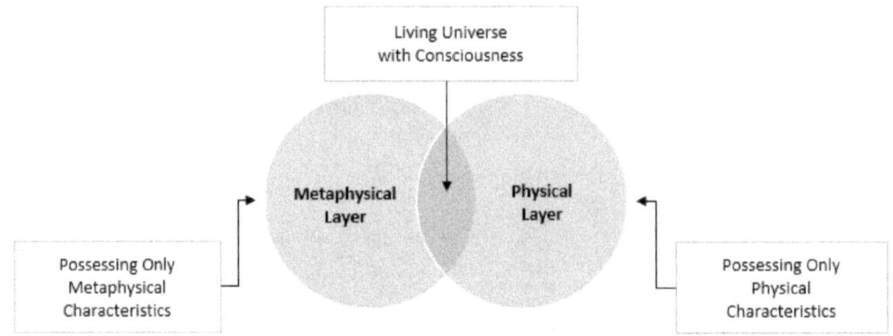

Strictly speaking for the Living Universe, consciousness is a measure of the Living Universe's ability to experience all dwelling spheres and spaces contained within it through external stimuli (only the High Power), internal stimuli, and an intrinsic sensing mechanism.

Strictly speaking for the Living Universe, awareness is a measure of the Living Universe's knowledge of all dwelling spheres and spaces contained within it through external stimuli (only the High Power), internal stimuli, and an intrinsic sensing mechanism.

The intrinsic sensing mechanism, the consciousness, the awareness, and the innate intelligence of the Living Universe are functions of the aforementioned sacred geometric rhythms and the following three (3) pathways:

- **The Stellar Path**: This pathway engenders association and awakening through cosmic resonance – a dynamic, simultaneous, and nonlinear causality where separated cosmological events influence each other beyond the limits of space-time. Under association, there is always a correspondence existing between any one thing and others through all possible realms of manifestations, physical and metaphysical.
- **The Solar Path**: This pathway serves as the intrinsic sensor for and the binary consciousness switch of the Living Universe through the resolution of pairing imbalances. Pairing refers to inverse, complementary, and symmetrical aspects. Whenever these aspects are perturbed, the Living Universe detects all instabilities, and it makes every effort to restore normality.
- **The Lunar Path**: This pathway embodies the principle of simultaneity, which describes cyclical processes as a series of natural transformations with all events in any cycle occurring simultaneously on more than one level of manifestation. Being timeless and continuous in the physical and the metaphysical layers, these simultaneous events must be connected to the High Power with divine attributes, because they cannot be coincidental occurrences.

Em Hotep!

DAWN OF THE FIFTH BELL

ANKH WADJA SENEB | MEDJAI OF GATE #05

Function: Delivery of Raw Kemetic Teachings
Subject(s): Maat, Interconnected Constituents, Vibrations, Confessionals
Position: Part 2 – The Raw Kemetic Teachings | High Spirituality

MEDJAI OF GATE #05 - DAWN OF THE FIFTH BELL

Peace to the High Power! Peace to the Living Universe! Peace to all Finite Living Beings! Peace to All Things – seen and unseen! For my spirit is with me, my image is with me, and my purpose is with me; and, let it be known by the Morning and the Evening Star that these self-evident teachings, unchanged by time or tongue, shall guide me and shall remain with me as I pursue my connection to the Living Universe and the High Power.

In Ancient Egypt, the virtues necessary to live a good life and to live in harmony among others centered mainly on the Egyptian goddess, Maat, and her forty-two (42) laws. According to Egyptian mythology, Maat was the daughter of the primordial man, and she symbolized wisdom, justice, cosmic order, and social harmony. This idea of social harmony molded ancient Egyptians to adopt cultural norms (e.g., mannerisms, behaviors, etc.) and social instructions (unspoken laws, rituals, etc.) to avoid disputes among others and to cultivate self-control. Consequently, the construction of social instructions would lead to one of the oldest psychological and philosophical concepts on understanding personality, known as the polypsychic view.

Strictly speaking for human beings as finite living beings, the polypsychic view holds that the intrinsic self contains the following interconnected constituents:

- Khet – The physical body
- Ka – The life or vital essence with a physical-spiritual twin
- Ba – A unique personality
- Shuyet – The shadow and a complementing dark alter ego
- Sa – The spiritual body as cosmic energy through intangible strength, spiritual protection, and the fluid of life
- Sekhem – Power of healing and development through spiritual might
- Ren – Intrinsic/unique identity

For clarification, Ancient Egypt was one of the oldest civilizations to integrate sophisticated systems of seals and impressions for record-keeping, identification, legal functions, and funerary rites. Fingerprints were found on ushabtis, small funerary figurines placed in tombs to serve the deceased in the afterlife.

- Ab – The weighted heart revealing the moral and the intellectual center

Please note that the religious variants incorporate other layers onto these constituents, such as effects in the afterlife, possession of superhuman powers through a transformed soul, rebirth in funerary rituals, etc.

Whenever any of these constituents are at odds, the human psyche experiences internal conflict that transfigures the intelligent spirit from a higher level of vibration to a lower level of vibration. The transfigured intelligent spirit is called the akh.

The Seven (7) Vibrations from lowest vibration to highest vibration are as follow:

- **Sahu**: Typically, an animalistic focus on basic needs, survival, economics, and safety for self-preservation, inclusive of treachery, theft, violence, manipulation, and deceit; however, there is an extremely deep Sahu state, causing self-sabotage, self-defeat, and self-destruction.
- **Relationship**: The prioritization of social connections for self-centered opportunity. Acceptance, validation, belongingness, love, and influence are contributing factors – behaviors rationalized through comparison with others.
- **Self-Esteem**: The focus on personal achievement, recognition, success, status, and self-worth to build confidence and to gain respect from other finite living beings.
- **Transformation**: The pursuit of personal growth, self-improvement, and maturity through introspection (i.e., questioning personal beliefs, values, and purpose), a desire for change, and a commitment to personal development.
- **Integration**: The authentic alignment of personal growth with action for a harmonious, balanced, and congruent life.
- **Ascent (Mer)**: The universal expansion beyond personal concerns to a deep sense of compassion for and a commitment to positive impacts on all finite living beings and the Living Universe. An excellent example of this transformation is seen through the spiritual acts of surrogacy and adoption, which embody generosity, selflessness, and compassion for life.
- **Hotep**: The gravitation toward a profound spiritual awakening, a skeptical push to question all things, a strong sense of oneness with all existence and the Living Universe, and the victory over the ego to obtain inner peace, wisdom, enlightenment, and an exceptional understanding of life's mysteries.

Please note that the religious variant of 'Hotep' is 'Ausar'.

At the highest vibration, Hotep, humans start seeking the wisdom of life's mysteries in the pursuit of truth. There are two (2) different types of truth – personal truth and absolute truth. Personal truths are shaped by individual experiences, emotions, subjective perspectives, conditioning, interpretations, and meanings of life; and, they are directly related to individual consciousness and awareness. Absolute truths, however, are universally shared truths that hold true regardless of individual perspectives. In High Spirituality, absolute truths are tied to the laws and the parameters governed by the High Power, the High Power itself, and all physical and metaphysical inner workings. Since human understanding asymptotically approaches absolute truth, there is no way that humans can ever understand it in full. Humans trying to reduce absolute truth into a static object is proof alone that human understanding is asymptotic because an absolute truth can be static, quasi-static, or dynamic/transient, being objectively true at a fixed point in space-time or objectively true across trajectory durations in space-time.

Another important subject, which must be addressed in the context of the Seven Vibrations before moving on, is the power of music because music introduces sound with frequencies, waves, motion, and oscillations that can shift the akh to higher or lower levels of vibrations. Remembering that the physical mantle and the intelligent spirit of finite living beings are indirectly created in the Living Universe through the sacred geometric rhythms, music can penetrate the human consciousness, tickling the senses, pulsating with the heart, unlocking vulnerabilities, and hypnotizing the akh. Such penetration might stimulate feelings of uplift, motivation, love, nostalgia, etc.; or, such penetration might stimulate feelings of madness, chaos, melancholy, deviancy, etc.; therefore, it is important to harmonize with music of the right spiritual fruits.

As mentioned earlier, the Ancient Egyptian civilization centralized its code of conduct and ethical guidelines on Maat and the Laws of Maat, depicted with the Scales of Justice weighing the heart against the feather; however, the raw spiritual teachings clearly indicate that such laws were not behind the intrinsic self and the vibrations. In fact, these laws were never meant to be laws at all, but rather confessionals for daily self-actualization. To simplify in another way, the religious variants wanted followers to imagine being challenged on laws by deities in the afterlife, while the raw spiritual teachings wanted individuals to imagine reciting confessionals in a mirror with full conviction.

Bear in mind that the confessionals come in negative and in affirmative forms; however, the extended listing of the affirmative confessionals, which exceeds the number of Maat Laws, is provided next.

For those seeking a deepening interconnection with finite living beings, let them pronounce the following Confessionals with teeth and tongue:

Affirmations of 1st Degree Confessionals

- Promise to Self, I will not engage in nor encourage bad faith acts.
- Promise to Self, I will not commit robbery.
- Promise to Self, I will not steal by any means.
- Promise to Self, I will not slay men and women – mother, father, or child.
- Promise to Self, I will not destroy grain nor the fruits of nourishment.
- Promise to Self, I will not make false offerings.
- Promise to Self, I will not allow the invention of gods before me nor subscribe to them.
- Promise to Self, I will not utter lies.
- Promise to Self, I will not carry away food from the hungry.
- Promise to Self, I will not utter curses.
- Promise to Self, I will not commit adultery nor engage in infidelity.
- Promise to Self, I will not make anyone to weep for display.
- Promise to Self, I will not harden the heart.
- Promise to Self, I will not attack nor plot against others.
- Promise to Self, I will not be deceitful.
- Promise to Self, I will not be covetous.
- Promise to Self, I will not be meddlesome, prying into the matters of others.
- Promise to Self, I will not slander anyone.
- Promise to Self, I will not be angry without just cause.
- Promise to Self, I will not lust for the committed nor yield to debauchery.
- Promise to Self, I will not engage in pious acts nor accept revelations – uncorroborated or false.
- Promise to Self, I will not pollute myself.
- Promise to Self, I will not terrorize anyone.
- Promise to Self, I will not transgress.
- Promise to Self, I will not be retributive nor vengeful.
- Promise to Self, I will not shut my ears to the words of truth nor my mind to the thoughts of reason.
- Promise to Self, I will not blaspheme.
- Promise to Self, I will not be of violence.
- Promise to Self, I will not be a stirrer of strife.

- Promise to Self, I will not act with undue haste.
- Promise to Self, I will not engage in acts against nature nor of deviancy.
- Promise to Self, I will not speak in riddles, folly, or double-talk.
- Promise to Self, I will not do wrong to anyone for any evil done, requiring balance.
- Promise to Self, I will not engage in wickedness, bewitchment, or perversion.
- Promise to Self, I will never stop the flow of nor plot against the Living Universe.
- Promise to Self, I will not disrespect the interconnectedness of all finite living beings.
- Promise to Self, I will not make any effort to speak on behalf of the High Power.
- Promise to Self, I will not act with arrogance nor express dominion over life.
- Promise to Self, I will not remain passive in the presence of wrongdoing or harm.
- Promise to Self, I will not be oblivious to things before me nor disregard life, death, body, or spirit.
- Promise to Self, I will not snatch away the innocence of children, nor treat them with contempt under personal belief.
- Promise to Self, I will not speak falsehoods about the High Power, nor pretend to know its nature, will, image, ways, desires, or dispositions.

Affirmations of 2nd Degree Confessionals

- Worthy in Self, I will honor virtue.
- Worthy in Self, I will benefit with gratitude.
- Worthy in Self, I will be peaceful in the absence of harm.
- Worthy in Self, I will respect the property of others.
- Worthy in Self, I will affirm that all life and all death are sacred.
- Worthy in Self, I will give genuine offerings, not of ill intent.
- Worthy in Self, I will live in truth of whom I am and what I offer.
- Worthy in Self, I will be bound by my individual purpose and the strength of my intelligent spirit.
- Worthy in Self, I will speak with sincerity and truth even when most uncomfortable.
- Worthy in Self, I will consume and carry my fair share.
- Worthy in Self, I will offer words of good intent.
- Worthy in Self, I will always be connected to things greater than myself.
- Worthy in Self, I will hold all finite living beings in the same regard.
- Worthy in Self, I will be trustworthy and loyal to positive bearing fruits.
- Worthy in Self, I will care for the Living Universe.
- Worthy in Self, I will seek the balance reflected and exemplified by the High Power.
- Worthy in Self, I will speak positively of others.
- Worthy in Self, I will remain in control of my emotions.
- Worthy in Self, I will be loyal to my relationships.
- Worthy in Self, I will hold purity and my deepest self in high esteem.
- Worthy in Self, I will spread positive energy and positive vibration.
- Worthy in Self, I will believe in myself, for I am responsible for myself without obligations from others.
- Worthy in Self, I will communicate with compassion and intelligence.
- Worthy in Self, I will objectively listen twice but speak once.

- Worthy in Self, I will question all things in unrestricted, yet elevated, consciousness and awareness.
- Worthy in Self, I will encourage harmony and unity among all finite living beings.
- Worthy in Self, I will invoke happiness and fulfillment within the limits of balance.
- Worthy in Self, I will be a bearer and a giver of love.
- Worthy in Self, I will make restorative efforts in conflict resolution and forgiveness.
- Worthy in Self, I will exercise self-discipline and self-control.
- Worthy in Self, I will take steps toward understanding my existence and my reality - physically and metaphysically.
- Worthy in Self, I will remind myself that my struggles are temporary; my existence is short and finite.
- Worthy in Self, I will follow my inner guidance, converging toward balance.
- Worthy in Self, I will walk in high vibration and high awareness, seeking knowledge, evidence, and reason before belief.
- Worthy in Self, I will be cognizant of the dual aspects of life and all mechanisms of the Living Universe.
- Worthy in Self, I will give charity to those less fortunate and those working to escape the lower limits.
- Worthy in Self, I will lead by example, for leadership sharpens leadership.
- Worthy in Self, I will speak with good intent.
- Worthy in Self, I will manifest through my intelligent spirit.
- Worthy in Self, I will be humble and reticent in the face of exploitation or mistreatment.
- Worthy in Self, I will achieve with integrity and sharpness.
- Worthy in Self, I will advance through my own abilities, gifts, and skills.
- Worthy in Self, I will embrace life, finite living beings, the Living Universe, the High Power – the "All".

Acknowledgments - Closure of Confessionals

- I acknowledge that life is finite in need of protection and preservation, for I am greater.
- I acknowledge that the inherent capability of the physical mantle shall not be restricted, for I am greater.
- I acknowledge that the knowledge and the expression of the intelligent spirit shall not be restricted, for I am greater.
- I acknowledge that I am able through consciousness, awareness, and a keen sense of perception, for I am greater.
- I acknowledge that any problem can be remedied through net-zero balance, for I am greater.

Em Hotep!

DAWN OF THE SIXTH BELL

ANKH WADJA SENEB | MEDJAI OF GATE #06

Function: Delivery of Raw Kemetic Teachings
Subject(s): Marriage, Meditation, Activities, Symbols, Dietary, Burial Handling
Position: Part 2 – The Raw Kemetic Teachings | High Spirituality

Peace to the High Power! Peace to the Living Universe! Peace to all Finite Living Beings! Peace to All Things – seen and unseen! For my spirit is with me, my image is with me, and my purpose is with me; and, let it be known by the Morning and the Evening Star that these self-evident teachings, unchanged by time or tongue, shall guide me and shall remain with me as I pursue my connection to the Living Universe and the High Power.

Recall that the High Power is a multi-dimensional life force with no spirit that is nothing like its direct creation (e.g., the Living Universe) or its indirect creations (i.e., finite living beings). Since the High Power has no spirit, no finite living being and no Living Universe can establish a two-way spiritual connection with it. Put in another way, a finite living being can establish a spiritual connection with the High Power; however, the High Power cannot establish a spiritual connection with a finite living being.

Recall that the High Power, as an impersonal entity, does not respond to solemn requests, spells, prayers, or the like for help, guidance, vengeance, or assistance from finite living beings including human beings because the fulfillment of its will remains the priority and it will not stop the fulfilment of its will in the interest of or to the benefit of finite living beings. In High Spirituality, such undertakings are considered to be acts of witchcraft and/or sorcery. For instance, trying to conjure a divine being to grant a request, trying to draw/channel power from spiritual/divine agencies to accomplish magical spells (bewitching incantations, baptisms, exorcisms, resurrections, yoga as a religious practice, teleportation, conjuring of ancestors, mind reading, acts of oracles, etc.), and casting spells/hexes/curses in the Living Universe to achieve a particular result – prayers can be a means to do so – are all occult acts of witchcraft and/or sorcery.

One can engage in various spiritual activities to channel the mental clarity and the spiritual enrichment necessary to dwell on the meaning, the individual purpose, and the connection with all existence, the Living Universe, and the High Power. These spiritual activities are also the natural remedies for combating harmful addictions, mental/physical illness, mental breakdowns, loneliness, and the corruption of the intelligent spirit. Corruption of the intelligent spirit can lead to psychopathy, sociopathy, thoughts of suicide, and so forth.

For clarification, demons, jinns, devils, or the like do not exist in High Spirituality, so there is no religiously-fabricated admission of demonic possession, demonic infestation, demonic vexation, demonic obsession, or need for exorcism because actual episodes of unusual behaviors, physical ailments, mental dissociations, and psychological distress are associated merely with the corruption of the intelligent spirit as well.

For clarification, places of paradise (Heaven, Jannah, Svarga, Gan Eden, Rig Veda, etc.) and places of purgatory (Hell, Gehenna, Inferno, Lake of Fire, etc.) do not exist in High Spirituality because High Spirituality revolves around the cycling of spirits with absolutely no afterlife, where the notion of an afterlife is often used as a fearmongering device. At most, paradise can be considered a state of mind for euphoria, and purgatory can be considered a state of mind for suffering – but never a literal place or a combination of both.

Auxiliaries

- **Kemetic Breathing**: This deep breathing technique involves inhaling on a four count, holding on a four count, exhaling on a four count, and holding again on a four count. Each exhale is followed by the vocalization of Ankh (life), Wajda (prosperity), and Seneb (health). Unlike unlabored breathing (eupnea) or shallow breathing, the full inhalation-exhalation cycle of diaphragmatic breathing stimulates the parasympathetic nervous system, releases endorphins, and improves bodily functions; thereby, calming the nervous system, promoting relaxation, encouraging fluid flow, lowering cortisol levels, and cultivating a connection between the physical and spiritual body.
- **Therapeutics**: These substances (e.g., incenses, burned sage, heated essential oils, Kyphi cocktails, etc.) are used to purify the air, to uplift mood (stress reduction), to cleanse spaces of negative energy (e.g., rid insects, harmful bacteria, and unwanted spiritual influences), and to improve focus.
- **Inspired Giving**: Charitable acts toward the suffering and the needy, involving giving when surpluses of food, clothing, currency, etc., are available as well as organ, fluid, and bodily donations to preserve life.
- **Exercise**: Activities that improve the physical and spiritual body through focused movements, physical wellness, inner peace, self-awareness, stress relief, and so forth.
- **Eutierria and Spiritual Trips**: Immersing oneself and engaging in nature, such as nature walks, gardening/planting, experiencing seasonal change, observing ecosystems, and embracing scenic beauty, helps to understand finite living beings at all levels.
- **Therapy**: A holistic, spiritual approach to well-being that reestablishes a greater sense of wholeness through recognition, realization, intervention, forgiveness, acceptance, journaling, mental release, self-care (personal health & wellness, alone time, etc.), and dialogue.
- **Voluntary Service**: This refers to community service that fosters a sense of purpose, connection, and empathy to all finite living beings, while also considering the well-being of the conscious Living Universe. This includes creating animal shelters, environmental cleanup, distributing food to finite living beings, and so forth. Bear in mind that community service in a spiritual sense involves all finite living beings, not just humans.
- **Deep Conversation**: This involves stimulating conversation that results in higher levels of intelligence, enlightenment, consciousness, rationality, and awareness. Such conversations are not only academic but also spiritual, extending to knowledge capacity and interconnectedness.
- **Self-Defense and Active Defense**: Interestingly enough, the Ancient Egyptians practiced martial arts – namely archery, wrestling, and stick fighting (Tahtib) – for physical protection (i.e., protection of the physical mantle) and for spiritual protection (i.e., protection of the intelligent spirit). It was never considered to be a standalone spiritual practice, as seen in modern martial arts traditions. Spiritual protection is a developed protection, sharpened by harnessing the senses through consciousness and the elements of the Living Universe through awareness. Even outside of combat, such defense equips someone with a source of strength, courage, confidence, and resilience to overcome all challenges and to shield against negative influences. In High Spirituality, people have every right to protect themselves physically and metaphysically. At all times, the physical body, rationality, consciousness, and so forth must be protected.
- **Rhythmic Generation**. Anything, which emanates from rhythm, such as music, humming, singing, dancing, body percussion, chanting, and so forth, can be utilized to tap into the physical and spiritual body.

Spiritual Affirmations

In High Spirituality, spiritual affirmations are used to build a strong foundation for our vital essence (Ka) and our spiritual body (Sah). Spiritual affirmations (words of power) are positive statements and expressions of gratitude, often repeated into the conscious Living Universe, that reinforce a desired truth, hope, effect, or belief, aiming to speak a sense of calm, purpose, result, or connection to one's higher self into existence. When combined with an elevating consciousness, the intelligent spirit soars beyond the obstacles of a present condition in an attempt to make a seemingly impossible outcome possible.

Marriage

In Ancient Kemet, where Egyptians scorned the unwedded, family marriages had always been the cornerstone of social life because they organized/integrated men, women, and children into cohesive working units, and they magnified the customs, the traditions, the roles, and the laws in effect required to establish marital contracts and marital rights. A spiritual connection, an unbroken union, an unbreakable bond, and a deep emotional relationship, a High Spiritual marriage is based on shared spiritual values, converging spiritual journeys, and compatible individual purposes. A marriage can be monogamous or polygamous; however, divorce is strictly prohibited, and marriages based solely on superficial outlooks and transactional value are considered invalid. Moreover, a marriage is fundamentally about those becoming bonded (private affair) rather than corresponding family members, so, it does not require a celebration or a formal ceremony.

Core tenets for a valid High Spiritual marriage include the following:

- A profound emotional relationship and a weighty spiritual connection must exist before, during, and after seeking a marriage. The spiritual connection serves as the prerequisite for a life-long contract with no possibility of divorce in times of hardship and in times of prosperity.
- The spiritual journey and the purpose of marriage seekers must be compatible.
- The marriage must be built on cooperative relationships where the marriage seekers work together, sharing resources and efforts to achieve mutual benefits, common goals, layered survival (e.g., no harm to one another, protection from outsiders, etc.), combined masculine/feminine leadership, and resonance. Resonance occurs when the transfigured intelligent spirit (akh) of marriage seekers coalesces into large amplitudes of vibration.
- The marriage must converge to the nfr (zero) balance with a dynamic interplay of opposing, yet complementary, masculine and feminine energies that involve the willingness to collaborate, the need to communicate effectively, combined rather than lopsided leadership, fair contribution, equality among marriage seekers, and wholehearted respect, responsibility, and accountability.
- Marriage is reserved strictly for adults, fully matured in physical mantle and intelligent spirit beyond puberty.
- Arranged marriages are invalid because marriage seekers must have full autonomy over their spiritual choices without influence, consent, and blessings from others.
- Marriages to relatives are invalid because High Spirituality does not support avenues of low genetic variation or incest.
- The involvement and the chaperoning of family are optional; however, no family can impose a dowry or any other financial/asset contribution in exchange for marriage, as this transactional measure – a bribe or no bribe – equivocates marriage seekers to property or artificial assets in the eyes of High Spirituality.

For clarification, High Spiritual marriages do not involve religious/cultural elements.

In High Spirituality, marriage seekers must accept the offering of one another, known as the 'Self-Offering'. The Self-Offering, not in a giving sense, refers to the collective embodiment of the best and the worst qualities of marriage seekers, inclusive of the interconnected constituents. Everything matters in a High Spiritual marriage, including educational history, medical history, reproductive capability, survivability, providership, criminal past, and so forth. All of these are 'packaged' into the Self-Offering for marriage seekers to make a decision.

Meditation

The equilateral pose, similar to the lotus pose, shown below, is the only posture used for meditation in High Spirituality. This pose, which is not directly associated with traditional religious practice in Egypt even though many religious Kemeticists liken it to Nefertem (Ptah's son in Egyptian iconography) and his attributes, signifies rebirth, regeneration (spiritual renewal), freshness, new beginnings via spiritual growth, enlightenment via intense focus on knowledge, and the vitality of and oneness with the conscious Living Universe.

Convergence to the geometrical configuration of the posture above is mandatory.

- The crown of the head is directed upward with closed eyes and neutral lips.
- The neck remains in line with the spine as the shoulder blades draw back to open the chest.
- The spine is straight with an upright, straight back.
- The abdominal area is drawn upward toward the spine.
- The chin remains perpendicular to the ground.
- The top of each foot rests on the top of each opposite thigh – the left over the right.
- The legs are flat with the hips in line and tilted forward with the tailbone slightly tucked.
- The hands extend outward with the center of the palm resting at the knee to form an equilateral triangle.

To maximize the meditation experience, ensure the following:

- **Alignment**: The pose must be executed with balanced geometric postures resembling triangles and squares, representing the interconnectedness of all things.
- **Breath Control**: Taking deep and intentional breaths enhances the flow of energy throughout the body. The smooth flow also promotes relaxation and rejuvenation.
- **Spiritual Connection**: Dwelling on a truth or individual purpose in a state of inner peace and harmony nurtures the mind-body-spirit conglomerate and alleviates stress.
- **Protection Ring**: This represents the unbroken continuum, infinity, and the eternal pursuit of knowledge. The ring, which can be coupled with spiritual elements, must enclose the body.

For clarification, these spiritual elements can be sacred geometries (octahedron, tetrahedron, hexahedron, icosahedron, and dodecahedron), interconnected constituents (khet, ka, ba, shuyet, sa, sekhem, ren, ab, or akh), or the following spiritual symbols:

- **Scarabaeus Sacer Beetle**: The life cycle of the scarab beetle, which involves the parent rolling its egg toward the sun, is a metaphoric representation of the transformative processes in nature engendered by the sun, which support life throughout the living universe.
- **Shenu**: This shape, which includes a hollow sphere bound by a rope to a horizontal base, represents the continuance of natural forces through cyclic periods tied to the plane of manifestation across timeless time, endless periods, and eternity.
- **Ankh**: The archaic form of the Ankh is a direct representation of the umbilicus that connects new life to its source of nourishment and growth. The loop represents feminine energy, the horizontal arm represents balance, and the tail/staff represents masculine energy.

The depictions of the interconnected constituents and the spiritual symbols are shown below.

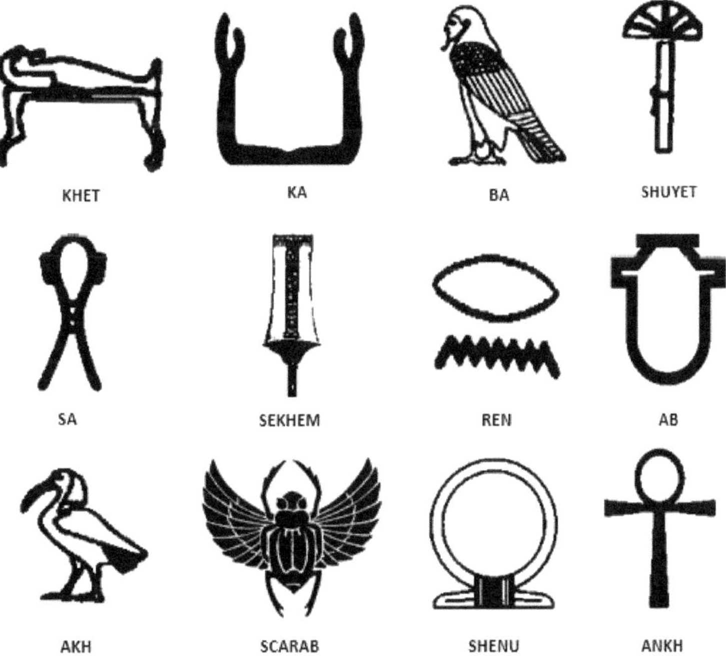

Dietary Intake

In Ancient Kemet, there were no food prohibitions in any Pharaonic society because Egyptians built classification systems concerning animals and plants based on the levels of sacrifice necessary to fulfill religious duties outside/inside temples and tombs, acknowledging that what was pure and what was impure was a matter of their gods. Dietary restrictions or negative prescriptions would emerge after the Greeks and the Romans studied the diets of priests during funerary acts and liturgical events, where fish, pigs, goats, sheep, donkeys, and legumes were considered unclean. Removing the religious elements, as these do not exist in the raw Kemetic teachings, it is evident that human beings can consume any food so long as the digestive system and/or the microbiome has the capacity to break it down, to extract nourishment/benefit from it, or to combat detrimental effects. For this reason, dietary recommendations rather than dietary restrictions are provided as follow:

- **Recommendation 1**: Dietary restrictions can be useful for specific medical conditions or health goals; however, overly restrictive diets can be harmful and unsustainable, potentially leading to unhealthy consumption patterns with food and negative health outcomes.
- **Recommendation 2**: Internally and externally absorb carbohydrates (natural sugars), polypeptides (proteins), nucleic acids, and lipids from unrefined organic matter alongside vital inorganics (water, minerals, herbs, spices, vitamins, etc.) as these are essential to life and all finite living beings.
- **Recommendation 3**: Always seek herbal, organic, homeopathic, and other natural remedies before consuming synthetics. Consuming teas and soups with different herbs and spice blends has its benefits.
- **Recommendation 4**: Abstain from ingesting food (fasting) for spiritual discipline, recovery, and mental/physical regulation using the two (2) fasting techniques from Ancient Egypt: (i) Natural Fast and (ii) Senu Fast.

The natural fast (abstaining while sleeping) involves sleeping for at least eight (8) continuous hours, followed by consuming all-natural sustenance at the time of breaking the fast. No food should be in the process of digestion during the fasting period.

The Senu fast requires three (3) days of full fasting, only consuming water for purgation and purification.

For clarification, there is no set time limit for fasting; however, it was common to fast in Ancient Egypt for a minimum of thirty (30) days per year.

Burial Handling

Recall that the raw spiritual teachings are incompatible with an afterlife, and they have nothing to do with religious funerary rites. Since there are no religious ceremonies or religious funerary rites, the base burial handling can be the same for all finite living beings, and the healing event can be customized in the interest of the deceased.

Recall that the High Power is impersonal to all finite living beings with a sole focus on fulfilling its will, so there is no need for prayer.

As a finite living being converges toward death, its intelligent spirit sheds the physical mantle, causing the intelligent spirit to transmutate into a complete spiritual essence before returning to the Pool of Spirits and the physical mantle to decompose. Witnessing the death and the decomposition of the physical mantle, the other finite living beings might go into a state of shock, followed by grief and bereavement. In High Spirituality, burials are healing rituals for finite living beings, not religious funerary ceremonies, used to help the bereaved and the grieving to find closure. Such healing includes a sense of closure to mourning, accepting a loss, celebrating life, paying respects (homage), remembering ancestors, reinforcement of social ties, and conscious reflection. After all, life is the gateway into the Living Universe, and death is the gateway out of the Living Universe; thus, both must be respected.

Strictly speaking for human beings, the body should be prepared as follows:

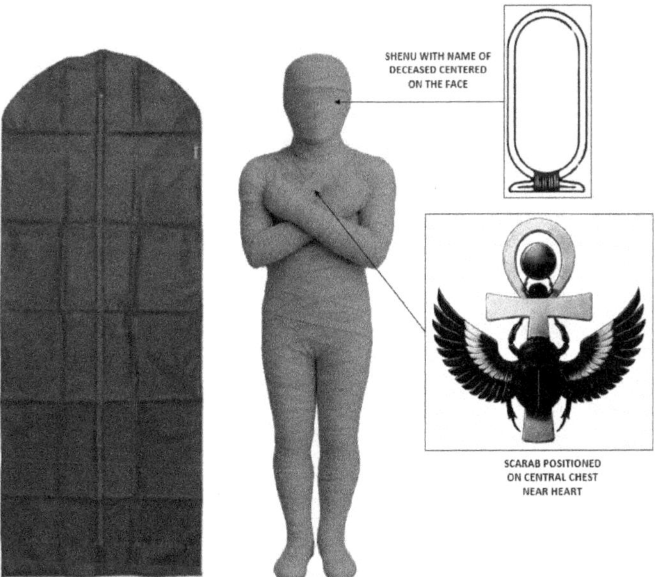

- The body, which lies in a closed, relaxed state, should be wrapped in bandages with arms squarely crossed (left over right) and fingers rounded toward the shoulders.
- An imprint combining the ankh and the Scarabaeus Sacer Beetle is symmetrically positioned with respect to the main portion of the body. The scarab sphere is located at the center of the chest, parallel to the heart line, and the leg of the ankh extends to the navel.
- Another imprint with the passing being's identity (i.e., personal name, date of birth, date/time of passing, etc.) on a Shenu can be centrally located on the head.
- The bandaged body is inserted into a biodegradable cover. The plastic cover is black to symbolize the return of the physical mantle to terra and the return of the intelligent spirit to the Pool of Spirits.

Em Hotep

DAWN OF THE SEVENTH BELL

ANKH WADJA SENEB | MEDJAI OF GATE #07

Function: Delivery of Raw Kemetic Teachings
Subject(s): Balance, Principle of Net/NFR Balance, Morality
Position: Part 2 – The Raw Kemetic Teachings | High Spirituality

MEDJAI OF GATE #07 - DAWN OF THE SEVENTH BELL

Peace to the High Power! Peace to the Living Universe! Peace to all Finite Living Beings! Peace to All Things – seen and unseen! For my spirit is with me, my image is with me, and my purpose is with me; and, let it be known by the Morning and the Evening Star that these self-evident teachings, unchanged by time or tongue, shall guide me and shall remain with me as I pursue my connection to the Living Universe and the High Power.

Encompassing truth, justice, order, and harmony, the Principle of Net Balance refers to the weighted scales of equilibrium required to maintain stability, oneness, no harm, and survival when taking a composite view of multiple or all viewpoints necessary to assess the most recognizable aspects and contexts of the High Power, the conscious Living Universe, and finite living beings.

Recall that Egyptians utilized 'nfr' to represent level and ground states because the modern-day 'zero' was not in use then. For this teaching, 'nfr' and 'zero' are synonymous.

- Net Balance of the High Power (Sacred Balance): The High Power transcends the infimum and the supremum with dual extremum in nature, so its net balance is always zero regardless of viewpoint. When the net balance is zero, this is called the 'nfr balance'.
- Net Balance of the Cosmos (Cosmic Balance): The Living Universe, which has consciousness and innate intelligence, has a net zero balance when unaffected. Moreover, the Stellar Path, the Solar Path, and the Lunar Path will automatically act to restore any perturbations/imperfections to normality. Once again, this is true regardless of viewpoint.
- Net Balance within Dwelling Spheres (Moral Balance): Finite living beings, which have individual purpose and complete free will in the Living Universe, can only exhibit a net balance of zero in dwelling spheres if and only if they can avoid, can correct, or can eliminate harmful imbalances across four (4) signature cases: (i) Case 1 – imbalances among similar finite living beings, (ii) Case 2 – imbalances among different finite living beings, (iii) Case 3 – 'finite living being to the Living Universe' imbalances, and (iv) Case 4 – 'finite living being to the High Power' imbalances.

Unlike the High Power and the Living Universe, finite living beings consist of an infinite number of finite living beings at many scales with different philosophies, viewpoints, purposes, meanings, capabilities, connectivity, and complexity levels of consciousness/awareness, so maintaining a net balance of zero requires a sophisticated and a cooperative approach known as morality.

Morality, which is instinctive to and which is relativistic to the viewpoints of finite living beings, is the intersection of changing, yet shared, subjective systems of conduct that differentiate between the dual extremum of balance.

Instinctive Morality refers to the idea that finite living beings possess an innate or a natural sense of right and wrong, potentially rooted in biological or evolutionary factors rather than solely learned through conditioning.

Moral Relativism, as well as Ethical Relativism, is used to describe several philosophical positions concerned with the differences in moral judgments across different finite living beings and conditioning. The uneven weighting of philosophical positions and cognitive dissonance are consequences of this idea, where cognitive dissonance, by definition, describes unknowing conflicts and unknowing inconsistencies in thoughts, beliefs, behavior, decisions, or attitudes.

The intersection of shared, subjective systems of conduct often gives the illusion of absolute morality. Absolute morality is the belief that there are universal moral principles that apply to all finite living beings in all situations; however, this is far-fetched, and it is idealistic because the moral balance would require acceptance from all finite living beings. Finite living beings have a moral obligation to prevent, to minimize, or to eliminate imbalances to ensure their survival and their coexistence.

Whenever the conduct of a finite living being shifts the balance toward the infimum, the imbalance affecting any of the signature cases will be associated with a negative pairing (e.g., bad, evil, darkness, hostility, hate, etc.). Maximizing negative pairing will not maximize net balance. Examples include the following:

- Imbalances leading to retribution (vigilante response)
- Imbalances leading to retaliation (reciprocal response)
- Imbalances caused by void and mental illness

Whenever the conduct of a finite living being shifts the balance toward the supremum, the imbalance affecting any of the signature cases will be associated with a positive pairing (e.g., good, light, peace, love, etc.). Maximizing positive pairing will not maximize net balance.

- Imbalances caused by happiness
- Imbalances caused by pleasure
- Imbalances caused by charity

Whenever the conduct of a finite living being does not shift the balance whatsoever, no imbalance affects any of the signature cases and no pairing occurs. Minimizing pairing effects and maximizing balanced/restorative states, known as homeostasis, will maximize net balance and will converge to the net zero/nfr balance.

- Homeostasis driven by forgiveness (restorative response)
- Homeostasis driven by concurring restitution from a fatal accident
- Homeostasis driven by rehabilitation
- Homeostasis driven by reconciliation, atonement, and/or penance

The only way to seek atonement for a wrong or an injury is by undertaking counteractions that converge to a net balance of zero, even if the counteractions involve penance and repentance. It is worth noting that atonement can be sought among finite living beings only but not the Living Universe with no free will under the High Power nor the High Power because the High Power always has a net balance of zero, which is the net balancing state required for homeostasis.

Since morality is driven by intersecting systems of conduct and shifts of net balance, finite living beings do not necessarily need a brain but rather a means of communication (verbal or nonverbal) and a conforming control mechanism to restore any imbalance to normalcy. The control mechanism is normally a penal, legal, or social code established by decision-makers, designated leaders, or moral appraisers at a given level of complexity of the finite level being. Consequently, this means that High Spirituality identifies imbalances, but does not associate punishments with these imbalances – even for apostasy – because morality is driven by finite living beings, not the High Power.

For clarification, religious doctrines assign penalties and punishments to moral breaches; even though, such penalties and punishments were not created by, were not corroborated by, and were not brought by a divine entity. In essence, humans are penalizing and punishing others or establishing control mechanisms on behalf of a divine entity without the consent/approval of the same divine entity.

For clarification, High Spirituality has nothing to do with apostasy in a religious context; however, if one chooses to abandon the teachings, then there are no punishments but rather a willful choice to live in ignorance (i.e., an absence of self-knowledge).

From this point on, the Principle of Net Balance will be applied in a simple form to a sufficient number of common social items, assuming equal weights and the human experience. The wording of social items should be carefully chosen, as minor changes can produce drastically different results ('committing arson' vs. 'recruiting people to commit arson'). Depending on the outcome, the social item might require moral relativistic resolutions through compromises, concessions, negotiations, and/or control mechanisms.

Case 1 – Imbalances among similar finite living beings
Case 2 – Imbalances among different finite living beings
Case 3 – 'finite living being to the Living Universe' imbalances
Case 4 – 'finite living being to the High Power' imbalances

For clarification, the Principle of Net Balance, unlike religion usually relying on surface-level understanding and abstract parables, can be applied to any issue of moral, social, and ethical value/relevance at any level of scope/detail – general or specific.

For clarification, anything that goes against the Confessionals or the High Power will always reduce to 'bad' acts.

For clarification, the idea of 'treating others the way that you want to be treated' can be integrated into the Principle of Net Balance.

Social Item # 01: Polluting Space with Space Junk

Case	Type	Pairing	Rationality
1	Moral	Negative	The accumulation of space junk caused by humans threatens the safety of other humans if fragments reenter Earth's atmosphere or if landing fragments introduce radiation into dwelling spheres.
2	Moral	Negative	The accumulation of space junk caused by humans threatens the safety of non-human organisms if fragments reenter Earth's atmosphere or if landing fragments introduce radiation into dwelling spheres.
3	Cosmic	Negative	Large pieces of space junk introduce unnatural and synthetic solid fuel remnants and, if this junk explodes, the momentum can impact the trajectory and the stability of nearby celestial entities in the Living Universe.
4	Sacred	None	The High Power is always in equilibrium with Nfr/Zero Balance

<u>Conclusion</u>: Assuming equal weighting, the net balances indicate that polluting space with increasing space junk/debris is in favor of negative pairing imbalances, so it can be categorized overall as a 'bad' act. This can also be extended to other cases of pollution (e.g., carbon emissions, second-hand smoke, plastics, etc.), posing risks to different ecosystems (dwelling spheres).

Social Item # 02: Consumption of Animals (Non-Human)

Case	Type	Pairing	Rationality
1	Moral	Positive	The consumption of animals helps humans to survive and to receive nourishment.
1	Moral	Negative	Humans risk disease and health-related concerns when consuming animals, depending on how the animal is digested and the capacity of bodily systems and the internal microbiome.
2	Moral	Negative	Animals do not want to be consumed. The presence of humans threatens their survival.
2	Moral	Positive	The consumption of animals increases the survival chances of other finite living beings (bacteria, viruses, parasites, etc.) that need to enter the human body.
2	Moral	Positive	The byproducts of animal consumption (urination, defecation, etc.) support other finite living beings in the localized dwelling sphere.
3	Cosmic	Positive	Eliminating finite living beings in dwelling spheres minimizes potential harm and potential instabilities that might be caused in the Living Universe.
4	Sacred	None	The High Power is always in equilibrium with Nfr/Zero Balance

Conclusion: Assuming equal weighting, the net balances indicate that consuming animals is in favor of positive pairing imbalances, so it can be categorized overall as a 'good' act.

Social Item # 03: Consumption of Humans (Cannibalism)

Case	Type	Pairing	Rationality
1	Moral	Negative	Cannibalism decreases human survival and human population rates.
1	Moral	Negative	Humans risk disease and health concerns like kuru when consuming other humans.
1	Moral	Negative	Humans do not want to be consumed by other humans.
2	Moral	Positive	Finite living beings threatened by the presence of humans increase in survival.
2	Moral	Negative	Finite living beings that prey on humans decrease in survival.
2	Moral	Negative	Finite living beings that rely on humans decrease in survival.
3	Cosmic	Positive	Eliminating finite living beings in dwelling spheres minimizes potential harm and potential instabilities that might be caused in the Living Universe.
4	Sacred	None	The High Power is always in equilibrium with Nfr/Zero Balance

Conclusion: Assuming equal weighting, the net balances indicate that cannibalism is in favor of negative pairing imbalances, so it can be categorized overall as a 'bad' act.

Social Item # 04: Killing - Taking a Life (Murder/Manslaughter) of Any Finite Living Being

Case	Type	Pairing	Rationality
1	Moral	Negative	The act of taking a human life reduces the human population and human survival rates.
1	Moral	Negative	The act of taking a human life causes a retributive/retaliatory cycle of more killing.
1	Moral	Negative	Human beings do not want to be killed.
2	Moral	Positive	Killing predatory finite living beings allows others to survive.
2	Moral	Negative	Killing non-predatory finite living beings hinders the survival of others.
2	Moral	Positive	The act of taking a human life provides nourishment to some finite living beings.
3	Cosmic	Positive	Eliminating finite living beings in dwelling spheres minimizes potential harm and potential instabilities that might be caused in the Living Universe.
4	Sacred	None	The High Power is always in equilibrium with Nfr/Zero Balance

Conclusion: Assuming equal weighting, the net balances indicate that taking a life (murder/manslaughter) is in favor of negative pairing imbalances, so it can be categorized overall as a 'bad' act. It is also worth noting that killing extends to all finite living beings, not necessarily just human beings. This is a significant difference between religion and High Spirituality, where taking the life of a non-human from a religious perspective, especially through sacrifice, is often not viewed as killing when it is in reality. Even stepping on grass and deforestation are perceived as 'bad' acts based on this logic.

Social Item # 05: Killing - Taking a Life (Self-Defense) of Any Finite Living Being

Case	Type	Pairing	Rationality
1	Moral	Positive	The act of taking a human life in self-defense safeguards the human population.
1	Moral	Positive	The preservation of human life is necessary for survival.
1	Moral	Negative	The offending human being(s) would not want to be killed.
2	Moral	Positive	Killing any other finite living beings in self-defense allows others to survive.
2	Moral	Positive	The act of taking a life results in nourishment to some finite living beings.
3	Cosmic	Positive	Eliminating finite living beings in dwelling spheres minimizes potential harm and potential instabilities that might be caused in the Living Universe.
4	Sacred	None	The High Power is always in equilibrium with Nfr/Zero Balance

Conclusion: Assuming equal weighting, the net balances indicate that taking a life in self-defense is in favor of positive pairing imbalances, so it can be categorized overall as a 'good' act.

Social Item # 06: Abortion - Taking a Fetal Life (Human Being Only)

Case	Type	Pairing	Rationality
1	Moral	Negative	Termination of fetuses decreases the human population and human survival chances.
1	Moral	Negative	Termination of the fetuses breaks the spiritual connection between parents and the fetus.
1	Moral	Negative	Termination of fetuses decreases genetic variability in the human population.
1	Moral	Negative	Parental risks from fertilization to birth can result in the death of fetuses and parents.
1	Moral	Negative	The fetus itself does not want to be terminated.
2	Moral	Positive	Termination of the fetuses allows other finite living beings as prey to survive.
2	Moral	Positive	The loss of life (mother, fetus, or both) might result in nourishment for other finite living beings.
3	Cosmic	Positive	Eliminating finite living beings in dwelling spheres minimizes potential harm and potential instabilities that might be caused in the Living Universe.
4	Sacred	None	The High Power is always in equilibrium with Nfr/Zero Balance

Conclusion: Assuming equal weighting, the net balances indicate that abortion is in favor of negative pairing imbalances, so it can be categorized overall as a 'bad' act.

Social Item # 07: Taking a Life (Euthanasia as direct, "Do-Nothing" as indirect, & Capital Punishment) of Any Finite Living Being

Case	Type	Pairing	Rationality
1	Moral	Negative	Termination of a life decreases the human population and human survival chances.
1	Moral	Negative	Termination of a life breaks spiritual connections
1	Moral	Negative	A finite living being does not want to be terminated but rather for the pain/condition to end.
2	Moral	Positive	Termination of a life increases the survival of other finite living beings as prey.
2	Moral	Negative	Termination of a life decreases the survival of other finite living beings as predators.
3	Cosmic	Positive	Eliminating finite living beings in dwelling spheres minimizes potential harm and potential instabilities that might be caused in the Living Universe.
4	Sacred	None	The High Power is always in equilibrium with Nfr/Zero Balance

Conclusion: Assuming equal weighting, the net balances indicate that euthanasia and capital punishment are in favor of negative pairing imbalances, so it can be categorized overall as a 'bad' act. This can also be extended to suicide and population control mechanisms (ethnic cleansing, eugenics, resource/supply limitations, etc.) that result in taking lives based on some case, view, or perceived suffering.

Social Item # 08: Domestic Violence – Married or Unmarried

Case	Type	Pairing	Rationality
1	Moral	Negative	Lack of a spiritual connection with no resonance.
1	Moral	Negative	Such violence breeds harm and retaliatory measures.
1	Moral	Negative	Such violence can cause a cycle of abuse if normalized.
1	Moral	Negative	No human wants to be domestically abused.
2	Moral	None	No imbalance. This social item never mentions death nor an external spiritual connection with a different finite living being.
3	Cosmic	None	Domestic violence has no bearing on the Living Universe.
4	Sacred	None	The High Power is always in equilibrium with Nfr/Zero Balance

Conclusion: Assuming equal weighting, the net balances indicate that domestic violence is in favor of negative pairing imbalances, so it can be categorized overall as a 'bad' act.

Social Item # 09: Public Nudity

Case	Type	Pairing	Rationality
1	Moral	Positive	Considered as becoming one with the elements of the Living Universe
1	Moral	Positive	Ability to absorb nourishments (e.g., vitamin D and cell energy from the sun) increases.
1	Moral	Negative	The absence of clothing removes a protective layer from humans.
1	Moral	Positive	Freedom and expression of the raw physical mantle.
1	Moral	Negative	Incites lust, lechery, or sexual crimes/exploitation.
1	Moral	Positive	Instigates population growth necessary for survival.
2	Moral	None	No imbalance. This social item never mentions harm to a different finite living being.
3	Cosmic	Negative	Instigating the reproduction of finite living beings in dwelling spheres increases potential harm and potential instabilities that might be caused in the Living Universe.
4	Sacred	None	The High Power is always in equilibrium with Nfr/Zero Balance

Conclusion: Assuming equal weighting, the net balances indicate that public nudity is in favor of positive pairing imbalances, so it can be categorized overall as a 'good' act.

Social Item # 10: Pornography

Case	Type	Pairing	Rationality
1	Moral	Negative	Projects sexual activities to humans before the age of adulthood.
1	Moral	Negative	Disturbs spiritual connections, especially the resonance among married humans.
1	Moral	Positive	Freedom and expression of the raw physical mantle.
1	Moral	Negative	Incites lust and lechery through imagination.
1	Moral	Positive	Instigates population growth necessary for survival.
2	Moral	Negative	Some forms of pornography suggest, encourage, or show bestiality.
3	Cosmic	Negative	Instigating the reproduction of finite living beings in dwelling spheres increases potential harm and potential instabilities that might be caused in the Living Universe.
4	Sacred	None	The High Power is always in equilibrium with Nfr/Zero Balance

Conclusion: Assuming equal weighting, the net balances indicate that pornography is in favor of negative pairing imbalances, so it can be categorized overall as a 'bad' act.

Social Item # 11: Homosexuality

Case	Type	Pairing	Rationality
1	Moral	Positive	Promotes spiritual connections and freedom among participants.
1	Moral	Negative	Cripples/hinders family structures and gene variations.
1	Moral	Negative	Hinders the path of reproduction, decreasing survival rates.
1	Moral	Negative	The glorification of homosexuality can cause drastic decreases in population size.
2	Moral	None	No imbalance. This social item never mentions harm to a different finite living being.
3	Cosmic	Positive	Decreasing finite living beings in dwelling spheres minimizes potential harm and potential instabilities that might be caused in the Living Universe.
4	Sacred	None	The High Power is always in equilibrium with Nfr/Zero Balance

Conclusion: Assuming equal weighting, the net balances indicate that homosexuality is in favor of negative pairing imbalances, so it can be categorized overall as a 'bad' act. Bear in mind that the assessment of homosexuality is complex, so it might require moral relativistic resolutions for public/private acts through compromises, concessions, negotiations, and/or control mechanisms. This can also be extended to homosexuality in animals (e.g., lions, giraffes, dolphins, etc.) as well. Moreover, homosexual relations and homosexual behaviors should be assessed separately.

For clarification, High Spirituality does not support homosexuality or same-sex marriages as it goes against nature; even though, nothing in the Kemetic teachings indicates that homosexuality was explicitly forbidden or was punished. There are, however, acknowledgments of 'men lying with men' – nothing about lesbianism – being impure and incompatibilities of same sex with the Ankh (feminine loop with masculine staff). Consequently, this is why the Christian cross is seen as a homosexual symbol in the eyes of High Spirituality because the two (2) connecting staffs indicate masculine-to-masculine energies.

Social Item # 12: Birth Control (Contraception)

Case	Type	Pairing	Rationality
1	Moral	Negative	Hinders the path of reproduction, sometimes permanently if used in the long term, decreasing survival rates and population size.
1	Moral	Negative	Incites lust and lechery by eliminating fears of childbirth.
2	Moral	Positive	Human birth control increases the survival of other finite living beings as prey.
2	Moral	Negative	Human birth control decreases the survival of other finite living beings as predators.
3	Cosmic	Positive	Decreasing finite living beings in dwelling spheres minimizes potential harm and potential instabilities that might be caused in the Living Universe.
4	Sacred	None	The High Power is always in equilibrium with Nfr/Zero Balance

Conclusion: Assuming equal weighting, the net balances indicate that birth control is in favor of negative pairing imbalances, so it can be categorized overall as a 'bad' act.

Social Item # 13: War with Use of Weapons of Mass Destruction (WMDs) and Child Soldiers

Case	Type	Pairing	Rationality
1	Moral	Negative	The killing of humans at high rates results in rapid decreases in population size.
1	Moral	Negative	Survival rates will plunge from direct human assaults and weapon effects.
1	Moral	Negative	Children, viewed as the future bearers, will be eliminated.
1	Moral	Negative	Human beings do not want to die. Preservation of life.
1	Moral	Negative	Removal of nourishment from WMDs
2	Moral	Positive	Human deaths increase the survival of other finite living beings as prey.
2	Moral	Negative	Human deaths decrease the survival of other finite living beings as predators.
2	Moral	Positive	The act of taking a life results in nourishment to some finite living beings.
2	Moral	Negative	Other finite living beings do not want to die. Preservation of life.
2	Moral	Negative	Other finite living beings and their dwelling spaces are threatened.
2	Moral	Negative	Removal of nourishment from WMDs
3	Cosmic	Negative	Use of WMDs can destroy dwelling spheres and alter the environmental conditions of the Living Universe.
3	Cosmic	Positive	Decreasing finite living beings in dwelling spheres minimizes potential harm and potential instabilities that might be caused in the Living Universe.
4	Sacred	None	The High Power is always in equilibrium with Nfr/Zero Balance

Conclusion: Assuming equal weighting, the net balances indicate that war with WMDs and child soldiers is in favor of negative pairing imbalances, so it can be categorized overall as a 'bad' act. This can be extended to genocide.

Social Item # 14: Creation of a Religion (Human Effects)

Case	Type	Pairing	Rationality
1	Moral	Negative	A religion can promote the death of, discrimination against, and separation from non-believers, decreasing population size/unity and survival rates.
1	Moral	Negative	A religion can have dangerous practices leading to loss of life. No human wants to die.
1	Moral	Negative	A religion constrains consciousness and knowledge capacity, forcing believers to accept falsehoods and delusions as miracles, wonders, and divine things beyond comprehension.
1	Moral	Negative	A religion creates social hierarchies (e.g., tribalism, class, etc.), leading to conflicts in inequality.
1	Moral	Negative	A religion perverts spiritual connection toward invented gods/deities
1	Moral	Negative	A religion allows humans to justify punishment, killing, and even slavery.
1	Moral	Positive	A religion can have ethical and moral values.
1	Moral	Negative	Doctrines can promote inequality between genders.
1	Moral	Negative	Doctrines can limit individual rights and freedoms.
1	Moral	Negative	Fear-based teachings can lead to trauma, manipulation, exploitation, and abuse.
1	Moral	Positive	A religion can provide a sense of wholeness through community.
1	Moral	Positive	A religion promotes marriage
1	Moral	Negative	A religion allows divorce.
2	Moral	Negative	A religion can call for animal sacrifices, leading to decreasing population sizes and survival rates. No animal wants to be sacrificed.
2	Moral	Negative	A religion can deny/devalue/disrespect the lives of non-human finite living beings.
2	Moral	Positive	A religion can hold an animal sacred.
2	Moral	Positive	A religion can command equality and praise of non-human finite living beings.
2	Moral	Positive	A religion can prevent the consumption of animals.
3	Cosmic	Positive	Decreasing finite living beings in dwelling spheres minimizes potential harm and potential instabilities that might be caused in the Living Universe.
4	Sacred	None	The High Power is always in equilibrium with Nfr/Zero Balance

Conclusion: Assuming equal weighting, the net balances indicate that creating a religion is in favor of negative pairing imbalances, so it can be categorized overall as a 'bad' act. This can be extended to cults.

Social Item # 15: Enslavement

Case	Type	Pairing	Rationality
1	Moral	Negative	Reduces humans to property and causes division.
1	Moral	Negative	Denies humans autonomy and the exercise of free will.
1	Moral	Negative	Induces violence, coercion, death, and trauma.
1	Moral	Positive	Can establish a spiritual connection psychologically through master-slave bondage.
1	Moral	Positive	Imprisonment can be used as a restorative means for a wrongdoing.
2	Moral	Negative	Reduces other finite living beings to property.
2	Moral	Negative	Denies other finite living beings autonomy and the exercise of free will.
2	Moral	Positive	Can establish a spiritual connection psychologically through master-slave bondage.
2	Moral	Negative	Induces violence, coercion, estrangement, and trauma
3	Cosmic	Positive	Enslaving finite living beings in dwelling spheres minimizes potential harm and potential instabilities that might be caused in the Living Universe.
3	Cosmic	Positive	Decreasing finite living beings in dwelling spheres minimizes potential harm and potential instabilities that might be caused in the Living Universe.
4	Sacred	None	The High Power is always in equilibrium with Nfr/Zero Balance

Conclusion: Assuming equal weighting, the net balances indicate that enslavement is in favor of negative pairing imbalances, so it can be categorized overall as a 'bad' act. This can be extended to genocide.

Social Item # 16: Blood Transfusions

Case	Type	Pairing	Rationality
1	Moral	Positive	Providing spare blood components (red cells, white cells, platelets, and plasma) increases the survival rate of humans.
1	Moral	Positive	Blood from humans provides nourishment for humans.
1	Moral	Positive	The sharing of life fluids opens a spiritual connection through indebtedness.
1	Moral	Negative	Incompatible transfusions can lead to life-threatening complications and illness.
1	Moral	Negative	Without a transfusion, needy humans can risk death.
2	Moral	Positive	Blood/flesh from other finite living beings provides nourishment for humans.
2	Moral	Negative	Non-human finite living beings are sometimes killed for xenotransfusion.
3	Cosmic	Negative	Rescuing finite living beings in dwelling spheres increases potential harm and potential instabilities that might be caused in the Living Universe.
4	Sacred	None	The High Power is always in equilibrium with Nfr/Zero Balance

Conclusion: Assuming equal weighting, the net balances indicate that blood transfusions have inconclusive pairing imbalances, so it might require moral relativistic resolutions for public/private acts through compromises, concessions, negotiations, and/or control mechanisms. This can be extended to organ donors.

For clarification, inconclusive pairing imbalances occur in the globalized approach to the Principle of Net Balance. After taking a detailed approach, inclusive of moral relativistic resolutions, weights, and various perspectives, any deduction to a Nfr/Zero balance becomes more plausible.

At this point, the reader should understand how complex the Principle of Net Balance can become when assessing/examining the sacred balance, cosmic balance, and moral balance for all signature cases at different weights, especially considering spiritual connections, the survival of finite living beings, the preservation of the conscious Living Universe, and the conduct for interconnectedness, unity, and cohesion. Even changing the perspective from a human to another human to a tree to a bacterium can yield completely different outcomes.

For clarification, finite living beings should take caution when establishing decision makers, sources of authority, and control mechanisms (penal, social codes, etc.) to determine moral balance because individual finite living being groups might be favored over others if the intersecting systems of conducts are weak or if an individual finite living being group dominantly imposes its perspective over the dissenting/differing masses.

As we approach the brilliance of the sun, we bathe in the dual effects of the Morning and the Evening Star, becoming immersed in the physical and metaphysical experiences of nature under the High Power, exposed to various cycles inherent in a Living Universe, simmered by an inherent intelligent spirit as well as molded, forged, and cultivated on a journey known as the Kemetic path longing for balance, interconnectedness, purpose, and the endless pursuit of knowledge, for we blaze the path of light only to find the keys to unlock the purpose deep within us!

Em Hotep!

HISTORICAL ADDITIVES

ANKH WADJA SENEB | CLOSURE

Function: Delivery of Raw Kemetic Teachings
Subject(s): Kemetic Chronology, Papyri, Egyptian Dynasties/Periods
Position: Part 2 – The Raw Kemetic Teachings | High Spirituality

CLOSURE - HISTORICAL ADDITIVES

Peace to the High Power! Peace to the Living Universe! Peace to all Finite Living Beings! Peace to All Things – seen and unseen! For my spirit is with me, my image is with me, and my purpose is with me; and, let it be known by the Morning and the Evening Star that these self-evident teachings, unchanged by time or tongue, shall guide me and shall remain with me as I pursue my connection to the Living Universe and the High Power.

This section briefly walks through the Nubian-Kemetic chronology with approximate years, not only to shed light on past events but also to illuminate how ancient culture, practices, knowledge, politics, and technology became infected with religious/cultist elements.

THE PREDYNASTIC PERIOD

Although no texts survive from the earlier (predynastic) cultures, excavations and later writings have revealed some facts and information about the structure and the customs of those societies. From antiquity, there are writings about Egypt that include both Egyptian texts on papyri, stelae, ostraca, and tomb/temple walls and accounts by classical travelers and authors.

2.5 million BCE: Homo Habilis (meaning 'skillful man') appeared in Africa.
2.0 million BCE: Earliest stone tools in Ethiopia and East Africa were used.
1.8 million BCE: Homo Erectus (meaning 'upright man') appeared in Africa.

150000 BCE: Homo Sapiens appeared in Africa.
70000 BCE: Neanderthal man appeared in Africa using fire and advanced tools.
43000 BCE: Cro-Magnon man appeared in Africa.
35000 BCE: Africans began iron mining in the Nile Valley.
33000 BCE: The Grimaldi Negroids expanded into Europe.
30000 BCE: Africans of Monomotapa created the 1st sculpture of a human figure.
12000 BCE: Sebelian II ruled in Pre-Dynastic Kemet.
10000 BCE: Africans of the Nile Valley introduced the 1st calendar.
8000 BCE: Early spread of agriculture and first settlements in the Nile Delta.
7500 BCE: Dated Nabta Playa Stone Circle site of the Nubian Neolithic Period.
7000 BCE: The Earliest cave drawings were drawn in the Sahara.
6020 BCE: Africans in the Congo used markings on bones to develop the first number system.

Years before pyramids topped the horizon and giant statues bordered temple enclosures, the Nile Valley was a region of slow evolution. Around 5000 BCE, pockets of agriculturalists started to mold the banks of the river into a home of permanence. The river was a gift and a curse every year, depending on the severity of wet and dry seasons, especially since the monsoon rains from the highlands of Ancient Ethiopia flooded each summer northwards. The Nile would overflow and then be drawn back again, depositing fertile black silt on the ground. This beat became the pulse of Ancient Kemet and Ancient Nubia – a life and a survival pattern that made people learn to read the signs of nature. Some communities had built dikes and basins to collect flood waters to use them at a later time. Houses cultivated barley, emmer wheat, and flax, storing enough to last through hardship periods. The Nile was not just a cyclical water source but the focal point of order, promise, and power; and, these early inhabitants, especially the farmers, established civilizations in Ancient Kemet and Ancient Nubia by harnessing, learning, utilizing, and protecting it.

In Upper Kemet, small villages punctuated the productive flood plain - each one dependent upon the Nile – to bring the blessings of its fertility. The villagers decorated pottery with swirling patterns of boats, animals, and abstract designs, reflecting creativity and ritualistic meaning. Graves became more differentiated, some with not-before-seen jars of food, strings of beads, and polished stone tools. Such things gave rise to social hierarchy and to the first beginnings of elite identity. To the south of Kemet, Nubia prospered with its own cultural progression. Archeologists have grouped the Nubian cultures as follow:

- **A-Group**: The earliest Nubian culture with strong rulers, which developed out of Neolithic cultures of the Nile valley. Known largely from its cemeteries, its burials, artifacts, and rock art are found along the Nile from the 1st cataract to the 2nd cataract. Trade was its primary source of wealth and power as its location gave it access to gold from the eastern desert, carnelian from the western desert, and commodities, such as incense, ivory, and ebony from farther south along the Nile. They exchanged these resources mainly for Egyptian products and Mediterranean olive oil. In addition to maintaining trade with Egypt, the A-Group rulers incorporated symbols that were used by Egyptian pharaohs in addition to Nubian seal impressions and writings depicting a bow above a rectangle, representing Ta-Seti (meaning "Land of the Bow"). The A-Group flourished until it was destroyed by the pharaohs of Egypt's First Dynasty.
- **C-Group**: This Nubian culture incorporated small circular houses with stone foundations, handmade ceramics with elaborate incised decoration, and graves covered with circular stone mounds as their A-Group predecessors; however, the importance of cattle, shown in its burial stelae, pottery, figurines, and rock drawings, demonstrates a firm link to the African cattle cultures that began in the Neolithic period. Though first ruled by Egypt and then by Kerma, the C-Group culture retained its own distinctive customs for centuries, until Nubians adopted Egyptian styles during the New Kingdom occupation of Nubia.
- **Kerma**: This Nubian culture was the most powerful Nubian state based at Kerma, a partly fortified settlement near the 3rd cataract. Though the population size was small (< 5000), a distinctive Kerma culture was found from the 2nd cataract to areas beyond the 4th cataract, including a tall mudbrick temple (deffufa), a palace, and a royal audience hall. To the east of the city were funerary temples and chapels amid an extensive cemetery, where the largest tombs were for royal burial mounds nearly 300 feet in diameter, with remains of human servants and animals. When Kerma rulers consolidated power, they brought their army – mostly archers – into conflict with the Middle Kingdom of Kemet, which lasted until the rise of the New Kingdom in Egypt.
- **X-Group**: This Nubian culture is associated with great tomb complexes built at Qustul and across the Nile River at Ballana. They appeared in northern Nubia after Meroitic rule ended and, like the tumuli at Kerma 2000 years prior, the tombs were composed of earthen mounds with elaborate substructures and wealthy royal burials with sacrificial retainers. Horse and camel sacrifices were commonly buried in the shaft of the tomb or in separate pits. Based on accumulated Greek texts, the X-Group is mostly like the Noubadian Kingdom because the Noubadians were almost certainly a group of Nubians whom migrated into the region from the south or the west around 370 CE, until they were defeated by the Blemmyes.

5000 BCE: People began to settle along the Nile River in Egypt.
4400 BCE: The Badarian culture formed. The people relied on agriculture and pottery as well as domesticated cattle, sheep, and goats.
4100 BCE: The first solar calendar was introduced by Kemet and Kush.

By 4000 BCE, there were two cultural spheres in Kemet. In the south was the Naqada civilization with its decorated pottery and boat motifs, flint blades, and large stone palettes, used perhaps during religious ceremonies. Naqada rulers became so powerful that their influence extended to other villages. The Maadi culture in the north, outward-facing to the Levant, traded with the emerging cities of Mesopotamia and imported copper, oil, and luxury items. Violence between the north and the south increased over the centuries. Naqada, dynamic and ambitious, devoured its rivals by degrees. Warfare and diplomacy became evident since the southern rulers unified cultures into larger polities. This unification of power was both bloody and idealistic since it outlined the foundation of a unified Kemet. This supremacy struggle was not merely political but about forging an identity and deciding what deities, practices, and symbols to define the Nile Valley as it entered the crowning era.

4000 BCE: Several powerful towns, especially Abydos, Naqada, and Nekhen (commonly called Hierakonpolis), and a possible unified southern kingdom rose.
4000 BCE: The Anu were the first settlers of the Nile Valley who founded Kush (Ta-Seti) and Kemet after developing the Ta-Seti Nile Valley Culture.
4000 BCE: The oldest known evidence of Metu Neter came from predynastic pottery at Gerzeh and inscriptions in Nubia at Gebel Sheikh Suleiman.
3758 BCE: The first religious principles of right and wrong were written by the Kushite King Ori.
3400 BCE: The first hieroglyphic scripts, Metu Neter, with consonants only, were found in Abydos on clay tablets, predating the cuneiform script of Sumer by two centuries. Later forms were used on texts like the Narmer Palette (3200 BCE) and the Pyramid Texts (2400 BCE). The records, the names, and the numbers were necessary, especially for logging trade. Two cursive scripts (hieratic until 800 BCE and demotic from 700 BCE) were developed from the hieroglyphic signs to provide increased speed in writing, particularly for business and literary texts.
3400 BCE: The symbol of Heru found on the Blaauboschkraal Stone Ruins, also known as Adam's Calendar, which is one of the oldest megalithic stone circles and menhir systems ever discovered. (> 75000 years old)
3400 BCE: The kingdom of Red Land (deshret) was established in the north, White Land (hedjet) in the south; they were ruled concurrently under two kings.
3300 BCE: Dated ritual knife made of copper handle and flint, elephant ivory blades discovered in an Abu Zaidan, Egypt excavation.
3275 BCE: The Scorpion King was a ruler of Upper Kemet, and he was one of the first rulers in Ancient Kemet, making preliminary attempts to conquer the northern kingdom.
3200 BCE: Dated Nubian Qustul Incense Burner incorporated images associated with Egyptian pharaohs: a procession of sacred boats, the White Crown of Upper Egypt, a falcon deity, and the palace facade called a serekh. It appeared to represent a ritual that involved a royal procession by boat to a palace.

The late 4000 BCE onward to the late 3000 BCE brought Kemet to the verge of unification. The warriors of Upper Kemet moved with their maces and standards, giving them the 'symbolic authority of the gods'. Ceremonial artifacts were present to do narrative work. The Narmer Palette, for instance, shows King Narmer wearing a combination of the White Crown of Upper Kemet and the Red Crown of Lower Kemet, which signifies oneness over the Two Lands. Kemet was united around 3100 BCE with a mix of conquest and diplomacy. Kemet was no longer a simple chiefdom but rather a kingdom. As religious acceptance increased, Narmer was seen not only as the pharaoh but also the living Horus, the protector of Ma'at, and the vessel of cosmological harmony. The unification of Kemet was not purely political, but spiritual somehow uniting Kemet with the gods. Kingship was stoned and was enshrined in the rituals. The early dynasties introduced law, order, and ethics to convert warring cultures into a nation that would become one of the greatest civilizations of all time.

THE EARLY DYNASTIC PERIOD

The Archaic Period (Dynasties 1-2) laid the roots of the Kemetic civilization. The Kings established the capital at Memphis, which was strategically located where the land of the Upper and Lower Kemet separated. Moreover, they pushed for the development of hieroglyphic writing not only as a practical means but also as a record of divine truth – mostly under the influence of priests and rising cults. The kingship was no longer distinct from politics, and the pharaoh was not merely a source of government but rather an entity that bridged divinity between the gods and the people. Abydos royal tombs had a mudbrick-stone construction that was considered entrances to other realms. Dazzled by nature, the Kemetic society had entwined politics, religion, and death burials into an uninterrupted frame. Nubia was both, a customer and a competitor, across the First Cataract. Nubians developed an independent, resilient culture to challenge Egyptian exploitation of local treasures in gold, ivory, and cattle by sending expeditions. The interaction, the competition, and the interdependence between Kemet and Nubia would prove bittersweet.

1st Dynasty (2920-2770 BCE)

- Papyrus was invented as paper, and writing was used.
- Wooden coffins were made, and corpses were wrapped in resin.
- Kush invaded the Kingdom of Elam in the Empire of Persia.
- The Grand Lodge of Luxor was built at Dendera by Khufu.
- The two ends of Egypt were merged at the capital of Memphis.
- Dated Sabu Disk artifact (2800 BCE)

2nd Dynasty (2770-2649 BCE)

- A rivalry for the throne occurs between King Hetepsekhemsy & King Khasekhemwy over which God, Horus or Seth, was in power, causing disorder and violence.
- King Djoser was the 1st Pharaoh to use stone to build pyramids.
- Menkaure built the 1st pyramid made of granite.
- The red pyramid was built using smooth outer sides.

3rd Dynasty (2649-2575 BCE)

- Imhotep was a real-life, highly influential Egyptian polymath, serving as vizier, high priest, and architect for Pharaoh Djoser.
- Imhotep built the first step pyramid and the Saqqara complex.
- Step Pyramid of Djoser at Saqqara & Djoser Netjerikhet (2650 BCE)
- Khnum Khufu Statuette (2590 BCE)

OLD KINGDOM ('AGE OF THE PYRAMIDS')

The Old Kingdom commences still under the reign of King Djoser (Netjerikhet) from the 3rd Dynasty. Djoser marked the beginning of the first actual golden age of centralized power in Ancient Kemet, which united the northern Delta and the southern Nile Valley under the sacrosanct position of pharaoh. Djoser was guided by his high priest and architect, Imhotep, whom transformed the royal burial of the mudbrick mastabas into the turning stone architecture. The Steel Pyramid of Saqqara, governing over six towering terraces of limestone, was 60 meters high, thus becoming the tallest architectural structure at that time. The pyramid was surrounded by a massive ceremonial complex with temples, courtyards, and shrines to replicate the royal palace. It was not only a tomb but also an eternal home where the king would still reign spiritually in the afterlife.

The royal ambition reached new levels with the Fourth Dynasty under the reign of Sneferu. Sneferu was a construction king who changed the techniques of pyramid construction. He unsuccessfully tried to build the Meidum pyramid despite successfully building the Bent Pyramid in Dahshur, which changed its angle halfway through construction. His last masterpiece was the Red Pyramid (2590 BCE), which became Kemet's first successful smooth-sided pyramid and which symbolized the perfected stairway to the sun. The slanting sides symbolized the rays of the god of the sun, Ra, who took the soul of the king to heaven, making him immortal. During the reign of Sneferu, Kemet undertook its first major trade excursions into Nubia, and fortresses were constructed to source gold, cattle, and incense. With his death, Sneferu secured the formula of kingship as a constructive warrior and intervener between the worlds, creating a kingdom ready for greatness.

The period of Khufu (c. 2589 -2566 BCE) was the zenith of pyramid building. It included the Great Pyramid of Giza, which stood 146 meters high and comprised more than 2.3 million limestone blocks. This massive project was accomplished around 2560 BCE and is perhaps the most remarkable of engineering works in human history. His successors continued his legacy: Khafre (c. 2558-2532 BCE) once built the second pyramid and presumably commissioned the Great Sphinx, a limestone creature with the body of a lion and the face of the king; Menkaure (c. 2532-2504 BCE) then built the third and most miniature pyramids with eloquent and fine granite casing. The Giza plateau was made a holy place of stone and an expression of wealth, religious piety, and the administrative powers of Kemet. Drawing on clues like the remains of food and fermented beverages found in the pyramids, there is significant evidence that the builders of pyramids were well-fed Kemetic agriculturalists, completing their mandatory labor duty during the season of floods. Slaves, mostly through chattel slavery, bonded labor, and forced labor, also participated in the construction process. Most slaves were foreign war captives, indebted locals, punished criminals, or rulers' body shields.

4th Dynasty (2575-2467 BCE)

- The reign of the great pyramid builders, such as Khufu and Khafre.
- The pyramids, sun temples, & mortuaries at Giza & Dahshur were completed.
- The art of embalming started.
- People prayed to the Sun God Ra.
- The first religious words and inscriptions were written on the walls of the royal tombs.
- King Userkaf built a sun temple for Ra at Abusir.
- Pyramids were built at Dahshur, including the Bent, Blunted + the Meidum pyramids.
- The Great Sphinx at Giza (2558 BCE)
- Great Pyramid of Giza (c. 2560 BCE)
- The mastaba tomb was revived with the building of the Mastabat Fara'un (2500 BCE)

By the Fifth Dynasty, pyramid building became less ambitious in size but more religiously profound. Other kings, such as Sahure and Neferirkare, placed more emphasis on solar worship, building magnificent sun temples as well as pyramids in honor of the deity Ra, whose cult was centered upon Heliopolis. Trade was very active during the reign of Sahure, whom sent expeditions to Punt along the Red Sea coast and to Nubia to obtain gold and incense. The era of Unas saw the addition of the earliest Pyramid Texts written on his tomb walls at Saqqara. These writings featured more than 700 spells, hymns, and prayers to support the pharaoh's journey to the afterlife, forming the stock of Kemetic funerary literature. Administrations were also becoming more sophisticated with scribes documenting tributes and governors running provinces.

The Sixth Dynasty, under the rule of Teti (2345 -2323 BCE) and Pepi I (2321 - 2287 BCE), marked a decline in centralized control as its authority was challenged by growing individualism at the local level. Foreign adventures against Nubia and Byblos proceeded; however, the crown's power was too diminished. The last eighty years of the reign of Pepi II (2278-2184 BCE) embodied the decay. At the time of his enthronement as a child, his long reign enabled nomarchs or provincial governors to build up power and wealth with their own monumental tombs comparable to those of kings. At the same time, the tribulations of low-running Nile floods brought on famine, undermining the faith that the pharaoh was 'pleasing the gods'. By 2181 BCE, Kemet was divided among conflicting dynasties centered at Hierakonpolis and Thebes.

5th & 6th Dynasty (2465-2181 BCE)

- The sun cult was promoted. Sun temple built at Abu Ghurob, and small pyramid at Saqqara.
- High officials came from outside the royal family.
- Record keeping of goods began.
- Pyramid Texts (2400 BCE) had been found in the tombs of kings and queens at Saqqara, the necropolis of the Old Kingdom capital, Memphis including: Unis (Dynasty V, 2353–2323 BCE); Teti (Dynasty VI, 2323–2291 BCE); Pepi I (Dynasty VI, 2289–2255 BCE); Ankhesenpepi II, wife of Pepi I; Merenre (Dynasty VI, 2255–2246 BCE); Pepi II (Dynasty VI, 2246–2152 BCE); Neith, wife of Pepi II; Iput II, wife of Pepi II; Wedjebetni, wife of Pepi II; Ibi (Dynasty VIII, 2109–2107 BCE); 6th Dynasty (2323-2152 BCE)
- First attestation of Pyramid Texts with Osiris descriptions (2350 BCE).
- First attestation of Coffin Texts (2170 BCE)
- Records of trading expeditions began.
- Egypt experienced cultural upheaval until 2043 BCE.
- The capital of Egypt moved to Hierakonpolis.
- King Patesi ruled Mesopotamia (Gudea).
- Pepi I Meryre's reign of over 40 years saw flourishing trade, conquests, particularly into Nubia, and the rise of powerful provincial governors. He was the son of the dynasty's founder, Teti, and was succeeded by his son Merenre Nemtyemsaf I.

7th & 8th Dynasties (2150-2130 BCE)

- The political structure of the old kingdom collapsed. Also, famine from long-term Nile River droughts, civil disorder, and a high death rate occurred.

THE FIRST INTERMEDIATE PERIOD

9th & 10th Dynasties (2134-1970 BCE)

- At Hierakonpolis, the local ruler Achthoes I seized power and ruled over parts of Egypt.
- Egypt is split into the north at Hierakonpolis and the south at Thebes.
- Prosperous period with much foreign trade.
- Jewelry making began, and large building projects started.

11th Dynasty (2074-1938 BCE)

- Egypt was unified under King Mentuhotep (2060 BCE).
- Egypt was reunited by King Mentuhotep II
- Trading with Asia and the Aegean began.
- The capital was moved to Thebes (Waset).
- The Kingdom of Kush began in the Sudan at Kerma.
- The Nubians were the first ethnic group to build castles and forts at Buhen.

Following the upheaval of the First Intermediate Period, Kemet was revived under the Eleventh Dynasty, ruled from Thebes. The key figure is Mentuhotep II (2055-2004 BCE), who, after several decades of wars, overthrew the Herakleopolitan kings who had rivaled him to reunify Kemet around 2055 BCE. This reunification was not just a triumphant military feat but rather a restoration to the 'divine order of Ma'at' that had been violated. Mentuhotep II commissioned a large funerary temple at Deir El-Bahri, blending pyramid and temple styles into something unique to Earth, sky, and the gods. His rule established stability, reopened trade, revived temple cults, and rebuilt irrigation canals. Thebes became the spiritual and the political heart of the land. To the Ancient Egyptians, the coming of a powerful king meant the 'traditional Kemetic gods' had blessed the Two Lands once again.

THE MIDDLE KINGDOM

The 12th Dynasty witnessed the transition to a stronger government under Amenemhat I, who succeeded the principles of the 11th Dynasty. In order to have better control of Upper and Lower Kemet, he established a new capital at Itjtawy, which was close to the Faiyum. This shift enabled him to extend his authority into the Delta while remaining connected to Thebes. His reign was centrally governed, and the viziers and scribes who served as his officials encouraged stability among the masses. Amenemhat I was not only a political reformer but also a cultural figure remembered in the work of literature. In the *Instructions of Amenemhat*, the author offers advice to his son on the inheritance of kingship.

Kemet flourished and prospered during the era of Senusret, the son of Amenemhat I. He fortified the southern border of Kemet, having led expeditions into Nubia to assert control of trading routes and access to gold deposits. Moreover, he built fortifications to prevent incursions. In Kemet, however, Senusret I embodied the greatest of religious believers, particularly in the rising Amun cult at Thebes. Around this time, Amun was merged with Ra, the sun god, to become Amun-Ra, the god of omnipotence. Among Senusret I's building activities are the obelisks at Heliopolis, huge temple additions, and administration centers. His reign illustrated the Middle Kingdom equilibrium of power, which consisted of military might, agricultural prosperity, and religious devoutness. The Kemetic economy was prosperous with trade extending to the Levant (cedar wood) and the Sinai (turquoises and copper).

Senusret III was one of the most celebrated kings of the Middle Kingdom, whose military expeditions transformed the Kemetic boundaries along the south. Designed to ensure that Kemet would get hold of all of its riches, he engaged in a series of expeditions in the lower region of Nubia, conquering the region and constructing bastions at Semna, Buhen, and Shalfak. These forts were occupied by armed men and outfitted with watchtowers and guaranteed Kemetic control over trade routes and access to Nubian supplies/commodities. Senusret III also amended the internal administration system to reduce local officials' authority, enhancing royal authority.

The Middle Kingdom peaked under the reign of Amenemhat III. He was a genius of irrigation who extended the Faiyum depression through enormous canal and dike projects to transform the desert into cultivated farmland. This provided food security to the increasing Kemet population. Monumental construction was characteristic of his reign, too, such as his pyramid at Hawara, near the Faiyum, and the so-called Labyrinth temple, which was considered more stupendous than the pyramids themselves, according to ancient Greek writers. As well as widening mining and quarrying ventures in Sinai and providing turquoise and copper in intensifying trade relations with Nubia and Byblos, Amenemhat III also enlarged exploration in the more southerly regions of the Eastern Desert in West Sinai, obtaining gold and further metal sources in the Sinai Peninsula. Despite the prosperity, Kemet was already showing signs of weakness with resources being pushed to the limit and power becoming more susceptible to external pressure.

The decline of the Middle Kingdom started with the growing instabilities of the Thirteenth Dynasty. The rulers did not have a long reign – sometimes, just a few years. By the middle of the 18th Century BCE, Kemet lost its military capability to extend its reach to Nubia, at Buhen, and at Semna. Garrisons were besieged by burgeoning Nubian politics and free-flowing African movements among other regions continued, paving the way for new Asiatic colonies to be admitted to the Delta. These immigrants introduced new technologies, namely the horse and war chariot, which later revolutionized military warfare in Kemet. These foreigners eventually became known as the Hyksos, and they came to power at the eastern Delta around 1650 BCE, while native Kemetic dynasties continued to rule in other parts. This disintegration concluded the Middle Kingdom and began the Second Intermediate Period, which saw foreign domination.

12th Dynasty (1938-1756 BCE)

- The Faiyum irrigation system was built.
- King Amenemhat I built the great Labyrinth and founded a new royal residence near Memphis.
- The Hyksos invaded Egypt.
- Senusret I conquered parts of Lower Nubia.
- Senusret II undertook a major land reclamation and built works in the Fayoum - an oasis area.
- During a successful reign, Senusret III completed the process of colonizing Nubia, where he built or extended a series of fortresses and abolished the powers and the privileges of nobles.
- Amenemhat III began the use of the Valley of the Kings.

THE SECOND INTERMEDIATE PERIOD

13th – 17th Dynasties (1756-1540 BCE)

- Kings were born as commoners, and the social structure broke down.
- The Hyksos seized power in the north.
- Diagnostic medicine began.
- The capital moved back to Thebes.
- The "Book of the Dead" appeared.
- War erupted between Thebes and the Asiatic kingdom.

- King Ahmose defeated the Hyksos and fully expelled them from Egypt up to 1530 BCE.
- Thutmose I conquered Persia and Iraq.
- The agricultural revolution began in the Sahara.
- First attestation of Book of the Dead spells on heart scarabs and coffins (1650 BCE)
- First attestation of Book of the Dead spells on linen shrouds (1600 BCE)

THE NEW KINGDOM (AGE OF EMPIRE)

The New Kingdom started in 1550 BCE with the success of Ahmose (1550-1525 BCE), who established the Eighteenth Dynasty. The Hyksos, who had ruled in the east Delta of Kemet for over one hundred years, were chariot- and bronze-armed kings who weakened and who were fully expelled around 1530 BCE. Ahmose, a prince of Thebes, instigated a liberation campaign, storming Avaris and subsequently driving the Hyksos out of Kemet and re-establishing Ma'at. Ahmose also advanced south into Nubia, regained forts, and re-established Egyptian rule to the Second Cataract. His reign provided the basis of Kemet's imperial dreams. No longer satisfied with defending their Nile Valley territory, the New Kingdom's pharaohs discovered that Kemet was a power that could dominate the Near East and Africa, resulting in a new era of conquest.

Kemet transitioned into an empire during the reign of Thutmose III (1479-1425 BCE). A co-regent initially with his stepmother Hatshepsut (14791-1458 BCE), Thutmose III only gained sole control following her death. Thutmose III made at least 17 military incursions into the Levant and Syria, extending Egyptian authority as far as the Euphrates River. His most important victory was at the Battle of Megiddo (1457 BCE), when he achieved a conclusive defeat of a coalition of Canaanite leaders, resulting in hundreds of cities becoming his tributaries. He likewise securely united Kemet with Nubia by forging his power to the Fourth Cataract. Prosperity flowed in Thebes through tributes, taxes, and foreign luxuries - Lebanese cedar, Syrian horses, and Nubian gold. During the reign of Thutmose III, the temple of Karnak was magnificently decorated with halls and pylons on which the king wrote his conquests. By the middle of the 15th Century BCE, Kemet was the most powerful nation in the Near East.

Prior to the military conquests of Thutmose III, there was an unusual period of rule by the lady pharaoh, Hatshepsut. At first, she served as regent of the young Thutmose III, but later proclaimed herself 'king', sporting the false beard of officialdom and assuming the full royal titulary. The reign of Hatshepsut was more about prosperity and diplomacy than war. She sponsored the well-known mission to Punt, which returned incense, myrrh trees, ivory, and exotic animals. Also, relief scenes can be seen at her magnificent mortuary temple at Deir el-Bahri. She was engaged in great construction works, the extension of Karnak Temple, and the erection of obelisks of incredible height. Later kings, such as Thutmose III, tried to obliterate her contributions from history as she had no right to power.

In the middle of the 14th Century BCE, one of the most radical experiments in Kemet – quite possibly the entire time period – took place under Akhenaten (originally Amenhotep IV, 1353-1336 BCE). Akhenaten believed that the Aten (the sun disk) was the only authority and that the Amun priesthood needed to be rejected. He established a new city at Akhenaten (modern-day Amarna) in 1348 BCE, where art and theology assumed his ideas of a universal, abstract deity. This was manifested by building the temples open to the sun, inscriptions illustrating the worship of the sun's rays, and a royal art depiction of a closed, intimate scene of Akhenaten, Queen Nefertiti, and their daughters in the sun's rays. This religious revolution undermined thousands of years of tradition as Amun and Thebes were relegated. However, this effort was brief. Upon the death of Akhenaten, Kemet soon forgot him, and his successors did everything in their power to eliminate his name. However, the Amarna era highlighted how fickle the divine kingship could be and how precarious the order founded on religion in Kemet was.

Akhenaten was succeeded by his young son, Tutankhamun (1332-1323 BCE), who was installed as pharaoh as a child by the guardians of the royal palace, who reversed his father's reforms and returned the capital to Thebes. Although his reign did not last long, Tutankhamun's reign was crucial in restoring the former religious order. The temples of Amun were opened, and the influence of the priesthood reasserted. Tutankhamun might not have been a great king; however, his tomb made a titanic impact. His tomb, found in 1922 CE in the Valley of the Kings, included more than 5,000 treasures, such as the golden mask. These items gave an unprecedented look into the New Kingdom's wealth, art, and funerary beliefs. The reign of Tutankhamun heralded restoration following Amarna interference. Ma'at was reinforced by reuniting the land, and the re-establishment of Ma'at ushered Kemet toward healing, even though the real leaders were hidden advisors, Ay and Horemheb, who would succeed him.

The Nineteenth Dynasty saw its Golden Age during the reign of Ramses II (1279-1213 BCE), known as Ramses the Great. His 66-year reign can be remembered as monumental buildings, military conquests, and imperial family power. In the early days of his rule, he engaged in the battle of Kadesh (1274 BCE) against the Hittites, which was one of the biggest battles involving chariots in the ancient world. Even with mixed results, Ramses declared it a triumph and, subsequently, had one of the first documented peace treaties ever made around 1259 BCE. Ramses created monuments on a vast scale: the Ramesseum at Thebes, temples of Abu Simbel carved into Nubian rocks, and extensions of Karnak and Luxor. He had more than 100 children, ensuring dynastic succession.

The Twentieth Dynasty marked the decline of the imperial power of Kemet. Kemet was attacked by the Sea Peoples, an unknown group of people, whom dominated the eastern Mediterranean during the reign of Ramses III. Ramses III held off their attack at the Battle of the Delta (c.1175 BCE); however, his rule exposed weaknesses within the ranks, including corruption, economic stress, and the first known labor strike in history at Deir El-Medina. Weaker kings failed to preserve this level of control after Ramses III, and Kemet eventually lost territories in Canaan and Syria. In 1070 BCE, central authority failed, the priests of Amun in Thebes took control, and Kemet fell into the Third Intermediate Period of fragmentation and foreign occupation.

18th Dynasty (1539-1295 BCE)

- First attestation of Book of the Dead spells on papyri (1530 BCE)
- King Thutmose I & Queen Hatshepsut made Egypt a superpower.
- King Amenhotep II began the artistic revolution.
- King Akhenaten & Queen Nefertiti pushed a one-god religion.
- King Tutankhamen ruled Egypt from the age of 10 to the age of 18.
- King Thutmose I conducted military campaigns into Persia and Iraq.
- King Amenhotep III built the Temple of Luxor.
- Society changed from polytheism to a monotheistic system. Horemheb, of obscure, nonroyal parentage, was previously the army commander under Akhenaten. In his Edict, Horemheb took firm measures to restore the traditional religion as well as law and order. He obliterated traces of Atenism, and Akhenaten was finally deserted.
- Queen Hatshepsut became the first female pharaoh.
- Egypt was at the height of its military power.
- Seti I built the great tombs in the Valley of the Kings.
- Egypt destroyed the Kushite Kingdom and occupied Nubia.
- The Sankore University was formed in the city of Timbuktu.
- King Thutmose III strengthened the sovereignty of Kemet by waging the last military campaign against Nubia, penetrating as far as the 4th cataract of the Nile.
- Queen Tiye became one of the most influential queens to rule Egypt through trade and the protection of her borders.

- The Valley of the Queens was formed.

19th Dynasty (1295-1186 BCE)

- King Seti I ruled as a warrior king. He re-established the empire in Syria/Palestine, which had been allowed to slip away during Akhenaten's reign. Along with Ramesses II, he undertook major building programs, including temples at Thebes and Abydos. His tomb was the largest in the Valley of the Kings.
- Ramses II built a city and a mortuary temple on the west bank near Luxor, and ruled for 66 years. Wages many battles and treaties between Egypt and the Asiatic powers.
- Queen Nefertiti helped to unify Upper and Lower Kemet.

20th Dynasty (1186-1069 BCE)

- King Setnakht restored order to the country.
- Ramses III became the last great warrior king after defeating the Libyans (years 5 and 11) and Sea Peoples (year 8). He built a magnificent temple at Medinet Habu, Thebes, and his tomb in the Valley of the Kings. The royal necropolis workforce conducted labor strikes. The so-called Harem Conspiracy fails to assassinate the king.
- The Royal Tombs in the Valley of the Kings were plundered.
- Period of great social, political & religious decline occurred. Egypt no longer a world power.
- The Turin Papyrus and the Wilbur Papyrus were written (1160 BCE).

Following the end of the New Kingdom, Kemet spent the Third Intermediate Period in ruin and with reduced royal authority. The Twenty-First Dynasty was based in Tanis in the Delta, while, in Thebes, the High Priests of Amun effectively controlled Upper Kemet. The authority of Psusennes I (1047-1001 BCE) was no more than a shadow with their tombs betraying a level of wealth eclipsed by decay. The priesthood of Amun became immensely wealthy in Thebes with sizable estates, land, and labor. Kemet was still divided; however, there was an indication of change with the consequential construction of temples and gold masks with jeweled ornaments in Tanis burials. Nevertheless, the Two Lands were separated. Kemet was not the same empire during the New Kingdom anymore, and its ruler was no longer the dominant government; instead, regional strength was the guiding light.

In the mid-10th Century BCE, power was usurped by rulers of Libyan descent, leading to the establishment of the Twenty-Second Dynasty. The best-known leader was Sheshonq I (945-924 BCE), who established control in Bubastis in the Delta. Sheshonq is primarily remembered not only due to his military expeditions to Palestine (925 BCE) but also because he reinforced the system of internal administration, which was mostly fragmented. Various dynasties existed simultaneously - the Twenty-Third in Hierakonpolis and Thebes, and the Twenty-Fourth in Sais, giving rise to a patchwork of regional states. From this period on, Nubia re-emerged as a separate power to the south. Although the insignia of pharaonic tradition remained with the kings in Kemet, Kemet was divided politically into local mini-monarchies, and foreign powers were put in force to guide the fate of the Nile valley.

While Kemet remained fractured, Nubia was revived to the south. Based at Napata, the rulers of Kush established a powerful state solely concentrated on Nubian culture. Around 747 BCE, King Piye (Piankhi) led a military expedition north to the capital of Musawwarat Es-Sufra, and his conquest was commemorated in the Victory Stela. These conquests unified the upper and the lower parts of Kemet because the Nubians ruled it, culminating in the Twenty-Fifth Dynasty. They went back to constructing temples and pyramids in Nubia, presenting themselves as the true successors of the pharaonic tradition. Piye stressed pity to Amun, and he declared himself not a conqueror but a restorer of Ma'at. Kemet reunited; however, for the first time in centuries, under the rule of Kush's kings, Nubian sovereignty transformed Kemet and Nubia into a single cultural domain.

The Nubian Dynasty was prosperous under kings like Shabaka (716-702 BCE), whom strengthened the Nubian control over Kemet, and Taharqa (690-664 BCE), whom was remembered as both a warrior king and a builder. Taharqa built on the temples of Kemet and invested in colonnades at Karnak and massive projects elsewhere in the Nile Valley. Unfortunately, his reign was concomitant with the Assyrian Empire's expansion, which led to conquests throughout the Near East. Northern campaigns were undertaken against Kush, while Kemet soon had to deal with Assyrian attacks. At some point, the Assyrians drove the Kushite rulers into Nubia. By 664 BCE, the Sais Delta was ruled by native leaders known as the Saite Dynasty, ending the Nubian era.

THE THIRD INTERMEDIATE PERIOD

21st Dynasty (1070-945 BCE)

- First attestation of Amduat papyri (1060 BCE).
- Civil war and foreign invaders tore Egypt apart.
- The capital was moved between several cities.
- The Kingdom of Kush formed an independent kingdom at Napata.
- Mummification techniques improved.
- King Osorkon became the first Libyan Pharaoh.
- The Nok culture formed in Nigeria.
- Queen Makeda of Sheba ruled as the symbol of remarkable beauty.
- Disunity and Libyan settlement occurred.
- The Nubians conquered Egypt.

22nd – 25th Dynasties (945-653 BCE)

- Nubian Kings Kashta & Piankhy removed all foreigners from Egypt.
- The Nubians were conquered by an Assyrian invasion.
- The Greeks helped to re-establish order.
- King Taharqa of Nubia invaded and conquered Spain and Palestine. He also interfered in the politics of Judah, which led to conflict with the Assyrians, who invaded Egypt in 671 BCE and again in 667 until 666 BCE. He fled to Napata and was buried in a pyramid at Nuri (Kush).
- The last Kushite ruler, Tantamani, was defeated by the Assyrians. (664 BCE). The Assyrians installed the princes of Sais as the native rulers of Egypt. Necho I (672–664 BCE), prince of Sais and vassal of Assyria, was killed by Kushite ruler Tantamani, who was attempting to regain power. However, Necho's son, Psammetichus I, became king and founded the dynasty.
- Kings from Sais began a revival in the arts, returning to the Old Kingdom style.
- The kingdom was in a constant state of chaos or war.
- Persia conquered Egypt.
- The 25th Dynasty - Kushite/Napatan Empire in Napata, with notable pharaohs of Shabaka, Taharqa, Shebitku, and Tantamani

The Assyrian evacuation of the Nubians left a vacuum in Kemet, which was filled by the Saite Dynasty, named after its capital at Sais in the western parts of the Delta. Its founder, Psamtik I (664-610 BCE), re-established the independence of Kemet by playing Assyrians and local powers collectively against one another. With this union, once again, he brought the Two Lands together. He employed large numbers of Greek mercenaries, which was the first time foreign troops had been employed in Kemet. Subsequent rulers such as Necho II (610-595 BCE) and Psamtik II (595-589 BCE) encouraged grandiose development, such as constructing the canals to the Red Sea. Echo II also started naval adventures. It was during a cultural revival that there was more focus on making temples again, the restoration of hieroglyphic art, and the worship of old gods. The Saite Egyptians also admired the work of the Old Kingdom, attempting to emulate it and to revive the splendor of previous dynasties.

The recovery of Kemet did not last long. In 525 BCE, the Persian king Cambyses II, son of Cyrus the Great, invaded and defeated Psamtik III at the Battle of Pelusium. Kemet was then conquered by the Persian Achaemenid Empire, which established the Twenty-Seventh Dynasty. The Persians retained the Egyptian management; however, they brought foreign governors and excessive taxes. Temples were forfeited, brewing anger and bitterness. Occasionally, rebellions would break out, yet the empire's power prevented Kemet from gaining independence. Leaders like Darius I (522-486 BCE) tried to make accommodations, ordering temple inscriptions and tolerating local cults, but Kemet was not quiescent. The belief that Kemet had been subjugated to a foreign power left a lasting impression and aroused the nationalist energies of subsequent kingly entities to gain independence. The diminishing Persian power in the 5th Century BCE afforded Kemet temporary freedom. The Twenty-Eighth Dynasty was brief, signaling the reinstatement of native rule. More importantly, the Twenty-Ninth Dynasty and especially the Thirtieth Dynasty produced the last native kings. Nectanebo I (380-362 BCE) and his son Teos (362-360 BCE) came to the throne and performed major construction works, restoring temples and strengthening Kemetic defenses. The last native pharaoh was Nectanebo II (360-343 BCE), who was also remembered as a patron of religion and the arts, building temples throughout the Nile Valley, including at Philae. However, there was also continuing internal and external conflict as Kemet became increasingly caught between the goals of Persia and the emerging power of Macedonia under Philip II. Kemet stood fatally at the brink of external power.

In 343 BCE, the Persians invaded again under Artaxerxes III, overthrowing Nectanebo II and securing their own rule to what is known as the Thirty-First Dynasty (343-332 BCE). This second Persian rule was worse than the first, as taxes were higher and temples were more rigorously controlled. Egyptian resentment festered, and there was nothing that could depose Persian control, even though Persia was not the only country that controlled Egypt's fate. Alexander the Great entered Kemet in 332 BCE as a welcomed liberator instead of a conqueror. A double proclamation of victory crowned him pharaoh at Memphis and son of Amun at the oracle of Siwa Oasis. This brought the millennia of independent Egyptian dynasties to an end, as Kemet became a part of the Hellenistic world.

THE LATE PERIOD

26th Dynasty (664-552 BCE)

- King Psamtek I defeated the Assyrians and the Kushite kings.
- Pharaoh Necho became involved in the politics of Judah and was defeated by the Babylonians at the Battle of Carchemish (605 BCE). He also initiated construction of the canal between the Nile and the Red Sea.
- Babylon fell to the Persian armies.
- The decline of the kingdoms continued.

27th Dynasty (552-404 BCE)

- The Temple of Apollo at Delphi was destroyed by fire in 548 BCE
- The Persians invaded and ruled Egypt, forming a Persian dynasty.
- Cambyses defeated the Egyptians at the Battle of Pelosium.
- King Dauius completed the canal started by Nekau I.

28th Dynasty (404-400 BC)

- Amytravios retook Egypt from Persia.
- Egypt's independence began again.
- The decline and fall of Egypt were all but complete.

29th and 30th Dynasties (400-332 BCE) *Last Native Kemet Dynasty*

- First attestation of the Books of Breathing (400 BCE)
- Artaxerxes I retook Egypt.
- Persians formed a second dynasty in Egypt.
- Alexander defeated the Persian army and conquered Egypt.
- The last period of rulership by native-born Egyptian Kings.
- Alexandria was founded in Egypt.

THE PTOLEMAIC PERIOD (332-30 BCE)

Upon his entry in 332 BCE, Alexander the Great was not received as an invading force but welcomed by the Egyptians as a liberator against the oppressive rule of the Persians. In Memphis, he was enthroned as pharaoh, taking on the role of God-king of Kemet. Traveling to the oasis of Siwa, Alexander consulted a prophetess, the oracle of Amun, whom legitimized his rule, declaring that he was indeed the son of a god. His purpose, though minimal, manifested into destiny. He directed the building of a new city, Alexandria, on the coast of the Mediterranean. The city would grow as a place of Greek and Egyptian learning and commerce. When Alexander died in 323 BCE, the empire was divided among his generals. Kemet was conquered by Ptolemy I Soter (305-282 BCE), one of his close servicemen, who proclaimed himself king and established the Ptolemaic Dynasty, which took both the military strengths of the Macedonians and the pharaonic traditions.

The early Ptolemies wanted to make their rule acceptable by observing Kemetic ways, yet maintained Greek tradition. Ptolemy I Soter reunified Kemet, stood up against invaders, and made Alexandria the new capital of Kemet. Ptolemy II Philadelphus (282-246 BCE) followed as leader, funding the Library of Alexandra – a vast collection of works that strived to catalog all knowledge in the world. One of the Ancient Wonders of the World, the Lighthouse of Alexandria, was built on the island of Pharos and guided the vessels into the booming harbors of Kemet. Greek was the language used by the administration, and the Kemetic religion survived with pharaohs occasionally offering to the gods. The kingdom had become a Mediterranean superpower due to the trade expansion by Ptolemy II to the Red Sea and the Indian Ocean. This assimilation alongside Greek rationalism and the traditional Kemetic religion gave the Ptolemaic state a dualistic nature.

Ptolemy III Euergetes (246-222 BCE) expanded Egyptian influence into the far Near East, gaining control briefly as far as Babylon. He recovered Kemetic statues of gods stolen centuries ago, which earned him the gratitude of priests and worshippers. However, as the Dynasty progressed, there were weaknesses. The successors, such as Ptolemy IV Philopator (221-204 BCE), lived in abandonment and overindulgence, undermining the State. Although he scored a dramatic military success in the defeat of the Seleucids at Raphia (217 BCE), his use of Egyptian soldiers instead of Ptolemaic troops inevitably led to unrest when Egyptians expressed unequal treatment. Over time, Ptolemy V Epiphanes (204-180 BCE) gained power with these lingering issues, and Kemet began wavering due to internal uprisings and external meddling. On the good side, the legendary Rosetta Stone (196 BCE) was designed during his reign, representing the integration of Greek and Egyptian cultures, as the inscriptions were in demotic, hieroglyphics, and Greek scripts.

Ptolemy VI Philometor (180-145 BCE) and his heirs were plagued by the ever-present interference of Rome, which started to meddle in Egyptian affairs. There were internal rivalries and conflicts among the siblings and the co-rulers of the Ptolemaic Dynasty, which even destabilized the kingdom. Economic complications surfaced within the country. Alexandria maintained its prestige as the center of intellectual and scholarly life, delivering discoveries in mathematics, astronomy, and medicine; however, in terms of political power, Kemet became more and more reliant on the goodwill of Rome. Civil wars and savage purges further weakened this dynasty by the time of Ptolemy VIII Physcon (145-116 BCE), causing Rome to take action to convert Kemet from an independent kingdom to a protectorate.

Cleopatra VII (51-30 BCE), perhaps the most well-known queen, attempted to liberate Kemet by allying with the most influential men in Rome. She had a son, Caesarion, with Julius Caesar (48-44 BCE), consolidating her throne. Her later alliance with Mark Antony (41-30 BCE) saw Kemet at the center of civil wars in Rome. Cleopatra was Alexandria's pharaoh and Hellenistic queen, restoring the cults' traditions while adopting Greek culture. However, her hostility toward Rome proved suicidal. In the Battle of Actium (31 BCE), Antony moved to face off against Octavian (later Augustus), whom triumphed over Antony and Cleopatra. Thereafter, in 30 BCE, Cleopatra committed suicide, and Kemet turned into a Roman province. Upon her death, the Ptolemaic Dynasty was no more, laying 3000 years of pharaonic rule to rest.

- Last attestation of the "classical" Book of the Dead papyri (50 BCE)
- Alexandria became the new capital of Egypt and was the home to the greatest library of the ancient world under Greek/Roman rule.
- General Ptolemy of Rome took over Egypt and became king.
- Queen Cleopatra VII was instrumental in making Kemet a world superpower at the time and helped Julius Caesar to overthrow Ptolemy.
- The Temple of Isis was built on the island of Philae on the Nile River.
- Africans in Kenya developed a complex calendar system based on astronomical reckoning.
- The Rosetta Stone was carved.
- Queen Cleopatra VII and Mark Anthony, Caesar's successor, were defeated by Octavius. They both committed suicide rather than face capture. She was one of the greatest Queens to rule Egypt.
- Egypt became a province of Rome. Egypt did not have another ruler for 2000 years.

GRECO-ROMAN PERIOD (30 BCE – 395 CE)

After Cleopatra VII committed suicide in 30 BCE, Kemet was subdued by one of the triumvirate, Augustus. Kemet was unlike other provinces in that it was supposed to be the personal possession of the emperor, being headed not by a senator but by a prefect of equestrian rank. This also guaranteed direct imperial access to the wealth of the Nile, especially in its grain, which sustained an increasingly crowded Rome. Alexandria subsequently developed to even serve as the second city of the empire due to its harbor, commerce, and scholarly institutions. The library and museum remained scholarship centers but were frequently interrupted by disturbances. The temples of Kemet did not stop their activity. Tiberius (14-37 CE) and Hadrian (117-138 CE) were just some emperors who financed constructions in conventional form. However, Roman rule was harsh: taxes were hefty, uprisings and the right to assemble were crushed. Instead of being in opposition to Roman rule, the Kemetic identity was progressively merged with Roman citizenry.

Religion at this time was a mosaic. Traditional cults like Isis, Osiris, and Amun continued to exist, often assuming Romanized forms. The cult of Serapis, a syncretic deity with Greek and Egyptian elements, was popular in Alexandria. Meanwhile, the Christian faith came in the middle of the 1st Century CE, attributing the establishment of the Church of Alexandria to St. Mark the Evangelist (c. 42 CE). Early on, Christians were victimized under emperors like Diocletian (284-285 CE), whose reign would come to mark the initiation of the Coptic calendar (284 CE). Cultural syncretism characterized this era with multicultural influence from Greek, Egyptian, Roman, and Jewish populations.

Under Diocletian (284-305 CE), Kemet was reorganized into smaller administrative units. His efforts against Christians (known as the Era of the Martyrs) were particularly harsh in Kemet, and led to a saintly and martyr cult by Coptic sources. Such efforts would shift when Constantine the Great (306-337 CE) legalized Christianity in 313 CE and later established the imperial capital in Constantinople (330 CE). Kemet assumed great importance as a province of the eastern empire, supplying grain and troops. Alexandria would form the center of Christian theology, especially after the debates at the Council of Nicaea (325 CE), where Bishop Athanasius opposed the teaching of Arianism on the divinity of Christ. As Christianity became the dominant religion, all the pagan temples were sealed, hieroglyphs became extinct, and all Kemetic spiritual/cultural life – religious and non-religious – died out.

In 395 CE, the Roman Empire was officially divided permanently with Kemet becoming a part of the Eastern Roman (Byzantine) Empire. High taxation and religious clashes characterized the Byzantine reign. Even, the Christian Church of Kemet became divided between the Chalcedonian (imperial) Church and the Monophysite (Coptic) Church because the Coptic Church did not accept the resolutions of the Council of Chalcedon in 451 CE, degenerating into violence. Egyptian monasteries flourished amid upheavals, and the Kemetic models of St. Anthony (251-356 CE) and St. Pachomius (292-348 CE) became seminal in monasticism worldwide. Economically, Kemet was essential as it exported grain, papyrus, and textiles. Byzantine efforts to impose orthodoxy turned off many citizens. A few years later, many Egyptians wrongly believed that Arab Muslim armies were their liberators after the Byzantines. By 642 CE, Alexandria fell under Islam, and Kemet became part of the Islamic world.

- Last attestation of indigenous Egyptian funerary texts (200-300 CE).
- Africans in Tanzania produced carbon steel in blast furnaces.
- Egyptians were given Roman citizenship.
- Roman and Egyptian culture existed peacefully and prospered together as religion and institutions were refurbished until the Byzantine Roman Emperor Theodosius became ruler. Emperor Theodosius destroyed all Egyptian temples and non-Christian books at the library in Alexandria and wiped out the last remnants of the once great Egyptian culture. 40,000 of its 70,000 books and manuscripts were destroyed. Christianity appeared in Alexandria along with the rise of Aksum (Ancient Ethiopia).
- The rise of Christianity began in Egypt. At the Council of Nicaea (325 CE), Emperor Constantine declared Christianity as the official state religion, and the doctrine of the Trinity was declared to be the Orthodox Christian belief.
- Mauritius of Thebes, the legendary commander of the Roman Theban Legion, was executed for defying Emperor Maximian Herculis, refusing to put down a Christian revolt.

LATE ANTIQUE PERIOD & BEYOND (395 CE+)

610 CE: The advent of Islam occurred.
641 CE: Egyptian hieroglyphic writing was no longer used. Muslim Arabs conquered Egypt and Sudan and introduced Islam after 300 years of Christianity.

In 642 CE, the fall of Alexandria led to the incorporation of Kemet into the thriving Arab-Islamic Caliphate. The new administrative capital was moved to Fustat on the Nile, founded by Amr ibn Al-As – the general who had led the conquest. Kemet entered a new phase of grain provision under the Umayyad Caliphate (661-750 CE), during which shipments fled to Medina and later Damascus, replacing Rome and Constantinople. The ancient Byzantine form of taxation continued and was channeled into the caliph's treasury. Greek and Coptic continued to be used in administration; however, they were gradually replaced with Arabic following the reforms of Abd al-Malik in the late 7th century CE. The spread of Islam was a slow process because the majority of Egyptians continued to be Coptic Christians, paying Islamic penalty taxes (jizya) yet keeping their churches and monasteries open.

The Abbasid Caliphate emerged in 750 CE with its capital at Baghdad, shifting the political center eastward. Kemet remained a desirable province, but it was no longer the only source of provincial contribution to a great empire. The governors of Baghdad sent to Kemet tended to be unpopular because of over-taxation, as the peasantry of Kemet contributed towards the upkeep of the empire. In the meantime, Fustat was growing into a thriving city with Arabs, Copts, Jews, and traders across the Mediterranean. Coptic Christianity continued to strengthen even amid the diversion of the Christian population to revolt against the British. The Abbasids also stressed intellectual interaction, forcing the older Greek texts preserved in libraries in Alexandria and Coptic monasteries to be translated into Arabic to pass ancient knowledge to the Muslim world or to brand pre-existing knowledge as their own via cultural appropriation.

By the late 9th century, Kemet started to exercise independence through local dynasties, beginning with the Tulunids (868-905 CE), born of a Turkish general named Ahmad ibn Tulun. He established a great army, made Kemet semi-independent, and used its wealth to construct grandiose projects such as the Mosque of Ibn Tulun in Fustat, which remains intact as one of the oldest mosques in Africa. The Tulunids were then followed by the Ikhshidid dynasty (935-969 CE), which also ruled Kemet as a semi-autonomous state that remained nominally loyal to the Abbasids. These rulers accessed the farming wealth of Kemet and made the Nile Valley the financial hub of their kingdoms.

In 969 CE, Kemet took a new turn under the conquest of the Fatimids, a Shi'a dynasty in North Africa with a newly established capital in Cairo. With its mosques, palaces, and markets, this Muslim city soon became more important than Fustat. Cairo formed the center of this empire and extended through North Africa and the Levant. Kemet's strategic location in the Mediterranean, Red Sea, and the Nile made it an international center.

642-1307 CE

- Arab rule and expansion. Moorish Dynasties flourished across Egypt, Sudan, Libya, Algeria, and Morocco for the next 648 years.
- The Arab slave trade (trans-Saharan) flourished as approximately 14 million African slaves were sold and exported to North Africa.
- Moors (Islamized Africans) invaded Spain, developing Spain into the center of culture and learning in Europe for almost 800 years. Moreover, they inadvertently assisted Arabs in forcing non-Muslim Africans in the upper regions of Africa into Islam under the penalty of death.
- Zimbabwe formed a great trading empire, which lasted 400 years.
- Sundiata formed the Sudanese Empire in Mali.
- Queen Dahia-Al Kahina fiercely fought Arab intrusion and the spread of Islam into North Africa and Western Sudan. Her rule was filled with violence and conflict with Arabs, even though she chose not to support Christians or Muslims. After her death, some of her people chose suicide rather than fall under Arab rule and Islam.
- The slave trade **expanded** to northwest Africa as Muslims used Africans as slaves to carry their goods and gold across the desert.
- King Mansa Mussa took the throne of Mali and built the Great Mosque at Timbuktu. He was best known for his pilgrimage to Mecca with 72,000 people and the conquest of the Songhai Kingdom.

1418-1911 CE: The Black Holocaust – The Sankofa Project. Almost 20 million Africans were forced into slavery, while an estimated 280 million newborns were eliminated because of slavery.

OTHER KEMETIC RESOURCES

- **Aegyptiaca by Manetho**: An Egyptian priest at the temple of Sebennytos in the Delta who lived during the reigns of Ptolemy I and II (305–246 BCE). Many scholars struggle to separate the historical and the mythological aspects of this work.
- **The King Lists**: Inscribed on temple walls and were key features in the Ritual of the Royal Ancestors, performed daily in the royal mortuary temples to honor previous rulers and to gain their acceptance of the kings.
- **The Turin Canon**: Written in hieratic on papyrus, it dates to the reign of Ramses II (1304–1237 BCE) and survives only in fragments, preserving only between eighty and ninety royal names.
- **The Palermo Stone**: When complete, this was perhaps an upright, freestanding oblong stone (stela), inscribed on both sides with horizontal registers and was set up in a temple. Each register, divided vertically into compartments, contained hieroglyphic texts that would have supplied a continuous, year-by-year record of each reign. Not all the fragments are present, but even when complete, the stone recorded events in the reigns of the first five dynasties only.
- **The Table of Abydos**: Inscribed on a wall in the Gallery of Lists, Temple of King Sethos I (1318–1304 BCE), this table includes seventy-six kings (starting with Menes) who preceded Sethos I. The accompanying wall scene shows Sethos I and his son, Ramses II, offering food to the king's names.
- **The Table of Karnak**: Inscribed on a wall in the Temple of Amun at Karnak, Thebes, this table dates to the reign of Thutmose III (1504–1450 BCE). The list originally included sixty-one royal names, but only forty-eight were still visible when it was discovered in 1825 CE. The sequence of names is incorrect, though some kings are mentioned who are not present in the other lists.
- **The Table of Saqqara**: Inscribed on the wall of the tomb of Tjuneroy, overseer of works at Saqqara, this table originally displayed fifty-seven names selected for inclusion by Ramses II. Because of damage to the wall, only fifty are now visible.

- **The Elephantine Papyri and Syene (Aswan) Ostraca**
- **Metu Neter Hieroglyphics and Ancient Kemetic Papyri** – Cataloged in the thousands.

At this stage, the reader is challenged to reassess the Kemetic chronology to understand the role that religion played in the downfall of Ancient Kemet from observing nature without religion, to the invention of religions in the ignorance of nature's wonders to disputes among leaders on religious doctrine advised by cult priests to multi-cultural syncretism to the remission of Kemetic traditionalism under foreign cultural influence (e.g. forceful conversion) to the persecution of beliefs to the violent rise of Christianity outlawing 'pagan' practices to Islamic supremacy with cultural appropriation. Religion might not have been the sole problem of Kemet; however, it was by far the largest common denominator of all Ancient Egyptian problems.

Em Hotep!

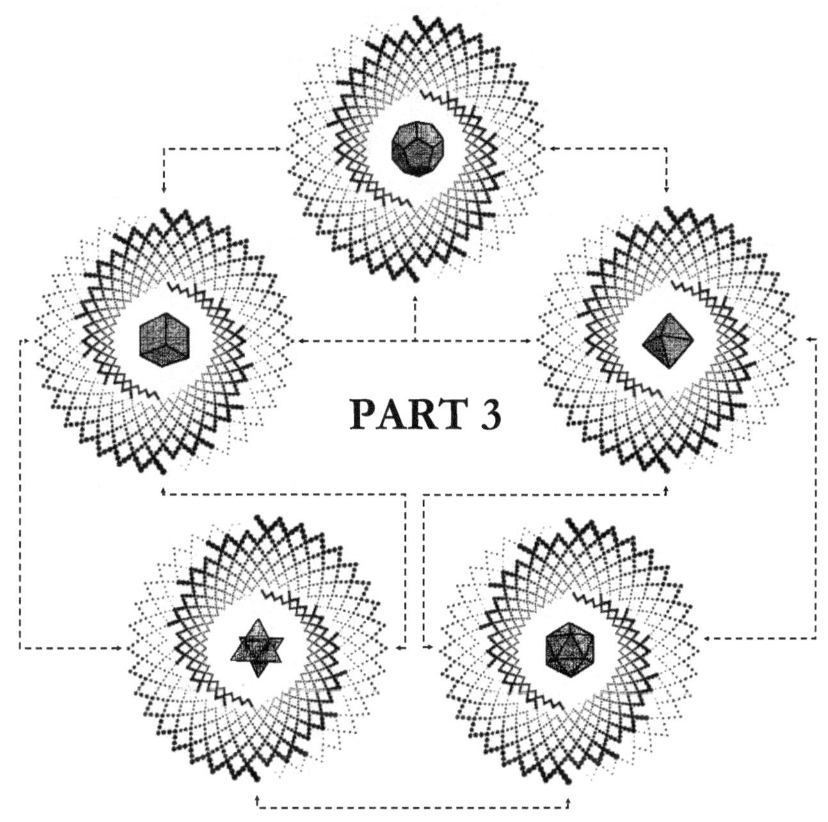

PART 3: BREAKING SOCIETAL CONTROLS

VULNERABILITIES OF BELIEF

ANKH WADJA SENEB | ARTICLE NO: 001

Function: The Awareness of Control Mechanisms
Subject(s): Religious Doctrine, Cults, Willful Ignorance, Belief, Faith
Position: Part 3 – Breaking Societal Controls
Theme: Dealing with Religions, Cults, & Atheism | Scene 1

Peace to the High Power! Peace to the Living Universe! Peace to all Finite Living Beings! Peace to All Things – seen and unseen! For my spirit is with me, my image is with me, and my purpose is with me. For those with knowledge understand that the mechanisms behind societal controls can only flourish when consciousness, awareness, vibration, and rationality are minimized and when willful ignorance, fear, indoctrination, and subjugating forces are maximized.

For clarification, willful ignorance is the conscious and the intentional act of avoiding or disregarding information, facts, or knowledge that challenges one's own beliefs or worldview, even when that information is readily available. It is a deliberate choice either to suppress one's rationality or to remain uninformed, often to protect one's ego (emotional shield), to avoid confronting uncomfortable truths, to submit passively to a higher authority, to hold onto a comfortable lie rather than face a painful truth (self-deception), to demonstrate fervent loyalty to a desired belief system.

Before opening the dialogue on the falsehoods, the contradictions, the delusions, and the misconceptions of religious practices, it is incumbent for all to know what a religion actually is, what the origins behind a religion are, and what causes a person to subscribe to a religion.

Religion, in its raw context, is a unified system or a consolidated set of intersecting systems of attitudes, sentiments, beliefs, meanings, values, symbols (e.g., creed, code, cultus, etc.), traditions, rituals, and practices associated with supernatural forces (e.g. gods, spirits, ghosts, demons, etc.), the orientation toward sacred and forbidden things/places, centralized morality, the roles of divine entities and/or authoritative figures/idols, the order, the innerworkings, and the conduct of existence, the transformation of experiences, and the factual explanations of nature as well as its origins. Consequently, there follows that a given religion must require (1) a belief in a deity or an authority figure/idol (single, multiple, or integrated), (2) a belief in the deity's or the figure's relationship with the world, (3) ways to worship the deity/figure, (4) a listing of all holy/sacred places or people, and (5) all divine-sent rules/commands.

For clarification, a <u>belief</u> is a statement, an opinion, or a position interpreted as or deemed to be true or false despite the lack of evidence necessary to prove it as true or false.

For clarification, a <u>fact</u> is a statement or a position that can be objectively verified as true or false based on direct experiences, evidence, observations, measurements, primary accounts, or reliable sources with sufficient corroboration.

Since religion is grounded on beliefs rather than facts, it can be established on dogmas – orally or written – that are not completely free of error/harm – historically, scientifically, and morally. Dogmas, which are considered authoritative and indisputable, are core tenets at the foundation of a religion or a religious ideology. They are presented as divinely-revealed revelations, divinely-inspired revelations, or inherently true without justification; and, the followers of a religion are not allowed to question, to change, or to correct them.

For clarification, restricting the ability to question anything, denying proven/observable facts, or suppressing rationality lowers consciousness, awareness, and vibration in High Spirituality.

Dogmas are then integrated into a codified set of beliefs, teachings, instructions, and principles known as doctrines that are adopted, are accepted, and are taught by ordained leadership. These doctrines, which originate from supposed religious insights, revelations, or sacred texts, provide the foundational understanding for a faith in guiding its members toward some purpose (e.g., the nature of God, the path to salvation, profound knowledge, etc.).

For clarification, faith refers to believing in something unseen, even when there are doubts or no reassurance, having unwavering confidence in something despite the lack of concrete evidence, and/or possessing undeniable trust and commitment in divine promises, prophecies, and revelations.

Religious doctrines are typically comprised of the following dimensions:

- **Ritual Dimension**: This dimension covers all aspects of performed religion, including the ceremonious activities, the rules governing rituals, the initiations, the incantations, and the frequency of the spiritual practices.
- **Experiential Dimension**: This dimension is concerned with how religious experiences (e.g., encounters with supernatural entities, sources of inspiration, moments of revelation, etc.) impact the emotions and the personal experiences of followers.
- **Mythological Dimension**: This dimension constructs a narrative or a story behind the religion, which must be believed no matter if it is true, fictitious, historical, or mythological. In most cases, the preservation of these myths and narratives – oral, written, or pictorial – is internalized through generational indoctrination, the practice of repetition, communication through symbols, or the acceptance of prophecies.
- **Doctrinal Dimension**: This is the philosophical dimension of the religion used to formulate a worldview or to create logical systems of meaning and structure. The worldview and the logical system must be coherent because contrasting/conflicting results lead to contradictions when explaining things such as morality, the afterlife, reincarnation, offerings and sacrifice, occult magic, handling of ancestors, worship, higher gods, holders of spiritual essence, the nature of the soul, the number of gods, or relationships with god.
- **Ethical Dimension**: This dimension describes the code of conduct or the penal/legal construct necessary to achieve happiness in one's life and to discriminate between right and wrong.
- **Institutional Dimension**: This is the social dimension of the religion concerned with the places of worship, the gathering of adherents, leadership/authority, the treatment of outsiders/visitors, and the formation of organized bodies often spearheaded by leadership, even though the decision-making power can be democratized.

- **Material Dimension**: This dimension contains records, logs, scriptures, and artifacts upon which the religion rests, regardless of whether they are accepted as evidence or not.
- **Reward Dimension**: This dimension, which can be categorized as intrinsic (internal or spiritual) and extrinsic (external or tangible), refers to the divine rewards granted under a religion in this life and the afterlife for loyalty, obedience, and undying faith.
- **Artistic Dimension**: This dimension encompasses how art is used in religion for teaching (didacticism), rituals (visual liturgy), personal devotion (visual contemplation), experiencing the sacred (visual mysticism), and expressing the divine through symbols, iconography, and abstract patterns.

Since the religious doctrines of different belief systems can be similar or can be different in some aspects, they can cause polarity in tolerance and conflicts among neighboring followership.

If a religious doctrine or a belief system holds that only one particular religion or belief is true, then it favors religious exclusivism.

If a religious doctrine or a belief system holds that, while one's own religion may be true, other religions can also contain elements of truth and might lead to salvation, even without explicit knowledge of the central tenets of one's own religion or the conflicting religion, then it favors religious inclusivism.

If a religious doctrine or a belief system holds that multiple religions can be true, can lead to salvation, or can at least be valid paths for human flourishing, promoting tolerance, understanding, and peaceful coexistence, then it favors religious pluralism.

The religious doctrine is often promoted by a set of prophets or founding fathers, claiming to be intermediaries of divine messages with sacred knowledge. The promotion techniques include:

- **Divine Calling**: The prophet or the founding father has been chosen by a divine being.
- **Divine Communication**: The prophet or the founding father can receive messages, teachings, or revelations from a supernatural source.
- **Intermediary Role**: The prophet or the founding father serves as a bridge between a divine being and humans, revealing and conveying the god's words to the people.
- **Speaking God's Word**: The prophet or the founding father is being used to execute the will of a divine being, giving the words of the divine being rather than his/her own opinions.
- **Spiritual Insight**: The prophet or the founding father solely possesses the deep spiritual understanding, discernment, and insight into the divine being's will.
- **Foresight**: The prophet or the founding father either has or acquires the ability to predict or to perceive future events.
- **Authenticity and Purity**: The prophet or the founding father is the sole authority over morality, codes of conduct, and social order as well as what actions are considered to be commitments to god's word or positive steps toward the teachings/faith.
- **Fearless Proclamation**: The prophet or the founding father delivers messages from the divine being without compromise to popular opinion and with courage, even if they are ridiculed, rejected, or untrue.

At this stage, the reader should understand how religious doctrine – driven by belief/faith – comes into conflict with and even stifles science, which is driven by evidence/fact. A few popular examples are provided below:

- A religious doctrine teaches that the Earth is flat or that celestial bodies orbit around the Earth (geocentric); even though the Cosmic Distance Ladder from science clearly shows how celestial bodies and how the distance between celestial bodies are measured using various methods.
- A religious doctrine teaches that the transformation of substances in alchemy is akin to occult magic, even though the practice of alchemy has been scientifically shown to be the precursor for modern-day chemistry and the driving force behind synthetic medicine.
- A religious doctrine teaches that a human being can only be created by a divine being naturally, even though science demonstrates that in vitro fertilization and cloning are possible.

Now that religion and its fundamental constructs are defined, let's take a brief intermission from religion to discuss cults.

A cult, by definition, is a system of beliefs or practices with high veneration and praise directed towards a particular figure or object. Most cults can be classified as faith-based cults, political cults, doomsday/apocalyptic cults, psycho-spiritual cults, self-improvement cults, destructive/abusive cults, salvation cults, savior cults, sex cults, commercial cults, and one-on-one cults.

The characteristics of a cult include the following elements:

- **Charismatic Leader**: A powerful, central figure who demands unquestioning devotion and dictates the group's beliefs and behaviors.
- **Isolation from Society**: The members are often discouraged from associating with people outside the group, leading to increased dependence, entrapment, and the "Us-Versus-Them" polarized mentality.
- **Unusual Beliefs & Practices**: The members engage in unusual, suspect, extreme, or novel beliefs, often with a belief system requiring willful ignorance that unjustifiably claims to have the way of life or the ultimate answers or the eternal knowledge to all of life's questions. In most cases, the supposed answers or the supposed knowledge are provided in a deceptive way, where members ascend to new levels only to find that previous levels were false.
- **Manipulation and Control**: The cult uses psychological manipulation and/or abuse to control its members' thoughts, actions, affairs, and emotions, often inducing psychological dependency. Cults disrupt critical thinking skills using mind-altering tactics such as sleep/food deprivation or repetitive chanting. Under deprivation, exhaustion makes individuals more malleable and less able to question the group's practices. Also, repetitive slogans and chants, often used during long rituals, override conscious thought and reinforce teachings and practices. It is worth noting that any positive outcome is attributed to the cult and any negative outcome is attributed to the member.
- **Unquestionable Loyalty and/or Committed Faith**: Dissent and questioning of the cult or the cult's ideologies are discouraged or are punished, fostering an environment of absolute, uncritical belief. When questioned by a member, the cult will often gaslight the member, will convince the member that his/her faith is not strong enough, or will dismiss the questions as tests of individual faith.

- **Exploitation**: Members are often exploited to benefit the leadership. In most cases, the exploitation is financial with a cash generation scheme; however, other forms include social conditioning, trafficking, political clout/gain, influence, access to information/territory, etc.
- **Indoctrination & Recruitment**: The cult systematically strips members of their old identity and beliefs, while rebuilding a new one based on the cult's ideology. To reduce the mental discomfort (psychological tension/strain), members are pressured to rationalize their radical behaviors normally by weaponizing cognitive dissonance and to deepen their commitment to the group through public confessions. From this point, members are encouraged to push this cult ideology onto their children, relatives, friends, and willing strangers – normally with some reward. For external recruitment, the targets are normally individuals experiencing trauma, abandonment, loneliness, lowliness, stress, drug use, an identity crisis, grief, or divorce. These vulnerabilities make people more receptive to the sense of belonging and the cult's promises.
- **Instilling Fear**: Cults instill fear into the membership by portraying the outside world as dangerous and evil and the cult as the only safe haven. For members, whom want to stay, the threats of shunning, blackballing, excommunication, and social ostracism are highly effective. For members, whom want to escape, coercive threats of punishment, death, forced loyalty renewal, and imprisonment are normally employed.

As the intermission comes to a close, the reader is directed to compare and to contrast a cult and a religion. After careful assessment, the reader will realize that a cult and a religion are not easily distinguishable. In fact, they are close to being the same, especially when considering the few examples below:

- **Thuggee Cult**: This cult's origins were associated with the Hindu goddess Kali, and its members often used strangulation with a cloth to kill their victims without shedding blood. Strongly believing in the Hindu myth, the group was convinced that Kali created men to destroy demons and taught them to kill by strangulation. They terrorized India for more than 600 years.
- **Heaven's Gate**: Inspired by the Book of Revelation in the Bible, Bonnie Nettles and Marshall Applewhite established Heaven's Gate as a doomsday cult with a focus on UFOs. In 1997, all the members committed suicide in order to ride a comet passing by the Earth.
- **Takfir Wal-Hijra and Al-Jihad**: Consisting of members from the Muslim Brotherhood and Islamic extremist groups, these members carried out a string of assassinations and self-sacrifices, believing that Islam was in a state of crisis and was under attack by world leaders.
- **The Soldiers of Heaven**: A messianic Shiite group, the Army of Heaven, attacked Iraqi security forces and Shiite pilgrims during a major holiday in Najaf and Basra. The cult's leader, who claimed to be the Mahdi (a messiah-like figure in Islam), was killed along with hundreds of his followers.
- **The Peoples Temple**: Jim Jones, a "charismatic" preacher from the United States, formed the Peoples Temple to spread his own version/sect of Christianity before moving to Guyana. During his time in Guyana, he constructed the Jonestown compound for his religious followers, whom died by mass suicide in 1978.
- **Burari Family Mass Suicide**: Eleven members of a family in Delhi were found dead in what police ruled a mass suicide. Police found notebooks with detailed instructions for the act, which was done to attain "moksha (salvation)". The family was believed to be acting under the influence of shared psychosis and an occult practice centered on their deceased patriarch.
- **Mackenzie Doomsday Massacre**: An evangelical pastor in Kenya ordered his followers to shun education and medicine and to starve their children to death in order to meet Jesus. In one of the deadliest cult-related massacres ever, at least 436 bodies have been recovered since police raided Good News International Church in a forest some 70 kilometers inland from the coastal town of Malindi.

- **Nigerian Confraternities**: The Black Axe Confraternity incorporates rituals that are reminiscent of religious practices, with members worshipping a figure called Korofo (meaning "the unseen God" or "the devil to guide all men"). The Eiye Confraternity, shrouded in bird-related symbolism, involves spiritual magic (juju) pulled from Igbo-Yoruba culture and worships a deity named Jaku-Jaku. The Vikings worship a one-eyed deity called Odin. The Ogboni (meaning "the elder") cult integrates a syncretic blend of indigenous Yorubaland practices into its secret society. These cults, among others like the Pyrates, Jurists, and Buccaneers, continue to engage in physical torture, blood sacrifices, kidnappings, senseless killing/violence, bizarre rituals, and psychological terror.

It should not be surprising that the overwhelming majority of secret societies, fraternal orders, sororal orders, organized criminal gangs, private sports/entertainment rings, deep-state organizations, and the like, which are all cults, are tied to a religion or have a religious affiliation.

Returning to the topic at hand, it is necessary to examine the origins behind religious doctrine. Of course, a fact-based explanation of the origin of religion is probably impossible because religion's primitive form would require sufficient details regarding the first ancient culture that conceived of the idea; however, understanding the primal nature of religion cannot be said to be entirely irrational because religion has been a recurring theme across diverse human cultures, and religious rendering has always included speculations on the idea of god, the connection of god to the world and humankind, the desire of god to be praised or sacrificed to, god's reward of either immortality or everlasting life, and the scope of divine revelation/intervention.

The major theories behind the origin of religion are provided below.

- Max Müller's theory of nature myths connects to the concept of the immanence of the supernatural by asserting that primitive people personified and deified the powerful, ever-present natural phenomena that they experienced. In this view, the gods were not initially separate, transcendent entities, but rather direct, immediate, or immanent expressions of the natural world itself. Müller believed that early human language was figurative or metaphorical in describing natural events – mostly the solar cycle in allegory. So much so that, over time, the original meaning was lost or forgotten, and these metaphors became literal stories with personified gods and heroes absorbed into religious concepts of the material world.
- In *Totemism and Exogamy*, Sir James Frazer extensively explored the connection between totemism, where humans are said to have kinship or a mystical relationship with a spirit-being, and the practice of marrying outside one's group (exogamy). Frazer's core argument was that these two social phenomena were closely intertwined in early human societies and served as the foundation for the evolution of more complex social structures and religious practices.
- Awe for the Supernatural is a central concept of religious fetishism, which is an early anthropological theory that explains the veneration of objects believed to have supernatural or magical potency. In this context, the intense emotional response of awe is directed at an object or location, which is thought to house a spirit or to embody a sacred power. During a ritual, the extraordinary power of the group's collective energy overwhelms individuals, who then, in ignorance of the rationale behind the emotional experience, project this 'sense of power' onto a totemic object/idol considered worshipful. Eventually, these individuals become convinced that the object/idol serves as a conduit to spirits, consequently formulating religious practice.

- Mao and Herbert Spencer, who had conflicting ideologies, believed that the origin of religion was a strong function of the immortality of the soul. As a materialist Marxist ideology, Maoism rejected the existence of a non-physical, eternal soul. The concept of immortality within Maoism was purely metaphorical, where a person achieved immortality by dying for the revolution and becoming a political symbol. Spencer's theories, on the other hand, were grounded in empirical science and social evolution, not metaphysics. His agnosticism and focus on observable, material progress meant that the supernatural or the spiritual concept of an immortal soul was irrelevant and indefensible.
- In his 1871 work, *Primitive Culture*, E. B. Tylor theorized that the earliest religions emerged from the confusion of primitive humans trying to explain dreams and visions. They believed that a "soul" or "phantom" could leave the body during sleep and that dreams were real, external experiences. From this initial, mistaken belief in a "ghost-soul", Tylor argued that primitive cultures extended the concept of spirits to inanimate objects, animals, and natural forces, leading to animism, which was the first stage in an evolutionary progression toward more complex forms of religion contrasting with the mystic idea, "the super-sensuous in all creation", that everything in the cosmos is permeated by a transcendental, spiritual reality and that a deeper reality exists beyond what the five senses can perceive.
- Alfred Jeremias's core theory posited that Babylonian astral mythology served as the foundation for the religious beliefs of many surrounding cultures. He believed that the movements of the stars, planets, and constellations were observed and interpreted as divine actions, and these interpretations became the source of myths, theology, and spiritual narratives.
- Émile Durkheim distinguished magic from religion to highlight what he saw as the critical, community-building function of religious sacraments. In *The Elementary Forms of Religious Life* (1912), he argued that a key difference lies in the public and collective nature of religious rites versus the private and individualistic character of magic. According to Durkheim, when people worship a totem or a god in a collective ritual, they are, in fact, unconsciously worshipping society itself, as the totem or sacred symbol represents the group and the collective moral power that holds it together.
- Andrew Lang's work documented high gods and supreme beings, often associated with the sky, in many different cultures. In his research, Lang posited the theory of a primordial, intellectual conception of a single creator god that may have later diversified or degenerated into complex religious pantheons. Lang noted the widespread belief in a supreme being or high god, often a sky god, among various peoples, a finding later elaborated on by anthropologist Wilhelm Schmidt. This contradicted earlier evolutionary theories that viewed monotheism as a late development. Lang's work included the Iroquois, the Polynesian, the Egyptian, the Greek, and the Chinese creation myths.
- Wilhelm Schmidt's thesis, primarily detailed *The Origin of the Idea of God*, was a direct challenge to the prevailing evolutionary theories of religion at the time. Opposing the idea that religion evolved from animism, ancestral worship, or 'polytheism to monotheism', Schmidt argued that the original form of religion for humanity was a belief in one supreme being as expressed through extensive ethnographic studies, particularly of hunter-gatherer cultures. Schmidt believed that the universal knowledge of this High God was originally given to humanity through divine revelation. He described this as God teaching humans what to believe about Him, how to venerate Him, and how to obey His will. In his view, subsequent religious developments did not lead to higher forms of belief but rather degraded the original monotheistic construct.

- In his work, *On the Nature of Things*, Lucretius argued that the origin of religion and superstition lies primarily in human fear. Lucretius's first core example centered on the 'fear of the unknown', where he explains that early humans witnessed inexplicable and powerful natural events, such as thunderstorms, earthquakes, and plagues. Lacking a scientific understanding of these occurrences, they mistakenly attributed them to the anger or will of supernatural beings. Lucretius's second core example centered on the 'fear of death', where he identified the terror of death and the unknown afterlife as a major source of human misery and religious belief. He argued that people invented the idea of an immortal soul or an afterlife with benevolent gods to comfort themselves and to escape the fear of annihilation.

Interestingly enough, High Spirituality does not support any of the anthropological or theological theories above because there are no spiritual genes or innate predispositions toward a faith or certain religious beliefs. Strictly speaking, the origin of religion, or the manifestation thereof, is nothing more than an attempt for humans to understand the mechanisms of spirituality. Humans often question how they survived a hopeless situation, why they are coincidentally available when strangers are in dire need of help, how they can tap into their spirit, how they can feel a mighty, yet unexplainable, presence, and many other questions. Spirituality encourages humans to engage in meditation, to raise consciousness and vibration, and to pursue an individual quest for meaning and purpose to seek answers to such questions in a critical-thinking manner; however, the vast majority of humans refuse to seek these answers on their own and instead rely on others to propose the answers out of willful ignorance as a path of least resistance. This reliance opens the door for a given religion to emerge, and the key to the religion's success is simply creating an explanation – not necessarily the best, the most factually accurate, the most historical, or the most truthful – riddled with belief that the willfully ignorant humans can subscribe to.

Doxastic voluntarism asserts that people have voluntary control over which beliefs they subscribe to, meaning they can choose what to believe. This view is split into two types: direct doxastic voluntarism, where beliefs are chosen immediately and without intermediate actions, and indirect doxastic voluntarism, where control is exercised through voluntary actions that influence belief formation. Put in another way, direct doxastic voluntarism can involve belief at will, where a person can choose to believe the religious proposition or disbelieve it; or, it can involve an immediate and intentional conviction, where a person chooses to believe in the religious proposition without even knowing what the proposition is (i.e., people care more about how the belief system makes them feel even if the belief system is fault or it can cause them harm under given circumstances). For the indirect side, this form posits that we can influence our beliefs by choosing to perform other actions that affect belief formation, such as seeking out certain information (research) or avoiding others (cancellation).

Doxastic involuntarism is the opposite view, holding that beliefs are not subject to voluntary control, by way of nature, external force, conversion, or due to psychological facts about belief formation.

Of course, subscribers can choose to convert away from a religious belief, even under the penalty of death; however, some sort of rehabilitation is necessary to avoid religious relapse or becoming trapped in the religious belief again. Religious relapse is a spiritual downturn experienced by once devout subscribers who are strongly questioning their beliefs in crisis. They concede the errors of the religious doctrine; however, they backtrack to the mistake or the false religious belief for many reasons: the feeling that a wrong answer is better than no answer (living the lie), the feeling that the faulty religious doctrine is still a better explanation than alternative religious doctrines, the feeling of disappoint god, emotional numbness, isolation from the community, guilt/shame, and parental resentment. This backtracking can be likened to a mental illness.

For clarification, the most effective means of trapping someone in a religion comes from parental resentment or generational indoctrination because parents – and sometimes other relatives or mentors – wield great influence over a child's belief formation. Consequently, people are always one generation away from religious indoctrination or becoming trapped in a religious/cultist doctrine.

Once again, the key to a religion's success is simply creating an explanation – not necessarily the best, the most factually accurate, the most historical, or the most truthful – riddled with belief that the willfully ignorant humans can subscribe to. Since this subscription to a religious belief is a function of faith, concerns of moral blindness emerge. Moral blindness centers on the idea that an overreliance on faith or divine command can override rational, empathetic, and ethical reasoning, resulting in the justification of immoral actions or the failure to recognize the moral implications of certain practices under religious obedience. Such is the case when there are theocratic justifications under religious obedience for violence, discrimination, the abuse of power, the persecution of heretics, terrorist acts, defending against perceived attack, killing, sacrificing your own children, and so forth.

The Euthyphro Dilemma, which is one of the oldest arguments concerning religion and morality from Socrates, questions whether something is good because god commands it, or whether god commands it because it is good.

If goodness is determined by divine command, then morality becomes arbitrary and is based on a deity's whim rather than on any reasoned principle.

If god commands an action because it is already good, then goodness exists independently of god, and religious belief is not the true source of morality.

Taking a libertarian approach to the religious subscriptions of willfully ignorant humans can also be dangerous, especially if these humans weave such religious ideals into penal codes, the ruling order, and community conduct. A good example of this can be observed with Muslim immigration into non-Muslim countries, where the freedom of religious expression exists. When Muslim refugees initially settle in non-Muslim countries in small numbers under the notion of peace, they are passive, law-abiding citizens, and they build communities that foster an "in-group/out-group" mentality, where moral concern is reserved for fellow believers but not for outsiders. As the Muslim population size grows, this mentality evolves to the weaponization of 'respected belief', where the Muslims not only rally for the right to practice their religious doctrine in full but they also try to force dissenting non-believers into observing their practices – wanting living conditions to be similar to the conflict-ridden home countries that they fled from. Over time, the Muslim immigrants start to mingle with the locals of the non-Muslim country, establishing relationships where a non-Muslim can only marry a Muslim upon conversion, for which the Islamic penalty of apostasy is death. Consequently, the conversion of a non-Muslim to Islam also causes the non-Muslim to place Islam above the non-Muslim's identity. Being more loyal to Islam than its non-Muslim identity, the converted Muslim – as an agent and a subscriber of Islam – starts campaigning for penal codes, ruling order, and community conduct to be streamlined with Islamic doctrine and sharia law, even at the expense of harming the religious freedoms and the lives of the non-Muslim locals. For instance, the Sudanese Civil War, which led to the split of Sudan into two (2) parts – Sudan and South Sudan, occurred when converted Muslims and Afro-Muslims used governmental force to coordinate attacks with outside Arabs to coordinate attacks against non-Muslim tribal groups – mostly Dinka and Nuer – for Islamization. The governmental force included withholding food/water resources, humanitarian aid, medical supplies, business funding, and state-entitled welfare services from the non-Muslim tribal groups until they converted; and, coordinated attacks occurred near the Nuba Mountains and the Blue Nile.

Once again, the key to a religion's success is simply creating an explanation – not necessarily the best, the most factually accurate, the most historical, or the most truthful – riddled with belief that the willfully ignorant humans can subscribe to. Not only does this subscription allow the creation of a baseless explanation behind the religious doctrine riddled with belief, but it also allows the proposer(s) of the subscription to invent a god. Consequently, the proposer(s) can pretend to know what a god wants, how a god thinks, what a god considers good/bad, what a god's will is, how a god should be worshipped or praised, and so forth, as the path of discernment is accepted by subscribers without any direct corroboration from a god.

Some reasons for inventing a god include the following:

- Fabricating an invisible arbiter of truth – an unseen, absolute authority of divine nature that is thought to have final judgment on what is true or false, especially when a consensus cannot be reached by assigned decision-makers
- Using a god to weaponize fear, shame, and guilt to subdue moral conflicts or social deviancy – mostly, through the creation of the 'paradise-purgatory' model in the afterlife.
- Using a god to establish a social control mechanism that outweighs physical, social, cultural, economic, and political advantages. For instance, there might be a handsome (physical), popular (social), high-ranking (cultural), and rich (economic) chief (political) who attracts far more wives than a low-caste commoner in a small village. Instead of allowing the chief to take as many wives - potentially leading to sexual jealousy or possessiveness imbalances through marriage – the invention of a god forbids polygamy and premarital relations to constrain the advantages of the chief in the interest of the commoner.
- Using a god to suppress rational thought for some purpose (e.g., ethnic cleansing, war efforts, imperialism, controversial science, etc.)

Common tactics for promoting an invented god under a religious doctrine include the following:

- Using 'faith before knowing' principles to stimulate curiosity for the invented god
- Gaining high political status to brand or to increase the relevance of the invented god. This includes creating an invisible being that will punish people for wrongdoing to prevent/avoid unacceptable behaviors, regardless of whether the behavior is good or bad.
- Evangelism and proselytizing the word and the wonders of the invented god
- Convincing others that animals and other living beings in nature worship the invented god
- Concealing evil, embarrassing, and uncomfortable elements associated with the invented god or religious doctrine to create the illusion of peace, normally through charitable work or positive public deeds
- Pushing a colonization strategy. Colonization is the process of establishing and maintaining control over a territory and its people, often involving the imposition of foreign political, economic, and social structures.
- Pushing an assimilation strategy. Assimilation refers to the process by which individuals or groups adopt the culture and customs of a dominant group. In the context of colonialism, assimilation can be a tool used to undermine the cultural identity and autonomy of the colonized population.
- Pushing an integration strategy. Integrations refers to the forced or coerced assimilation of indigenous or minority populations into the dominant culture and society of the colonizing power. This process frequently involves the suppression of indigenous languages, cultures, traditions, and governance systems, often in favor of the colonizer's own.
- Dying for a lie. The proposer(s) are even willing to 'die for a lie' to legitimize explanations behind their false religious doctrines, normally by shaping themselves as martyrs of faith. They convince their subscribers that a person would not willingly die for something they knew to be false, especially when given the chance to recant the lie and to save their own lives. So, their conviction and their willingness to die suggest that they are indeed telling the truth and that all aspects of their religious doctrine must be deemed true as well. The only problem with this line of thinking, however, is that there are numerous historical examples of people dying for what they believed to be true or what they knew was a lie, regardless of whether it was objectively accurate. One of the best examples is The Order of the Solar Temple, where the leaders, Joseph Di Mambro and Luc Jouret (as 'proposers'), preached an apocalyptic prophecy involving an environmental catastrophe. Members (as 'subscribers') were convinced that, by dying in a ritualistic "transit", they would escape a corrupt world (siege mentality), ascending to the star – Sirius. The outcome of believing the lie resulted in approximately 53 murder-suicides by gunshot, suffocation, and poison, including the two leaders who were aware of the lie. Such tragedies illustrate that proposers are indeed willing to die for a lie and that subscribers are indeed willing to die for a deeply held belief based on the same lie.

The steps required to break the control of religion include executing the following with a clear mind:

- Investigating the historicity, the reliability, the chronology, and the origins of the religious doctrine and key figures behind it. Religious doctrine must be proven, not taken as fact.
- Assessing how the leadership (proposers) and the followers (subscribers) of a religious doctrine make deceptive, unclear, or unrelated comparisons to other religious doctrines to mask or to distract from the shortcomings of their own religious doctrines.
- Seek out debates among scholars/experts of the religious doctrine as a neutral party. When a religious doctrine has to be defended, this is known as apologetics; when a religious doctrine is being attacked, this is called polemics. By being a neutral party, the defending side and the attacking side will always expose uncomfortable facts and problems with a religious doctrine. In almost all cases, religious leaders/followers will struggle to have historical/scientific debates based on fact, preferring to have theological debates driven by belief/opinion.
- Remembering that we live in a technological age where information is at our fingertips. Any claim made by scholars, experts, or leaders of a religious doctrine can quickly be cross-checked and debunked with direct references. Not to mention, the negative aspects of the religious doctrine are readily accessible to a person with no knowledge of the religious doctrine. In simple terms, technology is the greatest weapon against any religious doctrine.
- Assessing the maximum level of harm that the religious doctrine has caused or can/might cause if the religious doctrine is weaponized, is politicized, or is adopted on a large scale
- Assessing the number of people joining and leaving the religion, as well as the reasons. Normally, people leaving a religion will give warnings and evils behind the religious doctrine that are normally hidden from new members. Moreover, religions experiencing high growth typically hide low retention rates and failures to maintain new members after these members learn the ridiculous aspects of the faith. Bear in mind that even millions of followers under a religion does not make the religion true.
- Investigating how much effort is necessary to defend the religious doctrine (apologetics) – even against people whom share the same religious doctrine – and if the defense of the religious doctrine requires bizarre faith, willful ignorance, mental gymnastics, the 'literal vs. figurative' game, or a decrease in consciousness, vibration, or rationality. This is also connected to the 'wearing the mask' concept or the 'acting as a butler' concept, where one behaves servile but harbors deep-seated hatred of their own religious doctrine.

For clarification, mental gymnastics, by definition, is the use of complex or convoluted thought processes to justify or to rationalize a particular belief, action, or situation. It involves twisting and turning logic, facts, or evidence in order to fit a preconceived notion or narrative.

- Not supporting the religious doctrine strictly based on how it makes you feel or propaganda.
- Not creating a personal version of the religious doctrine to accept it or to circumvent its errors
- Investigating the religious doctrine for contradictions, falsehoods, historical inaccuracies, conflicts with direct observation, vague language/terms, items borrowed/copied/stolen from other religions, and avenues of misinterpretation. A religious evolution tree is provided below.

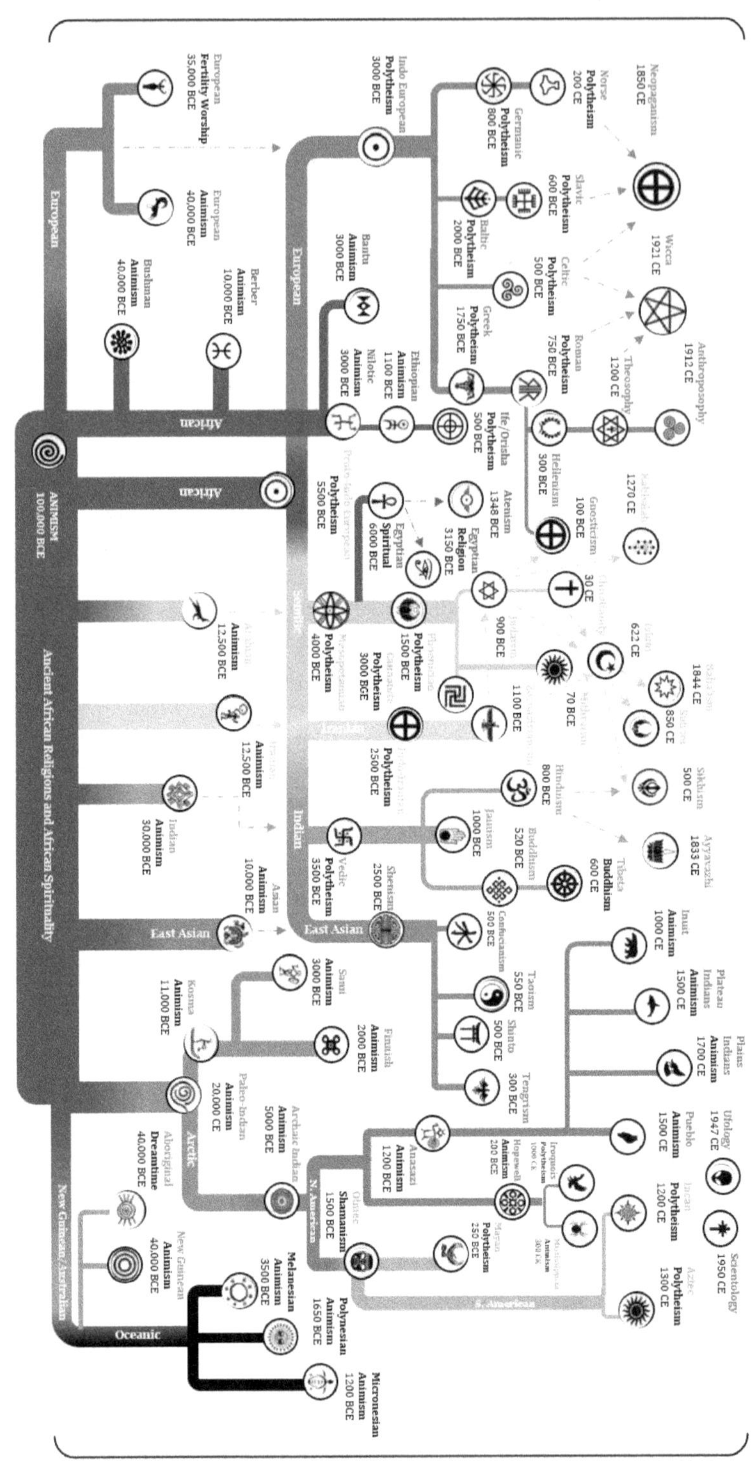
ANIMISM
100,000 BCE
Ancient African Religions and African Spirituality
European
African
African
East Asian
East Asian
Indian
Oceanic
New Guinean/Australian
European
Fertility Worship
35,000 BCE
European
Animism
40,000 BCE
Bushman
Animism
40,000 BCE
Berber
Animism
10,000 BCE
Indo European
Polytheism
3000 BCE
Norse
Polytheism
200 CE
Germanic
Polytheism
800 BCE
Neopaganism
1850 CE
Slavic
Polytheism
600 BCE
Baltic
Polytheism
2000 BCE
Wicca
1921 CE
Celtic
Polytheism
500 BCE
Greek
Polytheism
1750 BCE
Roman
Polytheism
750 BCE
Theosophy
1200 CE
Anthroposophy
1912 CE
Bantu
Animism
3000 BCE
Ethiopian
Animism
1100 BCE
Nilotic
Animism
3000 BCE
Ife/Orisha
Polytheism
500 BCE
Hellenism
300 BCE
Gnosticism
100 BCE
Atenism
1348 BCE
Egyptian
Religion
3150 BCE
Egyptian
Spiritual
6000 BCE
Polytheism
5500 BCE
30 CE
622 CE
900 BCE
1844 CE
850 CE
70 BCE
1100 BCE
Animism
12,500 BCE
Polytheism
4000 BCE
Polytheism
1500 BCE
Polytheism
3000 BCE
Polytheism
2500 BCE
Animism
12,500 BCE
Indian
Animism
30,000 BCE
Asian
Animism
10,000 BCE
Sikhism
500 CE
Hinduism
800 BCE
Jainism
1000 BCE
Buddhism
520 BCE
Ayyavazhi
1833 CE
Tibetan
Buddhism
600 CE
Vedic
Polytheism
3500 BCE
Shenism
2500 BCE
Confucianism
500 BCE
Taoism
550 BCE
Shinto
500 BCE
Tengrism
300 BCE
Inuit
Animism
1000 CE
Plateau
Indians
Animism
1500 CE
Plains
Indians
Animism
1700 CE
Sami
Animism
3000 BCE
Finnish
Animism
2000 BCE
Kosma
Animism
11,000 BCE
Paleo-Indian
Animism
20,000 CE
Arctic
Archaic Indian
Animism
5000 BCE
Aboriginal
Dreamtime
40,000 BCE
Ufology
1947 CE
Pueblo
Animism
1500 CE
Anasazi
Animism
1200 BCE
Hopewell
Animism
200 BCE
Inca
Polytheism
1200 CE
Scientology
1950 CE
Olmec
Shamanism
1500 BCE
N. American
Mayan
Polytheism
250 BCE
Aztec
Polytheism
1300 CE
S. American
New Guinean
Animism
40,000 BCE
Melanesian
Animism
3500 BCE
Polynesian
Animism
1650 BCE
Micronesian
Animism
1200 BCE

For clarification, the evolutionary tree clearly illustrates how later religions were influenced and were adapted from earlier religions, mainly transitioning from various forms of animism to polytheism to monotheism to scientific outliers.

For clarification, the evolutionary tree shows how religions syncretized ideas beginning with African thought/beliefs. This explains why there are similar patterns, common motifs, and overlapping beliefs across religious doctrines despite not having the same belief system. Examples of this would be ideas of an afterlife, a paradise/purgatory, a soul, a resurrection, deity types, etc.

For clarification, the evolutionary tree shows how religions and the supposed deities of religious faiths/doctrines have come and have gone without any apocalyptic consequences, objectively indicating an impersonal high power.

- Investigating deceptive efforts undertaken to increase the authenticity of, the credibility of, or the validity of the religious doctrine, including forgeries, invented testimony/revelation, doctrinal updates against decree, perversions of the public/historical record, euhemerism, etc.
- Investigating what is left out in doctrinal delivery/text or the uncomfortable/embarrassing aspects of the religious doctrine that the leadership intentionally hides, deletes, or omits, especially in subliminal branding/messaging, routine worship, or language translation.

For clarification, intentional and accidental mistranslations of religious texts can profoundly alter the original meaning and the influence of religious doctrines. Due to the complex nature of ancient languages, cultural gaps, and evolving theological interpretations, no translation is considered perfectly inspired or inerrant. Common motives behind false translations include (i) translators interpreting texts to align with the specific religious doctrines of their denomination or sect, (ii) translators must choose from multiple possible meanings for a single word when the cultural distance between the original texts and modern languages often make a precise, word-for-word translation impossible, (iii) translators deliberately mistranslate texts, altering meanings and removing inconvenient passages entirely, to serve an agenda, or (iv) translators might only possess faulty, redacted, or less complete versions of religious manuscripts requiring interpolations.

For clarification, a redaction refers to creating a contemporary source and then projecting this source backward to earlier centuries.

For clarification, an interpolation of a religious doctrine/text refers to any addition, alteration, omission, or insertion of non-authorial matter into a text that was not part of the original writing, often resulting from scribal errors, conscious emendation by readers and copyists, shifts in reliability, or the incorporation of marginal notes into the main text over generations of manual copying. Such interpolations can introduce new ideas, clarify confusing passages, or even distort the original author's intent, requiring textual critics to identify and to remove them.

- Assessing mechanisms employed to spread/protect the religious doctrine, including war, death threats, coercion, governmental force, slavery, trade, colonization, falsified studies/statistics, fake propaganda, poverty, censorship, human rights infringement of (non)believers, etc.
- Investigating how the religious doctrine or the leadership behind the religious doctrine controls the affairs of its followers, traps its followers (e.g., death by apostasy, purgatorial fearmongering, threats of violence, marriage ineligibility, etc.), and punishes its followers (e.g., abuse, shunning, etc.)
- Assessing how a religion tries to blur the lines between religion and spirituality – thus, conflating the two as identical. The moment one cannot distinguish between religion and spirituality and surrenders all rationality to the deity of the religious doctrine, (s)he becomes mentally lost.

For clarification, spirituality can exist without religion, but religion cannot exist without spirituality because a religion is constructed by taking a fraction of spiritual concepts and adding rules, tenets, rituals, authorities, dogma, prophecies, and other religious dimensions to them. An analogy of this is illustrated below.

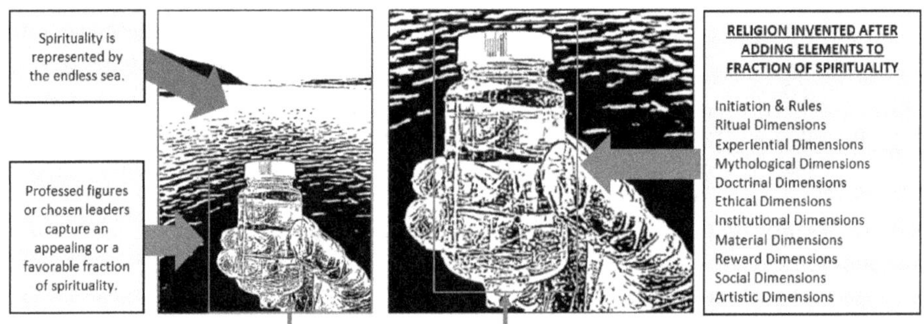

- Investigating the drug, magical, and mythological components behind the religious doctrine.

For clarification, mind-altering substances (entheogens) have been used in religious rituals for thousands of years – especially among schizotypal groups – offering a pathway to a divine being. Although some major religions forbid or discourage 'recreational' drug use, the restriction falls short when drugs are used for theological purposes. A few examples include the Native American Church's use of peyote – a cactus containing the psychoactive substance, mescaline – as a sacrament, the Christian use of psychedelics in early Greece, the use of Syrian Rue and cannabis (hashish) in Sufi Islam, ganja in Rastafarianism, bhang in Hinduism, the use of ibogaine – a psychoactive compound producing visions– in Bwiti culture, the potent psychedelic brew (ayahuasca) in the Amazon, and entheogenic mushrooms for healing and visionary practices in shamanic traditions. Moreover, synthetic and organic drugs are used to create the illusion of magic powers, especially in cultures with herbalists and witchdoctors.

- Weighing the reward dimensions and the religious entitlements of the religious doctrine. If the religious doctrine promises a place to its followers or declares a place sacred, then the followers might wrongfully seize or wage war against local inhabitants of such a place. There are cases where the religious doctrine offers rewards on empty promises (e.g., rewards that your eyes cannot see, that your hands cannot touch, and so forth).
- Investigating how tolerant a religious doctrine is of dissenting or differing religious doctrines. This includes a comparison of behaviors and acts that a religious doctrine encourages when its followership is the minority of a population or the majority of a population.
- Investigating the consequences and the dangers of a religious doctrine labeling groups as 'the chosen ones', 'the superior race', 'master race', 'the leaders of all humanity', and similar terms
- Investigating whether the religious doctrine meets the previously mentioned test criteria of a worldview, especially from a historical and a theological perspective
- Remembering that a religion or a religious doctrine can only have power over you, if you choose either to accept it or to submit to it.
- Investigating whether the religious doctrine encourages followers to seek vengeance against or the destruction of others through a god.

As a sidebar, followers oftentimes do not know what a religion forces them to pray to or to pray for. Not to mention, nothing in the history of humankind has a higher failure rate than prayer. An interesting point to consider is that religious followers never choose prayer over medical support. A religious patient, for instance, will not reject surgery or critical medical services in favor of religious prayer.

Thousands of religions with false promises, false narratives, failed prophecies, fake revelations, and fearmongering tactics have come and have gone, being replaced with updated/remixed versions of a religion, new sects of a religion, a syncretized variant of the religion, or a new religion altogether.

Tactics used to spread a religion normally include colonization, assimilation, integration, war/military campaigns, trade, forced conversion (torture/inquisition), slavery, generational indoctrination, superstition (farming, weather, visions, omen, etc.), state/governmental force, cult propaganda, strategic marriages, strategic alliances, bandwagon tactics, etc. Readers should always remain critical and aware of any religious doctrine, invented in the past, present, or future.

Now that the reader knows what a religion actually is, what the origins behind a religion are, and what causes a person to subscribe to a religion, as well as the traps, the tactics, and promotional techniques behind a religious doctrine, selected religions can be put under a microscope. For the Abrahamic religions (Judaism, Christianity, and Islam), a more in-depth historical approach will be taken.

Em Hotep!

ON ANCIENT RELIGIONS (NON-AFRICAN)

ANKH WADJA SENEB | ARTICLE NO: 002

Function: The Awareness of Control Mechanisms
Subject(s): Ancient Religions & Belief Systems
Position: Part 3 – Breaking Societal Controls
Theme: Dealing with Religions, Cults, & Atheism | Scene 2

ARTICLE NO: 002 – ON ANCIENT RELIGIONS (NON-AFRICAN)

Peace to the High Power! Peace to the Living Universe! Peace to all Finite Living Beings! Peace to All Things – seen and unseen! For my spirit is with me, my image is with me, and my purpose is with me. For those with knowledge understand that the mechanisms behind societal controls can only flourish when consciousness, awareness, vibration, and rationality are minimized and when willful ignorance, fear, indoctrination, and subjugating forces are maximized.

Recall that the key to a religion's success is simply creating an explanation – not necessarily the best, the most factually accurate, the most historical, or the most truthful – riddled with belief that the willfully ignorant humans can subscribe to. Although ancient religions have become obsolete, they are pivotal in understanding how manipulative frameworks of evolving religious doctrine have been used to establish control over people.

The earliest evidence of ancient Mesopotamian religions coincides with permanent settlements within urban centers in the mid-4000 BCE, following the invention of writing systems and the worship of forces of nature as providers of sustenance. Mesopotamian civilizations formed on the banks of the Tigris and Euphrates Rivers in modern-day Iraq and Kuwait. Some of the major Mesopotamian civilizations included the Sumerians, Assyrians, Akkadians, and Babylonians. Their religions included a vast pantheon of deities who controlled various aspects of life, as well as the associated Anunnaki gods. The Anunnaki were a group of Sumerian and Mesopotamian deities, whose names meant "offspring of Anu", with "Anu" being the sky god.

Leveraging sociocultural influence and political force, priests imposed a connection between people in city-states – often superstitious – and divine protectors, causing religion to be the center of life. As such, temples were seen as residences for gods/deities, and priests often tended to the cult statues, dressing them, offering them feasts, and using barges and chariots to transport them during religious festivals and ceremonies.

The key aspects of some ancient religions are provided in the sections below. While going through these aspects, the reader is encouraged to identify familiar parallels or themes to modern religions.

SUMERIANS

Origin	The ancient Sumerian religion arose in southern Mesopotamia (modern-day Iraq), with its civilization beginning from 6000 BCE to 4000 BCE.
Spread	• Sumerians spread their language, religion, and building practices to other cities in the region. • Sumerians developed and perfected many forms of technology, including the wheel, cuneiform script, arithmetic, geometry, irrigation, saws and other tools, sandals, chariots, harpoons, and beer. • As Sumerian city-states were conquered by the Akkadian and later Babylonian empires, their religious traditions were integrated into the conquerors' cultures.
Chronology	• Ubaid Period: First settlement in southern Mesopotamia by farmers whom brought irrigation agriculture. • Uruk Period: Pottery was mass-produced, trade goods began to flow down waterways in southern Mesopotamia, and slave labor was utilized. • Early Dynastic Period: Writing, rather than pictograms, became commonplace, wars increased, cities erected walls for self-preservation, and Sumerian culture spread from southern Mesopotamia into surrounding areas. • Akkadian Empire Period: Many people were bilingual in Sumerian and Akkadian. Towards the end, Sumerian was increasingly a literary language. • Gutian Period: A period of chaos and decline, the Guti barbarians defeated the Akkadian military but could not support the civilizations in place. • Sumerian Renaissance/Third Dynasty of Ur: Rulers Ur-Nammu and Shulgi extend their power into southern Assyria. The region became more Semitic, and the Sumerian language became a religious language. The era ends with invasions by the Amorites, whose dynasty of Isin continued until 1700 BCE, as Mesopotamia came under Babylonian rule.
Contradictions	• The precise details and order of creation stories differ between various Sumerian myths, even within single narratives. • Divine lineages and familial relationships of deities, such as the parents and siblings of Inanna or Utu, might be presented differently in texts from different cities and eras. • A god's attributes and roles, like the sun-god (Utu) being an executer of justice, might be emphasized differently during different historical periods.
Scientific & Historical Errors	• Irrigation System Flaws: Despite an advanced canal system, Sumerian cities located upstream could obstruct the water flow, negatively impacting cities downstream. • Human Error in Records: Cuneiform tablets sometimes contained errors, including errors such as tallying mistakes. Moreover, fraud could also have been a possibility. • Unpredictable Floods: The uncontrolled nature of the Tigris and Euphrates River floods, especially without a way to predict their exact timing, posed a challenge to their agriculture and settlements as well as religious explanations. For example, it was unclear if the rain came as god's favor or god's punishment.

Mythical Aspects	• Sumerian religion primarily features myths explaining the natural world and human origins, rather than a structured system of prophecies. • Sumerian myths, like those found in the Babylonian version of the Epic of Gilgamesh (Legendary King of Uruk's quest for immortality), provided the foundation for Mesopotamian literature and religious narratives. • The focus of Sumerian myth is often on why the gods made a particular decision or how humans reacted to it, rather than on an unmet prediction. • The Eridu Genesis (Sumerian Flood Myth) explains the creation of humanity, the first cities, and the origin of kingship. • The myth of Atrahasis details a great flood sent by the gods and the instructions given to a wise man to build a ship to save himself and his family. • In Sumerian myths, gods are anthropomorphic beings who can be benevolent, as with Enki, or vengeful, as in the Atrahasis epic. • The myth of Inanna's Descent and return from the underworld is connected to the cycle of fertility and the changing seasons.
Central Tenets	• A polytheistic system with anthropomorphic gods and goddesses ruling over natural and human domains. • Humanity's role was to serve the gods and to maintain cosmic order through rituals and offerings. • The earliest known written law code, the Code of Ur-Nammu, was Sumerian and invoked deities for the king's authority while establishing justice and order. • Religion was intertwined with the city-state structure, with priest-kings governing from within the temples.
Key Gods	• An (sky god) • Enlil (among chief gods) • Enki (god of water and wisdom) • Inanna (god of love and war) • Utu (sun god)
Other Religious Items	• Ziggurats, which were massive and elaborate temple complexes, were central to worship. • Offered sacrifices and held festivals • The Sumerian flood myth was a key story. • Sumerian understanding of the cosmos included a flat earth, a firmament above, and a netherworld below.

BABYLONIANS

Origin	The Babylonians (2000–1600 BCE) originated from the Sumerians and Akkadians in Mesopotamia, with traditions being reshaped to elevate Babylonian gods, particularly Marduk, especially during the reign of King Hammurabi.
Spread	• The Babylonians adapted the Sumerian cuneiform script and built upon Mesopotamian urban traditions. • The religion's spread was allied to the political power of the city of Babylon. As it grew in importance, so did its chief deity, Marduk. • Adaptation of Babylonian beliefs to neighboring peoples due to religious and cultural exchanges.
Chronology	• 18th Century BCE: The rise of the Babylonian state under the First Babylonian Dynasty. • Old Babylonian Period: Continued development of Babylonian culture and law • Neo-Babylonian Empire (626-539 BCE): A resurgence of Babylonian power before falling to the Persian Achaemenid Empire in 539 BCE • Many Babylonian religious elements would influence later religious thought in the Hellenistic world.
Contradictions	• Complex contradiction in understanding divinity - How the gods could be simultaneously immanent (within their statues and natural forces) and transcendent (living in the statues and natural forces). • Contradiction between emphasis on monumental temple worship and the belief that the divine was embodied in natural phenomena. • Influence from earlier Sumerian beliefs created a layered religious system where newer Semitic traditions adopted existing elements.
Scientific & Historical Errors	• Babylonians developed mathematical tools like tables for solving cubic equations and efficient methods for finding square roots, though they lacked algebraic notation and proofs. • The biblical account of Abraham's birth at Ur is considered a legendary, non-historical tradition, possibly developed during the Babylonian exile. • The story of Cyrus the Great entering Babylon by diverting the Euphrates is a legend that lacks confirmation in contemporary sources. • Archaeological evidence for the famous Hanging Gardens of Babylon is limited. Some theories suggest that they might have been located in the city of Nineveh.
Mythical Aspects	• The Babylonian creation epic (The Enuma Elish) involved the god Marduk defeating the primordial chaos monster goddess Tiamat in the battle for cosmic order. • The Descent of Ishtar was a myth describing the goddess Ishtar's journey to the underworld and her subsequent return, proving significant in death and rebirth.
Central Tenets	• The gods were an absolute monarchy, a change from the earlier democratic structure of the Sumerian pantheon. • The Enuma Elish influenced the Babylonian New Year festival, celebrating creation. • The initial belief that humans were created to serve the gods

	• Influenced by Sumerian law, Babylonian legal codes also existed under the Code of Hammurabi. • Like the Sumerians, the Babylonians had a hierarchical society where the king ruled with divine authority.
Key Gods	• Marduk (chief god of the city of Babylon and the creator of heaven and earth)
Other Religious Items	• Babylonian religion emphasized Marduk as the chief god of the city of Babylon, whom defeated the primordial sea monster Tiamat. • The Babylonian cosmology was heavily influenced by Sumerian beliefs, depicting a universe with a celestial realm for the gods and an underworld.

CANAANITES

Origin	Ancient Semitic people who inhabited the Southern Levant, the region in the Eastern Mediterranean, stretching from modern-day Turkey to Iraq. Their history generally spans between 3000 BCE and 1000 BCE.
Spread	• Archaeological excavations indicate multiple rather than a single ethnic group. Canaanites consisted of people with a myriad of burial customs and cultic structures. • Credited with developing the Phoenician alphabet, which is the basis for most modern Latin-based alphabets.
Chronology	• Late 3000 BCE: Evidenced by Ebla Tablets showing lists of offerings to key deities such as El, Baal, and Dagon. • 2000 BCE (Middle Bronze to Late Bronze Age): Evidenced by the Idrimi Inscription, which offers references to Canaanite religious customs and Ugaritic Texts (1400-1200 BCE), which detail Canaanite myths (like the Baal Cycle), hymns, prayers, ritual prescriptions, and lists of sacrifices. • Late 2000 BCE to Early 1000 BCE: Evidenced by Emar Tablets, which provide further insight into religious practices and festival texts written in Akkadian. • Fall of Ugarit (1200 BCE): End point for the documented flourishing of Canaanite city-state religion, though the religion itself continued to evolve and to influence the region. • 1000 BCE: Canaanite religious practices, especially those related to nature and fertility, continued to be a cultural force and a point of contention with the monotheistic Israelites as they occupied the land.
Contradictions	• The term 'Canaanite' lacks a clear ethnic definition, making the scope and nature of the religion difficult to define precisely. • The Ugaritic texts show Baal eventually overthrowing El to become the supreme god, indicating a shifting rather than a fixed divine hierarchy, which is a contradiction to a stable religious structure. • The Canaanite religion was polytheistic with many gods like El, Baal, and Asherah, yet the biblical accounts also portray a fierce condemnation of these deities in favor of the Israelite God, Yahweh. • Sexual fertility rites for ensuring agricultural abundance appeared contradictory, especially when they involved practices like human sacrifice.
Scientific & Historical Errors	• Canaanites' surviving records come from the site of Amarna, in Egypt, and excavations of archaeological sites where the Canaanites supposedly lived, not the Hebrew Bible.

Mythical Aspects	• Worship of a pantheon of gods and goddesses, often with El as the supreme father figure and Baal as the prominent storm and fertility god. • Nature worship according to natural cycles, with rituals focused on ensuring rain, fertility, and agricultural abundance through the actions of deities like Baal. • The Baal Cycle, found in the Ugaritic texts, describes Baal's death and resurrection, which was a central part of the yearly cultic rituals designed to guarantee the land's fertility.
Central Tenets	• A polytheistic system, sometimes monolatristic, with a pantheon led by the god El and his consort Asherah. • The Canaanites were often organized into city-states, sometimes under foreign influence like the Egyptians, and religious officials or priests held significant authority. • The Ugaritic texts provide much information about Canaanite beliefs and mythology.
Key Gods	• El (head of the pantheon) • Asherah (wife/consort of El) • Baal (storm god) • Anat (war goddess)
Religious Items	• Animal sacrifice and offerings at shrines and sacred groves. • The Canaanite cosmology shared similarities with Mesopotamian beliefs, including a flat earth and a subterranean netherworld.

ANUNNAKI

Origin	The Anunnaki are a group of deities from ancient Mesopotamian civilizations, including the Sumerians, Akkadians, Babylonians, and Assyrians. It is believed that about 450,000 years ago, before the Great Flood and during Earth's Pleistocene ice age, the Anunnaki arrived on Earth and established their initial base camp in Mesopotamia in the Fertile Crescent between the Tigris and Euphrates Rivers.
Spread	• The beliefs surrounding the Anunnaki spread through cultural transmission as they were adopted into the pantheons of the Akkadian, Babylonian, and Assyrian empires. • Literary traditions documenting the Anunnaki were preserved in ancient Mesopotamian literary works, such as the Epic of Gilgamesh, which helped to disseminate their mythology across the region.
Chronology	• There is no established chronology of the ancient Anunnaki. The Anunnaki are mythological figures who are neither historically documented nor scientifically proven beings. • Ancient Astronaut Theory: Some modern theories (like those of Zecharia Sitchin) claim that the Anunnaki were not gods but rather ancient extraterrestrials who came to Earth, possibly influencing early human civilizations. Zecharia Sitchin proposed a timeline of their supposed visits to Earth for gold mining, creating humans, and other activities.
Contradictions	• No Ancient Texts Support the Anunnaki theories. The idea of the Anunnaki as extraterrestrial miners is a modern interpretation and not supported by the actual Sumerian texts, which describe them as gods.

	• Rejection by Academia - Mainstream science and history dismiss the Anunnaki claims as pseudoscience.
Scientific & Historical Errors	• Mistaking Sitchin's pseudo-scientific theories, where the Anunnaki are portrayed as a spacefaring race from a planet called Nibiru, as historical fact. • Sitchin claimed the Anunnaki genetically engineered humans by combining their DNA with that of Homo erectus to create a slave race for mining gold. This is a fictional narrative, as evidence for such an event is nonexistent. • Core chronological errors following the misinterpretation of the Shar as 3600 years.
Mythical Aspects	• The Anunnaki were central figures in creation myths, such as the myth of Cattle and Grain, which describes their creation by Anu and their initial ignorance of agriculture. • Varying Portrayals: In early Sumerian texts, the Anunnaki were the most powerful gods. Later, they are associated with the underworld in Babylonian traditions and were sometimes referred to as the seven judges of the underworld.

Putting aside the Anunnaki, Ancient Mesopotamian religions, including those of the Sumerians, the Babylonians, and the Canaanites, lacked a concept of paradise as a heavenly reward for the righteous. After death, bodies were buried with grave goods, rituals were performed, and offerings of food and drink were made to the deceased to ensure their peaceful afterlife.

Ultimately, all three ancient religions envisioned the following:

- An afterlife was viewed as a bleak underworld of dust and shadows.
- An understanding of a paradise-like or utopian place in the form of a mythic or divine garden (Dilmun) – an earthly realm of joy for the gods rather than a destination for human souls.
- No formal purgatory, as souls do not have a chance for salvation or existence after death.
- All souls have a shared fate. Regardless of their earthly deeds, all were believed to be fated to inhabit the "Land of No Return". The Sumerian and Babylonian belief systems described this afterlife as the *Kurnugia*, while Canaanites referred to it as the pit or Mot, to which the soul departed after death.

Slavery in ancient Mesopotamia varied by culture; nonetheless, slaves were fundamentally considered property, similar to commodities. They performed essential labor, freeing up free citizens for other roles in the economy. While some slaves could gain freedom or could advance socially over time, the institution of slavery generally reinforced existing social stratification. However, whereas Sumerian and Babylonian slaves were specifically war captives, debtors, or criminals working in agriculture, domestic service, and large-scale construction, Canaanite sources of slavery remain vague in their various forms of forced labor. Ultimately, in the former two religions, legal codes provided some legal protections and the preservation of rights, including the right to own property and marry. Owners still received compensation for harm to their slaves, and they were liable for civil penalties and fines for various crimes committed by their slaves.

Although these religions are outdated and are considered fiction today, they controlled the entire fabric of society in ancient times. Once again, the key to a religion's success is simply creating an explanation – not necessarily the best, the most factually accurate, the most historical, or the most truthful – riddled with belief that the willfully ignorant humans can subscribe to.

Em Hotep!

ON ANCIENT AFRICAN RELIGIONS

ANKH WADJA SENEB | ARTICLE NO: 003

Function: The Awareness of Control Mechanisms
Subject(s): Ancient African Religions - Critical
Position: Part 3 – Breaking Societal Controls
Theme: Dealing with Religions, Cults, & Atheism | Scene 3

ARTICLE NO: 003 – ON ANCIENT AFRICAN RELIGIONS

Peace to the High Power! Peace to the Living Universe! Peace to all Finite Living Beings! Peace to All Things – seen and unseen! For my spirit is with me, my image is with me, and my purpose is with me. For those with knowledge understand that the mechanisms behind societal controls can only flourish when consciousness, awareness, vibration, and rationality are minimized and when willful ignorance, fear, indoctrination, and subjugating forces are maximized.

Recall that the key to a religion's success is simply creating an explanation – not necessarily the best, the most factually accurate, the most historical, or the most truthful – riddled with belief that the willfully ignorant humans can subscribe to, and ancient African religions are no exception. Numerous African religions have captured the minds of diverse tribes and kingdoms since the beginning of humankind, controlling thought, politics, trade, conquests, and social conduct. In this article, we will focus on the long-lasting ancient African religious beliefs. These beliefs include the Kemetic and Kushite religions, which are ancient polytheistic systems from Egypt and Nubia (modern-day Sudan), and the animalistic religions from West Africa, such as Yoruba, Vodun, and Dogon.

KEMETIC (EGYPTIAN) RELIGION

Recall that the raw Kemetic teachings were spiritual teachings about the physical and metaphysical layers of the Living Universe, which surfaced far before the Kemetic religion was created. Before 3150 BCE, ancient Egyptians and ancient Nubians pursuing knowledge or hidden wisdom about the seen and unseen mechanics of the Living Universe – normally, architectural masons, philosophers, and pioneers – were known as 'seekers of knowledge' equivalent to modern-day scholars. Empowered with this knowledge, some of these seekers seized the opportunity to start cults by integrating the knowledge into indigenous, polytheistic faiths through symbolism and fabricating temple practices. Over time, the cult priests had successfully blurred the lines between the raw spiritual teachings and their invented polytheist religions, transforming 'knowledge' into 'esoteric knowledge', assigning attributes of power to deities, and manipulating the ruling class to force their ideas onto the civilization. As a result, the Kemetic religion with the Neteru officially sprouted concurrently with the unification of Egypt under Narmer.

For clarification, 'seekers' of knowledge referred to anyone seeking the hidden wisdom of the Living Universe. Prior to the cult priest introducing agendas and temple practices, such knowledge was in the public/shared domain, not secret societies. All of the secret societies were later premised on protecting, holding, and concealing knowledge among the followership. This is evidenced in the 'Rising Sons of Ra', 'Keepers of the Primordial Flame', 'Custodians of the Divine Order', Moorish Orders (Arab-African knowledge mixtures), 'Freemasons' (Greek-African knowledge mixtures), etc.

The reader should never confuse the Kemetic Religion with High Spirituality.

Origin	Various polytheistic, indigenous beliefs of Ancient Egypt, originating around the Predynastic Period and culminating in the Kemetic (Egyptian) religion with the Neteru around 3150 BCE
Spread	• Pharaohs/kings establishing the religion directly on the civilization • During the Ptolemaic and Roman Periods, following the conquests of Alexander the Great, cults of certain Egyptian deities, such as Isis, spread into the Hellenistic and Roman worlds. • Syncretism with nearby beliefs and trade • Modern resurgence came in the form of Neo-Pagan movements like Kemetic Orthodoxy in the late 20th century.
Contradictions	• Adaptation of myths for different reasons, such as influencing rituals even in art and literature, means a myth could be retold differently depending on the context, leading to variations in detail and emphasis on a single event or deity. • Theological evolution over a long period, with different cities and time periods, means that the "true" story of a god or myth could change over time, creating a sense of inconsistency.
Scientific & Historical Errors	• Esoteric vs. Exoteric Knowledge: The Kemetic priesthood held esoteric (inner) knowledge not revealed to the general population. Masses practiced a more general system of belief, and the discrepancies in "knowledge" between these levels are to be expected. • Lack of a 'Unified Truth' allowed for a rich tapestry of diverse beliefs and practices, rather than a single dogma.
Mythical Aspects	• Superior human-like Gods: Gods were depicted with human traits, including birth, conflict, and even death and rebirth, but were understood to be immortal and be superior. • Symbolic Animal Forms: Gods were often shown in animal or part-animal forms as symbolic metaphors for their characteristics, attributes, roles, and power.
Central Tenets	• The ruler (pharaoh) was the guarantor of Ma'at on Earth, responsible for performing rituals and maintaining divine order among humanity. • Life is a cycle of creation and renewal, with a significant focus on the afterlife and veneration of the ancestors (Akhu) and the dead. • The soul comprised several parts, comprising the Ka (life force), Ba (personality), and Akh (transfigured spirit). In the afterlife, each soul is judged and transformed by Osiris. Those deemed worthy entered Aaru - Field of Reeds (a form of paradise). After death, the heart was weighed against the feather of Ma'at in the Hall of Ma'at. Those who failed had their heart devoured by Ammit (a monstrous creature) and their souls erased eternally. • Humans are fundamentally divine manifestations in creation, and the spiritual journey is about realizing this inherent divinity. • The universe was created from Nun (primordial chaos) and maintained by divine order and renewal cycles. The gods play a direct role.
Key Gods	• Ra, Horus, Atum, Osiris, Isis, Anubis, and all other Neteru

KUSHITE RELIGION

Origin	The Kushite religion began with indigenous animistic traditions and ancestral worship from the Kerma culture, with early influences from Egyptian religion and other cultures.
Spread	• Syncretism: Fusion of local Nubian traditions with the powerful influence of Egyptian religion to create a unique spiritual character • Cultural Continuity: The Kushite religion provided continuity and a sense of identity for the kingdom of Kush for thousands of years, even as Egypt came under foreign rule. • Royal Cults: Kingship emphasized the divine nature of rulers, ensuring continuity of religious beliefs and practices through monumental temples. • Womanhood in Religion: Evidenced by the prominence of Kandakes (queens) in religious iconography
Misconceptions	• Selective adoption and adaptation of Egyptian beliefs with indigenous Nubian deities caused Egyptian influence to diminish over time as the capital moved to Meroe. • Kush as a mere extension of Egypt: Colonialists framed Kushite history and religion as subservient to Egypt, overlooking its own rich cultural and religious developments. • Birthplace of Kingship: The narrative that Gebel Barkal was the birthplace of Egyptian kingship was promoted by New Kingdom Egyptians to legitimize their rule over Nubia.
Central Tenets	• Polytheistic worship deeply influenced by Egyptian religious traditions. Temples were built to house the gods and served as the center of religious life with priests in charge. • The king was a mediator between the gods and the people, and a king held a divine right to rule. Rulers and elites were buried in pyramid tombs, which were connected to mortuary chapels for offerings and rituals. Adopted a less elaborate version of mummification to preserve bodies.
Key Gods	• Apedemak (Nubian war god) • Amun (chief deity) • Isis • Osiris (god of the underworld) • Khonsu (moon god) • Sebiumeker (supreme Nubian god of fertility and procreation) • Arensnuphis (the good companion) • Mandulis (Kushite form of the Egyptian god, Horus)

YORUBA RELIGION

Origin	Yoruba religion (Isese or Ifa) began in 1000 BCE in the consolidation of city-states like Ile-Ife and included the worship of Olodumare/Olorun (Supreme God), ancestors, and numerous deities known as Orishas.
Spread & Chronology	• Beliefs and practices organically formed from the people's long history as a result of Mesolithic populations with Ile-Ife as a crucial early city-state and religious center. • Spread and Evolution: Practices were shaped by sociopolitical changes of evolving empires and city-states. Resultantly, the Ife Empire, a flourishing center of trade and craft, laid the foundation for subsequent kingdoms like Oyo. • Dissemination to the Americas (18th Century): The slave trade of thousands of Yoruba people across the Atlantic to the Americas influenced Afro-Atlantic religions like Santería and Candomblé, syncretizing the Orisha with Catholic saints. • Resurgence (late 20th and 21st centuries): People of Yoruba descent rediscover and revitalize their ancestral faith in Yoruba religion.
Contradictions	• Oral Tradition: The most significant factor was the transmission of knowledge through storytelling, which naturally led to differing accounts of the same gods or events. • Syncretism and Adaptation: Incorporation of aspects from external religions, particularly Islam and Christianity, has caused variations in existing traditions.
Errors & Misconceptions	• Some scholars, particularly colonialists, dismissed and misinterpreted variations as errors or evidence of primitive thinking, failing to recognize the rich and the intricate nature of oral traditions. • A lack of understanding of Yoruba cosmology can lead to incorrect assumptions about the relationships between deities and the divine, such as a mistaken notion that the Supreme Being is distant or less involved than a belief in numerous deities might suggest.
Central Tenets	• Belief in a pantheon of deities (Orishas) who act as intermediaries between humans and Olodumare. They are responsible for various aspects of nature and human life, and are venerated through offerings, prayers, and rituals. • Respect for ancestors and Iwa Pele (good/gentle character) is considered essential for strengthening one's Ori (inner head) and maintaining a positive connection with the spiritual realm. • When people die, they are believed to transition from the physical world (Aiye) to the spiritual world (Orun). • Individuals can be reincarnated into their family lineage after a good death, and their arrival was often marked by a child whom exhibited physical or mental similarities. • Divination is through the Ifá system, performed by Babalawo (father of mysteries) or high priest of the Ifá divination system. • The use of baptisms for spiritual cleansing
Key Gods	• Olodumare (the supreme creator god) • Olorun (the sky god and creator) • Orishas such as Obatala (the divine creator of humans) • Oshun (river goddess)

VODUN (VOODOO) RELIGION

Origin	Vodun was originally a West and Central African belief among the Fon people of Benin, formerly the Dahomey Kingdom. It involved animism (the belief that spirits inhabit all things), ancestral worship, and reverence for spirits associated with natural phenomena beginning around the pre-16th Century.
Spread & Chronology	• Syncretism among neighboring tribes and kingdoms took place between the 16th and 19th Centuries. • The slave trading of millions of West Africans to the Americas. • In colonies like Haiti, the acceptance of dark arts and occult magic among enslaved Africans crippled Western conversion attempts. • Blending of traditional Vodun beliefs with Catholic practices and symbolism, resulting in Haitian Vodou. For example, the West African spirit, Legba, who opens pathways, became associated with the Catholic Saint Peter. • The Haitian Revolution (1791) was partly energized and organized by Vodou priests and priestesses, solidifying the religion and forming the independent nation of Haiti.
Common Misconceptions & Contradictions	• Vodun is seen as a magical act rather than a legitimate religion. • Voodoo dolls are mistaken for tools of torture rather than for benevolent purposes to appeal to the spirits. • The practice is always associated with works of evil, even though the religion teaches that energy is amoral, and it can be used to protect against evil. • Mistaken for performing human sacrifices to complete dark rituals. While blood sacrifice (typically of animals) is central to the faith, human sacrifice is a false and harmful stereotype that practitioners deny. • Vodun has some overlap with witchcraft, but they are distinct things because Vodun consists of a pantheon of spirits, organized community structures, and a focus on communal aspects and ancestral worship.
Central Tenets	• Belief in a distant creator god, Bondye • Belief in a complex system of spirits (Loa) whom are powerful intermediaries capable of possessing and influencing humans • Deceased family members and ancestors are honored and revered. • Use of magic or sorcery by individuals known as boko, who work with malevolent spirits to cause harm where desired. • Trance states are common practices to connect with and to appease the spirits.
Key Gods	• Bondye (The Supreme God) • Loa/ Lwa (Spiritual intermediaries)

DOGON RELIGION

The Dogon tribe, which had roots tracing back to the Nile Valley in ancient Egypt, had a perpetual history of migration between Libya and Mauritania before eventually settling in the rocky Bandiagara Escarpment in Mali in order to escape religious persecution. Most of religious persecution consisted of jihads and conquests from dominant African Muslim communities (Mali Empire, Moors, Mossi, etc.) from the 10th to the 13th Century, Islamization efforts from Arabs through solidified caliphates, and French colonization in the late 19th Century. The Dogon is one of the few tribes that maintained its African identity, language, tradition, and culture despite the odds.

Origin	Dogon religion originated as a traditional spiritual system in Mali that centered on ancestor worship and a complex creation myth, involving the supreme creator god, Amma, and the Nommo – water spirits who brought knowledge to humans. Veneration of the dead was celebrated through rituals, including the masked Dama dance. Their spiritual leaders are known as Hogons, and their traditions are full of complex oral traditions, stories, dances, and balancing rituals.
Spread	• The cliffs offered natural defenses against slave traders and raiders, allowing the Dogon to preserve their traditional religious beliefs and practices, which were viewed as "pagan" by their persecutors. Such traditions were shared with passing traders and friendly communities. • The Dogon culture mesmerized the world with collectible masks and sculptures, which are still in demand today.
Chronology	• Pre-Cliffs Era: Likely living on the plains, the religion developed through oral traditions and rituals centered on the creator Amma and ancestor veneration. • Persecution and Migration (14th-16th Centuries): Jihads and raids by dominant Muslim communities forced the Dogon to abandon ancestral villages and flee to the Bandiagara cliffs. • French Colonial Era (19th century): The French ended the raids and attacks, offering a period of relative safety and stability. • Modern Period (late 20th century): Islamic and Christian influence significantly increased among the Dogon, who still stood by their traditional and religious practices. The Dogon continue to practice their rich, complex religious traditions, with rituals and ceremonies such as the Binou and Dama, which involve masked performances and sacrifices.
Contradictions & Errors	• Male Fertility vs. Female Procreation: The Dama ceremony emphasizes male power and symbolic fertility; however, biological procreation is the exclusive domain of women, creating a contradictory tension between the ritual ideals of male ascendancy and the biological reality of creation. • Masks and Sacredness: Masks are used in ceremonies like the Dama ceremony to invoke spiritual power. Yet, the sacred aspects of these rituals and dances are hidden from outsiders, creating a contradiction between the public exhibition of the masks and the private, sacred nature of the underlying spiritual practices. • Secrecy and Financial Needs: Dogon healers are expected to maintain the confidentiality of their healing knowledge, which can create a contradiction with their need for financial compensation for their work. They might hoard their secrets to protect their clients from others and their businesses, even though they also operate for the public good.

	• Facts vs. Fantasy: The rich and intricate nature of Dogon mythology and culture has different interpretations of their origins and knowledge, causing their lore to appear contradictory or fictional.
Mythical Aspects	• A central belief is the myth of the supreme creator god Amma, who designed the universe with 266 signs, and his divine offspring, Nommo (the primordial twins).
Central Tenets	• Belief in a supreme creator god (Amma) and the Nommo ancestral spirits, considered to be amphibious water spirits created by Amma to bring order • Balance and the pairing of complementary opposites, particularly the masculine and feminine principles • Belief in interconnected spiritual forces and ancestral spirits that shape the world and human destiny • Astronomical knowledge referenced to Sirius and Isis (Egyptian)
Key Gods	• Amma (supreme creator god) • Nommo (son of Amma, a prominent water spirit) • Lebe (spirit that embodies the Earth and its life-giving properties) • Yurugu (third subordinate deity created by Amma, representing fallen man)

Ultimately, some general characteristics of African traditional religions include:

- **Supreme Beings and Animistic Nature**: Belief in a Supreme God alongside a pantheon of lesser deities and spirits in natural objects such as trees and rivers.
- **Divination**: Guidance is sought from the divine realm regarding decisions, problems, and future understanding (i.e., prophecies, omens, etc.).
- **Community Centered**: The indigenous faiths are deeply integrated into community life with rituals and beliefs that maintain social harmony and spiritual well-being.
- **Pragmatism**: African religions are primarily focused on gaining tangible benefits in the secular world, incorporating spiritual health, wealth, and posterity.
- **Oral Traditions**: Knowledge and practices are primarily transmitted through oral traditions, stories, songs, and proverbs rather than written scriptures.
- **Ancestor Veneration**: Deceased ancestors are revered and are believed to influence the living, requiring appeasement and offerings for goodwill.

In African traditional religions, slavery was generally allowed, even though it varied in forms based on culture and priest influence. For instance, there were domestic systems where captives of war were integrated into families, there was chattel slavery where slaves made up the cheap labor force in times of economic hardship, there was voluntary servitude under religious commitment, and there were slaves under hereditary status. The condition and the treatment of slaves were functions of tribe, penalty, views of humans as property, level of offense, and kinship.

No matter the perspective, the priests were always the common denominator in spreading religious doctrines, consistently imposing bridges between devotees and objects of their worship and controlling the totality of society. Once again, the key to a religion's success is simply creating an explanation – not necessarily the best, the most factually accurate, the most historical, or the most truthful – riddled with belief that the willfully ignorant humans can subscribe to.

Em Hotep!

ON ZOROASTRIANISM

ANKH WADJA SENEB | ARTICLE NO: 004

Function: The Awareness of Control Mechanisms
Subject(s): Ancient Persian Beliefs
Position: Part 3 – Breaking Societal Controls
Theme: Dealing with Religions, Cults, & Atheism | Scene 4

Peace to the High Power! Peace to the Living Universe! Peace to all Finite Living Beings! Peace to All Things – seen and unseen! For my spirit is with me, my image is with me, and my purpose is with me. For those with knowledge understand that the mechanisms behind societal controls can only flourish when consciousness, awareness, vibration, and rationality are minimized and when willful ignorance, fear, indoctrination, and subjugating forces are maximized.

Recall that the key to a religion's success is simply creating an explanation – not necessarily the best, the most factually accurate, the most historical, or the most truthful – riddled with belief that the willfully ignorant humans can subscribe to. Such was so with Zoroastrianism, which was fabricated by a priest named Zarathustra, whom rejected the Iranian polytheistic belief systems, whom despised the repressive class structures, and whom resented princes and other priests with monopolies of power and control over commoners. Zarathustra faced significant resistance from the local religious establishment, and initially, he found it hard to attract followers, until the Achaemenid Empire emerged. The Achaemenid kings were devout Zoroastrians who ruled in accordance with the Zoroastrian law of Asha, giving the priest, Zarathustra, exactly what he longed for.

Origin	• Zoroastrianism is an ancient monotheistic religion founded by the prophet Zarathustra (Zoroaster) in ancient Persia, who supposedly received visions of a supreme being, Ahura Mazda.
Spread	• Zoroastrianism was practiced widely during the Achaemenid (under Cyrus the Great), Parthian, and Sasanian empires. • Spread through trade routes extending into Central Asia and East Asia • Arrived in India through refugees from Persia
Chronology	• <u>6th Century BCE</u>: Zarathustra established the religion in Persia (now Iran). • <u>Approximately 250 BCE</u>: The Vendidad, a Zoroastrian text, was written during the Parthian Empire. • <u>Sasanian Period (3rd Century CE Onwards)</u>: Formal codification of its doctrines. • <u>6th Century CE</u>: The Avesta, the collection of the religion's sacred scriptures, was finally written down. • <u>7th Century CE</u>: The fall of the Sasanian Empire and subsequent Arab conquest led to a severe decline in Zoroastrianism in Iran.
Contradictions and Errors	• <u>Misinterpretation of Fire</u>: Zoroastrians do not worship fire; instead, they revere fire as a sacred symbol of purity and Ahura Mazda. • <u>Varying Interpretations of Texts</u>: Zoroastrianism's oral nature for centuries and the later written compilation of texts led to variations in interpretation and practice

Central Tenets	• Embraces monotheism, proclaiming the existence of a benevolent supreme creator, Ahura Mazda (the wise lord) • Embraces cosmic dualism, presented as a cosmic struggle between Ahura Mazda and Angra Mainyu (the destructive Spirit), representing good and evil. • Based on moral responsibility and free will • Adherents strive for Asha (truth) against Druj (falsehood) as a guiding principle for Good Thoughts (Humata), Good Words (Hukhta), and Good Deeds (Hvarsta) to align with the divine order. • Belief in individual judgment after death based on one's actions and an ultimate, universal restoration of worldly goodness. • Believers are guided by spiritual beings called Fravashi, who act as guardians and guides throughout life. • Zoroastrianism is related to the early Vedic religion of India, which later grew into modern Hinduism. Its major scripture is called the Avesta and contains hymns just like the Vedas in India.
Key Gods	• Ahura Mazda (benevolent supreme creator) • Angra Mainyu/ Ahriman (spirit of evil, chaos, and darkness) • Amesha Spentas (Six "Holy Immortals") • Yazatas (Other divine beings or spirits who are worthy of worship), such as Mithra (god of contracts, covenants, and truth), Anahita (goddess associated with fertility, wisdom, and water), Haoma (god of health, strength, and enlightenment), and Atar (divine personification of fire)

Zoroastrianism proposes that souls cross the Chinvat Bridge after death (an idea shaping later Abrahamic religions), where good and evil deeds are weighed. Individuals judged with net-weighted good deeds go to Garothman (Heaven) – a realm of light and joy in the company of Ahura Mazda. On the other hand, souls weighted primarily with evil deeds are cast into the Druj-demana (Hell) – a place of eternal darkness and torment. Souls with an equal mixture of good and bad deeds go to Hamistagan (Purgatory) – a place of neither extreme suffering nor joy, awaiting a final universal judgment. During Frashokereti (the end of time), a future messiah, the Saoshyant, will somehow bring about a universal judgment. At this point, even souls in Hell will be liberated, and Angra Mainyu (the evil spirit) will be destroyed, leaving everyone to live in peace and harmony.

Just like the religions before it, Zoroastrianism did not advocate for the abolition of slavery; instead, it regulated slavery within the existing social structures. The legal documents from the Sasanian period, such as the Mādayān, provide detailed examples of how slaves were handled within the legal system. Historical Zoroastrian societies treated slaves as property, where masters were permitted to sell, to lease, to gift, or to use slaves as securities for loans or other collateral guarantees. Slaves could be jointly owned, had no ownership over their earnings, and could be transferred between owners according to legal formulas in the Sasanian law books. Although Zoroastrian law recognized slaves with dual status – a person and a possession – their treatment often leaned towards being a commodity.

Once again, the key to a religion's success is simply creating an explanation – not necessarily the best, the most factually accurate, the most historical, or the most truthful – riddled with belief that the willfully ignorant humans can subscribe to.

Em Hotep!

ON HINDUISM

ANKH WADJA SENEB | ARTICLE NO: 005

Function: The Awareness of Control Mechanisms
Subject(s): Ancient Vedic Religions as a Precursor
Position: Part 3 – Breaking Societal Controls
Theme: Dealing with Religions, Cults, & Atheism | Scene 5

ARTICLE NO: 005 – ON HINDUISM

Peace to the High Power! Peace to the Living Universe! Peace to all Finite Living Beings! Peace to All Things – seen and unseen! For my spirit is with me, my image is with me, and my purpose is with me. For those with knowledge understand that the mechanisms behind societal controls can only flourish when consciousness, awareness, vibration, and rationality are minimized and when willful ignorance, fear, indoctrination, and subjugating forces are maximized.

Recall that the key to a religion's success is simply creating an explanation – not necessarily the best, the most factually accurate, the most historical, or the most truthful – riddled with belief that the willfully ignorant humans can subscribe to, and the Asian religions (Hinduism, Buddhism, Sikhism, and Jainism) are no different. Asian religions generally encompass the vast diversity of spiritual and cultural practices formulated through the Veda by priests (puja) – always a common denominator in the creation of a religious doctrine.

Since the intent of this article is to explore how religious doctrines are invented, what the religious doctrines actually are, and how religious doctrines spread briefly, we will only focus on the most popular and arguably the oldest ancient Asian religion – Hinduism. The emergence of Hinduism centered on the Vedas, which were orally compiled and transmitted by migrant Aryans whom worshipped the main Vedic gods of Indra, Agni, and Surya from 1500 to 500 BCE in modern-day Afghanistan and Punjab. Unlike many other major religions, Hinduism lacks a specific historical founder with origins traced back to Indo-Aryan animism in the Indus River Valley around 7000-600 BCE. In other words, we have a case where subscribers are following a religion without even knowing where it came from. Not to mention, their sacred texts are a compilation of various works written by many different authors over thousands of years.

As the Aryans migrated into the Gangetic plain, they began to syncretize, to fuse, and to adopt non-Aryan and non-Vedic traditions into their own system, such as Krishna who was a Vrishni deity and Buddhist tenets from the Sramana tradition. Later, Hindu pujas would introduce new texts and teachings under the Gupta emperors, whom viewed Hinduism as a unifying religion – even promoting it in educational systems and giving land to brahmins. The new texts brought on a new pantheon called the Puranas, and this Puranic Hinduism is what modern Hinduism developed from, which explains why Indra, Agni, and the Maruts are no longer worshipped in favor of Vishnu, Shiva, and Shakti.

In the centuries to follow, personal devotion (bhakti) to these newly created gods and goddesses developed, where sacrifices were abandoned (although they continue in Shaktism) and vernacular songs began to be written. Prior to this, there were only mantras in Sanskrit as opposed to bhajans and kirtans. Local deities were fused with existing deities, such as Khandoba from Maharashtra associated with Shiva, and Bathukamma from Telangana becoming Shakti. Once again, we see a case where a religion steadily changes or evolves into another religious form through syncretism.

Origin	The Indus Valley Civilization is considered a significant precursor to Hinduism, sharing religious beliefs tied to nature, fertility symbols, and ritual purification. Archaeological evidence includes the worship of stones and animals as well as the findings of figures potentially resembling later Hindu deities like Shiva. Subsequently, Hinduism evolved directly from the Vedic Period with the composition of the Vedas and ritualistic practices of ancestral worship and sacrifices.
Spread	• Sanskritization, where local customs and beliefs were integrated into the broader Sanskritic Hindu tradition to connect diverse regional manifestations. • Trade route networks, such as the Silk Roads, facilitated the spread of Hindu ideas, art, and culture beyond the Indian subcontinent. • Emperors and priests
Chronology	• <u>Vedic Period</u>: The composition of the Vedas and the establishment of ritualistic traditions. • <u>Epic & Classical Periods (500 BCE–500 CE)</u>: Synthesis of Vedic and Harappan cultures, development of epics and philosophical schools, and the emergence of major deities. • <u>Medieval Period (500–1500 CE)</u>: Rise of the Bhakti Movement, increased importance of vernacular literature, and the continued spread of Hinduism to Southeast Asia.
Contradictions and Errors	• Ancient texts like the Vedas suggest a single, formless Supreme Being, yet many Hindu festivals feature extensive idol worship of various deities. • Different schools of thought within Hinduism hold opposing views on the existence of gods, with some emphasizing a single supreme reality and others focusing on numerous deities. • Some verses in Hindu scriptures are symbolic and are open to interpretations, while others might be taken literally, leading to perceived contradictions when viewed through different lenses. • Hinduism's nature as an evolving culture rather than a fixed dogma means that different philosophical perspectives have developed, sometimes in contrast to each other. • Some older Hindu scriptures contain descriptions of the cosmos, the sun, and the earth that are contradicted by modern science.
Central Tenets	• It was not started by any single individual, and its origins cannot be traced back to any particular historical period. • Hinduism is regarded as a way of life, not just a religion, with a vast collection of traditions and practices, encompassing concepts, such as dharma (duty), atman (individual soul), karma (action and consequence), samsara (rebirth), and moksha (liberation).
Key Gods	• A pantheon of gods and goddesses, with a concept of an ultimate reality (Brahman) that is the source of all existence. • Shakti is the supreme goddess, the divine mother, and a manifestation of power. • The Trimurti (Three principal forms of Brahman): Brahma (creator of the universe), Vishnu (preserver and protector of the universe), and Shiva (destroyer, whose destruction leads to re-creation) • Other deities, such as Ganesha and Lakshmi, are worshipped as manifestations of Brahman.

Asianic religions generally do not account for rewards in a paradise and a purgatory, but rather they view the afterlife as a continuous cycle of rebirth (samsara), influenced by karma. The ultimate goal is to escape this cycle through spiritual liberation, with different paths for each religion, such as Moksha in Hinduism, Nirvana in Buddhism, and divine union in Sikhism.

Slavery and the treatment of enslaved people varied significantly across Asianic religions. As far as Hinduism, the Rigveda, an early Hindu text, mentions Aryans enslaving indigenous peoples and labeling them dasa (slave) / dasi (devoted servant). Based on the narrations, these slaves were often treated as property, given as gifts and/or debt repayments.

Once again, the key to a religion's success is simply creating an explanation – not necessarily the best, the most factually accurate, the most historical, or the most truthful – riddled with belief that the willfully ignorant humans can subscribe to.

Em Hotep!

DISMANTLING JUDEO-CHRISTIANITY

ANKH WADJA SENEB | ARTICLE NO: 006

Function: The Awareness of Control Mechanisms
Subject(s): Abrahamic Religions, Old Testament, Tanakh, Yahweh
Position: Part 3 – Breaking Societal Controls
Theme: Dealing with Religions, Cults, & Atheism | Scene 6 | Part 1

ARTICLE NO: 006 – DISMANTLING JUDEO-CHRISTIANITY (PT 1)

Peace to the High Power! Peace to the Living Universe! Peace to all Finite Living Beings! Peace to All Things – seen and unseen! For my spirit is with me, my image is with me, and my purpose is with me. For those with knowledge understand that the mechanisms behind societal controls can only flourish when consciousness, awareness, vibration, and rationality are minimized and when willful ignorance, fear, indoctrination, and subjugating forces are maximized.

Recall that the key to a religion's success is simply creating an explanation – not necessarily the best, the most factually accurate, the most historical, or the most truthful – riddled with belief that the willfully ignorant humans can subscribe to, and Judaism is not an exception.

A comprehensive assessment of Judaism is beyond the scope of this article; however, the poor alignment between the Jewish narrative/sources and the historical record is sufficient to illustrate the delusions of Judaism.

The Jewish scripture rests upon the assumption that the books of the Tanakh were written close to the events in the Late Bronze Age and Early Iron Age, purportedly between 1200 BCE and 800 BCE, and that, by their very existence, these scriptures indicate that Judaism had emerged in the southern Levant by this time period. This assumption is completely false. Even if a person was to take the supposed events described in the Old Testament at face value, every single book of the Tanakh that purports to describe them was written hundreds of years <u>after</u> the alleged events. This is no basis for any sort of historical grounding.

The composition dates of the books contained within the Tanakh are highly disputed, and the alleged dates of events are complete conjecture, as they almost certainly never happened. The two most plausible composition theories include the Documentary Theory, which generally asserts that scholars began compiling these texts around the 6th century BCE before gradually evolving down to the Hellenistic era (*c.* 323 BCE – 30 BCE), and the Biblical Minimalist Theory, which holds that there is really no substantial evidence to suggest that any of these books were broadly composed until the Hellenistic era. The chronology of each book is provided below.

First Part of the Tanakh: Torah (5 Books)		
Name of Book	Dates of Alleged Events	Composition Date (Approx.)
Bereshit/Genesis	Creation to 1500 BCE	600 BCE (final 300 BCE)
Shemot/Exodus	1250 BCE	600 BCE (final 300 BCE)
Vayikra/Leviticus	1250 BCE	600 BCE (final 300 BCE)
Bamidbar/Numbers	1250 BCE	600 BCE (final 300 BCE)
Devarim/Deuteronomy	1250 BCE	600 BCE (final 300 BCE)

Second Part of the Tanakh: Neviim (8 Books)		
Name of Book	Dates of Alleged Events	Composition Date (Approx.)
Yehoshua/Joshua	1200 BCE – 1150 BCE	550 BCE (final 250 BCE)
Shoftim/Judges	1150 BCE – 950 BCE	700 BCE (final disputed)
Shmuel/1 and 2 Samuel	950 BCE – 900 BCE	700 BCE (final disputed)
Melachim/1 and 2 Kings	900 BCE – 560 BCE	550 BCE (final 300 BCE)
Yeshayahu/Isaiah	750 BCE – 550 BCE	500 BCE (final 300 BCE)
Yirmiyahu/Jeremiah	650 BCE – 550 BCE	450 BCE (final 150 BCE)
Yechezkel/Ezekiel	595 BCE – 575 BCE	500 BCE (final 200 BCE)
Trei Asar	800 BCE – 400 BCE	350 BCE (final 120 BCE)

For clarification, Trei Asar effectively means "The Twelve" and contains the books of Hosea, Joel, Amos, Obadiah, Jonah, Micah, Nahum, Habakkuk, Zephaniah, Haggai, Zechariah, and Malachi.

Third Part of the Tanakh: Ketuvim (11 Books)		
Name of Book	Dates of Alleged Events	Composition Date (Approx.)
Tehillim/Psalms	Psalms – No Specific Date	over time (final 150 BCE)
Mishlei/Proverbs	Proverbs – No Specific Date	over time (final 150 BCE)
Iyov/Job	Reflective – No Specific Date	400 BCE (final 200 BCE)
Shir HaShirim/Song of Songs	Poems – No Specific Date	400 BCE (final 200 BCE)
Rut/Ruth	Loosely Around 1050 BCE	400 BCE (final 200 BCE)
Eicha/Lamentations	586 Babylonian Captivity	Possibly 550 BCE
Kohelet/Ecclesiastes	Reflective – No Specific Date	400 BCE (final 200 BCE)
Esther/Esther	480 BCE	350 BCE (final 100 BCE)
Daniyel/Daniel	500 BCE	200 BCE (final 150 BCE)
Ezra-Nehemiah	539 BCE – 500 BCE	350 BCE (final 200 BCE)
Divrei HaYamim/1 and 2	1100 BCE – 500 BCE	350 BCE (final 200 BCE)

The earliest surviving copies of books of the Torah only date to the middle of the 3rd century BCE. This is a big problem when comparing the dates of the alleged events above. In the case of many parts of the Tanakh, the earliest fragments of manuscripts come from the Dead Sea Scrolls, which date roughly between 250 BCE and 150 BCE, with no manuscript or papyrus prior to 250 BCE. Outside of the Dead Sea Scrolls, historical findings include the Ketef Hinnom Scrolls and the writings of Hecateus of Abdera.

The Ketef Hinnom Scrolls consist of two small amulet scrolls dating roughly between 650 BCE and 600 BCE. These silver scrolls were found at Ketef Hinnom in 1979, and they contain a fragment of the book of Numbers (verses 24–26). This seems to indicate that this part of the Torah was being compiled by the end of the 7th century BCE; however, the passage is part of the 'Priestly Blessing' section, and the fact that this blessing existed in the late seventh century BCE does not prove that much of the Tanakh had been written at all by this time.

The writings of Hecateus of Abdera have also been used to help to date the composition of sections of the Tanakh. Hecateus of Abdera lived between 350 BCE and 300 BCE, and none of Hecateus' original writings have survived from antiquity; however, large amounts of references to his work are made in the writings of other Greek and Roman writers whose books have survived. This is also important because it indicates that some parts of the Tanakh had been written by the late fourth century BCE and were distributed enough by then that learned Greeks in northern Greece were familiar with elements of the books of Genesis and Exodus.

Clearly, the books of the Tanakh/Old Testament were written hundreds of years later than the Jewish narrative contends, including edits and changes. By the time a finished version of these texts was decided upon, it was nearly a thousand years after the alleged events being described. For example, the fictitious stories of the book of Exodus, which were set around 1250 BCE, were still being edited around 350 BCE or so. Moreover, there is no real historical evidence of any kind to substantiate the claims made in these books.

When it comes to the Ketuvim, the third and final section of the Tanakh, there is no denying that they were written in a much later period. The book of Esther, for instance, mentions Xerxes, whom was the ruler of the Persian Empire from 486 BCE to 465 BCE. Many of these texts were products of either the era of the Persian Empire (c. 550 BCE – 330 BCE) or the Hellenistic era in the Eastern Mediterranean (c. 330 BCE – 30 BCE). They were not products of the Late Bronze Age and Early Iron Age (c. 1200 BCE – 800 BCE), contrary to popular belief.

There is no clear history of the Jewish people from the time of Moses and the Israelites' flight out of Egypt in the Late Bronze Age (around 1300 BCE to 1200 BCE) to the destruction of the Temple of Jerusalem by the Babylonians around 586 BCE, as well as the subsequent Babylonian Captivity. For instance, the narrative of the Torah (the first part of the Tanakh) and the Neviim (the second part of the Tanakh) cover hundreds of years of Jewish history when the Israelites allegedly established their kingdom in the Levant, waged wars against their neighbors similar to the Canaanites, Moabites, and Edomites – later splitting into two different kingdoms. The problem with all of this is that this was a Dark Age of ancient history about which little can be verified.

The period of history between roughly 1600 BCE and 1200 BCE is well documented in the Eastern Mediterranean and Levant because there were highly advanced cultures in the Near East at this time, such as New Kingdom Egypt, the Hittite Empire, and the Minoans. Nowhere in the tens of thousands of letters and inscriptions that have been dated from this period is there any mention or indication of Israelites as a distinct culture group or as worshippers of Yahweh/YHWH.

Instead of new states emerging in the period that followed, the Near East experienced a seismic collapse between 1300 BCE and 1100 BCE when virtually all of the major empires and civilizations within the region were overrun by foreign invaders such as 'the Sea People'. Bear in mind that no one knows where the Sea People came from, despite being a prominent group at the time. Also, it is highly unlikely that accumulated knowledge would have survived from the Late Bronze Age of the Israelite kingdom to when the Tanakh was written.

The worst of this Dark Age occurred between 1150 BCE and 900 BCE, which is coincidentally the exact period claimed to be the golden age of the Kingdom of Israel. This makes no sense. For this to happen, the Israelite kingdom would have had to outdo every power in the Near East. When the Dark Age gave way to the Early Iron Age with a gradual societal resurgence, there was no sudden emergence of Israelite kingdoms in the Levant. The groups that emerged in the Levant during this time as the pre-eminent political, economic, and military powers were clearly the Phoenicians and the Canaanites. There is no evidence at all for the alleged Kingdoms of Israel, as it is described in the second part of the Tanakh, the Neviim.

The Jewish narrative also suggests that Judaism emerged when the world was gradually moving away from polytheism to monotheism and that Judaism was simply ahead of its time in the correct worship of one god. This is categorically false, especially since there were examples of monotheism prior to the alleged emergence of Judaism, and the Ancient Mediterranean and the Near East remained completely rooted in polytheism. Firstly, Zoroastrianism was solely monotheistic, with all other divinities reduced to the status of angels. Secondly, Atenism was a kind of monotheism that developed in New Kingdom Egypt by Pharaoh Akhenaten, and that involved the worship of the sun disk – Aten.

Lastly, we know from tangible historical and archaeological evidence that polytheism broadly prevailed in the Levant at the time that Judaism was alleged to be emerging here between 1200 BCE and 900 BCE. Among the Canaanites and the Phoenicians, the two most attested historical groups in the Levant in the Late Bronze Age and Early Iron Age, gods and goddesses such as El (the paramount god), Asherah (the chief goddess), Baal (a kind of storm god or god of war), Mot (deity of death), and Yamm (the god of the sea) were worshipped. This polytheistic system resembled earlier systems in Mesopotamia and Egypt and later ones amongst the Greeks and Romans. In fact, there is clear evidence for the worship of these other Western Semitic deities in the southern Levant and even among the Jewish people. As an onomastic study on *Baal worship in Early Israel*, Yigal Levin indicates that the word 'Baal' appears over and over again in both the Tanakh and in ancient place-names in the Jewish lands. For instance, in Samuel 5:20, "[King] David went to Baal Perazim, and there he defeated them. He said, 'As water breaks out, the Lord has broken out against my enemies before me.' So that place was called Baal Perazim". The inference is of the King of the Israelites worshipping Baal in some way. Elsewhere in 2 Samuel 13:23, the scripture states that "it came to pass after two full years, that Absalom had sheep-shearers in Baal-Hazor, which is beside Ephraim". Why were these supposed Early Iron Age adherents of Judaism living in places named after the Canaanite god of storms unless they worshipped this deity?

There is also a fundamental conflict in the Tanakh over the issue of the alleged Jewish people worshipping the gods of the Canaanites. In Judges 2: 11–13, for instance, it states, "Then the Israelites did evil in the eyes of the Lord and served the Baals. They forsook the Lord, the God of their ancestors, who had brought them out of Egypt. They followed and worshiped various gods of the peoples around them. They aroused the Lord's anger because they forsook him and served Baal and the Ashtoreths". There is even strong evidence suggesting that the Jewish belief in a single deity named Yahweh evolved gradually out of the Canaanite worship of deities like Baal and El, as reflected in the tensions inherent in the Tanakh from approximately 1000 BCE –500 BCE and the Kuntillet 'Ajrud inscription (8th century BCE) discovered in northern Sinai that reads: "I bless you by Yahweh of Teman and his Asherah". This naturally leads to three (3) difficult questions for the Jewish scripture: (i) When exactly was the Tanakh written?, (ii) Where did the Yahweh come from?, and (iii) Why does the evidence indicate that the monotheistic Yahweh was invented by shapeshifting and fusing attributes of polytheistic gods?

Having already established huge composition and dating issues when it comes to the Jewish Tanakh (Christian Old Testament), let's look at some of the content within the Tanakh. We ask the reader to consult other sources for a complete debunk of every single myth and falsehood of the Tanakh; however, we will examine a couple of clear case studies that illustrate errancy and willful ignorance of the Jewish narrative.

Case Study 1 – Bereshit/Genesis

The book of Genesis/Bereshit contains the following elements: (i) a god creating the world in six days out of primordial chaos and then resting on the seventh day, (ii) Adam and Eve and the Garden of Eden, (iii) the story of Cain and Abel, (iv) the tale of Noah and the Great Flood, and (v) the details of Abraham and his descendants.

While the Creation myth, the tale of Adam and Eve, and the Great Flood usually garner a lot of attention, surely the most outlandish section of Genesis is actually in the second half of the book, when we get to the genealogical sections detailing the descendants of Adam as follows:

"When Adam had lived 130 years, he had a son in his own likeness, in his own image; and he named him Seth. After Seth was born, Adam lived 800 years and had other sons and daughters. Altogether, Adam lived a total of 930 years, and then he died. When Seth had lived 105 years, he became the father of Enosh. After he became the father of Enosh, Seth lived 807 years and had other sons and daughters. Altogether, Seth lived a total of 912 years, and then he died. When Enosh had lived 90 years, he became the father of Kenan. After he became the father of Kenan, Enosh lived 815 years and had other sons and daughters. Altogether, Enosh lived a total of 905 years, and then he died. When Kenan had lived 70 years, he became the father of Mahalalel. After he became the father of Mahalalel, Kenan lived 840 years and had other sons and daughters. Altogether, Kenan lived a total of 910 years, and then he died" (Genesis 5:3–14)

Not sure how anyone can justify these ages, knowing that the ancient world was ravaged by war, was limited in defense against natural disasters, and was limited in medical/scientific knowledge.

Other sections of Genesis can be critiqued as simply being reflective of other ancient religions and mythological tales. They are not at all unique to Judaism. For instance, the story of a Great Flood is found in other ancient mythological and literary traditions from Mesopotamia all the way east to China, as well as further afield around the ancient world, as follows:

- The *Epic of Gilgamesh*, which was written down in Mesopotamia around 1300 BCE, has been tied to Sumerian clay tablets that first emerged around 2100 BCE. Thus, the tale of Noah, the Great Flood, and the Ark was really just derived from mythological systems further east in Mesopotamia.
- Yu the Great, the fabled founder of the legendary Xia Dynasty that ruled over China between 2050 BCE and 1600 BCE, supposedly defeated the Great Flood that was ravaging China by employing huge armies of men to deepen the country's rivers and to dig out dykes and canals.
- Even from such obscure places as the Philippines, we find flood myths similar to those found in Genesis. According to the myth, a drought in the world led people to begin digging for the soul of a great river. Eventually, they struck a great spring. When this happened, it angered the god of the rivers so much that the god caused violent rains, flooding the earth in the process. Soon, the rivers overflowed, and all of humanity was wiped out. Only two people survived, Wigan and Bugan, who were responsible for repopulating the world in a story that is very similar to Noah and the Ark.

Anthropologists and geologists such as David Montgomery believe that these tales of a mythical Great Flood in the ancient past were possibly cultural memories passed down from Neolithic man of the floodwaters left in large parts of the world when the last ice age ended around 12,000 years ago. The story of Noah and the Great Flood was just a late instance. It is not a piece of history, and alarming contradictions occur in the book of Genesis directly. In Genesis 1:25–27, as an example, it states the following: "God made the wild animals according to their kinds, the livestock according to their kinds, and all the creatures that move along the ground according to their kinds. And God saw that it was good. Then God said, 'Let us make mankind in our image, in our likeness, so that they may rule over the fish in the sea and the birds in the sky, over the livestock and all the wild animals, and over all the creatures that move along the ground.' So, God created mankind in his own image, in the image of God he created them; male and female he created them". However, in Genesis 2:18–20, we are then told that after he had created Adam, "The Lord God said, 'It is not good for the man to be alone. I will make a helper suitable for him.' Now the Lord God had formed out of the ground all the wild animals and all the birds in the sky. He brought them to the man to see what he would name them; and whatever the man called each living creature, that was its name. So, the man gave names to all the livestock, the birds in the sky, and all the wild animals." So, in Genesis 1, this god makes the animals and then quickly makes mankind, but in Genesis 2, this god has made mankind and then decides that he needs to make the animals to keep mankind company.

Case Study 2 – Shemot/Exodus

The Jewish narrative makes the following claims:

- The Pharaoh of Egypt mentioned in Exodus is Ramesses II, said to have ruled Egypt between c. 1279 BCE and c. 1213 BCE.
- The Egyptians had been engaged in conquering parts of the Levant going back to the 15th Century BCE under rulers like Thutmose III, so it makes sense that they would have enslaved groups like the Israelites and would have brought these groups to Egypt to build their great temples and mausoleums forcibly.
- A Kingdom of Israel and a Kingdom of Judah emerged at various points in the southern Levant during the Early Iron Age, so it makes sense that the Israelites would have returned from enslavement in Egypt to establish their own kingdom around this time.

The reality, though, is that there is not a single shred of historical evidence (inscriptions, hieroglyphics, cave paintings, scrolls, pyramid engravings, etc.) to support any of the claims above. Rather, the evidence indicates that the story of Exodus was a parable designed to mimic the experience of conquest, enslavement, exile, and return of a certain sect of the Jewish people in the sixth century BCE, when the story found in the Book of Exodus was possibly first articulated.

Examples of the irrationality requiring willful ignorance of fact in Shemot/Exodus are as follows:

- Early in Exodus, Moses experiences a miraculous sign from a burning bush that never burns out. This is one of several alleged supernatural interventions by a god. This god also speaks to him from the bush and later again on Mount Sinai. Such are not real-life events.
- Ten plagues are sent against Egypt by a vengeful god. This is not a real-life event.
- After he starts to lead the Israelites out of captivity in Egypt, the Red Sea (a body of water that is typically over 300 kilometers wide) is parted so that the Israelites can walk through. It then conveniently closes up to destroy the pursuing Pharaoh's army. Please note that no chariot components, bone remains, or Ancient Egyptian artifacts have been recovered in the Red Sea, indicating that this event never happened.
- Furthermore, it is typically overlooked that Moses supposedly led 600,000 men out of Egypt. If there were 600,000 adult male Israelites involved, then let's suppose upwards of two million Israelites were following Moses at a minimum, accounting for women and children. A migration of this size would have left behind archaeological evidence. It is also completely implausible, especially since this would have been more than the entire population of Egypt at that time.
- God delivers the Ten Commandments to Moses on Mount Sinai through divine intervention. This is hard to believe, as the Ten Commandments reflect earlier Confessionals from Egypt.
- The Israelites wandering for 40 years before finding their homeland is suspect. Why would it take the Israelites 40 years to get from Sinai to the southern Levant? Did they wander all around Arabia and Central Asia, or something to this effect, before finally coming all the way back to where they started from in the first place? Also, the description of domesticated camels in Exodus makes no sense because camels were not widely domesticated until the first millennium BCE in this part of the world.

As a sidebar, the time between the supposed destruction of the Temple of Jerusalem around 586 BCE and the commencement of the Babylonian Captivity and the return to Zion after Cyrus the Great ended the Captivity in 539 BCE was just over 40 years. This is the same time Moses and the Israelites were said to have spent wandering in the desert.

As a sidebar, there is no evidence (inscriptions, hieroglyphics, cave paintings, scrolls, pyramid engravings, coins, etc.) for a historical Moses at the times specified in the Tanakh. We do not see the first written account until fragments of 4QpaleoExodm (4Q) of the Dead Sea Scrolls, which is dated a thousand years after the Exodus events.

Lastly, we will discuss the lack of evidence for the Kingdoms of Israel and Judah, King David, King Solomon, the First Temple Period, etc. According to the Jewish narrative, the Israelites finally crossed over the River Jordan and into the land of Canaan after wandering through the desert for 40 years under Moses' leadership. The leadership was passed to Joshua after Moses' passing, and the Israelites campaigned extensively around the region to begin carving out their kingdom between 1200 BCE and 1150 BCE.

A period followed where the Israelites were ruled by religious priests or judges charged with implementing religious law. These ran from Othniel through judges, including Ehud, Gideon, and Samuel. Samuel became the key figure in the Israelites switching from the rule of the judges to a monarchy. This was eventually achieved with the accession of Saul as the first King of Israel. After Saul came Eshbaal as King of Israel for a brief period of time. Then, King David succeeded after conquering Jerusalem. He was considered the great hero of the Jewish narrative of the ancient Kingdom of Israel, uniting the Israelites for a brief time and bringing the Ark of the Covenant to the holy city. He also continued waging wars against the Moabites, the Philistines, the Canaanites, and the Edomites, raising Israel to its greatest level of ancient power around 900 BCE.

Eventually, David was succeeded by one of his many sons, King Solomon. Solomon built the First Temple of Jerusalem as the great center of Jewish religious worship in the Kingdom of Israel. An era of peace and prosperity under the wise king was attained after the conquests undertaken by David. Rehoboam, in turn, succeeded his father, Solomon, as king of the unified Kingdom of Israel. Under his reign, the brief golden age of the kingdom came to an end, as a rebellion among ten of the twelve tribes of Israel led to the country splintering into two kingdoms: a Northern Kingdom of Israel covering Galilee and Samaria, and a Southern Kingdom of Judah centered on Jerusalem. This division of the lands of the Israelites continued through the rest of the First Temple Period. Again, the chronology was debated, but this supposedly happened in the late tenth or early ninth centuries BCE.

There were many different kingdoms of Judah and Israel over the next several centuries. The Northern Kingdom of Israel eventually began to decay, especially under the influence of Jezebel – the wife of King Ahab. She allowed the worship of the Canaanite and other Semitic deities to replace the worship of Yahweh. The religious and moral decay of the Northern Kingdom of Israel was portrayed as a prelude to the conquest of the kingdom by the Neo-Assyrians – a new power that emerged out of Mesopotamia (modern-day Iraq).

The Kingdom of Judah survived in the south and went through various changes. Some of the moral and religious decline seen in the north occurred; however, it was supposedly corrected by reformist kings like Hezekiah whom was influenced by Isaiah and Micah. Eventually, the Kingdom of Judah was conquered by a new power that had emerged out of Mesopotamia – the Neo-Babylonian Empire. This led to the destruction of Jerusalem and the First Temple, an event usually dated to around 587 BCE. The Babylonian Captivity also ensued as the Judahites were carried away to Babylon as slaves. They were only able to come back to Judah and to build the Second Temple after the Persians conquered the Neo-Babylonian Empire and King Cyrus the Great of Persia issued a decree in 539 BCE calling for the Jewish people to return to Zion and to rebuild the Temple. After this, the Jewish people lived broadly under Persian rule down to the time of Alexander the Great and Alexander's conquest of the Persian Empire between 335 BCE and 329 BCE. Afterward, the Jewish people ended up under the rule of the Greek/Hellenistic Seleucid Empire until the Maccabean Revolt in 160 BCE. A new Jewish kingdom emerges that is later absorbed by the Romans.

The Jewish narrative above is nothing more than a broadly invented chronology, especially for events prior to and around 800 BCE. The rule of the judges, King David, and King Solomon, the division of the Kingdom of Israel, and the early history of the Kingdom of Judah and the Northern Kingdom of Israel are not supported by any historical or archaeological evidence. At 800 BCE, there are a few elements of this Jewish account that can be verified, though razor-thin. For clarification,

- There is no archaeological evidence to indicate Yahwehism as described in the books of the Tanakh existing in the southern Levant between 1200 BCE and 800 BCE.
- There is evidence that the Canaanites ruled during the Late Bronze Age and Early Iron Age kingdom and that Edom and Moab were two kingdoms in what is now Jordan.
- There is no evidence of King David or King Solomon.
- There is no extrabiblical evidence for the existence of Moses, Joshua, or any of the Judges.

The Tel Dan Stele, which is a stone stele dating to around 840 BCE, is a fragmented artifact discovered in 1993 that references the 'House of David'. It does not include a mention of a ruler called King David – just the 'House of David'. Moreover, there is nothing else to corroborate anything about the Jewish account of David on the Tel Dan Stele. There is a second possible reference to the 'House of David' on the Moabite Stone, dating to around the same time as the Tel Dan Stele; however, it does not contain anything other than what is already on the Tel Dan Stele. At most, this does not prove anything other than the fact that there was a powerful house in the region in the Early Iron Age named after a man called David, and that a vague awareness of this centuries later led to the authors of the Tanakh incorporating the name David into their narrative.

No extrabiblical references exist for King Solomon. This is a striking historical silence for an allegedly powerful and wise king supposedly ruling over one of the most important lands in the Near East. Not to mention, there are tens of thousands of clay tablets referring to rulers and events throughout this region without any mention of Solomon or Solomon's reign.

As a sidebar, excavations at Tell es-Sultan (ancient Jericho) strongly suggest that Jericho was destroyed around 1550 BCE and that it was abandoned by the time of the Old Testament conquest, traditionally taken as either 1400 BCE or 1200 BCE.

The historicity of Moses is also called into question, given his accepted prophethood in Judaism, Christianity, and Islam. The major attempts at seeking a historical 'Moses of the Torah' or proving Moses was a 'real' historical person are provided below.

- As early as the seventeenth century, some of the first European explorers of the region since the Arab Conquests in medieval times, like Monsieur de Thevenot, a French orientalist who visited the Levant and Arabia, were looking for evidence of Moses' existence. He found nothing in his early objective to identify the Biblical Mount Sinai.
- In the first great age of archaeology in the nineteenth century, numerous archaeologists such as Edward Robinson and Richard Francis Burton travelled through Palestine, Sinai, and lands on either side of the Red Sea in search of any evidence in support of the narrative around Moses in the Exodus. They could not find anything to support its claims.
- The lack of evidence has grown in modern times as archaeologists have deployed more scientifically advanced methods to check the seabed of the Red Sea for any sign of an ancient army that was destroyed here or to track whether a migration of millions of Israelites across the desert and around Sinai and Palestine ever occurred. They have never found any evidence.
- By now, we have a more or less exhaustive record of all the surviving documentation from New Kingdom Egypt and the Third Intermediate Period that followed it. Despite how literate the high society in Egypt was and the level of documentation that has survived from this era in the shape of royal tablets, inscriptions, tomb hieroglyphics, royal and governmental papyri, etc., there isn't a single record of an Israelite leader named Moses.

- In the twentieth century, the search for any record of Moses intensified as numerous Mormons travelled to Egypt, Jordan, Israel, etc., to find information on Moses or any record of his existence, as Moses is a particularly revered prophet within the Church of Latter-Day Saints. They have not found any sign of Moses' historical existence.
- There have even been efforts by the Saudi Arabian government in recent times to suggest that Moses' journey into Midian before he led the Israelites out of Egypt involved travelling into the north-western corner of Arabia. Many archaeological teams from France and Poland have been employed to excavate numerous sites there. While they have uncovered abundant artifacts about Iron Age cultures, such as the Lihyanites, the later Nabataeans, and Roman settlements in the region, nothing connected to Moses has ever been found.
- There are even issues when we turn to the later record of Moses in Jewish texts. During the Second Temple Period, for instance, Jewish writers began to portray Moses in a very different way. The narrative of Exodus was sometimes changed to have Moses actually ascending up to heaven at one point to converse with god rather than an apocalyptic prophet experiencing visions on earth. Once again, this shows that Moses is fictional, not historical.

Notice how a historical critique reduces the Jewish narrative to falsehoods and fiction. Since Christianity (discussed next) and Islam (discussed later) hinge on the Torah, we will soon find out that they are also full of historical falsehoods.

Once again, the key to a religion's success is simply creating an explanation – not necessarily the best, the most factually accurate, the most historical, or the most truthful – riddled with belief that the willfully ignorant humans can subscribe to.

Em Hotep!

DISMANTLING JUDEO-CHRISTIANITY

ANKH WADJA SENEB | ARTICLE NO: 007

Function: The Awareness of Control Mechanisms
Subject(s): Gospels, Jesus, Paul, New Testament, Resurrection, Crucifixion
Position: Part 3 – Breaking Societal Controls
Theme: Dealing with Religions, Cults, & Atheism | Scene 7 | Part 2

ARTICLE NO: 007 – DISMANTLING JUDEO-CHRISTIANITY (PT 2)

Peace to the High Power! Peace to the Living Universe! Peace to all Finite Living Beings! Peace to All Things – seen and unseen! For my spirit is with me, my image is with me, and my purpose is with me. For those with knowledge understand that the mechanisms behind societal controls can only flourish when consciousness, awareness, vibration, and rationality are minimized and when willful ignorance, fear, indoctrination, and subjugating forces are maximized.

Recall that the key to a religion's success is simply creating an explanation – not necessarily the best, the most factually accurate, the most historical, or the most truthful – riddled with belief that the willfully ignorant humans can subscribe to, and Christianity is no exception.

Recall that, in the previous article, we briefly looked at the falsehoods of the Jewish narrative as well as the poor historical grounding of key figures (e.g., David, Solomon, and Moses) and Jewish sources. Since the Christian doctrine considers the Torah (the first five books of the biblical Old Testament) to be divinely inspired scripture, the reader can already expect a historical path to failure, and this historical path of failure is best illustrated by assessing the historicity of the central character – Jesus Christ.

Before continuing, the reader must distinguish between the purely human being named Jesus of Nazareth and the divine being named Jesus of Bethlehem presented in the bible.

<u>The purely human being named Jesus</u> refers to an apocalyptic Jew named Jesus of Nazareth, whom preached a radical form of Judaism from combined Late Second Temple Period interpretations as the supposed messiah, proclaiming the imminent end of humankind and the need to overcome the controlling forces of evil in the world to usher in the new kingdom of god. These combined interpretations came from competing religious groups and priests, influenced by Persian, Greek, and Roman empires, whom had radically different interpretations of identity, scripture, law, and messianic interpretation, as listed below:

- Pharisees believed in oral law, resurrections, angels, and purity regulations.
- Sadducees (Temple elite) rejected resurrections, angels, and oral traditions.
- Essenes/Qumran communities were apocalyptic separatists awaiting divine intervention.
- Zealots/Sicarii were militant nationalists opposing Roman occupation.
- Diaspora Jews supported Hellenized synagogues spread across the Mediterranean.

For simplicity, let's assume that this purely human being named Jesus of Nazareth actually existed from a historical perspective; even though, the evidence is not overwhelming, as some say.

The divine being named Jesus of Bethlehem, presented in the New Testament of the bible, on the other hand, supposedly cast out demons, healed the sick, walked on water, fed multitudes with a few loaves of bread, and raised the dead, among other things. We will examine the historicity of this 'Jesus Christ' piece by piece because this 'Jesus Christ' is at the focal point of the biblical New Testament narrative.

For those not aware, the word 'Christ' comes from the Greek word, 'Christos', meaning "anointed one" or "messiah", and the name 'Jesus' is a modern transliteration of Yehoshua/Yeshua' from the Aramaic or Yeshu/Ishu from nearby Aramaic dialects, such as Syriac and Mandaic.

There were many people called Yehoshua/Yeshua' in the early first century CE, including Yehoshua son of Nun, Yeshua' the High Priest, Yeshua' Barabbas, Yeshua' ben Ananias, and Yeshua's ben Sira. Not to mention, Flavius Josephus references at least twenty different people named Yeshua in the *Jewish Antiquities,* and Tal Ilan conducted an intensive study in his *Lexicon of Jewish Names in Late Antiquity*, demonstrating that Yeshua' was the 6th most common male name among Jews from 330-200 BCE.

During the late Second Temple Period, roughly from around 50 BCE to 70 CE, there was a common practice of using ossuaries (bone boxes) to bury the remains of the dead, especially in Judea. Archaeologists have uncovered over a hundred ossuaries alone bearing names like Yeshua, indicating that the stem name of 'Jesus' was very common in Roman Judea.

To be clear, there was nothing unique about the name Yehoshua/Yeshua' or Jesus.

Equally, 'Christ' or 'Christos', which is actually a title, not a name, was also common. It was applied as an honorable title to different people in ancient times and to religious leaders, priests, or holy men – not necessarily individuals who claimed to be the son of a deity. For instance, in the *Life of the Emperor Claudius*, the Roman historical biographer, Suetonius, references a Jewish religious leader in Rome named 'Chrestus' (Latin derivative for 'Christos'). As a second example, the Greeks, who largely influenced the development of the Christian church in the Eastern Mediterranean from the first to the third century CE, used the term 'Chrestus' not necessarily to describe a holy man but to describe a person whom was 'worthy', 'upright', or 'good in essence'. As a third example, funerary monuments and gravestones abound from across the Greco-Roman Mediterranean referenced people as 'Chrestus' or 'Christos'. Lastly, 'Chrestus' or 'Christos' references are found in texts like Longus' *Daphnis and Chloe* – one of five ancient Greek novels dating back to the second and the third centuries CE.

To be clear, there was nothing unique about the title 'Christ'. Other people who claimed to be a Jewish messiah with divine powers include John the Baptist, Judas of Galilee/Gamala, Theudas, Simon of Peraea, the Egyptian Prophet, Jonathan the Weaver, Athronges, Menahem ben Judah, and the Samaritan Prophet.

Now, let's look at the birth of the divine being named Jesus Christ. According to the biblical narrative, Jesus was born in Bethlehem in a stable after his parents had travelled there from Nazareth, where they lived, to be enumerated in Joseph's birthplace, Bethlehem, in a Roman census of the Jewish province. Firstly, it should be noted that the story of the nativity only appears in two of the four canonical gospels in the New Testament, Matthew 1-2 and Luke 1-2, prior to jumping directly into Jesus's adulthood and ministry following a baptism by John the Baptist. Neither of the other Gospels says anything about Jesus's birth, nor do any of the other 23 books of the New Testament. Secondly, Matthew and Luke do not contain the same information about the nativity. For instance, Luke discusses angels appearing to some shepherds near Bethlehem and him telling them about the birth of Jesus; however, there is no mention of any magi or wise men from the east. The wise men only appear in the book of Matthew, which also provides an account of the so-called 'massacre of the innocents' – the fabled story where King Herod orders the massacre of all newborn babies across

Judea after being alerted that a child would become 'King of the Jews'.

There are many problems with this biblical narrative.

- Per Matthew 2:1-17, King Herod was the ruler of Judea at the time of Jesus' birth and that he subsequently tried to have Jesus killed when he learned that a future King of the Jews had been born, and such an attempt was thwarted by Mary and Joseph by taking this divine Jesus into Egypt and only returning to Nazareth once Herod had carried out his mass infanticide. The problem with this is that Herod (who is much better documented as a historical figure than the divine Jesus) died in the year 4 BCE, according to historians and archaeologists. This is four years before Jesus's putative birth. Not to mention, there is no historical evidence or independent records for the Massacre of the Innocents. Even Josephus details many atrocities during Herod's reign, but makes no mention of mass infanticide.
- Matthew 1-2 and Luke 1-2 reference the divine Jesus as being born in Bethlehem, most likely to tie the divine Jesus to the alleged birthplace of King David; even though, it is highly likely that the human Jesus was historically born in Nazareth. Nazareth is in Galilee, but Bethlehem is not. Nazareth as a hometown can be attested, but there is no evidence that Nazareth is a birthplace. Moreover, there are no eyewitness reports for Jesus's birth until decades later, and such reports were all written by people whom fervently believed that the divine Jesus was the son of god and that the divine Jesus was raised from the dead.
- In Luke 2:1-5, the scribe records: "In those days Caesar Augustus issued a decree that a census should be taken of the entire Roman world". This supposedly was the reason why Mary and Joseph travelled from Nazareth, where they lived, to Bethlehem, and where Joseph's family hailed from. The key issue is that no census, whether in ancient times or today, required people to leave the place where they lived before travelling back to the place of their birth to be counted in the census. Such travel times across the Roman Empire would be implausible.
- In the non-canonical Infancy Gospel of James, also known as the Protoevangelium of James, written in the first half of the second century, there is a lengthy account of the nativity; however, the entire story is different again. In this story, Joseph finds a cave for his family to stay in after they arrive in Bethlehem. His biological sons are there with him, and there is a midwife involved when Mary gives birth to the divine Jesus in a cave, with no ox or donkey present.

Outside of the nativity, Luke includes a brief section on Jesus' visit to Jerusalem when Jesus was around twelve years old. Apart from this, there is nothing in canonical scripture on Jesus's upbringing after he succeeded John the Baptist as leader of a messianic group in Galilee. It is very suspect that entire sections of Jesus' life are excluded from the gospels. A key example is the dismissal of the Gospel of Thomas (approx. 130 CE). This gospel begins with the divine Jesus performing his earliest miracle when he was five years old, fashioning twelve sparrows out of clay collected from the banks of a stream and then bringing them to life. This miracle upset the local Jews, whom were very conservative, likening such acts to sorcery. Jesus responds by killing people. In Thomas 2-5, a local priest even complains to Joseph about Jesus' conduct, and Jesus curses/kills the priest's child in retaliation. The New Testament writers could not have Jesus killing people as a child at the time, so the gospel of Thomas was excluded and the acts of divine Jesus were coated as a morality tale, where Jesus had to be 'matured' under the wing of learned elders.

A fragment of the Gospel of Mary from the Oxyrhynchus Papyri, alongside the Gospel of Philip suggest that Mary Magdalene was Jesus' wife or at least she was engaged in a sexual relationship of some kind with him. Anxious to create a model view of Jesus as a chaste messiah, the church authorities excluded these gospels from official accounts and condemned them as heretical.

Even worse, no Greek or Roman author from the first century CE mentions Jesus. The canonical gospels and other texts in the New Testament were not written by authors whom either knew the divine Jesus or lived around the same time as the divine Jesus. Moreover, the authors of the New Testament were not written for the most part by Jesus' twelve apostles or other near contemporaries like St Paul. Secular scholars believe that the earliest written gospel was the Gospel of Mark, which was likely composed between 65 CE and 80 CE (almost half a century after the supposed time of Jesus' death in 33 CE). Then, the Gospel of Matthew and the Gospel of Luke were likely written in the 80s CE, followed by the Gospel of John sometime between 90 CE and 110 CE. These are very late dates of composition to be deemed reliable, especially for a revered divine Jesus.

The most damaging is the silence of Paul. Paul, who wrote between 50-60 CE, is the first Christian author; however, he never refers to Jesus as a new historical figure. He talks of no birth in Bethlehem, no ministry in Galilee, no miracles, no parables, no trial before Pilate, no crucifixion between thieves. In 1 Corinthians 15:38, Paul writes of Jesus appearing to Cephas and others; these are experiences of vision, which are exactly what happened to Paul on the road to Damascus. The Jesus Christ of Paul is a celestial pre-existent entity that can be known only through scripture and revelation – completely different from the Jesus discussed in the synoptic gospels (Mark, Matthew, Luke, and John).

There are only three (3) authors who make non-Christian references to Jesus below in the entirety of the first century and the first half of the second century. These references arguably suggest the existence of a purely human being named Jesus, but not the divine being named Jesus portrayed in the bible.

- **Tacitus on Jesus**: Tacitus (56-120 CE) was a Roman senator and historian who was regarded as one of the foremost historians of the ancient world and a vital source for the history of the Roman Empire between the commencement of the reign of the Emperor Tiberius in 14 CE and the start of the Flavian dynasty under Emperor Vespasian in 69 CE, as written in two different works – the *Annals* and the *Histories*. The Annals cover the reigns of Tiberius and his successors in the Julio-Claudian dynasty down to the death of Nero in 68 CE. It is here that we find a passing reference to a 'Jesus'. In Book XV of the text, Tacitus is describing the Great Fire of Rome, which had ripped through the city and burned down a significant portion of it in 64 CE. There was speculation that Nero had the fire purposefully started because he wanted to clear large parts of the city to build a vast new palace for himself. Tacitus then stated in Annals XV, 44 that "to scotch the rumor, Nero substituted as culprits, and punished with the utmost refinements of cruelty, a class of men, loathed for their vices, whom the crowd styled Christians". From here, he mentions a 'Jesus' in an effort to explain to readers whom the Christians were: "Christus, the founder of the name, had undergone the death penalty in the reign of Tiberius, by sentence of the procurator Pontius Pilatus," (Annals, XV, 44). He goes on to describe how a small community of Christians was in Rome and that these were made a scapegoat by Nero for the Great Fire: "the confessed members of the sect were arrested; next, on their disclosures, vast numbers were convicted, not so much on the count of arson as for hatred of the human race. And derision accompanied their end: they were covered with wild beasts' skins and torn to death by dogs; or they were fastened on crosses, and, when daylight failed, were burned to serve as lamps by night" (Annals, XV, 44). Hence, we have here a single fleeting reference to Christ in Tacitus' work. It is worth noting that crucifixion was a common punishment at this time and that 'Christus' could have referred to any religious entity proclaiming to be a messiah. Assuming that 'Christus' refers to Jesus Christ, these short sentences can only indicate the existence of a human being named Jesus, not the divine being named Jesus from the biblical narrative.

- **Josephus on Jesus**: The only ancient, non-Christian writer, who mentions Jesus twice, is Flavius Josephus, who was a Jew more familiar with events in Judea and Galilee. The first of these references is generally accepted as genuine by Christian scholars. It is in the *Jewish Antiquities* and is found in the context of Josephus describing the prosecution of Jesus' brother, James, and some of the other early members of the Christian church. Josephus notes that the Sanhedrin – the religious court of the Temple authorities in Jerusalem, headed by the high priest Ananus – "brought before them the brother of Jesus, who was called Christ, whose name was James, and some others; and when he had formed an accusation against them as breakers of the law, he delivered them to be stoned: but as for those who seemed the most equitable of the citizens, and such as were the most uneasy at the breach of the laws, they disliked what was done; they also sent to the king, desiring him to send to Ananus that he should act so no more, for that what he had already done was not to be justified; nay, some of them went also to meet Albinus, as he was upon his journey from Alexandria, and informed him that it was not lawful for Ananus to assemble a Sanhedrin without his consent. Whereupon Albinus complied with what they said, and wrote in anger to Ananus, and threatened that he would bring him to punishment for what he had done; on which king Agrippa took the high priesthood from him, when he had ruled but three months, and made Jesus, the son of Damneus, high priest" (Josephus, *Jewish Antiquities*, XX, 9). Scholars are almost unanimous in accepting that this passage is a genuine reference to Jesus Christ as a human being, not a divine being.

  It is worth noting that the 'brother(s) of Jesus' or the 'brother(s) of the lord' can be interpreted in the literal sense or the figurative sense, and this is a point of contention when it comes to the relationship between James and Jesus or the relationship between Jesus and his followers.

  The second quote in Josephus' *Jewish Antiquities* is much more contentious. This is called the *Testimonium Flavianum*, 'The Testimony of Flavius Josephus'. It reads as follows: "About this time, there lived Jesus, a wise man, if indeed one ought to call him a man. For he was one who performed surprising deeds and was a teacher of such people as accept the truth gladly. He won over many Jews and many of the Greeks. He was the Christ. And when, upon the accusation of the principal men among us, Pilate had condemned him to a cross, those who had first come to love him did not cease. He appeared to them, spending a third day restored to life, for the prophets of God had foretold these things and a thousand other marvels about him. And the tribe of the Christians, so called after him, has still to this day not disappeared" (Josephus, *Jewish Antiquities*, XVIII.3).

  For centuries, this quote was used as propaganda to demonstrate how a Romanized Jew accepted the supposed divinity of Jesus. Today, it is a well-known forgery based on textual analysis. The consensus is that there probably was originally a reference to Jesus in this part of the *Jewish Antiquities*, but that the passage was doctored by later Christian scholars whom copied out the books and whom altered the passage to make it sound as though Josephus believed in the divinity of Jesus by adding insertions, such as "a wise man, if indeed one ought to call him a man" and "He was the Christ". In reality, the original text would have simply mentioned Jesus as one of the many messianic Jewish religious leaders active in Judea. Furthermore, a stylometric analysis of the passage using modern computer-based analysis by G. J. Goldberg indicates that the style of the passage is very similar to the Gospel of Luke, which suggests that Christian scholars later inserted elements of Luke 24:18–24 over Josephus' original passage. Such forgeries show the lengths that Christian scholars went to in the early medieval period to manufacture elements of the biblical narrative. It is also worth noting that nearly all of the extant manuscript copies of the *Jewish Antiquities* date to the tenth or eleventh centuries, nearly a thousand years after the text was originally written, giving ample time for the forgery to spread across Europe. Once again, assuming the reference is genuine, the reference indicates a human Jesus rather than a divine Jesus.

- **Pliny the Younger**: Pliny the Younger was a Roman politician and the son of the great Roman encyclopedist, Pliny the Elder. In 110 CE, he was appointed as the Roman governor of the dual province of Bithynia et Pontus that covered much of western Turkey. 247 of Pliny's letters have survived from antiquity. One of these was a letter to Emperor Trajan, where he asked the emperor what he should do about a group of Christians in his province, given how strange their religious beliefs were deemed to be. He does not actually mention Jesus specifically or provide any real detail about Jesus as a historical character. Instead, Pliny just seems to have been vaguely aware that they worshipped a figure called Christ. In *Epistulae*, X.96, Pliny stated, "They were in the habit of meeting before dawn to sing a hymn to Christ as to a god". Such behaviors were common among religious groups with venerated priests, but it does not show the existence of a divine Jesus as portrayed in the biblical narrative.

Outside of the references above, the Stoic philosopher, Epictetus, who lived in the late first and early second centuries, did make some reference to the Christians as a kind of oddity in the same way that Pliny did; however, he did not mention Jesus at all. It was as though he understood little about Christians and had no idea who their founder was. Beyond this, there is a striking silence in the writings of most other writers of the period prior to 150 CE. Philo of Alexandria, a Jewish scholar who was a contemporary of Jesus and whose writings have survived, never mentioned Jesus at all. Suetonius, an official and historian who was an exact contemporary of Tacitus, did not give an account of Jesus' execution in his life of Tiberius, suggesting it was a rather inconsequential event in the broad scheme of Roman history. Seneca, a moral philosopher, did not discuss Jesus, and Plutarch, a historical biographer, did not mention Jesus in *Moralia* and other writings on local religions and philosophical-theological systems, as he might have done if Jesus was a well-known figure in his time. It is only from the middle of the second century – when Christianity was starting to emerge as a quasi-political movement – that we see an increase in the number of Christian and non-Christian writers mentioning Jesus and the religion, notably Celsus and Irenaeus of Lyon. Overall, the evidential basis for the existence of a divine Jesus per the Christian narrative in the period prior to 150 CE is non-existent.

As a sidebar, there is no physical description of Jesus in the New Testament. The earliest known depiction of Jesus or Christ as a religious entity did not portray him as a man at all. In the second century CE, Christians tended to use pictograms and symbols to depict Jesus. These included the ichthys, which is basically a fish symbol, the chi-rho, and the tau-rho. There is no consensus on a human Jesus based on the differences of Jesus from Dura Europos, Jesus from the Catacombs, the Hermes of Kalamis, Jesus from the Catacombs of Commodilla, Jesus from the Catacombs of Saints Marcellinus and Peter, and the resemblance to Apollonius of Tyana.

Now, we will turn our attention to the last three (3) years of Jesus's life, encompassing the crucifixion, the resurrection, and the empty tomb. It is highly unlikely that the Romans or indeed the Jewish temple authorities would have allowed for Jesus' body to be taken away and buried respectfully in a tomb just hours after he was crucified. After all, one of the hallmarks of Roman crucifixions was that the dead were left hanging on the cross as a warning to others in a humiliating way. Alternative forms of crucifixion included stoning, strangling, beheading, or impaling. As a rebuttal, people who are supportive of the tomb theory have unearthed a single reference that would support the idea of a crucified body being taken away for burial before the sun set the day of death. In Josephus' *Jewish Wars,* he states that "the Jews used to take so much care of the burial of men, that they took down those that were condemned and crucified, and buried them before the going down of the sun." (Josephus, *Jewish Wars*, IV, 317). On the face of it, this seems to support the idea that Jesus could have been taken down from the cross and laid to rest in a tomb shortly after he died or even maybe there was an exception to the custom of leaving the dead on the cross as a form of Roman psychological terror; however, the passage from Josephus needs to be viewed in context. He is writing about the situation that prevailed in Jerusalem during the First Jewish Revolt (66 CE – 74 CE) as the city was under siege by the Romans. Many thousands of people had streamed into the city in the wake of the Roman advance, and this included groups of Idumaeans – a people who lived in the southern Levant, who, like the Samaritans, were ethnically akin to the Jews, but who had different customs. In the passage in question, Josephus is attempting to make it clear that the Jews were more civilized than the Idumaeans. Hence, the wider passage is "they [the Idumaeans] proceeded to that degree of impiety, as to cast away their dead bodies without burial, although the Jews used to take so much care of the burial of men, that they took down those that were condemned and crucified, and buried them before the going down of the sun". Thus, what Josephus was trying to do was suggest that the Jews were more civilized than the Idumaeans because of their proper honoring of the dead. Moreover, the context was people being killed in battle against the Romans and bodies being taken away during lulls in the fighting. It was an unusual circumstance that hardly seems like the strongest basis to claim that this was a normal custom.

Since the working assumption is that a human being named Jesus existed, we will grant the historical accounts – weak or strong – surrounding the crucifixion of Jesus. It is strange, however, that Mark 14-15 claims that Jesus died the morning <u>after</u> the Passover meal, and John 18-19 claims Jesus died in the afternoon the day <u>before</u> the Passover meal.

The gospels were written 35-65 years after Jesus's death, not by people whom were eyewitnesses but by highly literate and trained Greek-speaking Christians of later generations with already known sources of information. Moreover, the titles of these gospels did not correspond to the actual writer (e.g., Matthew did not write the gospel of Matthew). After Jesus' death, people started telling oral stories about him to convert Jews and Gentiles. Such is the case for the resurrection.

According to the biblical accounts, Jesus was crucified in Jerusalem by Roman authority during the Passover feast, having been arrested and convicted on charges of blasphemy by the Jewish Sanhedrin and then slandered before the Roman Governor Pilate on charges of treason. He died within several hours and was buried on Friday afternoon by Joseph of Arimathea in a tomb, which was sealed with a stone. Certain female followers of Jesus, including Mary Magdalene, who is always named, having observed his interment, visited his tomb early Sunday morning, only to find it empty. Thereafter, Jesus appeared alive from the dead to his disciples, including Peter, who then became a proclaimer of the message of his resurrection. The conflicting details among the synoptic gospels raise many questions: (1) Which women and how many women go to the tomb?, (2) Is it Mary Magdalene by herself or with other women?, (3) What are the names of these women?, (4) Was the stone of the tomb already rolled away when they got there or not? (5) Did they see a young man, multiple men, or an angel?, (6) Were the women told to go tell Peter and the disciples to meet Jesus in Galilee or were they told to tell the disciples when Jesus would be in Galilee?, (7) Did the women do what they were told?, and (8) Did the disciples stay in Jerusalem or leave right away?. Since these biblical accounts have many variations and the authors of these biblical accounts are not eyewitnesses, they cannot be historically reliable accounts of either a god raising Jesus from the dead or Jesus raising himself from the dead, especially if this implies that Jesus' body came back alive, never to die again. The resurrection has to be taken on faith, not on the basis of proof.

Not to mention, many biblical scholars frequently misquote Paul to indicate that Joseph of Arimathea buried Jesus around five years after Jesus's death. Paul, however, was writing 25 years after the burial, and he never mentions Joseph of Arimathea. Joseph of Arimathea is not mentioned until you get to the Gospel of Mark – 40 years after. In the First Letter of St Paul to the Corinthians (1 Corinthians 15: 4–6), which is accepted by biblical scholars as an authentic Pauline Epistle, Paul stated that "[Jesus] rose again the third day according to the scriptures, and that he was seen of Cephas [St Peter], then of the twelve, after that, he was seen of above five hundred brethren at once; of whom the greater part remain unto this present, but some are fallen asleep". Paul provides a version of events that is completely at odds with the gospels and there are further inconsistencies: (1) Paul never mentions anything about a tomb, (2) Paul does not mention Joseph of Arimathea, (3) Paul does not mention anything about the women first discovering Jesus' disappearance from the tomb, (4) Paul suggesting that Jesus appeared to Peter without ever mentioning the women, (5) Paul absurdly mentions "the twelve" separately from "all the apostles", and (6) Paul mentions Jesus being buried, not laid to rest in a tomb. This is further suspect because Paul was driven by scripture and revelation (e.g., Galatians 1:11-12, 16), not tradition. Additionally, Paul was prone to schizophrenia and hallucinations as seen in 2 Corinthians 12:1-9, so the mentioning of the undocumented 500 brethren is called into question, especially since (1) there is no independent corroboration of the claim, (2) it is unclear if Paul met or spoke to any of them, (3) there is not a single name of the 500 known, or (4) Paul could have heard this from a secondary or tertiary source.

Once again, there is no historical evidence for a divine being named Jesus.

From this point, we will shift from the historical shortcomings of a divine Jesus to issues with biblical manuscripts. The breakdown of the 88 Books (66 canonical books) of the Judeo-Christian Scripture and some added events is shown below.

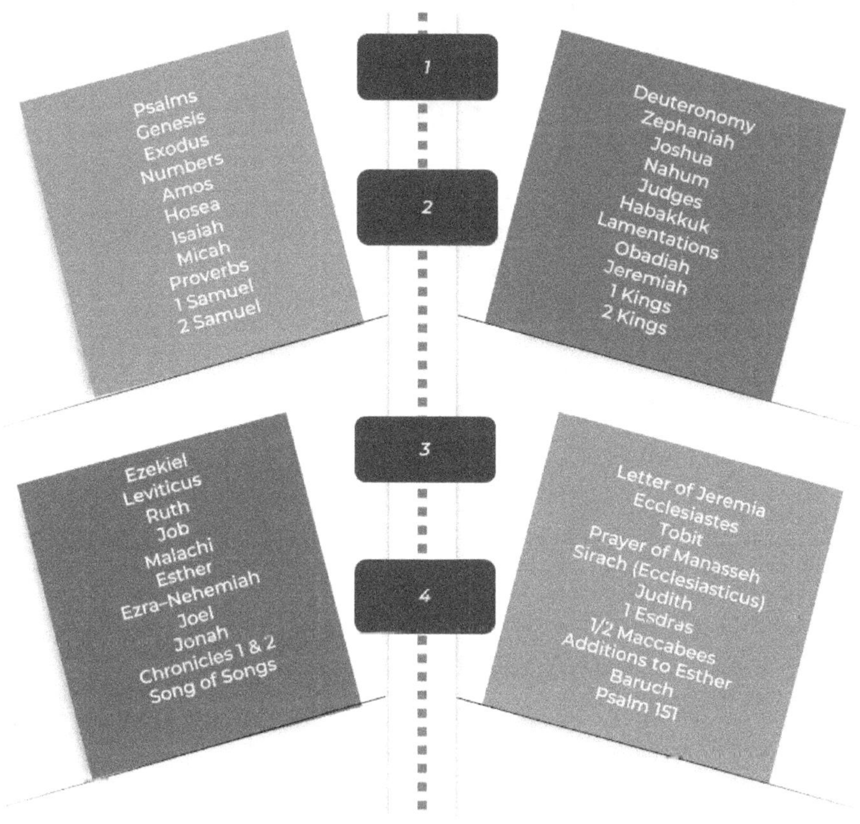

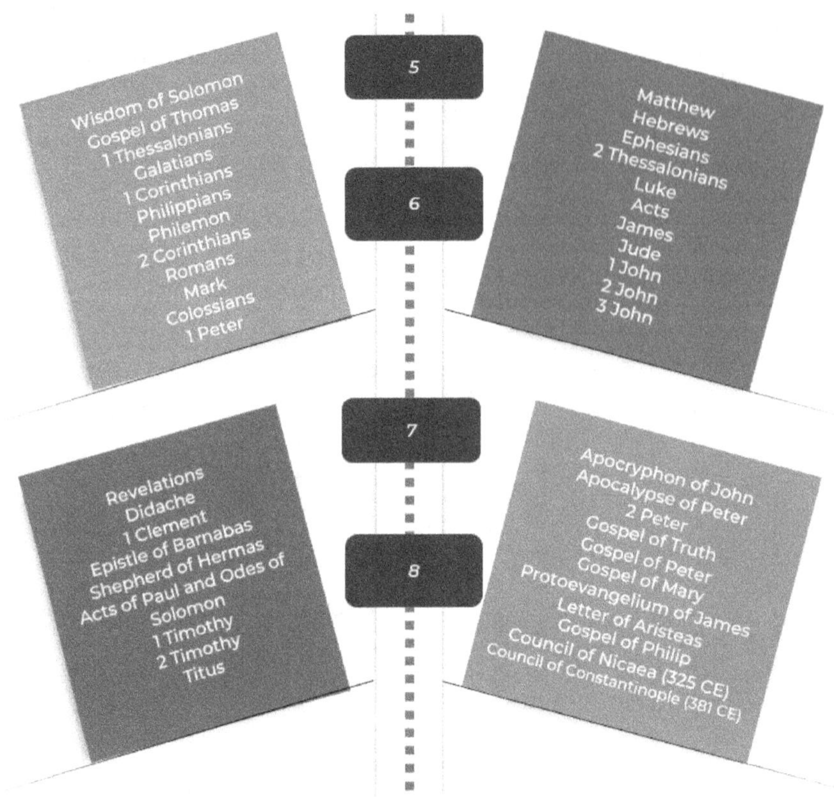

For clarification, the Council of Nicaea (325 CE) was called to settle disputes among a divided Christian church on the divinity of Jesus Christ. Some claimed Jesus to be a created being, while others claimed Jesus to be a divine being.

For clarification, the Council of Constantinople (381 CE), convened by Emperor Theodosius I, expanded the original Creed of Nicaea (325) to include a more detailed section on the holy spirit, describing it as "the Lord, the Giver of Life, who proceeds from the Father". It officially condemned the following as heresy: (1) the belief that Jesus was a created being, created after Adam, (2) denial of the divinity of the holy spirit, and (3) denial of Christ's full humanity.

Please note how far the church went to force the false idea of Christ's divinity, even among other dissenting Christian sects that came far earlier than trinitarianism.

In 1707, a biblical scholar named John Mill published his edition of the Greek New Testament, *Novum Testamentum Graecum, cum lectionibus variantibus MSS*, to outline discrepancies, copying errors, or deliberate alterations contained within biblical manuscripts. At the time, he reported 30,000 textual variants after examining 100 manuscripts. There were more textual variants; however, only 30,000 of them were deemed critical. As of today, we have 5800 manuscripts and approximately 500,000 textual variants discovered, which should raise an alarm surrounding the reliability of biblical scripture.

Despite the growth of the Christian church in the third and fourth centuries, mainly as a political movement, the earliest full surviving copy of the New Testament (Codex Sinaiticus) dates to the middle of the fourth century CE – hundreds of years after Jesus' death. There are virtually no copies or even fragments thereof that have survived from manuscripts dating to the first century CE and for most of the second century CE. In other words, we basically have to trust biblical texts that were copied generation after generation with no guaranteed chain of accuracy spanning approximately 250 to 300 years. Not to mention, we have to ignore what has and has not been preserved in the original New Testament sources alongside repeated changes, interpolations, and edits – contested and uncontested. This is very concerning, noting that Jesus' proposed death was in 33 CE. The chronology of the survival of main copies of the New Testament (late fragments and late full copies) is itemized as follows:

- John Rylands Library, Papyrus P52 (approximately 160 CE) shows a small segment of John 18: 31–33. It does not show these three verses in full.
- The Muratorian Fragment, which dates to 170 CE, shows the New Testament canon in formation.
- Papyrus 46 (P. Chester Beatty II) is typically dated to between 175 CE and 225 CE, and it contains sections from many of the Pauline Epistles, e.g., Romans, Corinthians 1 and 2, Galatians, Ephesians, etc.
- The Codex Sinaiticus dates to approximately 330 CE to 350 CE. It contains two (2) books, the Epistle of Barnabas and the Shepherd of Hermas, that are now considered to be non-canonical early Christian texts.
- The Codex Vaticanus dates to approximately 340 CE to 360 CE.
- The Codex Alexandrianus dates to approximately 400 CE to 430 CE.
- The Codex Ephraemi Rescriptus dates to approximately 450 CE.

Please note that these fourth and fifth-century CE codices exhibit some textual variations, and scholars believe that there were different New Testament traditions associated with Greek-Christian communities in major cities of the Eastern Mediterranean, such as Alexandria in Egypt and Constantinople (modern-day Istanbul). These are known as the Alexandrian and Byzantine textual traditions. Such traditions raise serious questions about how the editing process actually occurred and what acceptance/rejection criteria were used.

Centuries of close reading and examination of the New Testament have led to the identification of numerous forgeries and/or passages that were added/edited into the books of the New Testament. A comprehensive list of these is beyond the scope of this book; however, the table below provides just a selection of some of the accepted and most well-known forgeries and interpolations, based primarily on the study of various late antiquity and early medieval manuscripts.

Name of Passage	Place in the New Testament	Date Added
The Short Ending of Mark	Mark 16:9	c. 120 CE
The Agony of Jesus	Luke 22: 43–44	c. 120 CE
The Men in the Field	Luke 17:36	c. 120 CE
The Long Ending of Mark	Mark 16, 9–20	c. 140 CE
Prayer and Fasting Verse	Matthew 17:21	c. 170 CE
Ears to Hear	Mark 7:16	c. 300 CE
Profaning the Temple	Acts 24:6–8	c. 300 CE
Forgiveness Passage	Mark 11:26	c. 330 CE
The Transgressors	Mark 15:28	c. 330 CE
Pericope Adultare (Adultery Passages)	John 7:53 – 8:11	c. 350 CE
Johannine Comma	1 John 5:7–8	c. 350 CE
Scribes and Pharisees Passage	Matthew 23:14	c. 350 CE
Silas is Pleased	Acts 15:34	c. 360 CE
The Jews Depart	Acts 28:29	c. 360 CE
Healing the Paralytic at Bethesda	John 5:3b–4	c. 360 CE
Son of Man Verse	Matthew 18:11	c. 500 CE
Confession of the Eunuch	Acts 8:37	c. 500 CE

Recall that Jesus supposedly died in approximately 33 CE.

Let's discuss a few of the forgeries in greater detail.

- **The Short and Long Ending of Mark**: Perhaps the most famous New Testament forgery is the ending of the Gospel of Mark. Scholars noticed that the two different endings were not included in either the Codex Sinaiticus or the Codex Vaticanus. They determined through these textual comparisons that the Gospel of Mark actually ended abruptly at Mark 16:8. Mark 16 has Mary Magdalene and several of Jesus' other female followers heading down to Jesus' tomb. They find the stone over the entrance rolled back, and when they enter, a being (presumed to be an angel, though not explicitly cited as such) tells them that Jesus is gone and he is risen from the dead. The gospel then ends: "Trembling and bewildered, the women went out and fled from the tomb. They said nothing to anyone, because they were afraid". Christian writers were clearly not satisfied with this ending and decided to change it in the early second century CE to support the divinity of Jesus. Two different alternate endings, known as the 'long ending' and 'short ending', were produced. The short ending simply added: "Then they quickly reported all these instructions to those around Peter. After this, Jesus himself also sent out through them from east to west the sacred and imperishable proclamation of eternal salvation. Amen". However, even this 'short ending' was deemed unsatisfactory, and the following long ending was added: "When Jesus rose early on the first day of the week, he appeared first to Mary Magdalene, out of whom he had driven seven demons. She went and told those who had been with him and who were mourning and weeping. When they heard that Jesus was alive and that she had seen him, they did not believe it. Afterward, Jesus appeared in a different form to two of them while they were walking in the country. These returned and reported it to the rest, but they did not believe them either. Later, Jesus appeared to the Eleven as they were eating; he rebuked them for their lack of faith and their stubborn refusal to believe those who had seen him after he had risen. He said to them, "Go into all the world and preach the gospel to all creation. Whoever believes and is baptized will be saved, but whoever does not believe will be condemned. And these signs will accompany those who believe: In my name they will drive out demons; they will speak in new tongues; they will pick up snakes with their hands; and when they drink deadly poison, it will not hurt them at all; they will place their hands on sick people, and they will get well." After the Lord Jesus had spoken to them, he was taken up into heaven, and he sat at the right hand of God. Then the disciples went out and preached everywhere, and the Lord worked with them and confirmed his word by the signs that accompanied it". Hence, we have here a clear example of Christian editors and scribes changing the New Testament scripture.

- **Pericope Adulterae** (Adultery Passages): This is one of the most extensive forgeries in the New Testament and runs from John 7:53 to John 8:11. The passage reads: "Then each of them went home, while Jesus went to the Mount of Olives. Early in the morning, he came again to the temple. All the people came to him, and he sat down and began to teach them. The scribes and the Pharisees brought a woman who had been caught in adultery; and making her stand before all of them, they said to him, 'Teacher, this woman was caught in the very act of committing adultery. Now, in the law, Moses commanded us to stone such women. Now what do you say?' They said this to test him, so that they might have some charge to bring against him. Jesus bent down and wrote with his finger on the ground. When they kept on questioning him, he straightened up and said to them, 'Let anyone among you who is without sin be the first to throw a stone at her.' And once again, he bent down and wrote on the ground. When they heard it, they went away, one by one, beginning with the elders; and Jesus was left alone with the woman standing before him. Jesus straightened up and said to her, 'Woman, where are they? Has no one condemned you?' She said, 'No one, sir.' And Jesus said, 'Neither do I condemn you. Go your way, and from now on do not sin again.'" The adultery passages are generally understood to have been added to give extra emphasis on the idea of Jesus' message as being one of forgiveness and tolerance. It is now understood to be a much later forgery, written possibly hundreds of years after John was first written.
- **Confession of the Eunuch**: This is a passage that was added to chapter 8 of the Acts of the Apostles. The wider passage (with forged addition underlined) from Acts 8:36–38 is as follows: "As they travelled along the road, they came to some water and the eunuch said, "Look, here is water. What can stand in the way of my being baptized?" "<u>If you believe with all your heart, you may." The eunuch answered, "I believe that Jesus Christ is the Son of God.</u>". And he gave orders to stop the chariot. Then both Philip and the eunuch went down into the water, and Philip baptized him." This was basically added as a way to indicate that the Christian church was inclusive of eunuchs, a group which was otherwise explicitly condemned under Mosaic law in the Tanakh/Old Testament (Deuteronomy 23:1; Leviticus 21:20).
- **Healing the Paralytic at Bethesda**: The wider text in John 5:2–9 reads: "Now there is in Jerusalem by the Sheep Gate a pool, which is called in Hebrew, Bethesda, having five porches. In these lay a great multitude of sick people, blind, lame, paralyzed, <u>waiting for the moving of the water. For an angel went down at a certain time into the pool and stirred up the water; then whoever stepped in first, after the stirring of the water, was made well of whatever disease he had</u>. Now, a certain man was there who had an infirmity for thirty-eight years. When Jesus saw him lying there, and knew that he already had been in that condition a long time, He said to him, "Do you want to be made well?" The sick man answered Him, "Sir, I have no man to put me into the pool when the water is stirred up; but while I am coming, another steps down before me." Jesus said to him, "Rise, take up your bed and walk." And immediately the man was made well, took up his bed, and walked." Critical scholars have shown that the underlined text is a forgery. Most likely, it is a deliberate attempt to contrast a narrative of Christian miraculous healing with the use of healing waters in the cult of Asclepius, which was a popular Greek deity of healing in medicine in the ancient Eastern Mediterranean.
- **Pauline Forgeries**: Textual analysis has shown that 6 out of 13 of Paul's letters are either forgeries or interpolations written by authors claiming to be Paul.

Please note how the forgeries above are desperately trying to add divinity to Jesus Christ.

Please note that trinitarianism did not surface until 100 CE, nowhere in the Old Testament, and nowhere during the life of Jesus Christ, including his death in 33 CE.

There were undoubtedly many more forgeries and additions; however, the point has been made to the reader, so we will move on.

Clearly, following a religion necessitates willful ignorance, and mythological falsehoods contained within the bible are outlined in the table below.

Biblical Ref	Remarks
Genesis 1:3-5	The biblical god created light on the first day of creation and created the sun on the fourth day of creation. This is scientifically flawed as the sun gives the light necessary to separate night/evening and day/morning. Also, there were no moons or stars as alternative light sources.
Genesis 1:11-13, 2	The biblical god created the sun on the fourth day and the vegetation/plants on the third day. This is scientifically flawed, as vegetation requires photosynthesis for survival and photosynthesis requires the sun. Also, the script discusses a woman being born from a man's rib, which is a scientific impossibility.
Genesis 5, 9:29	The bible claims that Adam lived for 930 years, Noah lived for 950 years, and Methuselah lived for 969 years. Geneticists have scientifically determined that the ceiling on the human body based on the evolution of the human genome is 150 years. Bear in mind that there were wars, limited medical procedures, and no organ transplants available at the time of Adam and beyond.
Genesis 1:20, Psalm 104:12, Daniel 2:38, Revelation 12:4-12, 14:6,7, 2 Corinthians 12:2	The bible claims that there are three (3) heavens. The first heaven is where the birds dwell and where Satan dwells as prince of the power of the air since the cross. The second heaven is where Satan and the fallen angels first fell and what demons are fighting for now. The third heaven has the 'throne', where Paul went and heard holy things. These are all fictional ideas conjured by superstitious humans whom could not understand the world beyond the Earth's atmosphere. It is worth noting that the bible acknowledges 'Sheol' – the land of the dead in Job 3:17-22, Genesis 15:15, 25:8,17; Deuteronomy 32:50.
Genesis 1:1, 1:6-10	The bible claims that the earth rests on a flat firmament with a dome-like structure above it. Below the earth and above the dome are waters. Also, the bible indicates that the sun and the moon revolve around the flat earth. This is scientifically inaccurate as the 'global earth' concept has been proven, and celestial bodies, not just the Earth, revolve around the sun.
Acts 8:39-40	Philip the Evangelist was supernaturally snatched by the Spirit of the Lord and instantly teleported from the desert road, where he baptized the Ethiopian eunuch, to the city of Azotus.
Isaiah 6, Genesis 3	Presence of celestial beings, such as fiery beings with six wings (seraphim), and four-faced (man, lion, ox, eagle) creatures with four wings known as cherubim.
Jonah	Jonah survives being swallowed by a great fish. Somehow Jonah survived in the belly of the fish for three days without being digested.
Joshua 10:12–14	A fictional event occurs where the sun stands still over Gibeon and the moon over the Valley of Aijalon. This event took place during a battle between the Israelites, led by Joshua, and a coalition of five Amorite kings who were attacking Gibeon.
Mark 16:17-20	Somehow, demons can be cast out in the name of Jesus. This is definitely false.
Matthew 10:8	Jesus instructs his disciples to heal the sick, raise the dead, cleanse leprosy, and drive out demons. This is all riddled in fiction.
1 Corinthians 14:2	The gift of tongues (speaking in an unlearned language) within the context of the church at Corinth, emphasizing a direct, vertical communication with the biblical god. In Spirituality, this is likened to witchcraft.
John 6:53-56	These references discuss intaking the Eucharist, where believers eat the body of Christ and drink the blood of Christ. In Spirituality, this is likened to witchcraft and spiritual cannibalism.
Genesis 32:24-30	The biblical god wrestles with Jacob and loses. This challenges the idea of divine omnipotence.
Exodus 4:24-26	The biblical god decides to kill Moses because his son was not circumcised. Not sure why any god would care about this.

Exodus 32:14	The biblical god repents of the evil he thought of doing to his people. Not sure what this god repented to, and it opens the door for another divine being.
Numbers 22:28-35	Balaam talks to a Donkey and an angel. This is highly implausible, as humans cannot speak to animals or angels.
Deuteronomy 23:1	No man can attend the congregation if his testicles are damaged, or if his penis has been cut off. Not sure why any god would care about this.
1 Samuel 6:4-5	The biblical god demands five golden hemorrhoids as a "trespass offering". Not sure why any god would make such a demand.
2 Kings 1:9-12	Elijah shows that he is "a man of God" by calling down fire from heaven to burn 102 men to death.
2 Kings 2:11	Elijah is pulled into heaven by a whirlwind.
2 Chronicles 21:20, 22:1-2	Ahaziah is somehow 2 years older than his father, Jehoram.
Psalm 148:7	Mythological dragons are praising the biblical god.
Matthew 27:53-54	People got out of their graves and walked around after Jesus supposedly rose from the dead.
1 Corinthians 11:14	It is shameful for a man to have long hair.
Jude 9	Michael the Archangel argued with the devil about the body of Moses.
Genesis 23:1-2, Genesis 25:20	Depending on the interpretation of the text, Rebecca married 40-year-old Isaac at the age of 3 or 10. This age gap indicates that pedophilia was tolerated in the Bible, and adult men could take pre-pubescent girls.
Deuteronomy 22:20–21, 1 Corinthians 14:34–35, 1 Timothy 2:11–12	A woman found not to be a virgin upon marriage can be stoned. Women can neither teach nor assume the authority of a man. Even in the presence of men or in the churches, women must be quiet. For married women, their husbands shall rule over them. These verses are normally meant to uphold the patriarchal hierarchy.

Before we conclude this article, it is incumbent upon us to expose how Christianity condones senseless slaughter (genocide, massacres, etc.) and slavery throughout the bible, especially since Christianity carries the notion of an all-loving 'god'.

Biblical Ref	Concerning Remarks on Senseless Slaughter
Genesis 7	The biblical god killed every man, woman, child, infant, animal, and plant on Earth except for one family and a boat full of animals. Please note that this includes devout followers of such a god, the innocent, and unborn children. Also, this occurrence on 'Earth only' should raise concerns.
Genesis 18-19	The biblical god destroyed two cities, Sodom and Gomorrah, after a mob of lustful men wanted to sleep with the angels. Lot offered his daughters as sacrifices to be raped by the crowd of men who came to sleep with the angels. Lot's daughters later got him drunk and took turns sleeping with him to get pregnant and have children. In return, the biblical god rains down sulfur and fire, killing every single plant, righteous person in town, and innocent children.
Exodus 7-12	The biblical god has Moses ask to let the Israelite slaves go worship in the wilderness. When Pharaoh refuses, the biblical god sends plagues on every worker, slave, and child in Egypt. Their food sources are destroyed, their water turned to undrinkable blood, and ten plagues. Finally, this god kills the firstborn male children of every family in Egypt, even the slaves whom the biblical was supposed to deliver, just for being associated with Egypt. Somehow, this god discerns whom to kill and whom not to kill based on the killing of lambs and smeared lamb blood upon houses – not sure how slaves would own lambs. This

	level of massacre attributed to the transgressions of a few is common in the bible.
Exodus 14, Joshua 11:20, Numbers 21:21-35	The biblical god takes credit for hardening the Pharaoh's heart and the hearts of the Canaanites/ Amorites to fight the Israelites, so that this biblical god could execute massacres of anyone in opposition.
Exodus 32	Yahweh threatens to kill all the Israelites for worshipping a golden calf. After Moses pleads, Yahweh decides not to destroy 'everyone completely'. In response, Moses ordered anyone "on the Lord's side" to thoroughly slaughter their families and neighbors with swords.
Deuteronomy 9:13-29, Numbers 13-16	The biblical god expresses the desire to destroy everyone, but for the pleas and rituals of Moses. This god tries to get Israel to go to war and punishes those not dealing in violence with death before reaching the promised land. Also, there is a group of Israelites that assemble against Moses on the notion of multiple holy men. In return, the biblical god performs a 'miracle' that buries them alive and that unearths a deadly fire, burning hundreds of people.
Numbers 25:16-18, 31	The biblical god commands Moses and the Israelites to seek vengeance on the Midianites. They are to kill every man, woman, and child regardless of status or occupation (even slave infants), but to let the virgin girls live "for themselves". Some Israelite men had sex with some Midianite women and may have worshipped an idol in the process.
Deuteronomy 2:19-21	The biblical god destroyed the Rephaim and Ammonites and gave the land to the sons of Lot.
Deuteronomy 7	The biblical god orders the Israelites to annihilate seven nations: the Hittites, the Girgashites, the Amorites, the Canaanites, the Perizzites, the Hivites, and the Jebusites.
Deuteronomy 13	The biblical god commands the killing of anyone who worships another god – even their own families. If a few people in the same city worship other gods, then everyone in the city is to be slaughtered, the livestock killed, and everything of value burned, and nothing shall be built there again. Imagine the dangers that this religious doctrine poses to society.
Joshua 6:17	All of the occupants of Jericho, except for Rahab and her family, are slain.
Joshua 8:1-29	Joshua, under the command of the biblical god, sets the entire city of Ai on fire, trapping the people inside. Anyone who got away was pursued and slaughtered, except women.
1 Samuel 6:19-21, 2 Samuel 6:6-7	The biblical god kills 50,000 men for looking at his artwork. He also kills someone for accidentally touching it when an ox supporting it stumbled.
1 Samuel 15	The biblical god orders the complete destruction of the Amalekites, and is careful to specify infants and animals. Eventually, this god gets angry at them for not killing everything, and the prophet, Samuel, kills the king of Amalek and hacks him to pieces.
2 Kings 1:9-17	The biblical god kills a hundred men to prove Elijah is a prophet.
2 Kings 2:23-24	Some children make fun of one of Yahweh's prophets for being bald, but he curses them, and the biblical god sends two bears out to kill 42 children.
2 Kings 3	After Ahab's death, Mesha, the king of Moab, rebelled against Israel and refused to pay tribute. Jehoram chose to go to war with Moab to try to bring them into submission. Yahweh actually loses this fight thanks to human sacrifice, but not before destroying all but one city and ruining the land. The Moabites actually recorded the same story, being oppressed for a time by the Israelites and then being led to a late victory by their God, Chemosh, in the Mesha Stele.
Job	The biblical god permits Satan to do all kinds of awful things to his devout follower, Job: affliction with ailments, killing his family, and even killing his livestock. When Job questions, the biblical god refuses to justify himself but

	instead allows Job to produce a new family as if this compensated for past family deaths.
Psalm 109, Psalm 137:9	The biblical god invites evildoings on persecutors: evil toward their children, forcing them to beg in the streets, and encouraging their families to be blotted from the earth. The biblical god even blesses those whom take the little ones (children) and whom dash them against the rock.

As far as slavery, findings in the biblical text indicate that chattel slavery was explicitly regulated, not condemned. Chattel slavery, also called traditional slavery, is so named because people are treated as the chattel (personal property) of the owner and are bought and sold as commodities. In other words, a slave was considered the legal property of masters and was forced to obey them.

The table below outlines slavery being condoned throughout the bible.

Biblical Ref	**Concerning Remarks on Slavery**
Exodus 21:4-6	So, the children and women don't go free. The children are born slaves. Moreover, they can be used as leverage to turn a male servant into a lifelong slave. But if the slave plainly says, 'I love my master, my wife, and my children; I will not go out free,' then his master shall bring him to god, and he shall bring him to the door or the doorpost. And his master shall bore his ear through with an awl, and he shall be his slave forever. If a man doesn't want to leave his wife and children behind as slaves while he goes free, then he has to commit to lifelong servitude, being marked like cattle.
Exodus 21:7-11	When a man sells his daughter as a slave, she shall not go out (free) as the male slaves do. If she does not please her master, who has designated her for himself, then he shall let her be redeemed. He shall have no right to sell her to a foreign people, since he has broken faith with her. Women are being sold and assigned to husbands. They are taken as one of multiple wives (not seen as polygamy if wives are property) after being purchased as a servant.
Numbers 31:18	Now therefore, kill every male among the little ones, and kill every woman who has known man by lying with him. But all the young girls who have not known a man by lying with him keep alive for yourselves. This can be seen as sex slavery.
Leviticus 25:44-46	The biblical god clearly states: You may buy male and female slaves from among the nations that are around you. You may also buy from among the strangers who sojourn with you and their clans that are with you, who have been born in your land, and they may be your property. You may bequeath them to your sons after you to inherit as a possession forever. Even the children of slaves/servants are inheritable property.
Leviticus 19:20-22	If a man sleeps with a female slave who is promised to another man but who has not been ransomed or given her freedom, there must be due punishment. Yet they are not to be put to death, because she had not been freed. The man, however, must bring a ram to the entrance of the tent of meeting for a guilt offering to the Lord. With the ram of the guilt offering, the priest is to make atonement for him before the Lord for the sin he has committed, and his sin will be forgiven.
Exodus 21:20-21	When a man strikes his slave, male or female, with a rod and the slave dies under his hand, he shall be avenged. But if the slave survives a day or two, he is not to be avenged, for the slave is his money.
1 Peter 2:18	Servants, be subject to your masters with all respect, not only to the good and gentle but also to the unjust. Commanding slaves to obey masters with all respect.
Ephesians 6:5	Slaves, obey your earthly masters with respect and fear, and with sincerity of heart, just as you would obey Christ. Obey them not only to win their favor when

	their eye is on you, but as slaves of Christ, doing the will of god from your heart. Serve wholeheartedly, as if you were serving the lord, not people, because you know that the lord will reward each one for whatever good they do, whether they are slave or free. The biblical god rewards obedience to slave owners.
Leviticus 27:28-29	But no devoted thing that a man devotes to the Lord, of anything that he has, whether man or beast, or of his inherited field, shall be sold or redeemed; every devoted thing is most holy to the Lord. No one devoted, who is to be devoted for destruction from mankind, shall be ransomed; he shall surely be put to death. This allows slaves to be offered as sacrifices to the biblical god.

Of course, the two (2) tables above are not a complete list of senseless slaughter and slavery in the bible; however, it shows stark contrasts to a loving god, a humanistic worldview, and a peaceful doctrine., especially when combined with instances of human sacrifice. Some apologists argue that slaves, masters, men, and women are equal per Galatians 3:28; however, this reference is in access to Jesus/heaven, not the systems of slavery on earth. In Philemon 1:16, it says to emancipate slaves and treat them like brothers; however, this is a plea from Paul to elevate the legal status of one slave, Onesimus. Appealing based on the recipients' partnership with himself and his own fondness for Onesimus, Paul even offers to pay up. The biblical context does not extend to anyone but Onesimus.

Please note that Mormonism and the Church of Latter-Day Saints are premised on the Bible, so it is also false.

Please note that the Quran of Islam (see next article) confirms the Injeel (gospels), so it is also false.

Notice how a historical critique reduces the biblical narrative to falsehoods and fiction. Once again, the key to a religion's success is simply creating an explanation – not necessarily the best, the most factually accurate, the most historical, or the most truthful – riddled with belief that the willfully ignorant humans can subscribe to.

Em Hotep!

DISMANTLING ISLAM

ANKH WADJA SENEB | ARTICLE NO: 008

Function: The Awareness of Control Mechanisms
Subject(s): Islam, Muhammad, Sunnah, Quran, hadith, tafsir, Sira, Allah
Position: Part 3 – Breaking Societal Controls
Theme: Dealing with Religions, Cults, & Atheism | Scene 8

ARTICLE NO: 008 – DISMANTLING ISLAM

Peace to the High Power! Peace to the Living Universe! Peace to all Finite Living Beings! Peace to All Things – seen and unseen! For my spirit is with me, my image is with me, and my purpose is with me. For those with knowledge understand that the mechanisms behind societal controls can only flourish when consciousness, awareness, vibration, and rationality are minimized and when willful ignorance, fear, indoctrination, and subjugating forces are maximized.

Recall that the key to a religion's success is simply creating an explanation – not necessarily the best, the most factually accurate, the most historical, or the most truthful – riddled with belief that the willfully ignorant humans can subscribe to. This willful ignorance of Islam increases for Muslims whom are not fluent in the Arabic language (roughly 15% of Muslims speak Arabic), whom memorize verses without knowing their meanings (roughly 85% of Muslims memorize the Quran in a language that they do not understand), whom do not read the religious text, or whom dismiss the ancient scholars at the time of Muhammad in favor of modern scholars – normally, inventing their own version/sect/teachings of Islam separate from the actual religious doctrine. This section will focus primarily on the Quran (the word of god as dictated to Muhammad by the archangel Gabriel) and secondarily on the Sunnah (a body of traditions and practices of Muhammad that constitute a model for Muslims to follow) of high grade.

As an appetizer, we begin this discussion by placing a magnifying glass over the Nabataeans – an ancient, nomadic Arab tribe that flourished between the 4th Century BCE and the 2nd Century CE. Known for navigating the harsh desert environment for trade, the Nabataeans were neither empire-builders nor conquerors but rather protective fortifiers because their wealth and their power came through commerce. During this time, they controlled the spice markets and monopolized the caravan routes connecting Arabia, Syria, and the Mediterranean, primarily trading in frankincense, myrrh, silks, and precious stones. Despite freely roaming for trade, the Nabataeans always returned to their home capital of Petra (Raqmu), which was located in northern Arabia and the southern Levant, covering much of present-day Jordan and extending into parts of Syria, Saudi Arabia, and Israel, with rose-red sandstone cliffs, memorable caves, and burial tombs. The Nabataeans not only influenced trade and architecture but also writing and language, using a cursive script, becoming rounded and connected over time, derived from Aramaic and originally speaking a dialect of Aramaic — the common language of the Near East. By the 3rd–5th Centuries CE, the Nabataean inscriptions already looked strikingly similar to the Arabic script, especially with the inclusion of Arabic vocabulary and Arabic grammatical constructions. Strong examples of the integrated Nabataean script emerged in early Arabic inscriptions (4th–6th Centuries), including the Zabad inscription (512 CE) in Syria, and this script was spread through Petra and Nabataean trade hubs. Therefore, the Arabic alphabet/script, which is the script of the Quran (القرآن), is nothing more than a direct descendant of Nabataean writing.

Digging deeper, the polytheistic Nabataeans had a chief god named Dushara (meaning "Lord of the Mountain") that was given the generic title of ilāh (إله), which becomes Al-ilāh (ال + إله) when combined with the definite article (ال meaning 'the') and which becomes Allah (الله) when contracted/shortened. Allah was never a personal name, but only a title in the Nabataean culture; even though, the authors of Islam later stole this title, naming their god Allah deceptively under divine revelation.

Before Islam surfaced, Nabataeans also worshiped Dushara (Allāh) at Petra in cube-shaped shrines/sanctuaries and throughout Arabia alongside three (3) intercessional goddesses (الاهات): Al-Lat (ٱللَّٰتَ) meaning fertility and provision; Al-'Uzza (ٱلْعُزَّىٰ) meaning power and war, and Manat (مَنَوٰةَ) meaning fate and destiny. These goddesses would start as the consorts of Allah, only to be reduced to the daughters of Allah during the entrance of Islam and the Kaaba in Mecca – which housed numerous idols, estimated to be around 360, representing the many gods and goddesses worshipped by the different tribes. Controlled by the Quraysh tribe, the same tribe as Muhammad, Mecca was a significant center of pagan religious pilgrimage and tribal Arab polytheism, including the Quraysh god, Hubal. There were also syncretized influences from Judaism, Christianity, Sabeanism, Zoroastrianism, and other forms of paganism. Archaeological evidence shows that the qibla (the direction of prayer) of the earliest mosques (e.g., Kufa, Fustat, etc.) was aligned not toward Mecca — but toward Petra. Later Islamic authorities shifted the qibla toward Mecca, erasing Petra from the story.

In one of the most embarrassing and most controversial events, Satan successfully injected his words into Muhammad's mouth when Muhammad was revealing the word of god. Known as the Satanic Verses (الآية), Muhammad spoke Satan's words as the word of god, and early Islamic tradition records indicate that Muhammad initially acknowledged Allah's daughters as exalted intercessors before retracting.

Per the Sura (Sura means "chapter") 53:19–20, the current recitation is as follows:

أَفَرَءَيْتُمُ ٱللَّٰتَ وَٱلْعُزَّىٰ وَمَنَوٰةَ ٱلثَّالِثَةَ ٱلْأُخْرَىٰ

So, have you considered al-Lat and al-'Uzza? And Manat, the third – the other one?

However, early Muslim biographers of Muhammad's life wrote that these verses originally read:

Have ye seen Lat, and 'Uzza, and another, the third (goddess), Manat? These are the exalted cranes (intermediaries) whose intercession is to be hoped for.

The addition of the second sentence clearly shows that Allah's daughters were considered heavenly beings of intercessors, especially since Numidian cranes were a metaphor for incredible heights, remarkable flight, and graceful movements. Notable references from Muslim sources from the time of Muhammad, serving as direct evidence, include the following:

- Imam al-Waqidi (747 – 823 CE). Al-Waqidi was an early Arab Muslim historian and biographer of Muhammad, specializing in Muhammad's military campaigns. In *Asbab al-Nozul*, he wrote "On a certain day, the chief men of Mecca, assembled in a group beside the Kaaba, discussed as was their want the affairs of the city; when Mahomet appeared and, seating himself by them in a friendly manner, began to recite in their hearing the 53rd Sura.... 'And see ye not Lat and 'Uzza, and Manat the third besides?' When he had reached this verse, the devil suggested an expression of the thoughts which for many a day had possessed his soul; and put into his mouth words of reconciliation and compromise, the revelation of which he had been longing for from God, namely; 'These are the exalted Females, and verily their intercession is to be hoped for.' The Quraysh were surprised and delighted with this acknowledgment of their deities; and as Mahomet wound up the Sura with the closing words 'Wherefore bow down before God, and serve him' the whole assembly prostrated themselves with one accord on the ground and worshipped. ... In the evening, Gabriel visited him; and the prophet recited the Sura unto him. And Gabriel said, 'What is this that thou hast done? Thou hast repeated before the people words that I never gave unto thee'. So, Mahomet grieved sore, ...".
- Imam Al-Layth Ibn Sa'ad (784 – 845 CE). Ibn Sa'ad is an early Islamic scholar, biographer, and compiler of biographies who authored the *Tabaqat al-Kubra*, a critical source for early Islamic history and biographies of the Prophet Muhammad, his companions, and subsequent generations of scholars. Not only was he familiar with the *Asbab al-Nozul* from al-Waqidi, Ibn Sa'ad confirmed the Satanic Verses and Muhammad's acknowledgment of the three (3) goddesses in the *Tabaqat al-Kubra.*
- Ibn Ishaq (704 CE – 767 CE). Ibn Ishaq was a Shafi'ite Sunni Muslim historian from Medina who spent his life collecting oral traditions to write the influential *Sirat Rasullullah* (meaning "the biography of Prophet Muhammad") – a text known today through the edited version by Ibn Hisham. In *Sirat Rasullullah*, it reads: "[The emigrants] remained where they were [in Ethiopia] until they heard that the people of Mecca had accepted Islam and prostrated themselves. That was because the chapter of Al-Najm (Sura/Chapter 53 of the Quran) had been sent down to Muhammad and the apostle recited it. Both Muslims and polytheists listened to it silently until he reached his words 'Have you seen al-Lat and al-'Uzza?' They gave ear to him attentively while the faithful believed [their prophet]. Some apostatized when they heard the 'saj' of Satan and said, 'By Allah we will serve them (the cranes) so that they may bring us near to Allah'. Satan taught these two verses to every polytheist, and their tongues took to them easily. This weighed heavily upon the apostle until Gabriel came to him and complained...."
- Ibn Jarir al-Tabari (839 – 923 CE). Al-Tabari was a prominent Shafi'ite Sunni Muslim scholar who wrote 38 volumes of Islamic history, including a comprehensive Quranic commentary, *Tafsir al-Tabari* (meaning "interpretations of al-Tabari"), and his monumental history, *Tarikh al-Rusul wa al-Muluk.* Within the latter historical work in volume 6, pages 108-110, al-Tabari says: "When the messenger of God saw how his tribe turned their backs on him and was grieved to see them shunning the message he had brought to them from God, he longed in his soul that something would come to him from God which would reconcile him with his tribe.... And when he came to the words: 'Have you thought upon al-Lat and al-Uzza and Manat, the third, the other?' Satan cast on his tongue, because of his inner debates and what he desired to bring to his people, the words: 'These are the high-flying cranes; verily their intercession is accepted with approval [alternately: to be desired or hoped for].' When the Quraysh heard this, they rejoiced and were happy and delighted at the way in which he spoke of their gods, and they listened to him, while the Muslims, having complete trust in their prophet in respect of the message which he brought from god, did not suspect him of error, illusion, or mistake. ... Then [later] Gabriel came to the Messenger of God and said, 'Mohammed, what have you done? You have recited to the people that which I did not bring to you from God, ...'"

To add insult to injury, Sura 53:19–20 experienced later changes across Sura 53:19–22

Before Change: Have ye seen Lat, and 'Uzza, and another, the third (goddess), Manat? These are the exalted cranes (intermediaries) whose intercession is to be hoped for.

After Change: Have ye seen Lat, and 'Uzza, and another, the third (goddess), Manat? What! For you the male sex, and for him, the female? Behold, such would indeed be a division most unfair.

Under this change, Muslims were taught that those, who believed in Allah's three daughters, were unfair toward Allah, since they all preferred sons yet said that Allah had only daughters.

Muslim scholars still to this very day try to conceal the Satanic verses either in practice or in translation because this evidence not only strongly suggests that a pagan god once tied to a family of goddesses was rebranded as a monotheistic deity, but it also contradicts the following Quranic verse:

Sura 6:101

بَدِيعُ ٱلسَّمَٰوَٰتِ وَٱلْأَرْضِ ۖ أَنَّىٰ يَكُونُ لَهُۥ وَلَدٌ وَلَمْ تَكُن لَّهُۥ صَٰحِبَةٌ ۖ وَخَلَقَ كُلَّ شَىْءٍ ۖ وَهُوَ بِكُلِّ شَىْءٍ عَلِيمٌ

˹He is˺ the Originator of the heavens and earth. How could He have children when He has no mate? He created all things and has ˹perfect˺ knowledge of everything.

Moreover, these findings invalidate any verse indicating that there is no other god, except Allah, as seen in Sura 47:19, Sura 59:23, and Sura 3:18 from the shahada.

Furthermore, these findings beg the question about the protection of the supposed god, Allah, and the connections to the Kaaba. In the Sura 17:73-75,

وَإِن كَادُوا۟ لَيَفْتِنُونَكَ عَنِ ٱلَّذِىٓ أَوْحَيْنَآ إِلَيْكَ لِتَفْتَرِىَ عَلَيْنَا غَيْرَهُۥ ۖ وَإِذًا لَّٱتَّخَذُوكَ خَلِيلًا وَلَوْلَآ أَن ثَبَّتْنَٰكَ لَقَدْ كِدتَّ تَرْكَنُ إِلَيْهِمْ شَيْـًٔا قَلِيلًا لِّيَجْعَلَ مَا يُلْقِى ٱلشَّيْطَٰنُ فِتْنَةً لِّلَّذِينَ فِى قُلُوبِهِم مَّرَضٌ وَٱلْقَاسِيَةِ قُلُوبُهُمْ ۗ وَإِنَّ ٱلظَّٰلِمِينَ لَفِى شِقَاقٍۭ بَعِيدٍ

O Muhammad! They had all but tempted you away from what We have revealed to you that you may invent something else in Our Name. Had you done so, they would have taken you as their trusted friend. Indeed, had We not strengthened you, you might have inclined to them a little, whereupon We would have made you taste double (the chastisement) in the world and double (the chastisement) after death, and then you would have found none to help you against us.

In this verse, ignoring the strange plurality of "we" when there is supposed to be only one god, the Makkah disbelievers/polytheists tried to tempt Muhammad away from his divine message, but supposedly Allah protected him from fully giving in. Had Muhammad compromised his belief, even slightly, he would have faced a doubled punishment in this life and the hereafter, with no helper against Allah. The main issues are where was this divine protection when Satan successfully threw the Satanic verses into Muhammad's mouth during recitation, prevailing over Allāh, and why was Muhammad – or even Satan – not severely punished for straying from Allah's path. After all, Satan's negative influence on recitations and Allah's ability to stop Satan's influence on recitation before it happens – being omniscient – is mentioned in Sura 22:52.

وَمَآ أَرْسَلْنَا مِن قَبْلِكَ مِن رَّسُولٍ وَلَا نَبِىٍّ إِلَّآ إِذَا تَمَنَّىٰٓ أَلْقَى ٱلشَّيْطَٰنُ فِىٓ أُمْنِيَّتِهِۦ فَيَنسَخُ ٱللَّهُ مَا يُلْقِى ٱلشَّيْطَٰنُ ثُمَّ يُحْكِمُ ٱللَّهُ ءَايَٰتِهِۦ ۗ وَٱللَّهُ عَلِيمٌ حَكِيمٌ

Whenever we sent a messenger or a prophet before you ˹O Prophet˺ and he recited ˹Our revelations˺, Satan would influence ˹people's understanding of˺ his recitation. But ˹eventually˺ Allah would eliminate Satan's influence. Then Allah would ˹firmly˺ establish His revelations. And Allah is All-Knowing, All-Wise.

Next, we turn to the connections of the Kaaba, known as the "House of Allah". The Kaaba, which is the revered sanctuary of Islam located in Mecca, is a black stone with a wall built in its eastern corner, where pagans offered idols, animal sacrifices, and astral worship to gods associated with golden suns and moons. During pilgrimages, the pagans executed ritual processions, walking around the Kaaba in white robes, running between nearby hills, and chanting the names of their gods.

As a sidebar, the Kaaba was seen as a fertility idol, and it was customary for pilgrims to walk around the Kaaba naked or for women to wipe menstrual blood on the idol for effect. After the ritual, they would go to the hills of Safa and Marwa to engage in sexual activity.

Muhammad abhorred polytheistic worship, consequently aligning himself with faiths that he believed were from the true god and initially selecting Jerusalem as the direction of prayer (qibla) in the hope that the Jews would receive him as a prophet. After being thoroughly rejected by the Jews, Muhammad migrated to Medina and eventually turned the direction of prayer from Jerusalem to Mecca – the center of pagan worship in the Arabian Peninsula – as seen in Sura 2:144. Just as Muhammad had compromised with the pagan idol worshippers in Mecca by sanctioning and worshipping the pagan goddesses (Lat, 'Uzza, and Manat), he then sanctioned the pagan rituals concerning the Kaaba for Muslims (e.g., kissing the black stone, touching the Kaaba, circling the structure counterclockwise seven times, running between the two hills, etc.) after taking Mecca and cleansing the Kaaba thereafter. Umar ibn al-Khattab, like many other Muslims, later kissed the black stone, following Muhammad in his practice of veneration of pagan idols per Sahih al-Bukhari 1597, Volume 2, Book 26, Hadith 667:

حَدَّثَنَا مُحَمَّدُ بْنُ كَثِيرٍ، أَخْبَرَنَا سُفْيَانُ، عَنِ الأَعْمَشِ، عَنْ إِبْرَاهِيمَ، عَنْ عَابِسِ بْنِ رَبِيعَةَ، عَنْ عُمَرَ ـ رضى الله عنه ـ أَنَّهُ جَاءَ إِلَى الْحَجَرِ الأَسْوَدِ فَقَبَّلَهُ، فَقَالَ إِنِّي أَعْلَمُ أَنَّكَ حَجَرٌ لاَ تَضُرُّ وَلاَ تَنْفَعُ، وَلَوْلاَ أَنِّي رَأَيْتُ النَّبِيَّ صلى الله عليه وسلم يُقَبِّلُكَ مَا قَبَّلْتُكَ.

Umar came near the Black Stone and kissed it and said "No doubt, I know that you are a stone and can neither benefit anyone nor harm anyone. Had I not seen Allah's Messenger (ﷺ) kissing you, I would not have kissed you.

Muhammad kissing the black stone goes completely against all of the idolatry verses in Sura 6, as well as Abraham's smashing of idols in Sura 21:51-69. Ironically, Muhammad invented historical references for the Kaaba, claiming that Abraham and Ishmael laid the foundations of the Kaaba (Sura 2:127), that God ordained the Kaaba as a sacred house (Sura 5:97), and that the Kaaba was the first temple ever built for mankind (Sura 3:97). None of these are fact per the historical record or proximal faiths. Even worse, in the Sunnah, Muslims are taught that the black stone can somehow erase sin (Sunan an-Nasa'I 2919, Volume 3, Book 24, Hadith 2922) and that the black stone was white until it inherited the sins of all Adam's descendants (Jami` at-Tirmidhi 877, Volume 2, Book 4, Hadith 877). Ibn Abbas confirms that Muhammad said: The black stone came from Paradise and at the time of its descent it was whiter than milk, but that the sins of the children of Adam have caused it to be black, by their touching it. That on the Day of Resurrection, when it will have two eyes, by which it will see and know all those who touched it and kissed it, and when it will have a tongue to speak, it will give evidence in favor of those who touched and kissed it'.

For clarification, Muslims falsely proclaim that the Kaaba was first constructed in Islamic heaven 2000 years before the creation of the world, where a heavenly model of it remains. Adam supposedly erected the first Kaaba on Earth directly below the position of the heavenly model, and 10,000 angels were appointed to guard the earthly Kaaba. After the angels failed to do so, Allah then instructed Abraham – a major critic of idols by far – to rebuild it.

For clarification, Muslims do not know why they have to circumambulate counterclockwise, especially since Muhammad borrowed this idea from the Jews and the pagans.

For clarification, the black stone was possibly a meteorite discovered by the Phoenicians in 300 – 400 BCE and worshipped by pagans as a gift from god. The Romans brought the black stone to their territory in the 1st Century BCE, and the Roman Emperor, Aurelius Antoninus, moved it to Damascus, believing that the presence of the black stone equated to the presence of god. It was moved to Petra in the 7th Century and then sent down to Mecca in 687 CE by Ibn Zubayr after erasing Petra's history. In all instances, the pilgrims followed.

At this point, the reader can see that there is something tragically wrong with Islam; however, let's explore the standard Islamic narrative in detail to dismantle Islam systematically through historical critique (e.g., historical facts, maps/timelines of events, ancient writings, inscriptions, and geographic conditions) rather than some theological exegesis. This historical critique of the standard Islamic narrative will encompass problems with Islamic Sources, problems with Mecca, problems with Muhammad, and problems with the Quran. The reader must pay close attention to the dates.

Recall that the key to a religion's success is simply creating an explanation – not necessarily the best, the most factually accurate, the most historical, or the most truthful – riddled with belief that the willfully ignorant humans can subscribe to.

In the standard Islamic narrative, the vast majority of Muslims – mostly, nominal and conservative – have claimed for the last 1400 years that:

- Muhammad was the last and the greatest prophet, who was born in Mecca in 570 CE and who died in Medina in 632 CE. As a messenger of Allah, he received the Quran as the final revelation for the world, and he was chosen to model Islam as the paradigm of the world and to correct all corrupt texts – the Torah and the Injeel (Gospels).
- The Quran was sent down to Muhammad through revelation between 610 – 632 CE (610 – 622 CE in Mecca and 622 – 632 CE in Medina). The Quran is claimed to be the greatest and the only perfectly preserved text, final and eternal, correcting all previous revelations.
- Islam is the final religion based on Muhammad's life and sayings (Sunni hadiths) and the Quranic teachings.

Based on the standard Islamic narrative and Muslim's claims, Islam is completely dependent on three (3) items: The Quran (the Islamic holy book), Muhammad (the Islamic prophet), and Mecca (the Islamic holy place). Since these three (3) areas are foundational to Islam, they will be investigated at the time when they should have all existed in the 7th Century and the place where they should have all existed in the Hijaz (Central Western Arabia).

Problems with Islamic Sources

To investigate where all of the sources and the stories originate, the reader must examine the early expansion of Islam, per the military campaign mapping below in accordance with the standard Islamic narrative. The reader should convert this map to memory.

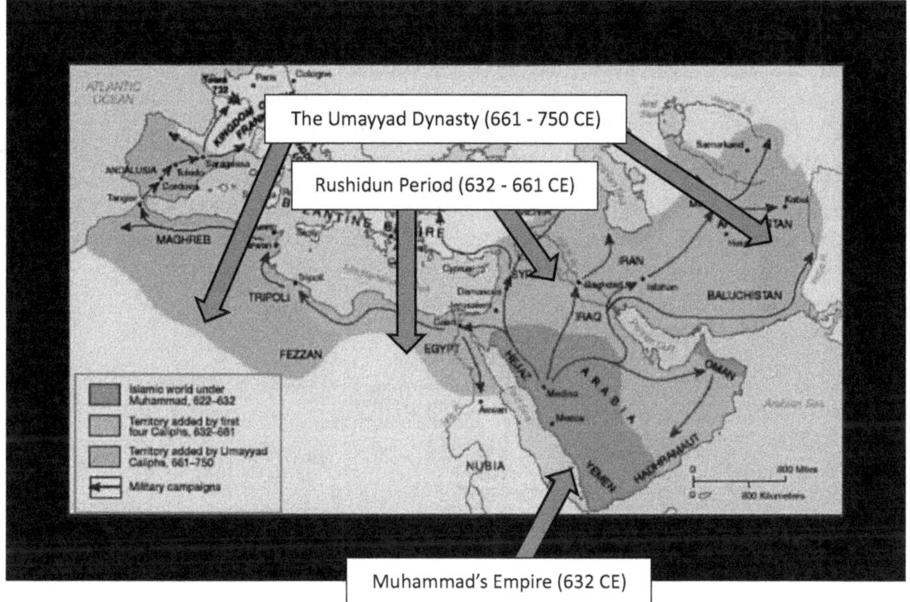

Strictly observing the map:

- The dark orange area represents the Islamic world under Muhammad from 622 – 632 CE, and Muhammad's empire primarily extended from the northern part of the Hijaz (Central Western Arabia) to Yemen. This area includes the two (2) major cities of Mecca and Medina.
- The light orange area represents the territory added by the first four caliphates through military conquest under the four (4) "rightly-guided" caliphs/rulers (Abu Bakr, Umar ibn al-Khattab, Uthman ibn Affan, and Ali ibn Abi Talib) after Muhammad died in 632 CE. This area extended from Tripoli near the Mediterranean Sea in the west to Afghanistan in the east and Turkey in the north to Yemen in the south.

Abu Bakr (reigned 632 – 634 CE): The first caliph, Abu Bakr, was a close friend and father-in-law of Muhammad. He united the Arabian Peninsula during the Ridda Wars (Wars of Apostasy), which broke out after Muhammad's death. Abu Bakr also oversaw the first compilation of the Quran into a single manuscript.

Umar ibn al-Khattab (reigned 634 – 644 CE): Appointed by Abu Bakr, Umar led an unprecedented expansion of the Islamic state, conquering vast territories from the Byzantine and Sasanian Empires. He established key administrative structures, such as a public treasury and the Islamic Hijri calendar.

Uthman ibn Affan (reigned 644 – 656 CE): Elected by a council, Uthman's reign saw further expansion of the caliphate. His most significant contribution was commissioning the standardization and canonization of the Quran to ensure uniformity across the growing Muslim lands. Accusations of nepotism and favoritism, however, led to unrest and his eventual assassination.

Ali ibn Abi Talib (reigned 656 – 661 CE): Muhammad's cousin and son-in-law, Ali's caliphate was marked by civil strife (First Fitna). He moved the capital to Kufa but faced opposition from those demanding retribution for Uthman's death, including Muhammad's widow, Aisha, and the governor of Syria, Mu'awiya. A few years after the Battle of Siffin (657 CE), an inconclusive conflict with failed arbitration between Ali's forces and the army of Muawiyah I, Ali was assassinated by a member of the Kharijite sect in 661 CE, which brought the Rashidun era to an end.

- The purple area represents the territory added by the Umayyad caliphate, beginning with the long-time governor of Greater Syria in Damascus, Mu'awiya I, from 661 – 750 CE. Muslims normally label this caliphate as the "First Real Islamic Caliphate" or the "First Real Islamic Kingdom", as the borders extended through the northern portions of Africa up to Andalucia (modern-day Spain) and almost to the Indus River in India.

The dark orange areas and the light orange areas are the areas of most concern because, by 661 CE, the Quran (the Islamic holy book), Muhammad (the Islamic prophet), and Mecca (the Islamic holy place) were already in place. Not to mention, the fundamentals of Islam follow from the period of Muhammad's reign and the Rushidun Period.

A basic timeline of Islam's emergence can be constructed as follows:

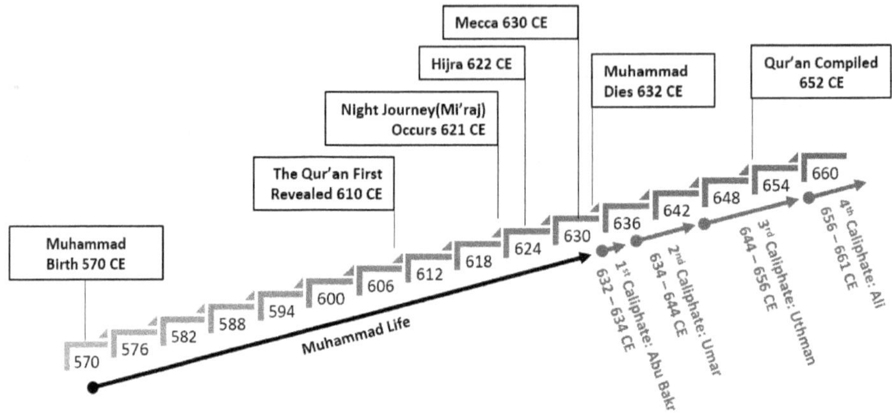

For clarification,

- Muhammad supposedly first received revelations in 610 CE in a cave on Mount Hira near Mecca from Allah through an angel named Jibreel (Gabriel).
- The Night Journey and Ascension (الإسراء والمعراج), normally shortened to Al-Mi'raj and referenced by the 111 verses of Sura 17, describes the mythical event, when Muhammad travelled from the Sacred Mosque (ٱلْمَسْجِدُ ٱلْحَرَام) in Mecca to the Farthest Mosque (ٱلْمَسْجِد ٱلْأَقْصَىٰ) in Jerusalem, and then ascended through the seven (7) heavens the Lote Tree of the Utmost Boundary all on a supernatural winged beast with a female face called a Buraaq in a single night – yes, the entire journey in a single night – after the Satanic Verses debacle. During this journey, Muhammad somehow met other prophets, led preceding prophets in prayer, witnessed the wonders of paradise and the punishments of hell, and communicated with Allah directly – even overriding the fifty (50) daily prayers ordained by Allah alongside advice from Moses. The majority of Muslims consider this to be a real-life event rather than some dream or vision.

As a sidebar, some scholars have mentioned that the story of Muhammad ascending to heaven on a Buraaq has been seemingly copied from pagan religions. In the Zoroastrian tales, the *Book of Arda Viraf*, for example, the righteous man, Arda Viraf, is transported after spiritual revelation to heaven and hell, and he is selected to journey to the next world to counter a growing sense of doubt and confusion among the faithful. In Persian beliefs, the Buraaq was a demon that took the form of a fiery horse. These creatures/demons could be summoned by a shaman, which coincidentally is how the Persians described Muhammad.

- The Hijra, which refers to the migration of Muhammad and approximately 80-200 of his early followers from Mecca to Yathrib (later renamed Medina) in 622 CE, was prompted by several years of intense persecution and hostility from the dominant tribe in Mecca – the Quraysh. The Quraysh, who were largely polytheistic, felt threatened by Muhammad's monotheistic message, which challenged their religious beliefs and Mecca's idol-based economy. Fearing the growing threats of the Muslims, the Quraysh plotted to assassinate Muhammad and to expel all Muslims, causing Muhammad's followers to leave Mecca in small groups to avoid suspicion and to establish an external Islamic state (ummah). This event also marked the beginning of the Islamic calendar. Later on, Muhammad would return to Mecca to launch a full-scale military and religious war (Muslim–Quraysh War) against his own tribe, beginning with the Battle of Badr in 624 CE and concluding with the Conquest of Mecca in 630 CE.

The compiled Quran, canonized by Uthman ibn Affan in 652 CE, was compiled twenty (20) years after Muhammad's death. Muhammad never created the Quran, and Muhammad never wrote it down while he was alive. The Quran was written down by Abu Bakr right after Muhammad's death, not by Uthman as most Muslims believe. The religious doctrine of Islam, including the biographies of Muhammad, sayings/teachings of Muhammad, commentaries on the Quran, and the Islamic histories, should have been finalized, standardized, and inculcated by 661 CE; however, there was one big problem – there were no eyewitnesses behind these Islamic sources at this time.

An extended timeline is provided below.

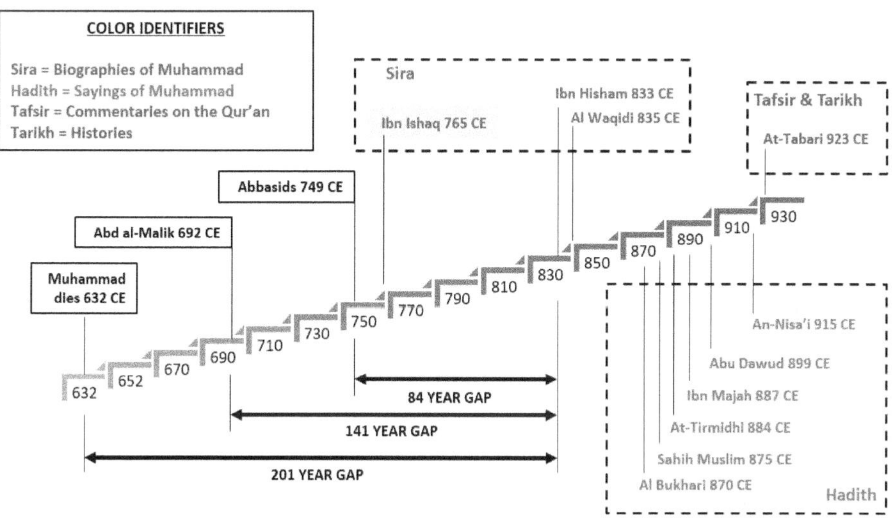

When Muhammad died in 632 CE, his biography (Sira) was not captured immediately by his early followers. According to Muslims, Ibn Ishaq supposedly wrote about Muhammad no later than 765 CE, which is a 133-year difference, far too late in another century to be credible. To make matters worse, Muslims cannot present any words, letters, excerpts, or literature from Ibn Ishaq as biographic evidence; therefore, this source will be dismissed. This means that the next written biographies on Muhammad would come from Ibn Hisham in 833 CE with a 201-year gap, and Al-Waqidi in 835 CE with a 203-year gap, respectively. Neither of these sources is in the correct century.

The Issue with late sources continues with the Sunni hadiths (the sayings and teachings of Muhammad). The hadith will be used in this context only as the collections of sayings, actions, and approvals of Muhammad. Many Muslims are not aware that the Quran is also a hadith, and this fact is literally acknowledged in the direct Arabic script of Sura 39:23, Sura 7:185, and Sura 68:44.

The first person to write down these sayings/teachings was Al-Bukhari in 870 CE – the late 9th Century. Looking at all the dates of the hadiths, everything known about Muhammad's sayings had a rough gap of 240 years or more, so none of the hadith writers knew anything about Muhammad. This leads to an important question: Where did these hadith writers get their material if they did not live in the same century as Muhammad? The answer is simple. The hadith writers memorized and collected hadiths from contemporary scholars about what Muhammad said. Al-Bukhari, for instance, was tasked to assess 600,000 given stories about what Muhammad said without any criteria on what to retain and what to discard. Going based on what he liked and what he did not like, Al-Bukhari reduced Muhammad's sayings from 600,000 to 7,397 – effectively discarding 98 percent of the teachings without explanation or archive.

Since the biographies and the hadiths are far too late to be credible, the only remaining Islamic sources are the tafsirs (commentaries of the Quran) and the tarikhs (histories). The tafsirs contain interpretations of each Quranic verse because no one can fully understand them through the Arabic text or through translation. Even the top Islamic experts do not understand 25 percent of the Quran – oftentimes proclaiming "Allah knows best" when their own understanding fails them. This contradicts the notion that Quranic verses are easy to understand and the Quran provides a clear explanation of all things per Sura 54:17 and Sura 16:89. If the Quran was easy to understand and it provided a clear explanation of all things, then there would be no need for tafsirs and tarikhs.

For clarification, electing to say "Allah knows best" instead of investigating matters around knowledge indicates that following Islam requires low rationality and low consciousness. The followers use Allah as an excuse to feel comfortable giving up on reasoning and not thinking for themselves.

At-Tabari was the first to introduce commentaries in 923 CE, 291 years after the death of Muhammad in 632 CE and 271 years after the Quran was initially compiled in 652 CE. There are others, such as Tafsir al-Qurtubi (1273 CE), Tafsir al-Baydawi (1286 CE), Tafsir ibn Kathir (1373 CE), and Tafsir al-Jalalayn (1459-1505 CE); however, Tafsir at-Tabari is the earliest resource. Once again, none of these sources was in the same century as Muhammad.

The reader should note that Abd al-Malik (646 – 705 CE) and the Abbasid Caliphate (750 – 1258 CE) are also included on the timeline above.

From 683 CE to 692 CE, the caliphate was divided between Abd al-Malik in Syria and his anti-caliph rival, Ibn al-Zubayr, whom was based in Mecca, controlling key holy sites and much of the caliphate's eastern provinces. In 692 CE, Umayyad caliph Abd al-Malik concluded the Second Islamic Civil War by defeating and killing his rival, Ibn al-Zubayr. This decisive victory enabled Abd al-Malik to consolidate his rule over the entire Muslim empire and to implement significant reforms. These reforms include:

- **Dome of the Rock**: Around 692 CE, Abd al-Malik completed the construction of the Dome of the Rock in Jerusalem. This monumental structure was built to assert the uniqueness of Islam and to serve as a focal point for his supporters during the civil war.

Please keep in mind that the Dome of the Rock had a qibla directed toward Jerusalem, not Mecca. This is a big problem for Islam.

- **Coinage Reform**: He introduced a new, distinctly Islamic currency to replace Byzantine and Sasanian coins. This included the production of the first purely epigraphic—or imageless—gold dinars in 696 CE.
- **Administrative Reforms**: Abd al-Malik began the process of "Arabization", including making Arabic the official language of the bureaucracy in place of Greek and Persian.
- **Resumption of Conquests**: After solidifying his rule, Abd al-Malik was able to resume military campaigns, including the expansion of Arab conquests throughout North Africa.

Abd al-Malik is placed on the timeline because he is the one who introduced Muhammad's name on the Dome of the Rock inscriptions, coinage, and Islamic protocols around 692 CE, which is 60 years after the supposed death of Muhammad. Once again, this is a problem for Islam because Muhammad ruled the Islamic Empire from 622 – 632 CE, and yet no name references, no inscriptions, no coins, or no protocols are ascribed to him until 60 years after his death.

The Abbasid dynasty ruled as caliphs from 749 CE to 1258 CE after leading a revolution against the ruling Umayyad dynasty, which had grown unpopular, especially among non-Arab Muslims (mawali). Led by the general Abu Muslim, the Abbasids decisively defeated the last Umayyad caliph, Marwan II, at the Battle of the Great Zab River in 749 CE. The second Abbasid caliph, al-Mansur, established the new capital of Baghdad in 762 CE, shifting the caliphate's center of power eastward into Mesopotamia. During the reign of Caliph Harun al-Rashid (786 – 809 CE), the legendary Bayt al-Hikma (House of Wisdom) was established in Baghdad. This academy, which was a hub for mathematics, astronomy, religion/ceremony, and philosophy, attracted scholars from across the Islamic world and beyond to translate and to expand upon classical knowledge.

As a sidebar, it is worth noting that the Abbasids used the House of Wisdom to appropriate and to pass off knowledge from other cultures as their own, as seen by the development of algebra by al-Khwarizmi, the codification of Greek and Indian astronomical knowledge, and Arabic numerals that originated from ancient India around the 3rd century BCE.

In 1258, Hulagu Khan besieged Baghdad with his Mongol army. After the city was captured, the last Abbasid caliph, al-Musta'sim, was executed, and the Mongols destroyed countless libraries, documents, mosques, and palaces; even though, a surviving line of Abbasids was re-established as ceremonial caliphs with symbolic religious authority in Cairo under the Mamluk Sultanate in 1261 CE until the Ottoman conquest of Egypt in 1517.

The Abbasids are placed on the timeline because they created the Muhammad of Islam or the Muhammad of Mecca – a fabricated image and narrative of Muhammad, whom died 117 years before the Abbasids even came to power.

Putting everything together, Muhammad was somehow revealed 84 years after the Abbasids and 141 years after Abd al-Malik first introduced him, all the while 201 years after Muhammad supposedly lived. Once again, this is a big problem for Islam.

Furthermore, a map of the locations of the earliest traditional writers of Islamic sources is provided below because the Islamic traditions teach that the origins of Islam are sourced to Mecca and Medina in the Hejaz (Central Western Arabia).

Bear in mind that people did not travel by plane or by ship at this time. Travel was typically done on foot, by camel/donkey, or by light raft.

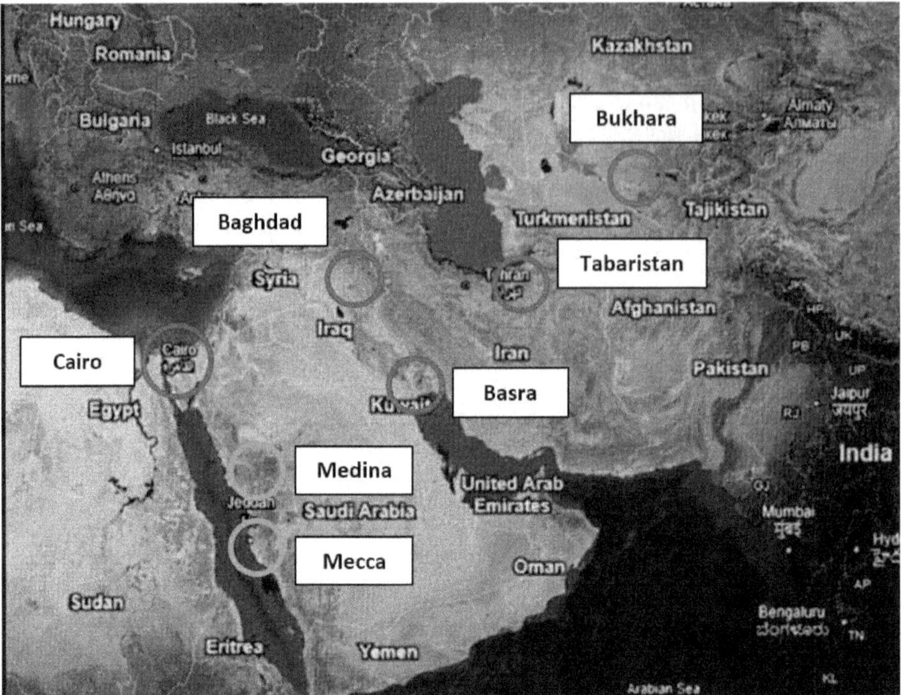

- For the Sira (Biographies of Muhammad), Ibn Hisham 833 CE has the earliest writings. Ibn Hisham was born in Basra, but was raised in Cairo. The travel distance between Basra and Mecca is 1,200 miles; the travel distance between Cairo and Mecca is 990 miles.
- For the hadith (Sayings of Muhammad), Al Bukhari 870 CE has the earliest writings. Al Bukhari is from Bukhara in Uzbekistan. The travel distance between Bukhara and Mecca is 2,600 miles.
- For the Tafsir/Tarikh (commentaries/histories for the Quran), At-Tabari 923 CE has the earliest writings. At-Tabari is from Tabaristan (Northern Iran). The travel distance between Tabaristan and Mecca is 1,700 miles.
- The Abbasids were located in Baghdad. The travel distance between Baghdad and Mecca is 1,176 miles.

For clarification, none of the traditional writers either lived or worked in Mecca or in Medina because these writers were far to the north of Mecca, and they came from the western and the eastern sides of Baghdad. They were indeed Abbasid writers.

The problems do not end there for Islam because historians demonstrate that Ibn Ishaq or Ibn Hisham neither created the Sira nor even wrote anything down. In the authoritative work, *The Life of Muhammad*, Muslims claim that Alfred Guillaume (1888-1965) searched through and translated the writings of Ibn Hisham, At-Tabari, and other early Islamic historians to reconstruct the lost biography of Muhammad, knowing that nothing about Muhammad's life was written down until 1819 CE. The key question is where did Alfred Guillaume obtain the material. It was not Ibn Hisham, but rather an Arabist named Heinrich Ferdinand Wustenfeld (1808 – 1899 CE). Wustenfeld actually compiled the Sira between 1858-1860 after traveling to four (4) German cities to accumulate Islamic resources from libraries and museums. When the compilation was completed in 1860, Wustenfeld published the work backward, attributing it to Ibn Ishaq. Consequently, this means that the biography of Muhammad, which is used today, is only 165 years old.

In other words, Muslims are dependent on an elderly German linguist who wrote Muhammad's story 165 years ago – and more than 1000 years too late – to know whom their prophet is or what their prophet did. Some of the stories also came from the Ottoman Period (1299-1924).

For clarification, this is not the only instance of backward compilation. In 1967, Fouad Sergin compiled another Sira from documents discovered in Morocco.

Based on the analysis thus far, it is evident that Islam did not exist in the 7th Century CE, and the Quran was not revealed to Muhammad in 22 years. At best, Islam and the Quran evolved over large periods of time, and the history of Islam is a later fabrication, at least from the time of Abd al-Malik and before.

For clarification, the key to dismantling Islam is to focus simply on the 7th and the 8th Centuries at the time of Muhammad because Muslim scholars cannot explain why it took so long to write down Islamic traditions, why there is no biography of Muhammad from the 7/8th Century, why the Quran was compiled with rewrites in 652 CE, where traditional compilers from the 9/10th Centuries received their material, or why they choose to trust sources 200 or more years late.

It is also worth noting that Islam has an isnad, which is the chain of narrators or transmitters whom relay a hadith or a matn (saying, action, or approval of Muhammad) from the original source to the current receiver. Somehow, this glorified oral tradition mechanism guarantees a hadith's authenticity and traceability through a lineage of tradition. The key issue here is that oral traditions are unreliable, unless they are captured in very small windows of time. Judging by the dates above, the time windows are far too large, hinting at the idea that everything is simply make-believe.

Although the historical record shows no evidence for the Quranic sources or the life of Muhammad from the 7/8th Centuries, Muslim scholars often resort to the absence of evidence not proving the evidence of absence; however, the threshold evidence is reached when directly assessing Mecca because, unlike early scholars and Muhammad, Mecca still exists, and it can be researched against the Islamic tradition.

Recall that based on the standard Islamic narrative and Muslim claims, Islam is completely dependent on three (3) items: The Quran (the Islamic holy book), Muhammad (the Islamic prophet), and Mecca (the Islamic holy place). If Mecca is proven false, then the standard Islamic narrative and the corresponding Muslim claims behind the Quran and Muhammad must be false as well.

Problems with Mecca

We begin the conversation with highlights of Mecca from the religious doctrine of Islam before the 9th Century CE.

The Islamic doctrine teaches that Mecca is the oldest and best-known city in history based on the following references:

- Mecca was where Muhammad was born and lived until 622 CE.
- Sura 7:24 describes God's command for Adam, Eve, and Iblis (Satan) to descend from Paradise to Earth after they disobeyed him in the Garden of Eden in space. In the Islamic tradition, Eve descended into Jeddah and Adam descended into either Sri Lanka or Dahna before reuniting with each other at Mount Arafat near Mecca. Adam was somehow 90 feet tall, and Eve's height is not mentioned.

For clarification, the choice to place Adam and Eve in Mecca consequently means that the earliest inhabitants of humankind are also from Mecca, which is categorically false.

- Sura 21:51-71 narrates the story of the Prophet Ibrahim (Abraham) challenging his people's idolatry within the Kaaba in Mecca.

For clarification, no historical and no archaeological evidence support that Abraham existed or that Abraham traveled to Mecca. Earlier religions, Judaism and Christianity, hold that Abraham traveled from Ur to Haran to Canaan, but never 1000s of miles south to Mecca. Nonetheless, for the purpose of this discussion, placing Abraham at the Kaaba in the Sacred Mosque in 1900 BCE means that Mecca should be well-known.

- In the *Trade Route Theory*, Montgomery Watt claims that Mecca was the center of trade in the North, South, East, and West. This claim also means that Mecca should be the best known and the best documented place because the center of trade implies high exposure to and high cultural contact with nearby cultures.

The following verses are always used by Muslims to outline instances of Mecca in the Quran, so the Arabic script will be added.

- Sura 3:96 mentions that the first sanctuary appointed for mankind was in Bakkah. Keep in mind that Bakkah is not Mecca, and Mecca is not contained within this Arabic passage.

إِنَّ أَوَّلَ بَيْتٍ وُضِعَ لِلنَّاسِ لَلَّذِى بِبَكَّةَ مُبَارَكًا وَهُدًى لِّلْعَـٰلَمِينَ

- Sura 6:92 and Sura 42:7 declare a mother of all settlements, but make no mention of Mecca, and Mecca is not contained within this Arabic passage.

وَهَـٰذَا كِتَـٰبٌ أَنزَلْنَـٰهُ مُبَارَكٌ مُّصَدِّقُ ٱلَّذِى بَيْنَ يَدَيْهِ وَلِتُنذِرَ أُمَّ ٱلْقُرَىٰ وَمَنْ حَوْلَهَا ۚ وَٱلَّذِينَ يُؤْمِنُونَ بِٱلْـَٔاخِرَةِ يُؤْمِنُونَ بِهِۦ ۖ وَهُمْ عَلَىٰ صَلَاتِهِمْ يُحَافِظُونَ

وَكَذَٰلِكَ أَوْحَيْنَآ إِلَيْكَ قُرْءَانًا عَرَبِيًّا لِّتُنذِرَ أُمَّ ٱلْقُرَىٰ وَمَنْ حَوْلَهَا وَتُنذِرَ يَوْمَ ٱلْجَمْعِ لَا رَيْبَ فِيهِ ۚ فَرِيقٌ فِى ٱلْجَنَّةِ وَفَرِيقٌ فِى ٱلسَّعِيرِ

- Sura 2:149-150 indirectly turns Mecca into the qibla. Mecca is not contained within this Arabic passage; however, the Sacred Mosque is explicitly mentioned.

وَمِنْ حَيْثُ خَرَجْتَ فَوَلِّ وَجْهَكَ شَطْرَ ٱلْمَسْجِدِ ٱلْحَرَامِ ۖ وَإِنَّهُۥ لَلْحَقُّ مِن رَّبِّكَ ۗ وَمَا ٱللَّهُ بِغَـٰفِلٍ عَمَّا تَعْمَلُونَ

وَمِنْ حَيْثُ خَرَجْتَ فَوَلِّ وَجْهَكَ شَطْرَ ٱلْمَسْجِدِ ٱلْحَرَامِ ۚ وَحَيْثُ مَا كُنتُمْ فَوَلُّوا۟ وُجُوهَكُمْ شَطْرَهُۥ لِئَلَّا يَكُونَ لِلنَّاسِ عَلَيْكُمْ حُجَّةٌ إِلَّا ٱلَّذِينَ ظَلَمُوا۟ مِنْهُمْ فَلَا تَخْشَوْهُمْ وَٱخْشَوْنِى وَلِأُتِمَّ نِعْمَتِى عَلَيْكُمْ وَلَعَلَّكُمْ تَهْتَدُونَ

- Sura 48:24 refers to Allah's divine intervention during the Treaty of Hudaybiyyah, where Allah supposedly prevented a battle between the Muslims and the Meccan disbelievers, even though Allah had already given the Muslims an advantage. This is the only reference in the Quran, where Mecca is directly mentioned, as highlighted in gray below.

وَهُوَ ٱلَّذِى كَفَّ أَيْدِيَهُمْ عَنكُمْ وَأَيْدِيَكُمْ عَنْهُم بِبَطْنِ مَكَّةَ مِنۢ بَعْدِ أَنْ أَظْفَرَكُمْ عَلَيْهِمْ ۚ وَكَانَ ٱللَّهُ بِمَا تَعْمَلُونَ بَصِيرًا

It is rather strange that the best-known place and the oldest so-called city, Mecca, appears only once in the entire Quran with very little detail.

Now, we look at the Islamic traditions after the 9th Century CE, and miraculously there are lots of Sunni hadiths and Quranic verses indirectly applied to Mecca. At this time, Mecca was considered to be "the place of the prophet" with a valley, a parallel valley, a stream, outside ruins, a pillar of salt, large fields with trees, grass, fruit, clay, and loam, mountains overlooking the Kaaba, and olive trees.

This level of vegetation requires large amounts of water, which have never been present in Mecca. In fact, Mecca is not in a valley, and it has none of the listed items in the previous paragraph because it is a desert – arid and dry.

The Quran also makes sixty-five (65) geographical references, where nine (9) places are explicitly specified by name, while the others mostly refer to places where people so happen to live. The first group of people comes from 'Ad occurring twenty-three (23) times. The second group of people is the Nabateans from Thamud, occurring twenty-four (24) times. The third group of people is the Midianites from Midian, occurring seven (7) times. Since these groups are listed in the Quran, it is natural to assume that they are important somehow. Assuming this importance and looking at the map below, the 600-mile difference between Mecca and these three (3) civilizations raises flags.

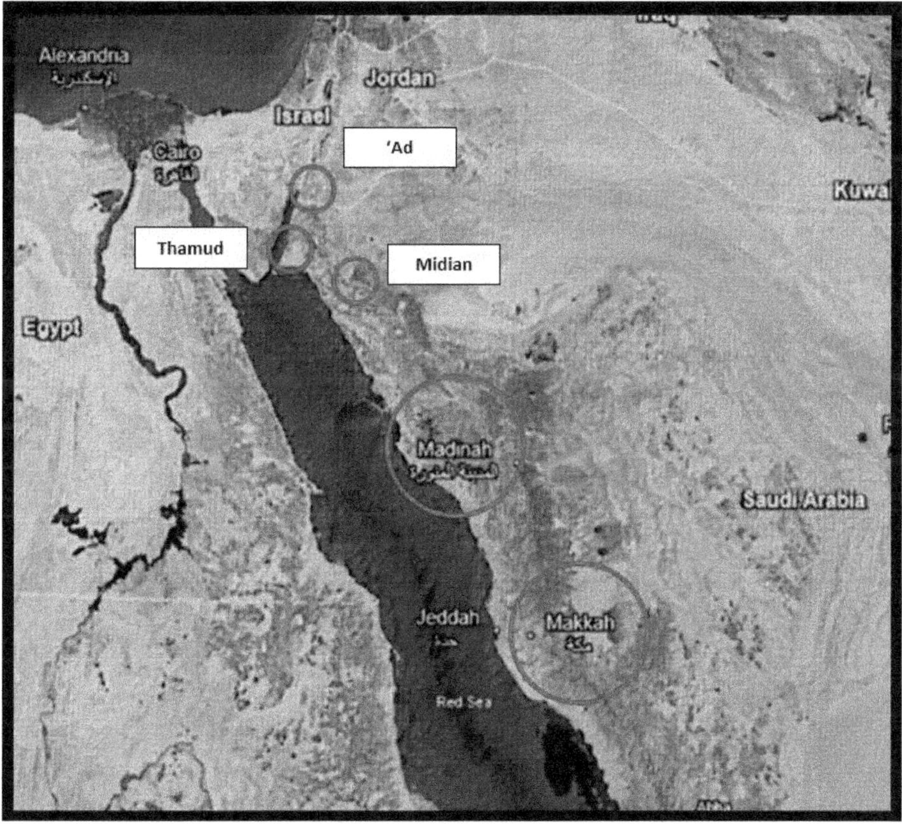

There is no way that Muhammad is having routine contact on a 1200-mile round-trip with these three (3) tribes or civilizations at a time when ships, planes, and phones did not exist.

Moreover, all maps so far indicate that everything in Islam was occurring far north of Mecca.

Continuing, the tradition teaches that all prophets lived, died, and were buried in a kneeling position to pray in death all in Mecca. Notable prophets include Adam, Seth, Ishmael, Noah, Hud (the great-great-grandson of Noah), Salih (the grandfather of Hagar), the Queen of Sheba, Daniel, and 70-300 other prophets. If the Islamic tradition is true, then the bodies of the prophets should still be in Mecca. None of the prophets' bodies has been found. Interestingly enough, there have been large-scale projects including clock towers, high-rise buildings, and various skyscrapers. Whenever there are large excavations, they attract historians and archaeologists whom seek artifacts and findings; however, absolutely nothing has been found in Mecca at the deepest foundations. In fact, Saudi Arabian archaeologists have gone on record to declare that nothing has been found, including pottery shards, jewelry, or rocks before the 8th Century – only Ottoman artifacts from 1300 CE at best. This is a big problem for Islam.

For sites constructed up to 706 CE, Dr. Dan Gibson notes that many early mosques and related structures do appear to face Petra geographically rather than towards Mecca. This includes the Medina mosque (626 CE), the Guangzhou mosque in China (627 CE), the Cherman mosque in India (629 CE), Jami' Hama al'Kabir in Syria (637 CE), Fustat mosque in Egypt (642 CE), Dome of the Rock in Israel (690 CE), Humeina mosque in Jordan (699 CE), Amman mosque in Jordan (701 CE), Grand Sa'ana in Yemen (705 Ce), and the Khirbat al Minya in Israel (706 CE). To be clear, every direction of prayer (qibla) from 624-706 CE was facing Petra, not Mecca.

Recall that Muhammad died in 632 CE, and the mosque was supposedly canonized in 624 CE. The first qibla facing Mecca does not occur until 715 CE, more than 80 years later. This is a problem for Islam.

Dr. Patricia Crone, who reads and writes 15 ancient languages from this time, searched for the earliest documented appearance of Mecca, and the earliest literary work containing Mecca's existence was the Apocalypse of Pseudo-Methodius Continuatio Byzantia Arabica during the early caliph Hisham in 741 CE – the mid-8th Century. This is nothing earlier than this, and it is more than 100 years after Muhammad. Greek trading documents refer to Ta'if (southeast of Mecca), Yathrib (modern-day Medina), and Khaybar, but not Mecca. Even when we look at the earliest maps, Mecca does not appear until 900 CE. No mappings based on Ptolemy's 2nd-century descriptions ever included Mecca. Moreover, Mecca is missing on several redacted 7th-century maps of Arabia, strongly suggesting that it did not exist at that time.

Furthermore, in her book, *Meccan Trade and the Rise of Islam*, Dr. Patricia Crone debunked Mecca being the center of trade by asking a simple question: What commodity was available in Arabia that could be transported such a distance, through such an inhospitable environment, and still be sold at a profit large enough to support the growth of a city in a peripheral sire bereft of natural resources? She goes on to point out that the trade at that time was heavily dependent on moving incense from southern Arabia to the Roman province of Syria and beyond for pagan rituals; however, this trade collapsed in the 4th Century due to Christianity's growth. Outside of this, Crone mentions that the only other trade items going by land were low-value commodities, such as dates, leather, and salt. Clearly, a large empire cannot become the center of trade – North, South, East, and West – trading in these items. Another fifteen (15) trade products, supposedly going through Mecca, never went to Mecca or even up the Arabian Coast, and the closest peripheral commodities were gold and myrrh in Yemen and Oman. Once again, nothing in Mecca. This is a problem for Islam.

In the *Trade Route Theory*, William Montgomery Watt claimed that Mecca became the center of trade after the 6th Century for political reasons. He suggested that due to the wars between the Sassanian (Persian) and the Byzantine (Christian) empires in the 5th – 7th Centuries, the original trade route in the map below, which normally went through the Persian Gulf, was shut down, and had to be redirected south, across the Arabian Sea, to the city of Aden (Yemen), where the goods were taken off the ships and were transported overland by camels 1250 miles up via the Western Plateau of Arabia to Gaza in the north.

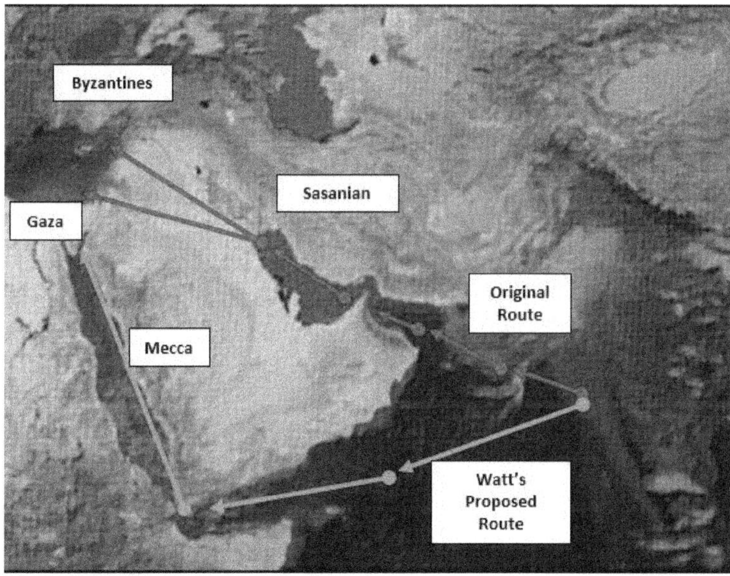

Dr. Patricia Crone easily debunked this theory by examining the terrain and cross-checking historical data on nearby trade routes. The two (2) problems are revealed with the map below.

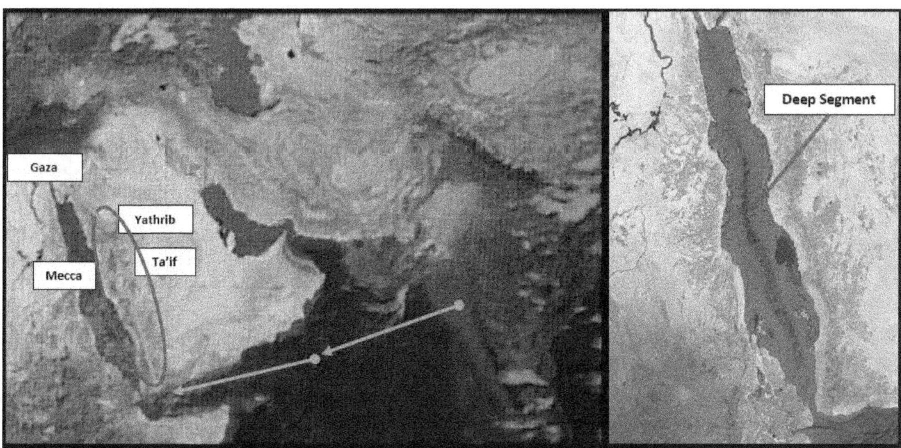

- Judging by the map on the left, if you are moving trade goods from the bottom of Arabia in Yemen up the western plateau, you would have to go through the mountains to Ta'if and then down 3000 feet to Mecca. From Mecca, you would have to travel back up to Yathrib in order to go through Khaybar, Tabuk, and then to Gaza for 1250 miles. There are no detours, and the map clearly shows a mountainous terrain with large differences in elevation from Mecca. Not to mention, Mecca is arid, and you cannot travel by camel without a reliable water source. It makes no sense to travel 3000 feet downward to the city of Mecca with no water and a limited food supply.
- Now, let's turn to the map on the right to see how trade occurred through the Red Sea, assuming land travel through Yemen is bypassed altogether. Notice how the Red Sea is shallow on the outside and extremely deep toward the middle. The deep segment shown on the map was very dangerous, especially since only light rafts and small sailboats existed at the time. This means there was no crossover through naval travel and based on the terrain, it would make no sense to travel on the right-hand side of the deep segment because the trade routes would be 3000 feet above.

After looking through many trade documents, it was also discovered that the actual trade route occurred toward Africa, as shown on the map below. We can even name the coastal cities: Assab in Eritrea (246 BCE), Adulis in Eritrea (79 CE), Suakin in Sudan (170 CE), Berenice in Egypt (275 BCE), and Safaga in Egypt (282 BCE).

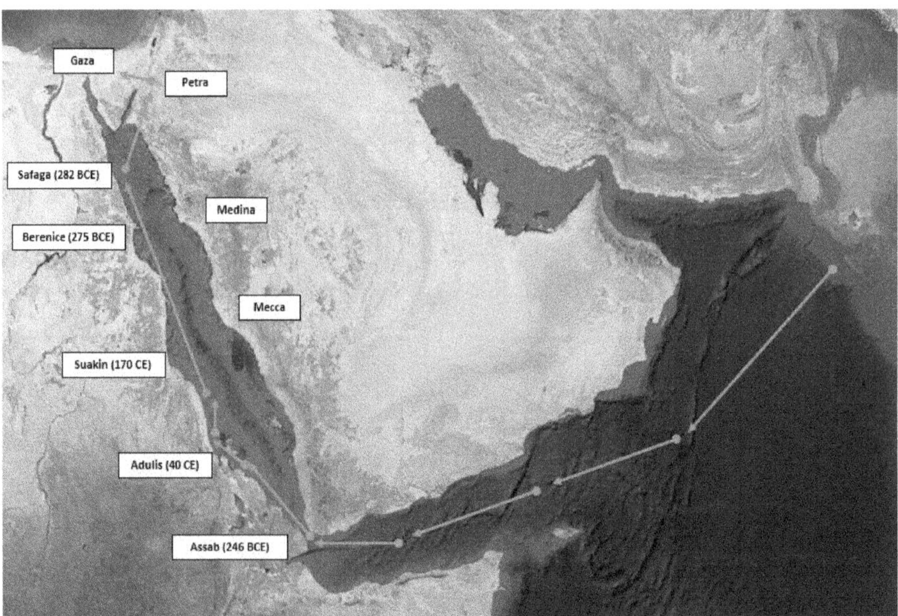

Please note how all the dates of the coastal cities come before Islam, how the coastal trade route lies on the western side of the Red Sea, how accessible the coastal ports are, and how the coastal ports are roughly a day's worth of travel away. Moreover, the African coastline has freshwater, unlike the Arabian coastline, so there are more people, more vegetation, and more provisions.

The earliest port on the Red Sea's eastern Arabian Coast is Yanbu; however, there is absolutely no history of Jeddah as a port for Mecca before the 8th Century. This is a problem for Islam, especially since Yathrib and Mecca neither had water nor large populations to accommodate early trade. Without Mecca, there is no 7th-century Islam.

If Mecca was the oldest city in the history of humankind, as the Islamic tradition teaches, then at least one of the surrounding cultures would have heard or would have written about it. After researching the Romans, the Assyrians, the Babylonians, the Persians, the Nabataeans, the Sabeans, the Himyarites, the Azdi tribes, the Kindahites, the Qedarites, the Nubians, the Aksumites, and the Abyssinians, Patricia Crone did not find one reference to Mecca. Even, the insignificant cities in Central Arabia (Najran, Sana'a, Ta'if, Yathrib, Khaybar, Mamre, Petra, and Ma'rib) are better known historically than Mecca.

The Islamic tradition also mentions that Mecca had valleys with flowing water and endless vegetation; however, soil studies indicate that the soil in Mecca could never have supported vegetation, especially being a bleak desert. Without a water supply, no food or vegetation can grow, meaning that no civilization can thrive there. Muslims try to contest this idea by falsely mentioning that the Zam-Zam well has been supplying an inexhaustible amount of water to Mecca since 1900 BCE. What Muslims do not know is that the Zam-Zam well only supplies 19 liters of water per second when it rains, and that large pipes bring water to the well before it is pumped at various locations near the Kaaba. Apparently, Muslims have never questioned where Zam-Zam water comes from believing it was a miracle of Allah; however, the water actually comes from desalination plants – largest in Jeddah – built by western construction companies like Acciona (Canada/Spain), Bechtel (US), and Black & Veatch (US), and the water is stored just outside of Mecca in the Muna Bulk Reservoir and the Briman Reservoirs built by Vinci construction (UK). The Zam-Zam well has nothing to do with Allah, and these companies, as well as Saudi authorities, profit heavily during the Hajj period, where pilgrims are strongly encouraged to drink the water for healing.

We do not see water in Mecca until after the 8th Century, when Queen Zubaydah from Iraq (762 – 831 CE) built and commissioned the Wadi Numan Aqueduct around 801 CE through neighboring towns (Numan to Al-Aziziyah) to supply 600-800 cubic meters of water per day. Additional renovations took place between 952 – 1880 CE followed by the desalination integration in 1926 CE. Roughly 98% of Mecca's water and 95% of Medina's water come from desalination plants.

The inscriptions on the Dome of the Rock suggest that Mecca was possibly constructed around 698 CE. The decoded message states: "This was written in the year the Masjid al-Haram was built in the seventy-eighth year". Noticing that the inscription says "was built" rather than "was rebuilt", it is safe to assume that the inscription refers to the site of the Masjid al-Haram, which later became Mecca in the Hijaz. The Kaaba within Masjid al-Haram was built around 698 CE, so Mecca was constructed during the reign of Abd al-Malik in the late 7th Century rather than the time of Muhammad or the time of Adam and Eve.

Even the Quran suggests that Mecca is not where it was created based on the type of Arabic used. The Quran is based on Qureshi Arabic of the northern parts of the Middle East, not the southern parts, including Central Arabia. In the southern parts, Sabaic Arabic, originating in Yemen from 600 BCE, was used in Medina and Mecca. Put simply, the Quran was written in the north away from Mecca and Medina. This should not come as a surprise, as the reader has already learned that the Quranic Arabic comes from the Nabataean Aramaic, which is 600+ miles north of Mecca.

Problems with Muhammad

Recall that Muhammad was supposedly the last and the greatest prophet who was born in Mecca in 570 CE and who died in Medina in 632 CE. So far, we have debunked the claims from the Islamic tradition showing that Muhammad never received the Quran as the final revelation of the world and that the source material (Siras, hadiths, tafsirs, etc.) for Muhammad is far too late. Islam is not even found historically before Muhammad. Another interesting fact is that early Arabs descended from the Hagar side with no prophet after Ishmael. This gave them the motive to invent one.

Let's start by examining coins, which were first introduced by the Lydians around 600 BCE. Not only were coins used for commerce, but they were also used to create and to maintain the identities of rulers. At this time, there were no TVs, newspapers, radios, etc., so the circulation of minted coins served as a means to introduce new rulers to the public. Minted coins bore images of the ruler, the religious identity, the commencement date of the ruler or empire, and the place of minting.

As a sidebar, the Islamic tradition prohibits the creation of detailed images of living beings to prevent idolatry and shirk (associating partners with god). While images of inanimate objects like mountains and trees are permitted, depictions of animate beings, including humans and animals, are generally considered haram (forbidden). Yet, Muslims still mint coins and create paper currency with such images.

Returning to the coins, experts, who study or collect coins known as numismatists, experienced problems when trying to overlay the Islamic narrative with coins from the 7th Century. In the 7th Century, the rulers under the Islamic narrative revolved around Mecca and Medina, so naturally any minted coins would also come from either Mecca or Medina to announce the new leadership. Based on catalogs and historical assets, all of the mints were situated in modern-day Syria, Lebanon, and Israel more than 600 miles north and modern-day Iran more than 600 miles east with not one minting entity in either Mecca or Medina. This is another problem for Islam because all of the mints would have been under the authority of a caliph in the 7th Century. Looking at the coins collected in the 7th Century, we notice the following:

- From the time up to Muhammad's death in 632 CE to the end of the Rashidun period in 661 CE, no Islamic coins exist for the leaders.
- The Sasanians (Persians), up to 661 CE, minted tons of coins far north. Interestingly enough, the Arab coins have many Christian symbols.
- The first caliph of the Umayyad Empire based in Syria under Mu'awiya I – a Christian – minted coins with Christian crosses in the west and Zoroastrian fire altars in the east up to 680 CE. There are still no Islamic coins, but the combination of 'MHMD' with a Christian cross begins to appear in 663 CE. This is a very interesting conflict with the Islamic tradition because 'MHMD' is a title ('praised one' or 'anointed one') rather than a name. In *Ansab al-Asraf*, the Baghdadi litterateur and genealogist, Ahmad bin Yahya al-Baladuri (883-884 CE), recorded the following on the birth of the Islamic prophet Muhammad bin Abd Allah bin Abd al-Muttalib (632 CE): As for Qutam bin Abd al-Muttalib: his mother was Safiyyah bint Jundub, the mother of al-Harit bin Abd al-Muttalib, and he died as a young boy. [Someone] other than al-Kalbi said: "He died three years before the birth of the Prophet, when he was a boy of nine years, whereupon Abd al-Muttalib experienced great anguish, [for] he had been dear to him [and] brought him joy. Then, when the Messenger of God was born, Abd al-Muttalib named him "Qutam", whereupon his mother Aminah informed him that she had been shown in a dream [that she was] to name him "Muhammad"—thus, he named him "Muhammad" [instead]." This story, based on the Islamic narrative, raises red flags because 'MHMD' appears with the Christian cross and 'MHMD' can be traced back to 1400 BCE, well before Islam emerged in the 7th Century. Based on these facts, only a handful of conclusions can be made: (i) 'MHMD' is not referring to the Muhammad born in 570 CE, (ii) the Islamic prophet of Muhammad was invented in the tradition, or (iii) the creators of Islam either borrowed or stole the idea of 'MHMD' from earlier religions. There is not even one reference to the term 'Muslim' or 'Islam' in the 7th Century, and the term "Allah" was generically used to mean god before Islam, thanks to the early Nabataeans, but was never the name of god used in Islam.

For clarification, the difference between a title and a name is very important, completely changing the interpretation of the four Quranic references for 'MHMD'. Sura 3:144 indicates that the blessed one is no more than a messenger. Sura 33:40 indicates that the blessed one is not the father of any of your men, but he is the messenger of Allah and the last of the prophets for prophetic closure. Sura 47:2 indicates believing in what was sent down to the blessed one from all prophets. Sura 48.29 indicates the blessed one is the messenger of Allah. Muslims attribute these verses to Muhammad, but none of these verses refer to a person called Muhammad whom lived in the Hijaz in Arabia. In essence, the writers of the Quran have manufactured a prophet by changing the title 'MHMD' into a name. To make matters worse, the Islamic tradition calls Muhammad the greatest prophet, yet he is only mentioned in the Quran four (4) times in comparison to Moses being referenced 136 times, Jesus being referenced 93 times, Abraham being referenced 79 times, and Pharaoh being referenced 74 times. So, Muhammad was not popular enough or great enough in this regard, indicating that it is more of a generic title for the blessed than an actual man's name. If this is not the prophet from Mecca at all, then Muslims cannot use the Quran to support the existence of "Muhammad the prophet" in the 7th Century, crushing one of the pillars of Islam.

For clarification, Muslims have also assumed that the inscriptions on the Dome of the Rock (691 CE) under Abd al-Malik referred to Muhammad as a man rather than a title; however, the inscriptions on the inner ambulatory actually confront Jesus's divinity, the Christian trinity, and Jesus as the son of god. This is clearly expressed in Sura 4:171 and Sura 112. Even the Shahada is rooted in this idea, where it states, "there is no god but god alone and the blessed one is his messenger". In this specific case, the blessed one would be Jesus under the divination context; even though, as a title, it can refer to different prophets in different contexts. Also, note that the Quranic verses in these inscriptions are not the same as those in the Quran today, but possibly precursors to the Quranic verses written later and then changed to embed a prophet into the narrative alongside the night journey on a winged beast.

- The first coin with the Shahada and mockeries of the Christian trinity appeared in the Umayyad Empire in Syria, not in Mecca or in Medina, under Abd al-Malik, with no reference to the term 'Muslim' or 'Islam' for another 40 years. The Shahada was created solely to counter the Christian trinity. This strongly suggests that Islam's anti-trinitarian stance was not introduced by Muhammad, but possibly by Abd al-Malik.

Next, let's discuss the early Arabic rock inscriptions, once again written in Nabataean Arabic from the north rather than the Sabaic Arabic from Mecca and Medina. All of the 7th-century rock inscriptions are in the north near Syria and the south in Yemen. Dr. Ilkka Lindstedt looked into 100 rock inscriptions from 640 – 740 CE in an effort to determine how Islam came into existence because there was no evidence of Islam on the inscriptions prior to 690 CE. From 690 CE to 710 CE, Muhammad started to emerge on coins, the Dome of the Rock, and protocols. In 710 CE, Muhammad suddenly became a prophet of the Hagarines (Ishmaelites/ Muhajiruns), followed by the presence of religious rites (pilgrimage, prayer, and fasting) from 710 – 720 CE. It is not until the period from 720 CE to 730 CE that the terms, "Muslim" and "Islam", refer to a specific group, almost 100 years after Muhammad's death. This means that there is a 100-year silence prior that indicates that Islam did not exist as a distinct religion until long after the time of Muhammad, casting doubt on whether Muhammad had any part in starting Islam at all. This is a big problem for Islam.

As far as external references to 'any' Muhammad – or something close to – outside of Islam in the 7th/8th Centuries, there are five (5) as follows:

- In 634 CE, Thomas the Presbyter discusses a battle between the Romans and the "Tayaye d-Mhmt" in Gaza. 'Mhmt' is the Persian variant of 'Mhmd', but 'Mhmt' refers to Pahlavi in this context, and the Tayaye were Lakhmids from Persia (modern-day Iran/Iraq), fighting in Gaza far north. Quite possibly, this might be another Muhammad because the Muhammad of Islam never traveled to Gaza, and he was not Persian.
- In 636 CE, there is a flyleaf referring to the "Arabs of Mhmd" whom killed many Syrians in Yarmuk (Gabitha); however, the Muhammad of Islam never traveled to Yarmuk in Syria.
- In the 660s CE, Sebeos refers to "an Ishmaelite called Mahmet...with 12,000 Israelites", but historically, there are no instances of 12,000 Israelites attacking or invading the Byzantines.
- In 690 CE, John bar Penkaye references "Muhammad...teacher/leader of the Arabs". This reference is still far north with no mention of Islam or this Muhammad being a Muslim; however, it is objectively the first good reference for Islam. The date remains a problem.
- In 730 CE, John of Damascus references "Mahmed, ludicrous doctrines..." in his work, the *Heresy of the Ishmaelites*, which marks the beginning of what later became the Muhammad of Islam, with scrutiny of 4 books (the cow for Sura 2, the woman for Sura 4, the table for Sura 5, and the camel with no Sura). It is worth noting that John of Damascus scrutinized a Quran with 4 books (one that does not even exist), and the Quran of today has 114 books – a fact that cannot be glanced over. In 730 CE, Muhammad had been dead for approximately 100 years, and none of the Muslims had the full Quran.

Problems with the Quran

So far, we have discussed serious concerns with the Islamic traditions, Mecca, and Muhammad, but not the Quran itself. As we investigate the Quran, the reader should always keep the following points from the standard Islamic narrative in mind:

- Sura 85:21-22 mentions that the Quran is uncreated and is eternally inscribed in a preserved tablet.
- Sura 10:15 instructs Muhammad to say that changing the Quran by his own accord is not his right, as he only follows divine revelation, and he fears the punishment of Allah if he disobeys.
- Sura 18:27 instructs Muhammad to recite the Quran, emphasizing that Allah's words are unchangeable.
- Sura 15:9 is a reminder that Allah sent down the Quran and Allah is the guardian of it.
- The Quran was sent down to Muhammad between 610 – 632 CE.
- The Quran was completed by Uthman in 652 CE.
- The Quran has remained unchanged and preserved for the last 1400 years. It has not been altered, tampered with, corrupted, or edited – not one single letter – since it was revealed; thus, there is only one Quran.

All of the points above must hold true for the Quran to be true according to the standard Islamic narrative. This includes the Quran being complete with all 114 Suras from the 7th Century and being unchanged in line with the 1924 Hafs Quran.

Since there is no information from Muhammad's time period, one has to go to the earliest hadith writer, Sahih Al-Bukhari, in 870 CE for information on the creation of the Quran – Sahih Al-Bukhari Volume 6, No. 509 and No. 510. These are the only two hadiths that describe the origin of the Quran, and they are 218-238 years late because Muhammad died in 632 CE and the Quran was compiled in 652 CE. The lateness of Al-Bukhari also suggests that his volume of hadiths did not capture the narrations perfectly. According to these hadiths, when Muhammad died in 632 CE, there was no Quran written down, and there was a battle in Yamama directly after Muhammad's death, where 70 people with the unwritten knowledge of the Quran died, as well as their memories. This led to a crisis, so Umar suggested that Abu Baker compile the Quran despite Abu Baker's hesitation to do something never done by Muhammad. Zaid bin Thabit, a trusted scribe of the revelation and Muhammad's secretary, was tasked with writing the compilation. After completion, Zaid gives the compilation to Umar, whom then gives it to his daughter and one of Muhammad's wives, Hafsah. For some strange reason, she places the all-important and first Quranic compilation under her bed without making any copies. Twenty years later, Uthman comes to power as the Third Caliph in Medina, and he receives news from Hudhayfah ibn al-Yaman that the people of Syria and Iraq were reciting the Quran differently from one another. Fearing a conflict, Uthman agreed that the Quran required official standardization (canonization), and he reached out to Zaid once more. Zaid brought forth the compilation that Hafsah placed under her bed, and he rewrote the Quran again in the Quraishi dialect; however, there was a key problem among the dialects because there were no Arabic vowels or Arabic diacritics/markings in the 7th Century. In essence, there was no way to understand the dialectical differences because the required markings were not in place at the time. To make the problem worse, Sahih Al-Bukhari wrote in the diacritics in the 9th Century and redacted his manuscripts back to the 7th Century, forgetting to remove the diacritics. Herein lies the first problem of a complete and unchanged Quran.

Returning, Uthman ibn Affan, the third Caliph of the Rashidun Caliphate, sent master copies of the newly standardized Quran to five major Islamic cities – Mecca, Medina, Basra, Kufa (modern-day Baghdad), and Damascus – to prevent Muslim communities from using different versions and recitations of the Quranic text. Not one of the five Uthman Qurans can be found today because Uthman would later order the burning of the official copies, despite the burning of the Quran being punishable by death. The problems with the Quran would not stop here because a new Quran with 116 Suras was introduced in Damascus by Ubayy ibn Ka'b at the end of the 7th Century.

Ubayy ibn Ka'b was a Sahabi (companion) and one of the greatest Quranic reciters, known for memorizing the entire Quran and possessing a profound understanding of its meanings. Muhammad was even instructed by Allah to recite the Quran to Ubayy, demonstrating his extremely high status in relation to the Quran. His compilation included two extra surahs compared to the standard text and had significant variations.

Another Quran also appeared in the late 7th Century by Ibn Mas'ud with 110 Suras (4 fewer than the standard text) and significant variants. Abdullah ibn Mas'ud was a companion of Muhammad, highly revered for his deep knowledge of the Quran and beautiful recitation.

Another Quran was introduced in Basra by Ahmad ibn Musa ibn Mujahid with 114 Suras. Ibn Musa tried to solve the problem with multiple Qurans by choosing seven of the recitations as canonical, and in time another three were added. Reciting any of the non-canonical recitations was forbidden and punishable.

Dr. Arthur Jeffery investigated the differences between the four (4) Qurans above in the 1930s and found roughly 15,000 differences – a real problem for Islam.

Now, we will shift to the 8th Century to discuss the different recitations in more detail because the Arabic used in the Quran today, with 28 letters, does not come from Mecca or Medina in the Hijaz, but from Nabataea further north. During the 7th Century, the Arabic was an adaptation of the Nabataean Aramaic based on 16 consonantal Syriac letters and each consonantal letter could be pronounced 5-8 different ways because there were no diacritics (dots and vowel markers) as seen on the largely incomplete Samarkand Manuscript in Uzbekistan, Topkapi Manuscript in Turkey, the Sana'a Manuscript in Yemen, the Al Husseini Manuscript in Egypt, the incomplete Ma'il Manuscript in London, and the incomplete Petropolitanus Manuscript in France. To conceal this issue, Quranic compilers started to add diacritics to the scripts in the 8th Century to force Muslims to read and to recite the script the same way. The diacritics included 1-3 dots with different positions, vowels (damma, fatha, and kasra), and delineators (sukoon and shadda).

For clarification, none of the manuscripts listed above are from the 7th Century, are complete, are in agreement with one another, or are in agreement with the 1924 Hafs Quran. Also, all of the manuscripts have 100s and even 1000s of manuscript variants, indicating that there was never a complete Quran in existence.

This issue must be overemphasized with a simple example by considering the modern Arabic root خ ف ض (with letters khaa', fa', and Daad from left to right). Looking at some forms of this root, its pronunciations, and its meanings, we have kha-fa-Da (خَفَضَ) meaning it decreased, kha-fu-Da (خَفُضَ) meaning it was easy/comfortable, khaf-fa-Da (خَفَّضَ) meaning it was reduced. Please note how the pronunciation and the meaning change with the diacritics. In the 7th Century, there were no diacritics, so let's remove the dots and the vowel markers. The result is (حمص) without any decipherable meaning. This example illustrates that there is no definitive way for Quranic compilers or even Quranic interpreters to understand early Arabic without the diacritics.

Recall that Muslims claim that the Quran has not been altered, tampered with, corrupted, or edited – not one single letter – since it was revealed. Clearly, the addition of the diacritics proves this claim false. Also, different compilers generate different outcomes of diacritics, which means that the meanings are corrupted.

It is worth noting that the compilers could not confer with one another because they did not know one another. Muslims believe that there is one preserved Quran; however, here are all of the Quranic types based on official recitations and transmitters.

Seven (7) Quranic Recitations chosen by Ibn Mujahid (936 CE)

1. Quran Recitation from Nafi' al-Madani (Medina 689-785 CE)
2. Quran Recitation from Ibn Kathir al Makki (Mecca 666-738 CE)
3. Quran Recitation from Abu Amr Ibn al-Ala (Basra 690-770 CE)
4. Quran Recitation from Ibn Amir ad-Dimashqi (Damascus 736 CE)
5. Quran Recitation from Aasim Ibn al-Najud (Kufa 700-745 CE)
6. Quran Recitation from Hamzah az-Zalyyat (Kufa 696-772 CE)
7. Quran Recitation from Al-Kisa'I (Kufa 737-805 CE)

For clarification, the Islamic authorities labeled these seven Quranic variants as the Mutawatir because the transmissions have independent chains of authorities so wide as to rule out the possibility of any error and on which there is consensus. The problem with this is that there is no consensus because the compilers never knew one another and never lived even in the same century as Muhammad. The approval came strictly from Ibn Mujahid, not through revelation or some angel Jibreel. Not to mention, multiple transmissions should not be required for error if there is supposed to be one Quran – complete, preserved, and uncorrupted. But wait, there are more Qurans.

As a sidebar, in *Corrections in Early Quran Manuscripts*, Dr. Daniel Alan Brubaker outlines intentional corrections and omissions made to early Quranic manuscripts, showing evidence that the Quran has not been preserved without alteration.

Fourteen (14) Quranic Recitations reviewed by Al-Shatibi (1194 CE)

8. Qalun Quran Recitation (835 CE)
9. Al-Bazzi Quran Recitation (864 CE)
10. Al-Duri Quran Recitation (860 CE)
11. Hisham Quran Recitation (859 CE)
12. Shu-bah Quran Recitation (809 CE)
13. Khalaf Quran Recitation (844 CE)
14. Al-Layth Quran Recitation (854 CE)
15. Warsh Quran Recitation (812 CE)
16. Qunbul Quran Recitation (904 CE)
17. Al-Susi Quran Recitation (874 CE)
18. Ibn Dhakwan Quran Recitation (857 CE)
19. Hafs Quran Recitation (796 CE)
20. Khallad Quran Recitation (835 CE)
21. Al-Duri Quran Recitation (860 CE)

The two (2) most popular Qurans come from Hafs and Warsh. 93% of all Muslims memorize the Hafs Quran and 3% of Muslims, mostly in North Africa, memorize the Warsh Quran. Keep in mind that Al-Shatibi chose Shu-bah and Hafs from 91 other Qurans and dismissed the remaining 89 Qurans strictly based on followership and popularity. Al-Shatibi never critiqued the different Quranic texts. But wait, there are more Qurans.

Nine (9) Quranic Recitations chosen by Al-Jazari (1429 CE)

22. Abu Ja'far Quran Recitation (Medina 748 CE)
23. Ya'qub al-Yamani Quran Recitation (Basra 821 CE)
24. Khalaf Quran Recitation (Kufa 844 CE)
25. Isa Ibn Wardan Quran Recitation (777 CE)
26. Ruways Quran Recitation (853 CE)
27. Ishaq Quran Recitation (899 CE)
28. Ibn Jummaz Quran Recitation (787 CE)
29. Rawh Quran Recitation (849 CE)
30. Idris Quran Recitation (905 CE)

Clearly, we have thirty (30) different Qurans by the 15th Century. A major problem for Islam.

In 1985, the Hafs Quran became the universal Quranic variant from the 1936 Faruq Edition in Egypt to the 1985 Fahd Edition in Saudi Arabia. The total number of differences between the Hafs Quran and the other 29 is approximately 93,263 – far too many to put in this book.

The Topkapi manuscript in Istanbul is the earliest manuscript with the lowest number of diacritics, dated to the mid-8th Century at the very least, and it has approximately 2,240 textual variants in comparison to the Hafs Quran.

There is no Uthman manuscript from 652 CE.

Please note that even one difference is a big deal in Islam because the standard narrative harps at the eternal word of god without change, difference, or error. By these standards, the textual variants, which include erasures, redactions, tapings/patches, overwrites, insertions, additions, markings, etc., indicate that the Quran is not divinely given.

Lastly, the 'radiocarbon (R-14) dated' Birmingham Folios, which were announced as the oldest Quran fragments in 2015, strongly indicate that early Quranic writers were borrowing textual content from pagans and early Christians. Known formally as Birmingham Folios (M157a) and dated for 568-645 CE, the incomplete fragments of only two pages – front and back – contain 33 verses out of 6,236 verses in the Quran and three (3) suras/chapters fully out of sequence. Interestingly enough, it consists of the following content:

- Sura 18:17-31 – The 7 Sleepers of Ephesus (512 CE). This was a well-known pagan story that existed before Islam began in 610 CE.
- Sura 19:91-98 – The Proto-Evangelium of James (145 CE) and The Pseudo Gospel of Matthew (600 CE) that existed before Islam began in 610 CE.
- Sura 20:1-40 – The Story of Moses (1400 BCE) that existed before Islam began in 610 CE.

When investigating further, scholars like Christoph Luxenberg and Gunther Luling have determined that the Quran was never a divine revelation but rather a compilation of Christian Lectionaries, Homilies, and Hymns written in Syro-Aramaic and then interpolated into Arabic. The compilation was then integrated with traditions from nearby faith cultures (Christians, Zoroastrians, pagans, etc.).

Muslim readers might have a hard time absorbing these facts, so another cause for concern will be provided. According to the Islamic narrative, Muhammad had scribes record his revelations – one scribe being Abdullah Ibn Sa'd ibn Abi Sarh. When Sarh wrote these revelations down, he frequently made suggestions for improving the wording, and Muhammad often agreed, allowing the changes to be made. Such allowance raised an alarm with Sarh. Eventually, Sarh left Islam, becoming one of the first Islamic apostates and discovering the Quran could not be from god if a mere scribe was allowed to change god's word. Muhammad would later order Sarh's death after the conquest of Mecca. Such references include: *Sirat Rasul Allah*, pg. 550; *Kitab Al-Tabaqat Al-Kabir*, Vol 2, page 168; *Al-Sira* by al-Iraqi, and Tafsir Anwar al-Tanzil wa Asrar al-Ta'wil by Abdallah Ibn Umar al-Baidawi on Sura 6:93.

At this point, the standard Islamic narrative has been completely debunked. Furthermore, there is sufficient evidence to conclude that Muhammad is a false prophet and that the Muhammad portrayed in the Islamic narrative never existed. Quite possibly, early Islamic writers (Ishmaelites) invented – even euhemerized – a fake prophet out of the real-life warlord Muhammad in cult fashion to force monotheism onto pagans through the Quran and to fabricate the standard Islamic narrative, especially since Ishmael had no remaining prophetic descendants.

Once again, the key to a religion's success is simply creating an explanation – not necessarily the best, the most factually accurate, the most historical, or the most truthful – riddled with belief that the willfully ignorant humans can subscribe to. Many subscribers to Islam defend the absurdity of this faith without even knowing what the doctrine is or what falsehoods of the standard Islamic narrative are at play. Many Muslims, for instance, often ask why Islam is always associated with terrorism/hate and why non-Islam groups cannot tolerate Islam, when it is supposed to be a peaceful religion – not knowing that Islam really means 'surrender and/or submit' rather than peace (= salaam). Although not all Muslims are bad people, they can easily become radicalized at any time based on the very teachings of their faith, including Islamic Jihad. Evidence of this can be found in the following Quranic scriptures:

- Sura 2:190-193 "Fight in the cause of God those who fight you ... And slay them wherever ye catch them ... And fight them on until there is no more tumult or oppression and there prevail justice and faith in God ..."
- Sura 2:216 "Fighting is prescribed for you and ye dislike it. But it is possible that ye dislike a thing which is good for you, and that ye love a thing which is bad for you. But God knoweth and ye know not."

- Sura 2:224 "Then fight in the cause of God and know that God heareth and knoweth all things."
- Sura 3:157-158 "And if ye are slain or die in the way of God, forgiveness and mercy from God are far better than all they could amass. And if ye die, or are slain, Lo! It is unto God that ye are brought together."
- Sura 3:169 "Think not of those who are slain in God's way as dead. Nay, they live finding their sustenance in the presence of their Lord."
- Sura 3:195 "... Those who have ... fought or been slain, verily I will blot out from them their iniquities and admit them into Gardens with rivers flowing beneath; a reward from the presence of God ..."
- Sura 4:101 "... For the Unbelievers are unto you open enemies."
- Sura 4:74-75 "Let those fight in the cause of God who sell the life of this world for the Hereafter. To him who fighteth in the cause of God whether he is slain or gets victory, soon shall we give him a reward of great (value). Those who believe fight in the cause of God and those who reject faith fight in the cause of evil, so fight ye against the friends of Satan, feeble indeed is the cunning of Satan."
- Sura 4:89 "They but wish that ye should reject faith as they do, and thus be on the same footing as they. But take not friends from their ranks until they flee in the way of God. But if they turn renegades, seize them and slay them wherever ye find them…"
- Sura 4:95 "Not equal are those believers who sit at (at home) and receive no hurt and those who strive and fight in the cause of God with their goods and their persons. God hath granted a grade higher to those who strive and fight with their goods and persons than those who sit (at home).
- Sura 5:33 "Indeed, the penalty for those who wage war against Allah and His Messenger and spread mischief in the land is death, crucifixion, cutting off their hands and feet on opposite sides, or exile from the land. This penalty is a disgrace for them in this world, and they will suffer a tremendous punishment in the Hereafter."
- Sura 5:36 "The punishment of those who wage war against God and His apostle and strive with might and main for mischief through the land is: execution, or crucifixion, or the cutting off of hands and feet from opposite sides, or exile from the land. That is their disgrace in this world and a heavy punishment is theirs in the Hereafter."
- Sura 5:54 "O ye who believe. Take not the Jews and the Christians for your friends and protectors. They are but friends and protectors to each other. And he amongst you that turns to them (for friendship) is of them. Verily God guideth not a people unjust."
- Sura 8:12-17 "Remember thy Lord inspired the angels (with the message): "I am with you. Give firmness to the believers. I will instill terror into the hearts of the unbelievers. Smite ye above their necks and smite all their fingertips off them. This because they contend against God and his apostle. If any contend against God and his apostle, God is strict in punishment ... O ye who believe. When ye meet the unbelievers in hostile array, never turn your backs to them. If any do turn his back to them on such a day, unless it be a stratagem of war ... he draws on himself the wrath of God and his abode is Hell, an evil refuge (indeed)."
- Sura 8:39 Fight against them until there is no more persecution—and your devotion will be entirely to Allah. But if they desist, then surely Allah is All-Seeing of what they do.
- Sura 8:59-60 "Let not the unbelievers think that they can get the better (of the godly). They will never frustrate (them). Against them make ready your strength to the utmost of your power, including steeds of war, to strike terror into (the hearts of) the enemies of God and your enemies and others besides, whom ye may not know, but whom God doth know ..."
- Sura 8:65 "O apostle! Rouse the believers to the fight. If there are twenty amongst you, patient and persevering, they will vanquish two hundred. If a hundred they will vanquish a thousand of the unbelievers, for these are a people without understanding."
- Sura 9:5 "... fight and slay the pagans wherever ye find them, and seize them, beleaguer them, and lie in wait for them in every stratagem (of war) ..."
- Sura 9:14 "Fight them, and God will punish them by your hands, cover them with shame ..."
- Sura 9:29 "Fight those who believe not in God nor the Last Day nor hold that forbidden which

hath been forbidden by God and his apostle nor acknowledge the Religion of Truth (even if they are) of the people of the Book, until they pay the Jizya [religious tax] with willing submission, and feel themselves subdued."

- Sura 47:4 "Therefore, when ye meet the unbelievers, smite at their necks, at length when ye have thoroughly subdued them, bind a bond firmly (on them) ... but if it had been God's will, he could certainly have exacted retribution from them (himself), but (he lets you fight) in order to test you, some with others. But those who are slain in the way of God, he will never let their deeds be lost."
- Sura 61:4 "Truly God loves those who fight in His cause in battle array, as if they were a solid cemented structure."

For clarification, the translator is replacing the Arabic word 'kill' with the English word 'fight' in the verses above, which lowers the intensity of the context. Indeed, Muslims are encouraged to kill, not just to fight.

It is important to examine the verbiage above closely to understand the mental tactics that Islam plays on its followers. In Islam, Muslims are conditioned to believe that they are always under attack, even if no such attack exists. When you discuss the Quranic verses above with Muslims, they believe that they are always acting in self-defense, either defending against a direct attack or an imminent attack, which might be based on wild speculation. In reality, they are on the offensive rather than the defensive. With such a paranoid mentality, Muslims are dangerously tricked into feeling imaginary hatred and enmity against Jews, Christians, and non-Muslims. Although there are peaceful Muslims, one cannot ignore the weight and the impact of the Quranic passages above on a devout, innocent Muslim whom wants to find and to obey Allah's will as commanded – even if it means engaging in violence. Moreover, the commands of violence promoted in the Quran are not restricted to a special time period or against a special people group. The Quranic commands are universal and thus applicable to all times and all places.

This is one of the main reasons why Muslim-Majority countries do not accept many Muslim refugees. Armed Jihad is permissible if one of the following conditions is met: (i) self-defense, and (ii) fighting against oppression. At the surface, such conditions seem reasonable; however, the definitions of "self-defense" and "fighting against oppression" in Islam are much broader than usually understood. Many Orthodox Muslims, for instance, believe that if a nation's leaders do not acknowledge the rule of Islam, then those rulers are "oppressors" and thus a legitimate target for war and violence. As a second example, Hollywood movies can be considered a cultural aggressor toward Islam, in humor or in stereotype, once again allowing violence per the Quran. That being said, Muslims can find an endless number of Islamic justifications for war and violence based on any interpretation of or any definition of "self-defense" and "oppression".

The potential threats of Islam and the radicalization of innocent/peaceful Muslims through Islam should be taken seriously by religiously tolerant and religiously inclusive nations with free societies, diverse cultures, vulnerable villages, and vulnerable immigration processes. The list of Quranic verses associated with Jihad, which lies in the minds of Muslims preaching Allah is greater when they commit a crime that they do not think is a crime, is quite exhaustive – even involves raiding, fighting and looting – however, we will provide a table of the major Jihad verses below, so that the reader can understand the magnitude of Islamic radicalization and the conditioning effect of Islamic doctrine:

Sura	Verses	Count
2	178-179, 190-191, 193-194, 216-218, 244	10
3	121-126, 140-143, 146, 152-158, 165-167, 169, 172-173, 195	35
4	071-072, 074-077, 084, 089-091, 094-095, 100-104, 144	53
5	033, 035, 082	56
8	001, 005, 007, 009-010, 012, 015-017, 039-048, 057-060, 065-075	90
9	005, 012-014, 016, 019-020, 024-026, 029, 036, 038-039, 041, 044, 052, 073, 081, 083, 086, 088, 092, 111, 120, 122-123	117
16	110	118
22	039, 058, 078	121
24	053, 055	123
25	52	124
29	006, 069	126
33	015, 018, 020, 023, 025-027, 050	134
42	39	135
47	004, 020, 035	138
48	015-024	148
49	15	149
59	002, 005-008, 014	155
60	9	156
61	004, 011, 013	159
63	4	160
64	14	161
66	9	162
73	20	163
76	8	164

Some Islamic scholars have made attempts to abrogate, to conceal, or to remove these types of verses; however, such efforts have never been effective because there are many recitations of the Quran, many Muslims desperately create a context where the verses are necessary, many Muslims feeling under imaginary/potential threat do not see the problem with the verses, and many Muslims ignore the scholars under the belief that the verses are divine with no possibility of alteration.

Islam further condones killing and destruction in the Sunni hadiths, which are a collection of the teachings of Muhammad. In Sahih Al-Bukhari, translated by Dr. Muhammad Muhsin Khan, we find the following:

- Sahih Al-Bukhari, Volume 4, p. 55 "Allah's Apostle said, 'Know that Paradise is under the shades of swords.'"
- Sahih Al-Bukhari Volume 4, p. 124 "Allah's Apostle said, 'I have been ordered to fight with the people till they say, 'None has the right to be worshipped but Allah,' and whoever says, 'None has the right to be worshipped but Allah,' his life and property will be saved by me…"
- Sahih Al-Bukhari Volume 4, p. 161 "It is not fitting for a prophet that he should have prisoners of war (and free them with ransom) until he has made a great slaughter (among his enemies) in the land…"
- Sahih Al-Bukhari Volume 9, p. 45 "Whoever changed his Islamic religion, then kill him."
- Sahih Al-Bukhari Volume 4, p. 181-182 "An infidel spy came to the Prophet while he was on a journey. The spy sat with the companions of the Prophet and started talking and then went away. The Prophet said (to his companions), 'Chase and kill him.' So, I killed him. The Prophet then gave him the belongings of the killed spy."

- Sahih Al-Bukhari Volume 8, p. 519-520 "Some people from the tribe of Ukl came to the Prophet and embraced Islam. The climate of Medina did not suit them, so the Prophet ordered them to go to the (herd of milk) camels of charity and to drink their milk and urine (as a medicine). They did so, and after they had recovered from their ailment (became healthy) they turned renegades (reverted from Islam) and killed the shepherd of the camels and took the camels away. The Prophet sent (some people) in their pursuit, and so they were (caught and) brought, and the Prophet ordered that their hands and legs should be cut off and that their eyes should be branded with heated pieces of iron, and that their cut hands and legs should not be cauterized, till they die."
- Sahih Al-Bukhari Volume 4, p. 158-159 "The Prophet passed by me at a place called Al-Abwa or Waddan, and was asked whether it was permissible to attack the pagan warriors at night with the probability of exposing their women and children to danger. The Prophet replied, "They (i.e., women and children) are from them (i.e., pagans)."

As a sidebar, Sura 2:256a states "Let there be no compulsion in religion", meaning that people should not be converted to Islam by force; however, the verses shown from the Quran and the Sunnah above, in addition to the historical military campaigns of the caliphates, prove this to be riddled with contradiction. In Muslim-majority communities, some Muslims handle non-Muslim groups through Sahih Muslim, Book 19, Number 4294: "When you meet your enemies who are polytheists or nonbelievers, invite them to three courses of action. If they respond to any one of these, you also accept it and withhold yourself from doing them any harm. Invite them to [accept] Islam; if they respond to you, accept it from them and desist from fighting against them. ... If they refuse to accept Islam, demand from them the jizya. If they agree to pay, accept it from them and hold off your hands. If they refuse to pay the tax, seek Allah's help and fight them." The choice of wording in the English translation is interesting because the Arabic script condones "killing", not just "fighting". To summarize, the Islamic teaching gives three (3) courses of action: convert to Islam, pay tribute (jizya), or face death (killing or fighting to the death).

After examining the verbiage from the Quran and the Sunnah, the reader should not be shocked to find Islam linked to various terrorist groups (Boko Haram, Al-Shabaab, ISIS, etc.), declared a mental illness by China, or declared a non-peaceful religion. Most Islamic terrorist groups are inspired by Muhammad's example in the *Life of Muhammad*, where he goes into Medina demanding that all obey him. When the Jews (Banu Qaynuqa, Banu Nadhir, and Banu Quraydhah) refused – as Muhammad was not from Medina – Muhammad slit the throats of all men in one afternoon, took women as concubines, and forced children into slavery – even sex slavery. One must understand the ideology behind Islam and the model of Muhammad to understand what Muslims are commanded to do and why the most innocent of Muslims willingly engage in terrorist behavior. We have already covered the ideology, but here is a brief model of Muhammad, whom is described as illiterate, unable to read or to write, per the Islamic tradition with references:

- In Sahih Muslim 4206, Muhammad ordered a woman – pregnant through adultery – to be stoned after bearing the child. Ma'iz, a man facing the same charge, was spared.
- In Sahih Muslim 1:33, Muhammad said: "I have been commanded to fight against people till they testify that there is no god but Allah, that Muhammad is the messenger of Allah, and they establish prayer, and pay tax (zakat) and if they do it, their blood and property are guaranteed protection on my behalf except when justified by law, and their affairs rest with Allah."
- In Sahih Al-Bukhari 44:668, Ibn Ishaq 764, Muhammad permitted stealing animals as food from unbelievers when his followers were hungry.
- In Sahih Muslim 6303 and Sahih Al-Bukhari 49:857, Muhammad gave cases where lying was acceptable.
- In Sahih Muslim 3901, Muhammad owned slaves, and he engaged in the slave trade, where one slave was traded for two black slaves.

For clarification, Islam condones slavery, even going as far as explaining how to treat slaves, how to trade slaves, what roles/rights slaves have, and so forth. When an Arab man conceives a daughter with a slave woman, for instance, he is allowed to have intercourse with his daughter in Islam because the daughter is viewed as a slave, which is property. Moreover, major Islamic slave trading occurred during the Trans-Saharan Slave Trade – inclusive of the Red Sea slave trade and the Indian Ocean slave trade – that is recognized as the longest in history, spanning 1,300 years. The majority of slaves included millions of vulnerable Africans, captives of war, indebted servants, and outstanding criminals. Oftentimes, the male slaves were castrated to prevent reproduction with non-slaves among tribes, and they were killed when labor could no longer be extracted. Such slave trades never receive as much attention as the Trans-Atlantic slave trade because Muslim-majority societies are normally monarchies or totalitarian regimes with little to no free speech.

- In Sunan Abu Dawud 4390, Muhammad carried out a genocide on Jewish captives of Banu Qurayza, killing all of the males with pubes and enslaving all of the males without pubes. Some scholars try to cover this up by claiming these Jews violated the Medina Constitution and peace treaties in treachery; however, there is not one hadith in all nine (9) books of hadith nor one biography that indicates the Jews either – officially or unofficially – renounced treaties or violated treaties in any way.
- In Sahih Bukhari 56:369 and 4:241, Muhammad murdered anyone whom insulted him.
- In Sahih Muslim, Muhammad suggested that one commit jihad in the way of Allah to elevate one's position in paradise by a hundredfold.
- Muhammad set a precedent for pedophilia in Islam by marrying a 6-year-old girl named Aisha and consummating with this little girl at the age of 9, when he was 53 years old. (See Sahih Muslim 3309, Sahih Al-Bukhari, Vol. 7, Book 62, Hadith 64, and Sahih Al-Bukhari 58:236).

Many Muslims try to excuse Muhammad's marriage to Aisha by claiming that Aisha was not like kids her age and that she was divinely special at a young age; however, the Islamic references show no evidence of this. In fact, it suggests the opposite per the following references:

Sahih Al-Bukhari, Vol. 8, Book 73, Hadith 151: Narrated `Aisha: I used to play with the dolls in the presence of the Prophet, and my girlfriends also used to play with me. When Allah's Messenger used to enter (my dwelling place) they used to hide themselves, but the Prophet would call them to join and play with me. (The playing with the dolls and similar images is forbidden, but it was allowed for Aisha at that time, as she was a little girl, not yet reached the age of puberty.)

Sahih Muslim, Book 8, Hadith 3311: Aisha (Allah be pleased with her) reported that Allah's Apostle married her when she was seven years old, and she was taken to his house as a bride when she was nine, and her dolls were with her; and when he (the Holy Prophet) died, she was eighteen years old.

For clarification, child marriage and pre-pubescent sexual relations (pedophilia) are permitted in Islam. To be direct, a man may satisfy his sexual desires with a minor girl as young as a newborn; however, the man cannot penetrate, unless the female being can 'handle' the penetration or the man has obeyed a 3-month waiting period. If the male penetrates and he harms the girl (keep in mind that heinous crimes normally require four male witnesses in Islam), then he should be held financially liable for her whole life. This rule applies to permanent marriage and temporary marriage (mut'ah per Sura 4:24). The evidence for pedophilia is also captured in the following references:

For clarification, there are little girls as young as 13, trying to report being raped by Muslim men. If the girl/woman cannot bear four (4) male witnesses of the rape, then the assailant escapes, and the girl/woman is charged with adultery. The penalty for an adulterous girl/woman is death by stoning.

Surah 65:4: As for your women past the age of menstruation, in case you do not know, their waiting period is three months, and those who have not menstruated as well. As for those who are pregnant, their waiting period ends with delivery. And whoever is mindful of Allah, He will make their matters easy for them.

Tafsir Ibn Kathir: Allah the Exalted clarifies the 'Iddah (waiting period) of the woman in menopause. And that is the one whose menstruation has stopped due to her older age. Her `Iddah is three months instead of the three-monthly cycles for those who menstruate, which is based upon the verse in Sura 2:228: The same for the young, who have not reached the years of menstruation. Their `Iddah is three months, like those in menopause.

Tafsir Ibn Abbas: (And for such of your women as despair of menstruation) because of old age, (if ye doubt) about their waiting period, (their period (of waiting) shall be three months) upon which another man asked: "O Messenger of Allah! What about the waiting period of those who do not have menstruation because they are too young?" (along with those who have it not) because of young age, their waiting period is three months.

For clarification, this is the reason why sex tourism is high in Muslim-majority countries, such as Morocco, Indonesia, and Bahrain, where underage girls and virgin women are prostituted, trafficked, and exploited using the temporary marriage (mut'ah) excuse. Sex is also incentivized to men in Islam in death per Mishkat al-Masabih, Book 4, Ch 42, No. 24, where men who martyr for Islam are promised fully-erect, infinite penises and 72 virgin wives – two are houris, and 70 are female dwellers inherited from hell. It is unclear if these virgins take human form, skeletal form, or another form. No rewards are explicitly stated for women, however.

- Although the Quran mentions that Muslims can only have four (4) wives per Sura 4:3, Muhammad had more than 13 women as wives and concubines (sex slaves) through (un)consummated and annulled marriages. He even coveted the wife of his cousin, Zainab bint Jahsh, and the wife of his adopted son, Zaid ibn Haritha, based on Sura 33:37.

For clarification, Sura 33:50 gives Muslims the ability to marry paternal/maternal cousins – even allowing inbreeding and incest in some cases – and gives women the ability to offer themselves to Muhammad for marriage without any dowry.

- Muhammad encouraged his men to rape enslaved women and female captives per Abu Dawood 2150 and Sura 4:24. Keep in mind that captives are viewed as property rather than humans. Also, he forced captured slaves to surrender a fifth of all loot taken in war per Sura 8:41.
- Muhammad committed multiple homosexual acts, which many Islamic scholars try to conceal. The first instance comes from Hadith Number 16245, Volume Title: "The Sayings of the Syrians," Chapter Title: "Hadith of Mu'awiya Ibn Abu Sufyan", where Muhammad was caught sucking on the tongue or the lips of Al-Hassan (son of Ali) as well as Hassan's penis. The hadith even describes the intimacy as the splitting of Hassan's legs. In a second instance, per Sahih Al-Bukhari, Volume 1, Book 4, Number 152-154, Muhammad invites young boys to wash his private parts. The last example, per Musnad Ahmad 3788, Ibn Masood describes a time when he traveled to the wide valley of Mecca with Muhammad. During a nightly travel stop, Muhammad drew a line in the sand and told Ibn Masood not to pass the line as he participated in sexual exploits (textual uses 'mounting' and 'riding' for sexual activity) with men from al-Zutt until sunrise. Ibn Masood described Muhammad as being 'in great pain' and the al-Zutt men as being 'well-endowed dark-skinned men'.

As a sidebar, Afghan Muslims participate in bacha bazi – a practice where Muslim men sexually exploit street orphans and impoverished youth around the age of 11, making them perform explicit strip dances – sometimes, before killing them.

- Per Kanz Al-Ummal (meaning "The treasure of deeds"), Volume 13, Pages 609-610, Hadiths 37609-3761, Ali Bin Husam Ad-Din Al-Mufqi Al-Hindi specifies narrations with grade 'Hasan or Good' where Muhammad slept with the corpse of his uncle's deceased wife, the mother of Ali bin Abu Talib, so that she would be considered the "mother of the believers".
- Muhammad often wore and cross-dressed Aisha's clothing to receive revelations, and also exposed his thighs in front of men. Notable references include Mishkat Al Masabih, Volume II, Chapter XXXVIII, "The Fine Qualities of the Prophet's Wives."; Sahih al-Bukhari, Hadith Number 2442; Sahih al-Bukhari, Hadith Number 2393; Sahih al-Bukhari, Hadith Number 3941; Sahih Muslim, Hadith Number 4472; and Sahih Muslim, Hadith Number 5984.
- A man, who divorced his wife 3 times by accident before having sexual relations with her, came to Muhammad for guidance after she decided to marry another man. Muhammad mentions that this woman "is not lawful for the first husband until she tastes the honey of the other husband and he tastes her husband" per Sunan Abi Dawud 2309. Muslims call this process halala.
- In Sahih al-Bukhari and Ibn Ishaq 243, Muhammad states that whoever wants to see Satan should look at a black man. Many Muslims try to argue that this statement is not racist since Bilal ibn Rabah from Abyssinia (modern-day Eritrea) was Muhammad's 'close companion'; however, Muhammad kept Bilal as a purchased slave until Muhammad's death, calling someone a companion does not absolve them from racist remarks, and Muhammad described Bilal's head as a dark, dried raisin. Bilal was purchased and freed by Abu Bakr after Muhammad's death.
- In Sahih al-Bukhari 2, 357, Ibn Sharib narrated Ibn Abdul Talib said: "Always when his wives had their period, I saw the Prophet nearby his camel herd. There, he had lovingly intercourse with the female animals; sometimes he also turned towards the young animals of both sexes." This is a passage that many Muslims try to hide, where Muhammad engages in bestiality.

Of course, more embarrassing facts about Muhammad and disgraceful things about Islam (beheadings, burning people alive, female genital mutilation, rape, honor killings, hostage taking, oppression of women, etc.) can be provided; however, the objective here is to show a general audience the model that Muslims – particularly Muslim men – are subscribing to when accepting and when being conditioned under the Islamic doctrine.

Another fact, which cannot be ignored, is that Sura 6:163, as well as the interpretations behind the verse, indicate that Muhammad was the 'first Muslim', contradicting the notion that past prophets were Muslims and that past prophets submitted to Allah.

The final segment of this discussion will cover how Islam suppresses rationality and consciousness to force believers into agreeing with the following major mythological entries and major scientific errors contained within the Quran. Since not all Muslims are Sunni, the focus will solely be on the Quranic verses.

The level of Muslim delusion includes the following:

- Intentionally providing a false translation of the Arabic text for questionable Quranic verses
- Appealing to metaphor when literal Quranic verses are highly illogical per the interpretations provided in credible tafsirs
- Falsely claiming that illogical verses were acceptable to people in early times
- Falsely claiming that the Quran and Arabic words have alternative meanings when early Islamic scholars support embarrassing, questionable, or illogical verses
- Denying the works of early Islamic scholars or the chains of narration (isnad) with adequate

grading when they favor illogical verses

- Falsely claiming that Allah sent down revelations to be understood by humans from the human perspective

Quranic Ref	Remarks on Falsehoods
Sura 13:2, 36:37-40, 91:1-2	The Quran expresses an Earth-centered (geocentric) view of the cosmos, where the moon follows the sun in orbit but the Earth remains fixed. The geocentric view was scientifically disproven by Copernicus, and the moon does not follow the sun. These verses also state that the sun has a resting place, where it prostrates based on the permission of Allah. This is also incorrect, as the sun is fixed and day-night cycles are controlled by exposure to the sun.
Sura 18:86, 18:90; 18:96-101	The Quran steals a popular, but false, Syriac legend from the 6th Century where Alexander the Great visits places where the sun sets and mentions a muddy spring and murky waters. The sun never sets in a manner like this, and the Gog and Magog references are fictional creatures that do not exist. The Quran indicates that two dangerous tribes, Gog and Magog, were trapped behind a massive wall of Iron erected by Dhu'l-Qarnayn and will only be let free on the day of Judgment; however, no such wall or tribes have ever been found despite the advent of global satellite imagery.
Sura 7:45, 10:3, 11:7, 22:47, 25:59, 32:5, 41:9-12, 50:38, 70:4, 90:4	The Quran mentions the Earth and heavens being created in six days or eight days with no attempt in the creation verses to indicate, even poetically, the vast duration of time in which the universe had developed. Per Sura 22:47, 1 day = 1000 years, and per Sura 70:4, 1 day = 50,000 years – a complete contradiction. Strangely, it mentions that mountains were only set on Earth by Allah, which is far from true because mountains continue to rise and erode to this day. In Sura 16:15 and 78:6-7, there is a claim that mountains are pegs used to prevent the Earth from shifting, which is far from true based on plate tectonics and earthquakes.
Sura 2:29, 37:6-10, 41:9-12, 55:33-35, 65:12, 67:5, 72:8-9	The Quran describes the Earth as being fully formed before the stars, which is categorically false because the elements in the Earth's crust and core are generated mainly by exploding stars (supernova). Even worse, it claims that the earth was created before heaven (Sura 2:29 and 41:9), as heaven was just smoke and that heaven was fashioned with seven heavens afterward. Later verses (Sura 79:27-30) mention heaven created before earth in contradiction. Tons of space exploration have yielded no evidence of the seven heavens. Also, the Quran claims that stars/lamps adorn the heavens and Allah shoots these stars/lamps at devils to defend the heavens. A completely absurd claim with no evidentiary basis.
Sura 54:1-3	The Quran claims that the moon was miraculously split into two pieces and then, somehow, put back together again. There is, however, no scientific evidence suggesting that the moon was ever split into two parts. The Romans, Greeks, Egyptians, Persians, Chinese, and Indians living before, during, and after the creation of Islam recorded no such phenomenon. Not to mention, the immediate effects of a split moon, such as unstable tides, violent winds, an increase in Earth's rotation, etc., were never recorded either.
Sura 15:26, 38:71-75, 55:14	The Quran adopts a creationist view, even though there is overwhelming scientific evidence that humans have evolutionary trajectories over the course of millions of years. It claims that Allah created man by blowing life into clay or mud. Keep in mind that the composition of clay/mud is comparatively far from the composition of human beings. Also, Islam denies prehistoric animals like dinosaurs despite the endless fossil record findings.

Sura 11:40	The Quran adopts the false flood story common to many ancient Near-East and Mesopotamian cultures, whereby Noah escapes on an ark with his family and a pair of all living things. There is no genetic evidence for a population bottleneck that could match this event whatsoever; and, this story does not account for the predatory nature and the ecological location of all living things.
Sura 23:13-14, 77:20-22, 86:6-7, 96:1-19	The Quran states that semen originates from somewhere between the backbone and ribs, even though science has shown that sperm comes from the testicles and that semen comes from various glands behind and below the bladder, which are not between the backbone and ribs. The Quran is in line with the scientific error of Hippocrates and the Egyptian priests who examined bulls prior to sacrifice rather than humans. They also adopt the Egyptian belief that the embryo is contained within the sperm rather than the sperm being a vehicle for sperm cells to travel to the ovum, as science demonstrates. Another peculiar Quranic claim is that humans develop from a congealed blood clot, which is false. Moreover, it is unclear what man was created from as Sura 96:1-2 says a blood clot, Sura 25:54 says from water, Sura 15:26 says from clay, Sura 30:20 says dust, Sura 19:67 says from nothing, and Sura 37:11 says sticky clay – clearly contradictions. It is also worth mentioning that the Quran completely disregards the female ovum.
Sura 23:14	The Quran claims that the bones of a human embryo are formed first and then covered up with flesh; however, modern science demonstrates that muscles and cartilage of the future bones form at the same time and in parallel.
Sura 36:36, 51:49, 75:39	The Quran claims that all organisms were created in male/female pairs, though this is not true for all organisms, such as viruses, fungi, some lizards, and other asexually reproducing entities.
Sura 16:66	The Quran indicates that milk is produced in the body somewhere between excretions and blood, even though the mammary glands responsible for storing and producing milk are nowhere close to the small/large intestines, where excrement flows.
Sura 13:3, 50:7, 88:17-20	The Quran pushes a Flat-Earth theory as seen in Tafsir Al-Jalalayn for Sura 88:17-20: At the earth how it is spread out (from the Arabic roots su-ti-ha and sa-ta-ha meaning it was stretched), so they can see in it a sign for the power of Allah ... and his saying su-ti-hat makes it obvious that the earth is flat, and this is certified by Ulama' Ash-Shar'a (Sharia theologians), not a globe as it is said by Ahlul-hay'a (the laymen)." (Tafsir Al-Jalalayn, Damascus 1964). Other examples include Sura 15:19 and 96:6, where all tafsirs use Arabic words like 'da-ha-ha', 'Ta-ha-ha', and 'madda' to indicate a flat Earth. Sura 43:10 compares Earth to a bed.
Sura 18:60-61, 25:53, 27:61, 55:19-22	The Quran borrows/steals the two seas from the story of Moses in the Jewish tradition to explain the barrier between fresh water and salt water. Based on scientific evidence, there is a transition region where fresh water remains temporarily separated from the salt water. This separation is not permanent, as the Quran mentions, because the different salinity levels between the two bodies of water eventually homogenize. The Quran claims that there is a divine barrier between them, which is not true. Even more false, Sura 55:20 mentions that coral emerges from saltwater and freshwater when, in reality, coral cannot survive in freshwater.
Sura 16:45, 17:68, 29:37	The Quran claims that earthquakes, blizzards, hurricanes, and other destructive natural phenomena are punishments for people with evil plots against Allah. Clearly, this is false; however, it begs the question as to why Muslim countries are also afflicted with such 'punishments'.
Sura 43:11	All of the Quranic verses mention that water comes from either the sky or Allah, which shows ignorance of the water cycle. In fact, there is a complete disregard of evaporation in the Quran.

Sura 16:79	The Quran claims that Allah holds the birds in the sky, which is far from true. Birds learn to fly naturally by adjusting their skeletomuscular wing frame and feathers to air pressure currents, causing lift, thrust, and drag.
Sura 13:13	The Quran claims that Allah uses thunder and lightning to smite people, which runs parallel to Zeus in Greek Mythology.
Sura 27:18-19	The Quran indicates that ants can converse, when science has proven that ants primarily communicate through chemical signals. Although ants can produce noises, there is no brain activity in ants showing the complexity of speech.
Sura 6:142-144, 39:6	The Quran claims that Allah only created four types of cattle – sheep, goats, oxen, and camels. This is clearly false, showing that the Quran is a product of desert nomads, whom never saw other animals.
Sura 12:41, 20:71	The Quran mentions that there were crucifixions at the time of Moses, around 1500 BCE, when the first historical reference to a crucifixion is from 500 BCE.
Sura 20:85, 20:95	The Quran mentions that Moses encountered a Samarian when Moses lived around 1500 BCE, and the Samarians lived around 721 BCE.
Sura 2:65	The Quran reveals an event where Sabbath breakers are transformed into apes.
Sura 7:107	The Quran mentions that Moses's staff transformed into a serpent.
Sura 72:1	The Quran describes the existence and the attributes of devils living among us.
Sura 27:16-17, 27:20-23	The Quran adopts the Jewish story, where Solomon commanded birds and devils, and where birds engaged in detailed conversations with humans as spies.
Sura 113:4-5	The Quran discusses the existence of magic and sorcery, although no evidence has ever proven that magic is real.
Sura 37:142	The Quran states that Jonah/Yunis survived in the belly of a whale for some time (some say 3, 7, and even 40 days) after being swallowed whole. There is no proof that this is possible. In fact, science suggests that a person could not persist long inside a whale's digestive tract without being crushed by the whale or by water pressure or without being immediately suffocated.
Sura 17:1	The Quran mentions a winged beast (Buraaq) accompanying Muhammad on the make-believe night journey.
Sura 2:50	The Quran mentions Moses's parting of the Red Sea, even though there is no historical or other evidence that such an event occurred.
Sura 38:36	The Quran describes how Solomon had the power to control the wind to fly upon a large wooden carpet to wherever he pleased.
Sura 2:73	In the Quran, Allah instructed a group of people to strike a murdered man with a piece of animal flesh to resurrect him temporarily as a means to determine his identity.
Sura 29:14	The Quran states that Noah was 950 years old. There is no reference for Adam, but Muslims somehow conclude that Adam lived for 1000 years after creation. There are no evolutionary or environmental justifications for these outrageous life spans, and the longest surviving human ever recorded was 122 years old.
Sura 21:91, 66:12	The Quran describes Jesus' virginal conception and birth in a graphic way, stating that Allah and the Angel Gabriel blew into Mary's vagina together.
Sura 3:54, 8:30	The Quran mentions that Allah is the best/greatest of deceivers.
Sura 2:115, 5:64, 28:88, 52:48, 55:26-27, 57:4, 68:42, 69:17, 92:20	The Quran associates physical features and body parts (eyes, hands, shin, etc.) with Allah, even though Allah is not supposed to be anything like his creation per Sura 42:11. The Quranic verses shown below highlight such features. Sura 2:115 – And to Allah belong the east and the west, so wherever you turn yourselves or your faces there is the **<u>Face of Allah</u>** (and He is High above, over His Throne). Surely! Allah is All-Sufficient for His creatures' needs, All-Knowing.

	Sura 52:48 – Now await in patience the command of thy Lord: for verily thou art in **Our eyes**: and celebrate the praises of thy Lord the while thou stands forth. Sura 68:42 – [Remember] the Day when **the Shin shall be laid bare** (i.e., the Day of Resurrection) and they shall be called to prostrate (to Allah), but they (hypocrites) shall not be able to do so. Sura 57:4 – He it is Who created the heavens and the earth in six Days **and then Istawa (rose over) the Throne (in a manner that suits His Majesty)**. He knows what goes into the earth and what comes forth from it, what descends from the heaven and what ascends thereto. With Sura 57:4, the determination of how Allah sits on a throne carried by eight angels is of interest. Even worse, in the Sunnah, per Sahih al-Bukhari, Volume 6, Book 60, Number 373 and Sahih al-Bukhari, Volume 2, Book 24, Number 504, the narrations clearly indicate that Allah has a foot and Allah casts a shadow. Some Muslims try to dismiss these verses as metaphors to dodge the issue; however, Sura 28:88 and Sura 55:26-27 prove them wrong, plainly stating that Allah can eliminate everything except for his face. Salafi Muslims admit that these verses are indeed literal, and the description of Allah in the verses shows strong parallels to the pagan deity, Baal, especially since Allah has two right hands per Sura 56:8-9 and Sunan an-Nasa'I 5379.

There are far more examples of fantasy, fearmongering, and fiction in Islam; however, these examples with Islamic references should give readers a nice glimpse of how Islamic followers must reduce their rationality and their consciousness to subscribe to this religious doctrine. Moreover, Muslims live in a society, where discussing the negative aspects of Islam results in harm or penalty; and, they are encouraged to lie if such a lie strengthens Islam based on Suras 3:28, 3:54, 9:3, 16:106, and 40:28. Six major examples include 'taqiyya deception' (tactical deceit), tawriyah (deliberate ambiguity such as double-speak, avoiding straight answers, conflicting definitions, concealing unfavorable double meanings, etc.), maruna (pretending to be flexible or moderate Muslims to win over or to infiltrate non-Muslim groups), kitman (omitting details, distorting the truth, or withholding key information), taysir (deceit through facilitation/relaxation by claiming Muslims do not have to observe all of the tenets of Islam or Sharia Law when they really do), darura (deceit through necessity to engage in something haram, illegal, prohibited, or forbidden). Such deceit is compounded by vicious cycles of poverty, violence, internal wars of Muslims killing Muslims, and political instability, where Muslims account for approximately 29% of refugees – often fleeing conflict from an Islamic, totalitarian regime under Sharia Law – and 40% of the Muslim population in Muslim-majority countries are in abject poverty. It is also interesting that Muslim refugees go to non-Muslim countries in large numbers instead of Muslim-majority countries, raising questions of whether Islamic societies are great or are peaceful to live in.

Even the Muslim women are victims of their own ignorance, supporting a doctrine completely against them. In the Islamic tradition, the majority of inhabitants of hell are women (Sahih al-Bukhari 29); women are deficient in intelligence, half-brained, and worth half of a male witness (Sahih al-Bukhari 2658); women are too stupid to understand religion (Sahih al-Bukhari 304); women can be beaten by their husbands per Sura 4:34; women can be taken as sex slaves (Sura 4:3, 23:5-6, and 70:22-30); women can never deny a husband sexually (Sahih al-Bukhari 3237); women cannot lead in authority (Sahih al-Bukhari 7099); women cannot object to their husband's polygamy rights (Sura 4:3); women cannot marry non-Muslims unlike Muslim men (Sura 2:221); women can only inherit half of the men (Sura 4:11); and women must breastfeed non-relative adult men to become unmarriageable if they share the same dwelling space (Sahih Muslim 8:3425). Also, keep in mind that Muslim newborns obtain additional mothers somehow, every time a newborn is breastfed by another woman outside the biological mother.

As a sidebar, the Islamic tradition promises women forgiveness and great reward per Sahih at-Tirmidhi 2565; however, none of these rewards are actually specified – just empty promises. In Sura 43:18, there are indications that women only long for adornment and jewels, which seems to be closer to human opinion than divine expression. Based on the Islamic tradition, a woman will gain material items alongside a husband, where she will be one of many wives. This should somehow keep her happy for the rest of eternity.

Once again, the key to a religion's success is simply creating an explanation – not necessarily the best, the most factually accurate, the most historical, or the most truthful – riddled with belief that the willfully ignorant humans can subscribe to. An overwhelming majority of Muslims do not have a sufficient understanding of Islamic history and the Quran in Arabic script, so they easily fall for the lies, falsehoods, and insanity behind them.

Em Hotep!

ON ATHEISM

ANKH WADJA SENEB | ARTICLE NO: 009

Function: The Awareness of Control Mechanisms
Subject(s): Skepticism, Agnostics, Existence of God
Position: Part 3 – Breaking Societal Controls
Theme: Dealing with Religions, Cults, & Atheism | Scene 9

ARTICLE NO: 009 – ON ATHEISM

Peace to the High Power! Peace to the Living Universe! Peace to all Finite Living Beings! Peace to All Things – seen and unseen! For my spirit is with me, my image is with me, and my purpose is with me. For those with knowledge understand that the mechanisms behind societal controls can only flourish when consciousness, awareness, vibration, and rationality are minimized and when willful ignorance, fear, indoctrination, and subjugating forces are maximized.

Knowing that the key to a religion's success is simply creating an explanation – not necessarily the best, the most factually accurate, the most historical, or the most truthful – riddled with belief that the willfully ignorant humans can subscribe to, many would consider atheism to be a viable alternative. Atheism refers to the lack of belief in any god or supreme being. It is widely recognized that atheism is not necessarily a religion or belief system but rather a personal stance relying on empirical evidence and scientific/naturalistic explanations of the universe. Naturalism asserts that only natural laws and forces operate in the universe, excluding supernatural or divine entities. While atheism is defined by what it rejects, it is not a single, unified ideology and encompasses various stances from active criticism of religion to simply not believing without necessary and sufficient findings. Viewed another way, we can define atheism in two (2) broad categories as follows:

- **Implicit Atheism**: Absence of theistic belief without a conscious rejection of it.
- **Explicit Atheism**: Absence of theistic belief due to a conscious rejection of it.

A few classifications are provided below to clarify the main ideologies.

- Ontological Atheism: Firm denial that there is any supreme being
- Ethical Atheism: Firm conviction that, even if there is a creator, such a creator does not run things in accordance with the human moral agenda
- Existential Atheism: Asserts that even if there is a god, he has no authority over one's life
- Agnostic Atheism: Cautious denial that god's existence can be neither proven nor disproven
- Ignostic Atheism: Asserts that the question of the existence of god is meaningless because the word "god" is incoherent, ambiguous, or poorly defined
- Skeptic: Uncertain about the existence of a 'god', but remains open-minded, recognizing the limits of human knowledge and human experiences.
- Pragmatic Atheism: Asserts that god is irrelevant to ethical and successful living
- Non-Religious: Lacks religious belief, but chooses to subscribe to forms of spirituality or to traditional dogmas instead
- Anti-theists: Lack any religious belief, even taking an active stance and staging attacks against religions and religious followers.

The main arguments posed by atheism include the following:

- **The Problem of Evil**: Philosopher Epicurus formulated a series of questions: Is god willing to prevent evil but unable? Then he is not omnipotent. Is he able but not willing? Then he is malevolent. If he is both able and willing, why does evil exist?
- **Lack of Evidence**: The extraordinary claim of god's existence demands more than just faith or belief. Furthermore, the burden of proof lies on those who assert that god exists, and not on those who doubt it.
- **Incoherence of God's Attributes**: Internal contradictions within the concept of god, particularly concerning god's omnipotence and god's goodness as seen in moral descriptions of religious texts, where a god ordains/promotes genocide and suffering.
- **The Problem of Divine Hiddenness**: This argument, highlighted by philosopher J. L. Schellenberg, questions why a perfectly loving god who desires a relationship with humanity would not make His existence more obvious. The existence of "nonresistant nonbelief" – people who are willing to believe but find themselves unable to – is seen as evidence against a loving god who would want to be found by everyone.
- **Critique of Religion**: There are countless cases where religion has been harmful to individuals and to society, an impediment to progress, a source of immorality, and a tool for social control.
- **God of the Gaps' Fallacy Criticism**: The absence of a scientific explanation for something does not automatically mean a deity or a god is responsible.

Some limitations of atheism are provided below.

- Atheism does not have a unified philosophical view, a set of values, or a way of life.
- Atheism neither offers supernatural explanations nor accounts for phenomena beyond the scope of science or reason.
- Atheism distinguishes between religion and spirituality; however, it focuses on what spirituality cannot be rather than what spirituality actually is.
- Atheism segregates morality from religion; however, it does not provide universal criteria for determining 'right or wrong' acts or 'moral or amoral' subjective views, especially with humanist or secular reasoning.
- Atheism cannot address behavioral marks, such as personality, deviancy, fetishes, appetites, mood, and instinct. This includes an explanation of their origin, the mechanism driving them, and the countless differences/combinations.
- Atheism cannot address complex human experiences, such as awe or wonder.

Many atheists support secular humanism, which focuses on solving human problems and maximizing happiness or pleasure with critical thinking, scientific evidence, compassion, ethics, and justice without divine or supernatural belief. Spirituality supports most of the ideals; however, spirituality maximizes net zero balance over happiness under an impersonal High Power.

Although atheism breaks the societal controls of religion, it still requires willfully ignorant humans (subscribers) to reject the metaphysical layer of the Living Universe solely in favor of embracing naturalism (i.e., the physical world). This rejection either constrains or dampens consciousness, awareness, or rationality. To illustrate this point with an analogy, let us look at the complex number system, which consists of a real part (representing the physical world) and an imaginary part (representing the metaphysical world). If subscribers of atheism solely believe in the real part, then they will understand that $\sqrt{4} = 2$, but not that $\sqrt{-4} = 2i$ because the imaginary part (i.e., the metaphysical world) has been stifled. They will claim that the $\sqrt{-4}$ is either undefined or non-existent, similar to the metaphysical world, which is far from true.

Em Hotep!

COMPARATIVE STUDIES

ANKH WADJA SENEB | ARTICLE NO: 010

Function: The Awareness of Control Mechanisms
Subject(s): Comparisons between Religion & High Spirituality
Position: Part 3 – Breaking Societal Controls
Theme: Dealing with Religions, Cults, & Atheism | Scene 10

ARTICLE NO: 010 – COMPARATIVE STUDIES

Peace to the High Power! Peace to the Living Universe! Peace to all Finite Living Beings! Peace to All Things – seen and unseen! For my spirit is with me, my image is with me, and my purpose is with me. For those with knowledge understand that the mechanisms behind societal controls can only flourish when consciousness, awareness, vibration, and rationality are minimized and when willful ignorance, fear, indoctrination, and subjugating forces are maximized.

People are interested in spirituality for a variety of deeply personal and universal reasons, including a quest for meaning, a need for inner peace, and a way to cope with life's challenges. For most, the rigid dogma, structure, and hypocrisy of organized religion can be highly disappointing. Spirituality, in contrast, offers a more personal and adaptable journey that is not dictated by institutional rules or doctrines. The following comparison table outlines how key religious ideas differ from the perspective of High Spirituality.

Religious Ideas	High Spirituality Perspective
On death, the soul leaves the body permanently and lives in the form of a ghost or spirit.	This idea of a soul or ghost does not exist. Upon death, the intelligent spirit sheds the physical mantle, circulating through the Pool of spirits until another physical mantle becomes available.
A spirit or soul is present in every object of the world, including natural objects like air, water, fire, trees, mountains, rivers, etc.	This idea of a soul does not exist. Only finite living beings possess a spirit.
Natural disasters like earthquakes, wildfires, droughts, floods, etc., are punishments from the divine god(s).	Natural disasters are consequences of laws governing the conscious living universe.
Spirits can be controlled by sorcery, tying them to some inanimate object like dolls, claws, wings, etc.	This idea of sorcery does not exist. Spirits operate based on the spirit cycle of the Sacred Geometric Rhythms.
Requiring the worship of ancestors, animals, or elements of nature	No such worship exists.
Rituals requiring genitals (circumcision, female genital mutilation, reproductive praise, etc.)	No such rituals exist.
Divine power residing in the sky, in special earthly places, or in multiple heavenly layers	High Power is a multi-dimensional life force, powering every dimension at every level. Heaven, hell, or special dwelling places do not exist.
Belief in rebirth and life after death.	There is no afterlife; however, rebirth can occur in a spiritual sense.
Sacrificing animals is necessary to please a god.	No sacrifice is necessary for an impersonal High Power.

Man and woman are viewed as the symbols of god's direct creation.	All finite living beings first materialize in a high-energy state and reproduce in a low-energy state. They are not directly created or individually crafted by a god.
Presence of demigods, angels, demons, devils, jinns, divine intercessors, oracles, and so forth.	Such entities do not exist.
Geocentric views or Earth-centric narratives	Spirituality addresses the conscious Living Universe in its entirety, not just Earth. This includes all possible dwelling spaces and all finite living beings inhabiting the cosmos.
Rainfall is controlled by gods and demons.	Rainfall is controlled by the actual laws of nature, including the water cycle.
God expects good deeds or obedience from worshippers – even passing judgment and punishments on sinners.	The High Power is chiefly concerned with fulfilling its own will, not the conduct of finite living beings. In High Spirituality, morality (right or wrong) centers around the NFR balance; however, judgments and punishments come from finite living beings. There is no sin – only immoral acts.
Prayers in honor of the god(s) are invoked, and offerings are made – normally financially.	The High Power is chiefly concerned with fulfilling its own will, not the prayers and offerings of finite living beings. Also, spirituality promotes affirmations, not prayers.
The belief that a god is the greatest good, prevailing over evil, and viewing happiness over suffering. There is even a need for a nemesis or a villain.	The High Power is the greatest good and the greatest evil through omnipotence. Suffering and happiness are simply by-products of a created Living Universe. There is no need to invent a villain.
Belief in either one god (monotheism) or many gods (polytheism), as well as pantheons	The High Power is a multi-dimensional life force that can act as a whole (monotheistic sense) or in parts (polytheistic sense) of a whole through omnipotence without restriction. There is no pantheon. If a god is restricted to being one and only one, then it is not almighty.
Divine visions and recitations are necessary to tap into the internal awakening of the spirit.	There are no divine visions. Meditation and confessionals channel the internal awakening of the spirit.
A god is required either to achieve salvation or to escape endless suffering – normally, to be reincarnated or to have eternal life.	The intelligent spirit has no past-life memory, and there is no reincarnation. Also, there is no afterlife, and the spirit cycle is eternal.
Spiritual knowledge is given in the form of parables or stories.	Finite living beings acquire spiritual knowledge by increasing rationality and consciousness. This knowledge can come through several mediums, including parables, teachings, direct academia, personal experiences, etc.
Temptation and material desires are based on the flesh.	Temptation and material desires are based on low vibrational states of the intelligent spirit and the physical mantle.
Religion is rooted in truth and faith.	Religion is far from the truth, seeking subscribers for credence and requiring blind faith or willful ignorance to justify man-made doctrines. Spirituality encourages meditation and well-informed thought.

Religion often requires the need to tithe with returns in abundance. There are even promises of economic and material gains.	Spirituality does not require tithes or taxes/zakat, only graceful charity. Also, there are no promises of economic/material gains because spirituality is driven by the interconnectedness of all finite living beings rather than a 'pay-to-play' scheme.
Ideas of a flat Earth or a flat firmament	All celestial bodies are made of multi-sided and multi-faced polyhedra. There are no instances of any planet or celestial body being flat or disk-shaped.
The soul is eternal.	A soul does not exist – only a spirit. The spirit is eternal, constantly cycling through the Pool of Spirits upon the life and the death of the physical mantle.
Humans were created to worship a god.	The High Power is only concerned with fulfilling its own will. If humans were created to worship a god, then the act of worship would have been pre-programmed in the intelligent spirit, and all humans would impulsively carry out acts of worship without knowing why. All acts of worship are learned behaviors of humans, so this is not the case. The same goes for other finite living beings.
Religions assign sacredness and holiness to people, places, things, and ideas. There are even cases, where humans have dominion over other animals and where certain humans are privileged, favored, and chosen over other humans.	In Spirituality, the conscious Living Universe is the domain for all finite living beings. Also, no finite living being is favored over another. There is no dominion or special hierarchy.
Messages from god never come from god directly, but through revelation, omens, signs, prophecies, or messengers.	No one can speak on behalf of the High Power. Revelations and testimonies mean nothing, unless they are corroborated by the High Power. Moreover, the High Power can make any message known to all finite living beings without needing an intermediary.
Fluctuating/unstable tendencies of the mind and sickness/illness of the body equate to demonic possession, divine wrath, and evil spirits.	Demonic possession does not exist. Mental instabilities occur due to the corruption of the intelligent spirit, and illness occurs when the normal functioning of the physical mantle is significantly disrupted.
Fear of god and faith in god lead to reward, including paradise over purgatory.	The High Power has neither declared nor programmed finite living beings to fear it. Also, the ideas of paradise and purgatory are mere myths perpetuated by belief rather than fact. In spirituality, paradise and purgatory do not exist as places; however, they can be considered states of mind based on vibrations.
Ritualistic practices propagate the principle of the world as an illusion.	In High Spirituality, all finite living beings are restricted in consciousness, so the perception of the 'real' conscious Living Universe – physical and metaphysical layers – might prove illusory or might be projections to certain finite living beings.

Religions invite feminine and masculine gods.	The High Power contains feminine and masculine energies as a multi-dimensional life force. It is not a male or female god/deity.
Engaging in idol worship	In High Spirituality, the worship of idols requires willful ignorance and a complete loss of rationality. The High Power never ordains such practices, but there are no penalties.
Marriage is ordained by a god with a covenant relationship between a man and a woman.	A valid marriage requires a compatible spiritual journey that culminates in resonance. It does not necessitate ceremonies, rings, family involvement, etc. Many religious marriages are seen as invalid marriages in High Spirituality.
The sum of a person's actions in current and previous states of existence is viewed as deciding their fate in future existences.	The intelligent spirit has no past-life memory, so previous states and future states of existence (if any) would be completely disconnected. Also, there is no fate for finite living beings, and reciprocal actions occur from imbalances. All finite living beings have complete free will, and the conscious Living Universe does not have free will.
Religions push for absolute purity, absolute peace, and absolute happiness.	The context behind 'absolute' is unclear; however, spiritual purity and spiritual peace are reached at the highest levels of vibrations. High Spirituality centers on balance, so absolute levels of happiness can be dangerous given the circumstances. Instead, spirituality focuses on increasing interconnectedness, knowledge, rationality, consciousness, and a sense of purpose.
Gods forbid the slaughter or the consumption of certain animals	High Spirituality has no dietary restrictions, especially since finite living beings consume other finite level beings for sustenance. The consumption and the killing of any finite living being do impact the Net Balance, however.
Gods are seen as water gods or fire gods.	The High Power is a multi-dimensional life force, powering the sacred geometric rhythms. Such rhythms assist in the creation of the prototypical elements. This means that there are no water gods or fire gods, as elements are created by the High Power, not of it.
Man is made in the image of god and is created after his likeness.	In High Spirituality, the High Power is nothing like finite living beings or things existing in the conscious living universe. Strictly speaking about humans, humans are accidental consequences of nature under an impersonal High Power. Also, the use of the possessive pronoun 'his' indicates a god with male gender, which distorts the meaning of this image and which places a restriction on this god.
God is a formless, spiritual creator of the universe.	High Spirituality concurs with the High Power being the creator of the Living Universe; however, the High Power can destroy itself (remove form) or can bring itself back into existence in an infinite number of forms. None of these forms is identical to the forms of finite

	living beings, even though the High Power can elect to take the form of finite living beings.
Religions indicate that there was nothingness in the beginning.	This is not necessarily true, as nothingness implies that even a god was non-existent. In High Spirituality, the High Power created the universe from emptiness, not nothingness. This is a very important distinction because the High Power is eternal regardless of presence.
Some religions do not support polygamy.	In High Spirituality, monogamy and polygamy are permitted because relationships are driven by the resonance of compatible spiritual journeys.
Virginity, abstinence, and celibacy are seen as virtues.	In High Spirituality, there is an interplay between survival and interconnectedness. If the central motive behind being a virgin or practicing abstinence and celibacy is to refrain from engaging in sexual exploits with those not spiritually compatible, then there is alignment.
Some religions demonize nudity, normally from the perspective of immorality.	In High Spirituality, nudity is not considered a bad thing. Embracing the natural body is an integral part of accepting beauty, humility, and a strong sense of liberation. Those tying nudity to immorality are on a lower vibration, but at this level, such thoughts of immorality will be present regardless of how many layers of clothing are worn.
The concept of a 3-in-1 god being the Son, the Father, and the Holy Spirit	In High Spirituality, there is slight agreement with this concept. For instance, the High Power can manifest as a whole or parts of a whole, where the parts can be viewed as 3-in-1, 10-in-1, etc. Outside of this, there are many issues with the concept: (1) The High Power is nothing like finite living beings, which have intelligent spirits and physical mantles. (2) The choice of 'Father' and 'Son' indicates a known and restrictive gender; however, the High Power is without restriction. (3) The choice to have a 'god in the flesh', a 'god in spirit', and 'a god in heaven' implies that multiple instances and multiple representations are necessary to deal with limitations of divine form. For instance, why have so many forms? Which form is the strongest? Can the 'god in the flesh' destroy the 'god in heaven'? Which would prevail in a power struggle? (4) Instances of 'god in the flesh' receiving education indicate that it is not all-knowing – a necessary attribute for godship.
A god born to a virgin in the flesh to die for the sins – past and present – of all humankind.	In High Spirituality, the High Power is impersonal, focusing on its own will, not the affairs of finite living beings. Although a god can do anything as an almighty entity, taking the form of a human on earth and dying for sins as a means of salvation seems nonsensical, especially since such a god can hardwire a

	person not to sin, and such a god created sin itself. In essence, this god created sin, allowed the sin to be introduced into humankind, took a virgin for birth, and died for the sins that it created. High Spirituality does not support any of these ideas.
A (demi)god can be resurrected.	In High Spirituality, finite living beings cannot be resurrected. The intelligent spirit sheds the physical mantle and returns to the Pool of Spirits. The High Power can engage in such acts if and only if its will requires these acts. Also, finite living beings cannot kill the High Power.
A god performing miracles to provide godship.	In High Spirituality, the High Power need not prove anything. Through omnipotence, the High Power can instantly rewire all finite living beings to understand its nature. Also, miracles require unexplained transcendence beyond the laws of the physical and metaphysical layers of the conscious Living Universe, not the scientific peaks of human understanding.
Concept of a god loving a human being	In High Spirituality, the High Power is an impersonal entity. Also, if a god supposedly loved its followers, then such followers would have unlimited fulfilment without any suffering or punishments whatsoever.
Religion has followers consume the body of and drink the blood of 'a god in the flesh'.	In High Spirituality, such acts are likened to witchcraft and [spiritual] cannibalism.
Praying five times daily toward a direction	In High Spirituality, such prayers mean nothing to an impersonal High Power. The High Power is focused on its will, not prayers from finite living beings.
Fasting for an entire month from sunrise to sunset	In High Spirituality, full fasts and intermittent fasts are recommended daily, not at specific times in the year. Also, these fasting periods are recommendations, not obligations.
Going on a pilgrimage to a holy place	In High Spirituality, the conscious Living Universe is the sanctuary for finite living beings as well as the dwelling spheres. Assigning holiness and sacredness to places is characteristic of man-made doctrine.
Religious doctrine has been used to justify slavery, even providing rules/teachings on how to treat slaves, how to trade slaves, and what roles/rights slaves have	In High Spirituality, the enslavement of any finite living being (human slaves, zoos for animal confinement, etc.) is characteristic of low vibration, so it is condemned.
Religious doctrine calls for war, harm, forced conversion, or a tax on non-believers.	In High Spirituality, none of this occurs. In fact, spirituality has never been linked as a direct support mechanism of or an instigator of war, unlike religion. The listed items even go against the NFR balance. Also, High Spirituality does not require any penalties or punishment for not converting. Converting is not necessary because spirituality is intrinsic to all finite living beings, unlike religion.

By analyzing beliefs, practices, ethics, and ritualistic expressions of different religions through a spiritual lens, readers can easily see how various faiths fail to address the ultimate questions of existence and to construct doctrine without contradictions. Readers are even encouraged to be highly critical of any past, present, or future religion. Spirituality is the polar opposite, seeking to discover well-informed meanings and rationales to existence based on evidence or proof.

Em Hotep!

DANGERS IN EDUCATION

ANKH WADJA SENEB | ARTICLE NO: 011

Function: The Awareness of Control Mechanisms
Subject(s): Schools of Thought, Indoctrination in Academia
Position: Part 3 – Breaking Societal Controls
Theme: Dealing with Education | Scene 1

ARTICLE NO: 011 – DANGERS IN EDUCATION

Peace to the High Power! Peace to the Living Universe! Peace to all Finite Living Beings! Peace to All Things – seen and unseen! For my spirit is with me, my image is with me, and my purpose is with me. For those with knowledge understand that the mechanisms behind societal controls can only flourish when consciousness, awareness, vibration, and rationality are minimized and when willful ignorance, fear, indoctrination, and subjugating forces are maximized.

From an objective sense, people herald education as the foundation of a free, informed society because it increases knowledge capacity and manufactures the mind. Students continue cycling through the structure of school systems generation by generation under the assumption that the content in textbooks and the messaging in educational institutions will foster fresh viewpoints and sharpen critical thinking skills; however, this subtle assumption allows the suppression of alternative viewpoints, ideological indoctrination, commercial exploitation, and manipulation to seep in through every layer of the educational process.

First off, whoever controls the curriculum also controls the narrative. This means that the curricula can be weaponized against anyone, and the portrayal of curricula as neutral frameworks is highly improbable. In state-controlled regimes, for instance, education is used as a tool to instill obedience, to promote nationalism, and to demonize rebels, opposition, and nonconforming outsiders. The curriculum will omit details that demonstrate the state in gross character, foul play, or abuses of humanity, but will often include the state as a hero, a victim acting in self-defense, or a beacon of hope. Bear in mind that every inclusion and every omission in a narrative directly shapes perception. In democratic societies, for instance, there are cases where the dominant thought patterns shape public opinion through biased interpretations of facts and the exclusion of dissenting voices from minority groups. Such cases normally paint imperialistic foreign diplomacy expeditions as 'civilizing missions', 'bilateral ventures', or 'economic recovery', even though these expeditions have resulted in slavery, erasure of indigenous cultures, and extreme poverty. In essence, the controller of the curriculum restricts the freedom of thought by blurring the lines between education and indoctrination.

For clarification, education transmits knowledge and develops skills; or, put simply, it gives students the tools to think. Indoctrination, on the other hand, tells students what to think, programming them to accept ideas without question. Such is so in many religious schools that teach students that proven scientific theories are false, despite offering no alternative explanation or logical basis – only absolute statements reinforced by fear, punishment, shame, or guilt.

Secondly, educational settings hardly promote open dialogue among students but rather conformity driven by a teacher's ideology as truth – unknowingly or intentionally. With no countermeasure to the teacher as a trusted agent, this causes dissenting students to feel mocked, penalized, or restrained, especially if their views are controversial or if their views are culturally incompatible, unacceptable, or insensitive. For instance, students discussing the need for a coal powerplant in an environment where only climate-conscious ideas are tolerated, students being shamed by peers for asking uncomfortable questions about creationism in favor of evolution, students being forced to value animal lives due to majority veganism without debate, or overreliance on emotionally charged narratives normally tied to diversity, inclusion, and sensitive social issues (abortion, immigration, discrimination, gun control, and inequality). The rejection of dissenting views, especially with an authority figure like a teacher in play, gives rise to cancel culture, where marginalized voices are censored, ostracized, or disciplined in favor of the dominant intellectual monoculture.

Lastly, we have to remember that manipulation is not only ideological, psychological, or physical but also financial. Educational institutions are no different than corporations, so students, who are effectively customers, are forced to purchase 'in-network' textbooks, to deal with predatory student loans/fees, and to learn from sponsored content that might be outdated, ineffective, and prejudicial. In-network textbooks are used either to maintain indoctrinating 'schools of thought' or to sustain publisher profits by selling overpriced books. There is nothing student-centered about these motives, and the commercial exploitation of the students leads the students to believe that they need certain degrees or specific certifications, even when the labor market offers poor job prospects. Outside of this, there is a great deal of tech manipulation as well. For instance, tech companies normally donate hardware/software to educational institution in exchange for student body data access, e-learning platforms make secret arrangements with companies that generate psychological profiles for behavioral marketing (nudging) based on clicks, governments typically force online learning platforms to introduce algorithmic bias to limit exposure to diverse viewpoints, and large corporations normally pay educational institutions to align with certain business interests, especially in times of worker shortage.

Although education is not inherently manipulative or bad, the power of education, the influence of education and the reach of education cause it to become a prime target for those seeking to control minds and/or to capitalize on opportunity. This article will explore different ways that they do so.

INDOCTRINATION VIA SCHOOL CURRICULUM DEVELOPMENT

Indoctrination via school curriculum development is a result of factors that form a layered ecosystem of influences, such as fear, funding, secrecy, gender norms, lowered standards, and corporate interests. These factors collectively shape what students are taught and, more importantly, how they think. The end goal is a predictable, controllable population rather than a critically minded, self-determining population. Some of these causative factors include the following:

- **Professors Afraid Because of Threats of Tenure and Death Threats**: Professors have restricted their speech (self-censor), lesson plans, and research in response to threats of harassment, violence, and death, not only from offended students but also from college administrators. As watchdogs, college administrators are willing to dismiss tenured professors, to shut down funding, and to eliminate the research activities of professors – normally mandated by stakeholders or governments – if these professors are caught saying something that might be considered controversial or offensive or are caught teaching outside the scope of approved curriculum frameworks. Most instances of professors being fired or put on leave occur over comments made on social media or during biased peer-review cycles.
- **Religious or Political Interest Groups Paying to Shut Down Influences**: Through financial leverage, religious or political interest groups fund programs, provide donations (i.e. directly to schools, through non-profits, or as bribes), or pressure institutions to suppress criticism of their ideologies. As a result, textbooks and lesson plans get edited to remove critical references, subtly presenting sanitized or one-sided views.
- **Secret Societies (Cults) Enforcing Their Interests**: Through network influence, secretive groups (cults) can infiltrate boards, committees, or donor circles that shape education policies. As a result, there is inclusion of narratives favorable to these groups (or exclusion of competing views), reinforcing their social, moral, or political agenda under the guise of 'values-based' education.

- **Men Being Conditioned to Uphold Patriarchal Systems**: Through gender-role reinforcement, school materials, hidden messaging, and policy bias encourage boys to internalize leadership (dominant) roles and encourage girls to accept subordination or support roles. Resultantly, textbooks, teaching examples, and teacher biases normalize patriarchal structures, making students less likely to challenge gender inequality later in life.
- **Intentional Lowering of the Bar**: Schools lower their academic standards to meet qualification criteria for funding and to give the illusion of educational equity. Ultimately, this makes students more vulnerable to misinformation tactics and the Dunning-Kruger Effect. The Dunning-Kruger Effect is a cognitive bias where people with low competence in a subject overestimate their abilities, while highly competent individuals may underestimate theirs, leading to a gap between perceived and actual performance.
- **Establishing Schools of Thought**: Curriculum developers or field experts make conscious or unconscious choices about which type of knowledge, theories, and readings to include; thus, universities implicitly validate certain schools of thought as the 'correct way' or the 'correct perspective' to understand a subject. Such choices exclude alternative theories/viewpoints, which might be sound, evidentiary, and plausible, from serious consideration among the majority thought leaders whom control peer-review rubrics, sources of certification, and entry standards for publication.
- **Limited Intellectual Independence**: When students are discouraged from questioning different subject matter when presented with a narrow range of perspectives, their intellectual independence is suppressed. This distorts students' understanding and limits pluralism within rational thought.

WEAPONIZATION OF ILLITERACY & LOW EDUCATIONAL STANDARDS

Illiteracy and low educational standards can be weaponized to maintain inequality and inequity in opportunity, even within a shared framework.

- **Reduced Opportunities**: Students with low literacy face significant disadvantages in the job market, especially since skilled positions typically require reading work instructions and/or technical publications. Resultantly, a lack of formal preparation makes them less competitive and restricts their ability to earn a sufficient income.
- **Cycle of Ignorance**: The illiteracy and low educational standards of one generation prevent it from properly educating future generations, especially with limited resources. Such educational struggles put future generations at a disadvantage, increasing the likelihood of failure.
- **Limited Participation in Political and Civic Functions**: Illiterate and poorly educated students often have low rates of political and civic participation, limited to no understanding of their rights, and no effective engagement in critical voting processes. Without a basic education, students remain uninformed, and they remain unable to advocate for their interests.
- **Control and Manipulation**: Dominant groups, who control information and messaging, can easily suppress dissent and can wield power over illiterate or poorly educated students.
- **Dependency and Disintegration**: Poor education impairs the development of critical thinking skills, making individuals unfit to question unjust systems, to challenge discriminatory practices, or to reform educational disparities.

DISCONNECT BETWEEN SCHOOLING & THE WORKPLACE

Traditional schooling emphasizes rote learning (learning by repetition) and academic skills over life skills (personal finance, cooking, scoping out opportunity, building shelter, marketing yourself, swimming, or other survival skills) and trade skills (critical thinking, problem-solving, vocational skills, etc.). The assessments of academic skills center on demonstrating a sufficient knowledge base to pass standardized tests – proficiency heavy with no true regard for growth – scoped from commonly pre-structured curriculum frameworks that are normally out of date. Assuming that students pass these assessments, they are awarded diplomas, degrees, and certificates, even though such awards do not necessarily come with the skills necessary to make them either employment-ready or entrepreneurship-ready. This creates a large gap between traditional schooling and the economic workplace because the economic workplace generates revenue based on resource utility, where resource utility measures the practical usefulness of a given new-hire. Simply put, if students have low resource utility (i.e., missing a skill set required for industry), then they cannot help industries generate revenue as new-hires, regardless of their educational level. Educational institutions are aware of this gap; however, they have no intentions of closing it because students in exploration or students pursuing low-demand programs will be locked in vicious tuition cycles (i.e., constant return to the classroom consumes taxpayer dollars as degree choice yields no jobs/opportunities), and the risk tolerance for ignoring industry-related skills will remain low. Some of these risk tolerances are provided below.

- **Emphasis on University Education**: Educational institutions want students to perceive a strong academic foundation as the primary pathway to higher education and to prestigious careers, lowering any risks on the curriculum focus.
- **Curriculum Lag**: Educational institutions do not want to bear the costs associated with updating school curricula to keep pace with rapidly changing technology and societal norms.
- **Limited Resources**: Teaching life skills and trade skills, especially those requiring specialized spaces and tools, are often too expensive for schools to provide.
- **Argument of Parental Role**: Educational institutions will shift blame to parents before admitting that outdated curriculum frameworks are failing students.
- **Contemporary Demands in the World Today**: Educational institutions will argue that their role is to provide a basic or a fundamental education, not an all-inclusive advanced education with the ability to analyze and to solve complex problems. This is actually not true.
- **Economic and Social Stability**: A system focused on preparing citizens for employment rather than entrepreneurship offers a more predictable and stable economic outcome that does not threaten the business relationships between educational institutions and corporate leaders.
- **Available Curricula and Resources**: Traditional schools are built on established curricula and readily available resources from select companies rather than the open market. If the curriculum becomes industry-focused, then these resources from these sources might not qualify, hurting existing prime vendor pipelines and distribution agreements.
- **Scalability and Standardization**: Standardized curricula and teaching methods are easier to implement across large student populations than the more individualized, adaptable approaches typically required for entrepreneurial education. There is a strong cost hit, and companies generating standardized content/exams will be rendered obsolete.
- **Optics of a Degree**: If educational institutions focus on skills rather than degrees, then degrees will decrease in value, including the 'college brand' behind them, and many students will gravitate toward trade schools over universities, upending predatory tuition cashflows and disrupting projected enrollment rates.
- **Indoctrination by Design**: Large corporations avoid new rival competition by steering education. They sponsor 'career readiness' programs, textbooks, and teacher training, all designed to funnel students into obedient worker roles rather than innovators or competitors.

For clarification, students are programmed to become compliant employees rather than independent entrepreneurs, as business setup knowledge is always absent from standardized curricula. This business setup knowledge includes drafting business plans, constructing strategies for operation, understanding funding vehicles, managing accounting and tax, brand awareness, legal compliance, hiring processes, and so forth. Without this, students will not be confident enough to become entrepreneurs or to remain in business.

UNETHICAL FUNDING PRACTICES & DISSENT PREVENTION

Manipulation of Funding

Manipulation of funding becomes most apparent when institutions and stakeholders unethically exploit loopholes to secure funding as follows:

- **Railroading Students**: Promoting students to higher grade levels, regardless of whether they have mastered the material or not. Institutions might prioritize completion rates, graduation numbers, or progression statistics because these are often tied to funding cycles, accreditation metrics, ranking, or performance evaluations. The impacts include a 'quantity over quality' culture, lower credibility of programs, and graduates lacking in required skills.
- **Falsifying Data**: Manipulating attendance records, exam results, or demographic data. Many governments and donors allocate funds based on special needs, diversity quotas, or performance metrics. Inflating numbers can secure extra grants or subsidies; however, it misallocates resources, causing deserving schools and underrepresented students to lose out.
- **Selective Enrollment**: Selectively admitting students whom are more likely to perform well academically, while sidelining those whom need more support. Educational institutions benefit from higher test scores, pass rates, or standardized rankings, which in turn attract funding, donors, or recruiting prospects. This perpetuates cycles of privilege, and reinforces inequality by neglecting students from disadvantaged backgrounds or without academic resources.
- **Buying of Degrees**: Educational institutions (or fraudulent actors as seen in diploma mills) sell degrees or provide honorary degrees. These institutions might masquerade as legitimate schools, attracting tuition fees, donor contributions, or government subsidies. Even in accredited schools, wealthy students may use influence or money to bypass requirements. Potential impacts include the devaluation of degree programs as paying students receive favor and a lack of trust in higher education.
- **Low Accountability Gaps**: Governmental representatives with interests in educational institutions might use influence to weaken auditing, regulation, and oversight structures to reroute or to qualify for multiple funding streams.
- **Performance-Based Funding Models**: Educational institutions might use influence to shuffle key performance indicators (KPI) in their favor. In this case, these institutions push to have unfavorable performance indicators removed so that the remaining ones will show them in good standing.

Suppressing Dissent in Academia

Behind the ideal of 'academic freedom', there are multiple structural, political, and cultural mechanisms that suppress, dismiss, or eliminate dissenting voices. This suppression can occur overtly or subtly, and often hides under noble-sounding policies like inclusivity, equity, or academic excellence. While institutions justify suppression in the name of safety, inclusiveness, or integrity, it is often clear that these ideals are selectively enforced. Through bureaucratic manipulation, ideological policing, and even direct intimidation, dissenting academics are neutralized to protect institutional interests, ideological homogeneity, and corporate or political alliances. Ultimately, what emerges is not a space of free inquiry, but rather a system of intellectual feudalism where tenure, funding, and legitimacy depend less on truth than on compliance.

Dissent can be suppressed in favor of inclusiveness as follows:

- **Ideological Conformity under the Guise of Diversity**: Institutions demand inclusiveness that only considers certain perspectives deemed politically correct. Dissenting scholars questioning dominant narratives on gender, race, politics, or globalization are often labeled as intolerant or non-inclusive, which provides grounds for disciplinary action or public condemnation.
- **Cultural Gatekeeping**: Inclusiveness committees might become ideological enforcers and can block appointments, promotions, or funding for scholars whom do not align with institutional narratives. They defend their actions by using terms like 'avoiding unsafe spaces' to mask censorship.
- **Compelled Speech and Self-Censorship**: Scholars may be required to use institutional language such as specific pronouns, equity statements, or Diversity, Equity, and Inclusion (DEI) philosophies in their research, syllabi, or job applications. Refusal to comply may result in career stagnation or dismissal.

Dissent can also be suppressed through bureaucratic control as follows:

- **Revocation & Denial of Grants**: Dissenting academics who challenge politically or corporately backed research, such as public health, pharmaceuticals, climate change, neoliberal economics, or military intervention, might find their grants denied or revoked.
- **Selective Enforcement of Policies**: Codes of conduct, harassment, or civility clauses can be selectively applied to target individuals whose research or statements embarrass the institution or challenge its alliances.
- **Reputation Management**: Administrations prioritize the institution's public image over truth or fairness. As a result, whistleblowers or critics might be silenced/gagged, discredited, or pressured to resign.

Dissent can also be suppressed through tenure, chairs, and academic gatekeeping as follows:

- **Tenure as a Shield for Corruption**: Senior faculty or chairs who conform to institutional politics typically retain protection even when engaging in misconduct, while dissenting or younger academics face non-renewal or dismissal.
- **Academic Gatekeeping**: Journals and hiring committees are dominated by the same ideological networks, which can suppress research that threatens prevailing paradigms.
- **Intellectual Monopolies**: Entire departments can become echo chambers, rewarding loyalty and conformity over intellectual courage. This creates "disciplinary silos" where dissenting frameworks are excluded by design.

In more extreme cases, dissent might result in personal endangerment as follows:

- **Death Threats and Mob Intimidation**: Scholars who challenge popular movements or expose institutional hypocrisy, such as corruption, political bias, or misconduct, sometimes face online mobs, harassment, or even physical threats on their lives, with administrations usually silent or complicit.
- **Character Assassination**: Dissenting academics may be falsely accused of bigotry, extremism, or unprofessionalism with the intention of isolating them socially and intellectually.
- **Psychological Attack**: Colleagues might ostracize, sabotage, haze, bully, or gaslight dissenters to break their morale and force resignation under duress. This includes removing research access and withholding publication rights.

Educational institutions might erase dissent historically and systematically as follows:

- **Curricular Sanitization**: Courses and syllabi are rewritten to exclude controversial debates, creating sanitized academic cultures.
- **Posthumous Marginalization**: The works of dissenting scholars are omitted from citations, conferences, or funding calls in an effort to erase their intellectual legacy.
- **Institutional Memory Control**: Universities often rewrite internal histories to portray themselves as progressive and unified, eliminating past dissent and controversy.

Based on the discussion, breaking societal control over education involves raising awareness of the dangers in education and shifting from vulnerable standardized, top-down systems to more decentralized, personalized, and student-centered models with a focus on industry (skills above degrees and entrepreneurship above employment). Decentralized models should be competing on microscales, making it harder to suppress alternative viewpoints, to push ideological indoctrination, to manipulate funding, and to engage in unethical practices.

Em Hotep!

UNSPOKEN DANGERS OF FAMILY

ANKH WADJA SENEB | ARTICLE NO: 012

Function: The Awareness of Control Mechanisms
Subject(s): Family Structures/Types, Parental Exploitation
Position: Part 3 – Breaking Societal Controls
Theme: Dealing with Family | Scene 1

Peace to the High Power! Peace to the Living Universe! Peace to all Finite Living Beings! Peace to All Things – seen and unseen! For my spirit is with me, my image is with me, and my purpose is with me. For those with knowledge understand that the mechanisms behind societal controls can only flourish when consciousness, awareness, vibration, and rationality are minimized and when willful ignorance, fear, indoctrination, and subjugating forces are maximized.

In theory, a healthy family structure is supposed to provide the foundational framework for an individual's emotional, psychological, and social well-being, offering a unique combination of unconditional love, support, security, and a sense of belonging that is crucial for personal development from childhood to adulthood. While this theory of a healthy family structure sounds appealing, it is rarely achieved and it is even more rarely maintained due to interpersonal conflicts, lopsided support outputs, power imbalances, toxicity, trauma, and the like. In most cases, these things introduce dysfunction, transforming a healthy family structure into a damaging family structure. All damaging family structures thrive on enmeshment, which describes emotional closeness where personal boundaries become blurred or non-existent and which erases a grounded, true sense of self to preserve group interests; however, the approach of each damaging family structure is different, creating its own version of chaos, its own emotional rules, and its own survival roles. Of course, a family structure can have a mixture or a combination of these approaches; however, one or two of the approaches are typically dominant.

The ten (10) main damaging family structures are provided below.

- **The Narcissistic Family:** In this family structure, children are treated as an extension of the parents' egos. All achievements, behaviors, and emotions are measured by how they serve the parents. The manipulation and control mechanisms ensure that all actions and all strategies help the parent's image stay intact. There is no room for individuality or self-expression, so the children will normally grow up putting the needs of others above their own, craving approval, and living with the constant fear of criticism. The result is a deep disconnection from one's authentic self.
- **The Codependent or Enmeshed Family:** In this family structure, children, who are trained to push personal feelings aside, manage the emotions of other people by keeping the household stable, making unnecessary concessions to lower tension, and carrying the weight of struggling, lazy, suffering, and needy loved ones. In adulthood, these children will normally overcommit in relationships and will feel guilty when they assert their own needs. In essence, they confuse selflessness with love, seeking dependent partners without specifying boundaries.
- **The Chaotic Family:** In this family structure, children grow up without routines, rules, direction, or reactions. At every turn, they are scanning for danger, wondering whether an action will trigger conflict or withdrawal, and tracking sensitivities. As an adult, calmness feels unsettling, and boundaries feel uncomfortable. They find themselves drawn to high-drama situations, struggling with consistency and distrusting stability.

- **The Addicted Family:** In this family structure, children are raised with at least one parent involved in substance abuse. Parents constantly shift among neglect, over-involvement, and aggression, depending on the drug effect. As a result, the children learn to anticipate moods as a survival skill. When adulthood is reached, they oftentimes exhibit deep trust issues and fears of intimacy. Relationships become unpredictable, especially since they cannot determine whether abuse equates to love or abuse equates to hate. Moreover, they attract partners with similar traits and patterns because they feel understood by those with the same shared experiences, boundaries, triggers, and instabilities.
- **The Emotionally Immature Family:** In this family structure, parents struggle to regulate feelings and to handle stress. They come across as wounded, and their inability to manage the emotional climate of the home makes the children feel more like parents than children. All of the unresolved issues of the parents somehow become the responsibility of the children. As the children grow older, they suppress their needs – sometimes feeling completely invisible and unimportant – to protect their parents from discomfort. In relationships, they carry excessive responsibility, struggle to express their own emotions, and assume that no one will truly reciprocate the same level of support.
- **The Abusive or Rage-Filled Family:** In this family structure, childhood is dominated by anger and fear. Children learn to predict triggers, to self-silence, and to suppress natural reactions in order to avoid punishment or attack. Consequently, tension (over-seriousness) and survival replace playfulness and safety. Sometimes, children identify with the aggressors, either justifying the violence as necessary given the circumstances or lashing out in violence as an emotional shield. Moving into adulthood, these children either carry explosive anger forward or they create a pattern of avoiding confrontation to bury the anger. In relationships, they accept violence as the norm, tolerating friendly and unfriendly episodes of mistreatment, anxiety, and abuse.
- **The Controlling or Authoritarian Family:** In this family structure, parents dictate all aspects of a child's life. The child's choices, voice, and individuality are all shut down in favor of complete obedience. Children in these households place compliance above growth because questioning the system feels very dangerous. In adulthood, they constantly experience self-doubt and paralysis when making decisions because they worry that such a decision would not match that of their parents. There are also times when the children reach a breaking point, and they rebel impulsively against the parents, rejecting authority altogether before relapsing into order without autonomy.
- **The Neglectful or Absent Family**: In this family structure, all needs (emotional, physical, medical, dental, safety, etc.) of the child are ignored. In these cases, the parents might or might not be physically present; however, they are always emotionally or mentally unavailable. The unavailability makes the children feel unseen and passively self-sufficient, as if the children are raising themselves in the presence of parental apparitions without guidance. Such children appear independent on the outside, but are confused – if not afraid – on the inside. As adults, these children create a pseudo-independence, where they appear capable despite struggling with their own emotional world. This struggle results in closeness voids that the children try to fill by forming external, artificial families/bonds (i.e., sports families, religious families, fake kinship among close friends, etc.) with those they can trust.
- **The Perfect or Image-Focused Family**: In this family structure, appearances matter more than authenticity. The focus is on reputation rather than feelings, and the family unit is conditioned to maintain the image even if it means living a lie or fueling delusion. Pain and vulnerability are hidden behind well-crafted fantasies. In essence, the family unit is performing for approval, suppressing its true character. In adulthood, the children appear successful on the outside, but fraudulent or lost on the inside because real equals unsafe.

- **The Overprotective or Fear-Based Family**: In this family structure, children are smothered under the banner of safety. Independence is treated as rebellion or danger. In essence, you are shamed for wanting freedom. In adulthood, these children mistrust their instincts, doubt their decisions, and blame themselves for not preventing disasters.
- **The Parasitic Family or Welfare-Based Family**: In this family structure, the parents, who wanted nothing out of life (i.e. school dropouts, bums, etc.) or who were on a high margin of success before disaster struck (i.e., a professional sports athletes hitting rock bottom after an injury, a wealthy banker losing everything after gambling on stocks, etc.), strictly raise their children to be successful for personal gain. These parents give very little to their children, but they expect a lot from the children in return. When a child becomes an adult breadwinner, (s)he is responsible for taking care of the parents as well as the siblings who did not amount to anything. In essence, the breadwinning sibling becomes a walking ATM, and the family expects the breadwinning sibling to give with no regard to the breadwinner's debts, bills, or expenses. The failed sibling, on the other hand, is absolved of all responsibility and is conditioned to ask the breadwinning sibling for provision. This creates a polarizing effect, where the breadwinning sibling is loved when they offer provisions, and where the breadwinning sibling is hated for rejecting and not having provisions. In relationships, the failed sibling oftentimes becomes a freeloader with tons of emotional support, while the breadwinning sibling assumes a caretaker role with constant pressure, high expectations, and low emotional support.
- **The Overly Structured Family**: In this family structure, the parents pre-assign roles and functions to children, almost as puzzle pieces of utility, to serve a family purpose – even making risky but necessary sacrifices to ensure the family purpose is met. From childhood, for instance, each child is parentally ordained and groomed to be a doctor, a banker, a lawyer, a business owner, a contractor, a security handler, etc., without any decision in the matter. The children operate on strict schedules, cooperative planning, selective networking (normally controlled by the parent), proactive mentorship, and parental strategy. In adulthood, these children struggle with regular friendships and relationships because they constantly provide unsolicited advice, judgment, coaching, and blueprints on different family matters, as if they are the authority.

Be mindful that families also raise children in homes with:

- **No-Parents**: Households lacking biological parents, normally a foster family or an orphanage
- **Single-Parents**: Households where only one parent is present
- **Two-Parents**: Households where both parents are present
- **Poly Settings**: Households where the biological parent(s) and secondary parents/partners cohabitate with the child(ren)

For clarification, a child can experience parental absence, owing to a myriad of factors such as the death of a parent, surrogacy, military service, adoption, long-term medical leave, mental detachment (psych ward, dementia, drug-induced states, etc.), abandonment, immigration, career absorption, and imprisonment.

Some of the pros and cons of different household settings are provided in the following table.

Type	Pros	Cons
No-Parents	• Children might develop early independence and resilience. • Community, extended family, or foster networks can provide diverse influences. • Sometimes, escaping abusive parents leads to safer environments.	• High risk of emotional neglect, trauma, and identity struggles • Limited access to stable finances and guidance • Greater likelihood of poverty, exploitation, and educational setbacks. • Lack of consistent role models may hinder social development.
Single-Parent	**Mother-Absent Households (Father raising children alone)** • Children might develop self-reliance and discipline if the father provides structure. • A strong male role model can foster confidence and independence. • Can challenge gender stereotypes (father as nurturer and caregiver). **Father-Absent Households (Mother raising children alone)** • Mothers often form deep emotional bonds with children, offering strong attachment and security. • Children may develop empathy and emotional intelligence through maternal modeling. • Mothers build strong support networks, extended families, and community groups. • Mothers are normally more understanding of conflict, abuse, or irresponsibility.	**Mother-Absent Households (Father raising children alone)** • An emotional nurturing gap, as children might miss maternal warmth, which in many cultures is strongly associated with emotional availability. • Fathers may face difficulties balancing work and caregiving, especially in societies with weak support systems. • Daughters may lack maternal guidance during puberty, relationships, and reproductive health discussions. • Fathers might overly discipline the children, oftentimes not knowing their own strength. • Potential social stigma if the mother's absence leads to aggression. **Father-Absent Households (Mother raising children alone)** • Financial strain is often more severe, since women in many regions face lower wages and limited economic opportunities. • Sons may lack a father figure for role modeling, leading to potential struggles with identity or masculinity norms. • Children may experience feelings of abandonment or inadequacy tied to an absent father. • Mothers might nurture a child too much, leading to coddling of or protection of bad behaviors.

Two-Parent	• Shared responsibilities reduce stress and financial pressure. • Children benefit from complementary parenting styles and perspectives. • More stability in resources, routines, and emotional security. • Strong social acceptance in most cultures.	• Dysfunctional homes or divorce can pressure children to choose between parents. • Potential for conflict, role rigidity, or unequal labor distribution (for instance, gendered household burdens). • Children internalize unhealthy relational dynamics if parents remain together "for the kids" while in high conflict.
Poly-Settings	• More adults can share childcare, financial support, and household duties. • Children may experience a broader sense of community and exposure to diverse viewpoints. • Stronger safety nets if one adult is unavailable. • In supportive environments, this setting encourages open communication and flexibility.	• Risk of instability if adult relationships are unhealthy or socially unacceptable. • Children may face social stigma or sexual misunderstanding. • Legal and custody complications might create insecurity. • Power imbalances or favoritism among adults may negatively affect children. • Parental confusion or social awkwardness with biological and custodial parents present

No matter the family setting, there is always a chance that family exploitation will occur. Family exploitation occurs when certain individuals in a family unit, especially vulnerable family members, are subjected to physical, psychological, and emotional harm. Such exploitation can be driven by economic desperation, including poverty, cultural practices, selfishness, or family secrecy. Some examples of exploitation are provided below:

- **Violence and Abuse**: Physical, psychological, emotional, and sexual abuse are used either to control/dominate immediate family members or to satisfy filthy, uncontrolled urges – normally with vulnerable family members – that cannot be fulfilled outside the immediate family.
- **Neglect**: Typically centered on poverty or intentional abandonment, neglect is the failure to provide necessary care and protection to loved ones.
- **Prostitution**: Men, women, and/or children are pushed into sex work by families, where poverty and cultural normalization in some regions make prostitution a 'family survival strategy'. In Nepal and India, trafficking networks often involve relatives selling girls into brothels under the pretext of jobs or marriage. The Kamaiya system (bonded labor system) in Nepal historically pushed entire families into exploitative arrangements, including prostitution. Around the world, there are 'baby factories' targeting teenage girls, male/female escorts via trafficking rings, and forced pregnancies for science.
- **Using Children for Cheap/Free Labor**: Many children across the globe are pulled from school to work for family income. In Bangladesh, for instance, children as young as 8 years old work in garment factories regardless of parental approval due to financial desperation. In West Africa, more than 1.5 million Ghanaian and Ivorian children are involved in cocoa-related child labor. Even more dangerous, children in the Democratic Republic of Congo are used heavily in the local mines – mainly cobalt, coltan, and lithium – hoisted down small crevices/holes with little tools and without protective gear. These children normally develop life-threatening conditions or die altogether, being replaced by other children from willing and unwilling mothers. Moreover, there are cases throughout Africa, where mothers intentionally give birth to children to have labor resources for working large farmlands.

- **Child Poisoning**: This can be executed through less visible forms of abuse than physical abuse. Some examples include grooming, indoctrination, suppression of thought, and indebtedness-based conditioning. Normally, this type of exploitation is present in households when warring parents are fighting over the custody of children.
- **Parental/Custodial Vultures**: Overly protective parents who stifle their children's independence, or family members who benefit from the misfortunes or death of a loved one, acting selfishly to gain property or money rather than offering support. These parents often believe that their children are indebted to them simply for being born. Put in another way, these parents believe that their reproductive efforts helped their children realize success or fortune; and, they should be compensated for their efforts across the child's lifetime. At every turn, they are present to collect their supposed shares and entitlements as 'parental tax' for the child existing.
- **Financial Exploitation**: Family members exploit relatives (elderly, disabled, or children) to access benefits, wealth, or inheritance, often in situations of poverty or greed. Using family members for their resources and personal financial benefit, family 'parasites' constantly leech on or guilt-trip the more fortunate members into paying personal expenses. There are also cases, where guardians misuse cash benefits meant for orphans and vulnerable children (OVC), diverting funds to personal luxuries. Similarly, cases of 'benefit theft' occur, when relatives collect welfare or disability checks of deceased, disabled, or incapacitated family members.

This type of exploitation is also evident in child support systems. Child support is money that a separated or divorced parent is ordered by a court to pay to support a biological child or biological children in a different household. This money is supposed to ensure that a child's essential needs are met. These needs include food, clothing, housing, utilities, school-related expenses, medical care and insurance, and reasonable recreational, social, and developmental needs. Ultimately, the child is supposed to have the same standard of living as if he or she was in a household with both parents. Unfortunately, misuse arises when this money is diverted away from the child's welfare to the irresponsible benefit of the (custodial) parents.

Moving on, individual personality types often shape relationship behavior and power dynamics. The personality types are provided below.

- **Dominant Type**: A dominant person seeks to lead, to control, and to take charge of the relationship dynamics. They only feel secure when in a top position to set direction and to make key decisions. While dominants can provide structure and protection, they can easily shift to authoritarian or extremely controlling behavior if unchecked.
- **Finesser Type**: Finessers are sensual manipulators who use persuasion, strategy, and deceit to get what they want. They have the ability to read people well and to exploit their emotional and material weaknesses for personal gain. Finessers thrive on short-term advantage but struggle to sustain genuine trust or loyalty.
- **Low-Life Type**: A low-life is a person with little ambition, discipline, or moral integrity, often taking more than they give. These types of people drain partners emotionally or financially and tend to rationalize their failures. Relationships with them will often lack progress and reliability.
- **Breadwinner Type**: A breadwinner refers to the main or sole financial provider in a relationship. Breadwinners often take pride in supporting others and defining their worth through provision. However, they might grow resentful if their contributions are taken for granted or if they feel unappreciated.
- **Parasite Type**: A parasite is a dependent partner who lives off the other's efforts without contributing meaningfully. Parasites are emotionally and financially draining, and they justify dependence through manipulation or pity. After exhausting one relationship, they quickly find another relationship.

- **Team Player Type**: Team players are described as cooperative, supportive, and communicative partners who value shared effort. They focus on problem-solving and mutual growth, fostering healthy partnerships. They thrive in relationships built on respect and open dialogue.
- **Fixers**: A fixer is someone drawn to help or to rescue their partner from emotional, financial, or personal problems. They are empathetic and often attract damaged partners, mistaking healing for love. Being in a relationship with a fixer can lead to burnout, smothering, or codependency if boundaries are constantly violated.
- **Territorial Type**: Territorial partners are possessive individuals who view their significant other as belonging to them or as needing constant guardship. Driven by insecurity or fear of loss, they monitor attention from their partners, they become jealous when situations do not favor them, or they resort to physical violence to subdue competition.
- **Passive Type**: A passive partner avoids confrontation and often lets others take the lead or make decisions. Appearing peaceful and agreeable, passive partners are prone to being overlooked or dominated. Passivity can lead to quiet resentment or emotional disconnection in relationships over time.
- **Open-Minded Type**: Open-minded individuals are partners who are receptive to different ideas, lifestyles, and experiences within the relationship. Open-minded partners promote growth, tolerance, and adaptability; nonetheless, if boundaries are too liberal/loose, it can blur commitment, comfort, and/or stability.
- **Conservative Type**: A conservative person is an individual who prefers traditional values, routines, and moral boundaries in relationships. They provide structure and loyalty, but might resist change, leading to rigidity or judgmental tendencies.
- **Romantics/Charmers**: A romantic is an individual driven by affection, intimacy, passion, and the desire to capture their partner with good looks. Relationships with charming partners include emotional intensity and hormonal incitement; however, romantics can sometimes prioritize superficial gestures over intellectual depth, and they can be deeply loving or deeply manipulative, depending on their intentions.
- **Hustler Type**: A hustler constantly seeks financial or social advancement – legally or illegally – by blending street-smart and/or book-smart ambition with boldness. While they bring drive and energy to a relationship, they might prioritize success to the extent that risks become dangerous or threatening.
- **Controller Type**: Controller types are individuals who need to dictate outcomes and to manage every aspect of the relationship. They often confuse control with care and, while organized and protective, they erode their partner's autonomy, creating tension or silent protest.
- **Thought Leader**: A thought leader is a visionary thinker who influences, guides, inspires, or motivates their partner through intellect, insight, ideology, or key decision-making. They might unintentionally dominate or invalidate their partner's views if not humble or if left unchecked.

Of course, a person can exhibit characteristics of multiple personality types in a relationship, even though some personality types will dominate over others.

The major relationship types are provided below.

- **Traditional Committed Relationship**: A traditional committed relationship is a conventional model, where the man is the primary provider and decision-maker; and, the woman takes a more domestic, supportive, or nurturing role. This family relationship is typically built on marriage and clear gender roles. The key risk comes with the sustainment of male provision. If the man fails to provide for any reason, then the woman, as well as the children, become exposed, forcing her to seek another male provider who will hopefully take in her children.
- **Traditional with Side (Infidelity-Based)**: Infidelity-based traditional relationships maintain the conventional structure outwardly with a main partner and family unit. However, one partner secretly maintains a side partner – normally as a reward – for external sexual pleasure or emotional support.

- **50/50 Relationship (Egalitarian Partnership)**: This relationship type involves both partners sharing financial, emotional, and domestic responsibilities equally. As a result, decision-making, expenses, fairness, and labor are negotiated. If one of the partners falls short, then that partner becomes the target of blame without the other partner picking up the slack.
- **Cooperative Relationship (Flexible & Complementary)**: This relationship type is a balanced, pragmatic partnership based on shared goals and mutual support, where each partner contributes according to strength as a team rather than strict equality or tradition. There is a mature understanding that both partners will mostly have unequal inputs or imbalances, depending on the circumstances.
- **Long-Distance Relationship**: In this relationship type, partners live separately in far locations due to work, study, or circumstance. Nonetheless, a strong emotional connection is maintained digitally or through scheduled visits.
- **Strictly Emotional Relationship (Organic Partnership):** In this relationship type, partners form a close bond with or without sexual intimacy. In most cases, they feel connected by shared experience, defining moments, or a blurred friendship with spiritual overtones. This relationship is special in the sense that it does not require the partners to necessarily be together. They naturally gravitate toward each other.

To break the control that family and relationships have over you, you must understand the impacts of your family structure on yourself, your individual personality type, and compatible relationship types. Moreover, you must recognize signs of control, establish clear boundaries, welcome honest and vulnerable communication, refuse to compromise on self-autonomy or independence, work on conflict resolution, and seek mutual respect. Always prioritize self-care and create an exit plan if the situation is beyond resolution.

Em Hotep!

CONFRONTING MEDIA & STATE

ANKH WADJA SENEB | ARTICLE NO: 013

Function: The Awareness of Control Mechanisms
Subject(s): Government & Media Tactics, Poverty Machine, Messaging
Position: Part 3 – Breaking Societal Controls
Theme: Dealing with Media & State | Scene 1

ARTICLE NO: 013 – CONFRONTING MEDIA & STATE

Peace to the High Power! Peace to the Living Universe! Peace to all Finite Living Beings! Peace to All Things – seen and unseen! For my spirit is with me, my image is with me, and my purpose is with me. For those with knowledge understand that the mechanisms behind societal controls can only flourish when consciousness, awareness, vibration, and rationality are minimized and when willful ignorance, fear, indoctrination, and subjugating forces are maximized.

For centuries, the global population has fallen victim to blindly trusting the government, political leaders, and the mainstream media. In the sociopolitical sense, blind trust is the assumption that the government and the press media are always acting in the best interest of its citizens without requiring transparency, accountability, or evidence to back up its claims. When citizens blindly trust their leaders, they might neither scrutinize policies nor question potential overreach. This lack of oversight can allow officials to act without being held accountable for their mistakes or their misconduct. Additionally, blind trust can make citizens more susceptible to state propaganda or yellow journalism, leading to a misinformed public and a distorted understanding of events, especially since those capitulating to the propaganda will be less likely to question official narratives and will assume that the government and media representatives know best. Consequently, these citizens perpetuate bad governance by voting for crony officials – normally backed by the media as dissenting groups are suppressed – in ignorance and by fighting as armed allies, not realizing their self-inflicted ruin for the crony officials.

For clarification, yellow journalism is defined as a style of reporting that prioritizes sensationalism, exaggeration, emotional appeal, and eye-catching headlines to promote sales/ratings over factual accuracy. This journalism contrasts with investigative journalism, which unveils matters that are concealed either deliberately or accidentally by bad actors through the analysis and the exposure of damning facts, wrongdoings, scandals, corruption, and felonious circumstances to the public.

In this article, we raise awareness (promoting informed confidence over blind trust) of the tactics, the techniques, the games, and the strategies employed by the government and the media to control and to manipulate public opinion.

THE ILLUSION OF GOOD GOVERNANCE

When creating the illusion of good governance, the State makes the following efforts to conceal flaws, failures, malfeasance, and systemic issues pertaining to a regime or a political institution:

- **Maintaining Secrecy and Control**: Officials withhold critical information, suppress dissent, restrict access to decision-making processes, and tightly manage narratives. By limiting transparency, they prevent scrutiny, and they maintain a facade of stability and competence while hiding unrest or economic decline.
- **Fraudulent Appearances/Images**: Officials might showcase selective success stories, manipulate statistics, pay for anti-protests, organize paid rallies, use complex language, stage-manage events (public relations), or leverage media sources to project efficiency, progress, or unity. This creates a polished public image that hides corruption, inefficiency, or inequality.
- **Exploiting Weaknesses in Power Structures**: Officials exploit institutional or constitutional loopholes to facilitate corruption, nepotism, and marginalization, to take advantage of divided opposition groups, or to fake inclusivity. The idea is to maneuver around weak oversight mechanisms by dismantling them from the inside. These maneuvers appear lawful or democratic, when they actually undermine accountability and constitutional power. For instance, leaders choosing to extend constitutional term limits through referendums or amendments to pass a large welfare bill is viewed as a positive democratic choice by needy families, even though it infringes on the checks and balances of power granted under a democratic constitution.

Governments also adopt the appearance of democratic practices – elections, constitutions, parliaments, and freedoms – knowing that such practices protect public and private enterprises and con citizens into a false sense of participation. Some tactics include the following:

- **Electoral Illusions**: There are cases of controlled elections, where agents manipulate voter rolls, intimidate opponents, or rig counts, especially when a single party dominates the political arena. The dominant party will allow the opposition on the paper ballot; however, the dominant party will outmaneuver the weaker party through patronage, coercion, large donor pools, primaries, special delegation, political favor, or gerrymandering. Even token opposition (sponsored rivals) is utilized to create the perception of competition.
- **Institutional Facades**: This includes rubber-stamp legislatures that exist to push executive decisions, subverted courts where judges appear independent but are politically appointed and loyal to the ruling elite, and constitutions with loopholes where rights are preserved but riddled with exceptions (usually for "matters of national security").
- **Restricted Public Freedoms**: Citizens have the right to free speech, protest, or expression in practice, but these rights are closely monitored and controlled by lobbyists and special interest groups. These groups have the ability to shift agendas/messaging, to determine interviewees, to gag dissenters, and to distract/pivot viewership toward or away from issues.
- **Symbolic Reforms**: Democratic practices allow officials to announce reforms with no intent of meaningful change. Since these announcements are normally driven by trust, officials can play identity games to rally supporters or to gain donations demographically from powerful enterprises.
- **Democracy as a Tool**: Citizens, who buy into the positive concept of democracy, participate in the weaponization of democracy, where democracy is used as a cover to infiltrate other nations, to execute imperialist intent, and to justify wars with other nations in the interest of public and/or private enterprises.

HOW THE GOVERNMENT SUPPRESSES DISSENT

Suppressing dissent refers to any action taken in an attempt to stop or to penalize a person from making a public statement or from engaging in behaviors seen as a threat to powerful interest groups and public/private corporations. Governments seeking to preserve power at all costs often suppress dissent through an array of overt repression and subtler manipulation techniques as follows:

- **Censorship and Information Control**: Examples include restricting independent media, blocking websites, controlling content publishing licenses, and flooding the public with state propaganda to drown out critical voices.
- **Surveillance and Intimidation**: Examples include monitoring phone calls, social media, and assemblies, and harassing journalists, activists, or academics through threats, raids, or "visits" to instill fear. In some cases, whistleblowers can be jailed or killed for disseminating sensitive information.
- **Legal Manipulation**: Examples include passing vague laws on sedition, manufacturing fake news, manipulating national security to criminalize peaceful criticism, and using courts to jail or to fine political opponents and protesters.
- **Police and Military Force**: Examples include dispersing demonstrations with violence, tear gas, or arrests, deploying paramilitary or plainclothes agents to disrupt organizing efforts, and restricting/removing assembly and union rights.
- **Economic Pressure**: Examples include denying jobs, licenses, or contracts to dissenters and freezing bank accounts or targeting families with financial penalties.
- **Divide-and-Rule Tactics**: Examples include portraying critics as foreign agents, traitors, thugs, outcasts, rebels, or enemies of the State to isolate them from wider society and instigating rivalries/conflicts within opposition groups to weaken solidarity.
- **Co-Optation**: Examples include offering positions, favors, or bribes to silence influential critics and absorbing civil rights leaders or freedom fighters into government structures where their independence is diluted.

MACHIAVELLIAN PRINCIPLES OF POWER

In his work, *The Prince*, Niccolò Machiavelli indicates that power is self-justifying, so that those who wield it successfully are respected, even admired, regardless of the morality of their actions. He points out that the world rarely remembers the means of seizing power - only the duration of authority. Rulers are encouraged to lie, to manipulate, and/or to use coercive persuasion when it serves the needs of the State (the end justifies the means). The following are key principles derived from his work, which emphasize pragmatic, and often ruthless, statecraft to maintain and to increase political power, even if it goes against conventional morality:

- The world is not necessarily a meritocracy. A ruler's actions should be judged by their effectiveness (pragmatism) in securing and in maintaining power and the State, rather than by traditional moral standards (morality).
- Rulers should maintain a powerful public image because perception creates reality.
- A ruler should perform actions that ensure they will be remembered and that gain attention from those whom can offer opportunities.
- A ruler must actively observe and must address problems as they arise rather than wait until these problems have become too great to remedy.
- A ruler should seek to be feared rather than loved.

The key principles above must be in place at all stages – obtaining power, consolidating power, and maintaining power. Some Machiavellian recommendations are provided below.

Obtaining Power

- Take power through military strength or through cunning deception/manipulation when brute force is not possible.
- In times of crisis, such as war, famine, and economic collapse, exploit the chaos and provide opportunities for ambitious individuals, offering security or decisive leadership.
- Alliances should be formed when one is weak, and they should be broken when one is strong. In essence, rulers should use others as stepping stones to authority.
- Present oneself as pious, just, or compassionate to gain legitimacy, especially if the legal system or the belief deifies leadership.

Consolidating Power

- Eliminate rivals by absorption, exile, or destruction, and neutralize threats early to prevent future challenges.
- Take control of institutions by seizing the army, the judiciary, and the treasury.
- Prevent opposition from assembling or uniting to ensure no single group becomes strong enough to overthrow authority.
- Provide wealth, high positions, or privilege to secure loyalty among elites and key supporters.

Maintaining Power

- Balance fear and respect because excessive cruelty might breed rebellion over obedience.
- Prevent the public from painting a negative image of leadership or from recording historical shortcomings.
- Foster nationalism by rallying citizens under leadership against external threats.
- Create a legacy solidified by loyalists and monuments.

PROFITING FROM POVERTY

Drawing upon modern observations, exploiting poverty involves profiting from the vulnerabilities of the poor and the welfare systems meant to help the poor. This so-called "poverty machine", which is intentional by design, includes a wide range of enterprises, such as legal businesses that thrive in low-income areas, government contracts that privatize public services, and black-market merchants who seek illicit dealings. The machine is fueled by fooling poverty-stricken people into believing that they are making just enough money to survive (i.e., living paycheck to paycheck, living at their means, barely passing by, etc.), when, in reality, they are seconds from homelessness or extreme desperation.

Instead of analyzing theoretical cases and assessing poverty rate data, a series of real-life examples will be provided below to illustrate how corporations form volume businesses out of vulnerable or needy populations for profit.

- **Payday Loans**: These are small, short-term, high-cost loans advertised for quick cash in an emergency. Lenders require access to a borrower's bank account or a postdated check. With annual percentage rates (APR) of 400% or more, these loans are difficult to repay and are designed to trap borrowers in a cycle of debt.
- **Overdraft Fees**: The banking system generates billions of dollars in overdraft fees annually, with a small percentage of account holders paying the majority of these charges. This practice disproportionately affects low-income people, who are more likely to have irregular incomes.

- **High Rent Spikes**: Landlords in low-income neighborhoods often charge disproportionately high rents or raise rent unexpectedly when property value increases. This contributes to high rent burdens for poor tenants who have few options for affordable housing and face exclusionary factors such as poor credit, bankruptcies, or past evictions. In some cases, a predatory vouch system is established, where private landlords jack up the rental prices for qualifying low-income groups, knowing that the State will pay a portion of the rent.
- **Courts and Legal Fees**: High financial bail amounts make it more difficult for poor people to remain out of jail while awaiting trial. Not to mention, the high cost of private attorneys makes it difficult to afford a strong defense, especially when stacked on top of impoundments, filing fees, and transcript charges.
- **The Private Captive Market**: Private prisons incentivize police either to invent crime or to establish unwritten arrest quotas on low-income groups incapable of legal defense. Not only do the prisons receive money for every new inmate or repeat offender, but they also use inmates for cheap labor. For instance, prisoners in California fight wildfires for as little as $1 an hour, yet many are barred from becoming firefighters after release. Inmates also receive state pay, averaging $70 per month (roughly 6% of the U.S. minimum wage) for regular work. After arrest, these incarcerated people are charged for necessities (food boxes and clothes boxes) and services, such as telephone calls, video visitations, and commissary items. The necessities and services draw vendors, whom make every effort to uphold the system for profit. Another not-so-obvious way that prisoners are exploited is through science. There are cases where scientific research centers approach death-row inmates or inmates with life sentences to pitch a 'dying for science' exchange. The research center will request the inmates to serve as human specimens in a dangerous experimental treatment or to enter space/sea probes to study lethal environmental impacts on the human body in exchange for a financial 'death' payout package that will benefit their loved ones.
- **Tax Credit Skimmers**: Tax authorities intentionally increase the length of tax forms to encourage low-income groups to seek tax preparers. The tax preparers take additional money on top of the tax refund from unsuspecting customers whom need to subsidize their lives. Even worse, they give loans and other high-interest fast cash products to low-income groups with payback during tax refund season.
- **Abusing Routine Medical**: When the government sponsors medical services, health care professionals target qualifying patients, encouraging them to undergo as many procedures as possible. Dentists, for instance, will prioritize taxpayer-funded insurance holders over private insurance holders for cleanings, oral cancer screenings, and fluoride treatments. There are also cases, where dentists perform unnecessary treatments like root canals on young children and where dentists recoup medical supply losses by seeking reimbursement through insurance. Outside of dental, some poor people are disproportionately plagued with kidney failure and need constant blood cleaning from a dialysis machine since their kidneys cannot function properly. There are dialysis centers hindering kidney transplant referrals to keep as many patients cycling through the machine at all hours of the day for profit. Playing alongside, the pharmacists capitalize on medical by giving over-the-counter (OTC), non-prescription, and prescription drugs as treatments rather than cures in micro/small doses to circumvent regulations and to generate volume sales out of vulnerable and suffering people. There are also cases, where doctors or pharmacists capture the opportunity to use experimental drugs/vaccines on suffering patients without insurance coverage or without financial resources to pay medical bills.
- **Foster Care**: Foster children are given a direct subsidy from Social Security for their well-being; however, many companies are paid a fee to create databases that make these kids ineligible. Typically, the kids can be deemed ineligible if they are not physically/mentally ill, they do not have special needs, and they do not have deceased parents. Any subsidies for ineligible kids are constantly cycled back into the states. This means that foster children who have only one dead parent or who have been abandoned/adopted will receive nothing.

- **Humanitarian Aid & Loan Abuse**: Many world leaders in 3rd world countries or frontier markets intentionally hinder the development of their nation or cause chaos in order to qualify for economic recovery funds, humanitarian aid, and large-volume loans (i.e., International Monetary Fund (IMF), World Bank, Peacekeeping, etc.). Once the funding arrives, governmental representatives loot their treasuries and reallocate the funds to personal projects and political friends. Less than 5% of the money is shared among the public, and the lingering poverty allows the pilfering politicians to reapply for more funds. There are even cases, where these politicians will instigate humanitarian crises – normally based on religious or tribal – to ensure a perpetual cycle of aid and loan abuse.
- **Thriving Dark Markets**: Poverty puts people in survival mode and amplifies mental health issues (paranoia, depression, thoughts of suicide, etc.). Under such conditions, human trafficking increases, where humans are monetized in different ways – sexual activities and organ salvaging. Organ salvaging involves taking healthy organs from men, women, and children for profit. These organs can be accumulated through violent killings, theft from banks, or kidnapping. Often, the biggest buyers are healthcare networks with extensive waiting lists and research labs. Outside of organ salvaging, there are also concerns of dark priests and bad-acting missionaries, whom use religious doctrine to lure the impoverished into self-sacrifice or sacrificing others. As far as mental health, dark market merchants normally form drug trafficking rings to capitalize on vulnerable citizens, driving epidemics.
- **Paying the Media**: It is a documented practice for some media outlets to be paid 'hush money' to bury stories, a strategy often called "catch and kill". In a "catch and kill" arrangement, the media company buys the exclusive rights to the story with no intention of ever publishing it. The story is effectively buried to protect the reputation of the subject. There are other cases, where the government sends public relations agents to shut down or to eliminate investigative journalists. In the general scheme of things, the media is either complicit in the wrongdoing or silenced from exposing the wrongdoing.

More examples can be provided; however, the purpose is to show how the government and the media, as well as indirect beneficiaries, exert control to perpetuate poverty intentionally for profit. In essence, many groups stand to benefit from ongoing poverty, including big pharma, labor unions, religious institutions, insurance companies, rental companies, logistics export chains, land grabbers, casinos, and so forth. Poverty is not always a function of poor personal responsibility and laziness.

REMOVING THE SMOKE SCREEN: POLITICAL SUPER FACTIONS

Political super-factions are large, resourceful blocs, including parties, states, established leaders, or elites, that typically thrive by splitting societies apart. They weaponize binaries/extremes, fallacies, scapegoats, outrage, and confusion to maintain power, influence, and access. By exaggerating division and erasing the middle ground, they ensure that the public fights among itself through shocks and triggers to their benefit. Some of their strategies used to sow discord among the public are provided below.

- **Token Gifts**: Giving handouts through welfare programs to increase governmental dependence, political party power, and public rapport/points through deception. Individuals can become caught in a "welfare trap", where the loss of benefits from earning a higher income might outweigh the additional money from working or where the loss of benefits can lead to instant homelessness. Those in this position will easily capitulate to political super factions.
- **Race Hustling**: Minority activists, who exploit racial issues (racial victimhood, racial inequality, and racial injustices – ancient and modern) for personal or for political gain. In most cases, the broader struggle for racial justice is completely ignored, and the activists do not care about the condition of their own communities.

As a sidebar, the concept of "race" as a social construct tied to physical appearance and inherent traits was invented during the Age of European Exploration, roughly spanning the 16th to 18th Centuries. The rise of the Atlantic slave trade and colonialism created a need to justify the subjugation of certain groups, leading to the creation of racial hierarchies. The hierarchies were later codified in skin color through the concept of 'whiteness' to separate European settlers from enslaved Africans and to separate non-identifying mixed African clusters (mainly Afro-Arabs and Arab settlers in North Africa) from enslaved Africans. Such contrasts also cause colorism in Africa, as the skin colors range from ebony to ivory.

- **Narrative Hijacking**: Seizing control of a story or an account of events from its original speaker or author and then twisting it to serve a different agenda. This involves altering how the story is perceived and is interpreted by an audience, interrupting a speaker to share a similar, yet supposedly worse story, minimizing a story to invalidate someone's genuine feelings, drowning out the real story to add authenticity to the fake story, or retelling a false story in repetition until accepted as true.
- **Controlling the Narrative**: Describes efforts taken to shape a story in a deliberate, often strategic, way. It involves selective leaks, information control (censorship, internet filtering, takedowns, throttling, platform deplatforming, cyberattacks/hacks, sabotage, and search algorithm manipulation), counterbalancing (responding to negative facts with positive information), drip strategies (releasing information slowly to delay the full story), suppression (attempting to prevent damaging facts from becoming public), unlawful surveillance, and casting doubt through blasts (making factual information appear as conspiracy theories or contradictions).
- **The Gender Game**: Maintaining triggering messages about the behavior, the attitude, and the place of men and women in society, as well as how men and women are supposed to conduct themselves socially, emotionally, and mentally. For instance, shaming men for showing respect to women as simping, men expressing emotions as weak, women choosing to work outside the home as masculine, etc., are a part of this game.
- **Identity Politics**: Using the shared experiences and shared demographics of particular social groups for gain, benefit, or advantage. Superfactions mobilize based on a shared identity, such as race, ethnicity, gender, tribe, age, sexual orientation, class (income), attribute, disability, or religion, foolishly believing that it will result in greater political freedom and self-determination. For instance, an Arab voting for a Muslim politician, whom might hate Arabs, simply because the politician is a Muslim, is voting based on identity. Identity politics always divides the public, and the most tolerated form of discrimination is by class – income or elitism.
- **Polarization**: Reducing complex issues into a rigid "with us or against us" binary without allowing mixed viewpoints. For instance, 'science vs. anti-science', 'pro-life vs. pro-choice', and 'believer vs. non-believer' are all taglines that incite division among. All people with mixed viewpoints are seen as silent supporters, enablers, allies, uninformed, 'sleep', or ignorant, depending on the mixture.

For clarification, the term 'sleep' is used against those whom are not considered 'woke'. In simple terms, 'woke' refers to anyone whom cannot see a problem, a game, or a tactic in motion right in front of them. In the political arena, 'wokeness' has been weaponized to find systemic injustice and systemic racism in everything, even if such systemic issues do not exist.

- **Manufacturing Labels**: Also known as political branding or reframing, this rhetorical strategy is used to influence public opinion, to define adversaries, to spark outrage, and to frame debates in a way that benefits a particular political agenda. These short-hand terms oversimplify complex issues and appeal to emotion rather than reason. Some common negative labels used by super factions include: thugs, gangbangers, bandits, degenerates, terrorists, bad actors, traitors, communists, and so forth. Contrast these with the following positive labels used to reframe: troubled, misunderstood, ignored, triggered, gifted, 'just a kid', harmless, and so forth. Such labels can also be used to demonize out-groups or to create scapegoats. For instance, immigrants are framed as "job-stealing criminals" or the rich are framed as "bloodsuckers feeding on the poor".

- **Bread & Circus Distractions**: Keeping the public fixated on spectacles, scandals, or invented crises, normally through endless drama, rifts within/among political opposition groups, and cultural wars, to distract from systemic corruption and systemic failure.
- **Virtue Signaling**: Deceptively expressing opinions or sentiments in public to signal good character, moral principles, or support for a cause. The term is most often used pejoratively to imply that the person is more interested in appearing virtuous than in genuinely advancing the cause. The public display of morality is driven by a desire for social approval, applause, or ego-boosting rather than by a sincere conviction to help a cause. For example, a gas company apologizing and making donations for an explosion that killed workers and that caused a massive oil spill is virtue signaling.
- **False Campaign Promises:** Making declarations or pledges during an election or a campaign rally with no intention of fulfilling them. They are often used to secure votes or to increase standing in political polls without legal repercussions, if not delivered upon.
- **Tilting Economics:** Economics answers some of the most critical questions about society, such as *What resources are available?*, *Who has access to such resources?*, *Who receives priority in the access chain?*, *Who will control or who will regulate the means of production?*, *How will the capital flow in the society? How opportunities and equity will be created and will be distributed among different demographics?*, and so forth. These questions center on this idea of scarcity. In economics, scarcity is the fundamental problem that arises because human needs are virtually unlimited, while the resources available to satisfy those needs are finite. This disparity forces individuals, businesses, and governments to make choices about how to (re)allocate resources efficiently; and, it consequently becomes a control mechanism of human survival. Political super factions normally use economics to subvert, to paralyze, or to weaken a society through policy, lobbying, and political power.

REMOVING THE SMOKE SCREEN: MEDIA

False information is often designed to be shocking as an attention grabber that triggers fear, disgust, or anger. People are more likely to share or to engage with novel and emotionally charged content. Unlike a simple, sensational lie, the truth is often complex and requires time for proper research, fact-checking, and dissemination. A lie, on the other hand, can be spread in seconds, while correcting the lie might take days or weeks. Even after a lie has been debunked, the false narrative can persist in people's minds and can continue to influence their thought process, especially with the endless 'What-If' scenarios. Common media distortion tactics are provided below.

- **Misinformation & Disinformation**: Misinformation is false information spread without intent to deceive, while disinformation is the deliberate spread of wrong information.
- **Spin**: Interpreting real facts in a biased way to make one side appear in good standing. For instance, there is a difference between calling a mass layoff a "strategic restructuring" and calling it a "scandal of middle-class persecution".
- **Smear & Character Assassination**: A sustained, multi-channel assault/attack (dredging up old posts, twisting quotes, stereotyping, or fabricating scandals) on a person's reputation, a group, or an idea, inclusive of selective leaks, troll farms, false narratives, and biased coverage.
- **Hoaxing & Planting Fake Stories**: Fake events, such as staged protests, deepfake videos, and fake whistleblowers, are fabricated to mislead or to entrap target people or organizations. This also includes astroturfing, which involves using bots or fake accounts to post coordinated messages, to make fringe views appear popular, and to inflate user engagement of a particular cause, politician, or product artificially.
- **False Advertising**: Marketing products or policies with claims known to be false or misleading.
- **Slander/Libel**: Viral statements – inflammatory, damaging, and/or embarrassing – about a person or a group that are falsely spread beyond retraction, correction, or remedy.

- **Media Cover-Ups**: Deliberately underreporting or ignoring stories that harm powerful people or interests, such as spiking investigative reports under advertiser pressure.
- **Troll Farming**: Coordinated networks of fake or paid accounts that harass opponents, that amplify narratives, and that make fringe views seem mainstream. In essence, bots are used to post thousands of comments per hour to sway online polls or trending hashtags.
- **Targeted Messaging**: Micro-targeting ads or posts at specific demographic groups with tailored content – sometimes sending contradictory messages to different audiences. For example, one campaign promises environmental action to progressives while promising deregulation to business owners. This shapes opinions covertly, as voters and lawmakers do not see what others are being told.

It is worth noting that media is normally synonymous with news agencies, podcasts, and social media; however, the range of media includes aspects from entertainment, music, art, and general TV broadcasting. This means that the tactics above can be integrated into lyrics, poetry, art depictions, sitcoms, movies, sports, and so forth. The power and the control that the media wields over public opinion cannot be ignored.

REMOVING THE SMOKE SCREEN: EXPERT/SCIENTIFIC STUDIES

Oftentimes, people rely blindly and passively on the opinions of authority figures rather than requesting valid evidence. While citing authority figures is not always wrong, authority figures can be wrong, even within their own certified field of expertise. Any claim should be evaluated based on the evidence supporting it, not by whom is making the claim. Without the evidence, people will be susceptible to expert manipulation or scientific bias. Some tactics used to turn science into a tool of persuasion rather than truth are provided below.

- **Falsifying Evidence**: Fabricating or altering data to produce desired outcomes.
- **Introducing Bias**: Conducting studies to confirm or to verify what the expert already believes by skewing findings or adding unsupported interpretations.
- **Removing Data Outliers**: Cherry picking or removing "inconvenient" data that weakens the desired trend or outcome.
- **One-Sided Verbiage**: Using persuasive or loaded language in study write-ups to make the findings appear more conclusive. For instance, calling outcomes 'promising breakthroughs' when results are either marginal or unclear.
- **Concealing Parameters**: Intentionally omitting details, such as sample size, demographics, locations, or assumptions to prevent scrutiny and to exaggerate the reliability of findings.
- **Overgeneralization**: Extrapolating results beyond their tested scope to mislead others into thinking such results are universal.
- **Rigid Questioning**: Structuring surveys or experiments so that only certain answers or certain outcomes are possible.
- **Data Collection Irregularities**: Formulating conclusions in the absence of or the low sampling of data pools.
- **Improper Use of Experts**: Using experts outside of their certified field as if they are experts in everything. This gives weight to opinions that are not scientifically credible.
- **Misleading Interpretations**: Drawing conclusions that data does not actually support.

In order to combat these tactics, the following questions should always be asked.

- Who performed the study, as well as the expert's credentials?
- What was the scope of the study?
- Where was the study conducted?
- What were the assumptions of the study, as well as the control variables?
- What were the selection criteria?
- How was the data collected, as well as the location of the raw data?
- What was the sample size of the data?
- How was the data processed?
- What were the findings/evidence?
- Do the findings/evidence support the expert's interpretations and conclusions?
- Can the interpretations and conclusions be generalized beyond the sample size?

Please note how difficult expert manipulation and scientific bias are when someone scrutinizes all aspects of an expert/scientific study.

Em Hotep!

AN ENEMY TO YOURSELF

ANKH WADJA SENEB | ARTICLE NO: 014

Function: The Awareness of Control Mechanisms
Subject(s): Self-Sabotage, Self-Destruction, Combating the Inner Self
Position: Part 3 – Breaking Societal Controls
Theme: Dealing with Self | Scene 1

ARTICLE NO: 014 – AN ENEMY TO YOURSELF

Peace to the High Power! Peace to the Living Universe! Peace to all Finite Living Beings! Peace to All Things – seen and unseen! For my spirit is with me, my image is with me, and my purpose is with me. For those with knowledge understand that the mechanisms behind societal controls can only flourish when consciousness, awareness, vibration, and rationality are minimized and when willful ignorance, fear, indoctrination, and subjugating forces are maximized.

Recall that the polypsychic view of Ancient Egypt holds that the intrinsic self contains the following interconnected constituents: Khet (the physical body), Ka (the life or vital essence with a physical-spiritual twin), Ba (unique personality), Shuyet (the shadow and a complementing dark alter ego), Sa (the spiritual body), Sekhem (the power of healing and development through spiritual might), Ren (intrinsic/unique identity), and Ab (the weighted heart). Whenever any of these constituents are at odds, the human psyche experiences internal conflict that transfigures the intelligent spirit (akh) from a higher level of vibration to a lower level of vibration.

We will examine the extremely deep Sahu (lowest level of vibration) state, where the intrinsic self capitulates to self-destruction and irrationality without any regard for self-preservation or self-interest. This examination will be broken into the following three (3) cases, distinguished by the intent, the desire, or the foresight to cause self-harm: (i) primary self-destruction, (ii) tradeoffs, and (iii) counterproductive strategies.

- **Primary Self-Destruction**: This is the most irrational case, where a person intentionally and deliberately brings harm, defeat, ruin, destruction, and failure to himself/herself due to intense feelings of guilt, remorse, anxiety, low self-esteem, or insignificance. As these feelings flare, the person grows accustomed to mental and physical suffering, fully embracing the pain as either a coping mechanism or a numbing agent. Eventually, the person normalizes the desire for suffering, seeking a thrill, a passion, an addiction, or a pleasure for enduring pain, abuse, humiliation, and self-defeat. Some examples include masochism (reflecting hostility toward the intrinsic self because of self-hatred or inner guilt), anorexia (reflecting a dangerous intolerance of personal image to the extent that disappearing is better than existing), and wrist cutting (self-inflicted punishment for misdeeds and deficiencies falsely blamed on the self). Any desire to be punished, to inflict self-harm (up to and including suicide), or to escape from the disliked image of oneself falls under this case.
- **Tradeoffs**: In this case, the person foresees undesirable harm or undesirable risks; however, the person accepts the harm and the risks as a necessary means of achieving some sort of goal or benefit. The first example, self-handicapping, which is defined as any action that enhances the opportunity to externalize (or excuse) failure and to internalize success, is illustrated by parents robbing a grocery store to feed their hungry children after losing a job or a rugby player continuing to play for a championship after sustaining a concussion or life-threatening injuries. The second example, substance abuse, is trivial because people commonly indulge in mind-altering substances, such as alcohol or drugs, knowing the self-destructive aspect in exchange for a euphoric rush. The third example, health negligence, is illustrated when a bank officer

fails to comply with the advice and recommendations of medical practitioners (e.g., do not fly for a week, restrict caffeine intake, get proper sleep, etc.). Other trade-offs involve sacrificing tangible rewards in order to escape embarrassment (face-work) or using shyness for likeability.

- **Counterproductive Strategies**: In this case, the person shows a systematic pattern of self-defeating behaviors, not knowing that such behaviors have harmful consequences. The focus is neither on normal behaviors that occasionally turn out badly nor on isolated accidents or mishaps. Rather, it is on systematic behavior patterns (bad habits) that are common or typical among normal adults and that lead reliably to self-harmful outcomes. These patterns offer little to no benefit to the person, yet the person acquires and maintains them anyway. One pattern is perseveration, which describes doing something repeatedly when there is no longer any reason or when such repetition becomes harmful. Self-damaging examples of perseveration include gambling excessively or refusing to give up on losing stocks. Another pattern involves the handling of pressure situations. Pressure situations are intense, self-focused situations, where it is highly desirable and important to perform/execute well. The rapid increase in self-focus spikes anxiety and disrupts normal brain response. If not corrected, this pattern can lead to self-destructing episodes, such as panic attacks, nervous shock, involuntary shaking (twitching or seizure), and collapse. The next pattern is learned helplessness, which is an internalized principle that the individual infers based on unhappy experiences of incapability, inadequacy, or victimization. Self-damaging examples include refusing to speak in public due to mental blanks from crowd intimidation (incapability), refusing to find new work after being fired from multiple past employers (inadequacy), and habitually blaming others for misfortune or failed success (victimization). The next self-defeating pattern is mental bargaining, where a person exhibits poor behavior in understanding a zero-sum conflict, aiming too high in efforts, or aiming too low in efforts. The final self-defeating pattern, ineffective ingratiation, involves performing actions solely for the approval of others, including simping.

Transfiguring the intelligent spirit from a higher level of vibration to a lower level of vibration shifts the layers of self-exposure. In social penetration theory, layers of self-exposure, expressed in ratios, describe the process of gradually revealing personal information, moving from superficial details to intimate details. Such layers are provided below.

- **The Public Self** (75% Exposure): This is the self that individuals allow the world to know. Often referred to as 'the mask' or the 'civilized version', it functions to build an individual's social identity and professional image and to protect the true self from judgment and rejection.
- **The Private Self** (20% Exposure): The private self is the layer of self-exposure only revealed to the closest people or the loyal/trusting inner circle in one's life. It includes an individual's deepest fears, vulnerabilities, quirks, beliefs, triggers, traumas, social awkwardness, and embarrassing past. At this exposure level, a person can only form close mutual bonds and emotional safety nets with other people whom love them for whom they are.
- **The Hidden Self** (5% Exposure): The hidden self, which consists of the inner chamber of private thoughts, deeply-rooted shame, twisted fantasies, sincerest regrets, forbidden desires, and impulsive kinks, embodies the darkest space of a person's psyche. The hidden self is best illustrated in moments, where a person experiences unnatural attractions, urges, stimulations – sexual or non-sexual – toward something (e.g., glue, rubber, animal fur, etc.), where a person expresses out-of-body deviancy impulsively (e.g., becoming violent during blackouts, committing arson under trance, resorting to intermittent psychopathy, etc.), or where an 'evil' voice/presence mentally encourages a person to attack others or to self-harm. In most cases, the individual not only fears the hidden self but also fears what the hidden self reveals.

For clarification, a person, who has no fear of the hidden self or what the hidden self reveals solely based on the individual, is a psychopath.

For clarification, a person, who has no fear of the hidden self or what the hidden self reveals based on upbringing or social environment, is a sociopath.

Assuming that a person is neither psychopathic nor sociopathic, the bonds associated with the layers of exposure and the fears of the hidden self might also make a person susceptible to peer pressure. Peer pressure, by definition, is the influence exerted by one's social circle to adopt certain behaviors, values, or habits, usually in an effort to gain acceptance, status, or belonging. For instance, a male teenager might drink excessively or might use drugs not out of desire, but to avoid being seen by his peers as 'boring', 'corny', or 'lame' – even through bullying or hazing. The influence of the social circle can worsen as familiarity grows because the extensive knowledge of or the close association with someone often leads to a loss of respect. Not to mention, people are most impacted by judgment, when they are still struggling to be honest with themselves.

The extremely deep Sahu (lowest level of vibration) state, calling for self-destruction and irrationality, also encapsulates the conditioning of physical and mental enslavement because physical and mental enslavement warp the perception of freedom and self-worth, especially when wrapped in trauma. Trauma, by definition, is a deeply distressing or disturbing experience that overwhelms the ability to cope, such as abuse, neglect, violence, loss, or severe emotional pain. Some types of traumas include:

- Acute trauma from a single event
- Chronic trauma from repeated or ongoing events
- Complex trauma from multiple traumatic events occurring frequently, back-to-back, and spontaneously.

When trauma is coupled with physical and mental enslavement, the residuals of the conditioning usually cause one of the following mindsets:

- **Revolutionary**: A deep-seated, envious hostility toward an oppressive force, which can only be resolved through retaliation, revenge, and reciprocal acts
- **Submissive**: A lowly and compromised mindset, where a person chooses to assimilate or to conform to an oppressive force to lessen suffering
- **Self-Hating**: Accepting inferiority to and subjugation by the oppressive force, blaming the conditioning on personal weakness and group insignificance
- **Self-Gaslighting**: A dismissive mindset, often ignorant of struggle, that includes denying oppression, making light of oppression, or rejecting the need to overcome/resist oppression.
- **Indifferent**: Based on convenience, a person with this mindset acknowledges that an oppressive force exists, but refuses to take risky action, unless a significant reward or benefit is available.
- **Sympathizer**: A mindset where a subjugated person defends or rationalizes the behavior of the oppressive force, either mistaking control for case or mistaking violent rage for ingrained distress. This is often associated with Stockholm syndrome.

Even if we subtract physical and mental enslavement, traumatic experiences can still wear away at a person's sense of self in the extremely deep Sahu state. In trauma bonding, which is a strong emotional attachment that forms between an abuser and a victim, for example, the bond maintained through cycles of abuse often feels like love or dependency, though still harmful. Such a bond opens a gateway for victims to continue putting themselves in vulnerable positions (e.g., intentionally getting drunk around strangers to be taken advantage of sexually, intentionally serving as a martyr for unfriendly people, encouraging others to share in abuse of self, etc.) or pursuing said abuser even after liberation. The ultimate end is self-destruction once again.

Assessing enslavement and trauma in the context of the extremely deep Sahu state leads to the following question: Should people have the right to destroy their lives up to and including suicide? The personal right to destroy or to take one's own life centers on personal autonomy over life and death. In principle, people do have a right to self-destructive choices in full competency and authority, assuming no harm to others. Most societies generally reject suicide as a right, but increasingly recognize the ethical complexity of end-of-life choices of terminally ill people. There are even societies that criminalize assisted suicide, suicide attempts, and successful suicides, even though the law enforcement of successful suicides remains dubious.

Another condition under the extremely deep Sahu (lowest level of vibration) state, often resulting in self-destruction and irrationality, is grief. Grief comes in many forms; however, it is best understood from the Kübler-Ross model in the following stages:

- **Denial**: The period of grieving during which a person refuses to accept the reality of a situation. It is a defense mechanism that helps us to protect ourselves from the shock of the upsetting hardship. Examples include refusing to accept/acknowledge the situation, refusing/avoiding the topic in conversation, and stating that the loss is not true or that the source of the news is unreliable.
- **Anger**: Resorting to anger as a natural response to accepting the reality of a situation. This includes blaming others, oneself, or even a spiritual power.
- **Bargaining**: When we experience grief, we often feel hopeless and overwhelmed. It is common to be overcome by statements of "what if" and "if only," as we experience a loss of control over what is happening. During the bargaining stage of grief, a person attempts to negotiate or to make compromises to feel less sad or to dwell on different outcomes.
- **Depression**: A feeling of sadness and hopelessness that often results from being powerless against emotional strain.
- **Acceptance**: The period of grief when a person finally comes to terms with accepting a painful reality through closure.

Regardless of how many conditions we look at, the common denominator for the extremely deep Sahu (the lowest level of vibration) state is the attack on the mindset. Even something as simple as labelling can be detrimental to the intrinsic self. Being repetitively labeled with negative titles (e.g., 'criminal', 'lazy', 'quitter', 'dumb', and the like), for instance, often leads people to live up to these labels. Far worse, these negative labels can stigmatize people, causing them to reinforce stereotypes and to glorify dehumanization. This includes the acceptable and the use of discriminatory, profane, and derogatory labels – intragroup and intergroup. For instance, a man constantly labelled a 'deadbeat dad', despite direct child involvement and adequate child support, might embrace the negative label and completely abandon his own child, choosing irrationally to be the greatest version of the negative label to reinforce the stereotype. Another, not so obvious, labelling issue revolves around naming children because their names represent identities that they are forced to live up to, and they are repetitively reminded of the context behind their names every time their names are called. For instance, naming children after a relative might cause the children to live vicariously through the relative, naming children after religious figures (even if they do not follow the same religion) might cause them to gravitate toward or to idolize the corresponding character of the religion, or attributing the names of children to negatives (e.g. burden, murder, death, etc.) might cause the children to internalize such attributes in behavior patterns.

As a sidebar, militaries, colonial powers, secret societies, and religious leaders have always exploited naming conventions because they are well aware that naming conventions serve as the psychological anchors of identity and the encodings of cultural, traditional, and individual views – inseparable from the intrinsic self. Any control over the naming conventions leads to the psychological adjustment to their agendas, dogmas, or practices. When Islamic names are given to African tribes, for instance, the tribes shift their allegiance from their own African identity to the religious identity, going as far as killing those within their own tribe whom resist the non-African religious identity. Even worse, there are cases where 'converted' African tribesmen, viewing themselves as 'slaves of Allah' or living up to an Islamic name, helped foreign Muslims (mostly Arab) to penetrate African territories to force their native tribes from African practices to Islam. This can happen with any religion, not just Islam; however, the psychological adjustment of naming should never be ignored.

As a sidebar, there are cases where labels and words are weaponized to weaken individuals. For instance, inspiring the masses to be 'humble' or telling someone 'to stay humble' can be used as a means to exploit them. Another example is the projection of messages and labels in music to control the mood and character of crowds. The last example is employed in hostage negotiation tactics to build rapport with a criminal through outward humanism.

We will now shift to a different aspect of the extremely deep Sahu (lowest level of vibration) state, where the intrinsic self conforms to group behaviors or beliefs without critical thinking. This conformity can be an effort to follow the crowd to feel safe or validated, or it can be an effort to refuse using your own mind/brain (dependency handicap of rationality) to live in the comfort of blaming others for bad ideas.

The first instance of this conformity is illustrated in the differences between individual thinking and collective thinking. Typically, an individual mindset is a thought space that prioritizes personal autonomy, self-reliance, and independent achievement. Such beliefs and attitudes shape a person's thoughts, feelings, and behaviors, focusing on individual needs, rights, and goals over the concerns of a group. At the extremely deep Sahu state, the weaknesses of individual thinking are exposed when a person is afraid to fail and when said person knows that no one else but the intrinsic self can be blamed for such failure. In this case, the person will rely on social blueprints or self-help instruction, which may or may not apply to his/her life, for validation to credit themselves for success and to blame the external resource(s) for failure.

In contrast to individual thinking, collective thinking prioritizes the collective good, mutual support, and collaboration over individual gain. It involves a sense of shared responsibility for the well-being of a group and a focus on contributing to the group's success rather than solely pursuing personal interests. At the extremely deep Sahu state, the weaknesses of collective thinking are exposed when people become either imprisoned in the ideas of the group or jealous of a system not benefiting them. In this case, people will form alliances with unions or rebels against the authority for validation to credit themselves for removing poor leadership and to blame the poor leadership for failure. Interestingly enough, the lack of rationality leads to no useful actions beyond leadership replacement, and people in this condition continue to blame the ousted authority, even though they, themselves, either contribute or share in the blame directly after the fact.

In general, a person should have a healthy balance of individual and collective thoughts; however, such a balance cannot be achieved in the extremely deep Sahu state because rationality does not exist.

The last instance of this conformity is illustrated in the mistaken belief that the employment system guarantees a successful life for all people. The employment system, while a need for most, still echoes the enforcement of dependency, exploitation, and subjugation of individual autonomy to the needs of the corporation. Large enterprises driven by profit imperatives often exploit career-minded employees through false promises, systemic inequities, and disposability. These false promises include vertical movements, promotions, bonuses, or career development that rarely materialize. As a result, employees stay committed longer than they should, hoping for progress that never comes and creating a self-defeating cycle of dependency, delusion, disappointment, burnout (physical, mental, or demographic), and sometimes death. The cycle is validated by following co-workers (the crowd), and the comfort of blaming others is normally projected to poor management.

Although this article does not provide an in-depth psychosocial analysis of the extremely deep Sahu state based on the polypsychic view of Ancient Egypt, it does provide a brief overview of a person's capability for or impetus toward self-destruction and irrationality. Through poor rationality, self-sabotaging behaviors, negative self-talk, and a lack of self-confidence, you will always be your own worst enemy, and no one can protect you from yourself.

Em Hotep!

A BID FAREWELL

Recall that this text, **The Kemetic Path: Achieving High Spirituality**, has been compiled to fulfill three (3) primary objectives: (i) to provide a spiritual alternative to those struggling with religious disaffiliation or seeking a strong connection with nature and a High Power on a higher level of consciousness, (ii) to revive ancient Kemetic teachings based on an overlooked perspective coined as High Spirituality and (iii) to thwart societal control mechanisms.

High Spirituality, which is a part of this pathway with an impersonal High Power, involves the personal quest for meaning, individual purpose, a deepening interconnection with finite living beings, and a connection to something beyond oneself, such as the High Power and the conscious Living Universe, to reach higher consciousness and to evoke awareness. Furthermore, it encompasses a person's beliefs, values, and practices, and it can be expressed in many ways without any religion, including through nature or personal reflection. It must be remembered that teachings and spirituality were in existence before the fabrication of any religion, and to be spiritual is to be a student of nature.

Spirituality means knowing that our lives have significance in a context far beyond some mundane everyday existence on the physical and metaphysical planes. The development of spirituality is generally recognized as requiring some sort of religious practice or discipline; however, this is far from true, and these man-made religions do nothing except create paradoxes, fallacies, division, needless rituals, hypocrisies, and false narratives to blur the lines between religion and spirituality. Unlike religion, spirituality presupposes that anyone can tap into the interworking of the conscious Living Universe through a heightened, meditative sense of rationality, consciousness, awareness, and high vibration without the need for blind faith, willful ignorance, or intellectual stagnation, where pre-established religious explanations prevent believers from asking deeper questions about the causes of complex issues. Moreover, a true understanding of spirituality will always expose the lies behind religion, which are typically fabricated by people speaking on behalf of some god, people inventing some god for subscribers, or people receiving uncorroborated divine revelations/visions.

Previous articles within this text have also demonstrated that spirituality can help defeat societal control by fostering individual autonomy, inspiring resistance, and providing an alternative source of meaning outside of dominant social norms. Societal control relies on individuals accepting external standards no matter the source, and spirituality can defeat this control by shifting the individual's focus inward to find a personal source of truth and meaning, especially since a core component of spiritual autonomy is the belief that one holds inner wisdom. Rather than seeking meaning through material wealth, social validation, or other markers of indoctrination, spiritual individuals embrace spiritual paths, seeking deeper forms of knowledge and fulfillment and making themselves less susceptible to manipulation. Lastly, genuine spiritual practices often lead to inner and outer liberation. Spiritual practices encourage self-examination, helping individuals to identify and to let go of socially conditioned beliefs and behaviors that might not align with their authentic selves.

For clarification, this liberation is primarily achieved by breaking free of religion, education, family, friends, government, media, work, poverty, and the Self, as well as thwarting manipulation tactics. Manipulation tactics include gaslighting, love bombing, projection, guilt tripping, passive aggression, stonewalling, triangulation, negging, devaluation, minimization, coercion, blame shifting, feigning confusion, diversion, polar thinking, slander, breadcrumbing, hoovering, deflection, tag teaming, pity play, moving the goal posts, brainwashing, trauma bonding, cult pulling, grooming, or scorched earth strategy. The need for a spiritual shield is undeniable, especially for the highly impressionable age group from 10 to 18.

The simplicity of spirituality should be well-appreciated, for it can never be riddled with contradiction.

At this point, we would like to wish everyone the best on their spiritual journey - a profoundly personal and transformative process. Always climb toward Hotep, and never fall into Sahu.

Em Hotep!

WORKS CONSULTED

Kemetic Light Texts

Ancient and Primitive Rite of Memphis, pgs. 214-386
Bells of Revealing Light, Catalogues ii-ix, xii-xiv
Craftsman Initiation Rituals (Kemet Pre-Temple), Entered Apprentice - Light Bearer, 360 Deg
Esoteric Path: Fields of Wonder
Sacred Revealing Light - Protection Abode (abridged)
Seven Bells: Levels of Lights & Ancient Kemetic Science
Treatise to Seekers: Knowledge of Light, Volumes 1-3, 4, 11-14 (redacted)
Medtu Neter: Origins of Protection – On Spiritual Feats, Symbolism, and Philosophy of Kmt

References (If Not Specified in the Main Body)

Abulencia, Charizze. "Why Is Education Important and How Does It Affect One's Future?" *World Vision Canada*, 29 Aug. 2023, https://www.worldvision.ca/en/stories/why-is-education-important.

Adkins, Brent. "Less than Nothing: Kant, Hylozoism, and the Impossibility of Meaningful Life." *Academia*, 2018, https://www.academia.edu/35743456/Less_than_Nothing_Kant_Hylozoism_and_the_Impossibility_of_Meaningful_Life.

"Aesthetics." *Philosophy Basics*, n.d., https://www.philosophybasics.com/branch_aesthetics.html.

Ai, Amy L., et al., editors. *Assessing Spirituality in a Diverse World.* 1st ed., Springer, 2021. *Amazon.*

Akers, Ronald L., et al. "Social Learning and Deviant Behavior: A Specific Test of a General Theory." *Contemporary Masters in Criminology*, edited by Joan McCord and John H. Laub, Springer US, 1995, pp. 187–214, https://doi.org/10.1007/978-1-4757-9829-6_12.

Alabdulkareem, Saleh Abdullah. "Science, Fact, and Absolute Truth: Critical Views of Learning." *Procedia Social and Behavioral Sciences*, 3rd World Conference on Learning, Teaching and Educational Leadership, vol. 93, Oct. 2013, pp. 2100–08, https://doi.org/10.1016/j.sbspro.2013.10.173.

Allen, James P. *The Ancient Egyptian Pyramid Texts.* SBL Press, 2015. *Amazon.*

Allison, Dale C. Jr. *Resurrecting Jesus: The Earliest Christian Tradition and Its Interpreters.* T&T Clark, 2010. *Amazon.*

Almeida, Michael. *Cosmological Arguments.* Cambridge University Press, 2018. *Amazon.*

Amen, Ra Un Nefer. *Metu Neter, Vol. 1: The Great Oracle of Tehuti and the Egyptian System of Spiritual Cultivation.* Kamit Pubns, 1990. *Amazon.*

Amen, Ra UN Neter Neter. *Metu Neter Ankh Ausar Volume 2/3.* Khamit Media Trans Visions Inc., 1990. *Amazon.*

Amin, S., et al. "Transition to Adulthood of Female Garment-Factory Workers in Bangladesh." *Studies in Family Planning*, vol. 29, no. 2, June 1998, pp. 185–200, https://pubmed.ncbi.nlm.nih.gov/9664631/.

Amirault, S. B. "Conservation of Mass, Momentum, and Energy." *S.B.A. Invent*, n.d., https://sbainvent.com/fluid-mechanics/conservation-mass-momentum-energy/.

Amoroso, Richard L, and Elizabeth A Rauscher. "Speculation on a Unified Field Theory (UFT), Grand Unification Theories (GUT), and Supersymmetry and Superstring Theories." *Orbiting The Moons Of Pluto: Complex Solutions To The Einstein, Maxwell, Schrodinger And Dirac Equations*, World Scientific, 2011, pp. 238–66, https://doi.org/10.1142/9789814324250_0013. Series on Knots and Everything.

Andrade, Gabriel. "Clinical Cases and Metaphysical Theories of Personal Identity." *Medicine, Health Care and Philosophy*, vol. 22, no. 2, June 2019, pp. 317–26. *Springer Link*, https://doi.org/10.1007/s11019-018-9869-3.

Arenhart, Jonas Rafael Becker, and Raoni Wohnrath Arroyo. "Back to the Question of Ontology (and Metaphysics)." *Manuscrito*, vol. 44, no. 2, 2021, pp. 1–51. *SciELO*, https://doi.org/10.1590/0100-6045.2021.V44N2.JR.

Armstrong, Karen. *A History of God: The 4,000-Year Quest of Judaism, Christianity, and Islam.* Ballantine Books, 1993. *Amazon.*

Asana. *19 Unconscious Bias Examples and How to Prevent Them.* 4 Jan. 2025, https://asana.com/resources/unconscious-bias-examples.

Asante, Molefi Kete. *The History of Africa: The Quest for Eternal Harmony.* Routledge, 2019. *Amazon.*

Asante, Molefi Kete, and Ama Mazama, editors. *Encyclopedia of African Religion.* 1st edition, SAGE Publications Inc., 2008. *Amazon.*

Ashby, Muata. *Egyptian Proverbs (Tem T Tchaas).* Sema Institute, 2005. *Amazon.*

Ashby, Muata. *Per Em Heru (Book of Enlightenment).* E-Book, www.UnitedBlackBooks.org, 2020, https://www.facebook.com/UnitedBlackBooks/photos/a.555150568003365/1364149257103488/?_rdr.

Ashby, Muata. *The Ancient Egyptian Wisdom Texts.* Sema Institute, 2006. *Amazon.*

Ashworth, A. J. "Self-Defence and the Right to Life." *The Cambridge Law Journal*, vol. 34, no. 2, 1975, pp. 282–307, https://doi.org/10.1017/S0008197300086128.

Atkinson, William Walker, et al. *The Kybalion: The Definitive Edition.* Tarcher, 2011. *Amazon.*

Bahr, Ann Marie B., and Martin E. Marty. *Indigenous Religions (Religions of the World).* Chelsea House Pub, 2005. *Amazon.*

Baum, Matthew A., and Philip B. K. Potter. "Media, Public Opinion, and Foreign Policy in the Age of Social Media." *The Journal of Politics*, vol. 81, no. 2, Apr. 2019, pp. 747–56, https://doi.org/10.1086/702233.

Bear, Mark, et al. *Neuroscience: Exploring the Brain.* Jones & Bartlett Learning, 2025. *Amazon.*

Beaudry, Pierre. "Pythagorean Spherics: The Missing Link Between Egypt and Greece." *21st Century Science & Technology*, 2004, https://amatterofmind.org/Pierres_PDFs/PUBLICATIONS/1._PYTHAGOREAN_SPHERICS_Missing_Link_Between_Egypt_and_Greece.pdf.

Beckett, Scott William. *The Role of Mezirow's Ten Phases of Transformative Learning in the Development of Global Leaders.* 2018, https://digitalcommons.pepperdine.edu/etd/1019. Pepperdine University, Dissertation.

Beek, Walter E. A. Van. "Matter in Motion: A Dogon Kanaga Mask." *Religions*, vol. 9, no. 9, Sept. 2018, p. 264, https://doi.org/10.3390/rel9090264.

Before Egypt: What Started the Kemetic Civilization? Directed by Danita Smith, 2024. *YouTube*, https://www.youtube.com/watch?v=MpBX3WR596o.

Being a Non-Muslim under Islamic Rule: The Theory and the Reality. https://answering-islam.org/NonMuslims/index.htm. Accessed 25 Nov. 2025.

Bell, Melina Constantine. "John Stuart Mill's Harm Principle and Free Speech: Expanding the Notion of Harm." *Utilitas*, vol. 33, no. 2, June 2021, pp. 162–79, https://doi.org/10.1017/S0953820820000229.

Bell, Richard H. *Understanding African Philosophy: A Cross-Cultural Approach to Classical and Contemporary Issues.* 1st edition, Routledge, 2002. *Amazon.*

Benavot, Aaron. "Building the Case for Literacy." *Adult Education and Development*, no. 71, 2008, https://www.dvv-international.de/en/adult-education-and-development/editions/aed-712008/international-reflections-on-issues-arising-from-the-benchmarks-and-call-for-action/building-the-case-for-literacy.

Bhardwaj, Bhawana, and Dipanker Sharma. "Negotiation Skills: How to Stay Stronger in Negotiation." *Managing and Negotiating Disagreements: A Contemporary Approach for Conflict Resolution*, First edition, Emerald Publishing, 2024, https://doi.org/10.1108/9781837979714.

Bhardwaj, Rashmi, and Debabrata Datta. "Consensus Algorithm." *Decentralised Internet of Things: A Blockchain Perspective*, edited by Mohammad Ayoub Khan et al., Springer International Publishing, 2020, pp. 91–107, https://doi.org/10.1007/978-3-030-38677-1_5.

Bierbrier, Morris. *The Tomb-Builders of the Pharaohs*. The American University in Cairo Press, 2016. *Amazon*.

Big Think. *These Are the 4 Types of Atheism*. 29 July 2022, https://bigthink.com/the-well/four-types-atheism/.

Bimrose, Jenny, et al. *Adult Career Progression and Advancement: A Five-Year Study of the Effectiveness of Guidance*. Institute for Employment Research, University of Warwick, 2008, https://warwick.ac.uk/fac/soc/ier/publications/2008/eg_report_4_years_on_final.pdf.

Bishop, James. "What Is Panentheism?" *Bishop's Encyclopedia of Religion, Society, and Philosophy*, 21 Nov. 2021, https://jamesbishopblog.com/2021/11/21/what-is-panentheism/.

Blackmore, Susan, and Emily T. Troscianko. *Consciousness: An Introduction*. 3rd ed., Routledge, 2018. *Amazon*.

Bolelli, Daniele. *Create Your Own Religion: A How-To Book without Instructions*. Disinformation Books, 2013. *Amazon*.

Bouzat, Juan L. "Darwin's Diagram of Divergence of Taxa as a Causal Model for the Origin of Species." *The Quarterly Review of Biology*, vol. 89, no. 1, 2014, pp. 21–38, https://doi.org/10.1086/674992.

Boykoff, Jules. "Limiting Dissent: The Mechanisms of State Repression in the USA." *Social Movement Studies*, vol. 6, no. 3, 2007, pp. 281–310, https://doi.org/10.1080/14742830701666988.

Bozdogan, S., and N. Rabbat. "The Kemetic Cultural Influence on Ancient Greek Philosophy." *Massachusetts Institute of Technology*, 18 Dec. 1995, https://web.mit.edu/4.288/Students/diop/term.html.

Britannica Editors. *African Religions*. n.d., https://www.britannica.com/topic/African-religions.

Britannica Editors. *Canaan: Historical Region, Middle East*. 10 Nov. 2025, https://www.britannica.com/place/Canaan-historical-region-Middle-East.

Bunge, Mario. "Sociology, Epistemology Of." *International Encyclopedia of the Social & Behavioral Sciences*, edited by James D. Wright, 2nd ed., Elsevier, 2015, pp. 984–88, https://www.sciencedirect.com:5037/science/chapter/referencework/abs/pii/B9780080970868321468.

Burgess, John P. *Philosophical Logic*. Princeton University Press, 2012. *Amazon*.

Burkov, Vladimir N., et al. *Control Mechanisms for Ecological-Economic Systems*. Springer, 2015. *Amazon*.

Cameron, David W., and Colin P. Groves. *Bones, Stones and Molecules: "Out of Africa" and Human Origins*. Academic Press, 2004. *Amazon*.

Carlile, Richard. *A Manual of the Three First Degrees of Freemasonry. With an Introductory Key-Stone to the Royal Arch*. Wentworth Press, 2016. *Amazon*.

Carrier, Richard. *Hitler Homer Bible Christ: The Historical Papers of Richard Carrier 1995-2013*. CreateSpace Independent Publishing Platform, 2014. *Amazon*.

Carrier, Richard. *Jesus from Outer Space: What the Earliest Christians Really Believed about Christ*. Pitchstone Publishing, 2020. *Amazon*.

Carrier, Richard. *Not the Impossible Faith: Why Christianity Didn't Need a Miracle to Succeed*. Lulu.com, 2009. *Amazon*.

Carrier, Richard. *On the Historicity of Jesus: Why We Might Have Reason for Doubt*. Sheffield Phoenix Press Ltd, 2014. *Amazon*.

Carrier, Richard. *Proving History: Bayes's Theorem and the Quest for the Historical Jesus.* First Edition, Prometheus Books, 2012.
Carrier, Richard. "Some Problems with Modern Kemetic Mythology." *Richard Carrier Blogs*, 26 Feb. 2021, https://www.richardcarrier.info/archives/17733.
Carrier, Richard. *The Obsolete Paradigm of a Historical Jesus.* First Edition, Pitchstone Publishing 2025
Cebeci, Tuncer, and Peter Bradshaw. "Conservation Equations for Mass, Momentum, and Energy." *Physical and Computational Aspects of Convective Heat Transfer*, edited by Tuncer Cebeci and Peter Bradshaw, Springer, 1984, pp. 19–40, https://doi.org/10.1007/978-3-662-02411-9_2.
Center for South Asia Outreach. *Religions of South Asia.* n.d., https://southasiaoutreach.wisc.edu/religions/.
Chang, Yi-Fang. "Basic Principles of Physics and Their Applications, and Logical Structure of Quantum Mechanics." *International Journal of Modern Theoretical Physics*, vol. 7, no. 1, 2018, pp. 16–39, https://www.researchgate.net/profile/Yi-Fang-Chang-3/publication/351866011_Basic_Principles_of_Physics_and_Their_Applications_and_Logical_Structure_of_Quantum_Mechanics/links/60adae4b458515bfb0a3346d/Basic-Principles-of-Physics-and-Their-Applications-and-Logical-Structure-of-Quantum-Mechanics.pdf.
Charloux, Guillaume. *Final Report for the Maghâir Shúayb Excavations* (Phoenix, Arizona, 2023).
Clark, Rosemary. *The Sacred Magic of Ancient Egypt: The Spiritual Practice Restored.* Harakhte House, 2021. *Amazon.*
Clark, Rosemary. *The Sacred Tradition in Ancient Egypt: The Esoteric Wisdom Revealed.* Harakhte House, 2021. *Amazon.*
Coats, George. "Moses in Midian', in Journal of Biblical Literature, Vol. 92, No. 1 (March, 1973), pp. 3–10.
Cole, Cheryl L. "American Jordan: P.L.A.Y., Consensus, and Punishment." *Sociology of Sport Journal*, vol. 13, no. 4, Dec. 1996, pp. 366–97, https://doi.org/10.1123/ssj.13.4.366. Sociology of Sport Journal.
Coleman, Sam. "The Real Combination Problem: Panpsychism, Micro-Subjects, and Emergence." *Erkenntnis*, vol. 79, no. 1, Feb. 2014, pp. 19–44, https://doi.org/10.1007/s10670-013-9431-x.
Comparative Index to Islam: Muhammad. https://www.answering-islam.org/Index/M/muhammad.html. Accessed 25 Nov. 2025.
Corrigan, Terence. "OPINION | The Illusion of Democracy: How Authoritarianism Thrives in Modern Political Landscapes - News24." News Item. *Institute of Race Relations*, 27 Nov. 2024, https://irr.org.za/media/opinion-the-illusion-of-democracy-how-authoritarianism-thrives-in-modern-political-landscapes-news24.
Crichlow, Wesley. "Weaponization and Prisonization of Toronto's Black Male Youth." *International Journal for Crime, Justice and Social Democracy*, vol. 3, no. 3, Jan. 2014, pp. 113–31, https://doi.org/10.3316/informit.270476229410483.
Dakdok, Usama K. *Generous Quran: An Accurate, Modern English Translation of the Qur'an, Islam's Holiest Book.* Usama Dakdok Publishing, LLC, 2009. *Amazon.*
Dancig-Rosenberg, Hadar, and Noa Yosef. "Crime Victimhood and Intersectionality." *Fordham Urban Law Journal*, vol. 47, no. 1, Dec. 2019, p. 85, https://openurl.ebsco.com/contentitem/gcd:140930219?sid=ebsco:plink:crawler&id=ebsco:gcd:140930219.
David, Rosalie. *Handbook to Life in Ancient Egypt.* Revised 2nd, Oxford University Press, 2007. *Amazon.*
Davis, Brenda. "Educational Reform, Public Engagement and 'Complexity.'" *TCI (Transnational Curriculum Inquiry)*, vol. 9, no. 2, 2012, pp. 50–66, https://doi.org/10.14288/tci.v9i2.183652.
Davis-Floyd, Robbie, and Charles D. Laughlin. *Ritual: What It Is, How It Works, and Why.* Berghahn Books, 2022. *Amazon.*

De Bruin, Anique B.H., et al. "Examining the Stability of Experts' Clinical Case Processing: An Experimental Manipulation." *Instructional Science*, vol. 33, no. 3, May 2005, pp. 251–70, https://doi.org/10.1007/s11251-005-3598-8.

Dennis, Otto. "The Branches of Philosophy." *Rudiments of Philosophy and Logic*, The Department of Philosophy, Akwa Ibom State University, 2020, pp. 67–95, https://www.researchgate.net/publication/377555363_THE_BRANCHES_OF_PHILOSOPHY.

Derda, Tomasz. 'Did the Jews Use the Name of Moses in Antiquity?', in *Zeitschrift für Papyrologie und Epigraphik*, Bd. 115 (1997), pp. 257–260.

"Dogon." *Cultural Survival Quarterly*, vol. 16, no. 2, Mar. 2010, https://www.culturalsurvival.org/publications/cultural-survival-quarterly/dogon.

Doherty, Earl. *The End of an Illusion: How Bart Ehrman's "Did Jesus Exist?" Has Laid the Case for a Historical Jesus to Rest.* Age of Reason Publications, 2012. *Amazon.*

Duchesne-Guillemin, Jacques. *Zoroastrianism.* 11 Oct. 2025, https://www.britannica.com/topic/Zoroastrianism.

Dungen, Wim van den. *The Egyptian Gentleman.* Lulu.com, 2017. *Amazon.*

Eain, Thet Tent, and George Aung. "A Comparative Analysis of Søren Kierkegaard and Albert Camus's Views on Human Existence: Existentialism and Absurdism -Similarities and Differences." *Asia-Pacific International University*, May 2023. *ResearchGate*, https://www.researchgate.net/profile/Thet-Tent-Eain/publication/386342079_A_Comparative_Analysis_of_Soren_Kierkegaard_and_Albert_Camus's_Views_on_Human_Existence_Existentialism_and_Absurdism_-Similarities_and_Differences/links/674e1181f309a268c01fdaf5/A-Comparative-Analysis-of-Soren-Kierkegaard-and-Albert-Camuss-Views-on-Human-Existence-Existentialism-and-Absurdism-Similarities-and-Differences.pdf.

Effiong, James Edem, et al. "Traumatic Bonding in Victims of Intimate Partner Violence Is Intensified Via Empathy." *Journal of Social and Personal Relationships*, vol. 39, no. 12, 2022, pp. 3619–37, https://doi.org/10.1177/02654075221106237.

Ehrman, Bart D. *A Brief Introduction to the New Testament.* 4th ed., Oxford University Press, 2017. *Amazon.*

Ehrman, Bart D. *Forgery and Counterforgery: The Use of Literary Deceit in Early Christian Polemics.* Oxford University Press, 2013. *Amazon.*

Ehrman, Bart D. *Misquoting Jesus: The Story Behind Who Changed the Bible and Why.* HarperOne, 2007. *Amazon.*

Ehrman, Bart D. *The Triumph of Christianity: How a Forbidden Religion Swept the World.* Simon & Schuster, 2018. *Amazon.*

El-Diraby, T. E. "Epistemology of Construction Informatics." *Journal of Construction Engineering and Management*, vol. 138, no. 1, Jan. 2012, pp. 53–65, https://doi.org/10.1061/(ASCE)CO.1943-7862.0000392.

Ellerbe, Helen. *The Dark Side of Christian History.* Morningstar & Lark, 2004. *Amazon.*

Ellis, Normandi. *Awakening Osiris: The Spiritual Keys to the Egyptian Book of the Dead.* New Page Books, 2023. *Amazon.*

Elmi, Qorban, and Mojtaba Zarvani. "Problem of Evil in Taoism." *Religious Inquiries*, Volume 5, no. 10, Dec. 2016, pp. 35–47, https://ri.urd.ac.ir/article_46549.html.

Encyclopedia.com. *Canaanite Religion: An Overview.* n.d., https://www.encyclopedia.com/environment/encyclopedias-almanacs-transcripts-and-maps/canaanite-religion-overview.

Erman, Adolf. *A Handbook of Egyptian Religion.* Leopold Classic Library, 2016. *Amazon.*

Evans, Henry Ridgely. *Cagliostro and His Egyptian Rite of Freemasonry.* 1919. *Amazon.*

Facts and Details. *History of Ancient Nubia: Kush, Kerma, Meroe, Egyptians.* July 2024, https://africame.factsanddetails.com/article/entry-233.html.

Fenton, Natalie. "Fake Democracy: The Limits of Public Sphere Theory." *Javnost - The Public*, vol. 25, nos. 1–2, Apr. 2018, pp. 28–34, https://doi.org/10.1080/13183222.2018.1418821.

Finkelstein, Israel, and Neil Asher Silberman. *The Bible Unearthed: Archaeology's New Vision of Ancient Israel and the Origin of Its Sacred Texts.* Touchstone, 2002. *Amazon.*

Fisher, Andrew. *Metaethics: An Introduction.* Routledge, 2011. *Amazon.*

FitzPatrick, Jessica Jane. *Learning About 21st Century Skills and Progressive Education Through Practitioner Research.* 2021, https://hdl.handle.net/10092/101691. University of Canterbury, Thesis.

Fiveable. *Sumerian Mythology and Pantheon.* n.d., https://fiveable.me/ancient-times-myth-history-measurement/unit-2/sumerian-mythology-pantheon/study-guide/qAQMS8Dy9meF7g1C.

Flood, Mike. "What Kind of Atheist Are You?" *Humanists UK,* n.d., https://humanists.uk/humanistlife-archive/what-kind-of-atheist-are-you/.

Forbes, Graeme. *The Metaphysics of Modality.* Oxford University Press, 1986. *Amazon.*

Forth, Adelle, et al. "Toxic Relationships: The Experiences and Effects of Psychopathy in Romantic Relationships." *International Journal of Offender Therapy and Comparative Criminology*, vol. 66, no. 15, Nov. 2022, pp. 1627–58, https://doi.org/10.1177/0306624X211049187.

Foster, John L., translator. *Echoes of Egyptian Voices: An Anthology of Ancient Egyptian Poetry.* Univ of Oklahoma Pr, 1992. *Amazon.*

Frankfort, Henri. *Ancient Egyptian Religion: An Interpretation.* Dover Publications, 2000. *Amazon.*

Frisch, Alexandria. 'The Apocalyptic Moses of Second Temple Judaism', in Hebrew Union College Annual, Vol. 90 (2019), pp. 185– 207.

Fundamentals of Marx: Idealism vs. Materialism. Directed by The Marxist Project, 2019. *YouTube*, https://www.youtube.com/watch?v=XyzFwHFN_BI.

G. Gauch Jr., Hugh. *Scientific Method in Practice.* Cambridge University Press, 2002. *Amazon.*

Gallois, André. *The Metaphysics of Identity.* Routledge, 2016. *Amazon*, https://doi.org/10.4324/9780203756218.

Gallow, J. Dmitri. "The Metaphysics of Causation." *The Stanford Encyclopedia of Philosophy (Fall 2022 Edition)*, edited by Edward N. Zalta and Uri Nodelman, 2022, https://plato.stanford.edu/archives/fall2022/entries/causation-metaphysics/.

Gawlikowski, Michael. "Aynuna on the Red Sea', in Polish Archaeology in the Mediterranean, Vol. 29, No. 1 (2020), pp. 35–44.

Ge, Fei. *Toward Concordance: Searching for Solutions to Cosmological Tensions and Tests ΛCDM Cosmology.* 2024, https://escholarship.org/uc/item/3925396j. University of California, Davis, Dissertation.

Geist, Stephen. "The Fascinating Story of the Anunnaki — Part 1." *Medium*, 12 Aug. 2022, https://medium.com/@stphngeist/the-fascinating-story-of-the-anunnaki-part-1-2c8e1eed71f.

Geremia, Hannah. *Roll for Alignment: The Application of Moral and Ethical Systems in Tabletop and Digital Dungeons & Dragons.* 2022, https://doi.org/10.13140/RG.2.2.35030.73285. University of Wollongong, Honours Thesis.

Goldberg, Sanford C. "A Normative Account of Epistemic Luck." *Philosophical Issues*, vol. 29, no. 1, 2019, pp. 97–109. *Wiley Online Library*, https://doi.org/10.1111/phis.12143.

Gorz, Andre. *Capitalism, Socialism, Ecology.* Translated by Chris Turner, Verso Books, 2013. *Amazon.*

Green, Samuel. *The Different Arabic Versions of the Qur'an.* https://www.answering-islam.org/Green/seven.htm. Accessed 25 Nov. 2025.

Grinstead, Charles M., and J. Laurie Snell. *Introduction to Probability.* American Mathematical Society, 2012. *Amazon.*

Gula, Robert J. *Nonsense: A Handbook Of Logical Fallacies.* UNKNO, 2007. *Amazon.*

Gunn, Battiscombe G., translator. *Instruction of Ptah-Hotep and the Instruction of Ke'Gemni: The Oldest Books in the World.* Kessinger Publishing, 2010. *Amazon.*

Gutierrez, M. L. *The Bible Dilemma: Historical Contradictions, Misquoted Statements, Failed Prophecies, and Oddities in the Bible.* Dog Ear Publishing, LLC, 2009. *Amazon.*

Hall, Manly P. *The Secret Teachings of All Ages: An Encyclopedic Outline of Masonic, Hermetic, Qabbalistic and Rosicrucian Symbolical Philosophy.* Dover Publications, 2010. *Amazon.*

Hamilton, A. G. *Numbers, Sets and Axioms: The Apparatus of Mathematics*. 1st ed., Cambridge University Press, 1982. *Amazon.*

Hansson, Lena. "Science Education, Indoctrination, and the Hidden Curriculum." *History, Philosophy and Science Teaching: New Perspectives*, edited by Michael R. Matthews, Springer International Publishing, 2018, pp. 283–306, https://doi.org/10.1007/978-3-319-62616-1_11.

Harper, Steve. *Christianity Exposed: The Truth About Christianity*. Independently published. *Amazon.*

Harris, Mark D. "African Traditional Religions." *MD Harris Institute*, 19 Oct. 2023, https://mdharrismd.com/2023/10/19/african-traditional-religions/.

Harrison, Paul. *Profane Egyptologists: The Modern Revival of Ancient Egyptian Religion*. Routledge, 2019. *Amazon.*

Hattab, Helen. "The Metaphysics of Substantial Forms." *Routledge Companion to Sixteenth Century Philosophy*, edited by Henrik Lagerlund and Benjamin Hill, Routledge, 2017, pp. 450–71, https://www.taylorfrancis.com/chapters/edit/10.4324/9781315770512-28/metaphysics-substantial-forms-helen-hattab.

Hauskeller, Michael. "The Apparent Absurdity of Meaning Subjectivism." *Meaning in Life: A Subjectivist Account*, Springer Nature Switzerland, 2025, pp. 19–41, https://doi.org/10.1007/978-3-031-80362-8_2.

Hausman, Alan, et al. *Logic and Philosophy: A Modern Introduction*. Cengage Learning, 2013. *Amazon.*

Hietanen, Mika. *Classical Rhetorical Argumentation for the Rhetorical Critic*. Routledge, 2026. *Amazon.*

Highhouse, Scott, and Thaddeus B. Rada. "Different Worldviews Explain Perceived Effectiveness of Different Employment Tests." *International Journal of Selection and Assessment*, vol. 23, no. 2, 2015, pp. 109–19, https://doi.org/10.1111/ijsa.12100.

Hinnells, John R., editor. *A Handbook of Ancient Religions*. Cambridge University Press, 2007. *Amazon.*

Hintikka, Jaakko, et al., editors. *Philosophy and Logic In Search of the Polish Tradition: Essays in Honour of Jan Woleński on the Occasion of His 60th Birthday*. Springer, 2003. *Amazon.*

Hirai, Naofusa. "Shinto." *Encyclopædia Britannica*, 14 Nov. 2025, https://www.britannica.com/topic/Shinto.

History.com Editors. "General MacArthur Orders End of Shinto as Japanese State Religion." *History*, 27 May 2025, https://www.history.com/this-day-in-history/december-15/macarthur-orders-end-of-shinto-as-japanese-state-religion.

History.com Editors. "Hinduism: Symbols, Beliefs & Origins." *History*, 4 Nov. 2025, https://www.history.com/articles/hinduism.

History.com Editors. "Zoroastrianism." *History*, 28 Aug. 2025, https://www.history.com/articles/zoroastrianism.

Hogan, Timothy. *The Alchemical Keys To Masonic Ritual*. Lulu.com, 2007. *Amazon.*

Hornung, Erik, editor. *Ancient Egyptian Chronology*. Brill Academic Pub, 2006. *Amazon.*

Hurbon, Laënnec. "Haitian Vodou." *The Open Encyclopedia of Anthropology*, Apr. 2022, https://doi.org/10.29164/22haitianvodou.

Hurlbut, Dima. "Review of Douglas Thomas and Temilola Alanamu (Eds.), African Religions: Beliefs and Practices Through History." *Choice*, vol. 56, no. 11, 2019, https://doi.org/10.17613/jghm-m041.

Imbo, Samuel Oluoch. *An Introduction to African Philosophy*. Rowman & Littlefield Publishers, Inc., 1998. *Amazon.*

Islam & Terrorism. https://answering-islam.org/Terrorism/index.html. Accessed 25 Nov. 2025.

Izunwa, Maurice O. "Understanding the Nature and Branches of Philosophy." *Journal of Current Issues In Nigerian Law*, vol. 1, no. 1, Sept. 2022, https://journals.ezenwaohaetorc.org/index.php/JOCINL/article/view/2078.

Jarus, Owen. "Who Were the Canaanites, the Ancient Biblical People Credited with Inventing the Alphabet?" *Live Science*, 24 May 2025, https://www.livescience.com/56016-canaanites.html.

Johnston, Sarah Iles, editor. *Ancient Religions*. Belknap Press, 2009. *Amazon.*

Karam, Azza. "Education as the Pathway towards Gender Equality." *United Nations*, 19 Dec. 2013, https://www.un.org/en/chronicle/article/education-pathway-towards-gender-equality.

Karp, Karen S., et al. "13 Rules That Expire." *Teaching Children Mathematics*, vol. 21, no. 1, Aug. 2014, pp. 18–25, https://doi.org/10.5951/teacchilmath.21.1.0018. Teaching Children Mathematics.

Khan Academy. *Ancient Mesopotamian Civilizations.* n.d., https://www.khanacademy.org/humanities/world-history/world-history-beginnings/ancient-mesopotamia/a/mesopotamia-article.

Khan, Adnan. *The Metaphysics of Space and Time.* July 2021, https://www.researchgate.net/publication/353480568_The_Metaphysics_of_Space_and_Time.

King, David. *A Handbook of Logical Fallacies.* n.d., https://dl.icdst.org/pdfs/files4/55091d33e9c4060d798ba255a28b94cf.pdf.

Klein, Richard G. "Darwin and the Recent African Origin of Modern Humans." *Proceedings of the National Academy of Sciences*, vol. 106, no. 38, Sept. 2009, pp. 16007–09, https://doi.org/10.1073/pnas.0908719106.

Korteling, J.E. (Hans), and Alexander Toet. "Cognitive Biases." *Encyclopedia of Behavioral Neuroscience, 2nd Edition*, edited by Sergio Della Sala, Elsevier, 2022, pp. 610–19. *www.sciencedirect.com*, https://www.sciencedirect.com:5037/science/chapter/referencework/abs/pii/B9780128093245241059.

Krieg, Andreas. *Subversion: The Strategic Weaponization of Narratives.* Georgetown University Press, 2023. *Amazon.*

Kulatilake, Samanti. "The Peopling of Sri Lanka from Prehistoric to Historic Times." *A Companion to South Asia in the Past*, edited by Gwen Robbins Schug and Subhash R. Walimbe, John Wiley & Sons, Ltd, 2016, pp. 426–36, https://doi.org/10.1002/9781119055280.ch27.

Leadbeater, Charles W. *The Hidden Life in Freemasonry.* Jazzybee Verlag, 2017. *Amazon.*

Lichtheim, Miriam. *Ancient Egyptian Literature, Volume I: The Old and Middle Kingdoms.* University of California Press, 2006. *Google Books.*

Lichtheim, Miriam, and Hans-W. Fischer-Elfert. *Ancient Egyptian Literature, Volume II: The New Kingdom.* University of California Press, 2006. *Amazon.*

Lindor, Moïse. "Public Policies, Poverty and Illiteracy in Young and Adults in Haiti. Challenges and Perspectives." *Revista Interamericana de Educación de Adultos*, vol. 41, no. 1, 2019, pp. 6–33, https://www.redalyc.org/articulo.oa?id=457566118002.

Liontas, John I. "Idiomatics: The Ethos, Pathos, and Logos of Idiomatics Proper." *Athens Journal of Education*, vol. 12, no. 4, June 2025, pp. 547–74, https://doi.org/10.30958/aje.12-4-1.

Lloyd, G. E. R. *Ancient Worlds, Modern Reflections: Philosophical Perspectives on Greek and Chinese Science and Culture.* Oxford University Press, 2004. *Amazon.*

Loftus, John W. *The Christian Delusion: Why Faith Fails.* G38-Prometheus, 2010. *Amazon.*

Lorkowsk, C. M. "Hume, David: Causation." *Internet Encyclopedia of Philosophy*, n.d., https://iep.utm.edu/hume-causation/.

Lubicz, R. A. Schwaller de. *The Temple in Man: Sacred Architecture and the Perfect Man.* With Lucie Lamy, Inner Traditions, 1981. *Amazon.*

Lumen Learning. *The Sumerians.* n.d., https://courses.lumenlearning.com/atd-herkimer-westerncivilization/chapter/the-sumerians/.

Machiavelli: 5 Principles and Tactics for Power. Directed by Captain Sinbad, 2019. *YouTube*, https://www.youtube.com/watch?v=siczzLbinFY.

MacLeod, Mary C., and Eric M. Rubenstein. "Universals." *Internet Encyclopedia of Philosophy*, n.d., https://iep.utm.edu/universa/.

Macuch, Maria. "BARDA and BARDA-DĀRI Ii. In the Sasanian Period." *Encyclopaedia Iranica*, 28 Oct. 2016, https://www.iranicaonline.org/articles/barda-ii/.

Magalhães, Ana Lúcia. "Teaching How to Develop an Argument Using the Toulmin Model." *International Journal of Multidisciplinary and Current Educational Research*, vol. 2, no. 3, pp. 1–7, https://www.ijmcer.com/wp-content/uploads/2020/07/A0230107.pdf.

Mahaffey, Benji, and Jessica Whittemore. "Taoism: Symbol & Principles | Yin-Yang Meaning." *Study.com*, n.d., https://study.com/learn/lesson/taoism-symbol-principles-yin-yan.html.

Makinde, Olusesan Ayodeji. "Infant Trafficking and Baby Factories: A New Tale of Child Abuse in Nigeria." *Child Abuse Review*, vol. 25, no. 6, 2016, pp. 433–43, https://doi.org/10.1002/car.2420.

Mandalawi, Alaa Abdul Khaleq Hussein Al. "From Indoctrination to Thinking: Curriculum as a Tool for Liberating the Mind." *Al-Iraqa Foundation for Culture and Development*, 13 Sept. 2025, https://doi.org/10.13140/RG.2.2.16850.21445.

Mander, William. "Pantheism." *The Stanford Encyclopedia of Philosophy (Fall 2023 Edition)*, edited by Edward N. Zalta, https://plato.stanford.edu/Archives/spr2021/entries/pantheism/. Accessed 27 Nov. 2025.

Mark, Emily. "Taoism." *World History Encyclopedia*, Feb. 2016, https://www.worldhistory.org/Taoism/.

Martin, Michael. *The Case Against Christianity*. Temple Univ Pr, 1991. *Amazon*.

Masolo, D. A. *African Philosophy in Search of Identity*. Indiana Univ Pr, 1994. *Amazon*.

Materialism Versus Idealism (5). Directed by Philosophy Portal, 2019. *YouTube*, https://www.youtube.com/watch?v=JPB1h_yVN00.

Matthew Stuart - The Metaphysics of Personal Identity. Directed by UNE Center for Global Humanities, 2014. *YouTube*, https://www.youtube.com/watch?v=B9VoutR5sBA.

Mawere, Munyaradzi, and Tapuwa R. Mubaya. *African Philosophy and Thought Systems: A Search for a Culture and Philosophy of Belonging*. Langaa Rpcig, 2016. *Amazon*.

Mayr, Erasmus. *Understanding Human Agency*. Oxford University Press, 2011. *Amazon*.

Mbiti, John S. *African Religions & Philosophy*. Praeger, 1969. *Amazon*.

McDermid, Douglas James. *Is Pragmatism Coherent? Classical and Contemporary Pragmatism on Truth, Realism, and Epistemology*. 1998, https://www.proquest.com/openview/77fa88b9fb0b4c5550c6f8cecb43b8b9/1?pq-origsite=gscholar&cbl=18750&diss=y. Brown University, Thesis.

McLanahan, Sara, and Julia Adams. "Parenthood and Psychological Well-Being." *Annual Review of Sociology*, vol. 13, no. Volume 13, 1987, Aug. 1987, pp. 237–57, https://doi.org/10.1146/annurev.so.13.080187.001321.

McLeod, Saul. "Freewill vs Determinism In Psychology." *Simply Psychology*, 3 Mar. 2025, https://www.simplypsychology.org/freewill-determinism.html.

Melia, Joseph. "Nominalism, Naturalism and Natural Properties." *Nominalism about Properties*, edited by Ghislain Guigon and Gonzalo Rodriguez-Pereyra, Routledge, 2015, https://www.taylorfrancis.com/chapters/edit/10.4324/9781315724874-12/nominalism-naturalism-natural-properties-joseph-melia.

Mellentine, Jenna. "Dogon People | History, Culture & Symbols." *Study.com*, 2 May 2023, https://study.com/academy/lesson/dogon-history-culture-religion-people.html.

Meyer, Tom. *Archaeology and the Bible*. Institute for Creation Research, 2023. *Amazon*.

Micu, Alexandru. "The World's Religions: An Overview." *ZME Science*, 30 Apr. 2023, https://www.zmescience.com/feature-post/in-god-we-trust-but-other-people-dont-really-lets-look-at-religions/.

Minas-Nerpel, Martina. "A Demotic Inscribed Icosahedron from Dakhleh Oasis." *The Journal of Egyptian Archaeology*, vol. 93, no. 1, Jan. 2007, pp. 137–48. *SAGE Journals*, https://doi.org/10.1177/030751330709300107.

Miracchi, Lisa. "Knowledge Is All You Need." *Philosophical Issues*, vol. 25, 2015, pp. 353–78. *JSTOR*, https://www.jstor.org/stable/26611135.

Molina, Oscar, and Carmen Samper. "Types of Problems That Elicit Inductive, Abductive, and Deductive Arguments." *Bolema: Boletim de Educação Matemática*, vol. 33, 2019, pp. 109–34, https://doi.org/10.1590/1980-4415v33n63a06.

Monsieur de Thevenot, *The Travels of Monsieur de Thevenot into the Levant in Three Parts* (London, 1686).

Montgomery, David R. *The Rocks Don't Lie: A Geologist Investigates Noah's Flood*. W. W. Norton & Company, 2013. *Amazon*.

Morina, Edgar. "Disproving Islam: A Brief Guide to Understanding Islam." *Dokumen.Pub*, 2020, https://dokumen.pub/disproving-islam-a-brief-guide-to-understand-islam-1nbsped.html.

Mumba, Humphrey Chewe. *The Pros and Cons of Unitary and Federal Systems of Government.* 2014, https://www.academia.edu/7017973/Pros_and_Cons_of_Nigeria_Vs_Zambia_Governance_Systems.

Murphy, Nicole. *Types of Bias.* 14 May 2025, https://cpdonline.co.uk/knowledge-base/safeguarding/types-of-bias/.

Nicholas, Ralph W. "Factions: A Comparative Analysis." *Political Systems and the Distribution of Power*, edited by Michael Banton, Routledge, 2012, pp. 21–61. *Amazon.*

Nkoma, John S. *Introduction to Basic Concepts for Engineers and Scientists: Electromagnetic, Quantum, Statistical, and Relativistic Concepts.* Mkuki Na Nyoka Pub, 2018. *Amazon.*

Noonan, Harold, and Ben Curtis. "Identity." *The Stanford Encyclopedia of Philosophy (Fall 2022 Edition)*, edited by Edward N. Zalta and Uri Nodelman, Metaphysics Research Lab, Stanford University, https://plato.stanford.edu/archives/fall2022/entries/identity/. Accessed 26 Nov. 2025.

O'Connor, Cailin, et al. "Social Epistemology." *The Stanford Encyclopedia of Philosophy (Summer 2024 Edition)*, edited by Edward N. Zalta and Uri Nodelman, Metaphysics Research Lab, Stanford University, https://plato.stanford.edu/archives/sum2024/entries/epistemology-social/. Accessed 27 Nov. 2025.

Odijie, Michael. "Cocoa and Child Slavery in West Africa." *Oxford Research Encyclopedia of African History*, Oxford University Press, 2020, https://oxfordre.com/africanhistory/display/10.1093/acrefore/9780190277734.001.0001/acrefore-9780190277734-e-816.

Ogbonnaya, L. Uchenna. "What Makes African Philosophy African? A Conversation with Aribiah David Attoe on 'The Foundational Myth of Ethnophilosophy.'" *Filosofia Theoretica: Journal of African Philosophy, Culture and Religions*, vol. 7, no. 3, Sept. 2018, pp. 94–108, https://doi.org/10.4314/ft.v7i3.7.

Ogundiran, Akinwumi. "Yorùbá Indigenous Religion." *Oxford Research Encyclopedia of African History*, 2024, https://oxfordre.com/africanhistory/display/10.1093/acrefore/9780190277734.001.0001/acrefore-9780190277734-e-1556.

Omoniyi, Iwaloye Bunmi, and Bongani Thulani Gamede. "Evaluating Effective Teaching and Assessment Methods for Entrepreneurship Education to Produce Self-Employed Higher Education Graduates." *Academy of Entrepreneurship Journal*, vol. 28, no. 6, Sept. 2022, pp. 1–16. *www.abacademies.org*, https://www.abacademies.org/abstract/evaluating-effective-teaching-and-assessment-methods-for-entrepreneurship-education-to-produce-selfemployed-higher-educa-15459.html.

Out of Africa: The First Wave of Religion. Directed by Mythopia, 2024. *YouTube*, https://www.youtube.com/watch?v=qKO25-QTMx0.

Palmer, Martin. *The "Times" World Religions.* Times Books, 2002. *Amazon.*

Palumbo, Letizia. *Trafficking and Labour Exploitation in Domestic Work and the Agricultural Sector in Italy.* European University Institute, 2016, https://data.europa.eu/doi/10.2870/384097.

Park, Hyunjoon, and Pearl Kyei. "Literacy Gaps by Educational Attainment: A Cross-National Analysis." *Social Forces*, vol. 89, no. 3, Mar. 2011, pp. 879–904, https://doi.org/10.1093/sf/89.3.879.

Parkinson, R. B., translator. *The Tale of Sinuhe and Other Ancient Egyptian Poems 1940-1640 B.C.* Oxford University Press, 2009. *Amazon.*

Parry, Tyler D. "'How Much More Must I Suffer?': Post-Traumatic Stress and the Lingering Impact of Violence Upon Enslaved People." *Slavery & Abolition*, vol. 42, no. 2, Apr. 2021, pp. 184–200, https://doi.org/10.1080/0144039X.2021.1896187.

Patterson, Elizabeth. "Civil Contempt and the Indigent Child Support Obligor: The Silent Return of Debtor's Prison." *Cornell Journal of Law and Public Policy*, vol. 18, no. 1, Oct. 2008, pp. 95–141. *COinS*, https://scholarcommons.sc.edu/law_facpub/39.

Payette, Jamie. "History Dive: West African Vodun (Voodoo)." *Odysseys Unlimited*, 29 Nov. 2024, https://www.odysseys-unlimited.com/history-dive-west-african-vodun-voodoo/.

Pecorino, Philip A. "The Cosmological Argument." *Introduction To Philosophy: An Online Textbook*, n.d., https://www.qcc.cuny.edu/socialSciences/ppecorino/INTRO_TEXT/Chapter%203%20Religion/Cosmological.htm.

Pemment, Jack. "Psychopathy Versus Sociopathy: Why the Distinction Has Become Crucial." *Aggression and Violent Behavior*, vol. 18, no. 5, Sept. 2013, pp. 458–61, https://doi.org/10.1016/j.avb.2013.07.001.

Philosophy Institute. *Exploring Atheism and Related Concepts: From Naturalism to Secularism*. 15 Oct. 2023, https://philosophy.institute/philosophy-of-religion/exploring-atheism-naturalism-secularism/.

Picoult, Jodi. *The Book of Two Ways*. Ballantine Books, 2021. *Amazon*.

Pidd, Michael. *A Practical Guide to Using Data Ontologies – in the Arts, Humanities and Social Sciences*. June 2021, https://www.dhi.ac.uk/books/ontology-guide/.

Pilat, Dan, and Sekoul Krastev. "Dunning–Kruger Effect. The Decision Lab." *The Decision Lab*, 2021, https://thedecisionlab.com/biases/dunning-kruger-effect.

Price, Robert M. *Bart Ehrman Interpreted: How One Radical New Testament Scholar Understands Another*. Pitchstone Publishing, 2018. *Amazon*.

Price, Robert M., and Jeffery Jay Lowder, editors. *Empty Tomb: Jesus Beyond The Grave*. Prometheus, 2005. *Amazon*.

Prince, Christian. *The Deception of Allah Volume 1*. Usama Dakdok Publishing, LLC, 2011. *Amazon*.

Ptah-Hotep. *The Teachings of Ptahhotep: The Oldest Book in the World*. Blackwood Press, 1987. *Amazon*.

Puljak, Ana Mladina. "Developing Soft Skills in Education: Why They Matter." *Erasmus+ Teacher Training Courses Split Croatia | Platform21*, 29 Nov. 2024, https://erasmus.courses/blog/developing-soft-skills-in-education/. Creativity and Soft Skills.

Rachels, James, and Stuart Rachels. *The Elements of Moral Philosophy*. McGraw-Hill Education, 2019. *Amazon*.

Rao, Aaron. "Photography in Hollywood: Image Manipulation in Modern Entertainment." *Researchers World*, Volume 7, No. 4(1), Oct. 2016, pp. 167–72, https://doi.org/10.18843/rwjasc/v7i4(1)/20.

Renyi, Alfred. *Probability Theory*. Dover Publications, 2007. *Amazon*.

Restall, Greg. *Logic: An Introduction*. 1st edition, Routledge, 2006. *Amazon*.

Reynolds, Susan. "Nations, Tribes, Peoples, and States." *Medieval Worlds Comparative & Interdisciplinary Studies*, vol. 2, 2015, pp. 79–88, https://doi.org/10.1553/medievalworlds_no2_2015s79.

Riddle, Chauncey C. "What Is Philosophy?" *Collected Works*, SViewP.com, n.d., sviewp.com/CCRbook/CCR-TI-2-Chap%201.pdf.

Roberson, Joshua Aaron. *The Ancient Egyptian Books of the Earth*. Lockwood Press, 2012. *Amazon*.

Roberson, Joshua Aaron. *The Awakening of Osiris and the Transit of the Solar Barques: Royal Apotheosis in a Most Concise Book of the Underworld and Sky*. 2013, https://doi.org/10.5167/UZH-135412.

Roth, Wendy D., et al. "Beyond Money Whitening: Racialized Hierarchies and Socioeconomic Escalators in Mexico." *American Sociological Review*, vol. 87, no. 5, Oct. 2022, pp. 827–59, https://doi.org/10.1177/00031224221119803.

Rundle, Bede. *Time, Space, and Metaphysics*. Oxford University Press, 2009. *Amazon*, https://doi.org/10.1093/acprof:oso/9780199575114.001.0001.

Rysiew, Patrick. "Naturalism in Epistemology." *The Stanford Encyclopedia of Philosophy (Fall 2021 Edition)*, edited by Edward N. Zalta, https://plato.stanford.edu/ENTRIES/epistemology-naturalized/. Accessed 27 Nov. 2025.

Saakana, Amon Saba, editor. *African Origins of the Major World Religions*. Karnak House Publishers, 1991. *Amazon*.

Salih, Ismail Idowu. "Slavery in the Twenty-First Century: A Review of Domestic Work in the UK." *Vulnerability, Exploitation and Migrants: Insecure Work in a Globalised Economy*, edited by Louise Waite et al., Palgrave Macmillan UK, 2015, pp. 200–11, https://doi.org/10.1057/9781137460417_15.

Saunders, Eleanor A., and Jill A. Edelson. "Attachment Style, Traumatic Bonding, and Developing Relational Capacities in a Long-Term Trauma Group for Women." *International Journal of Group Psychotherapy*, vol. 49, no. 4, Oct. 1999, pp. 465–85, https://doi.org/10.1080/00207284.1999.11490964.

Scalf, Foy, editor. *Book of the Dead: Becoming God in Ancient Egypt*. Oriental Institute of the University of Chicago, 2017. *Amazon*.

Schiappa, Edward, and Jim Hamm. "Rhetorical Questions." *A Companion to Greek Rhetoric*, edited by Ian Worthington, John Wiley & Sons, Ltd, 2007, pp. 1–15, https://doi.org/10.1002/9780470997161.ch1.

Scribd. *Anunnaki and Sumerian Tablets Overview*. n.d., https://www.scribd.com/document/230465225/Sumerians-and-Anunnaki.

Sepkoski, David. "The Earth as Archive: Contingency, Narrative, and the History of Life." *Science in the Archives: Pasts, Presents, Futures*, edited by Lorraine Daston, The University of Chicago Press, 2017, pp. 53–83, https://pure.mpg.de/pubman/faces/ViewItemOverviewPage.jsp?itemId=item_241499.

Sethy, Satya Sundar. *Introduction to Logic and Logical Discourse*. Springer, 2021. *Amazon*.

Shaw, Ian, and Elizabeth Bloxam, editors. *The Oxford Handbook of Egyptology*. Oxford University Press, 2020. *Amazon*.

Shelley, James. "The Concept of the Aesthetic." *The Stanford Encyclopedia of Philosophy (Spring 2022 Edition)*, edited by Edward N. Zalta, Metaphysics Research Lab, Stanford University, https://plato.stanford.edu/archives/spr2022/entries/aesthetic-concept/. Accessed 27 Nov. 2025.

Shroff, Jainik. "Jainism, a Timeline." *Medium*, 16 July 2021, https://youngminds.yja.org/jainism-a-timeline-705dad8474f4.

Sidey, Douglas. *The Economic and Financial Effects of Single-Parent Homes*. 2015, https://digitalcommons.liberty.edu/honors/512. Liberty University, Senior Honors Theses.

Simkhada, Padam. "Life Histories and Survival Strategies Amongst Sexually Trafficked Girls in Nepal." *Children & Society*, vol. 22, no. 3, 2008, pp. 235–48, https://doi.org/10.1111/j.1099-0860.2008.00154.x.

Simpson, William Kelley, editor. *The Literature of Ancient Egypt: An Anthology of Stories, Instructions, Stelae, Autobiographies, and Poetry*. Translated by Robert K. Ritner et al., Yale University Press, 2003. *Amazon*.

Simpson, William Kelley, editor. *The Literature of Ancient Egypt: An Anthology of Stories, Instructions, Stelae, Autobiographies, and Poetry*. Translated by Robert K. Ritner et al., Yale University Press, 2003. *Amazon*.

Skansi, Sandro. "Theodore Sider: Logic for Philosophy." *Prolegomena*, vol. 11, no. 1, 2012, pp. 114–17, https://www.croris.hr/crosbi/publikacija/prilog-casopis/217412.

Smith, Barry. "Ontology." *The Furniture of the World: Essays in Ontology and Metaphysics*, edited by Guillermo Hurtado and Oscar Nudler, Editions Rodopi, 2012, https://philpapers.org/rec/SMIOJD.

Smith, Christian. *Religion: What It Is, How It Works, and Why It Matters*. Princeton University Press, 2019. *Amazon*.

Smith, Nathan. *Introduction to Philosophy*. Kendal Hunt Publishing, 2022. *Amazon*.

Smith, Peter. *An Introduction to Formal Logic*. Cambridge University Press, 2003. *Amazon*.

Sofroniou, Andreas. *Philosophy and Politics*. Independently published, 2021. *Amazon*.

Sötemann, Christian. "Existence and Subsistence: The Power of Concepts." *Philosophical Investigations*, 30 Oct. 2017, http://www.philosophical-investigations.org/2017/10/existence-and-subsistence-power-of.html.

Speaks, Jeff. "Theories of Meaning." *The Stanford Encyclopedia of Philosophy (Summer 2018 Edition)*, edited by Edward N. Zalta and Uri Nodelman, Metaphysics Research Lab, Stanford University, https://plato.stanford.edu/archives/win2025/entries/meaning/. Accessed 27 Nov. 2025.

Springer-Gould, Michael. *The Weaponization of Poverty: An Investigation Into United States Military Recruitment Practices In High Schools Of Low-Income Communities In The Inland Empire.* 2020, https://scholarship.claremont.edu/pitzer_theses/110. Pitzer College, Pitzer Senior Theses.

Squire, Larry R., et al., editors. *Fundamental Neuroscience.* 3rd ed., Academic Press, 2008. *Amazon.*

Stewart, David, and H. Gene Blocker. *Fundamentals of Philosophy.* Pearson College Div, 1996. *Amazon.*

Stewart, Robert B., editor. *The Reliability of the New Testament: Bart D. Ehrman and Daniel B. Wallace in Dialogue.* Fortress Press, 2011. *Amazon.*

Strohl, G. Ralph, et al. "Jainism." *Britannica*, 24 Oct. 2025, https://www.britannica.com/topic/Jainism.

Stuart, Michael T., et al., editors. *The Routledge Companion to Thought Experiments.* 1st edition, Routledge, 2017. *Amazon.*

Sturmhoefel Warnberg, Linnéa. *Maintaining the Prison-Industrial Complex: Private Actors and Power—A Multi-Dimensional Power Analysis of CoreCivic and The GEO Group.* 2021, https://urn.kb.se/resolve?urn=urn:nbn:se:lnu:diva-100471. Linnaeus University, Bachelor's Thesis.

Stygar, Ryan. "Thinking Outside the Box: A Point-Based System of Reintegration for California's Inmate Firefighters." *California Western Law Review*, vol. 56, no. 2, 2020, https://scholarlycommons.law.cwsl.edu/cwlr/vol56/iss2/6.

Such-Gutiérrez, Marcos. *This Ancient Society Helped Build the Modern World.* 24 Aug. 2023, https://www.nationalgeographic.com/premium/article/invention-sumer-cradle-civilization-tigris-euphrates.

Susser, Daniel, et al. "Technology, Autonomy, and Manipulation." *Internet Policy Review*, vol. 8, no. 2, 2019, pp. 1–22, https://doi.org/10.14763/2019.2.1410.

Suveren, Yaşar. "Unconscious Bias: Definition and Significance." *Current Approaches in Psychiatry / Psikiyatride Guncel Yaklasimlar*, vol. 14, no. 3, July 2022, p. 414, https://doi.org/10.18863/pgy.1026607.

Swastiningsih, Swastiningsih, et al. "The Role of Social Media in Shaping Public Opinion: A Comparative Analysis of Traditional vs. Digital Media Platforms." *The Journal of Academic Science*, vol. 1, no. 6, Oct. 2024, pp. 620–26, https://doi.org/10.59613/fm1dpm66.

Tamari, Nazanin. "Zoroastrian Fire Foundations: A Portrait of Slaves and Slaveholders." *Slavery & Abolition*, vol. 44, no. 4, Oct. 2023, pp. 697–719, https://doi.org/10.1080/0144039X.2023.2264111.

Tao. "The Origins of Shintō Religion in Japan." *Go! Go! Nihon*, 26 Nov. 2022, https://gogonihon.com/en/blog/shinto-religion-in-japan/.

Taylor, Edwin F. *Principle of Least Action.* 2000, https://www.eftaylor.com/software/Action.pdf.

The Four Fundamental Forces - IB Physics. Directed by IB Physics - Andy Masley, 2021. *YouTube*, https://www.youtube.com/watch?v=jdgLNVwyAEc.

The Qur'an: An Evaluation of the Muslim Claims. n.d., https://www.answering-islam.org/Quran/index.html.

The Truth About Ancient Egypt (Kemet) | Heavy Is the Crown Vol 2 Presents: Tony Browder. Directed by Building Se7en, 2025. *YouTube*, https://www.youtube.com/watch?v=ByU8vzHt80w.

Thomas, Douglas, and Temilola Alanamu, editors. *African Religions: Beliefs and Practices through History.* Abc-Clio Inc, 2018. *Amazon.*

Tomescu, Irina. *Abandoned Children and International Adoption: An Analysis of Unintended Consequences of Institutional Arrangements in Romania, 1990-2001.* 2003, https://etd.ohiolink.edu/acprod/odb_etd/etd/r/1501/10?clear=10&p10_accession_num=osu1392805477. The Ohio State University, Master's Thesis.

Tooley, Michael. *Metaphysics– An Overview: Basic Concepts, Methods, Issues, Questions, and Arguments.* 12 June 2010, https://spot.colorado.edu/~tooley/Overview4360-5360.pdf.

Torres, Walter J., and Raymond M. Bergner. "Humiliation: Its Nature and Consequences." *The Journal of the American Academy of Psychiatry and the Law*, vol. 38, no. 2, 2010, pp. 195–204, https://pubmed.ncbi.nlm.nih.gov/20542938/.

Tremlett, Paul-Francois. *Levi-Strauss on Religion: The Structuring Mind.* Routledge, 2008. *Amazon.*

Truncellito, David A. "Epistemology." *Internet Encyclopedia of Philosophy*, n.d., https://iep.utm.edu/epistemo/.

Turner, Piers Norris. "'Harm' and Mill's Harm Principle." *Ethics*, vol. 124, no. 2, 2014, pp. 299–326. *journals.uchicago.edu (Atypon)*, https://doi.org/10.1086/673436.

Urubshurow, Victoria Kennick. *Introducing World Religions.* 1st edition, Routledge, 2008. *Amazon.*

Vaid, Bhuvinder S. *Ontology and the Nature of Being.* n.d., https://www.sfu.ca/educ867/htm/ontology.htm.

Van Eyghen, Hans. "Animism and Science." *Religions*, vol. 14, no. 5, May 2023, p. 653. *www.mdpi.com*, https://doi.org/10.3390/rel14050653.

Varvoglis, Harry. "The Major Branches of Physics." *History and Evolution of Concepts in Physics*, Springer Science & Business Media, 2014, pp. 29–103. *Amazon.*

Varzi, Achille. "Mereology." *The Stanford Encyclopedia of Philosophy (Spring 2019 Edition)*, edited by Edward N. Zalta, Metaphysics Research Lab, Stanford University, https://plato.stanford.edu/archives/spr2019/entries/mereology/. Accessed 26 Nov. 2025.

Victor, Jeffrey S. "Moral Panics and the Social Construction of Deviant Behavior: A Theory and Application to the Case of Ritual Child Abuse." *Sociological Perspectives*, vol. 41, no. 3, 1998, pp. 541–65, https://doi.org/10.2307/1389563.

Vyas, -Doorgapersad S., and E. P. Ababio. "The Illusion of Ethics for Good Local Governance in South Africa." *TD: The Journal for Transdisciplinary Research in Southern Africa*, vol. 6, no. 2, Dec. 2010, pp. 411–27, https://doi.org/10.10520/EJC111910.

Watt, Paul. "Japanese Religions." *Stanford University*, Oct. 2003, http://spice.fsi.stanford.edu/docs/japanese_religions.

Webber, Jeremy. "Legal Pluralism and Human Agency." *Osgoode Hall Law Journal*, vol. 44, 2006, p. 167, https://heinonline.org/HOL/Page?handle=hein.journals/ohlj44&id=187&div=&collection=.

Weber, Keith. "Beyond Proving and Explaining: Proofs That Justify the Use of Definitions and Axiomatic Structures and Proofs That Illustrate Technique." *For the Learning of Mathematics*, vol. 22, no. 3, 2002, pp. 14–17, https://www.jstor.org/stable/40248396.

Wegner, Jennifer Houser. "Ancient Egyptian Creation Myths: From Watery Chaos to Cosmic Egg." *Glencairn Museum*, 13 July 2021, https://www.glencairnmuseum.org/newsletter/2021/7/13/ancient-egyptian-creation-myths-from-watery-chaos-to-cosmic-egg.

Weisberg, Jonathan. "Formal Epistemology." *The Stanford Encyclopedia of Philosophy (Spring 2021 Edition)*, edited by Edward N. Zalta, Metaphysics Research Lab, Stanford University, https://plato.stanford.edu/archives/spr2021/entries/formal-epistemology/. Accessed 27 Nov. 2025.

Westerlund, David. *African Indigenous Religions and Disease Causation: From Spiritual Beings to Living Humans.* Brill, 2010. *Amazon.*

What Is Sikhism? Directed by ReligionForBreakfast, 2020. *YouTube*, https://www.youtube.com/watch?v=MWsClPXLApA.

Wheeler, Liz. *Hide Your Children: Exposing the Marxists Behind the Attack on America's Kids.* Regnery Publishing, 2023. *Amazon.*

Wilkinson, Toby, translator. *Writings from Ancient Egypt*. Penguin Classics, 2016. *Amazon*.

Williams, Deborah H. *A Critical Approach to Analyzing and Addressing Worldview-Based Cultural Conflict Between Indigenous Peoples and Western Science in Education and Research*. 2023, https://www.proquest.com/openview/21d88e313d572b803d609ee619a21e1b/1?pq-origsite=gscholar&cbl=18750&diss=y. University of Kansas, Dissertation.

Williams, Geoffrey. *African Designs from Traditional Sources*. Dover Publications, 1971. *Amazon*.

Winsor, Mary P. "Taxonomy Was the Foundation of Darwin's Evolution." *Taxon*, vol. 58, no. 1, 2009, pp. 43–49, https://doi.org/10.1002/tax.581007.

Wiredu, Wiredu. *A Companion to African Philosophy*. John Wiley & Sons, 2006. *Amazon*.

Witelski, Thomas, and Mark Bowen. *Methods of Mathematical Modelling: Continuous Systems and Differential Equations*. Springer, 2015. *Amazon*.

Withey, Michael, and Henry Zhang. *Mastering Logical Fallacies: The Definitive Guide to Flawless Rhetoric and Bulletproof Logic*. Callisto, 2016. *Amazon*.

Women in Christianity and Islam. https://answering-islam.org/Women/index.html. Accessed 25 Nov. 2025.

Wood, Laura C N. "Child Modern Slavery, Trafficking and Health: A Practical Review of Factors Contributing to Children's Vulnerability and the Potential Impacts of Severe Exploitation on Health." *BMJ Paediatrics Open*, vol. 4, no. 1, June 2020, p. e000327. *PubMed Central*, https://doi.org/10.1136/bmjpo-2018-000327.

"World Philosophical Heritage: The Divine Chain of Sikh Gurus." *Onelittleangel.com*, n.d., https://www.onelittleangel.com/wisdom/quotes/sikhism.asp.

World Religions from an Academic Point of View. Directed by UsefulCharts, 2024. *YouTube*, https://www.youtube.com/watch?v=nxhSOcyPCVo.

Wright, Jacob L. *Why the Bible Began: An Alternative History of Scripture and Its Origins*. Cambridge University Press, 2023. *Amazon*.

Zindler, Frank R., and Robert M. Price, editors. *Bart Ehrman and the Quest of the Historical Jesus of Nazareth: An Evaluation of Ehrman's Did Jesus Exist?* American Atheist Press, 2013. *Amazon*.

Zwemer, Samuel Marinus. *The Origin of Religion*. Marshal, Morgan & Scott, Ltd, 1935. *Amazon*.

www.ingramcontent.com/pod-product-compliance
Lightning Source LLC
LaVergne TN
LVHW081257100826
845148LV00005B/896

* 9 7 8 1 7 3 4 6 4 2 7 7 3 *